A Few Steps Too Far

A Few Steps Too Far

Mike Collins

With best wishes to good neighbours, Sandra, Ken and Paul.

[signature]

Memory Lane

First published in Great Britain by Memory Lane
ISBN 978-0-9567697-2-5
Printed and bound by Good News Books, Essex, England.

To Jo, for half a century of love and support.
And for Al and Dörte, Nicky and Derek, Jan and Max.
Great family.

Also for Peta, my trekking companion in Tibet,
who enjoyed (I hope) some of these stories,
thus inspiring this book.

Acknowledgements

The author would like to acknowledge the help and assistance
of Prontaprint of Wolverhampton for the expert collation of many
photographs and express his appreciation of the original interest
in this book shown by the publishers Memory Lane, particularly Julia,
and for their subsequent advice, hard work and
expertise during the publication process.

But, especially, he would like to acknowledge the help and
encouragement of all the outstanding people who have led and
guided him over the hills and the other rocky paths of life.

Foreword

I first met Mike Collins when he joined the Royal Society for the Prevention of Accidents in 1982. It was a challenging time in road safety but he soon got his teeth into the job and occasionally into me. Mike has made it plain that he doesn't like journalists much so I think he expected to have to fight me from time to time. Over the years a mutual respect grew into affection as we both realised that the other was trying to do a good job.

Reading the book I found a lot of things about Mike which I didn't know but didn't surprise me. He always wants to get the job done. He has written many articles about his foreign adventures in RoSPA's road safety journal, *Care on the Road*. At times he seems to have the energy of ten men but I think he just doesn't want to waste a minute of his existence.

But I am glad he has found the time to write it all down so the rest of us can share it.

Janice Cave MBE
Director of Public Affairs at RoSPA and Managing Editor of Care on the Road

CONTENTS

Chapter 1	First Steps	*1*
Chapter 2	Wolverhampton,Police, Sport and the Far East	*27*
Chapter 3	A Few Steps Up The Ladder	*87*
Chapter 4	Being Paid To Fly – At Last!	*99*
Chapter 5	Steps In The Dark	*177*
Chapter 6	Travel Writing, From Vancouver To Montreal Via Mexico	*283*
Chapter 7	Some more true traveller's tales for Jan and Max, South America, Atlantic to Pacific Coasts and Back	*321*
Chapter 8	Some serious safaris - The South Pacific, Australia, New Zealand, and round the world, 1994	*353*
Chapter 9	The Himalaya, first, second and third time and a few other high places! - Sagarmatha/Chomolungma, 1995/6	*401*
Chapter 10	Round the world again, the other way this time - Russia, Mongolia, China and Vietnam	*429*
Chapter 11	Trekking in Uzbekistan, Tajikistan and the Pamirs - Kilimanjaro, Mount Meru and Ngorongoro	473
Chapter 12	The Pilgrimage to Santiago de Compostela and the Cretan Gorges	*493*

Chapter 1

First Steps

Not so long ago I was arrested by the Chinese Army in Lhasa and handed over to the Chinese Police. This was definitely several steps too far!

The arrest was a direct result of a compulsion that I have always had - a curiosity to find out what lies on the other side of the hill - whether the obstruction in question is a physical, mental or imaginary barrier. I believe that anyone who possesses an enquiring mind should try to find out what lies on top of, over, or around these obstacles. Trouble is, I want to see the view from the summit. If not the curiosity remains, with regret at not having taken that step - as it persists with me about a few things. The impulse has resulted in some stimulating situations. Alarming rather than stimulating was the arrest in Tibet. Undeniably a chance taken, which did not come off!

A number of steps too far, in the following year, were necessary to complete a five hundred kilometre trek, the Camino Pilgrimage, from the Pyrenees to Santiago de Compostela, arriving with severely dilapidated feet. However, more about these steps, and others, in a bit.

I joined Wolverhampton Borough Police in 1953, after being called up in 1949 for National Service in the Royal Air Force. Before National Service I had been one of the new breed of Police Cadets, in Wolverhampton, for two years.

Many years later the Chief Constable said to me, 'You were an experiment as a Cadet. I think that we can say that the experiment was successful'.

This, I guess, did not diminish my ego, - never a fragile organism. I reached seventeen whilst a cadet, and managed to pass the driving test, probably through having driven an older friend's sports car, a gorgeous two-seater drop-head Wolseley Hornet, from the age of about fourteen. Probably the first step too far, although there were not a lot of other cars, or police patrol vehicles about in those days. Upon my passing the test my parents bought a BSA three wheeler, almost certainly, I now realise, to keep me off a motorbike.

The BSA was a sporty little car, with a BSA Scout 10 horsepower engine, also a drop-head and a two-seater. It was so light that one could pick up the back end to turn it round. A twin seater bench seat made it very convenient for, and quite attractive to, various girl friends (one at a time). I hand-painted it crimson, removed the windscreen and replaced it with two small semicircular screens in front of each seat, in the fashion of Fangio's racing cars of that era. Summer evenings, driving around Shropshire, on virtually empty roads with petrol at about two bob a gallon is a remembered delight. It also produced a feeling of being the cat's whiskers. With a sporty engine and weighing not a lot the car must, I now realise, have been terribly unstable. The one wheel was at the back, like the early Morgan three wheelers. It had a manually operated windscreen wiper, legal at that time, but pretty dangerous, as one had to turn a handle for each swipe across the screen. This was like the US Army Jeeps, but I am not sure if they or BSA had the idea first. The car was bought from my cousin, whom I think had severely frightened himself with it. We risked taking it on holiday to South Wales, my Father travelling with me, and Mother sensibly going by train!

Few other members of the Borough Police owned a car at that time apart from the Chief Constable. This certainly got me noticed, and was probably the reason that, on rejoining as a Constable I was quickly nominated for a driver training course. This eventually led to my subsequent police career and most of my occupations since.

I still have a sports car, a classic Jensen Healey, brilliant yellow this time. It has a very satisfying growl, and I find it interesting that, after more than fifty years, coming up behind a group of girls the noise still makes them turn their heads. Unfortunately when they see who is driving it they turn back! There is a distinct gender difference in relation to vehicles. It is rumoured that the Romans were less worried by the knives on the wheels of Boadacia's chariot than by her habit of pointing with her left arm then turning right. I won't get any further into that, but I do know that the gender distinction is apparent, even at a very early age. When the Jensen is parked outside my house and the kids are on their way home from school, the little girls say, 'Ooh, what a pretty car!' The boys say, 'Cor, how fast will that go then?'!

I used to park the BSA in a street near the Police Station (only the Chief was allowed in the yard) and often found a little boy playing in the gutter near the one rear wheel. That little boy, a policeman's son, grew up to play Rugby for England, so it was lucky that at the age of seventeen and knowing not a thing about real grown-up driving, I managed to avoid driving over his feet. We sold the car on my joining the Royal Air Force. The new owner despatched it to the great garage in the sky very soon afterwards. I do have very happy memories of, and gratitude towards, the BSA, and wish that I still had it. They were made in my Mother's home city of Brummagem. I later found that some of the Three Wheelers had been used by the Metropolitan Police as Traffic Patrol cars in the 1930s. The mind definitely boggles – but the past is a different country!

While I do have some less than fond thoughts about the former Birmingham City Police, I very much regret the demise of the Birmingham Small Arms Company. Later in my life we were to borrow competition prepared trials motor bikes from that great factory on the hill at Small Heath. (My parent's ploy to keep me off motor bikes was not successful). It was an inspiration to watch the old craftsmen caressing their machinery, actually I am sure with love, and to inhale the wonderful smell of Castrol 'R', racing oil. It was possible to see exactly the same loving attitude amongst the older craftsmen at the Jenson factory in West Bromwhich. As a police officer I once sat in on a test drive in a Jenson Interceptor from the factory. I was sitting on an upturned wooden crate where the passenger seat would eventually go, and the speed – what speed limit? And what officious Health and Safety? It was very exciting though, and quite incident free. I have recently completed a fairly accurate model of my BSA, painted the correct colour, which sits proudly alongside an accurate model of the Jensen Healey, also dressed in the right yellow, and a rather nice Austin Westminster, ('Bella machina'- see later!) in police livery.

In the same cabinet is a Wolverhampton Police 'Black Maria' van – more also about 'Black Maria' later. I am pleased to have this one, as we used, very riskily, to hang out of the back of it's grown up counterpart to put out hundreds of 'No parking' cones when Wolves were playing at home. I am glad to say that there was little Health and Safety input in those days and we controlled the parking far more effectively than happens today. Nobody ever fell off!

I opted to do my National Service in the Royal Air Force, as I had always wanted to fly, perhaps to see better over the hills. In 1949 the Service was still in the process of slimming down after the war, and did not much want to expensively train aircrew who, as National Servicemen, had only an eighteen months commitment. It would have been different had anyone known that Korea was just around the corner. However I completed all the aircrew selection tests at Royal Air Force Hornchurch, and was offered aircrew training as a Navigator or Flight Engineer, if willing to sign on for eight years. As a cousin close to my parents had been lost in the war, not returning from a bombing raid over Germany, this was not a popular option with my Mother. I still greatly regret that I did not take the opportunity to find out what was over this particular mountain, but was not prepared to put my Mother through that specific hoop. It might have been different these days, with perhaps less sensibility to parent's wishes.

I quite enjoyed basic training, squarebashing, at Royal Air Force Padgate, near Warrington. Having been an Air Training Corps Cadet from the earliest possible age, it was not totally strange. Warrington was in those days totally overlaid with the smell of soap from the factories, the beginnings I suppose of the Unilever Empire. After my having turned down the aircrew opportunity, the Air Force rather surprisingly put a square peg in a square hole, noticed that I had been a police cadet, and promoted me to Corporal in the Royal Air Force Police. The RAF Police was not a trade which I would have chosen, but no other choice was on offer. However, I felt fortunate while doing my police training at RAF Pershore to be part of a parade marching through the city centre of Worcester to the Cathedral.

We were accompanied by a Royal Air Force Band, and the thrill of being in time to military music, with several hundred other young men was a thrill which I can still remember. Military music is important, as a bond and an inspiration, and I am sorry for those who have not felt the stimulus that it can produce. I also have to say that I am proud of the RAF Police site at the National Memorial Arboretum near Lichfield, which I think is one of the best on that tremendously stirring site. It is a black marble obelisk with lettering in gold and the Royal Air Force Police shield showing an heraldic griffin under the crown and the motto 'Fiat Justitia' - 'Let justice be done'. However, the detail which makes the back of my neck tingle is the bed of snowdrops planted behind the memorial and the coloured engraving of a bunch of snowdrops on the obelisk. Someone on the designing committee had a wonderful sense of humour, since we wore peaked uniform caps with a white cover and white webbing belts and were known as ... !

I did quite well on the course and was posted to Royal Air Force Hednesford. This was surprising, as high up on Cannock Chase, it was not that far from my home in Shropshire. In fact it is only a few minutes flying time from my over thirty years flying base at Wolverhampton Airport. In those days, however, using a mixture of train and several buses it might as well have been a hundred miles away. I became stranded one night in Walsall, trying to return to duty. Walsall was not the nicest place in the world then to be marooned in, and I spent the night - after a fashion - in a Salvation Army Hostel used, it seemed, mainly by tramps. A new experience anyway!

The Senior NCO in charge of the Police Flight (the RAF term for a unit) at Hednesford was a rather fearsome Glaswegian, known behind his back as Chiefy. He had been a Services champion boxer in his younger days, and looked it. Nearly all we junior NCOs were teenage conscripts, who did not see the need to be very serious about guarding prisoners or RAF property, or life in general. Looking back now we must have been a big responsibility and a worry as he came towards the end of his service, and I rather regret that we did not serve him better. I respect him now for what he was and what he did.

It was not uncommon for two or three WRAF girls from a nearby Air

Force Station to join us at night in the Guardroom, which was totally out of order. As they were regulars they were usually older than most of us, and, shall we say, had more experience! It was also not uncommon, when no girls were present, for those on night duty to take up the challenge of climbing up the icy Station Water Tower. Being high on the Chase it was mighty cold at 2am, and even mightier at the top of the tower but there was a great view in all directions. Any prisoners were either polishing the Guardroom floor (which was supposed to be our night job) or making toast, fried eggs and coffee on the coke stove for the NCO left to answer the telephone.

Chiefy soon cottoned on to this and caught us one night in flagrante delicto.

He telephoned in, and said that he was just off to bed, and asked if all the prisoners were secured and everything in order.

'Oh yes, Flight Sergeant, all locked up...'

Three minutes later he walked in. We did not do this again. He had of course served through the war, and was quite capable of instilling terror into conscripts.

Two incidents did head me towards his more friendly side however. The Station was one of the several Initial Training Centres for National Service conscripts. Part of the training was to run regular Boxing Tournaments between the Training Wings. On one occasion there was space on the programme for a bout between two of the permanent staff. I volunteered to fight a rather large individual from the cookhouse. It was fairly obvious that I was expected to lose by Chiefy, the former champion. This would have been extremely popular with the recruit audience, but a blow to the Police Flight's carefully fostered reputation of being fearsome hard men! He did not know at that time that I had been a very active member of the Bridgnorth Boxing Club since the age of fifteen and whilst a police cadet, and had also won a fight in a similar tournament at RAF Padgate during my initial training. Fortunately for everyone's reputation and Chiefy's pleasure, I won again!

I continued taking part with the Bridgnorth Club as often as possible, and was getting reasonably well known, with a cartoon of myself in the ring in the local paper. The Club was formed in 1946 by Dr. Tony Hodges, a GP from the Bridgnorth area, who had been British Hospitals boxing champion before the 39-45 world war. He was a lovely man, a real gentleman, and in middle age still very difficult to hit! The main trainer was Jim Garbett, another super guy who had been a Wolverhampton police officer. Bridgnorth was the site of yet another Royal Air Force initial training station. This was still active, training National Service personnel, so the Club benefited from a succession of RAF physical training instructors, some of whom had been professional boxers. Sparring with them was a huge learning curve, because it was almost impossible to lay a glove on them. We also had two PT instructors appearing for us who went on to become Royal Air Force amateur champions at different weights, Corporals Danny O'Shea and Dennis Morris.

On one occasion, getting a couple of days leave from the RAF, I joined in an inter-club contest in Ludlow Town Hall. Our trainer, Jim, told me afterwards that he had said to my opponent, 'Don't be too hard on him, he's a young lad and hasn't been able to train much lately'. This was slightly unfortunate as I knocked the guy out of the ring with a left hook - my best punch - which landed, probably more by luck than judgement, smack on the button. His look at Jim, and me, as he climbed back in, was a good example of ring rage!

I was honoured to be sometimes on the same programme as an amateur from Smethwick, Pat Cowdell, who eventually turned professional and became British professional featherweight champion, and European Super-feather weight champion. He was 'The Warley Wonder'. Pat went on to challenge for the world featherweight title against a Mexican, Salvador Sanchez, in Houston. He lost, but only on a split decision over the full fifteen rounds. He fought a second time for the world title but again just could not take that final step.

Another world class boxer on the same amateur programmes as myself was Tommy Nicholls, from the Works Club at Sankeys, a very big engineering factory in Wellington, which is now a suburb of Telford. Tommy was a delight to watch, an artist, and proved himself to be one of the best amateurs in the world by beating every one put against him in the International Tournaments which were just resuming after the war. I am reminded strongly of Tommy by the young professional Amir Khan, another artist, both so fast that you could barely follow their gloves. It was about this time that I was matched with a miner, who became British Mineworkers Championship finalist. He was a short, very powerfully built young man, who possessed no technique or finesse, but relied on eventually delivering one tremendous punch. I was told later that I was so far ahead on points after the first two rounds that it was becoming laughable. But then I found myself waking up on the canvas from that one big punch that I never saw coming! I later saw him on television, using exactly the same system in the final of the Miner's Championships.

The second thing in my favour with Chiefy was the recapture of an escaped prisoner. Escaping was not difficult for those so inclined, as the Guardroom cell walls were made of (wait for it) a double thickness of plaster board! One of the junior NCOs on duty was required to sign for the prisoners when taking over from the previous shift. None of us took this particularly seriously, until, having taken my turn to sign the sheet I discovered a large hole in one previously occupied cell outer wall. We all ran in various different directions, and fortunately, perhaps as a foretaste of my future police career, I chose the right direction, and caught the guy, well outside the Station perimeter fence and on his way to Brindley Heath railway station. I marched him back up the long steep hill from the little station which, not surprisingly was known as 'Kitbag Hill'! I had to be charged with losing a prisoner of course, but because I had recaptured him was not punished.

However, Chiefy called me into his office and accused me of orchestrating the escape so that I could cleverly make the re-capture! I was outraged by this, and, in his own office, called him every name I could think of. I am sure that these were fairly tame by the Gorbals end of Glasgow standards, but I always felt that he liked my standing up to him.

Soon after this the Korean War broke out and all National Service periods were extended from eighteen months to two years. I remember, during my extra six months, that he and I inspected the gardens of the Sergeant's Mess, which were tidied and weeded by our prisoners.

Chiefy, looking at some lazy plants, said, 'I thought that these would be out by now.'

I just could not help saying, 'I had hoped the same', which I believe he also appreciated. I suppose that most people would say that I was lucky not to have been posted to Korea, and I would not have wanted it then, but regret this now.

Like most of our prisoners awaiting punishment or Court Martial, the escapee was a National Serviceman who found it all too much for him, and stayed at home after a leave. I had had to travel down to Hampshire to pick him up, and, I thought, treated him with politeness and consideration on the train journey back to the Midlands. The hole in the plasterboard did therefore come as a bit of a shock. Another airman was in a much worse state, and somehow got hold of a bottle of blue 'Blanco' which was used to clean and resurface RAF webbing belts and backpacks. Blue Blanco is rather a contradiction in terms, but that is what it was called! Anyway, this youth drank the bottle one night in his cell. It did not kill him, but he did look an awful sight after being sick!

Another person, much more bizarre than our normal prisoners, never saw the inside of the Guardroom, as we had been instructed to leave him alone. He was a tramp-like figure, roughly as broad as he was high, and wearing the tattered remnants of a military uniform. He was always bareheaded and wandered around the Station roads, never speaking, and carrying a tame raven on one shoulder. He worked, more or less, at labouring jobs within the perimeter of the Station. Being middle-aged and with a fearsome, always unshaven visage he was a sight to rather worry the young recruits in an area subjected to whitewash and military discipline. He was untouchable however, and as we were all mainly occupied with our own discomforts, not really of much concern then.

I would love to know, now, the history behind his unusual appearance and behaviour, and why he was left alone. Whether he was a man shell-shocked by war time experiences and mercifully allowed to see out his life in the Service environment without hospital treatment, whether he was being protected by a person of rank or whether all the 'Brass' were too frightened about what he might do, I did not, do not and never shall know. It was a bizarre and unusual situation and I am sure that there was a unique story in there waiting to be uncovered.

It had a parallel later in my life, when a white-bearded homeless old man was allowed to live for years until his death in a ramshackle tent on a grassy section of the Wolverhampton Ring Road, unbothered by Police or Council officials. He was of Polish origin and was believed to have suffered to such an extent during the war that he could not bear to be inside a building. Maybe their stories were the same. Maybe the wanderer with the raven and the lonely camper on the Wolverhampton Ring Road were one and the same. Maybe the ghost of my bizarre man from Royal Air Force Hednesford still stalks the windy hills of Cannock Chase. It remains a mystery.

Like most National Servicemen I could not wait to get on with my life, but I am glad now that I did those two years, and feel that although they were an interruption, they were also an introduction to the real world. Even in the initial training squad I met such a variety of my peers, from the boy who boasted of having been to the same public school as the Duke of Edinburgh to real teenage villains from the slums of London, Liverpool and Manchester. For some reason unknown to me I was appointed 'Senior Man,' a sort of Acting Corporal, who was required to try to get the other twenty or so in the hut to do what they were supposed to do. This was not easy and the Senior Man quickly became unpopular.

One evening, just before 'lights out' I found that my iron bedstead, complete with blankets etc, had been carried about fifty yards from the hut! However I survived. Some of the less robust characters became targets of the villains, and did not have a pleasant time.

One of my colleagues in the Service Police Flight was the son of a Ghillie from Drumnadrochit, an estate near the shores of Loch Ness. After returning from leave with luggage consisting entirely of bottles, he could drink prodigious amounts of undiluted whisky. He was also a skilled operator on the bagpipes. Mac, when topped up and energised from one of his bottles, was much in demand to give a short and sharp skirl on the pipes outside the Sergeant's Mess bedrooms at about 3 a.m. This was probably a chant too far, but we never got caught. The two Air Force years helped me to grow up. Eventually via later service in the R.A.F. Volunteer Reserve they led to the ability to pilot both gliders and powered aircraft, and to the most interesting part of my police career – more of this later. I do think that the generations since who have missed the Service experience would, in most cases, have benefited from it.

Part of the duty of the Police Flight was to mount an armed guard over the pay parade. Pay parade, every Friday, was made in cash to all airmen on the Station, and would have been a considerable amount, even in those days. It was collected from a Bank in the nearest town, Rugeley, by the Officer i/c pay. One of the Police Flight was tasked to stand outside the Bank, with a loaded .38 service revolver holstered on a webbing belt, and then accompany the cash back, by service car, to the Station Headquarters. We had completed some small arms training, but I don't remember being briefed about this, and in fact don't believe that there was a briefing. 'Stop the cash being stolen' I suppose it would have been! I do remember at the time being not too sure what I would have done in the event of a hold up.

Remembering myself at eighteen I would probably have shot someone. Putting a loaded revolver in peacetime into the hands of immature eighteen year old conscripts surrounded by friendly people was a trifle irresponsible, I now think. But this was not that long after World War Two, when thousands of eighteen year olds were using much more firepower, and of course in 1949 we loved it! Wow, the wild west in Staffordshire! This was not all that many years before the 'Great Train Robbery' – had the revolver ever been fired I guess the headlines would have been even more lurid.

Before my Royal Air Force service ended the Station became a P.D.C. - the last place in the UK before Airmen posted abroad left the country. With the Korean War in full swing many were going there or to other countries in the Far East. Contrary to the myths of Hollywood not all the United Nations troops were American. Some of these airmen had volunteered, others had not, but both categories seemed determined to make their last days in the UK memorable ones. There was quite a lot of drunkenness by those who could get off the Station to the nearest pub, and it was quite usual to find big holes in the wire perimeter fence. One night one of my colleagues waited, in the dark by one such hole, and eventually marched about twenty drunken airmen back to the Guardroom. We had a job to accommodate them, and I thought then, and still do, that he must have had a drop to drink himself to undertake such a task. Brave, anyway. He too became a civilian police officer, eventually in the same Force as myself.

I had noticed a very smart young Royal Air Force Regiment junior officer at Hednesford, whom we knew was also a National Service man like ourselves. Bob also joined the Wolverhampton Police Force, and we served together for many years and became good friends. Another job for the Police Flight was to meet the late night trains arriving at Rugeley Trent Valley Station. These were usually full of airman, reluctantly returning from their last leave in the UK, and either being not very happy at all, or in a state of being far too happy. This was a task, unlike the armed pay parade, that was definitely not a one man job!

We had a good relationship with the Staffordshire Police in Rugeley and Hednesford, probably because we were on hand to take care of our own off the late trains, and we often had a visit from the local man on his bicycle, needing refreshment after wheeling his bike up Kitbag Hill. Chiefy invoked their professional help on one occasion though, when he spotted a coke delivery lorry leaving the Station with a fair proportion of it's load still on board. Either he had had a tip, or was gifted with extra-sensory perception – good police work anyway. I was on duty and was called to witness the attempted theft.

The coke was regularly delivered by a local merchant and provided the almost incombustible fuel for the horrible coke stoves used to heat every hut. Oh, the frustration of trying and regularly failing to set light to the bloody things. There was a regular black market in kindling. And the stoves had to be polished in the Recruit's Wings huts until you could shave in the reflection. We had the prisoners to do it!

I guess that sneaking away with a proportion of what was being paid for was a good scam at the time – Chiefy may have suspected that it was going on, as he was very much on top of all the Station goings-on. This provided my first professional contact with the civilian Police, as a (more or less) adult, and led to the Coke Contractor being prosecuted at Staffordshire Quarter Sessions. He said that it was a mistake, so they let him off! This was where I first rubbed noses with the rooted inbred objection of Staffordshire juries to convict anyone of anything, as I found to my annoyance in later cases of my own.

I parted on good terms from Chiefy, who rather to my surprise gave me a good discharge character, but not before I had definitely taken another step too far.

At home for a weekend off, and glorying in my Corporal's stripes I was rash enough to threaten to charge two airmen walking through the town. Being minus service caps, they were certainly improperly dressed. However, these were two 'old sweats', who had certainly been through the war, and probably up to the rank of Sergeant and down again several times. Despite being temporarily in 'down' mode there was no way they were going to take that from a teenage National Serviceman. I learned a good few new words, descriptions of my parentage and future, and a lesson about looking before leaping! Also, as another pre-view of life as a police officer, I learned the value of the occasional 'Nelson touch', the blind eye!

Later, as a young police officer I wanted to carry out some Territorial or Volunteer Reserve duties in my spare time. However the only branch of the services that a police officer could then join was as an instructor to the Cadet Forces. This did not carry a liability for call-up in an emergency, so was acceptable to Chief Constables. Many police officers did serve the country in this way.

In1961 I applied for and was granted a commission as a Pilot Officer in the Royal Air Force Volunteer Reserve (Training Branch). I served in this branch for over fifteen years, and was awarded the Cadet Forces Medal. I was a Flight Lieutenant, carrying out Squadron Leader's duties as an Inspecting Officer when I had to resign the commission when sent by the Foreign and Commonwealth Office to Africa. Although trying to fit in RAF duties with my job as a police officer was sometimes difficult, I did have some great times. There was the opportunity to attend full time RAF Courses, which I was able to do by taking some police annual leave. Five such occasions stand out, the first being an admin and officer training course which gained me promotion to Flying Officer.

I then did a full time gliding course at RAF Kirton-in-Lindsey, which I was able to complete to solo standard during weekends at Royal Air Force Cosford, near Wolverhampton. This enabled me to join the Wrekin Gliding Club, run by and for RAF personnel at Cosford. In turn this led to flying at the Long Mynd Gliding Club in Shropshire, which is one of the premier gliding and soaring sites in the UK. I also spent a wonderful week at a civilian gliding club at Perranporth, at a former RAF airfield perched on the edge of the Cornish cliffs. Getting an auto-tow launch, up and out over the cliffs, with the blue Cornish sea underneath, and soaring along the line of the cliffs is a very enjoyable memory. My wife Jo, and my Mother, with the new baby were meantime having a great time on the beach below!

I never met Chiefy again after leaving RAF Hednesford, which perhaps is a good thing. I suspect that it would have been painful for both us if he had needed to salute me after I received the RAFVR commission. Being a long serving 'old soldier' I know that he would have performed the salute meticulously and with precision, but with perhaps a bit of Gorbalese under his breath!

In 1969 I was selected to go, with 30 other Training Branch officers, on an RAFVR visit to the Royal Air Force Station at Luqa, Malta, now Malta's main airport. We were flown out by RAF transport, landing in Nice to refuel. It felt rather good to walk across the tarmac at Nice Airport, in full RAF uniform, and to know that all the waiting holiday-maker passengers and everyone else in the Airport, were wondering who we were and what was going on, an invasion of France, no less!

The fact that I was by then a police Chief Inspector attracted a lot of attention from the press in Valetta, and I was hauled out of several lectures and meetings to be interviewed. I believe that this caused the senior RAF officers at Luqa to also wonder what was going on! This was a really wonderful visit, with the intention of demonstrating the work of an operational Royal Air Force base overseas. We were taken out one day on an RAF Sea Rescue Launch, achieving the memorable and enjoyable speed of 35 knots in Marsaxlokk Bay.

There was plenty of free time as well, to explore Valetta and the rest of Malta. I and another officer, in civvies of course, managed to visit one of the island casinos, and on my first ever casino gamble, on my first ever game of Roulette, picked up quite a bit of money on one number, still outlined in gold in my mind, number 38! The odds against that happening must be fairly high, and naturally, despite trying my best in Las Vegas years later, it has never occurred again!

A Navigation Course at RAF Gaydon is the fourth course standing out in memory – extremely enjoyable and useful when I was involved in the Midlands, Scottish and Welsh Police/Army helicopter experiments in 1968. In fact being able to quote a Royal Air Force navigation course helped me to get onto the experiments in the first place. During this course, and having by now qualified as a private pilot I had the controls of a twin engine Vickers Varsity at night over the North Sea. This was, to the say the least, a new experience and many steps too far had I not been closely supervised! Also enjoyable, in the same aircraft, was flying over Jo's parent's home on the Somerset coast, over the Bristol Channel and the Black Mountains of South Wales. On a day when the horizon seems unlimited they are actually very green!

The fifth really enjoyable course during my Volunteer Reserve service came in 1974. It was sea-survival training, based at the RAF School of Sea-Survival and Rescue, Mount Batten, Plymouth. I was the only VR officer on the course, and was sharing it, at the age of 43, with a number of young, very young, aircrew. Strange to think that now they will be either extremely senior officers or retired. Or, perhaps, dead, and a name inscribed at the National

Memorial Arboretum in the beautiful commemoration to all service personnel killed on duty since the end of the 1939-45 war. Needless to say, they were a lot more agile than myself at climbing from the sea into the tossing inflatable dinghy, especially as we were wearing full flying gear, including parachute harness and bone-dome. They were however, pretty kind and relatively non-sarcastic! I was also trying to manipulate, and keep dry, my camera, and surprisingly managed to get some shots which I prize mightily. At the end of the course we were each given a certificate, also much prized, stating that we had satisfactorily completed the course and 'with fortitude had undergone the rigorous requirements of the School'.

A jungle-survival course followed sea-survival, but as it is rather more difficult to find jungle than sea in the UK it was not so realistic. It was attention grabbing though, and may yet be useful! One of the interesting features of those days, in both RAF and Police courses, was the opportunity to liven up a technical lecture with a 'mistake' in the slide projector carousel which most speakers used to illustrate points.

One of the best versions of this was to bring up a slide which showed an upside down naked female and then say, 'Oh hell, I apologise, she'll have to go. My secretary keeps inserting pictures of herself into the carousel – she is obviously trying to tell me something'. This bit of light relief went down best with an all-male audience and improved a talk about widgets, sprockets or valves. It is not quite the same with the laptop that we now all use! Another useful boring lecture technique that I have employed was to glue pictures of two open eyes on the inside of a pair of old spectacles. One could then close ones real eyes for a moment or two in safety!

I was extremely fortunate and elated to be given a long flight in the two-seat version of the Gloster Meteor jet fighter, the first operational aircraft to fly supersonically, again on a day when the visibility went on for ever. From a few thousand feet over Newcastle the Scottish Highlands were easily visible. Before strapping into this aircraft it was necessary to wear full kit, including parachutes.

The pilot, briefing me said, 'If I say jump and you say 'what' I shan't be here to answer you!'

A good flight though, as was an hour in a Hunting Jet Provost, where again I was privileged to have control for quite a time over the Vale of York. This aircraft was then the RAF standard advanced trainer, but was also used as an operational ground attack and fighter by a number of overseas Air Forces. Considering the gulf between an amateur private pilot and professional military aircrew, the amount of credence given to my licence was a pleasant surprise. Perhaps they were impressed with the trouble and expense taken to achieve it on one's own. Other joyful moments include aerobatics from RAF Shawbury, in a Chipmunk, the RAF basic trainer. This was flown by a friend, a former RAF Typhoon fighter pilot, to whom I had given encouragement to get re-commissioned into the VR.

Two bizarre incidents whilst gliding also stand out. RAF Cosford is now the home of the Midlands Royal Air Force Museum and the 'Cold War Exhibition'. At that time, it was possible to drive through a gate kept open during the day and onto the airfield. A group of us, in flying kit, were standing by a glider at the end of the tarmac runway.

A car drove onto the field, the driver got out and, pointing to the runway, said, 'Excuse me, is that the main road to Shrewsbury?'

Well, no, not really! The second was at the Long Mynd, the gliding site being at the edge of a very steep scarp slope. This produces the superb lift found when the wind is from the west. As there are sometimes occasions when a glider cannot make it back to the site there is an emergency landing field at the bottom - some thousand feet down - of the scarp. When someone gets it wrong it is the job of the professional instructor to take a tractor and glider trailer down the one extremely steep road and lug it all the way back up. The slope is 1in 3 in parts, so is not to be trifled with. Naturally the pilot is not incredibly popular, and may have to stand a few rounds in the Club bar later. This happened one day while I was there and I volunteered to go down with Jack the instructor to help bring the aircraft back. We set off in good order, with Jack driving the Ferguson tractor and myself standing on the trailer hook behind him.

As we neared the one in three bit I realised that we were rapidly increasing speed, and going much faster than seemed safe or normal.

Jack stood up on the seat and shouted, 'The brakes have gone!' and did a really beautiful swallow dive onto the grass at the edge of the road.

It was at that point that I realised that perhaps I should get off too. This was not easy, being perched between tractor and trailer, but somehow I extricated myself and did what I am sure was a less elegant dive. Needless to say, the tractor carried on without us, and was not improved by the bend at the bottom of the hill. Very luckily neither of us was hurt physically apart from bruising, but received a certain amount of suggestions about parachutes being needed when driving the tractor, etc. Perhaps this was a ride too far!

It would probably surprise many people to learn that aerobatics in a glider are quite possible (given enough height). I was privileged to experience this at Cosford, and also at RAF Gaydon with Tony, a friend who was a Volunteer Reserve gliding instructor there. Loops, spins and chandelles – the gliding version of a stall turn - were exciting, but I was never very good at them, preferring to keep the right way up. I later did a lot of flying with Tony after we had both become power pilots.

I did enjoy my time in the VR and regretted leaving, but in 1976 I was asked by the Foreign Office to go to the Sudan to reorganise the Police communications system. It was also becoming increasingly difficult to combine it with growing responsibilities as a police officer, and to my family. The courses I have described always entailed living in the Officer's Mess, where I met many interesting and pleasant people. It frequently emerged that my full time life was in the police service, which would usually evoke interest (especially from Women's Royal Air Force officers!) but also some good natured leg-pulling and anecdotes about unfair speeding convictions.

However the only unpleasant Royal Air Force officer that I have ever met came about in a different context. Whilst I was still serving on motor and motor-cycle patrol, I chased a sports car travelling at well over the speed limit. It was a case for prosecution, not a ticking off. The driver, an officer from RAF Bridgnorth, was not very happy, but had no valid excuse, and I put the offence report through. It was, although we never use the phrase, a 'fair cop'!

Not long before this incident we had formed a Force Rugby team, composed mainly of guys, including myself, who had not played the game before. Wolverhampton, being the home of 'The Wolves' is very much a soccer town. We were not, despite some coaching by a former Welsh international, Gwyn Bayliss, very good. About three weeks after my meeting with the RAF speeder, we had a rugby fixture (extremely brave, or foolhardy of our fixture secretary) with Royal Air Force Bridgnorth. Naturally, and of course, and who could have expected otherwise, their captain was my speeder, who turned out to be a Cambridge rugby blue. He noticed me but did not so much as nod, and proceeded to walk all over us. That, in itself, was not a problem, and up to him. No one could touch him and they beat us by a score that I am not going to quote, because it is probably a Guinness Book of Records job!

Unfortunately that was the one time that my Father came to see us play. We did not mind being beaten, as it was a very regular occurrence. However, I was surprised, and a little shocked when the captain, my speeder, stalked off at the end of the game, without saying a word to anyone, and did not join us in the after-match meal. It must say something about this man's sportsmanship, in that he was obviously unable to separate the sport from the speeding. In the case of our team it was very definitely a case of a fixture too far! I am reminded by this incident of the story, (apocryphal I think) of the police officer who pulled over a Vicar for speeding. The Vicar insisted that the police officer must do his duty, and to prove that he bore no ill-will invited him to tea at the Vicarage on his next day off.

As he drove away, duly ticketed, he put his head out of the window and said, 'Don't forget, four o'clock on Friday. Bring your Mother and Father as well, and I'll marry them!'

Reading the above descriptions of enjoyable experiences it does sound as if serving in the Volunteer Reserve was all fun. In fact we did do a lot, I hope, of useful work, in trying to inculcate citizenship values into teenagers, and also offer them the option of a career in the Forces. One example, of which I am proud, was starting boxing classes as a regular part of the training at the Wolverhampton Squadron, in which I served for several years. This was rather a step too far for me, as we had some large West Indian boys, the biggest of whom broke one of my ribs!

However, one lad, also a West Indian, was good enough to enter the national Air Training Corps championships. In the final he forgot all that I had been trying to teach him and allowed his natural instincts to take over. He won, conclusively, perhaps more positively than if he had tried to box calmly. However, the look of pleasure on both his and his Father's faces when he was presented with the trophy made it all worthwhile. I felt at the time, but hope that I was wrong, that this boy was not going to succeed in too much else in his life, but at least, thirty five years on, he has one success to look back to. The Wolverhampton Squadron Commanding Officer, Doug, had been aircrew in a Lancaster as part of the elite Pathfinder Force during the war, and had been awarded the Distinguished Flying Medal. We got on well, and are still friends. I had the privilege of once flying him and his son from the former Royal Air Force airfield at Halfpenny Green, in a much smaller aeroplane than a Lancaster.

We also took the boys canoeing on the Midlands canals, played Wolverhampton Police Cadets at soccer, and on one never to be forgotten day I got about thirty of them to the top of Snowdon. It wouldn't be allowed now without a ton of paper work and months of Criminal Record Bureau checks, but we never lost or hurt one, and gave a lot of teenagers, mostly from the poorer back streets of the city, something different to remember. I wonder if they do? Meeting some of them a few years ago (one, would you believe in the Transit Lounge at Moscow Airport) I think that they do.

Returning, after the above digression, to my National Service days, I did eventually, in 1951, get 'out' but was still undecided about whether to rejoin and take the option of signing-on for aircrew. I had been pressured several times during my two years service to sign on as a regular and apply for a commission, which I was told could be almost guaranteed. Suddenly, recruits were wanted, more than they had been two years earlier! My main career was never going to be anything but a choice between flying in the RAF or rejoining the police, and it took me a long time to make up my mind.

I still have huge regrets that, with the regulations as they then were, I could not do both. Had a crystal ball been available, perhaps I could have found out that the mandatory top age limit for joining the police would be extended for those with a military background. I could have had my cake and eaten it! I guess however that with fifteen years of gliding and flying in the Volunteer Reserve and nearly forty years as a private pilot I did get some way towards that ideal. I do think of myself as having been very lucky.

Whilst making up my mind, and as a temporary expedient I took a job as a Farm Management trainee at the Home Farm of a big local estate. It was a useful physical experience and a meeting with men, manual workers living a tough poorly paid life, for whom I still have a great respect. I had an uncle by marriage who had been invalided out from the Metropolitan Police, and on learning this one of the workmen realised that it was my Auntie that he had been in love with many years before.

'But when George came home in his police uniform I never stood a chance!'

This set me thinking a bit about the benefits of joining the police and realising that a uniform, even (or fast forwarding a few years, perhaps 'especially') a police one, does strike a chord in the female heart! Despite having been raised in a small country market town I did not know a lot about farming. My response of , 'er, black and white ones' to the question, 'What sort of cattle are kept on the farm?' during an interview for a place at a Farm Management College did not impress the panel too much. Retrospectively I doubt very much if my subsequent life would have been as interesting had I given a better answer, so actually it was the right one.

Nothing much exciting happened during the time on the farm, except that I was called back for two weeks Royal Air Force Reserve duty in 1952. The Korean War was still in progress, and the world had begun to divide into the two armed camps. One response of Britain to the 'Cold War' was to set up several underground nuclear bunkers, which could be used as Regional Centres of Government in the event of Westminster being wiped out. I was recalled to guard the one at Hack Green in Cheshire for a fourteen-day exercise. Just me against the Russians.

During the exercise I was noticed by a visiting gold lace covered senior officer, who asked loudly why that Corporal was wearing the wrong pair of trousers; - 'best blue' instead of battledress. I overheard it being explained to him that I was now a civilian masquerading as a Royal Air Force Policeman.

I should have shot him. They had loaned me a gun. I doubt if the Russians would have minded about my trousers!

Hack Green has now been turned into a Museum about the Cold War, and signs advertising 'This way to the Secret Nuclear Bunker' are situated around Cheshire. I do wonder what visitors from America or other countries might think about this.

Visiting the site of our Guardroom on Cannock Chase, and the holy of holies, Station Headquarters in the twenty-first century, I find it weird to see how nature has almost entirely taken over. Where the smallest blade of grass would have been mercilessly put to death, probably with scissors or a table knife, and the smallest pebble white-washed to death, probably with a toothbrush, the Cannock Chase jungle reigns supreme. However, we were there and the memories remain. I was quite affected to see the memorial boulder marking the old main entrance, and inordinately pleased that it bears a photograph of the Police Flight, lined up outside the Guardroom, Snowdrops all. Am I on it? Can't tell, the fifty year old photograph is blurred, and I have changed a bit, but it's nice to see. Fiat Justitia.

As well as the signs showing the way to the secret bunker another total anachronism which must have caused overseas tourists to blink twice was the absolutely beautiful 1930s British racing green Lagonda. This was the type, open top of course, with a bonnet half a mile long, held down by leather straps, super-charged (what a lovely noise) and the handbrake on the outside of the driver's side. It was owned by the Lancashire Constabulary, having been given to them before the 39-45 War by Lord Cottenham, a well known racing driver of that era. He, together with Sir Malcolm Campbell, had been involved in the setting up of police driver training, and the writing of Training Syllabi, and had owned three Lagondas. He gave a Lagonda each to Lancashire, Essex and the Metropolitan Police, the first three British police driving schools.

These were the days of the aristocratic, and rich, racing drivers! Soon after this most generous gift the war began, and the Metropolitan and Essex cars had been lost sight of when peace broke out. One has one's suspicions. However, Lancashire had treated theirs with tender loving care, and it was eventually refurbished as a project by their police cadets and was used occasionally - on sunny days - as a training car by the driving school. I saw the car while doing a motor cycling course with Lancashire and it really was beautiful. What the American tourists in Southport or Blackpool thought when seeing four officers in uniform sitting in the open cockpit about six feet above the road surface is an interesting concept. It even had a 'Police Driver Training' plate on the back.

'Well, we thought the Limeys were a bit backward, but ....'

Of course though, if you could drive that you could drive anything. Part of the art of advanced driving is to make progress unobtrusively. Difficult to do this using double-declutches in a racing green super-charged Lagonda! It was used by Lancashire in this way until the end of the twentieth century.

Another British response to the Cold War was the provision of Police Mobile Columns. In the event of Westminster being flattened these would have been deployed in support of the decentralised Regional Seats of Government. The latter would have been an alternative to, or an expansion of, the secret nuclear bunkers. Every so often an exercise to test the preparedness and viability of the Columns was held, and some years after the Hack Green exercise I was involved in one such.

The Column consisted of twelve Ford Personnel Carriers and Cook's Vehicles, two Radio control and maintenance lorries plus water carriers and five smaller 4X4s, all painted 'Police blue' and with, for that era, reasonably efficient Home Office communication facilities and living equipment. With motor cycles the column amounted to thirty one vehicles, with 'Police Mobile Column' painted in white on the side of each vehicle, - quite an impressive sight. Personnel were to be one hundred and thirty police officers, of all ranks up to Superintendent, who commanded from the lead vehicle. He (for sure in those days!) was required to map-read his way using a grid reference to a remote country site and set up all the facilities. This seemed to me to be rather in the style of the wild west covered wagons in a defensive ring against Red Indian warriors.

The column which I had volunteered for - (it seemed to offer the prospect of a bit of fun) - was led by a Superintendent from Birmingham City Police. We had been tasked to head west, into the Shropshire hill country. I strongly suspect that our leader had never been further west than the Birmingham City boundary. As time went on it became obvious that he was totally and irretrievably lost in the maze of partly unmapped and very narrow Shropshire lanes, somewhere between the two Clee Hills. We had a motor cyclist at the front end, but he was lost as well.

Having walked, cycled, driven and flown all over this area I knew exactly where we were, and it was becoming very interesting to see where we would finish up. The thirty one vehicles went round in a number of circles, and I think that at one time the lead lorry was in danger of catching up with the rear of the last one. Certainly we went through one tiny village three times. By the time we got there for the last time the children had been decanted from the village school to cheer, and had all been supplied with little union jacks to wave as we passed through!

'Where am I going?'

'I don't know.'

'When will I get there?'

'I ain't certain.'

Lee Marvin's gritty song from *Paint Your Wagon* in real life! Very late, we arrived at our destination, Farlow Common, below Titterstone Clee Hill, and laagered up. I have a nice photograph of several of us pushing another officer in an antique and derelict Bath Chair, which we found in a deserted cottage. Perhaps it is as well that the Russians did not flatten Westminster.

There is a family follow-up to the Mobile Column experience through my son Alasdhair. As a 19 years old very junior 2nd Lieutenant in the Royal Corps of Transport he was placed in command of a column of Tank Transporters to be moved from A to B in northern Germany. Like my erstwhile commander on the police column he got absolutely lost and led the transporters into a housing estate and thence into a cul-de-sac. As one cannot do a three point turn with a Tank Transporter they had to grindingly reverse back out through the estate. This was much to the amazement and bewilderment of the number of fathers doing the Sunday morning duty of lovingly polishing the BM, Audi or VW! No doubt something was also said about junior officers by the squaddy drivers!

I found throughout my police service that policemen did not respond well to exercises. In a real, live, situation they would work unstintingly for days on end with minimum rest and food, sometimes in personal danger and always in personal discomfort. But exercises, we did not take very seriously. During the period of the 'cold war' the majority of police officers would have had war service or national service experience. Perhaps this explains something.

I recently discovered from a police colleague from elsewhere in the UK that they used to sound the 'Last Post' by bugle when filling in the latrine trench after their mobile columns. I believe that a further factor of this attitude is the knowledge that in a genuine emergency the police will be there, doing real work and usually first, in contrast to the men in suits who turn up later.

A different exercise, also as part of the cold war planning, involved testing the response of the local authority. Based in Wolverhampton Town Hall I acted as the police liaison officer with the Fire Service, Ambulance and Borough Engineer's staff. The joint control room did not, to be polite, work well. I remember receiving a message that the Town Clerk (who was obviously fireproof) had been hit by an unexploded atom bomb which had bounced off him and struck down the Mayor. I am rather cynical nowadays about Government schemes to combat terrorism, having seen how plans and instructions are devolved down to ground level.

But perhaps, as terrorism is a realistic and immediate threat now, more than was the thought of nuclear bombs demolishing the Town Hall, they will work more effectively. The West Midlands Police have just built such a combined control room.

Perhaps others writing about service in the police would deny, or debate, my assertion that make-believe situations were not always taken seriously. I am sure however, that those of my generation did have that attitude. Maybe it was an antidote to the times when you could be on your own, without any other help or means of communication except the whistle, and in physical danger. Perhaps it is analogous to the notoriously relaxed wartime feelings of aircrew when off duty, most then living just for the moment. But when flying, self-discipline was rigid and they were a tightly knit team with every member playing his full part. I do think that it is true that we were also, when doing a real job, a tightly knit team.

I also believe it to be a fact that a minority group, like the police, will instinctively band together against attack or criticism from outside the group. This can be, and sometimes is, a bad thing if carried to extremes. However, it is certainly true, or at least was in my day, that even if one did not particularly like or respect a colleague, everything possible would be done to get to his assistance when it was needed.

This is a similar effect to the military ethos that there is no comrade as good as the one that you have fought alongside. The US Marines say, 'Once a marine, always a marine' and, 'Old soldiers never die' is a well-known British aphorism. I think, also true, and proved by the number of former colleagues who came to our re-union in 2007 is, 'Once a Wolverhampton Police Officer, always a Wolverhampton Police Officer'. I believe these words to be true of police officers, who have, or perhaps more correctly, had in those days, a sense of a separate identity from the 'civilian' population.

I have always preferred, in referring to the police, to use the word Service, rather than Force. There are a number of definitions which can apply to 'service'. One is 'to be useful', and another is 'to do what is necessary.' The most appropriate is, I believe, 'an exertion made on behalf of someone else.'

Alexander the Great, probably the greatest military tactician that the world has ever seen, only demanded of his soldiers that they had 'dynasmus' which meant 'the will to fight.'

Alexander's tactics and battle plans are discussed at Sandhurst to this day. Many of the police officers that I knew, and served with, had dynasmus. In their cases I interpret this as intelligence, a 'nose' for a criminal, the will to work, to risk themselves if necessary and, if it were needed, the ability and the will to fight. I wonder, I just wonder, if in the twenty first century one could genuinely say the same about people in imitation police uniforms - Community Support Officers and Special Constables? These are placed, by Government economies and muddled policies, into sometimes impossible situations. A number of reported incidents suggest that it cannot so be said.

A point of view which has a bearing on the above comment is that I am quite certain that I would make a much better police officer now, over thirty years since I retired, than I was fifty years ago. This is, of course, apart from the inevitable deterioration of strength, hearing and vision. The inescapable problem with police work, and with police/public relations is that those who have learned the most about people and life, are almost invariably pounding a desk, rather than the pavement, or about to retire. I do welcome recent moves to get senior officers out on the streets, but still the police officer that the public are most likely to meet is a young one, not yet finished learning his trade. That trade is learned on the streets or in the countryside and cannot be taught in training centres, or by dressing up in a uniform, but is gained in dealing with people in all their innumerable manifestations and complications.

Alexander had an influence in the West even in the nineteen seventies, as we were then learning how to use, in a riot situation, the techniques that he invented for his foot soldiers, the 'Wedge' and the 'Trudge', to break up a riot. We were also learning, and using, his tactic of allowing the cavalry to come through from the rear to the front line. This involved the line of foot officers moving at a signal to make just enough room for the horses to come through, at what felt like a gallop. This was very effective, and made one realise just how big and frightening a mounted horse can be. Alexander used the technique for the first time when he beat the Persians of King Darius at the battle of Issus, and changed the course of history. We used it in Birmingham at the battle of Digbeth in 1978. We won as well. The latter battle certainly got into the newspapers, but probably won't be in the history books, so I record it here!

After being retired for longer than I served, I still react to many situations as a policeman, and still receive some benefits from that service. The truth of the adages was also proved when in 2007 a former colleague, Joe, and I organised a 'forty years on' re-union of those who had served in Wolverhampton Borough Police. There were over a hundred responses and over sixty men and women, including some widows of former officers, turned up at the National Memorial Arboretum in Staffordshire on a beautiful day in April. Some had travelled from as far away as Penzance, Essex and Sunderland, and many of course were not particularly fit or mobile. We got the Mayor of Wolverhampton to dedicate a plaque and raised enough money to give a substantial donation to the police charity C.O.P.S. – Care of Police Survivors.

During his dedication the Mayor said, 'I stand here in quiet pride to give thanks for the lives of the men and women who served our society.'

There was quite a lot of attention from the Press, both local and that specialising on the police, and an item in the magazine of the National Association of Retired Police Officers referred to Joe and I as having had 'long and distinguished careers.' I felt that this was a satisfactory conclusion to my main vocation.

I met Jo, my wife to be, towards the end of my National Service in the summer of 1951. Unfortunately she lived in West Somerset, which was a long long way, before the M5 was built, via Worcester, Gloucester, Bristol and Bridgewater. So, I bought my second car, a drop head Hillman Minx. The soft top leaked, so she carried an umbrella when we went out in it during the occasional weekends when I could get down there.

Five hours each way.

There was practically no tyre legislation at that time, and with very little money, all of which was being spent in much more interesting ways, I let the tyres get quite bald but painted them black, so they at least looked new. I remember being half way to Somerset and on stopping for fuel being surprised to note a sliver of pink inner tube visible where the tread should have been. No money for a new tyre, so nothing much else to do but carry on gently and hope. Following this the brakes gave up on a steep hill called Paradise Lane, on the outskirts of Bristol, where Jo was by this time a trainee Nurse. We swooped down and onto the main Bristol to Weston- super- Mare road between two buses.

Another two cases where a 'thank-you' was due to my fairy godmother, guardian angel or whoever, the first being an economy too far and the second definitely being a hill too far! Despite these moments of concern I quite loved the old Hillman – my second 'Topless Beauty'. It had to go, in a good cause, however when I eventually sold it to buy an engagement ring for Jo, which I am very pleased that she still has, and will, in the fullness of time pass on to Nicky, our daughter. I admit now that I did some very silly things in the Hillman, before growing up.

We had met first while I was on leave from the Royal Air Force. I was spending a holiday with my parents at a 'Holiday Fellowship' Guest House in Lynmouth. Jo and several of her school biology student colleagues were undergoing a field trip, under the supervision of a senior mistress, and staying in the same guest house. There was a mutual attraction, although she has disclosed since that at first sight she thought I was very miserable looking! Still does. We got together, despite the chaperonage of the teacher, who when I met her years later exclaimed, 'Ah, it's the young man from Lynmouth!' I guess that she had realised at the time what was going on! My parents and I had travelled to Lynmouth by train, and 'bus, but I managed to involve cars in this as with most things since.

After the school party had left, half way through our week, I wanted to see Jo again. Without telling anyone I got myself to Minehead, which was the nearest town of any size to the remote village on the edge of Exmoor where she lived. I had intended to rent a car but there were none to be had in Minehead, and the only possibility was at a garage at Roadwater, an even more remote village. How I got to Roadwater is a mystery now, but I must have been fairly determined. I was able to rent a decidedly ancient car, and found my way through the hills of Exmoor to the very beautiful village of Wootton Courtenay where she lived.

Having got there - it was now late afternoon - I succumbed to a panic attack, with no idea of what was the next step to take. It was, at that stage, definitely a potential step too far! I remember sitting in the car near her house, and pondering the next move. It was a lovely summer's afternoon (weren't they all in those days). I had got her address from the local shop – a good bit of pre-police work, but was being regarded with grave suspicion by one of the neighbours, who kept coming out of his front door to see if I had moved off. He also had a pretty daughter, and regarded any unknown young men hanging about as not particularly welcome.

Eventually I plucked up courage and knocked the door. The cry of pleasure when the door was opened made the journey and the wait worthwhile. The family, Jo, her parents and younger sister were having their tea, and I was quickly made to sit down and have a piece of cake and a cup of tea to settle my nerves. I suspect that her parents knew how I was feeling. Fortunately I was not regarded with the same suspicion that the neighbour had shown, and we were able to take a short drive around the very beautiful area between the little town of Dunster and Exmoor. By the time darkness was falling I was beginning to realise that I had serious difficulties in getting back to Lynmouth. Public transport, even in those days when it was much more user-friendly than today, had finished for the night.

Having promised to return to see Jo as soon as possible I luckily found my way back to Roadwater, on very dark winding roads, and prevailed on the garage owner to drive me the 20 odd miles to Lynmouth. He agreed, reluctantly, as the only feasible route was up Porlock Hill and down Countisbury, two of the steepest hills in England. Even with modern cars they are not to be trifled with. There was a water butt then half way up Porlock Hill for cars that were boiling! Well, we got back, but only to find that I was in total disgrace for not having told anyone where I was going and that I would be late back. I had to apologise to everyone at breakfast time the next day.

However, it was worth it. If I had not done that drive too far I am pretty sure that any possible romance would not have survived the long distance and infrequent opportunities to get together. Both our lives would have been so, so very different.

Chapter 2

Wolverhampton Police, Sport and the Far East

Having realised that I was not going to be the best Farm Manager in the world in 1953 I decided to apply to rejoin Wolverhampton Borough Police.

I had to take the education test to be accepted, which was a problem since maths, even the most basic, has always been a difficulty. Fortunately I had to take it in the small Shropshire Constabulary station in Bridgnorth, under the supervision of a sympathetic Sergeant. There were some kindly ones, even in those days. Despite assuring me that I was joining the wrong Force, he did the maths paper for me. I suppose that my eventual career would have pleased him, particularly as I ended up with a communications budget of millions, but I was able to repay the help in a roundabout way.

Some years later I was supervising a very nervous applicant for our Force in the Wolverhampton Office. His mind had gone completely blank when asked to write an essay about his best moment in life so far. He told me that he had been an Amateur Boxing Association UK Championship finalist at the Albert Hall, and with a bit of prodding we turned this into an acceptable essay. Bob later brought a British Police Boxing Championship home to Wolverhampton. So, I have absolutely no bad conscience about either of these events.

Bob was quite deceptive in appearance, only just making the required height, and slight of build. In the days when fitness and physical ability were necessary attributes for a police officer in towns like Wolverhampton he must have surprised quite a few villains. Boxing still had a part to play in my life in those days, as a retired officer called Isaac (Ike, of course) ran our uniform stores.

Ike had the most broken nose that I have ever seen. He had been a professional in the days of the Black Country roughhouse fairground boxing booths. The steel workers and miners were offered a pound a round to stay upright against him - 'We take on all comers', and he was well known throughout Wolverhampton. At the age of 60 he was still good enough to take on most people, and was interested in Bob and myself. We fixed up a little gym with a punch bag in a corner of the stores and Bob and I, plus a few others, used it, under Ike's tuition. I am proud to still have Ike's boxing gloves. I remained involved with Bridgnorth Boxing Club, although shift work was making this difficult.

Time off for sport had to be for a very good reason, such as the Force cricket team, and individual hobbies did not really count. I managed to continue the involvement at Bridgnorth, until, as a senior police officer I was asked to appear in the ring at a Tournament to present a young boxer with the same rose bowl that I had won and held for twelve months many years before. Later still I was asked to join, also in the ring, a group of former boxers from the Club. We were described in the press as 'former champions'. Two real Royal Air Force champions, Danny O'Shea and Dennis Morris, were in the group, but in my case this was an exaggerated step too far. I had actually managed to put Dennis on the floor during sparring years before, so have never worried too much about the embellished description, and the cutting is nice to have! Also a good memory is the surprised expression on Dennis's face at the time the knock-down happened.

A wedding in Malaysia - Singapore and Thailand

In a strange, roundabout way, boxing led to international friendships, which have gone on into the next generation. It led also to work abroad, and travelling for experience and pleasure as well. My nose was quite badly damaged – perhaps by that one punch from the mineworker's champion, and in 1962 I went into Hospital to have it rectified. In the next bed, and having the same operation, was a student teacher from the nearby Malaysian Teachers Training College.

The Brinsford College had been set up after the war as part of a Commonwealth Assistance Programme. Hira Singh, who was a Sikh from a family settled in Penang, became a friend, and many of his friends became our friends. Jo was expecting our first child, Alasdhair, and when he arrived later that year his first visitors were Hira Singh, and Kulwant Singh. The Sikhs called the baby 'The Warrior', a Sikh tradition for boys.

We remained friends after he returned to Malaysia and out of the blue I was invited to Hira's wedding in Ipoh, Penang, in January 1975. We had both been invited to Kulwant's wedding in 1965 in Taiping, and to Gordon Hooi's in Ipoh in 1968, and had reluctantly decided that neither was affordable. However by '75 promotions had brought a better income and although we could not afford both air-fares (they were a lot higher then) Jo persuaded me to go. As it coincided so well with my desire to see over the hills, perhaps not too much persuasion was needed.

We had taken a few European holidays by then, but I had never been anywhere as far away, exotic and exciting as Malaysia. We had been invited to many parties and festivals at the Training College, made friends and developed some understanding of Malaysian (and Sikh and Chinese) culture, but finding myself in the Far East in reality was earth shattering. I chose to take a stopover in Bangkok, and on descending from the aeroplane in an English winter weight raincoat realised that I had quite a lot to learn about 'east of Suez'.

Travelling in a thirty-foot long canoe with a powerful outboard motor strapped to the stern on the Klongs - canals - of Bangkok and seeing the way that the river people live was another eye opening experience. Eventually I arrived in Kuala Lumpur, rather wilted, and made my way by train to Ipoh, which was quite a big city even then. The wedding reception was held in the Town Hall in Ipoh and attended by over a hundred guests. They were all, except one expatriate couple from Birmingham, Indian, Chinese or Malay, in glamorous and colourful clothing and jewellery. As Hira and his family were well known and very well respected in Ipoh there were some Malaysians of the rank of Dato among the guests. Being important and honoured people they had to be treated like minor royalty.

As I had travelled from the furthest distance, and my initials being M.C., Hira ordered me to act as the Master of Ceremonies at the reception. And this was my first time in the Far East! At the time I felt like running away, but now I realise what an honour it was. In a Malaysian wedding the MC is in charge of the whole event, choosing the music, organising and introducing the speeches, making sure that the food was presented properly and literally being the master of ceremonies. I can still easily recall the flashing lights, the glittering jewellery and colourful saris of the ladies, and also my feeling of inadequate terror!

And the heat!

Jo and I had already met Asbir, Hira's wife to be, in England, where she was doing her law degree, and she and Hira's Mother were extremely supportive of the stranger in their midst. However, I did feel in need of further backing and wished that we had struggled to somehow find the second airfare. The inerasable Birmingham accents of the expatriate couple were actually quite a comfort, as I thought, 'Well, at least two people will understand what I am rabbiting about'. I was placed, as befitted my status as MC, at the top table, next to Asbir's brother, who was also due to make a speech.

He was in a much worse state of terror than myself, similarly a stranger to many of the guests, and had also come a comparatively long distance, from Sarawak on the island of Borneo. He had absolutely no idea of what to say to the many guests. I found myself having to write his speech, hands under the table, between courses, of which fortunately there were many. I do remember thinking at the time this is rather an odd situation for a Wolverhampton Policeman to be in. In the event we both survived!

Hira and Asbir had booked a traditional honeymoon at a Hotel in the Cameron Highlands, a very beautiful, forested plateau in central peninsular Malaya. The village where they were staying, Tannah Ratta, was high up and therefore, for me, blessedly cool. To my surprise Hira had booked a room for me in the Hotel, so that I could drive them there, in his car – not quite so traditional! I remember an interminable winding road up into the Highlands, and catching a glimpse in the mirror of an aboriginal tribesman. He was a tiny figure complete with feathered head-dress, loincloth and bow and arrow, running across the road and into the trees behind us.

After a couple of days I left Hira and Asbir undisturbed for the rest of their honeymoon, and returned to Ipoh by train. Apart from coping with the stress of being the M.C. I had the chance to meet other old friends from Brinsford College, and spent a night at the home of Gordon Hooi Khong Cheong, who also lived in Ipoh, although of Chinese ancestry. It was extremely interesting to find the difference in cultures between people of the same nationality but different ancestry. It was good to meet Gordon's parents, neither of whom spoke more than a word or two of English, but we managed! When going to bed I was warned not to leave anything valuable near the window, as thieves were known to operate with a sort of fishing rod to 'hook' up anything they fancied. I wait to hear of a similar technique in the UK; no doubt it will be tried. (Since writing this, it has!) Hira had arranged for me to be driven north to Fort Butterworth on the Straits of Malacca by a young friend of his and then take a ferry to the beautiful island of Penang.

The beaches on the Straits side of the island were something to be seen, and I am not surprised that it became very popular as a wedding location. In 1975 they were unspoiled and beautiful, and I hope, though with not much confidence, that this is still the case. We visited the huge reclining Buddha and the Snake Temple, where the unwary visitor quickly finds that he is a host to three snakes, one in each hand and a third on his head! The snakes were friendly though, and the Temple keepers enjoy the fun! There was also the chance to meet an elderly veteran of the Japanese occupation, and hear stories of that time, straight from a person of experience. Another absorbing look into an exotic culture and traditional hospitality.

I was treated extremely well by Hira and Asbir's families and friends and learned much, including, from Gordon, the Chinese toast 'Yam Seng' or 'bottoms up' – you have to do it, sink the lot, or lose tremendous face. It does mean the bottom of the glass! After rashly talking about my cricketing experience, I was invited to take part in a cricket match at the rather lovely and very professional looking Ipoh Cricket Club. Fortunately, and much to my relief, it rained! I strongly suspect that I might have been out of my class facing

Indian fast bowlers, and it would have been another step considerably too far.

I also met Santokh Singh, the Chief Police Officer of the State of Selangor, and an Honorary Prince. He was a very handsome and impressive man, and a friend of Hira's family. I had by this time reached the rank of Superintendent, which was enough to earn me respect from the Malaysian police officers that I met, some of whom had attended courses in the UK or America. I was treated very well, both in Ipoh and Kuala Lumpur. I made subsequent visits to Malaysia, and on one occasion was seen off at Kuala Lumpur Airport by Santokh, after his son's wedding, to which I had been invited. I was flying on Malaysian Airways, as far as Singapore, standard class of course.

He came out to the aircraft with me, and said to the Captain, 'This man will travel first class.' And I did! This does not happen at Heathrow or Gatwick. Santokh was a not infrequent visitor to the UK, as he was a lawyer as well as Chief Police Officer, and we spent some memorable times in his company.

During Hira and Kulwant's stay at the College, we had taken them both to an International Police Association dance at the Birmingham Police Training School. As there were no police officers other than those of Anglo-Saxon ancestry, and Kulwant in particular being a very handsome young man with a flamboyant taste in turbans, they attracted a lot of attention! Many of the Malaysians had no concept of how cold England can be in wintertime, and did not seem to have been very well briefed. Clothing was not always suitable, and we heard tales of earlier arrivals having failed to realise that in England we sleep under the bed clothes, not on top of them. Hira was a year ahead of Kulwant and when he went home we were introduced to Amarjeet and Gordon Hooi Khong Cheong who were starting their college courses.

Amarjeet was a very pretty girl, of Sikh ancestry. None of the three had seen snow before, and on one occasion, when we had invited them all to our police house for a meal, it snowed heavily. I got as near to the College as possible in my car, but eventually Kulwant and I had to carry Amarjeet through the snow, as her flimsy shoes and sari were not capable of coping with a real English winter! When the weather got a bit better, the three were keen to see as much as possible of the UK, and did travel around a lot. I suggested that we could all go and have a look at the Snowdon area. Unfortunately the chosen day became very 'welsh' and we all got soaked. I expect that near our mountains, but it was a bit of a shock for the others. This applied to Gordon in particular, as he fell into the river at Bettws-y-Coed. The river Conwy tends to be very cold, even in summer and poor Gordon travelled home in my sweater, at least three sizes too big, and then wore a pair of Jo's furry slippers to warm up his feet in front of our fire. However I have a nice photograph of a pre-immersion Gordon taking a photograph of Amarjeet taking a photograph of Kulwant posing before a wet boulder!

After being taken to Penang Island and a grand tour around Ipoh (meeting some rather mystified junior police officers I flew down to the southern tip of Peninsular Malaysia at Johor Bahru, to spend a few days with Amarjeet and her husband Mahendran and their two small daughters. Mahendran was then a Malaysian Government Immigration Officer in Johor, just across the Straits from Singapore. Finding their house after flying in to Singapore was an interesting exercise, but the welcome and hospitality were wonderful, and I stayed with them for three nights. Singapore, with its wartime history overtaken by a vibrant and exciting present was a wonderful place to visit.

We went as a group to the zoo, where an Orang Utang (the wild man of the forest) leapt unannounced and without invitation, into my arms, giving the two girls much pleasure at my surprise and slight horror! It was the subject of a number of photographs by giggling Singaporeans. The vast collection of weird statues in Haw Par Villa were a good backdrop for more photographs of poses in weird positions. Tiger Balm Gardens were delightful, and provided a chance to buy a little pot of Tiger Balm, which is reputed to cure any pain anywhere through external application. Now, some people might say that this was due to a placebo effect, but I do know that using it to massage my temples would cure a headache. Believe what you will! Many other parts of Singapore were also delightful, although as a big city with an international port it obviously had parts that were not so squeaky clean. The city centre was so clear of litter and graffiti – a result of the 'no tolerance' policy enforced by the then Prime Minister, Lee Kuan Yew. This went along with a no tolerance for other anti-social acts, and I felt, and still feel, a great regret that it was not possible to swap him for our useless bunch at Westminster, or at least to take a leaf from his book. Amarjeet and Mahendran and I also had a day out to Kota Tinggi, on the eastern coast, facing the South China Sea, where there are spectacular waterfalls.

This stay was another very happy few days, and it was with considerable sadness that I was lifted off from Singapore Airport by Air France for the long long journey home. I returned from Hira's wedding to duty in Wolverhampton with my appetite thoroughly whetted for work and travel in what were then mysterious, even to English eyes bizarre, countries. I had been treated unbelievably well, met so many friends, old and new, and seen a part of the world that not many English people of my generation and income, apart from soldiers, had then been given the opportunity to visit.

I am very glad to say that over forty years on we are still in touch with them all, apart from Hira, who sadly died in 2005. I and my son Al have stayed in their homes in Malaysia, whilst most of them have visited us in Wolverhampton. After a few years teaching Hira decided to qualify as a lawyer, and came back to the UK to do so. He eventually started a legal firm in Ipoh with his wife Asbir. We were rather taken aback one day when Hira telephoned to say that he was bringing his uncle, Judge Gill, to visit us. The Judge was in the UK for a time on legal business. They arrived in a very big and blindingly white Mercedes, which effectually blocked our cul-de-sac. It was a summer afternoon, so we had an English tea in the garden, but our deck-chairs ('budget buys' at that time!) were not particularly robust. I spent the afternoon convinced that the Judge would be deposited without warning onto our lawn. Fortunately it didn't happen, but the visitors were interesting for our children when they arrived home from school.

Kulwant and his wife Mohinder had moved to Tasmania after teaching for a while in Malaysia, and he was one of the first Sikhs to be accepted by Australia as an immigrant. I met them for the first time for many years during a wonderful visit to Australia, and stayed in Sydney with their son Roshan, who was then in the Australian Navy. I was taken, of course, to Bondi, and having also swum off a Hawaiian beach in Honolulu, Copacabana in Rio and on both sides of the Indian Ocean, feel that I have been very lucky to experience such places. Kulwant, also a visitor to Sydney, was not familiar with the city and Roshan was on sick leave and not able to drive. So we set off to Bondi, with Mohinder and Roshan in the back continually telling Kulwant to be careful and where to turn and so on.

Eventually, getting a bit tired of this he said, 'Oh, I am so glad that Mike is the only one not telling me what to do!'

A swim at Bondi was, however, well worth it. We are very pleased to welcome Mohinder to our home on her occasional visits to the UK. Kulwant usually stays at home in 'Tassie' to look after their smallholding, but came with her in 2009, which was great. I hope that one day it may be possible to visit them there.

An overnight journey on a Malaysian train is another interesting situation, not quite as glamorous as Bondi. The train that I caught on one visit was classed as a sleeper, but the beds were tiny compartments, approximately the size of a coffin, with no gender separation. One crawled in, struggled out of as many clothes as possible, and as one was surrounded by other coffins containing giggling Chinese girls, hoped not to have to get out again until morning! My son Al, having won a Scholarship from Wolverhampton Grammar School to study a foreign legal system at the age of seventeen chose Malaysia, and was hosted by first Hira and Asbir, and then Amarjeet and Mahendran. He also had a wonderful time, seeing a lot of Peninsular Malaysia and Singapore, but that is another story which I shall leave him to tell himself!

I should now rewind to 1953 – a time when sleeping surrounded by giggling Chinese girls was far from the expectations of most Englishmen. (Maybe the experience would not be quite so exceptional over fifty years on).

My initial police training had been at the Regional Centre at Mill Meece, near Stafford, a former Armed Forces training camp. It had not received much modernisation, and instead of fairies at the bottom of the garden we had the main Trent Valley railway line to London. Coal fired expresses pounded noisily past through most of the night. Drill and discipline were big features of the twelve week course, together with detailed lectures on how to deal with outbreaks of epizootic lymphangitis, other bovine illnesses and fowl pest. As an officer destined for the industrial area of Wolverhampton this was not tremendously essential knowledge, although, to be fair, not totally impossible to encounter. The fairly ferocious instructor who took drill also took unarmed combat. It was obvious that he felt that the worst thing that had ever happened to the Police Service was the introduction of women as uniformed officers. 'Bloody women' was a frequently used expression until one of the girls managed to put him on his back during an unarmed combat practice, to cheers from recruits of both genders.

Actually we had very little self-defence instruction, as my squad contained the ten thousandth recruit due to pass out from Mill Meece. We were scheduled to do a physical training display for the Home Office hierarchy and the Chief Officers who were attending, and it was thought more important to train for this and to learn about fowl pest than to be taught how to defend ourselves. Perhaps an odd set of priorities for prospective police officers, but rather in tune with the rest of the course, 'It's in the book, so that is the way you do it.' I did not, and do not, subscribe to this, and throughout the rest of my police career 'did it my way'. I would not dare to suggest that 'my way' was always right, but most of the time it seemed to work.

I also think that it is true to say that I learned more about being a police officer during a week or two of being 'shown round' by an experienced colleague than in the twelve weeks at the training centre. Obviously the academic learning was, and is, essential, but I did wonder at the time, and still do, if the 'mix' was right. We did, of course, do some role-play with instructors taking the parts of villains, but it never seemed to me that the practical needs had been thought through. For example we were not given any guidance whatsoever about how or why to protect a crime scene from damage by ourselves or through intrusion by others. Since the first police officer at a serious crime scene – say a murder – is almost always a uniformed Constable, sometimes very junior, one would have expected this to be basic and elementary. No, it was left to be worked out by oneself, or by word of mouth from colleagues. Surprising.

I think now that almost certainly the Home Office had an interfering hand in the Training Centre syllabi, which, if true, says something about the practical common sense in that Department of State. Then as now. In fact as a Constable I was the first at the scene at two murders, a manslaughter, several suicides and sudden deaths which could have been murders, and many lesser crimes. However, I knew a lot about fowl pest! As a more experienced Constable I was involved in doing role-play myself to train our Special Constables. There was an annual competition, held in the Town Hall, and attended by the Mayor and Chief Constable.

It was run very much on the lines of a TV show, 'Thank God you're here' where 'celebrities' are put into an unrehearsed and unexpected scene and have to try to play it through with other actors who know what they are doing! Our poor 'Specials', not usually as articulate as the celebrities in the game show, were faced with some sort of unrehearsed crime or disorder, and were marked on how they dealt with it. This gave those of us who had volunteered (for a bit of fun and a change) to be the victims or villains, an absolutely wonderful chance to ham it up. We were supposed to work to an approximate script prepared by the Training Inspector, but I have to say that this did not always happen. Well, in defence, real police work is always unpredictable and rarely runs to a script! I do remember running after one Special, who was gallantly marching his prisoner off the stage. I brandished a plateful of absolutely horribly congealed mess of left-over fish and chips which we had begged from the canteen. He heard me crying, 'Don't forget the evidence Officer', but the poor guy really did not know whether to loose the prisoner and grab the plate or tell me to sod off. Hopefully it taught him to consider priorities!

The display at Mill Meece for the Chief Officers, followed by a march past, consisted of a series of PE exercises without verbal orders by about fifty recruits, male and female, timed to co-ordinate with a well known marching song, *Imperial Echoes*. Even now I cannot hear that music without needing to swing my arms above my head or touch my toes or both. I am quite glad to say that it isn't played very often nowadays.

The highlight was the whole fifty jumping one after the other over an immense vaulting horse. One recruit 'made a back' by kneeling on top of the horse, raising the height to be cleared to fearsome proportions. I am still not decided whether the mildly psychopathic Instructor hoped that it would be a faultless display of physical fitness, training and skill, or an instrument of revenge on the women recruits. Perhaps he felt that it would introduce some light relief for the assembled brass if most of us knocked the kneeling man off his perch. Being both a PE and self-defence Instructor and a Drill Sergeant he was almost certainly a sadist as well!

Needless to say this really was a frightening prospect, more of being made fools of in front of our Chief Constables rather than being hurt. We had a springboard at the foot of the horse, but it was still a hell of a height, and regularly failing in practice did not calm the nerves. Again needless to say, the one man who could do it easily, being a slim six foot two and a school athletics winner was the man who was let off the jump to 'make the back'. In the event we all did it, to much applause, but wow, I don't think that I have ever been so frightened by a prospect, even by the Chinese Army and Police in Lhasa. (More about this even later still)! In the fullness of time, my son Al appeared in an Oxfam fundraising photograph with the England footballer Gary Lineker jumping over his back, leapfrog style. Great publicity but, I have to say, not as high a jump!

Having completed the initial police training undamaged I returned to Wolverhampton and was housed in the single men's quarters, Penn Hall, which stood in the highest part of Wolverhampton, with a splendid view south to the Malvern Hills. It had been the mansion of one of the Victorian industrial magnates, and was taken over by the town council. It is now, in the twenty first century, in use as a special school, so the city are still benefiting from the industrial boom which sent goods from Wolverhampton all over the world and made it one of the most prosperous towns in England. In 1953 it housed ten single men, all full of energy and high spirits. Rather as I had found in the Royal Air Force, there was not too much that could not, or had not been done – at least when off duty!

At this time cricket came back in to my life. Wolverhampton, for a small Force, had a very effective cricket team, led by a Sergeant (later Chief Superintendent) who was a former Naval Officer and a very good and stylish batsman. I had played for the team as a Cadet, being good enough for a place through my fielding, and was welcomed back with open arms. As a Cadet I had also taken part in some swimming relay races for the police team, and qualified as a 'life saver' during the Mill Meece training. I was awarded a rather nice badge to be sewn onto my swimming trunks, that our border collie 'Pip', who lived with my parents, managed to get hold of and savaged to death! Cricket however has had a place in my family since before the end of the nineteenth century. My Grandfather was a player, a bowler, and the Secretary of Bridgnorth Cricket Club. My Father, a batsman, was also Secretary in his turn although his playing days were interrupted by the First World War.

Our house in Bridgnorth was on the edge of what was, and still is, a very beautiful ground, with facilities good enough for Shropshire to regularly play Minor Counties Championship fixtures on. In 2009 and 10 it was nominated as the best ground in Shropshire. All I had to do was to pass through a convenient gap in our garden hedge to get onto the ground. Bridgnorth has a place in cricket history, as Sidney Barnes the famous England bowler played for them as a professional in his later years. Cyril Washbrook, who was opening bat for Lancashire and opened many English Test innings with Len Hutton, was educated at Bridgnorth Grammar School, and married a local girl. He played many times for Bridgnorth, until snapped up by Lancashire, for whom he had a birth qualification.

Many international cricketers have played at Bridgnorth, apart from Washbrook, who was one of our own. The Club often hosted County sides, like Warwickshire and Glamorgan who frequently included English Test players, and nowadays the Birmingham League sides have First Class Counties players available. In the fifties the club was an excellent training ground for young cricketers, some of whom went on to play in County Cricket. The Club regularly took a team on tour in the West Country, and in 1952 went on tour in Somerset.

Having met Jo the year before, and both of us feeling by then that it was serious, I decided to make the most of being in the West Country once more. I rented a car again, more easily than in the previous year and took a couple of days leave of absence. It was too tempting, and too easy to neglect the cricket to make sure that I saw her during that week. Perhaps if it had not been for that week the romance might not have prospered – we were a long way apart, there was no M5 and not much money. Contact had been principally by letters and 'phone calls, and even the latter was difficult then. They had no telephone so she had to go, with permission, to the Manor House, one of the few families in the village to have a telephone. I used to call at a pre-arranged time from a 'phone box with a pocket literally full of change.

However, I think that my absences from the cricket tour helped to cement our affair. I did get into trouble for neglecting practice, but had decided where my priorities lay. I was able to be present though, with the team, on one interesting occasion. We had all purchased very smart scarlet blazers with the club badge on the pocket, in order to make a show. We had a fixture with a Somerset Eleven on the County Ground at Taunton. As the Australian Test team, with a host of world famous names - Ray Lindwall and Keith Miller for example - were due to play Somerset a couple of days later we were ambushed, in mistaken identity, by the whole of the juvenile population of Taunton. It was rather nice to be able to masquerade as Lindwall or Miller. The moral is don't believe everything you might read in an autograph album!

From the age of thirteen or fourteen I had regularly gone through the gap in the hedge every Spring and Summer evening to use the nets, to help with rolling the pitch, cutting the grass, getting ready for the next match, and take part in pretty well everything else going on in the Club. Many of the playing members had recently returned to Bridgnorth from the Armed Forces and were somewhat of heroes to me. I was still hoping for a flying career when called up, and shared interests between cricket, boxing and the Air Training Corps, for the latter cycling the twenty eight miles round trip to Wolverhampton. I was also a Rover and King's Scout, and through this attended a Parade and Service at St. George's Chapel, Windsor.

All this probably explains why I just, just, just scraped through the Oxford School Certificate. I do rather wish, now, that I had been more interested in schoolwork, but cannot believe that I could have foregone those wonderful summer evenings. The sun always shone, the grass was emerald green and when newly cut smelled gorgeous, and it was possible to be still in the nets, with like-minded people, at 10 p.m. I have now rejoined the Club as a Vice-President, to enjoy sunny weekend afternoons, and was asked to propose the toast to the Club at the 2008 annual dinner. I used those remembered summer evenings as the basis for my toast. I'm told that Cyril Washbrook's grandson also played for the Club as a professional. Full circle again.

With a Grandfather who was a bowler, a Father who was a batsman and all those evenings of practice I guess that I should have been an all-rounder. This however, was not to be. My strength was in fielding, and I can say truthfully that on a good day, with the wind behind me, I could be very good, indeed being described as 'brilliant' in the press over one piece of work (the cutting still exists, for those who doubt!) I am proud that I have some photographs of myself in the first eleven, selected for my fielding and the occasional innings where I stayed in while other people got some runs. I played more regularly for the second team though, from about fourteen until police shift work made it impossible some ten to twelve years later.

I also played for Bridgnorth Grammar School Old Boys team (for whom Cyril Washbrook was also qualified – wow!). Some of these were on the Bridgnorth Club ground in the annual knock-out competition. However, I was involved in a 'knock-out' of my own, in a match against the School X1, on the school pitch, which was less than perfect. Facing a young man who had had a recent trial as a fast bowler for Worcestershire, I completely failed to spot one which reared up and was laid flat out. This was well before batsmen's helmets became a la mode! (Softies now, I reckon.) I still have the dent in the middle of my forehead, which I was able to exhibit with pride whilst chatting about cricket to a former Indian Test star in Kuala Lumpur years later. I did manage to pick myself up, and 'retired hurt', but was rather surprised to be called on to thank the school for their hospitality during the tea interval. I hate to think what I might have said, still being rather far away with the fairies!

Penn Hall was a good place to be. There was a tennis court, I had parking for the Hillman and there were a number of ladies who cooked and ran the place for us very effectively. Being young, all ex-armed forces, and fit there was quite a lot of surplus energy to be dissipated, with often not too long a time allowed for sleeping. Early Turn, as it was called, started at 5.45 a.m. and you had to be there. No excuses were allowed, and one that I had frequently used in my school days, 'I found my bicycle with a flat tyre, Sir,' would have been met with a response of, 'You must get up early enough to walk here if necessary'. One of our number owned a huge old pre-war car, which, with a pinch could accommodate six or seven bodies.

Parking near the police station was very restricted so we tended to all pile into this, and the sight of seven uniformed officers scrambling for a seat, helmets flying all over the place, with about three minutes to cover the three miles from Penn Hall would have certainly been good for an episode of the Keystone Cops. Getting on Parade, adjusting uniforms and usually yawning would also have been a sight. 'Produce Appointments' was called by the Duty Sergeant, when all present had to produce their notebooks, handcuffs and staff. (Oddly enough it didn't seem to matter whether one had a writing implement or not!) The media seem to invariably call the staff a truncheon - perhaps this is the correct historical term, but I have yet to meet a police officer who would call it that.

The fact of our consistently hurried departure from Penn Hall often meant that one or the other 'appointment' got left behind. As this was another cardinal sin, on a level with being late on parade, some last second panic scrabbling and bargaining for a spare in the Parade Room was quite common. After parade we were marched out by the Duty Sergeant into the town centre, then to disperse to our beats. This let the public know that we were around – not done nowadays, but not a bad idea? I have discussed later, in the section about the South Pacific, the smartness, pride and dignity of the police band in Western Samoa as they march each morning to the daily flag raising ceremony in Apia. They are obviously very proud of their country, - and why not? Is there a lesson there somewhere for our police chiefs?

Another regular irritating unreality in film or TV programmes is where a police car is driven as fast as possible up to premises where suspects are believed to be, with the sirens and blue lights on full blast. This is the exact opposite of how it was done in real life, where 'softly softly' was much more likely to 'catchee monkey'. Even the engine and normal lights would be turned off for the last few yards, in order to sneak up to the building. Unfortunately I was starting to see, towards the end of my service, that real life was beginning to ape fiction, with young police officers having been brought up on a visual diet of incorrect, and rather stupid, techniques. It sets my teeth on edge to see a prisoner or suspect put into the back seat of a police car, behind the driver. In real life you don't ever do that, they go in the back on the passenger side, for reasons which seem to me to be obvious, and even then must be handcuffed and escorted.

A different modern exasperation comes from crime novels, and film and TV programmes, where the investigating police officer meticulously calls the suspect or even prisoner 'Sir' after almost every word. In twenty five years service I did not have occasion to use that honorific much, and certainly not to prisoners or suspects. It was not usual either for anyone being reported for a summary offence to be addressed in that way, unless there was a reason for doing so. One might use 'Sir' or 'Madam' occasionally in the early stages of an enquiry or interview, or where it might help to build a bridge, but there was no requirement to do so and certainly not repeatedly. I do not think that mine was a unique attitude amongst my colleagues.

How do the various myths in programmes featuring the police arise? I know of one former police officer who advised on films and TV. He was asked why he was giving incorrect advice.

The reply was, 'I tell them how it should be, but they say that the public would not expect it that way!'

It certainly isn't, or wasn't, real life. A police officer was required to be polite, but not servile. In normal conversation, with people other than those arrested or under suspicion, the respectful title was given to people who appeared to deserve it, as well as police officers of a higher rank, and those of status such as Royalty, senior military officers, Lord Mayors, local dignitaries or senior politicians. I doubt that, if still serving, I would include many of the latter two nowadays, and they would have to be content with Mr.

Almost every author writing a crime or detective story seems to think that policemen are addicted to using the phrase 'bang to rights', as in 'we've caught you bang to rights'. I have news for them! I have never, ever, heard it in the real world, either during my service or during the many contacts with the police since. I cannot imagine any genuine police officer using such synthetic language, and it certainly is not 'police jargon'. What does it mean anyway? We did not all drop our 'aitches', or 'proceed' to wherever we were going and I never heard, 'It's a fair cop' either! Some of us actually had an IQ of over 160, which is likely to be unbelievable news to most fiction writers, many of whom seem not to live in, or to have experienced, the real world.

Another irritating misconception amongst the writers of detective stories is that uniformed officers did not get involved in investigations, and that these are solely the prerogative of detectives. Save for serious crimes this was simply not true, and it was not a 'promotion' to be nominated a detective. My colleagues and I investigated many crimes as uniformed officers, including serious assaults, riots, sexual crimes, theft, housebreaking and of course motor vehicle crime. There were times when CID involvement became a hindrance and an encumbrance, and I could get better results on my own. Writers of crime fiction or screen plays, even well known ones, all seem to be hooked on another myth, that police officers, detectives especially, cannot exist for more than an hour or two without a serious intake of alcohol. Whilst it is no doubt true for some, it certainly was not, and, I believe, still is not a universal habit. Journalists usually do rather better than novelists in the accuracy stakes, except for muddling police ranks and responsibilities, which my local paper seems quite unable to grasp.

A similar situation in regard to myths exists with novels about war. My RAF Volunteer Reserve friend Doug, whom I mentioned earlier, was a member of the Royal Air Force Pathfinder Force in Lancaster bombers during the 1939-45 war, and completed fifty two sorties. He could, I think, be expected to know how things were during bombing raids. I asked for his comments about one particular, highly praised and well reviewed, novel about the Pathfinders. He said that the main theme of the book was quite impossible, and that it had many inaccuracies throughout. Perhaps one can expect a film or TV programme to dramatise and compress events, but surely a book could stick closer to the truth? The argument that events have to be dramatised to make them interesting is correct as far as it goes, but there has to be a core of believable truth. I have seen enough events that needed no dramatisation. This is rather like the 'dumbing down' which has taken place in so many so-called comedies, which are actually only pratfall slapstick or offensive unpleasantness. To be genuinely funny there needs to be a contrasting theme of sadness or pathos, something that seems to have been almost entirely lost sight of.

Helmets! British police helmets, as worn in film or TV, are invariably shown with the incorrectly described chinstrap under the chin, where it looks silly. In fact the correct method is to have the strap just under the lower lip, and I only ever saw one real police officer do otherwise. Since the wretched thing fell off anyway whenever one had to run there was a real point in making it as comfortable as possible while walking. Although they were a handicap in a chase or a struggle I know that I was proud to wear one and to be following the historical precedent. I strongly resent the imitation policemen who seem to be now allowed to wear them.

In the fifties and sixties police officers were also kitted out with an extremely thick and heavy greatcoat, which did keep out the cold on a winter's night, but did not help one to run fast. It weighed a ton when wet. Getting a much shorter driving coat when joining the motor patrol was a bonus, as the legs could move! The traditional policeman's cape was also thick and heavy, and did, until completely soaked, keep off the rain pretty well. We had a drying room at the Station, which was a bonus on a wet January night shift! The cape actually had a considerable additional value. Carried folded over one shoulder, with the heavy collar, metal numbers and 'dogs' (lion's head and chain used to fasten the cape) at the end, it could be used as a shield against a knife or club attack. It could even, when swung hard, be used in an offensive role. I doubt very much if the Home Office had even thought of this. Perhaps it was when they did that we lost the cape. While I am, perhaps cynically, not sure that the police service has moved forward from those days, I do envy the modern Constable his lighter weight weather protection. You needed to be fit to carry ours when it got wet. Of course, we did not have to carry so much ancillary equipment as the twenty first century man struggles with, until the big and heavy portable radios came into use. Nowadays perhaps, if the question were asked, 'What are policemen?' the answer might be, 'Someone to hang things on!'

On the subject of helmets, one quickly discovered their one huge disadvantage on duty at Molineux, the Wolverhampton Wanderers football stadium. In the 1950's Wolves were a First Division team (the First Division was then the top flight – the equivalent of the Premiership today). They had proved themselves to be unofficial world champions and the best club team in the world against international opposition, beating Real Madrid, the Russian Spartak and Dynamo teams and the Hungarian Honved, who previously had been considered the best of the best. These matches were under the newly installed floodlights. They won the League championship three times between 1950 and 1960, were runners-up three times and third twice and won the FA Cup in 1949 and 1960. They also regularly provided three men, sometimes more, for the England team – simultaneously!

We were very pleased to be associated with them and prided ourselves on keeping trouble to a minimum and getting the regular 40,000 crowd away quickly. The helmet disadvantage came about a few minutes before the half and full time whistles, when we put officers up onto the edge of the pitch to stop crowd invasions. There were no barriers in those days; it was down to physical presence and the respect for the police which generally still prevailed. During those two or three minutes before play ended it was crucial to watch in one direction for the ball as it might easily be rocketing towards you at full speed, whilst still keeping an eye on the crowd. It was also a requirement to keep moving, as the crowd were not too impressed with anyone blocking their view. If there was snow on the terraces it was essential too to keep an eye wide open in the other direction for snowballs, which occasionally (especially if we were playing Chelsea) had a stone in the middle. Anyone unfortunate enough to lose a helmet from either cause quickly found out what it was like to be laughed at (and cheered) by 40,000 people. As we had a few comedians I think that this may have occasionally happened deliberately.

When the teams had left the field we provided the half time entertainment on snowy days. One learned how it felt to be a duck in a fairground shooting gallery. It was a relaxation for most of the crowd to see who could knock a helmet off. It was impossible to stop or prevent it, and one just had to keep a very wary eye on the crowd and be prepared to do a sidestep or duck. Doing either whilst retaining some semblance of dignity was not easy. I should say that, in those days, with most visiting teams this half time show was fairly good natured, and an agile bit of footwork would usually get a cheer. The bobby was not really seen as an enemy. However there were some teams that we did not enjoy having as visitors. I had to walk through and up a gangway in the 'Away Supporters Stand' once when Wolves were playing Chelsea. At the top I found that the back of my uniform overcoat was covered with thick gobs of spittle. Again, nothing to be done about it – it is not possible to arrest over a thousand people.

A soccer fixture definitely needing riot control in the town centre was when Glasgow Rangers came to play a 'friendly' and brought half the Gorbals with them by train! We 'borrowed' some Staffordshire horses for that one, not having our own, and they were invaluable. I believe that the Mounted Branch has now been discontinued in a number of Forces. I cannot understand this, unless it is purely on financial grounds, as the horses were certainly of use during crowd disorder, and yet were a splendid Police/Public relations factor at open days, or when on patrol, at least amongst decent people.

The Molineux Stadium was on a beat which frequently fell to me, and one night, about 2 a.m., I found one of the doors unlocked. After checking out the offices and before calling out the key-holder, I walked all round, and went onto the pitch. Being completely deserted of course it was a bit eerie, but I shot a couple of penalties past Bert Williams, of Wolves and England, who was reckoned to be certainly the best keeper in England, and arguably in the world, at that time. I heard a huge cheer when I scored. He doesn't mention those two penalties in his recent book – guess he never even saw them! I am tempted to say that I used my helmet in lieu of the imaginary ball that night, but that would be stretching an otherwise true story a bit too far!

I was present at the floodlit matches against Spartak, Dynamo and Honved, and can remember the 'electricity' that flowed around the capacity crowd, particularly when Wolves scored the winning goal against Honved, after being two down. It was tangible enough to bite on, it raised the hairs on the back of your neck and ran shivers up and down the spine. I think that sparks could almost have been seen as people hugged each other. I have been in some strange, even bizarre situations since then, but have never felt quite like that again.

Police headgear came into focus again when I became responsible for the police arrangements at West Bromwich Albion – another First Division (pre-Premiership) team at that time. I used to take my son, then aged about fourteen and perennially hungry. I could get him a good place in the front row of the wing stands. As senior police officer one was invited into the Director's Room at half time for coffee and (invariably) salmon and cucumber sandwiches. It was easy to grab a handful, wrap them in a paper napkin, put them inside my uniform cap, stroll down the touchline and, as surreptitiously and nonchalantly as possible hand them to Al, whilst trying to look as absolutely normal as I could. Nobody ever complained, but I did sometimes wonder what the people on either side of him made of it. I reckon that one can get away with almost anything if you look confident and as if it is meant to be!

The Constable's uniform helmet did have an advantage over the officer's flat cap, in that there was a usable space inside it. It was not unknown for certain PCs on night shift to sneak thirty minutes shut-eye on a cold and wet night shift – there was always some sort of shelter to be found, but they had to be sure of waking up after not too long a snooze. This was where an alarm clock, carried on parade inside the helmet, was essential. The alarm clocks of the 1950s were not the sleek sophisticated ones of today but miniature 'Big Bens'. They would have been too obvious in a tunic pocket but could just about be fitted inside the helmet.

However this practice ceased after one hilarious occasion when a wound up alarm clock went off, just as the Duty Sergeant called, 'Attention, produce appointments!'

I saw an unusual, but valuable, use of a police horse, outside the stadium after one of the matches at West Brom in the '70s. A fan boasting a long woollen football scarf had been causing trouble, and a mounted officer had managed to seize both ends of the scarf, lift him up and carry him, legs dangling a good foot above the ground, towards the police van. Not policy but very appropriate and effective, so I said nothing! It was a pleasure to find that Wolves and West Brom would both be in the Premiership for the 2010/11 season, as I had a lot to do with both of them. Also that the other two West Midlands big teams, Birmingham City and Aston Villa would be in the Premiership during that season. I did some air traffic control for Birmingham City, but my only connection with Villa is that they would have been my maternal Grandfather's home team!

The Early Turn finished at 2 p.m. or if necessary whenever you were through, and went on for fourteen days. At the end of that time there were two days off, Saturday and Sunday, before starting fourteen nights, 9.45 p.m. to 6am. Even with our fitness and energy the two days off were a necessity. I did use the Hillman, and later the Panther motor cycle, that I bought when the Hillman turned into an engagement ring, to travel down to the West Country. I hope that I was not too bad tempered on those weekends. As Early Turn was followed by nights we had the equivalent of an extra day tacked on to the two days off, making it a reasonable weekend. However this was paid for by the quick changeover from nights onto Late Turn, which was 1.45 p.m. to 10 p.m. The change over itself was tiring, and Late Turn was the one on which incidents tended to happen, so you worked until you finished. We did not have any clocking on or off, but you did have to be signed off. This was sensible, as Inspectors had to be sure that all their officers had returned safely to the Station.

Having passed the car licence test at seventeen I naturally considered myself to be an extremely experienced driver, but had no knowledge of motor bikes, as my parents had bought the BSA three wheeler to keep me off them. However, I now realise that I was earmarked as a potential patrol car driver, as our Police car fleet became expanded and modernised. It was apparently thought necessary that several of us should be put through the motor bike licence test with a view to future deployment. We had an 'in-house' examiner, and a motor cycle combination, with a wooden box as a sidecar. The examiner, another former Naval Officer, who knew and used quite a few interesting words of abuse, took us to an area of common ground near Penn Hall and sat back to let us find out for ourselves how to manipulate it. What a good training technique! In theory, with three wheels instead of two a 'combo' does not require any sense of balance, but the police bike, old and tired, was an evil piece of machinery, and did not always go where it was pointed. One of our number, Ken, who had been a prisoner of the Japanese on the Burma Railway, was first to go, and rode it straight into a nearby duck pond. More interesting language, some of it submerged and some, I think, Japanese. Eventually I got the hang of it, and later swapped the solo Panther for a Norton 'Big Four' and Watsonian sidecar which Jo and I took to Paris in 1959 via the ferry and some cobbled French roads. No Chunnel!

The sidecar was not very well sprung, and she had a large bruise on her bottom on arrival. We did actually cause quite a stir in Paris, as at that time the French only used motor cycle combinations to carry working tools etc, in a box on wheels, rather like the evil Wolverhampton Police machine. Perhaps that's where it came from, as a bit of war booty. A passenger, especially a female one, in the sidecar was very definitely an unusual event to the Parisians, and we gathered interested crowds every time she got in or out, as if we were off to the moon! In view of the length of the journey to Paris I rigged up a communications system, using a length of old gas tubing with a tun-dish(a funnel!)taped to each end. Passed through the roof of the sidecar this worked surprisingly well, the only snag being that we could not both talk at once, and it had to be 'over to you' after each query or comment. This was also of interest to the Parisian crowds. I have thought since that I should have patented this device. Might have been worth a fortune before mobile 'phones.

The 'Big Four' was a very reliable but slow old beast, designed for a sidecar. Keeping up with the racing traffic from traffic light to traffic light in the Champs Elysees was a challenge, despite my expertise learned with the evil machine near the duck pond. The French method was, and is, to go full revs away from every light, then stamp very hard on the brakes at the next red one. The Norton could not cope with this, neither throttle nor brake wise. This was perhaps not so much of an interest to the Parisians as an irritation. They drove with panache, even then!   I do not have to look for sinister causes for the death of Princess Diana; the French style of driving provides enough reasons.

The Norton was behaving well, and we drove out of Paris to Chartres to visit the old town and the Cathedral one day. We also managed to do the proper tourist things in Paris, like a visit to the Moulin Rouge and going up the Tower. Two particular things are memorable. Going out for a meal one evening we found our way to the Café de la Paix. Money was not plentiful, so we carefully examined the menu outside before going in, and decided that it could just be done on that day's budget. The Head Waiter bowed and scraped (we were not in motor cycling gear) and Madame's coat was carefully put away and after being ushered to a good table we revisited the menu. Shock, horror! It bore no relationship to the one outside, and we could afford virtually nothing! What we did not know was that at that time (and may still be, but I have never dared to go back) there were two ends of the Restaurant, one reasonably and the other unreasonably priced. We had entered through the unreasonable entrance. We could only escape with as much dignity as possible. I hope that I gave the impression that we had decided to go somewhere better, but I doubt it.

The other memory is similar, as Nortoning through the Bois de Bologne we spotted an attractive open air Restaurant under some beautiful trees. Just the place for lunch. After taking off all the motor-bike gear and sitting down, again with a bow and a scrape, we found that this time we could actually afford something from the menu. Unfortunately it was only a banana and a glass of lemonade each. Still, we made them last, and enjoyed the ambience! It was a good holiday, despite the prices!

On the way home, as the Norton was still thumping away nicely, we diverted to spend a couple of days at Dovercourt, near Colchester, ostensibly for the beach but actually to find some food that we could afford. Having got to and from Paris with never a problem we got lost on this bit. Our visit to Paris co-incided with a State Visit by President Eisenhower to France, and we were lucky enough to see him and President De Gaulle process down the Champs, with an escort of beautifully groomed and accoutred horses, and extremely smart motor cycles, both from the Guard Republicaine. As both Presidents were still very news-worthy, the escort was picked up by the British Press and named 'Ike's Bikes'. I have never been a Francophile, but have to say that I was impressed by the smartness, courtesy and efficiency of both the Agents (city police) and Gendarmes during this holiday.

'Ike's Bikes' were particularly interesting as by then I was alternating Squad Car duties with motor cycling. We had a team of scarlet B.S.A.500 cc solos, with big windshields and leg shields – the nearest thing available then to a full fairing. They did look very smart, especially used in pairs, and, I think, as good as De Gaulle's escort. We were tasked to operate, as much as possible, as a 'Courtesy Patrol', to pick up on bad road behaviour, and either to issue a word of advice, a warning or a summons as appropriate. Motor cycles were being fitted with radios at that time, with the radio pack behind the rider and above the rear wheel. This did tend to make the bike unstable and ninety was about the most it was safe to do on them. In most circumstances this was fast enough, as they were only used within the urban area. It seems unbelievable now, but when I first got onto the police bikes we rode them without helmets, just a flat peaked cap, with the strap down under the chin to hold it on. Then came the legislation, and we got the 'corker', not very good looking but certainly safer. Clothing had also been informal – it was in order to ride without a tunic, just shirtsleeves on a hot day. Minimal protection, no health and safety issues!

A few years later, having completed the police advanced motor cycling course, (during which I became used to falling off, on the grass) I became involved in some competitive motor cycling, with a colleague, Joe, also a police motor cyclist. He and I were involved together in a number of later occasions, both on and off duty, and he is still a friend. Joe had been a motor cyclist for, I think, most of his life, and was very much into trials riding. He was very well known in this sport, and also the faster world of motor cycle racing, particularly motor cycles and sidecars. I am sure his name is still well known amongst those with similar interests. Joe had thought that it would be a good idea to start a Wolverhampton Police Trials Team, and with myself and one or two other people interested, we started practising on the 'pit-bonks' where old open-cast mining had left scarred, undulating muddy ground, with pools in wet weather and short but extremely steep slopes.

Joe had a bike which I used to practice on, and on which I had many a spill while trying to accumulate some expertise! Trials are not competitions involving speed, but accuracy in slow, very difficult riding over the trickiest course that the organisers can find, and a requirement to stay aboard the machine. Points are lost for every time a foot touches the ground, with every section being closely observed. They are described as 'The Olympics of motor cycling' in one current advertisement on the Internet! The bikes are highly specialised, lightweight, with minimal or no seats as one has to stand on the footrests to negotiate the sections. It was disconcerting to be heading up a 1 in 3 slope and suddenly by getting the balance wrong, to be heading downhill at speed! Scrambling, or motocross, is doing a similar thing on a much smoother course, racing the other competitors so that speed is of the essence. Both sports teach great throttle control, balance and machine handling. The UK and Spain are the two countries where Trials riding is most popular – seems rather a strange combination.

We continued practising on the pit-bonks and in an old quarry – the Black Country abounds with such ideal places, and entered some trials locally, with Joe usually getting either a prize or a mention, but the rest of us docked too much for 'paddling', i.e. feet touching the ground too many times. Just occasionally it was good to complete a section 'clean'! (Although invariably no-one comes away from competing in a trial 'clean' in the conventional sense!) We also entered the Services Trial several times in the early 1960's as the Wolverhampton Police Team. The Services Trial was quite a prestigious event, held at Bordon in Hampshire on the very rough tank training ground of the Army School of Mechanical Transport, and open to all the armed forces and emergency services. Predictably the army dominated this, and we did not win any prizes, but we had some great times and made a lot of friends, particularly amongst the Metropolitan Police team. We all slept in Joe's small caravan one year, parking it in the middle of the barrack square at Bordon. As the army seemed to be always going home for the weekend in those days, nobody bothered us! I was on holiday with Jo at her home in Somerset the next year, so drove up to Bordon, taking her Father and cousin Terry with me as supporters. As her Father had been a despatch rider at one point during his wartime army service I am sure that he enjoyed it, and would probably have liked to have taken part!

We borrowed - drawing on Joe's extensive contacts in the sport - specialised machinery from the BSA factory in Small Heath, Birmingham. This was another great experience, to meet the old craftsmen who loved their job. What a tragedy that such a British icon went, along with so many others due, I believe, partly to inept and short sighted management. Regrettably in 1966, with the amalgamation of the Police Forces in the West Midlands, our team had to be disbanded, all of us going to different areas and responsibilities, Joe as the second in command of the new Force Traffic Department. He was required by the Chief Constable to initiate, recruit, train and command a police motor cycle display team, including an officer from each Division of the Force, and, using regular police bikes, standing on each other's shoulders and similar mad stunts! This was to promote police/public relations and to help bind the Divisions from the constituent Forces together. It was extremely successful for a time, until the men in suits, the bean-counters put their oar in. Who knows, if we could have stayed together as a trials team we might even have beaten the Army or Royal Marines! However, we competed, and tried.

I had rather more individual success with another venture into extra-curricular motor cycling, at around the same period, whilst a Sergeant. At that time there was an annual national competition 'The Motor Cyclist of the Year', with heats held in various towns and cities around the U.K. A colleague and I were allowed to enter the Wolverhampton heat, using regular police bikes, in competition with 29 other entrants. There was an observed five miles road run, plus some manoeuvring such as figure of eight slow riding, balancing on a narrow plank, an obstacle course with oil drums, clearance judging and an emergency stop, followed by some questions. I am quite pleased to record that I won the heat, which excited the 'Express and Star' tremendously, as I had done so with dropping a point! They reported it, but unfortunately using a photograph from their archives, showing an extremely dishevelled policeman emerging from a house just after being attacked with a sword. They could have asked for an heroic winning pose! Once more I do not think that it did my career any harm, the publicity, even the `photo with uniform cap somewhat askew, providing good reading for the Chief Constable and Watch Committee members. I was allowed to use the same police machine to get to the final, held at Brands Hatch racing circuit, where I had already done some single seater car racing training. It was, I suppose, a bit unusual to take a police motor bike all the way on public roads and through bits of London, but the police signs, front and rear, were covered up so that I could not get involved in anything. I did not cover myself with glory by winning the final, but it was a great occasion, and I did not disgrace myself or the Force. Some you win . . . .!

In the mid 1970s I had progressed through the ranks sufficiently to get involved in more motor sport, this time on four wheels. No one should ever doubt that motor racing is a very quick way of becoming a minor millionaire. Provided that you start as a major millionaire! All motor sport is expensive, and racing and rallying especially so. Although I was flattered to be invited to teach at a rally school, and actually did so, I was never able to enter a rally myself, as one has to be able to stand the total write-off costs of your steed, through one's own resources or factory sponsorship. The same applies to single seater track racing, except that as a member of a Racing Driver's Club it is possible to pay to use their well insured machinery. There have been a few special people who made it directly into a sponsored team, former garage mechanic and World Champion Graham Hill probably the best known Brit to do so. I did not possess that extraordinary talent.

The other essential ingredient is to start early enough. At over forty I quickly discovered that I no longer had the immortal sense of invulnerability or aggression that goes along with being nineteen or twenty. The mind set now is 'If I turn this over it's going to hurt.' The young do not think this way! Experience can (given the right attitude) compensate for increasing reaction times and older eyesight on public roads. High speed racing, even if everyone is going the same way for most of the time, is very different. However, I had enough skills to survive through several seasons of competitive Formula Ford single seater racing at Silverstone and Snetterton. I even achieved a prize – on this occasion a third place. I was far enough ahead of the rest of the field to be convinced that I was winning. Unfortunately two other cars were even further ahead! The prize presentations that year were at a black tie dinner dance at the very plush De Vere Hotel in Coventry, so Jo had a nice evening as well.

I did well enough to obtain the RAC National Racing Competition licence, which has to be earned. To be eligible one has to finish in at least six Club races at two different circuits with no adverse report from the RAC Stewards. I took my 14 year old son to one or two of these. I expect that, as a spectator, they did not seem very exciting to him, but with your bottom about three inches above the track at 120mph, the corners come up very quickly indeed, and the guy in front seems only inches away from your front wheels. In the rain it gets really exciting, as you can no longer see the guy in front, or the corners! So, I did not turn one over or hurt myself, and it was an enjoyable, if expensive time. But, in 1978, with retirement from the police service, and a new job, the world changed. There is a Yiddish proverb, 'Men tracht und Gott lacht'. Man plans and God laughs. About right I guess.

Many years after our Norton and sidecar trip to Paris I revisited the Champs Elysees as Chief Driving Examiner for the Royal Society for the Prevention of Accidents. A Company with whom we had an advanced driver training contract had posted a man to Paris. He was less than happy about Parisian driving habits and standards. I was flown from Birmingham Airport to Charles De Gaulle in the early hours, met the client and we spent the day driving up and down the Champs, and round and round the Peripherique until he was a bit more relaxed. I returned to Birmingham the same day, at a cost of £266 for the flights, plus the cost of my time. This appeared in the 1987 Guinness Book of Records as 'the most expensive driving lesson ever'!

At around that time, whilst working for RoSPA, the BBC asked me to do a road safety talk on driving abroad. I decided to use a commentary, that is talking aloud while driving about the hazards that are in view and the action that the driver intends to take. This is a very effective way of concentrating the mind and recognising dangers. I agreed to drive around Birmingham City Centre with a reporter holding a mike, and myself commenting as if we were driving in the centre of Paris. This was quite interesting as it required talking about things as if driving on the right, whilst actually being on the conventional left. (And substituting the Arc de Triomph for the Birmingham Law Courts). Good for improving concentration! It obviously worked quite well, as a couple of days later I bumped into (on foot) the RoSPA Chief Executive who said that he had enjoyed my broadcast from Paris but hoped that the BBC had paid the fare!

While working for RoSPA at this time I was quite well known to the media, and was asked to do a series of broadcasts to go out on the BBC World Service. These were aimed at new drivers in the developing countries of the Commonwealth, and intended to interest them in proper techniques. We completed a number of programmes in different situations, - town traffic, fast roads, country lanes and hills, and discussed bad weather and proper steering and braking techniques. I understand that they were well received in, for example, parts of the Middle and Far East and some of the Pacific Islands.

Years later I needed to apply for a driving licence in Tonga, but sadly they did not seem to have heard my talks! I was also asked to make a film on the hazards of winter driving for Yorkshire TV, which I still have on video. It does get wintry up there, and the advice was good, but viewing it now I wish that I had had a better hair cut! More interesting was being asked to do the driving for a Quiz Show on Independent Television, where two teams competed to get the right answers to questions about various specialist subjects. As the subject when I was involved was 'Driving' I was described as an expert, and filmed doing various manoeuvres wrongly and rightly. The interest came from seeing the number of people, the time and the amount of equipment needed to make just one twenty second film clip, of, for example, a 'kangaroo' start. The filming was started in the Granada Studios before going out on the road, and I was taken around the set of *Coronation Street* and watched some of the very well known cast arriving for the day's shooting. The set was an eye-opener, as none of it was higher than about seven feet, 'Rovers Return' walls and all. Very clever.

Rewinding now to the time when I returned from Mill Meece Training Centre, this was when I began to learn properly how to be a police officer. Recruits, although in theory fully operational, were 'shown round' the different beats on their Division by an experienced officer, starting on Night Turn. In 1953 many, perhaps most, experienced Constables had war service, quite a number as Officers, and I think that contact with, and learning from them was also a useful part of 'growing up', perhaps extending what I had learned in the Royal Air Force. I was posted to 'B' Division, which covered a little of the town centre, but also some rougher areas and some huge post war council estates. These did contain, along with some lovely salt of the earth Black Country working people, quite a few villains.

One street, near the town centre, now long demolished to make way for the University and Ring Road, was the embodiment of Dickensian tenements, with top floors within handgrasp of the house opposite, cobbles and no street lighting. I usually walked down Charles Street and Tin Shop Yard at night with my right hand touching the top of my staff in the specially long trousers pocket, and the hairs on the back of my neck alert. This area of the town contained some dreadful back-to-back housing; a left over from the terrible conditions of the 19th Century, when the towns of the Black Country suddenly expanded during the Industrial Revolution and were flooded with immigrants from the countryside.

Professor Carl Chinn of Birmingham University describes the appalling conditions that these people endured, both in the factories and mines and in what were their homes. In his book *Black Country Memories* he includes a quote from someone who was a child in one of the back-to-backs that, 'no-one could exaggerate the horror of living in such places' and that their demolition in the Nineteen Fifties was an infinite improvement. I could not argue with that, but have wondered if, with a bit more foresight the tenements could not have been evacuated, improved or rebuilt and made a living museum of the terrible life of the working class in the early nineteenth century. The life expectancy for that part of Wolverhampton was nineteen years and one month, and we should not forget what people endured to make this country the richest in the world. I agree with Carl's correspondent that these conditions produced some tough and unique characters, not all of whom felt affection for the passing policeman!

My first night on duty co-incided with the night of Queen Elizabeth's Coronation. This was a learning curve, being a demonstration of how silly people can get when drunk en-masse. The town centre streets were full of women dancing with skirts around their waists, and men climbing lamp posts or anything vaguely climbable. Everyone was friends with everyone else that night, including policemen, and it was rather difficult to remain dignified in the face of women begging to be kissed! As I had realised earlier from the comment by my farm worker colleague, a police uniform can be seen as quite erotic by some women. In fact there was one officer during my early service who was well known for the 'offers' that he received and for being constitutionally unable to turn any of them down. He was believed to have made a number of last minute escapes from bedroom windows whilst on official night duty.

One of the Beats that I was shown round contained a notorious public house called 'The Three Tuns'. This was on a road adjoining one of the big council estates and was the scene of many Saturday afternoon wedding receptions. As attaining complete drunkenness in the shortest possible time was the main object of most men attending, (and some of the women) the receptions at this particular pub almost always deteriorated into open warfare between the relatives of the bride and groom. Blood for supper was to be expected by whoever was on Late Turn on that Beat. However, being shown round at night by Tom, a veteran of both the 39-45 war and the warfare in the 'Tuns', I learned a valuable early lesson in policemanship. A girl on a bicycle rode towards where we were standing waiting outside for the landlord of the 'Tuns' to call time. If we had not been there it might have been a delayed call, and a big part of night duty was to walk through as many bars as possible to make sure that drink was not being served after 10.30 p.m. Tom stopped the girl, who had no lights on her bike, and instead of producing his notebook as I expected, said, 'You get off and push it home, because there might be a policeman round the corner.' A good example, I think, of the Nelson touch, and almost certainly more instructive than a Court appearance to the girl, who giggled and pushed her bike away.

The 'Three Tuns', I should say, is still standing over fifty years later, but is now a much more respectable Chinese Restaurant! I later watched Tom inflict some instant punishment on a man who had been very brutal to his wife, saying repeatedly 'Champion of Malta 1942'. When justice had been done and better behaviour promised he turned to me, who had been called as back-up but not needed, grinned and said, 'Never been to Malta in my life!' Conduct not approved of nowadays, or then either, but I believe that, in those times, much more effective than the Magistrates, and a lot quicker. Two different faces of 'policemanship'.

'Domestics' as they were known were a regular part of police duty on Late and Night Turns on the big housing estates and were often very difficult to deal with satisfactorily. A domestic quarrel could turn into a murder or grievous bodily harm very quickly unless nipped in the bud. It was not at all unusual for husband and wife to mend their differences and both attack the police officer that the wife had earlier sent the kids to find. With a two-man patrol car crew this could be handled, and as fast response vehicles we were often tasked to sort out the quarrel.

On one occasion a colleague and I were dispatched to a house at about 11.00 p.m. where the man had come home drunk and was taking out all the frustrations of his life - he was some sort of low-level labourer - on his wife. She was a poor little soul, obviously beaten many times, and with two small girls cowering in a corner of the room. We decided that something had to be done about it, but he was quite beyond any reason or of responding to the mantra that sometimes worked, 'Come on, both of you, get off to bed and have a good cuddle.' In my early twenties, saying this to a working couple in their forties felt very much like teaching Granny how to suck eggs, but it was surprising how often they took the advice.

On this occasion it wasn't going to happen, and as the wife had not suffered anything except common assault, inside the home, there were no legitimate grounds for arrest. There was only one way to ensure that the woman and children got at least one night of peace, and we both retreated out of the house calling him a 'yellow coward'. By the time we got to the pavement he was provoked enough to take a swing at me, which was all we needed. In Court next morning he accused me of calling him 'A yellow belly', which fortunately I was able to truthfully deny. After Court he came up to me and said that I had broken his nose, but obviously realised that he had been badly at fault, and, as was often the case in those days, held no grudge, but even perhaps a modicum of respect. The people that we rather scornfully called the 'nine o'clock brigade' then took over that family, and may have been able to help the wife and children, but I rather doubt that it came to a satisfactory conclusion. The drink habit on a Friday night was far too well ingrained, and most wives would have little choice but to stay in the home. Such incidents were very common, and of course my action was not approved police conduct. But, at that time, there was no other way. I have never had a problem with this, and indeed am proud that I got this woman, and her children, and others like her, the one night of peace at least, which she manifestly needed. Maybe the man learned a lesson, and he may even have been quite a good provider when not drunk.

As well as not taking exercises very seriously, I think that it is true to say that a lot of police officers - men more specifically - had a great sense of humour. Whilst still on foot patrol I enjoyed taking part in a bit of fun with the mounted statue of Prince Albert, which still stands in the city centre, and which Queen Victoria had unveiled when she eventually came out of mourning. It shows Albert as a romantic horseman, slightly over life-size, and originally gallantly brandishing a sword. Unfortunately the sword was stolen years ago, and never replaced so he looks as if he is expecting a tip. However, little Vicky was so enthralled by it that she knighted the Mayor on the spot. This was also a bit unfortunate, as he had had nothing to do with the statue, which had been another Councillor's brainchild entirely. The Mayor did accept the knighthood, surprise surprise! I hope that the snubbed Councillor was philosophical enough to say to himself, 'Well, that's life!' Is there a moral there somewhere? Could be 'Get yourself in the right place at the right time!' Any road up, as we say in these parts, in the early fifties there were still a few brewery dray horses around, working to top up the pubs in the early hours before opening time. Naturally the horses would deposit large loads of horse product during their journeys, and if the Beat Officer could get hold of a suitable receptacle it was quite fun to empty a pile of this under Albert's horse's tail, and then watch the reaction of the early morning crowds off to work, especially if it was still steaming. One rather naughty but amusing way of hastening the end of the Night Turn, particularly on a dark, preferably foggy wintry morning was to clamber up behind Albert, remove one's helmet and call out to the rather sleepy early workers, in as sepulchral and deep voice as possible, 'Good morning – how is the Queen today?'

The West Park in Wolverhampton has a quite large boating lake and it was not unknown for two officers on nights on the beats adjoining the Park to scale the railings, borrow one of the boats tethered for the night and pass away half an hour on the water. The Sergeant would, of course, be elsewhere, outside the railings! The lake was a magnet for ducks, and I heard at a recent reunion of the time when a live duck was caught, put into a box and handed in at the Central Station as 'found property'.

We used to do a lot of school visits, to talk about road safety and try to show that the police officer was a friend, a person to go to if lost or worried, and not a threat. It was amazing how many harassed or impatient (or just thick) mothers would talk about 'giving a naughty child to the policeman'.

How stupid can one get? However, we eventually and gradually found that the N.U.T. could be even more stupid than that, as through their blind and bigoted left wing views we found it more and more difficult to gain access to schools to talk. This has been mirrored recently by the same union voting to refuse entry to schools to army careers officers.

One job on Night and Late Turns, which seems to have completely disappeared with the virtual demise of the man on a foot or bicycle beat was the 'special attention.' People leaving their houses empty (usually the more expensive houses) would request that the beat officer would pay attention to their property during darkness. There would be a list of such places on each beat which had to be noted during parade. If you were doing the job properly you would vary the time at which you checked the property, so a prospective burglar would never be sure, unless he was following the officer, that the coast was clear. As most of the suburban beats were patrolled by bicycle, anyone following would have been a bit obvious. This system seemed to work, and it was not unknown to result in a good arrest.

I remember being on a beat, not far from where I live now, which had a big and expensive house, often on the special attention list. It was very pleasant at 5 a.m. on a summer morning, work almost over, to sit on one of the swings in the back garden and watch the sun coming up, sometimes even joined by the patrolling Sergeant or Inspector. I suppose that this would have made a nice photograph by a nosey neighbour! It was surprising though how many times an intending or actual burglar was taken aback by an officer having a rest in this way. One appropriate arrest took place as an unlucky man climbed out of the back window of a Co-op Store and fell over the night turn beat man having a quiet smoke underneath it.

One night about 11.30 p.m. I was on bicycle patrol in a fairly affluent suburban area. I was joined by Joe, my trials riding colleague, now a Sergeant and confined also to a bicycle. A badger scurried across the road in front of us, and Joe called out, 'Look at that bloody old thing!' in an audible voice. Unfortunately this was heard by a lady at the front door of one of the nice houses, presumably putting out the milk bottles. She lost no time at all in telephoning the Station to complain that she had been called a 'bloody old thing' by two policemen. Quite difficult to deny this, without the badger!

Less pleasant jobs on nights or late turn was the checking of all commercial properties that were vulnerable or worth being broken into. This was known as 'shaking hands with door knobs' and was where a confrontation with a gang might occur. With no way of communication except a whistle this could be a problem. However, I did find that that ancient call for help, started by the Bow Street Runners, could work. I had started to question two men and two women lurking by a car in the town centre in the early hours, when I found myself on the pavement being kicked by all four. Managing to use the whistle, and town centre beats being close together, I quickly had a colleague on the scene, and then it was containable and arrestable. How nice that in 2010 I had a message from that particular colleague, Brian, now living in New Zealand, who had heard on the bush telegraph that I had made it to Everest Base Camp, and could not believe it!

Later, at the time when separate policewomen's departments had been consigned to history, as an Inspector I was running a mixed shift of male and female officers. This was due to the agitation for women to be on the same pay scales as their male colleagues. As a quid-pro-quo the women had to undertake the full range of police duties, including shaking hands with door knobs. Although violence against woman officers was then comparatively rare, it used to worry me that in the shadows behind a factory, and especially if the girl was wearing trousers, as permitted on nights, she would be mistaken for a male officer and attacked. The demise of the specialist department had another consequence. Our policewomen had kept a comprehensive list of all local known, or suspected, sex offenders, which at times had proved very useful indeed. This was, remember, well before computers or the National Sex Offender's Register. When the women had to go on shifts, this became no-one's job and it either died a death or became less reliable.I was told by several policewomen that they would have preferred to stay with the status quo, and retained the different pay scales, but a vociferous minority and the political climate of the time, forced through the change.

We did have a very persistent burglar who was using, and evading capture by means of a bicycle, although this was not known until he was eventually caught. He was targeting good class houses in the western suburbs of the town, or just outside the town, gaining entry to the ground floor and then stealing anything small of value, even going into bedrooms where the occupants were asleep, and taking cash, wallets, jewellery etc. After this had been going on for too long, the local press were getting very agitated and we were all very exercised to catch this guy. Eventually he took the one step too far by getting into a house where a fit young man, a member of the Wolverhampton Rugby team, lived. He was heard, and laid out and although the house was outside the Borough in the Staffordshire Police area, our control room got the 999 call. I was on Squad cars at that time, and realising that this was probably 'our' burglar got there well before the nearest Staffordshire car, and took him to Wolverhampton Police Station before Staffordshire could get their hands on him! We discovered that he had been using a bicycle to travel between houses, sometimes two or three a night, at the hours when workmen on their way to early morning shifts were starting to appear on the streets. Carrying a small bag apparently full of tools on the handlebars, which also served as a receptacle for the small stolen items, he had never been challenged. This was a good example of how the police need help from the public, and also that the town boundaries needed to be enlarged, which eventually did happen.

My interest in cars and driving steered me away from a role in Criminal Investigation, although I did find out that I could do the interrogation of some prisoners that I was involved with as well, or better, than some detectives. However, uniform branch did do some plain clothes work, and I was tasked, not long after the 'showing round ' process was finished to try to catch a very persistent street bookmaker red handed. Betting laws have been relaxed tremendously since, but unregulated street bookmaking was then a frequent and comparatively serious offence. Ill-afforded money from working men could be made at it. I still had the Hillman Minx - the one with the leaky roof, so kitted myself out in overalls left over from the farming days, muddy boots, and a dirty face, and sat in it using a full page newspaper with a small peephole cut out to hide behind. This worked beautifully, and Alf was quite put out when I arrested him. He obviously felt that he should have spotted me. When I reported to the Duty Inspector, (a former Army Officer), muddy boots and face and all, I was told, 'You are a disgusting sight, get out of my office'. I think that he was grinning though! Another enjoyable bit of plain clothes work, and unmarked car use was to bring into play a very up-market Bristol coupé, borrowed from a dealership, to catch a persistent car thief.

Soon after this the Hillman turned into Jo's engagement ring, and I bought the first of the two motor bikes of that period of my life. The second, the Norton combo, was second hand and needed some welding work on the sidecar. There was a small welding shop owned and run by a reasonably friendly West Indian, who agreed to do it for me. He did, in what I would now describe as 'after a fashion', but we were quickly looking for him officially. Having found that his wife was 'playing away from home' he became less than friendly, the mother of all domestics erupted and he eventually set fire to her with a can of petrol. Although she did not die the rest of her extended family did not appreciate this, and my welder disappeared from sight before we could arrest him. Some months later two men were fishing in the very deep local Bushbury Pool, when they appeared to have made a really heavy catch, a big pike at least. After a struggle, up came my welder, wearing concrete boots.

Near this pool was a building which had to be examined very carefully during Night Turn, as it, the Gas Workers Canteen and Club, had been broken into many times. If it had not been checked and was found broken into by the Steward in the morning all hell broke loose, as everyone kicked everyone else down the chain of command until reaching the beat PC, where the buck stopped, (unless he was married or had a cat). He was likely to be rudely awakened and recalled to the Station at about 10 a.m. So, one night I was checking meticulously all around the building. My Sergeant was a very experienced and wily old Scotsman, well respected by the criminals in that area. He gave me the most tremendous fright, by jumping out at me, as I walked close to the wall around the corner of the Club. I learned about practical policing from that – his intention of course. At night, you do not keep close to the wall near a corner without good reason! Whilst teaching town and city officers about fowl pest or making us jump over each other they did not have time to cover practical skills like that at Mill Meece. We were never taught or practised in how to put handcuffs on a struggling prisoner either – an unbelievable omission.

Whilst still on foot patrol duties I attended a suicide, where a pub landlord had killed himself by putting a plastic bag over his face while lying in bed. I took possession of the bag of course, and during the inquest the Coroner asked me to demonstrate the position in which I found the body. To my great horror and definite reluctance he then insisted that I put the bag - which had not been washed - over my own head. I still cannot see the purpose of this and it is my belief that the Coroner had been recently caught over the speed limit in his Daimler, or was a sadist, or rather weird – or perhaps all three. Several of us had a narrow escape from serious trouble with another local dignitary. The part-time police doctor, a spectacularly unpleasant GP, a man with his charisma put on backwards, was called to a canal towpath where we had pulled a teenage boy from the water. I and two other officers had worked very hard for some time to bring him round, using manual resuscitation. Nowadays a para-medic with breathing equipment would have been on the scene very quickly, but not then. The Doctor turned up, eventually, poked his shiny toecap into the boy's side and said, 'Dead as a nit!' I am sure that he was right, but he very very nearly went into the canal, by accident of course. I can still see the boy's face.

Another very unpleasant job was when my squad car was sent to the scene of a man who had seen fit to lay himself across one of the main railway lines in the town. This should have been a job for the Railway Police but it was down to us to get the remains to the Mortuary. He had been quite a big man, and had been exactly, but not neatly, bisected by the train. We had to pour what was left into the 'box'. All part of the day's work I guess.

A colleague and I found ourselves responsible for bringing a baby into the world one late evening. The Asian mother was, very unusually, totally on her own apart from the elderly neighbour who had dialled '999'. She was in a barely furnished and almost dark one room flat with no sign of the father, who had probably done a runner. I believe that it was another case of a girl disowned by her family through involvement with a man disapproved of by them. We struggled a little indecisively until the Ambulance personnel arrived, but actually I think that she did most of what was necessary herself.

A call to a back-to-back house in a poor part of the town caused a bit of a stir one morning, as my Squad Car was directed to a reported murder. There was a weird scene waiting for us. In very small cupboard the body of a middle aged man was literally crammed – knees drawn up to his chin, so that his jaw was resting on them and a rope looped and knotted round his neck and down to his feet. He was folded up like a toy, and there was just room in the cupboard for him. He had been found by one of his relatives – imagine the shock. It certainly looked like a murder, and we did the necessary things, but it was eventually found that this was a very unusual, bizarre (and, I would think, unpleasant) way of committing suicide. He had folded himself into the cupboard and then choked himself through pressure with his feet on the rope loop.

Another incident, in the same under-privileged area of the town still sits in my memory. We were called to the sudden death of an elderly lady, found dead by a neighbour. The small house was cold, almost bare and lacking in any comfort. The neighbour told me that the lady had been a widow for many years, and had lost two children, a boy and a girl, through illness in the early years of her marriage. This was not, of course, uncommon for needy people in the nineteen twenties and thirties. What struck me then was a picture on the wall of the otherwise almost unfurnished room where she died. This was a painting, not a photograph, of a small boy and girl, hand in hand on a sunny beach. I wondered about the comfort, or perhaps the torment, that she had had from that picture, over the long lonely, empty years. This empathy, and wondering, was to me at least part of being a police officer. Now, in the twenty first century, still being able to remember the bare bedroom and the painting and comparing the comparatively very rich and advantaged life that I have had, one wonders, 'Why?'

The sight of a very small baby, starved to death by his Ukrainian peasant parents, both of whom were convicted of manslaughter, was not enjoyable either. The nearest that we could get to a reason for this was the man did not believe that the child was his and had forced the woman not to feed it. I had started off being sorry for the woman, after being called to the death, until the Duty Inspector and I unwrapped what remained of the baby. It looked like a skinned rabbit.

I knew during the early part of my two year probationary service that I was being considered for a police driving course, having been taken out during 1954 with another Constable for a test drive by the Traffic Inspector. At this time the Force had just taken delivery of some new cars, the 'Morris Six'. I wrote off one of these in stopping a lorry stolen from Birmingham – more of this later!

The Six looked the part, but had the gearshift projecting from the steering column. This was described by male drivers as being there for women to hang their handbags from, but it also meant a lot of jointed linkage, and when the joints inevitably started to wear, silent gear changing became an art. I remember the Traffic Inspector saying to me after one calamitous change in JDA 999 (a car never to be forgotten!) 'Why can none of you buggers drive when I'm in the car?' They did not get a good reception from the British motoring press either, being described as like riding on a cloud, but steering with a piece of wet fog!

We then bought some Austin Westminsters which were just coming onto the market, with a police variant. These were beautiful cars, nice to drive, powerful and, for the time, quick, and styled by Pinin Farina for Austin, in advance of their time. I took a photograph of one to Italy, where Jo and I had arranged to meet some Vigili Urbani Traffic Officers in Milan and they were very appreciative of the styling. 'Una bella machina' was nice to hear.

As a Traffic Inspector at the time of the police amalgamations in 1966 I had a Westminster handed over to me from the Staffordshire Constabulary. When it became known that the Government were going to enforce amalgamations amongst many forces the equipment and police buildings likely to be handed over were allowed to deteriorate. It seems that the Staffordshire Police Authority were not very gruntled at losing part of their Force area. An Inspector fell through a rotten staircase in the Wednesfield Police Station after we moved in! Staffordshire had not shown the Westminster handed over to the West Midlands Constabulary much tender or loving care either and the floor had a large hole between the seats, through which the road was visible.

They were a nice car though, and I liked even that one. Before the Westminsters were available and alongside the Morris Sixes we still had a few of the traditional 'Dixon of Dock Green' era cars, big Wolseley 18/85s, built like a tank and a pleasure to drive, as long as there was not too much hurry. At least the driver was well protected. Flashing blue lights and two tone horns were not yet in use, and all that we had to help on a rush job was a tiny amber light on the roof and a bell in front of the radiator, which could be heard quite well - after the car had passed! There was however a very effective loudspeaker, operated by the observer, and in a hurry he would use this, calling 'Police, clear the road' or occasionally something even more positive like 'Shift it', or words to that effect. The downside of this was that it was quite easy to leave the loudspeaker switched on, thus broadcasting the observer's private comments about dozy civilian drivers to the whole of Wolverhampton.

A car which turned out to be useless for 'hurry up calls' was a Ford Zephyr, which was bought through a bit of political pressure in the Watch Committee, the controllers of police finance. We put a paving slab in the boot to keep the rear wheels attached to the road surface on sharp turns.

Another failure as a patrol car was a Humber Hawk, which looked nice but was underpowered. It was quickly retired to VIP escort duties. I was driving it with a colleague while it was still being used on patrol, and descended a hill with packed snow on the road. I made a rather rough gear change down to second gear in order to turn left (the gearshift was also one of the type that projected from the steering column. That at least is my excuse, which would be difficult to disprove now). Before I knew what had gone wrong we were neatly descending the hill backwards, having provoked a lot of rear wheel spin. Fortunately it was the middle of the night, but my colleague revealed his Anglo-Saxon ancestry, with a few short sharp words. I learned a bit more about driving from that.

Not long after, in the same car and doing an 80 mph VIP escort very near (in order to close out paparazzi) to the rear of Princess Margaret's Rolls, it suddenly occurred to me that one mistake, by me or her chauffeur, could get my name on the front page of every newspaper in the world. I was relieved that it didn't, as I am quite sure that she would have been a fearsome lady to deal with, if inconvenienced. Of course the French police did not do such an escort for Diana, so perhaps in this way, as in others, we were in advance of our time, as well as being part of the best in the world!

I was involved in three other Royal occasions - the first as a Cadet and the last as a Superintendent, so they neatly spanned my career. As a 16 year old Cadet I was given the fairly important job of telling the Borough Organist, who of course had his back to the audience and to the entrance to the Civic Hall, when to strike up the National Anthem. This had to be timed precisely as the Duke of Edinburgh, newly married to Princess Elizabeth, entered the Hall. I was told to look at the Chief Constable, who would touch his lapel when he judged the time to be right. I hate to think what the Duke would have said if I had mistimed it, because rumour has it that he was asked for his autograph by one of the local dignitaries. 'Do you think I'm a bloody film star?' was the reported reply!

Mind you, at that time he did look like one! That was also the first time of several that I appeared in the local paper, the 'Express and Star', but actually they were filming the Organist! Only a few years later, as a PC, I was tasked to guard the two official maroon Rolls Royces overnight. They were brought up from London the day before the Queen's visit, and garaged overnight in the police garage. Her Rolls was locked, but the identical one to convey the Aide de Camp and Ladies in Waiting was left open. I sat in the back of that one all night, practised gracious waves and wondered whether it would be noticed if I ate my fish and chip supper in the Rolls.

I did not risk it.

Jo and I turned out the next morning to see the Queen arrive at the Town Hall, and were struck by how small and beautiful she was. I was rather proud to have made sure that her car was safe, and to be wearing the crown on my uniform. That pride stayed with me for the whole of my police service. The last occasion, only a year or so before I retired was the Queen's visit to Walsall, which by that time we were policing as well as Birmingham and the rest of the Black Country. A section of the route into Walsall was my responsibility, with my officers lining it. I had the use of a general purpose car in which to patrol my section, and this was definitely a full uniform, cap on straight and medals (of which by then I had three) occasion, so I got a cheer from the big crowds every time I drove up and down. Seeing an official car appear would have suggested that the long wait for the royal party was over, but eventually they cottoned on to the fact that I was the dustcart before the Lord Mayor's Procession, and the cheers became ironic. That was the point when I decided to start waving! I did expect to get at least a knighthood for this service, but it didn't happen.

After the 1966 amalgamation I had several MGB GT two seater hard top sports cars under my aegis as the Wolverhampton Division Traffic Inspector. Great – very professional looking, fast, manoeuvrable, lovely to drive, but what do you do with a prisoner? I suppose the answer is that you sent for the Paddy Waggon or Black Maria. The origins of Paddy Waggon are pretty obvious, but Black Maria is a bit more obscure. However, I reckon that I have met the lady, or at least her descendant!

In the early days of policing in Jamaica, whenever the Constables met a problem that was too much for them they sent for an extremely large and fierce local lady called Maria. She sorted it out in quick time, and eventually that became the generic name for the prison van. After leaving the police service and while travelling across America by Greyhound Bus (one meets a lot of interesting people that way) a lady who absolutely fitted the description of Maria got on board in Vegas. She had a very pretty little girl with her called Ebony. Mum took up the whole of one bench seat, so Ebony sat in the back, near me.

Every so often Mum would shout, 'Ebony, Ebony, what you doin' Gal?'

Every time Ebony replied, quite correctly, 'Nuffin, Mam'.

'Well, you stop it Gal, you hear?'

You do meet interesting passengers on a Greyhound Bus. Further into that journey, during the long ride from Laramie, across Wyoming, we took turns to lie flat in the aisle to assuage bottom fatigue. Maria and Ebony had got off by then, fortunately.

On the occasion of our visit to Milan in 1961 to visit the Vigili Urbani Traffic Police, arranged through the International Police Association, we had driven through France and crossed the Alps through the San Gotthard Tunnel. This was a long way in the Morris Minor Traveller that had by now replaced both the Panther solo and Norton combo motorcycle. We descended onto the plains of Lombardy, and approached Milan as it was getting dark. At this point we realised that we had no idea where our Hotel was, or a map of Milan, which is no mean city. There had been a failure of planning on my wife's part! It was also thundering. Taking a cool and calculated approach, i.e. in a panic, I decided to find the largest police station possible, and ask for our Vigili Urbani contact. This was not easy, and involved at one point driving onto, and quickly off, an operational urban railway line.

Finally locating a police station we asked for Signor Sabotti, only to get the response, 'Domani matina, Domani matina' at a gradually increasing tempo and volume. The bubbles rising visibly from their heads clearly read (in Italian) 'Stupid Foreigners'. As neither of us spoke any Italian, and in the circumstances of being wet, bedraggled and shell-shocked this took some time to translate. It is surprising that we were not locked up.

Eventually the light dawned and we disappeared once more into the thundering night, no doubt to the relief of the whole Station. However, our Hotel was still an unknown, and the only thing to do was to drive around hoping to find it. We could at least remember the name! At about midnight, by an absolute fluke we did, found that they were expecting us and had kept a hot meal ready. We have both loved Italy ever since, and have returned many times.

Domani matina dawned a beautiful Italian blue, and by some miracle we retraced the route to the Police Station. Imagine our relief to find that Signor Sabotti was there expecting us, and speaking understandable, if fractured, English. He had been a prisoner of war in England and had become an Anglophile. This may say something about the way we treated our wartime prisoners. We had a thorough tour of the Vigili Headquarters, with an entourage of Signors Mariani, Innocenti and Cobianchi and I was impressed with their traffic planning and congestion control.

After a very hospitable lunch, during which Jo was introduced to Campari and had enough of it to put her off it for life, (she discreetly emptied the glass into a flower pot) Signor Sabotti asked if we would like to see a rehearsal at La Scala. Naturally we jumped at this, so he suggested that we drove him across the city in our car. This was my first introduction during daylight to Italian city driving habits, and although I have experienced it many times since it remains a vivid memory. In particular being in a foreign, big city, with an Italian traffic officer who believed, in common with most of his compatriots, that cars were designed to go fast, and should always do so, and who spoke at best Italian flavoured English, was a bit of a strain. I did feel that the Minor was a bit down market, as the Vigili were using Lancias. However, I did have the photograph of the Westminster, 'bella macchina', as a makeweight. 'Avanti, Avanti, no stop for them, they wait' as we flew through central Milan is a memory, not of steps too far, but miles an hour too far.

Well, we did arrive unscathed at La Scala, which was just about to close to the public. Our guide commenced a voluble argument with the Custodian until the last straggler had departed, and then with a very conspiratorial and expressive wink took us inside. (Who did he say we were? Good international policemanship anyway!) We had the privilege of hearing a rehearsal of the 'Tales of Hoffman', and got safely back to Vigili HQ, then our Hotel, and a collapse after a wonderfully interesting but slightly stressful day. Who we saw in the rehearsal I was too shell-shocked to retain, but I guess it might even have included friends of Pavarotti or his Father.

The next morning we set off south east, to Rimini on the Adriatic coast, where our International Police Association host was a motor cycle police officer named Guerra. He spoke very good English, having spent time in Australia, but shocked me by taking us into a café for a meal whilst on duty and in full Police uniform. This was lawful as long as he was wearing a flat cap and not the helmet, which at that time was similar to a British police helmet. Such things were not done in Wolverhampton. It also seemed strange, in the Rimini climate that 'shirt sleeve order' was not in force. We got on well with Signor Guerra, who was about our age and seemed to have about the same standard of living, with a small car. Rimini then was very different to what it has since become, and had only a small Force of fifty officers. Again their HQ was well appointed and furnished. We hoped that we secured more IPA members there by the time we left.

This holiday left us with many good memories – the Carabinieri in full dress uniform, including cocked hat and sword in Venice, a point duty policeman directing traffic amongst the clouds in the mountain Republic of

San Marino, the workmanlike road patrols of the Polizia Stradale and above all the hospitality and friendship that the words 'Polizia Inglesi' called forth among Italian officers.

We had been interested in photographing police officers of other countries in uniform since our first visit abroad, to Spain. The Guardia Civile, with their strange hats were very photogenic, but also looked quite tough, and it was understood that taking their photograph was prohibited. I decided however to ask for permission, hoping that my limited French might be understood. I asked one particularly severe looking officer if it could be permitted, and pointed to my camera. He did not smile, but delivered a torrent of Spanish and made it obvious that we should follow him. He marched off round several corners, we following meekly and wondering where we would finish up. Eventually, somewhat to my relief we found ourselves in a camera shop, being supplied with a new film which I did not need! I cowardly said, 'Gracias,' and abandoned the idea of a uniform photograph.

Having satisfactorily impressed the Traffic Inspector during my driving test in the Morris Six I was nominated for a Driving Course at the Regional Police Driving School at Stafford. This began one of the three best times of my police career, from August to September 1954. (The other two were a motor-cycling course with Lancashire Constabulary and getting paid to fly at last in the Police/Army helicopter experiments).

I had been driving legally, for six years, and illegally before then, and like most young men, of that and every generation before and since, (and probably those still to come) thought that I knew all there was to know about driving. I quickly discovered that I knew nothing, perhaps even less than nothing, if over-confident ignorance could be defined that way. I had been nominated by Wolverhampton for an advanced course, which was unusual as the normal progression was from a standard or basic course, through intermediate to advanced. I have to think that this was my possession of the BSA still kicking in. Because of this and as I was still a probationary officer, still within my first two years, I imagine that I was looked at fairly closely.

There were nine male (of course, at that time!) officers from different Midland Forces, on the five week residential Driving Course. I loved it from the start, although taken down a peg or two on the first day by a fairly ferocious Sergeant, who made me return the wire rim of my cap to it's proper shape. I had savaged it into something resembling a Luftwaffe Officer's cap. Pity, I had thought it looked quite dashing!

We were split into three groups of three, each group with it's own Instructor. The course was a well-balanced mixture of study, practical driving and some basic mechanics. There was a lot of writing as we copied out by hand some of the lectures from the Metropolitan Police Driving School, which were eventually to form the basis of 'Roadcraft' and 'Fleetcraft', now used by all service and civilian advanced driving schools. If one writes the contents of a book out by hand it does commit it to memory. A rather old-fashioned teaching method perhaps, but it worked. I can still, over fifty years on, quote a lot of the original 'Roadcraft' even though it has been changed and modernised and indeed criticised by myself many times since. There was an advantage in having a mix of Forces, as we got to know something about the Police areas surrounding our own and the personalities within them. Perhaps a bit like a University, where one can make friends for life.

Police Driver Training of that era and 'Roadcraft' have been criticised for being too rigid. In fact a flexible approach was a 'sina qua non' of the course, as taught. The criticism has inevitably been by people involved in driver training, who have never experienced a police advanced course, but only read the book. Perhaps they are jealous.

Another reason for the criticism may have been that some quite well known people were keen to advertise their own methods and publications. A certain titled gentleman who is still around comes to mind. I can honestly say that in the years since 1954, with involvement in all forms of driving and training from motor cycles, trials riding, single-seater racing cars and rally cars to off-roading, double decker buses, large articulated goods vehicles and a Centurian Tank that I have experienced nothing which even approached those weeks at Stafford, or the later motor cycling course with Lancashire. I am eternally grateful to them for the pleasure, the knowledge and the long undamaged life that they gave me. I really do not think that, for the time and the facilities available, that either the course, or the instruction, could have been improved.

There is also another factor at work here. It is an accepted maxim in the British armed forces that a well trained member has a high level of morale with confidence in their own ability and that of their colleagues. They will be secure in the knowledge that any assigned duty will be within their training and competence. I do know that I had this level of morale at the conclusion of both my driving and motor cycling courses, knew that I could drive and ride properly and was happy, and indeed eager, to go anywhere and do anything. I believe that my colleagues felt the same. We were fit, well trained, capable, and I think, had Alexander the Great's dynasmus. Unfortunately this factor was lost sight of by the actual and political leaders of the police service when training budgets were cut to save money. There was a huge loss of morale in the 1970s leading to the haemorrhaging of trained men, and I believe that this, as much as the low pay, was one of the major reasons.

The days of late summer of 1954, out on the road for six to eight hours, were delightful. Each Instructor was an authentic expert, and it was then that I realised just how little I knew about real driving. We covered the whole of Staffordshire and sometimes beyond, using some old but beautiful machinery that had been retired from normal police use. I remember a big Lanchester and a huge Humber, both very powerful, and quick enough to be demanding, but not particularly easy to drive, being equipped with very primitive synchro-mesh gear boxes or so called 'crash boxes'. I learned about gear changing from these. The nowadays untaught art of double de-clutching is still useful today on my 1972 Jensen-Healey.

One particular Instructor, Jack, had a very dry north Staffordshire sense of humour, and I can remember some of the stories that he used to keep the two students sitting in the back interested and awake. I borrowed this technique from him and still use it today in my advanced training work. Jack was still a Constable at the time, but obviously due for promotion, and eventually became, as a Chief Superintendent, the head of the Staffordshire Traffic Department. He supervised the motorway police training as the M6 was unrolled down through Staffordshire.

Training had developed a lot since the pre-war days of Lord Cottenham, the donor of the Lagondas, whom I mentioned earlier. In the nineteen thirties there were cars around which would travel very fast indeed, but also took a long time to come to a stop. This led to the idea, originally thought up by the Metropolitan Police School, of the driver giving a verbal commentary, about what he could see in the distance, and what he was going to do about it, if necessary. One of the 1930s Instructors told me that all his colleagues were anxious to know that the student driver had actually seen the level crossing gates, or whatever lay ahead, for their own health and safety. This developed into a very useful training aid, where one sees more because one is searching for something to say, fixes the potential hazard ahead in the mind and improves concentration no end. It is still used as a valuable aid by the emergency services and the armed forces and all advanced driving organisations. It was a big part of our training at Stafford.

Also important was the correct use of the brakes in dealing with corners and slippery roads in the days before ABS or other stability control accessories. The instructors had installed a sneaky little red light on all the cars, which blinked on the Instructor's side whenever the brakes were applied. Thus it was not possible to have a sly dab on the brake pedal at the wrong time or place without bringing down wrath on one's head. I recently came across, from an American police trainer during one of our transatlantic electronic chats, the following advice that he uses. 'Remember that the brake is not your friend after you have entered the curve'. Too right! Another conversation with the same person, Jeff, has led to a campaign to change the name of 'Pull and push' to 'Synchronised Steering'. The Americans call it 'Shuffle Steering' which is even worse than pull and push, but the discussion led to the idea of suggesting a change. This will take years, but from small acorns.......!

Two exercises that were designed to make the driver think well ahead, and which I still use in training, were to drive as far as possible on a difficult winding road without using the brakes, and to try to drive through an urban area without the wheels ceasing to revolve. Both involve a certain amount of luck with other traffic, but they do make you work and look. To successfully do the second exercise through a fair sized town like, say Shrewsbury, is quite a feat!

Towards the end of the course we practised 'bandit chases' with one car trying to get away from the other two. This was quite fun, as we were allowed to go quite quickly. Much later, and retired from the Service, I was in Staffordshire with a civilian trainee when we got caught up in the current version of these chases. They were hamming it up a lot more than we used to, with the driver and passenger in the 'bandit' car both wearing balaclavas. For a few moments I thought that it was the real thing, but the game was given away when we caught up with the bandits waiting in a side road to be spotted!

We trainees, borrowing a Staffordshire patrol car and driver to act the part of a villain, also practised the three car stop, boxing him in with police cars in front and behind and the third closing in from the offside, to slowly force the bandit towards the kerb.

I was involved in such a real stop when on squad car duty, when a taxi was hi-jacked from Wolverhampton Railway Station, with the thief holding a knife to the driver's throat. We caught up with him on the very busy Wolverhampton to Birmingham dual carriageway, and formed the box with myself, another Wolverhampton car and a Staffordshire car.

The training paid off, as this worked perfectly, and we arrested the thief with no damage or throats cut. This was actually a good result for the time, as although the two Control Rooms could talk to each other by radio, my observer could not talk to the Staffordshire car. In fact we could only talk to another car of our own Force by requesting 'talk through' which was not very efficient. It meant that all cars were 'on the air' and left the Control Room struggling to retain control. Mobile communications have come a long way since then, in which I later played some part.

Another real incident, after the driving course, and whilst on night motor patrol duty did not go quite so smoothly as the 'box'. This involved a lorry stolen from Birmingham. At that time before the 1966 and '74 police amalgamations, there were five police areas between Birmingham City Police and Wolverhampton County Borough. The A4123 passed through parts of Birmingham, Staffordshire, Worcestershire and Dudley Borough before ending in Wolverhampton. The lorry, stolen by means of a garage breaking and entering was seen by a Birmingham car, and followed onto the A4123, refusing to stop. As it progressed towards Wolverhampton the police presence was strengthened by Staffordshire, Worcestershire and Dudley cars.

We had two cars available to join in, of which mine was one. I believe (the situation did get a bit confused) that at one time there were no less than ten police cars trying to stop the lorry, the driver of which was determined not to be stopped. The A4123 is a wide dual carriageway for most of it's length, about fourteen miles, and whilst an urban road had at that time no speed restriction of any sort. Cars did travel fast upon it, there being no National Speed Limit. It was an early (1930s) attempt to build a motorway, although badly flawed, dangerous, and nowadays restricted to 40 mph. The lorry was able to get up a good head of steam, about sixty miles an hour, not worrying about red lights or side roads, thus making any attempt to stop it very dangerous indeed. The car crews not being able to talk to each other also made this pretty well impossible.

It was not until it reached the narrower streets of Wolverhampton town centre that it slowed enough to make stopping it a possibility, although still difficult. The foot duty men in Wolverhampton had mostly been alerted, via the flashing police pillars, that he was apparently on his way to us. We still had no idea where he was going or what he was trying to do, apart from escape. Being part of the chase by this time, I remember seeing officers on foot jumping from shop doorways, and throwing their staffs, handcuffs, torches or anything else heavy at the lorry's windscreen.

This had absolutely no effect, they bounced off! Whilst being quite brave it was also dangerous. If the windscreen had broken I am sure that carnage would have resulted, as the vehicle was still going too fast for town centre streets. The whole episode was incredibly dangerous, as although after midnight there were still private cars and pedestrians about, and he had been followed along a road which commonly held cars travelling at up to (or over) 100mph. It was about this time that, being young and foolish, (and perhaps with dynasmus!) I decided that something needed to be done. The lorry made a right turn and I knew that a little way ahead the road narrowed to go under a railway bridge. Knowing the Wolverhampton streets and having been able to get to the front of the other pursuing cars I was able to squeeze past the lorry, and slewed the patrol car round to the right so that it blocked the road under the bridge.

I remember shouting to my colleague in the passenger seat, 'That'll stop him!' But it didn't! We had both managed to jump out before he hit us, anticipating being the ones to make the arrest when he stopped. The lorry was big enough and heavy enough to shove my car, one of the new Morris Six's, aside, and careered on, heading back towards the A4123. Amazingly, although subsequently written off, the Morris was still driveable, and we rejoined the chase, although now at the tail-end. The doors were flapping, bits were falling off and later that night I was ceremoniously (and sarcastically) handed a wheel trim by one of the Birmingham City Police drivers. It was not really much use by then, and thus began my love affair with Birmingham City Police!

However, the collision had brought down a mudguard on to one of the lorry's front wheels, slowed him down and severely restricted his ability to steer. Somehow, and I really do not remember how, as we approached the main road again, I had got back to the front of the pursuit, doors banging and scattering bits of the car all over the place. I imagine, with hindsight, that the other police drivers had decided that we were now disposable, and that they could leave it to us. The lorry careered across the dual carriageway of the A4123 (totally without any speed limit to other vehicles remember) and into a side road opposite. Fortunately this had a steep upward incline that slowed him down considerably, and the driver managed to turn left into another minor road, not knowing that this was a cul-de-sac. The lorry stopped at the 'sac' end, the driver flung open his door, jumped down and ran into a gap between two of the houses.

My blood being somewhat up by now I was the first to follow, but there were still between fifteen and twenty men, in various stages of fitness, behind me. The driver jumped over a number of garden fences - it was still all a bit hectic, with no opportunity to count the fences, but he eventually fell over. I fell on top of him. That was not quite the end of the chase, as fifteen or so bodies then fell on top of me! Not knowing what we were dealing with and thinking that he might be armed and had certainly been desperate to escape, I hit him as hard as I could with my fist. I believe that most of the other fifteen landed blows on my back.

We took him back to Wolverhampton, not in my patrol car, as the doors could not be shut, and Birmingham City CID officers came over to collect him, at about 3 a.m. They put him in front of the Birmingham Magistrates that morning, and - quite unbelievably - he was given bail! Nowadays I would have expected this, but then it was definitely unusual. Despite the fact that my Mother originally came from Birmingham this definitely continued my love/hate affair with the City and it's police force. Needless to say the guy was not seen again for about three months, when he was spotted, in disguise, by a sharp-eyed Birmingham foot patrol officer, and re-arrested. OK, one face-saver for Birmingham!

Meanwhile, back in Wolverhampton I had gone home to change and brush up, knowing that I would be required, when the nine o'clock troops came to work, to explain a car standing in the police yard, it's days of police duty only too obviously over. I am told that the Traffic Inspector cried when he saw it, but this may be apocryphal! It was one of the new Morris Six's though. I had rather a lot of writing to do over this incident, but think that I was right in the action I took, as the way that the lorry was being driven could easily have caused multiple fatalities.

We were very lucky that no civilians or police officers were hurt at all, and although I suspect that my fate was for a time in the limbo between the sack and a commendation, eventually it was agreed that I was justified. Nowadays, with 'stingers' and the incredibly better communications, it could have been stopped in other ways, or even followed at a good distance, and tracked by a helicopter until it ran out of fuel. However, we had to work with what we had, and the policies relating to stopping vehicles of the time.

I was awarded a Certificate of Commendation for bravery and skilful driving by the Watch Committee, and a monetary award of roughly the equivalent of a week's pay. We are still using the cutlery, for best, that we bought with this! More satisfying I think to me was, still being a young Constable in my fourth year of service, that I became known throughout the Force. Being a good policeman was about the highest accolade possible from one's peers. 'Good' in this context did not mean being a nice person, but effective and a thief-taker. There were others of my colleagues on motor patrol who were better thief-catchers than I.

Jim, for example, made an arrest almost every time he went out of the Station in uniform, but this affair did help my reputation. Another of my colleagues, spotting a car looking very down on it's rear suspension, stopped it and found the boot full of stolen lead from a nearby Church roof. Lucky maybe, but good police work to be interested enough to stop the car in the first place. I would call that dynasmus as well.

When the lorry driver came before Birmingham Quarter Sessions (the fore-runner of the Crown Court), charged with theft, breaking and entering and dangerous driving, I was the principal witness.

When asked if he wanted to put any questions to me he asked, 'How did my nose get broken?'

I replied, 'In view of his dangerous efforts to escape, and not knowing if he was armed, I hit him as hard as I could to subdue him'.

'Yes', said the Recorder, (the Judge at Quarter Sessions), 'Any more questions?'

Try giving that reply nowadays, after a similar or even more dangerous situation. The sky would be dark with the shit about to rain down on me from the media, the Civil Liberties brigade, the Courts and probably my own Chief. At that time, 1957, when we did things reasonably sensibly, I was again commended by the Court on my actions, and also for the maps which I had produced showing the whole of the dangerous driving route. However I did begin to wonder if fragile noses were a product of genetics in the Black Country.

We were not trained for an incident of this type involving heavy vehicles during the Staffordshire driving course. Practically it would have been impossible, so it was often a case of trying to use initiative and common sense in unusual situations. However, I thoroughly enjoyed the five weeks, and came top of the course in every subject, gaining the much sought-after advanced qualification of class one high, and being recommended as an Instructor.

On return to Wolverhampton I was posted quickly into motor patrol, driving 'Squad Cars'. Nowadays these might be called 'fast response' cars, and we were available to deal with anything, not just traffic accidents or incidents. Whilst I was still a Squad Car driver the BBC commenced the series called 'Z Cars'. The 'Z' came from the phonetic alphabet 'Zulu' which was their designation within the Lancashire police radio scheme. Our designation within the Midlands was 'YY' so officially we were 'Yankee' cars. The 'Zulus' were shown doing exactly the job that we did with our Squad Cars, and it made a good programme, still remembered by a surprising number of people. The theme tune, very catchy and memorable, is now the Everton FC anthem. One of the main characters, a Z Car driver called 'Fancy Smith' was played by the then young, but now very well known actor Brian Blessed. Years later I had the chance to talk to Brian and said to him, 'When you were acting it I was doing it'. He laughed very heartily!

I was also asked to train our dog handlers and other specialist officers to advanced driving level, so although never a member of a regional driving school staff I was de-facto a police instructor. I enjoyed the operational driving too much to apply for a full time instructor's post, but was very pleased to have started what eventually became Wolverhampton's own police driving school. This continued running full time car and motor cycle courses until the Force was amalgamated in 1966. It then became part of the driving school for the bigger West Midlands Constabulary, and so on into the even bigger West Midlands Police. While involved with the dogs I became quite interested in their work, and volunteered to act as a 'suspect' to be chased and brought down. We did this a few times at Police Open Days, and although wearing a thickly padded 'sleeve' (the dog was trained to go for the arm) it remains an interesting memory - being chased and attacked by a fully grown Alsatian!

During my service in the late fifties and sixties the prospect of police officers having to be armed was becoming an increasingly important topic. As the supply of recruits who had completed National Service in the Armed Forces was drying up we began getting firearms training at a nearby Royal Air Force range, with a small supply of .38 and .45 ex-army revolvers held at the Central Police Station. The instructor, using the Range at RAF Cosford, was a police officer who had ended the second world war as a Sergeant in the Grenadier Guards. At the re-union of Wolverhampton Officers at the Memorial Arboretum in 2007 he was present, although of course elderly and not very mobile. He got a great cheer and a laugh when, using his Sergeant's voice and presence, he shouted, 'Stand up straight' before the group photographs were taken!

In later years I was in charge of an armed party searching for a dangerous and armed criminal. Perhaps fortunately he was not on our patch, but I was partly involved in the custody of a member of a dangerous London gang who had been arrested in Wolverhampton. I can remember now the appearance of this man, and how it struck me at the time that he had the untamed look of a tiger in a cage. Whilst never having taking part in the discharge of a firearm except in training, I was however involved in two incidents that could have resulted in fatalities. In 1956 Wolverhampton was the destination of many of the Hungarians who had revolted against Soviet rule, and been given asylum in this country. Some of them had been prisoners in criminal jails in Hungary, and did not change their spots on arrival here.

One such, nicknamed 'Poughy' which I learned means 'Softy' was rather a trouble maker, and persisted in annoying various young women. Three of us went to bring him in, which should have been quite enough, but 'Softy' had armed himself with a very long and apparently sharp knife and declined to come with us. This was a bit of a stand off, with 'Softy' brandishing his knife over his head and we three wondering how best to tackle him. It was solved by one of my colleagues, who had been a Commando during war service, by suddenly rushing him, and grabbing the knife, considerably surprising all of us in the process. The same officer had been my observer in the police car wrecked by the stolen lorry, so I reckon that he either had a very active guardian angel or was a lucky man.

The other incident involving long sharp objects ended well, at least for the police, and once more featured myself on the front page of the Midlands evening paper 'The Express and Star' in 1960. Crewing a Squad Car, my observer colleague, Ernie, and I were told to go to what had been reported as a 'domestic' – lots of shouting, screaming and broken glass from a house on one of the council estates, at the fairly unusual time of 9.30am. Ernie and I, who although older than me is still around and still a friend, approached the back of the house, via what was meant to be a back garden. Knocking the front door, when one doesn't really know what is going on, is not good procedure. In fact it would have been more technically correct to have one of us stay at the front while the other went round to the back, but in this case it was fortunate that we stayed together.

As we approached the back door, over a scruffy patch of grass, a well-built man in his mid-twenties rushed out towards us, shouting, 'Bugger off!' and brandishing what appeared to be a sword over his head. He brought the sword down towards my head and fortunately I was able to raise my right arm and take the blow, from the flat of the sword, on the elbow. It knocked me to the ground, but my serge uniform jacket withstood a lot of the force and my arm was bruised only.

The sword, which we later discovered to be a 27 inch long sword-bayonet issued to the British infantry regiments in the 18th and 19th Century, was sharp at the point. Luckily for Ernie and I it was not very sharp along the striking edge. Bayonets were issued and the infantry trained to use them against Napoleon's army, despite their having been first made in the French town of Bayonne! It was a lunging or stabbing weapon like the gladius carried and used so effectively by the Roman legionaries. Luckily our assailant did not know this! He was trying to use it as a cutlass with a sharp edge.

He then swung the sword at Ernie's head, and luckily it was deflected by his uniform peaked cap, which was actually destroyed and later used as an exhibit in Court. They then grappled, Ernie trying to deflect further blows at his head with his staff, until they both fell into a hedge. By this time I had picked myself up, and saw that the man was on top of Ernie and about to hit him again on the head with the sword. He was obviously totally out of control, demented, and fortunately for Ernie not able to exploit the sword enough to make use of the point. If he had done so it would have been a killing situation.

I needed something, preferably longer than a staff, with which to equalise things. Again fortunately there was a short washing-line prop standing nearby, and I grabbed this and hit our assailant, who was sitting astride Ernie, as hard as I could on the head. It broke the line prop in half and subdued the man enough to get handcuffs on him. He remained violent and neighbours helped to restrain him. We than asked for back-up via our car radio and when this arrived and the man had been taken away, tried to investigate what had been happening. Baughen had a history of illness and aggression. Before the neighbours called the police he had fallen out with his elderly parents and virtually wrecked the house of which they were the tenants.

The case was opened that day in Court and was front page news! Eventually Baughen was sent to prison, and, I hope, medical treatment for his mental condition, but in those days I am not so sure that this took place. Very distressing to think of a son behaving like that, and a depressing history. I remember his parents as being pathetic old people. In those days I imagine that I did not dwell for long on the sadness of such a case, but now, being both a Father and Grandfather, I cannot help wondering how it was when he was a small boy, perhaps a loved and wanted son.

I later had the chance to examine the weapon closely, and research the history, as it was passed to me to dispose of. Those bayonets were very different to the short 'pig-stickers' issued to me during my RAF service and still in use, I believe, today. The long sword type bayonet had a handgrip and guard and therefore could be used as a stabbing or slashing sword separate from the musket or rifle.

Ernie and I were both commended by the Wolverhampton Stipendiary (professional) Magistrate and a few months later I was in bed after a late shift on the previous day when Jo brought up the post. Amongst it was a letter from Buckingham Palace, telling me that Ernie and I had both been awarded the Queen's Commendation for Brave Conduct. This was totally unexpected and a complete shock. It was, of course, due to a recommendation from the Chief Constable, Norman Goodchild CBE, and his Deputy, Tom Marsh. I had a great respect for both these officers (apart from the recommendation, although I can't deny that I was pleased about it!) and I still do have that respect although of course both have now passed on. I was very pleased to pay tribute to them both, in the hearing of their families, much later in my life at our Force re-union in 2007.

The award of the laurel leaf medal to Ernie and I was made by the Lord Lieutenant of Staffordshire, at Penn Hall, on the outskirts of Wolverhampton, where I had been in single man's quarters earlier in my service. Both our wives, Her Majesty's Inspector of Constabulary, other senior officers and the press and photographers were invited, with a lunch to be held after the award ceremony.

The Deputy Chief Constable, Tom Marsh was in charge of the ceremony, with Ernie and myself in full uniform, white dress gloves and helmets of course. (I was then used to wearing a peaked cap for driving, but had retained a helmet for the occasional football match duty, so it is quite lucky that it did not fall off through unfamiliarity!) The plan was that the Lord Lieutenant was standing behind a table with a microphone and our medal cases on it. We were at the side, to be marched out, turning towards the table to salute. As it was a nice day the ceremony was held outside, at the front of the rather beautiful Hall. Mr. Marsh, who had held the rank of Major during the War, gave us the order to 'Quick march' then 'Halt' in front of the table. Ernie was in front of me. The order then came 'Left turn'. This would have turned both of us with our backs to the Lord Lieutenant, and facing the Malvern Hills!

I am prepared to swear that all the following thoughts passed through my mind in a microsecond, and Ernie will say the same! 'Does he mean it and does he intend to follow it with an About Turn?', 'Was it a mistake?', 'Should I obey or disobey?', 'Is Ernie going to obey or disobey?', 'It will be a farce if he turns one way and I turn the other.', 'There is a press photographer here.', 'Oh shit.'

Well, if we had both been serving in the army we might have obeyed the last order, and turned to salute the Malvern Hills. But policemen aren't (or weren't) like that and we both used a bit of common sense, came to the same conclusion and after a moment's hesitation both ignored the command and turned right to face the Queen's Representative. After that all went well. I was even able to stand in an adjacent stall to Mr. Lawrence, Her Majesty's Inspector of Constabulary, the most senior position in the British Police, in the men's toilet at Penn Hall. Quite a privilege.

However, the split-second of indecision remains, I think, the worst moment of my police career, and over fifty years later I can see the back of Ernie's helmet extraordinarily clearly and relive the thoughts that were speeding through my brain!

Reverting to some personal history, in June 1956 Jo and I were married in the little Church in her home village of Wootton Courtenay, with the Reception in the Village Hall. In July 2006 we had our Golden Wedding celebration also in the Village Hall, on the same site, but a new and much grander building. Our parents could not be present of course, but a number of the original guests were there, including Jo's brother and sister. Our daughter Nicky with her husband Derek were very much involved and worked very hard indeed to make it a success. Our son Al and his wife Dörte plus one grandchild with the second one due to arrive at any moment appeared unexpectedly, which was a joyful moment. A very happy occasion on a lovely summer day, looking out at Dunkery Beacon on Exmoor.

In 1956 I had rented a car to travel up to the Isle of Skye, our honeymoon destination – it took three days then, no M6, and you went through just about every urban area in the north of England and Scotland. We stayed at the Royal Hotel in Portree, did a lot of walking in the magnificent scenery, and some climbing in the Cuillin Mountains. I climbed Sgurr Alastair and Sgurr Na Gillian, and on wet days, of which there were naturally a few, practised climbing knots in bed! We were also shown around Dunvegan Castle by the wonderful old Laird of the McLeods, Dame Flora, herself. When our son arrived, we decided to call him after the mountain, but we had a Doctor from the Scottish Highlands, who told me, 'If you are going to do that, do it properly,' so it is Alasdhair, which seems to be unique. He has never objected!

As I had been in the single men's quarters at Penn Hall, we had to find somewhere to live, and luckily managed to rent two rooms, one up and one down, in a house belonging to an elderly widow. She was very straight-laced, and could be quite severe if she thought something was not 'ship-shape and Bristol fashion'. We had had to provide references, and were informed that no drunkenness or rowdy behaviour would be tolerated. At this time, the drink and drive laws were pretty lax, and police dances, I am ashamed to say, did involve quite a lot of drinking. This was an experience of the time and the culture. We got back to our digs on the Norton combo very late after one Christmas Ball, pushing the bike as we neared the house to avoid waking up the whole street. This was OK, but I was incapable of climbing the stairs to our bedroom. I sat on the bottom step for what seemed hours, with Jo expecting us to be turned out by our landlady, bag and baggage, at any moment. However, she never knew! On another occasion Jo had failed to clean the shared cooker satisfactorily when our landlady was expecting family guests, and she was torn off a mighty strip – probably being taught things in the process.

After about eighteen months we were very lucky to be allocated a new police house at Aldersley, a nice suburb to the north west of the town. Before that we had been offered the chance to share a house with one of the Wolves first team players. We turned this down as it was a small terrace house (now long gone), near to and the property of the Club. In a way I regret having turned this down, as it might have led to some interesting friendships, but then we may not have been allocated the police house.

Aldersley was a comparatively remote suburb, and had almost the feel of a village. Certainly, although I was still doing normal shift duties our house, with the 'police' sign above the office door, did become rather like a village police station. As Jo was known to be a Nurse, we had a lot of callers for a variety of reasons. I dealt with a knifing incident whilst off duty, and quite a few 'domestics' amongst the neighbours.

The house had a huge back garden, totally wild when we moved in, with builder's rubbish scattered willy-nilly. We did manage to tame it reasonably well before we moved on, and some of the trees that we planted are now monsters. I did several periods of duty in the Chief Constable's Office – the Force admin centre, and with my previous experience there as a Cadet, was usually pulled in when they were short-handed. During one such period I found an old Home Office memo to all Chief Constables, suggesting that police houses should be planned with big gardens, so that the occupant would have to spend a lot of his off-duty time at home, keeping the garden in good order.

Sneaky, or what?

We got on very well with Bill and his wife Audrey in the other police house, and co-operated in keeping the office clean and tidy. This was a requirement, and the office was inspected regularly, with the house and garden also being inspected on a more occasional basis. We were discovered to have taken the electric kettle from the office into our own use during one occasion, and I was very severely told off! The inspections were accepted then as a part of the privilege of having a police house, but I wonder if they would be now. The two houses have been sold privately since, and ours extensively enlarged – unthinkable to have got permission for this when we were there. The office is now removed from police use, as the houses are not necessarily occupied by police officers, but I think that it provided a service for the community. Perhaps that depended on who was living there.

Wolverhampton had engaged on a programme of building a number of police houses in various areas, in pairs, separated by the small office. They were intended to be used when necessary by the beat officer, and actually became little local police stations, which I am sure was a very good policy for the time as personal radios did not exist. If the Control Room needed to contact a beat officer a beacon mounted on a blue police telephone pillar was flashed. There were seventy two of these sited throughout the town. If on a night shift one was bored with shaking hands with door knobs it was a relief to see the flashing light on the pillar on your beat. Something, somewhere, possibly interesting, was up! On the other hand the officer inclined to be idle could say that he had not seen the light, as there certainly was not one on every street corner.

We moved up to Aldersley, bit by bit, by the motor cycle combo! As we had managed to maintain a good relationship with our landlady, I also took her up in the sidecar to see our house. She did enjoy the visit, but I am not so sure about the ride. We actually did make quite a few friends amongst the neighbours whilst living in her house, and are still in touch with some of these. One of our neighbours a street or two away was William Ambrose Wright, Billy Wright CBE, Captain of Wolves, and ninety times Captain of England.

A professional footballer who was never sent off and one of the very very few who were never even cautioned or booked. And a Shropshireman as well. Billy was the first player in the world to earn a hundred international caps, and still holds the record for the longest unbroken run of international appearances. And he used to travel to and from town on our bus – Jo travelled on the same bus many times. No Lamborghinis or Bentleys for soccer players in those days.

One incident at Aldersley to which I was called turned out to be both amusing and pathetic. A neighbour told me that there was a military deserter hiding in a ruined building near the canal, a couple of fields away from our house. I decided to go down there myself rather than call it in, while Jo, who was at home, had visions of some hardened warrior, ex S.A.S., at least seven feet tall and probably armed. In the event he was not hard to find, and turned out to be a poor little shrimp of a teenager, wet through, shivering and very hungry.

We gave him a hot meal and let him get warm before getting a car to take him to the Station, and thence back to Royal Air Force Bridgnorth. He had been on leave, overstayed it and then panicked about going back. In the days of National Service it was quite usual for the military to ask us to check the home address of someone who was AWOL. Sometimes the soldier or airman would be there and quite glad to be taken in. On one occasion however, the family denied that the absconder had come home. There was a young man in the house, about the right age, but in civvies. Mum said, on being questioned, that he was a lodger. The army form gave the deserter's first name as Michael and I noticed that he had 'Mick' tattooed on the finger of one hand. It also appeared that the family dog was very familiar with him, very affectionate, and after a bit of pressure he admitted being the man and that he had decided that the army was not for him. I was quite pleased with this bit of detective work, but it was really just a case of 'man's best friend' being not quite true!

A sad incident to which both Jo and I were called out from home at Aldersley was a motor cyclist who had been thrown from his machine in a collision with a car. He was obviously dying and there was nothing that either of us could do except try to keep him warm and comfortable until the arrival of the Ambulance. No para-medics on fast motorbikes then. We both felt very useless, especially with a crowd around all expecting us to produce some sort of miracle.

Other incidents included a woman wearing only a nightdress at midnight, who had heard that her husband had escaped from prison, where he resided for beating her up. Jo had to deal with that one, together with Audrey from the other police house, as both Bill and I were on duty. That often happened, and she also dealt initially with two reports of indecent assault, a child knocked off his bicycle, a boy with a broken arm, a woman with a broken leg and a woman who wanted to hand in a revolver. Was I ever there?! A really bizarre thing that she also coped with was a man who fallen off his bike in front of a bus, just outside our house. Fortunately he was missed by the bus, but Jo found that he had fallen because a large moth had flown right inside his ear, and got stuck there. He was lucky.

The police houses provided, I maintain, a service effectively free of charge, to the community, that is not found nowadays.

However, back to 1956. Having been married in June, and taken the wonderful honeymoon on Skye (which was still a real island, reachable only by ferry) I was posted to an Advanced Motor Cycling Course with Lancashire Constabulary, residential for two weeks, from the middle of August! Not wonderful timing, and we did think that my Traffic Inspector had a macabre sense of humour. Still, a course at Hutton, near Preston, was a real prize, as it was regarded as probably the premier British Police Driving School, which in effect meant one of the best in the world. I was very lucky to get on it, and again went straight onto an advanced course, without the usual preliminary standard or intermediate one. This was, despite the unfortunate timing, one of the three best periods of my police service. The Instructor, was extremely well known, and a great character, renowned as 'Goldie'.

On the arrival of two Lancashire officers and myself he greeted us with the words, 'When you fall off, and you will, the first thing to do is to make up your mind whether to report it or pay for it!'

After retirement he made a good second career as an after dinner speaker. We were on Triumph 500s, no screen or leg shields, and I think that it rained every day – at least that is how it feels now. I have not worried too much about getting wet ever since. But it was a wonderful fortnight, covering most of Lancashire, which is a pretty big county. We went up and down on the grass of Winter Hill near Bolton, where we did all fall off. Up and down the incredibly steep slopes of Hardknott and Wrynose Passes, and into every nook and cranny of the Lake District.

All day was spent on the road, or on the grass, getting a break occasionally at one of the numerous cafes where Goldie was known and obviously loved. He would sometimes lead, challenging us to keep up, or follow so that he could criticise the inept bend lines or panic stricken braking. As we discovered after the first day, at every stop the bikes were examined, and if anyone had forgotten to turn off the fuel tap or otherwise fail to park properly according to the Goldie code, that person paid for the food!

We had a theory and law exam at the end of the course followed by the fearsome practical ride. Each of us did a route of about an hour, followed by the Head of the Driving School in one of the Lancashire Jaguars (the actual 'Z Cars'). The Chief was another great character, who demonstrated playing 'Car football' on the skid pan. This was to score a goal by 'kicking' an old tyre between two goal posts, through a rear end movement of the Jaguar, using the accelerator and handbrake to provoke wheel spin and thus sliding the rear end in the direction needed. It doesn't sound very easy, and I don't think that it was, but he could do it, time after time! To my surprise, since Lancashire did not give them away easily, I again achieved a Class one, and really felt that I now knew something about motor cycling.

Sadly Goldie has passed on, and I lost touch with the two guys from Lancashire, but I still see Phil, one of the Instructors from the Driving School occasionally, through functions of The Royal Society for the Prevention of Accidents. He has advised on parts of this narrative.

Eventually after some happy, sometimes eventful, years at Aldersley we decided that it was time to get on the housing ladder. We had done quite a bit to the house, and I think that my Inspector triggered the move by telling me that there comes a time when you have spent enough on someone else's property. He had done the same thing himself.

One of the things that we had done was to get permission to buy a garage and erect it in the garden for the combo, and then the Morris Traveller which succeeded it. We bought a pre-fab DIY garage, which one erected oneself. It was made of asbestos sheets in a wooden framework. With a concrete base, the walls went up quite well, but putting on the roof was a pig! Eventually I broke, completely, one of the roof panels, which made the garage rather ineffective. However, we had some very good friends among the neighbours, Owen and Ann and their three children, and Owen volunteered to help me to mend the broken panel. I doubt if the money was available for a new one. We laboured mightily with glue and sheets of sticky backed plastic fablon, and managed to get the asbestos re-aligned and stuck together. We laid the panel on the ground prior to positioning it on the roof, and as I said, 'That's a good job done then,' stepped back and put a foot through all the repaired work!

I am told that Owen's face was a picture, but he was a nice man and not prone to violence! We did eventually complete the job, and it was more or less waterproof, but not a particularly well inspired design. Owen and Ann have passed on, but we are still in touch with their children, now of course well grown.

We moved to our own house in 1964, where we still are. Having accumulated a houseful of furniture by then the move was by much more conventional means. I think that, had we known that it would eventually come on to the private market, we might have stayed at Aldersley, but such a possibility was not even to be considered in 1964. Once again the crystal ball to see coming events would have been a bonus. It was a nice house, but cold. One of our 'improvements' was a remote control so that the wall mounted electric fire could be switched on whilst still in bed. This consisted of a length of wire, running under the carpet from my side of the bed, to the fire with an end hooked round the on/off switches, which fortunately pulled downwards for 'on'. Heath Robinsonish, like my gas pipe communication system for the combo I suppose, but they both worked.

One incident while a squad car driver has a strange relationship to my life today and the house that we moved to. My colleague and I were tasked to go to one of the main roads in the western suburbs, where a very large sow was running amok. The 999 lines into the Control Room were red hot. It did not take long to find the sow – work backwards along the line of fleeing women and children!

Pete and I approached it (to cheers I think from those bystanders brave enough to remain). It really was big, and a large sow, apparently frightened into ferocity, looks very dangerous and not to be talked to! Despite my brief farming experience I had, and still do not have, any idea of how a farmer deals with a pig on the loose. I imagine he uses a pitchfork. This we did not have, and a staff was not a lot of use. If you think about it there is very little to catch hold of with which to arrest a reluctant pig. We tried an ear each, and were shaken off with a glimpse of some rather nasty teeth. Eventually we both managed to get a grip on her tail, which she did not like either and were pulled along the road for several hundred yards, followed by the cheering crowd.

Fortunately the God of police officers in need had provided a farm towards the outskirts of the town, with a nice green field, and with the expenditure of a lot of physical energy on the part of Pete and I, (and the pig), we managed to interest her in it, and bar the gate. By now the owner, who kept a smallholding from which she had escaped, had arrived so we turned her over to him. This was one incident which did not make the local paper, although I would love to have seen a video of Pete and I both attached to her tail and being pulled along at a rate of knots. The strange thing is that the farm was eventually sold for building plots, and one of those houses is where I now live. Sometimes I think that I see the ghost of the sow rampaging round the field whereon my back garden now lies.

Another incident that I am quite proud of took place when a colleague and I in a squad car were cruising the town centre car parks one dark evening, looking for opportunist thieves. A guy standing in the shadows by a parked car looked 'wrong'. As I pulled up, he moved away, and then started to run. I bailed out, chased him on foot all round the narrow streets surrounding the car park (which is still in use by the way, bringing back happy memories). Being pretty fit I soon found that he was a member of a well known local family, in possession of an expensive brief case, of which he was definitely not the owner.

I was still writing up the arrest later at the Station when the owner came to report his car door forced and a brief case stolen. We were able to have the very satisfying experience of saying, 'Could this be the one?'

I did expect to at least get a letter of thanks from the owner, but this did not happen. Perhaps he thought we were just doing our job, which I suppose we were.

However, life often seemed to have 'swings and roundabouts' built in, and not long before I had received a commendation for tracing the offender in a non-stop collision, more by luck than anything else. The offending car had left paint traces on his victim's vehicle, which fortunately had yielded a sample and which had given us an idea of the colour we were looking for. It therefore seemed worthwhile, although dark, to cruise round the big council estate which lay further out of town and to the side of the main road. We found a car of the right colour parked untidily on the estate, and lo and behold, it was damaged in just the right place! The driver, although in his house by now, was well under the influence of drink. Forensic science proved that the paint trace was from that car.

Some luck, but I suppose the commendation was for knowing the best place to look. Local knowledge of thieves, families and their habitats was, and I think, is, vital to successful police work. With the amalgamated bigger Forces, I suspect that it has now largely disappeared, or is not as detailed as it was.

Another non-stop, later when I was no longer on Squad cars but a foot patrol Sergeant, proved the swings and roundabouts principle, because this one really deserved a word of praise at least, which never came! It was a big collision, on a major cross roads late at night, with the victim's car being written off and he quite badly injured and taken to Hospital. The road which the offender had apparently taken leads north to the M6, and it seemed a fair chance that he had gone that way. As we had a small general-purpose car available I and a Constable followed in the hope of finding something damaged by the side of the road. We went as far as Keele Services, way, way out of our area and using my Squad Car driving skills to go as fast as possible, but found nothing relevant.

Returning to the scene we scoured the area, and some distance away found small bits of a broken number plate and a headlamp rim. Enquiries the next day of various motor dealers identified the type of car from the rim, and again thinking that a housing estate in the right direction - a different one this time - might contain the offender I commenced a trawl of the local small repair shops in the north of the town. It was a considerable pleasure to find a car of the right sort being repaired in a small workshop, with a missing headlamp rim and a damaged number plate, which our bits fitted! Local knowledge again - at least this time the injured owner did thank me from his hospital bed!

Chapter 3

A Few Steps Up The Ladder

Between being posted to the Squad Cars in 1954 and promotion to Sergeant in 1963 I was definitely on a roll. There were a number of arrests and incidents, together with the bread and butter jobs of chasing speeders and other bad driving, and clearing up the results of the latter. Some of the arrests were serious ones, woundings, affrays, burglaries and breakings and enterings, while some of the incidents were funny.

On one occasion, one summer evening we were called to the main town cemetery, where we found a youth lying in a grave which had been freshly dug and was awaiting it's legitimate occupant. He was face down in the grave which was about eight feet deep. As he was semi-conscious it was not an easy job to get him out and into an Ambulance. We found that he had been walking with his girl friend, had had a quarrel and seeing the grave, moved the boards covering it and threw himself in headfirst! He had tried to get out but could not turn over due to the narrowness at the bottom of the hole. No charges on this one, and I do not know if he made it up with the girl. Hopefully not, for her sake!

A rather unusual case for a uniformed officer to take to Court was a young man that I charged with sending obscene literature through the post. It took a lot of interviews and questioning before he admitted it – this again was the result of girl friend trouble. That and drink was the cause of much of our work. But, it was a good time – something different every day, almost always interesting and often rewarding, and what I had joined the police service to find.

The swings and roundabouts factor kicked in at about this time, with an arrest in which luck played a big part. On one off-duty day, Jo and I were visiting a relation, Mary, her husband and small son Mark, who lived in Coventry. Coventry, now in the West Midlands Police area, was then policed by it's own Force, Coventry City Police. Jo and I offered to take Mark for a ride in our Morris Minor Traveller into the City Centre. In one of the crowded and busy main streets I spotted a man that I had had dealings with in Wolverhampton, and whom I knew was now wanted on warrant by the Staffordshire Police. I guess that is why he was in Coventry.

Absolutely fortuitously I was able to park the car in a reasonable place, left Jo and Mark inside it and grabbed the man. He was actually a big softy, and did not resist. I then began the process of deciding that this was probably another step too far, and what was the next move going to be, as I no idea where Coventry Police Station was. Then out of the blue (literally) I spotted one of the 'Dr Who' type police boxes, (the Tardis) which Coventry used. Wow, saved again! A phone call on the public side `phone brought a Coventry car for my prisoner, and directions to Coventry Central Police Station, where I was greeted by a rather surprised Custody Sergeant.

I received a nice letter of commendation for this from the Chief Constable of Staffordshire, which did not do my career any harm. Much to my disappointment, Mark, who now lives in Canada and is a Doctor of Philosophy and a Professor at McGill University does not remember this at all. However, his Mother does, and although I imagine she was not too happy about the incident at the time, seems to have forgiven me!

After the second police amalgamation in 1974 I came to know Coventry Central Police Station very well indeed. As head of communications for the West Midlands Police it was my responsibility to link the three areas of Coventry, Birmingham and the former West Midlands Constabulary towns of the Black Country together, communications–wise. This entailed putting in a modern Control Room in what had been the Coventry City gymnasium. This was not popular with the local officers, but after months of preparation and perspiration we did it, on time, for the 1st of April 1974. It worked well enough until it was possible to build one Force-wide Control Room.

I was in Coventry the night of the Birmingham 'pub' bombings by the I.R.A., sped back to the central Control Room in Birmingham, and did not go home for three days! This was very soon after the amalgamation, in April '74, and to be honest, neither we, nor the Ambulance Department, Fire Service nor the City authorities were prepared for such a big terrorist incident. A lot went wrong, through, for example, taxi drivers trying to help by ferrying injured people to the nearest Hospital. This led to some Hospitals being desperately over-loaded whilst others were left undisturbed. The Ambulances would have been directed to the best places.

My job was to run the Casualty Bureau, - identification of the dead and injured, information to relatives, and to the Press. Despite the Birmingham Police avowals, during the amalgamation planning, that all their systems were perfect and nothing needed to be changed, we quickly found that their existing Casualty Bureau was totally inadequate for a major incident of this type and size, and we struggled. There were many joint post-incident inquests by all the emergency services, and City authorities, where it seemed to me that a lot of defensiveness and back-protection was going on, but I suppose that this was inevitable. It was then the biggest provincial terrorism ever in the UK, and could not really have been timed to be more difficult to manage. My post-attack role was to modernise and enlarge the Casualty Bureau. The Birmingham Control Room itself had, I think, coped pretty well.

I think that it is true that the Metropolitan Police and the Forces of the big cities, Manchester, Birmingham, Liverpool, tended to look down on those of us in smaller urban areas, thinking that we had a relatively quiet life. I know that we ourselves thought this of the County Forces around us, neither being really true. I am quite sure that everything that happened in London also happened in Wolverhampton, not perhaps with the same frequency, but turn over a stone and you could find it. I too have been on multi-officer, 'bursting down the door and going in through the windows' drug raids in the 1960s.

In the 1960s Wolverhampton had one of the first 'race riots'. This was a battle between West Indian and Pakistani immigrants, the origin of which is now lost in the mists of time. I was involved in trying to sort out what had happened and who had done what. One Pakistani lady, who lived in a small terrace house, which has now been replaced by multi-story University accommodation, told me, 'This man, he come bursting in my house, so I hit him with the chapatti pan'. I imagine that this was quite effective.

Two macabre incidents also come to mind, the first being an extremely overweight man who sat heavily onto a porcelain toilet. The toilet bowl shattered into jagged pieces, one of which penetrated the part of his body that could be expected, causing death, and a lot of blood.

My colleague on Squad Car duty and I were called to another scene, where a neighbour reported that an elderly lady had been brutally murdered. In fact her death was completely natural, a massive haemorrhage, but we were literally paddling in the blood which covered the floor of the downstairs room where she was lying. It is just amazing how much blood even a small body contains.

One morning, after promotion to Sergeant, at 5.15 a.m. I was cycling in to work on Early Turn, and passed a licensed bar whose lights were still on. Investigation revealed a crowd of merry makers still being served! The Licensee, a Mr. Khan, told me that they were all his friends. If we had believed that we would have believed anything. This really was a bit blatant, and the place has been a nuisance in the town every since, despite being closed down several times and re-opened under different ownership and different names. Recently the Licensing Justices, in their undoubted wisdom, decided not to concur with yet another police appeal for permanent closure.

Then there were the prostitutes, plenty of them then and the West Midlands Police are still trying to deal with them and their clients. This is like trying to get a large snake into a small sack – you cope with one bit and it bulges out somewhere else. What was becoming very apparent was that there was a growing pimp culture, women being 'run' by one man who lived on their earnings, and beat them up if they did not perform. This was a new, perhaps transatlantic, import. I took one such man to Court, who had the same surname as a very famous Scotland Yard detective of the time, which earned me a bit of leg-pulling. In Court he accused me of kicking him, and produced a pair of trousers with a black mark impressed on the seat. This impression did not make much impression on the Magistrates. I could not possibly comment.

Most women 'on the game' were unsavoury characters, and it was quite difficult to see how they earned any money, even by moonlight. The beautiful Christine Keelers of the time did not of course work the streets. There was one West Indian woman who was quite attractive - in her early days - and I remember, as a very young Constable, being warned by a Sergeant, 'Don't ever let that one get you on your own – she'll have your trousers off before you know where you are.'

The strength of the smaller Forces, now all done away with, was the immense amount of local knowledge which was built up, not only about the town (now a City) itself, but about the local villains, weirdos, yobs - yes, we had them too - and other types of trouble makers. As a foot patrol Constable one would be visited during nights by the Duty Inspector, part of whose remit it was to see that his relief or shift were doing their job. One Inspector, who had been a very effective detective before promotion, carried a pack of photographs of local burglars, shop-breakers and violent people, (all three often combined in one man). He would quiz each Constable he met, 'Who is this then?' or, 'What's his alias?' Woe betide you if you could not give a reasonable answer. As his best mood was one of vague annoyance and went downhill from there one naturally tried to get it right.

By stopping to talk to people one could learn from them and give them confidence and often friendship. I remember speaking to a rather sad old tramp whilst on nights during the fifties. I gave him half a crown – quite a respectable sum in those days, and this sort of action was not at all uncommon amongst my colleagues. Yes, I know, he quite probably drank it, but just maybe it carried him on over the miles to the next 'Spike'.

Another strength of the smaller Forces was that all the motor patrol officers knew each other, and had an idea of each other's strengths and weaknesses. As foot patrol officers were attached to us as observers or to gain experience as future drivers we knew a lot of them as well. Also the Force was compact enough to run an annual police children's Christmas party. We had a couple of real comedians, Jim and Johnny who dressed up as clowns, Tom, an accomplished magician and Dave who lacked only the white beard to be the archetypal Santa Claus. I volunteered one year to be 'Puss in Boots'. Somehow I got hold of a black cat costume with a papier-mâché head. We worked out a sort of pantomime, during which the cat would appear on stage. It was hot in the suit and I had to keep retreating to the wings to take my head off. When we got to the cakes and sweets time the kids were invited onto the stage to collect their presents. All the little girls wanted to stroke the cat, which was OK, but all the boys decided it would be fun to give him a bonk across the head, which was not, since papier-mâché is hard on the inside. Also it took quite a time to clean the sticky chocolate and icing sugar off the fur before returning it to whence it came!

Many years later I was running a staff driving course at a local Young Offenders Prison. One of the Warders, knowing my background, said, 'I suppose you know a lot of the people we've got in here?'

My reply was, 'I doubt it, but I bet I know most of their Fathers and Grandfathers.'

This would be true, since a criminal tendency runs in families. You could see that a sixteen or seventeen year old boy was heading for disaster, following the family tradition, and try to talk him out of it, but very very rarely with any success.

Of other incidents which stand out in retrospect, one was a collapse of the Sadlers Wells Ballet Company! They had been allocated a building for rehearsal, remote from the Grand Theatre, and heated by a coke stove which was found later to have leaked carbon monoxide fumes. The dancers began to keel over, one by one, so we and the Ambulance Service were alerted. There was a definite race to get there, get into the building and carry out the girls, which as they were not dead but just limp, yielding and disorientated, was quite an enjoyable job. I am pretty sure that we beat the Ambulance personnel to it. Mouth to mouth resuscitation was under consideration when, in the open air, they unfortunately began to recover! The Duty Inspector was alerted to what could have been a major disaster. This was our cricket captain, the former Naval Officer, who did have the ability to use interesting language. Being on foot he was one of the last to arrive, and commented unhappily, 'You buggers got there so quickly there was no-one left for me, only the men, all jockstrap and balls!'

I came across a nurse at the Royal Hospital, who unusually for that profession was a rather unpleasant lady. I had charged her boyfriend with a fairly serious case of fraudulent use of documents and she promised me that should she get the chance I would be treated in Hospital with a rusty knife! Didn't ever happen, but rather atypical, proving I suppose that even nurses are human. I did feel that she was rather ungrateful though, as on Fridays and Saturdays from early evenings into early mornings we were regular attenders at the Royal's Casualty Department to throw out the aggressive, unwashed, unlikeable and unwanted.

In 1958, as the M1 was being built I was asked by Hertfordshire Police to interview the pilot of a local Flying Transport Company, who had been seen landing a twin-engined aircraft on a nearly completed section! He admitted it without argument but would admit no guilt, since the aeroplane was misbehaving. Must have been interesting avoiding the newly built bridges though. It never came to Court anyway.

We had two very sad incidents involving dead children. The first took place on Boxing Day, on one of the big housing estates. A very young boy had been given a little tricycle for Christmas. It was obviously not new; money on the estates was not plentiful, but had been carefully repainted red and white by Dad, and had a shiny new Mickey Mouse bell on the handle-bars. It must have been a joy and a delight to the child. And, I am sure, to his parents. But on Boxing Day someone had left the front garden gate open, and he rode it out into the road, behind a lorry which was about to reverse, completely out of the sight of the driver. I had that tricycle in my garden shed for months, and can still see it very clearly, as I could not face taking it back to the parents. I had to ask them in the end of course, but not surprisingly they told me to get rid of it. That hurt as well, thinking about the work that had gone into getting it and painting it. Also hurtful, still, is thinking about the lorry driver, who was not in any way to blame. You wish, if you think about these things that you could have done something to help, but of course, there was nothing. Decades later I can still get upset about this.

The other death that is still very clear in my mind involved a girl, of about nine, run over by a Council lorry while cycling home from school. It was the policy that a police officer accompanied the Mortuary Van to the Mortuary, so that a chain of identity was preserved. The girl was still wearing her green school raincoat and green woollen gloves, knitted I guess by Mum or Gran. Her body, the raincoat and gloves were unmarked, but she had no head. Only a bit of white bone. This was bad enough for me, but really terrible is the fact that my colleague from the Squad Car was performing the same service for the girl's sister, of a similar age. Two small girls, cycling home from school, both killed by a lorry. How do you tell the parents what has happened? How do you get the identities confirmed in such a situation? These are the hard and brutal facts of policing, which despite all the technology and modernisation still have to be carried out by human beings. Those human beings have to suffer as well.

Of course there are techniques – it was never blurted out, despite what you may see on films or TV. Always one would seek out a sympathetic neighbour or relative, infinitely preferably female, gradually lead up to the facts, and then try to organise as much help as possible. 'Counselling' by professionals, which is now part of my daughter Nicky's work, just did not exist.

It was not uncommon to have women, being told of a close relative's death, to refuse to believe it. I have been accused of being mistaken or worse, playing a cruel joke. This was also difficult to resolve, but you had to find a way round it. This was another area where a woman officer was invaluable. When breaking news I sometimes, to my horror, found an almost irresistible urge to laugh. This would be described now as a defence mechanism to protect myself, I guess, but it worried me a lot at the time.

One way of breaking death news was only used if it was absolutely unavoidable, and this was to do it by telephone. I had to do so once and it was difficult. A small airliner had crashed onto houses on its final approach to land at Wolverhampton Airport. There were only the crew on board, but both were killed instantly. I was one of the officers dealing with this, and was asked to answer a telephone call being put through to the nearest police box. This was from the father of the young co-pilot, who lived in the south of England, and who had learned that the plane had crashed, but not the fate of the crew. I had to tell him, of course, although I could now perhaps debate whether a white lie, suggesting serious injuries, would have been better. The best and normal way would have been to get an officer from the father's local force to go round in person, and this was in process when he telephoned, having been told, by a well meaning person I suppose, of the crash. I am still not sure whether the truth or a lie was the better option, but it was a difficult duty.

Another case of death still worries me, nearly fifty years on. We were called one evening to a car salesroom. This was the small showroom of a private car sales company. Suspended by a rope round his neck, over one of the cars, was the dead eighteen year old son of the owner. He was a strong well built young man, and it was impossible to believe that he could have been strung up by another person without some evidence of a struggle. The parents were of course devastated, and so were all the boy's college friends and girl friends. The post-mortem showed nothing except that he had choked to death. I spent a lot of time on this but could find nothing to suggest that the boy was other than a normal, well liked teenager. The inquest eventually came to the conclusion that this was an auto-erotic experiment that had gone tragically wrong. However, I have wondered ever since if there was anything that I missed, or anything more that I could have done. Well, he would have been a State Pensioner himself by now, and I shall never know the truth, but I still wonder.

A case leaving me even now uncertain that I got at the whole truth was a complaint by two small girls (both about ten) that the owner of a shop had taken them into the back of his shop, given them some chocolate and indecently exposed himself. They had told their mothers, who complained to us. A policewoman took statements from the girls, but the case was mine, as the beat officer. The shop owner denied it vehemently, both when interviewed and right up to and after conviction, but there were certain things that inclined me to believe the girls. They could describe the back of the shop very accurately, which could not be seen from the public part, and had kept the chocolate. It was decided to prosecute, and I was impressed with the way the Magistrates dealt with the girls. The Chair was a woman, who questioned the girls very thoroughly but sympathetically, and the hearing was not in the normal Court Room, but a small private one. The shopkeeper, a middle aged, apparently respectable man, was convicted, which I guess was the ruin of his life. There was certainly no way that he could have maintained his shop on a big council estate, as he would probably have been strung up by the local vigilantes. I have never been entirely happy about this, although the Magistrates were. I would dearly love to question the two girls, who are now late-middle aged women of course, as to whether they were really telling the truth or acting out a fantasy. One expects that in later life they would be aware of the damage that such a lie could do. However, I guess that such a course would not be ethical, even if possible. Perhaps it is better anyway that I shall never know.

I also wonder whether the general public, for whom we worked, realised, or realise nowadays, the impact that cases like these can have on the involved officer. It wasn't, never was, and never will be all fun and rescuing pretty ballet girls, or handing in ducks in cardboard boxes as found property. There are many scenes that I can still see.

On the other hand I think that counselling should be only very rarely necessary for a well balanced person who has been involved, otherwise than as a victim, in traumatic events. It was unknown in the nineteen fifties and I do not think that they get more traumatic than a small girl with no head, or a lot of bodies under a railway carriage. The growing culture of compensation for involvement in a traumatic situation disgusts me. It is a part of the job for a police officer, fireman or soldier. The word 'compensation' should I believe be changed to 'greed' and I have no time for the police claimants involved in some of the high profile cases that have happened since, for example, at the Hillsborough football disaster.

In the fifties and sixties England was subject to very dense fogs – 'pea-soupers' as they were called, and Wolverhampton, being a heavily industrialised area suffered badly. The motor patrol was tasked to try to get the traffic stuck in fog in the town centre moving safely. The only way to do this was to forget the Squad Cars and use motor cycles to guide a queue of drivers at a safe speed following the bike, the rider having a better view. As there were never enough bikes available other drivers on duty were deployed to point duty at strategic places.

What this did to our lungs I hate to think, and after a couple of days motor cycling like this one would be coughing up black sputum for weeks. Somehow, in those days, no-one seemed particularly worried about the health aspect, so you just did it and tied a handkerchief over your mouth and nose. I was caught out once driving one of the Morris Sixes on a solo assignment, and was right out on the outskirts of the town. The fog rolled in very suddenly, thick and heavy, and I needed to get back to the Station. There was only one possible way, and that was to sit in the front passenger seat, swing my legs across to the clutch, brake and accelerator, and steer with my right hand, while following the nearside kerbline through the open passenger window. Again, not good for the lungs, and the problem came when arriving at a junction! I knew the town well enough by then to cope with this, and got back safely, but I don't recommend it as a way of driving. A fog too far. Fortunately those days disappeared when the Clean Air Act arrived.

An important part of Late and Night Turns was to keep an eye open for drivers under the influence of drink. Possibly drugs as well, although these were a lot less common then. We would sometimes get the number or description of a suspect vehicle from a call by a foot patrol officer or occasionally from a member of the public. It was then a question of local knowledge, likely areas to search, or to head towards the direction in which the vehicle was travelling. We did get quite a few successes that way, and on one occasion stopped and arrested the driver of a rather nice Rolls Royce. It fell to me to bring it to the Station, the driver going by free police transport. Strangely it took quite a long time to find the way back to the Station!

Proving a drunk-in-charge was a lot more difficult then. No breathalysers or forensic evidence. The officer had to be able to show cause for stopping the vehicle, such as erratic, or very slow or very fast speeds. The condition of the driver was then given in evidence. 'Breath smelling of drink (alcohol doesn't smell -another media myth), face flushed, voice slurred, unsteady gait, aggressive conduct etc'. All this gave enough ground for an arrest and, if the custody Sergeant agreed, the driver was seen by the Police Doctor, at the Station. The success or failure of a prosecution was then very much in the hands of the Doctor – this was in the days of 'walking the line' which was painted on the charge room floor. Very primitive really, and we lost some cases due to poor medical evidence.

One such still rankles, since the guy was as drunk as a lord. I was travelling to work, on nights, in uniform and standing on the open rear platform of a double-decker trolley bus. These buses were very quiet, no engine noise, so that I was easily able to hear the sound of grinding gears and an engine being revved very hard as we got into the town centre. The bus slowed to a walking pace, so I jumped off, to see what was happening. In front of the bus, travelling very slowly, still at high revs and obviously in first gear in the centre of the road was a small van.

I ran up to the driver's door, and through the open window could see that the driver was slumped over the wheel. I was able to open the door, pushed him away from the wheel towards the passenger seat and grabbed the handbrake, stalling the van. The driver was virtually blotto, stank like a brewery and was apparently incapable of speech. He could possibly have been ill, but there were plenty of grounds for arrest, so with the van now stationary I was able to manhandle the driver into the passenger seat and drove the van into the police station yard. In retrospect this was actually pretty risky in case he became violent, but it was only a few hundred yards, and mobile 'phones were not even a twinkle in the inventor's eyes then. So, I did it my way. It took three of us to get him into the charge room, not because he was violent but because he was practically unconscious, unable to walk, and had to be carried. The Doctor was called and certified that he was not ill, but so much under the influence of drink that he could not do any of the standard tests, walking the line.

This man happened to be a quite well off farmer, living in a village out of town, and he opted to be tried at Quarter Sessions. He was able to afford a Barrister, one who was quite a successful defender, and was known for attacking the police officer concerned in any case he defended. It also happened that the driver was committed to Staffordshire Quarter Sessions, where at that time juries were known to have such a dislike of voting to convict that they would have let Jack the Ripper and Dick Turpin the Highwayman go! With such evidence the lawyer's only chance was to say that I had made it all up. Several friends of the farmer swore that he had been as sober as a judge when getting into his van just before I arrested him. The Doctor was often a weak witness in Court, which was a bit strange as he could be a bully to individual patients.

Although I could see my case going down the swanee, it was actually quite enjoyable to see him wilting under ferocious questioning, and getting some of his own medicine, so to speak! Well, the Staffordshire jury lived up to their reputation, but I did receive a leak from the jury room. Apparently one woman juror had said that she knew that part of Wolverhampton and at 9.30 p.m. it was always very busy. As I had said that it wasn't, I must have been telling lies throughout!

It does still annoy me, but at least I stopped him killing himself or anyone else, and the Barrister would have cost him a lot of money. This was one of the swings and roundabouts cases, some you lose, some you win, but in another of those strange co-incidences the wheel has circled round. Many years after the driver's death we have friends who bought and magnificently redeveloped his farmhouse so that I can sit there on occasion and silently toast his memory, wherever he now may be.

I had a regular and welcome partner on Squad Cars, Ray, who was hoping for a chance to join the motor patrol. We were looked upon as an elite, and there was always a waiting list. Ray had qualified as a Grade 2 driver on his driving course, and was allowed to drive under supervision. One morning he and I were on Early Turn, Ray driving, when we got a call that a body had been discovered on the tennis courts at the town's second Hospital, New Cross. Ray got the bit well between his teeth, and we flew down the Wednesfield Road. I remember that my right foot was pumping on a non-existent brake pedal, but we got there.

We found that it was the body of a middle aged Assistant Nurse, who had clearly been murdered, stabbed in the neck and breast and battered with a rock. We were very much the first there, apart from the Hospital gardener who had found the body. Our job was therefore to protect the scene, and keep everyone else away, until CID senior officers could arrive. Scotland Yard was called in and Chief Superintendent Ernest Millen of the Murder Squad put in charge, and I acted as his driver several times. Oddly enough I was on duty in the Control Room a day or two later (drivers used to also do regular duties in there, which was a good way of gaining experience) when I answered a 999 call. The caller, a female with an obviously disguised voice, named an Indian Doctor at the Hospital as the killer. I tried to keep her on line, but she was quickly gone, with no way to trace the call. The good doctor was arrested and after attempting to commit suicide by a drug overdose was charged with murder. He was committed to Staffordshire Assizes where the reluctance to convict even Jack the Ripper factor kicked in again. A defence witness had claimed that bloodstains on his clothing, overcoat, shoes and in his bathroom could have come from his dealing with emergency cases.

If you believe that.....!

What a pity that DNA evidence was not available then. After his acquittal the police stated that no other person would be sought. It is therefore easy to make 2 plus 2 equal 4. The Doctor did not stay in England. This case attracted a lot of national publicity, and still, fifty years on, is referred to from time to time in the press.

I was also first at the scene of a rather more macabre murder, where in a very quiet cul-de-sac in one of Wolverhampton's leafy suburbs a parked car was found to contain the bound and gagged body of an Asian man on the back seat. This did give rise to the thought that there had been foul play (how I hate that silly phrase) and the culprit was fairly quickly identified.

Another murder, this time involving one of our own took place in daylight in the very centre of the town. Detective Sergeant Jim Stanford was knifed to death by a man that he was trying to arrest. The man – only a youth really, was well known to many of us, and just about everyone in the Force turned out to search for him, whether on or off duty. He was caught fairly quickly and sentenced. Jim's funeral, at Bushbury Crematorium was a massive affair, with officers in uniform lining the route and the Chief Constables of neighbouring Forces leading the cortege with our Chief, and town dignitaries. On a beautifully sunny day, with a view over Shropshire and as far as the Wrekin it was an impressive, moving and imposing spectacle. Jim had a wife and small children, so the sadness was there in full measure, but there was pride as well. He was posthumously awarded the Queen's Police Medal for Gallantry. Jim is commemorated by a plaque in the rebuilt Wolverhampton Central Police Station, together with another Wolverhampton Officer, who was shot by a gang before the Second World War.

Chapter 4

Being paid to fly – at last!

In 1967, a year after the amalgamation of the three Black Country Borough Forces and areas of Staffordshire and Worcestershire into the West Midlands Constabulary, I was nominated for the six months Inspector's Course at the Police Staff College at Bramshill in Hampshire. Not all new Inspectors were able to get on this course, which was much sought after, and I was lucky to be selected. Bramshill was, and is, the only Police College. Hendon was the Police College before the 39-45 war, set up to produce and fast-track senior officers but it then reverted to being the Metropolitan Police training centre. Bramshill was designed to do the same job in a similar fashion to the Army and Air Force Staff Colleges. I get hot under the collar that Training Centres, designed to carry out recruit training, are frequently called 'Colleges' by the uninformed!

Another junior Inspector and I travelled down to Hampshire together. Dave had, unusually, a Jaguar, so we journeyed in style. The first sight of Bramshill, which is a genuine Elizabethan Mansion, glowing golden in the setting sun, with the blue police flag flying, was a delight and is a happy memory. We were greeted, along with other new arrivals, by senior officers in the beautiful entrance hall, made to feel welcome and at home. The six months was divided into two terms of three months each of general studies and police professional studies. I enjoyed both terms.

My general studies tutor was a former Oxford professor, a rowing blue, who still coached crews on the Thames at Henley. He and I got on well and I learned a lot from him. Tutorials, one to one, were held regularly, and I remember surprising him at least once by talking about Ulan Bator, the capital of Mongolia! The College was run on Officers Mess lines, with a very formal dining-in night once a week, to which one could invite a guest. Every student had to spend one of these dinners on the 'top table', where the staff dined. As they were all academics or senior police officers it was difficult to keep up with the conversation, or to get a word in, and I remember feeling like a spectator at Wimbledon – head swivelling!

We had good sports facilities, cricket, tennis, and archery on the lawn in front of the house and sailing on the lake in the grounds at the back and were able to have regular swimming sessions in the pool at nearby Sandhurst, the Army College, where I was introduced to water polo. It was a very pleasant way to serve six months, but was also designed to widen horizons, get people thinking and as a preparation not only for the supervisory role of an Inspector but to trawl for talent for the higher ranks. I think that for most people it worked, but perhaps not everyone enjoyed or appreciated the General Studies term. I had previously been nervous when speaking in front of an audience, but came away enjoying it and looking forward to the next opportunity, and felt that I had grown, in many ways.

The professional studies involved a lot of role-play, recorded on closed link TV so that one could see one's own mistakes and weaknesses, as well as lectures, and debates. We also visited Parliament and places like Broadmoor, the Establishment for the criminally insane, where I met the comedian Jimmy Saville, also there on a visit as a benefactor. My police eye noted that the perimeter fence had been erected the wrong way round, so that it kept people from getting in, rather than getting out. It was fascinating to see, many years later at a prestigious Army College near to the home of my daughter and son-in-law, that the fence had also been erected back to front – this time to keep people in rather then keep them out. Absolutely amazing! To give the Army credit they reversed the fence eventually, but Broadmoor may be – probably still is – the same.

At Bramshill there were regular concerts given by the staff and students, to which many well-known personalities were invited. I remember taking part in a sketch, watched from the front row of the audience by an extremely well known and popular author and playwright. Unfortunately I have to say that he looked bored, but perhaps that was his normal expression.

At the conclusion of the Inspector's Course there was a big passing out parade, as it was combined with the passing out of one of the first Special Courses, the one designed to find and train young 'high flyers' who would go on, hopefully, to senior positions. We were inspected by Her Majesty's Chief Inspector of Constabulary, the highest position in the British Police Service. This is a political post, but filled by a career police officer. He was wearing a uniform the headgear of which was a very large plumed and cocked hat. It was strongly rumoured that he had designed it himself. I could not resist the thought that he looked like the Duke of Wellington on the battlefield at Waterloo, and a bit daft without a horse. Also inspecting us was the Home Secretary, Roy Jenkins. He stopped before me and paused for a moment, searching for something to say I hoped for something like, 'My word you do look magnificent Mr.Collins,' but instead it was the question, 'Have you been here before?'

As I was part of the Inspector's Course, none of whom would have been to Bramshill before, this revealed a certain lack of knowledge of the situation. However, mustn't expect too much I suppose. We were not honoured to have a white horse on parade, but I was later privileged to see this tradition when my son passed out from his short-service commissioning course at Sandhurst.

Whilst having been treated to luxury in Dave's Jaguar on our initial journey to Bramshill, I felt that I should reciprocate, but did not want to put a lot of miles onto our elderly Morris Traveller. I made enquiries around Bramshill and found a farmer who had an old Ford Popular for sale. It worked, sort of, and he only wanted £20 for it. It carried me, and on widely separated occasions Dave, up and down from Hampshire for six months, and then it became known as 'Mum's car'. It was a terrible old thing, top speed about fifty, but getting into a speed wobble at more than forty! Dave wisely declined to ride in it most of the time. We kept it for about another six months and then sold it for £25. This is the best car deal that I have ever made or am likely to make.

We had a free afternoon once a week, and another Inspector and myself made good use of the Ford Pop to see as much of Southern and South Eastern England as possible. Swimming at Brighton and seeing beautiful Buckler's Hard are two Wednesday afternoons that stand out, but I was also very lucky indeed, on one trip to London to get into one of the first London performances of 'Fiddler on the Roof' with Topol, at the Haymarket Theatre. I had to queue for a standing ticket of course and was about the last one to squeeze in. The theatre was choc-a-block, and as this was just after the Israeli-Egyptian Six Day war I am sure that most of the audience were Jewish. The patriotism was so thick that you could bite on it, the hairs on the back of my neck were raised and I felt shivers run up and down my spine. It was a tremendously emotional experience, not unlike being present when Wolves beat Spartak and Honved.

I was again lucky to be selected for a place on the Intermediate Command Course in 1972, which was for prospective senior officers. It was pleasant to be greeted by my previous tutor, 'Well hello, *Chief* Inspector'. This was a more intensive three months, delving into world politics and psychology. One lecturer described the United States as the country posing the most potential danger to world peace. The jury is still out on that one.

There was again plenty of time to enjoy sport. It was the soccer season, and I did take part, but by now this was a step too far for me, or perhaps a step too slow. You had to be seen doing some extra-curricular activity, and it was definitely a black mark not to take part in anything. So, as there was a choir, I joined that. This was a bit of a con, as I have never been able to sing an accurate note. However, my mistakes were drowned out by younger and stronger voices! In the run up to Christmas we gave a number of recitals at Old People's Homes, Hospitals and the like, and no one complained about me. We also gave a concert to an invited audience. Now, on an occasion like this, those in the choir wanted it to be seen that they were in the choir. I had weaselled my way into the front row, before the curtain came up, well visible. By the time the curtain was fully up, I found myself in the back row, several members of the choir being bigger and perhaps pushier than myself!

During these three months a number of future very senior officers were students, including, in the next room to me, the future Chief Constable of the Royal Ulster Constabulary. On both courses there were a substantial number of overseas officers from Commonwealth or former Commonwealth Forces. The shared experiences were invaluable, if sometimes a bit strange:

'In Pakistan, we always shoot to kill.'

'Why is that?'

'Because bullets are expensive'.

There was usually a bit of horseplay at dining-in nights, and one officer from an African country had a salt cellar emptied into his mess jacket pocket. He did not like this at all, and later produced a revolver with which to shoot the offender. He was persuaded against this, physically, but I have always wondered how he got it into the country.

An English tradition that did puzzle our Commonwealth colleagues was the County badge worn by some Forces on the uniform jacket lapel. The prancing white horse of the Kent Constabulary was not too difficult:

'Ah, this man, he is looking after the horses?'

This was not taken too well by the person referred to, a Detective Inspector, put into uniform for the course only, but was understandable, sort of. However, the fiery dragon, worn by the officers of the Somerset County Police, did raise some questions, perhaps not all of them answered seriously. The bear and ragged staff of Warwickshire caused a bit of a stir as well. The stick was to control the bear!

We had a great end-of-course Christmas Ball, to conclude the Intermediate Command Course, to which Jo was able to come, visiting Bramshill for the second time. This is still a good memory.

In 1966 I had been promoted to Inspector to be in charge of the Wolverhampton Division motor patrol. As this was the time of the formation of the amalgamated West Midlands Constabulary office space was at a premium and I have a nice cartoon of myself sitting in a broom cupboard, which doubled as my office for the first few weeks. In 1967 word spread that the Force was to provide an Observer, to work on the Midlands phase of the first serious attempt at evaluation of the use of aircraft by the Police.

For some time there had been wistful thoughts amongst the police hierarchy concerning the possibility of establishing PAWS (Police Air Wings!)

to emulate our transatlantic colleagues. Finance and the non-availability of army units had prevented any previous trials, but now the Home Office, the Army, the Royal Air Force and various police forces had got their act together. Four middle ranking police officers from Staffordshire, West Midlands, Birmingham City and West Mercia were to take over from the Metropolitan Police, who had provided the observers for the first phase of one month in, or over, London. Local knowledge was of course essential for the police observer, as the pilots would not have it and our work was likely to be too detailed for map reading.

I had by now attained quite a bit of gliding experience, and been on various Royal Air Force courses, navigation and a lot of flying, amongst them. I wasted no time at all in putting pen to paper, and magnified my flying history (which did actually go back to the age of fourteen as an Air Training Corps Cadet) and knowledge of the Midlands as far as I dared. As I was chosen I guess the point had been made that I was the outstanding and inevitable choice. The case boiled down to, 'C'est moi, c'est moi, 'tis I' extracted from the song by Lancelot du Lac in the musical *Camelot*! So began the third period of special enjoyment during my police career – cars, motor bikes and now helicopters! The first task, on meeting the other observers at Royal Air Force Cosford, in December 1967, was to find out how we would react to the three Sioux helicopters with which the Regimental air platoon was equipped. We were quite a mixed bag, with the most senior, George, holding a Distinguished Flying Cross as a navigator in Lancaster bombers during the war, to myself as a glider pilot and Derek and Harry with no, or very little, flying experience. After being introduced to the three pilots (a Captain and two Sergeants) and their ground support staff we were given a pretty rough ride, which included auto-rotation (frightening the first time) and the helicopter equivalent of a stall turn being the pièce de résistance. As everyone survived with Official Dignity dented but still intact we were given the go-ahead for a month's trial.

George however, was heard to say later in the experiment, 'These bloody little things turn a lot quicker than a Lancaster!' The Sioux was a very manoeuvrable two-seater machine, with extremely good all round visibility, but looked a little like a birdcage tied on to a balloon. In the later phases we used four-seater Scouts, which were rather more conventional.

The Air Platoon had recently returned from a tour of very active duty in Aden and were all dead keen to get back into action. The mix of soldiers and policemen was an instant success, and Captain (now Major) John, Derek and I still have a re-union every so often. I note with pleasure that Major John writes that the Army personnel enjoyed their stay in the Midlands more than they had earlier with the Metropolitan Police. During the most recent re-union we were able to visit the police helicopter base at Wolverhampton Business Airport and spent a fascinating time being shown over the current aircraft, a four seat Eurocopter.

The machine and its communications and observation equipment are a world away from what we had in 1968, and so is the observer selection and training process. 'C'est moi' would not be enough nowadays! This is real progress that I can understand and appreciate, compared with much of what has happened during the last forty years. We were all impressed with the enthusiasm and expertise of the crew, and the visit has gone a long way to restore my faith in the Police Service of today.

The timing of our Midlands phase, in January 1968, coincided with a vicious outbreak of foot and mouth disease, a prolonged snowfall, freezing blizzards, fog and widespread flooding. The weather affected us considerably, and the Siouxs and crews had to land in a bath of disinfectant after each sortie because of the foot and mouth. The Army Air Corps provided a back-up fixed wing aircraft when necessary, and I can claim to be one of the very few British Policemen who have flown in a De Havilland Beaver on both skis and conventional wheels on duty, and (later in Canada) on floats. I guess that the Mounties did it all the time, but it was not done over here!

After some initial procedures, ground handling and familiarisation training we were tasked to attend everything possible, being scrambled by any of the four Force Control Rooms. The observer's duties were detailed navigation, incident control as necessary, including liaison with police on the ground, and communication with the Control Rooms. The Home Office had provided a reasonably (for the time) workable air to ground Pye Vanguard radio net. We also did a formal evaluation of each sortie with the pilot. We had our own police radio controller, Reg, a Sergeant from Staffordshire Constabulary, who had been carefully chosen. I think that the selection procedure, although certainly not as thorough as that of today, must have been quite efficient, as all of us did reach higher rank. We had to temporarily 'promote' Reg, as the four observers were billeted, and fed, in the Officers Mess at Cosford, and at RAF Kinloss when we did the Scottish phase of the experiment. Reg, being a Sergeant, was persona- non-grata in the Mess. This struck us as not quite fair, since the difference in status is rather different in the police to that in the armed forces. He was therefore, on occasion, given an instant but temporary promotion by borrowing my or Derek's uniform jacket. We were invited to a party in the Sergeants Mess one evening and thoroughly disgraced ourselves by winning the jackpot!

The dramatic part of the trial started early, with a train crash reported twenty miles from base at a station on the outskirts of Birmingham, in my area. It was from this sortie that I learned what flying in a service helicopter in adverse conditions was all about. When we were alerted visibility was down to 50 to 100 yards in fog. My pilot on this occasion was Rod, a Staff Sergeant, and he elected to try it. Fortunately a railway line leading to the accident site passed close to our base. We got on track, almost literally, and managed to find the right line through the complex of junctions surrounding the target area.

Happily the crash was a minor one, a rear end shunt, with limited casualties. After landing nearby, (to the huge delight and astonishment of the assembled crowd) and giving some assistance and traffic state reports, we started our return to base. Rod (six foot three, with collar and shirt size to match) had not been able to be much help to me on the ground. He had been entirely occupied in swatting small boys and reporters, all of whom seemed to regard the helicopter as a shot-down enemy aircraft, ripe for souvenirs. This was quite a sight, and as most of the small boys were Asian obviously he was spiritually back in Aden.

By now the urban smog was down to 20-30 yards, and it was necessary to fly very low indeed to keep sight of the ground. Our base had no homing service, so it was entirely a question of Mark 1 eyeball on his part and local knowledge on mine, the main and potentially fatal hazard being power lines. For me it was a wonderful display of controlled slow flying. On our eventual safe return we found that the platoon commander, Captain John, had alerted the railway, who had responded by reporting our progress to him, signal box by signal box!

Two days later, with the weather much improved, we were committed to one of the games of scrabble which filled much of the waiting time in the scramble room, when the call came to another train crash, on the Trent Valley express line. This was in Staffordshire, but I knew where and the visibility was excellent, so I took off with Rod. We soon saw that this crash was a real one – a big one. The express train was derailed and spread-eagled over the fields adjacent to the line, having crashed at high speed into a very large and heavy low loader transporter. It had become stuck going over one of the new half barrier level crossings and weighed 130 tons, being loaded with a heavy electricity transformer, and was 148 feet long. The express had been travelling at about 80 mph, drawing twelve coaches with about 250 passengers. Eight of the coaches were derailed, the first four being thrown thirty yards past the impact site.

There were a number of fatalities, eventually totalling eleven, some hideously flattened under the derailed carriages. Many passengers were injured, forty two of them seriously. Local police were already on site, and we identified that the main and urgent need was for a medical team, as injured passengers were wandering about, shocked and barely conscious.

I remember asking an Inspector what we could best do and his reply, 'Get me some Doctors and Nurses for God's sake'.

This site was in a very rural area, with no immediate medical help, and the approach roads were jammed – the crossing of course being unusable. We made for Stafford, the nearest town, with our base alerting the major hospital. Here I saw again a wonderful display of judgement and control, as the nearest feasible landing place was a petrol filling station forecourt next to the hospital. This was long before helipads at hospitals, but helped to lead to them.

Rod went straight in, without any guidance from the ground. The petrol pumps and signs seemed to me to be no more than inches outside the rotor circle. As the Sioux could take three at a pinch I evacuated and bundled two of the waiting nurses into the cockpit, snatching at their caps as they approached to avoid them being sucked up into the rotor. It was at this point that I learned for the first time, despite being married to one, that nurses pinned on their caps.

One mature and fierce Sister told me just what to do. The astonishment of the garage staff and the inevitable crowd, (none of whom knew about the crash), whilst viewing these proceedings can easily be imagined. Air Ambulances were unheard of in those days. We were joined by the two other aircraft and although I was able to indicate wind direction and rotor clearance, and with difficulty keep the crowd away for all but the first one with Rod, each approach was a superb demonstration of pilot skill. We got a shuttle service going, Doctors and Nurses, six at a time and quickly delivered all the necessary medical teams, and their equipment, to the crash site. After the medics had been delivered we were occupied with traffic control and diversions to get the ambulances to the site. We also plotted a cross-country route for a Coal Board heavy-duty crane to reach the scene.

By now the movement of the helicopters were being hampered by the number of media chartered light aircraft circling the crash. When darkness forced our return to Cosford we found that we were extremely newsworthy, and almost local heroes. It was just the boost that the experiment needed, and which went a long way on its own to justify the trials. Of course, one would have preferred that the justification could have been without death or injury. The sight of the bodies trapped under the derailed carriages is one that I can still see. A railway carriage on one side in a field is a huge, macabre and frightening, even sinister, object

This collision was almost literally the impossible case of an immovable object and an unstoppable force. The train driver, whose last few seconds of life can only be imagined with horror, had tried to jump out of the cab, but failed to get clear. There was not a lot left to bury. One can only imagine the thoughts of the lorry driver too, and the shock of the police officers escorting the long load by patrol car, as they realised what was inevitably about to happen.

This crash did lead to changes in the Regulations about heavy goods vehicles passing over level crossings, and widened knowledge of the dangers of the new unmanned ones. It also stirred the curiosity of the NHS about the possibility of helicopter transport for casualties and a helicopter based emergency medical service. This latter consequence was fuelled by the work that we were able to do soon after in delivering urgent blood supplies in bad road conditions. Routine now, but not thought of then.

We then attended a series of lesser events, some with success, others less so. One nice operation over a crowded street, directing a policeman on foot by radio to arrest a suspect, went, 'That's it, right a bit, now straight on, now left, and he's the only one who isn't looking up at us!'

On another occasion we were able to substitute for the thirty officers who were not available, by circling a warehouse where a suspect was holed up. He stayed there until collected. We all operated at times over each other's territory, and learned that with good communications we could work well anywhere. George on his home ground in Worcestershire, having flown to respond to a break-in call noticed an area of down trodden grass leading to a lane near the premises. This quickly led to the burglar's arrest by the troops on the ground.

On one return to base we found ourselves flying over my house, and naturally did a couple of beat-ups. Twenty minutes later my neighbour's chimney collapsed. Absolutely unconnected of course, but I was expecting the bill for weeks. Also enjoyable was flying over the local infant's school that my small son attended, just at playtime. There was a lot of jumping up and down, and I imagine he got a lot of brownie points by saying, 'That's my Dad up there!'

Another exercise was the flying of a police Alsatian to see if it was possible without being attacked – fairly hairy this episode. The dog loved it but the handler was terrified!

One Saturday we were tasked to fly to a First Division football ground around which about two thousand visiting fans were taking the town apart. Quite what we could do did not seem to have been envisaged by the Control Room who asked for help. It was perhaps hoped that the sight of the Helicopter with Police marking would turn their thoughts to higher things.

However, we did learn from this, and some years later, in 1978, I was tasked to keep an eye on what we knew was going to be a violent and racially motivated demonstration in Birmingham City Centre, which became known as the 'Battle of Digbeth'. On this occasion we used a rented 'Jet Ranger' helicopter – a rather more contemporary looking machine than the Sioux but lacking the superb visibility from the cockpit bubble. I found that a helicopter, used skilfully, can have a remarkable effect on a hostile crowd. We spotted a gang picking up bricks and rubble from a building site, obviously with which to attack the police cordon. The pilot and I looked at each other, nodded simultaneously and he dropped it like a stone, fast and noisily to just above their heads. They scattered like rabbits. Now, I don't know if this technique has been used since, but it worked then. Perhaps, hopefully, it infringed their civil rights. This was effectively my last operational job within the police service, and like many of the other jobs it did get headlines, 'The police helicopter hovered menacingly above the crowd'. The press didn't see us not hovering! Also like so many other jobs it gave great satisfaction to have the equipment and the ability to do it properly. And we did win the battle! I am pleased to say that my grandson Jan has a model Jet Ranger, with Police markings, which flies extremely well, and simulates dropping on to the rioters nicely when the power runs down!

Not all the incidents we attended ran totally smoothly. Captain John and Derek had been briefed to take part in a pre-planned exercise, assisting police vehicles to tail a van involved in 'criminal activity'. The planning had ensured that the exercise would not involve the helicopter straying into commercial flight paths. Unfortunately however John and Derek's aircraft was diverted to a genuine report of a stolen lorry on the M6 where two Cheshire police officers had been set upon with pickaxe handles. The air and ground search that followed did result in the arrest of one of the assailants. Rod and either Harry or George (identities now lost in the mists of time but it was not myself, as I was looking down at a fire in Wolverhampton) were tasked to replace the first aircraft, but were not told that this was a planned exercise and that there was no need to follow the 'criminal' van into Birmingham. With admirable tenacity Rod was hot on the heels of the van, whilst the tailing police cars had lost sight of it! However, the Air Traffic Control staff at Birmingham Airport were getting hot under the collar as the slow moving trace on their screens darted and dodged about in their restricted air space. One would have to say that Rod, recently back from Aden, would have seen arresting the criminal as a priority – that was the nature of the guy anyway! He returned to Cosford after a successful operation, a bare minimum of fuel, and quite unaware of the furore at Air Traffic Control. With a lot of conciliatory (honeyed) words the ATC staff were appeased, so all ended well, with a good arrest on the Staffordshire – Cheshire border.

We found that at the majority of incidents we attended our role would conclude with some traffic reporting, control and perhaps diversions. This had a side effect of giving our pilots a police officer's interest in vehicles, and they began to enjoy the dramatic reaction when the Sioux, nearing it's top speed, gradually overhauled at low level a car doing 80 to 85 mph. When our Police sign became visible there was a sharp reduction in speed and a look of guilty surprise. In fact it was quickly apparent that the use of helicopters for purely traffic duties was extremely un-cost-effective. The only time it could be justified was for a really big event, or when clearing up the traffic after some other incident, and in the UK there has not been any other regular use, up to the present time.

In 2008 however it was announced that when the Essex police helicopter is airborne it might be used to check traffic speeds, with signs warning drivers that this may take place. It will not be used solely for checking speeds, again because of the cost equation. It is different in the States, who have more money available. I once drove from Montreal, in the east of Canada, to Vancouver in the west via Mexico, and was very impressed indeed with the attitude and behaviour of motorists, outside the big cities of course. I suspect that this may have a lot to do with the stronger level of enforcement, aided by airborne police.

When the snow set in properly we were not only asked to deliver blood supplies to hospitals, but also to seek out trapped livestock. These were tasks which were not necessarily police ones but which evaluated well in the general 'service' role. We were all, soldiers and policemen alike, really motivated to justify the evaluation, and get the use of aircraft accepted by the police and public, and perhaps to bring about a national 'copper chopper fleet'. (If transporting police dogs they would be 'copper chopper snappers').

The relations with our RAF hosts continued to be extremely good. There was an RAF Gliding and Soaring Club at Cosford, of which I was a member by virtue of my RAF Volunteer Reserve commission, and it was very good for my morale to get myself strapped into a very potent looking Olympia sailplane under the professional noses of our pilots. I believe that it was the high spot of the month for the platoon commander, John, when he soloed in a rather more primitive glider! As the month long trial drew to a close, with regrets on both sides, we did several stand-bys for anticipated armed robberies, which regrettably did not materialise. John filled in time during one stand-by in balancing the Sioux on a deserted wall. It must have looked rather like a huge rook, with Meccano tail feathers, but the Press did not get to film this.

Perhaps the word had got out to prospective robbers – there had certainly been plenty of publicity, both written and broadcast. It was strange, reading my local paper in 2006 to find my photograph, together with the rest of the Cosford team, in the 'pictures from the past' section. Rod, the very big Staff Sergeant, later made his name known in the aviation world by flying underneath one of the Thames bridges. I doubt not that he could do it easily. We celebrated the end of the trial by forming the most exclusive club in the world, the 'Midlands Police Helicopter Association' complete with a unique tie. It still exists, although sadly now with just three members, John, Derek and myself. The Cosford Gliding Club presented me with a cartoon showing myself hanging head downwards from a Sioux, focusing a very large magnifying glass at the ground!

In February the same winter we four police observers travelled by train to Royal Air Force Kinloss, alongside the Moray Firth on the north east coast of Scotland. We were invited to pass on our experience to the police officers from several Scottish Forces, taking part in the Scottish phase of the trials. This army unit were from Carter Barracks, Bulford in Wiltshire. They were equipped with Scouts, faster and with a bigger payload than the Sioux, but like the Jet Ranger, lacking the incredible all round visibility from the perspex bubble. We found that the pace of crime, and life in general was far slower in the north of Scotland than in the industrial Midlands, but the scale of the country and the chances of becoming temporarily uncertain of one's position (i.e. lost) among the snow covered mountains were immense.

However, it was explained that this posed no problems with an Army helicopter. 'If necessary we'll go on until we find someone and then land and ask him the way'. We never needed to, but it was a comforting thought! The army were exempt from the normal rules about low flying, and this was a tremendous advantage in any police operation. We were hoping to have a rescue to carry out, but no one fell off a mountain during our week's stay. I did carry out a cross-country exercise, over the Grampians from Inverness to Aberdeen, with nothing but white below apart from the long black gash of Loch Ness. It looked exactly as if a giant had slashed at the hillsides with a sword, to create a fit and proper home for a monster. We also did a cross-country to the Hebrides to evaluate air travel for supervisory purposes. Land and sea transport to remote posts might easily take many days. This demonstration helped to lead to the huge Force of Strathclyde becoming one of the first in the UK to have it's own machine.

The hospitality of the RAF and the 'polisse' was again tremendous. There was a NATO exercise taking place at Kinloss while we were there and the visiting Canadian and European aircrews were fascinated (if that is the right word) to find eight flying policemen in the Mess. I do believe that I heard a couple of Canadians saying words to the effect that they had not believed in stories about flying pigs, but by and large relations were good. This was especially so after the very senior police officer who was with us introduced the Canadians to snuff. So, we got our own back!

A tour of Bell's Distillery laid on by the local Superintendent (there was some off-duty time!) was a delight, and brought an entirely new aspect of the duties of Customs and Excise Officers into focus. A lemonade bottle full of the kind of whisky that money cannot buy was hidden in my home (for personal consumption only) for many months. Smooth? Wow! We had been promised by an RAF Shackleton pilot that we could join one of the routine North Sea/Artic cold war patrols carried out from Kinloss. As these were at least twelve hours long it was more a threat than a promise, but unfortunately could not be arranged before our week came to an end. The flights were later carried out by RAF Nimrods - Nimrod, 'the mighty hunter'.

Our involvement in the experiment ended with the same four travelling to a Regimental Depot near Abergavenny, for trials with the police in South Wales. Again the hospitality was lavish, with the Regimental silver being brought into use in the Mess. It is a sobering thought, while enjoying a good meal in good company, to consider the sacrifices and traditions that the silver represents. We also discovered and appreciated the local pub custom of locking the front door at 10.30 p.m. but opening the back, through which the village policeman was wont to enter for his regular refreshment. The flying was of the same high standard, but there were no highlights during our short visit.

The four evaluation trials (London, Midlands, Scotland and South Wales) did not lead to the instant creation of P.A.Ws., but certainly did do a great deal to advertise the potential of aircraft to the police service as a whole, and particularly to those Forces taking part. It also, I believe, led to better procedures at unmanned level crossings, and the beginnings of Health Service airborne operations. I became nominated as the West Midlands Constabulary, (and later the West Midlands Police) official air observer, and was given a number of interesting and valuable tasks for my Force and neighbouring areas. Once I found myself on a murder enquiry for Warwickshire, searching farmland to look for signs of a suspect's movements through growing crops.

On another occasion we used a helicopter to search for two small boys who were missing from home. Sadly both were eventually found drowned in a sewage farm, near their homes on the outskirts of Wolverhampton. Having three major football clubs in the area led sometimes to serious traffic congestion. In 1968 when Wolves, West Bromwich Albion and Birmingham

City all landed home ties in the FA cup, we begged the use of the AA twin engined aircraft, piloted by Captain Bill Lewis. He must have been ex-Royal Air Force, as he had the most magnificent handlebar moustache! In 1968 Birmingham was still policed by the Birmingham City Force, and they provided their own air observer, while I was to cover the roads around Wolves and the Albion. Unfortunately this entailed a lot of serious banking and tight circles, and the need for the observers to look down at the roads below. This became too much for my colleague, who had to disembark at Birmingham Airport in a very unhappy condition, while I carried on trying to report on all three grounds, with the aid of an 'A to Z' for Birmingham! I am sure that today at least one of those matches would be played on a Sunday, but that was unheard of then. I was intrigued to learn, when visiting the current helicopter base, that they do still carry an 'A to Z'!

I was also nominated as the West Midlands Air Observer for Civil Defence duties, which entailed flying a number of sorties in a De Havilland Chipmunk, a Royal Air Force two seater trainer, in order to retain navigation and observation skills. This Cold War plan was that, together with the Police Mobile Columns on the ground, we could help to set up alternative seats of local Government, if the bomb was ever dropped. A nice bonus too for me, even though the prospect of doing it for real was not a happy one. Perhaps we could have been useful to lead a lost Mobile Column to the right place!

We continued to have very good co-operation from both the Army and Air Force, and in 1968 used an R.A.F. Westland Wessex (a large personnel carrying helicopter) on a complicated enquiry, which became known as the 'torso murder'. The middle half of a young, apparently Asian, woman's body had arrived in a suitcase on a train from London Euston to Wolverhampton, found with some shock by the carriage cleaners. The owner of the suitcase had, unsurprisingly, decided not to accompany it. We needed to find, amongst other things the missing head. The legs were found in another suitcase near the River Lea in Essex. It had been decided, by those who know about such things, that the head might have been thrown out of the train somewhere between Wolverhampton and Euston. To walk the line was likely to be dangerous and very time consuming, so we begged the Wessex from Royal Air Force Odiham, in Hampshire.

I put on my rather smart Police Helicopter Unit flying overalls, with prominent shoulder flashes, and met Squadron Leader Tarwid as he landed on Wolverhampton Racecourse. The Squadron Leader was of Polish nationality. The Poles were notorious during the 1939-45 war for being action-orientated, hating bureaucracy and for getting on with the job. The Squadron Leader seemed to be of the same mould and was obviously keen to go head-hunting. The question of the tunnels between Wolverhampton and Euston came up and I think that he would have volunteered to fly through them, had it not been decided to walk these with a railwayman as a guide!

I was accompanied by a Detective Sergeant and we both sat in the open hatch in the fuselage of the Wessex, secured by a safety strap and with our legs dangling over the side. Because of the complications of following the line into Euston it was decided that we should go only as far as Watford and the rest would be walked. We started at Wolverhampton Railway Station, very low and with the wheels just above the electric cables, and crabbed down the line sideways, hatch foremost. My colleague and I had a very good view of the several parallel railway lines sliding towards and underneath us.

My Force had alerted the railway authority to the planned intention, but it seemed that the word had not got through to all the drivers. The expression on their faces as the large Wessex came flying sideways towards them and about twenty feet above, was, shall we say, 'interesting'. One could even lip-read a few words, usually short, sharp, mostly in Anglo-Saxon but occasionally Punjabi. We took four hours on the down leg, landing several times by the side of the line to investigate suspicious objects. Funny what gets thrown out of railway carriages. A dead cat looked very hopeful from the air, but turned out to be just a dead cat. I do not know how difficult it was to fly the aircraft in such an unusual manner, but I was again tremendously impressed with the skill, professionalism and friendliness of the pilot and crew.

As the Wessex needed to refuel at its base at RAF Odiham it was decided to stop overnight and do a return leg the following day. The Police Staff College at Bramshill is, by co-incidence, quite close to Odiham, so arrangements were made for my colleague and I to sleep there. We were landed by Squadron Leader Tarwid just in time for dinner at the College. The fact of walking into the very large dining hall, with around two hundred officers of various senior ranks already seated, plus the academics, is one of the happiest memories of my police career. I was still in flying kit and the 'Police Helicopter Unit' was then only a vague rumour or a remote future possibility for most of them. Heads turned! There was huge interest, and I felt very much like a visitor from the next century, descending as a time-traveller in a sci-fi film. This was not far off from the truth! My CID colleague, in jacket and flannels was comparatively second team, and, I am sure, slightly miffed about not being provided with a flying suit and badges as well!

The next morning, after explaining to all and sundry what the Helicopter Unit was all about, we were picked up from the front lawn of Bramshill, flew to Watford, and then repeated the search, this time going north. By now all the engine drivers seemed to have got the message, as had the media. When

I was eventually disembarked at Birmingham Airport, a BBC news camera team were waiting for a picture and a comment! After eight hours of watching railway sleepers sliding underneath, a state of disorientation existed. I do not remember what was said, but the filming must have been acceptable as it appeared on the 'News at Ten'.

The girl's head was eventually found, leading to identification, but not by us. It was found, gruesomely hidden in a duffel bag under a bush, by some walkers just about to have a picnic in Epping Forest, weeks later. The case was brought to a successful trial and the conviction of the girl's father for murder. He had not approved of her choice of boy-friend and decided to end their friendship by killing her. Whilst the use of an air search had no direct relevance to the conviction, it did eliminate the railway line and saved a lot of man-hours, which were then available in other ways.

The Army held a very big exhibition, Armex, in West Bromwich in July 1972. We used the Sioux and Scout helicopters again to do major surveillance and airborne traffic observation over four days. The Army came in force, with the head of the Air Corps Demonstration and Trials Squadron flying with me, and the ground crew coming up in a big troop carrying Puma. My helicopter unit flying kit had been put back into storage, ready for the far distant day when PAWs became the norm rather than an oddity, but I was able to surprise the Air Corps Ground Crew with my Royal Air Force Gliding and Soaring Association wings on a Royal Air Force flying suit – this was quite enjoyable. There was plenty of coverage and some good photographs in the local papers.

More pleasing though was a memo to my boss from the Chief Superintendent of West Bromwich Division, praising the, 'excellent and invaluable work'. This was particularly pleasing as I had fallen out big time with him while I was the Chief Constable's Personal Assistant a few years before. It had devolved upon me to organise a major Church Parade and march past for the new West Midlands Constabulary, in West Bromwich. Police Horses, and the Force Band et al, showing the flag to the people of the Black Country. The Chief Superintendent was an old fashioned policeman, afraid of nobody. His 'patch' was hallowed ground and he was the King of it. He had decided on the route, in detail, that the parade should take through the town, and I changed one small bit without consulting him.

When he found out the roof blew off. He telephoned me, the conversation beginning with 'You buggers at Headquarters', and went downhill from there. This was a long diatribe on his part, and at one point we were cut off - (must have been one of my former staff on the switchboard) - and when we were reconnected it was obvious that the flow of invective had continued without a pause. Being full of injured pride on behalf of his patch he had not realised that I was no longer on the receiving end!

As I progressed from the lowly rank of Inspector however, I came to have a lot of time for this man. He would snarl like a wounded tiger if you were at fault, and inflict horrible punishment. But, he always fought for his own men in the face of higher authority and gave generous praise when he thought it was due. He could certainly be compared to the old fashioned ferocious Hospital Matrons. I am very afraid that their like do not exist any more, probably never will again, and I revere their memory.

All we four air observers and Reg, our communications man, realised that the work we were doing in 1967-8 would not bear fruit quickly enough to affect our own careers. By the time that it did start to impact on the police service we had all moved on to other things. Our involvement, however, certainly did none of us any harm, and I am very proud that eventually a major change in police strategy and operations was effected, which we helped to initiate. Helicopters are now as indispensable to police work in the UK as in the States and other countries and we helped to get it going. The expression 'what goes around comes around' has been true many times for me. In July 2008 at the annual 'Care of Police Survivors' service, I had the chance to talk to the current Chief Constable of Staffordshire. While discussing the 1968 helicopter experiments he told me that plans were being examined to have a combined airborne team for the whole of the Midlands. This is many steps further than we envisaged in 1967/8.

Being part of the experiments also persuaded me to upgrade my gliding certificates to a private pilot's licence in order to fly powered aircraft. I had nearly forty years of intense joy, pleasure and occasional gut-wrenching fright from this, flying over some of the most beautiful country in the UK, to the west of Wolverhampton and the Welsh Marches.

Incidentally one is never lost when flying, just temporarily unsure of one's position!

The fright could happen due to our position just east of one of the R.A.F.'s fast and low training routes. It was not unusual to be flying over something below that was travelling at 400 knots in the opposite direction! Halfpenny Green, from where I flew, situated in a 'bowl' between hills, is also known to attract sudden banks of fog. Once I got caught coming back with a passenger with only about a hundred metres forward visibility. Receiving worried queries about our position by radio was, at the time, a bloody nuisance.

Fortunately almost every field was familiar, but the wide grey runway suddenly appearing ahead out of thick fog was very welcome indeed, and actually just where it should have been. I had just enough height to hop over the boundary hedge, round out and land, sweating but safe!

When Wales got it's own Parliament it was good to go international (so to speak) to Welshpool or Caernarvon Airports for coffee. In the days before Birmingham Airport became as big and busy as it now is one was announced over the loudspeakers in the Terminal Building when approaching to land in a single engined four-seater! Wow, big time!

It was a pleasure to take both children flying when they were small, and also their friends and partners in later years. One flight that was memorable was when we rented an aeroplane from Guernsey, where we were on holiday. After my being checked out as safe, Al, aged twelve, and I set off for Cherbourg Airport. Not a long or particularly difficult flight, finding France was easy! Finding Guernsey on the way back was a little more tricky. The problem was the French Air Traffic Controller, whose English was not quite as good as it was supposed to be, English being the international ATC language. He passed me several increasingly frantic messages, which when we got on the ground I discovered were intended to keep me away from Cherbourg Harbour. The message should have been, 'Do not overfly the nuclear submarine pens, or they will shoot at you!' I have had a few reasons during my life not to be too fond of the French, but perhaps my interpretation was at fault. Anyway, I didn't and they didn't, but it might have been a flight too far!

Another intensely enjoyable flight in 1975 was taking Al, aged 13, to Mona Airfield in Anglesey. We followed the North Welsh coast from the Mersey over Llandudno and the other holiday towns to which we used to take our camper van. At that time I was flying a French built Rallye Club which was part owned by Mick, who with his wife Maureen became very good friends of ours. Mick kept the plane in an innocent looking shed in a farmer's field near Wolverhampton, which was irresistibly reminiscent of a scene from a World War Two resistance or spy film. The whole of the front of the shed could be lowered or raised, and the aircraft winched outside or back in, using a pulley. When the door was closed the fact that there was an airworthy aircraft inside was totally hidden! The field sloped quite sharply downhill, with telephone wires across the bottom end, so we forgot about the wind, took off down hill and landed uphill, leaving plenty of height over the wires, both ways. I did think that I was learning about flying from this, until seeing some Australian crop duster pilots on local farm work fly *under* the wires after take-off. It was occasionally necessary to get rid of sheep before departure in the aeroplane, or to frighten them off before landing, but it was a rather wonderful time. On the occasion of the flight to Mona I was picking up Steve, a flying instructor friend of Mick's, and his young son, as he had been working there. At that time Mona was a satellite airfield for Royal Air Force Valley, the home of the RAF's fast jet operational training base. It was very necessary to get everything as it should be on the approach and landing. Fast jets from Valley can still be seen - and heard - screaming down the Welsh valleys underneath one, when half way up a mountain in Snowdonia! I was pleased not to have upset the RAF Controllers, but by the time we started back over Snowdonia darkness was not too far away and virtually with us as we approached Wolverhampton. With two small boys on board this was one occasion when I did not take the step too far, and let Steve land us safely over the wires and uphill onto the sloping field.

There were many other intensely enjoyable flights in the Rallye, including one solo when I spent a wonderful hour amongst and above the clouds, coming down to see the street and house lights starting to glimmer and flicker in Wolverhampton to the south and Shrewsbury to the north, as the sun sank in the west. This time I did take the step, but survived it. After landing I sat for a long time in the cockpit, thinking about it, listening to the engine ticking and clicking as it cooled, and feeling very happy and privileged. My mind went to the poetry written by a World War Two fighter pilot:

'Oh, I have slipped the surly bonds of earth, and danced the skies on laughter silvered wings.'

'Sunward I've climbed and joined the tumbling mirth of sun-split clouds – and done a hundred things you have not dreamed of.'

It ends:

'I've put out my hand and touched the face of God.'

That has meant a lot to me.

Mick, who had a senior position with an international construction company, was by a strange co-incidence, sent to the Sudan in 1976, to build a dam. I was there to build up the Police Force and I am not sure which of us had the most difficult job. We both learned a number of Arabic words involving fate, tomorrow, perhaps, go away and, 'Yes, of course it can be done!' The one that I have always liked best is, 'Maafi mushkelin' – 'No problem'! We managed to see quite a bit of each other while I was there, although Mick was in the Sudan for much longer, and was accompanied by Maureen and their small daughter Louise for a time.

At one time I was effectively private pilot to the Wolverhampton Clergy, having a Curate friend who was a keen flier of large model aeroplanes. I agreed to take him, plus another Curate and the latter's fiancée for a sight seeing flight over Shropshire. On the aircraft we were using that day, a Piper Cherokee, the pilot gets in first, and the front seat passenger squeezes in last. When we were all tucked in I discovered that I had forgotten something essential. Completely forgetting myself, I said something aloud in Anglo-Saxon that would have been quite acceptable in police company but not otherwise. Profuse apologies as we untucked ourselves. Very unprofessional behaviour, but they did enjoy the flight. I guess that I should, to be honest, record the embarrassing times as well as the good ones, but this was, regrettably, two words too far.

There were times however when it all went right, and in 1975, in company with Tony, my gliding instructor aerobatic friend, now also a power pilot, we won the 'Tacair' Navigation Trophy at Halfpenny Green Airfield. Tony and his wife Carol became very good friends of ours. He and I formed the West Midlands Police Flying Club in 1974 and entered a team in a number of the Police National Air Rallies that were starting to be held in the early seventies. With Tony, who was an honorary member, we won the Police Review Challenge Trophy at White Waltham, the 'Tacair' Trophy at Denham in 1975 and were runners-up at Staverton (Gloucestershire Airport) in 1976.

Coming back from a rally at Biggin Hill with Tony, we were privileged to fly low-level right across the centre of London. I think that it must have been easier on that occasion for air traffic control to keep us down low out of the way, but whatever the reason it was a good experience.

Tony and I hosted the National Police Air Rally at Coventry in 1978, and ran a Navigation and Map Reading Competition. One of the pretty horrible clues was 'find a peculiar academic' - Gaydon Airfield of course! We were lucky enough to persuade the leader of the Red Arrows Royal Air Force Display Team to fly in and land, (in his red Hawk display aircraft) and to get a very well known BBC Commentator to do the schpiel over the loudspeakers for us. A good day.

Another good day with Tony was joining a Police Air Rally at Hove Airport, and flying along the Sussex coast in beautiful weather. Another happy memory. I also have a nice recollection of landing at Welshpool Airport with Jo, an international afternoon coffee stop trip - and another pilot in the café commenting on the smoothness of the touch down. 'Right on the numbers too,' was the compliment I think. Doesn't always happen!

Winning the Trophy at White Waltham in 1971 is a good memory, but getting there is not! The journey down was in horrible visibility. We had a team of two aeroplanes, Tony flying one and leading the way and I following. One of my passengers was a Royal Air Force Squadron Leader, an aircrew navigator, with whom we were very good friends. Despite this professional input we both became uncertain of our position (lost), and the flight time to White Waltham was one hour forty five minutes.

Coming back, in much improved viz, was just one hour. To be fair to our professional, he had been used to finding his way in a Canberra, which was a considerably faster aircraft than a Cherokee and with extremely different avionics. We later found that both our aircraft had been circling, in very poor viz, over the big brickworks near Bedford, trying to fix our position. This could have been a flight too far, but like many things in my life, we got away with it, and the day improved from that point. The friendship which Jo and I had with Stan, the Squadron Leader and his family gave us many enjoyable evenings in the Mess at Royal Air Force Cosford. I was able to reciprocate by inviting him to a Dining In night at Bramshill, the Police Staff College during my time there.

Halfpenny Green Flying Club enlarged the air-racing programme in which Tony and I had entered in 1975, and it began to attract national publicity. I volunteered to act as a Marshal at one of these gatherings, and watched Prince William of Gloucester, ninth in line to the Throne, who was an entrant, waiting outside his aircraft in a queue for fuel. He was very rudely pushed aside by someone who either did not recognise him or did not care. The Prince merely stepped aside, and quietly smiled. I thought that this was pretty good, but literally minutes later he and his co-pilot were charred corpses, having spun in moments after take-off, trying to turn too low and slow. Although it is green again now the hedge where they crashed was barren and brown for many years afterwards. Well, this part of Shropshire is traditionally royalist – the original Royal Oak where King Charles hid is about three minutes flying time from Halfpenny Green.

One another incident with a helicopter occurred in 1989 at my daughter's wedding. The reception was held at a Hotel in a small village near Wolverhampton, and unknown to most of us, including myself, her bridegroom, Derek, had arranged for a helicopter to fly them from the village cricket field to the Hotel where they were spending the first night. As I had spent the whole of a drive in mentally constructing and rehearsing my speech whilst taking a lorry load of steel from Birmingham to Sheffield, I was determined to deliver it uncurtailed. I did notice that Derek and Tony, my flying friend who was one of the conspirators, were getting a little agitated.

As this was late September dark fell in the early evening and the pilot had specified that he needed to take off by a certain time, which was fast approaching. Eventually I did deliver all the speech (and it was a good one, I think) and Derek announced to the considerable surprise of the party that we had to trek out of the Hotel to the cricket field. On arrival of course all was explained, but my small Godson, being in possession of his own camera, loudly demanded that the bride and groom should move out of the way, so that he could photograph the helicopter!

I have to admit that composing a wedding speech whilst driving a heavy weight of steel rods is not best safety practice – rods too far maybe. Taking steel from Birmingham to Sheffield is almost exactly the equivalent to taking coal to Newcastle, but I did it a few times. On another occasion I was being helped to load up by a locally born youth of Asian parentage. Half way through he stopped, looked at me and said in best Brummie, 'Yow ai a proper lorry driver, am yer?' This was a bit disconcerting, as no, I suppose that I was not, but doing it for the experience more than anything else. I had not thought that I was such an obvious amateur though. On being asked why he thought that, the reply was rather scornful, 'Cos yow'm warin a tie of cos'. Another learning curve!

I should make it clear here that the Birmingham and Black Country accents are in no way similar – another fact that the film and television industries entirely fail to recognise. Perhaps it is a case of mistaken identity. After carrying out an advanced driving test recently for an elderly man with a delightful and genuine Dudley accent he rang me up the following day to thank me. I had not been able to award him the top grade, so his message was, 'Yo'm an 'ard mon, but yo'm fair.' I was pleased with this accolade in authentic Black Country spache! Please note the difference, film producers. Birmingham, 'Yow', Black Country, 'Yo'!

Part of the work that I was doing well into my seventies was teaching 'Banksman' and 'Banksman Assessor' courses to people involved in the manoeuvring of large lorries in very confined spaces. The origin of the word 'Banksman' goes back to the days when, especially in the industrial Midlands, all heavy loads were moved by canal barge. One man was deputed to stand on the towpath to help the 'oss to position the barge. We are still using the term and I find that historically fascinating.

We had a delightful neighbour, Sam, when living in our police house at Aldersley. He had a quite senior position in the Midlands Waterways, responsible for the area between Wolverhampton and Llangollen.Being a typical ex-bargee with a wonderful combination of Shropshire, Cheshire and Black Country accents he was sometimes invited to talk about the canals on the radio. On one such occasion, when asked how the canal folk would repair damage to a barge below the waterline Sam's reply was 'Ossmukantar'. You work it out - we had to, and the accent goes on the 'an'!

We had a lot of barges still moving through Wolverhampton in the fifties, and though the bargees were tough, very self-reliant characters I do not remember us ever having any trouble from them. They did not cause any, and any that was caused to them would be sorted out by themselves. To sit in a very warm, cosy cabin, and hear some of the stories that both men and women could tell, the women often drawing meantime on a short, very black and evil smelling pipe, was a delight. Although there are still plenty of barges moving through the Midlands the people are not the same, and I much regret their passing.

In 1966, following the amalgamation of the towns and Police Forces of the Black Country ,which formed the West Midlands Constabulary, I had been promoted to Inspector to head the Wolverhampton Division Traffic Department. I was presented by colleagues with an Inspector's walking stick. Rather regrettably, in returning immediately to traffic I did not have the chance to use it for some years! Then followed a couple of good years, with a lot of rewarding work to do and some good troops to do it with.

In 1968 promotion followed to Chief Inspector. The new job was to run the Force wide Control Room – the controlling body for the fast response cars, motor cycles and other vehicles on the Force radio net. Part of the job was also responsibility for all other Force communication facilities; personal radios, telex, teleprinters and land lines. I had a lot to learn, with new equipment urgently needed for the new larger Force. A new central Control Room at Brierley Hill, near Dudley, had been partly planned. It was my job to get the planning completed, the installation done, train a larger staff and ensure a smooth move from Wolverhampton. This all went well, with the Chief Constable declaring that it was his 'Starship Enterprise'. I have to say that it did no harm for him to find me there at 9 p.m. one night, putting in some final touches to the, as yet, unmanned consoles.

Truly, I did not know that he was in the building!

As the opening of the Control Room more or less coincided with the inception of a massive new Force wide switchboard, my name became known at the Home Office Telecommunications Branch as a technical wizard. Little did they know! I was still feeling my way, and very much relying on expert help, but it was a very interesting time, and seemed to work. At this time I was asked to join a committee of scientists and police communications officers from other Forces to plan and supervise the Mobile Automatic Data Experiment, or 'MADE', which was being conducted for the Home Office by Marconi. This was the forerunner of the impressive technical communications now available to the emergency services and shown to us in the Eurocopter.

One pleasant feature of my new post at Brierley Hill was my entitlement to use the Senior Officer's Mess for lunch. We were usually joined by the Force

Solicitor, a rather abrasive man who I did not have a lot of time for. One day at lunch however, he took me completely and utterly by surprise by asking across the table, 'Do you remember once having a girl friend called Shirley?'

My mouth must have hung open for several seconds as my mind quickly re-wound twenty five years to the time when I took my Father in the BSA on holiday to Mid Wales – the one where my Mother sensibly went by train! Shirley, also on holiday in the same house with her Auntie, and I had enjoyed a nice little romance, especially in the bench seat in the BSA, and we kept in touch for a time. It was never going to go anywhere, as I was due to be called up, and she lived in Halifax – a long way from Wolverhampton in those days, especially by three-wheeler! However, she had known that I was a police cadet in the Midlands, and the Solicitor being a family friend had asked him if he knew me.

He told me that he had replied, 'We have an absolutely splendid Superintendent called Mike'. I somehow doubt this, but I was quite flattered that she had thought to ask, twenty five years on! There was a tailpiece to this story, as during a Force Ball at Brierley Hill soon afterwards, the Solicitor carefully introduced Jo and I to his wife, saying maliciously, 'This is Shirley's boy friend'. Very fortunately I had told Jo about the incident in the Mess, so we had a good laugh at his attempt to make mischief! Typical of the man, I think.

I was never too impressed with Birmingham City. That's the Police Force (as was), not the Football Club!

During the preparation phase for the enlarged West Midlands Police Force, due to commence on 1st April 1974, I was appointed to the planning team and promoted to Superintendent in 1973. The post of communications officer for the new Force, which now included the two cities of Birmingham and Coventry, based at the new Force Headquarters in Birmingham city centre, was given to me. I think that a good analogy for this amalgamation is that of a shotgun wedding, where the parties had been intimate but now hated each other. However, shotgun it was. Almost immediately after the new Force inception day, I was deluged with requests for improvements from all over the Birmingham area. This was a little strange, as Birmingham, throughout the planning, had insisted that all their systems were perfect, and should not be changed. But we coped.

One of my ancillary responsibilities was to ensure that everyone had evacuated the multi-story building in the event of a bomb alert, of which there were quite a few at that time. They were always hoaxes following the IRA bombing in the city centre, but each one had to be taken seriously. We were a prime target of course. Since the lifts could not be used if there was the possibility of an explosion, I had to clear every office on every floor, using the stairs. I suppose that this was vaguely a communications job, or perhaps I just looked fit enough. Unfortunately each flight and each landing had a large plate glass window set into the outside wall, which was between us and the next door building, the offices of the Birmingham Post & Mail – another prime target! It never did happen, but I can still feel the hairs on the back of my neck lifting as I charged up and down – definitely eight stories too far!

I have been delighted to see, in 2010, that there is a prospect of the Crown Prosecution Service having to hand some prosecuting decisions back to the Police. I know, from colleagues who served after me, how difficult and inefficient they were to work with, and how reluctant to put any case before the Courts which was not a virtual cast iron certainty. Cost and 'losing' a case seemed to be the overriding factors. Many of us who made decisions about whether to prosecute or not before the inception of the CPS thought differently. The inconvenience and expense of a Court appearance to a malefactor, even if the prosecution 'lost' was a form of justice, and I was quite happy to leave this to the Courts, rather than shirk the issue.

I was never as happy in my job after the 1974 amalgamation as I had been before. I found that the senior personnel of the former Birmingham City Force, with a few notable exceptions, were exceptionally arrogant and quite unprepared to admit that their Force had been anything but perfect. In fact, in the view of a number of us, it hadn't been. One of the reasons why Arthur Scargill was able to deploy his flying pickets with success and mobilise other unions in support of the disastrous miner's strike was at least partly due to Birmingham. He tried out his mobile flying pickets at Saltley Gas Works, and won the day. The then Chief Constable ordered the police to close the works gates, fearing injuries, thereby ceding victory to Scargill. It is my view, with hindsight of course, that a more determined effort to keep a clear passage for the fuel lorries entering the Works might have been made. Accepting the possibility of injuries, this could have saved a lot of bitterness, wounded people and financial hardship amongst the miners as the strike progressed and lasted so long.

One innovation during the new job led to an improvement in police motor cycle communications throughout the UK. The practice had been to place the bulky handset and control box on top of the fuel tank, above and between the rider's legs. It was realised that in the event of a collision the rider was likely to lose an irreplaceable part of his anatomy (there were no female police motor cyclists in 1974, or very few anyway) and I was tasked to sort this out.

With the help of the local branch of the Home Office Telecommunications Department we arrived at the use of an earpiece and mike fitted into the helmet. They were connected to a remote control box, thus taking everything off the tank. This was, I have to say, a more sophisticated device than my old gas pipe on the Norton combo. An obvious solution given that suitable headsets were now available, but it was strange that no one, including myself who had been a motor cyclist, had thought of it earlier. I suppose that everyone blanked out the fact that one could be thrown over the tank and handlebars and just accepted the risk. I discovered recently that Lancashire Police, who had their own telecoms department and were not as reliant on the Home Office as ourselves were working on the same changes for motor cycle communications – great minds.......!

Expert advice to the Government of The Sudan

The planning work and the MADE committee probably led to my being invited to visit the Foreign and Commonwealth Office in 1976.

On arrival I was told, 'The Government of the Sudan have asked us to send an expert to improve their police communications. Well, we can't afford an expert, but we wondered if you would like to go'.

This (despite the tongue in cheek opening remarks) was a flattering and exciting offer, and gave me the chance to see over another hill or two, so after a quick family discussion, and agreement from my Chief Constable, I said, 'Yes'.

Events then moved very quickly indeed, I had to be there as soon as possible, preferably yesterday. We had to curtail a family holiday, and I found myself landing at Khartoum Airport just before the beginning of Ramadan, the month of fasting. This turned out to be an example of lack of thought and planning by the Foreign Office, since to carry out any constructive work during Ramadan is time consuming and difficult.

Ramadan is the observance of the fourth of the Five Pillars of Islam. The first pillar is that Allah is the one God and that Muhammad was his messenger. The second instructs Muslims to pray five times each day, once before sunrise, once after midday, once between midday and sunset, once immediately after sunset and finally one hour after sunset. The third pillar is to give a percentage of what one owns to charity. The fourth is the month of fasting, Ramadan, taking no food or drink between dawn and dusk, unless a bona-fide traveller or a pregnant or nursing woman. The fifth and final pillar instructs Muslims to make a pilgrimage to Mecca once in their lifetime, after which they can become known as a Hadjji.

It seems that the Foreign Office were either not aware of the five pillars, or had forgotten, or did not care. I have not been too surprised to read of shortcomings by the wizards in that huge ornate building in King Charles Street during the years since. Naïveté is the word that comes to mind. The problem with work during Ramadan was that as it was irreligious to eat between sunrise and sunset everyone becomes very tired – not surprisingly. At sunset the practice is to break the fast and eat as much as possible to sustain the body during the next twenty-four hours, staying awake until four or five am in order to do so. By early afternoon the streets are littered with sleeping bodies anywhere there is room to lie down. One can understand why people do not feel up to working hard after a few days of this regime. At the end of the month of fasting is the four day festival of Id-Al-Fitr, with a build up of excitement at bit like, 'three shopping days left to Christmas.' Not much work gets done then either!

I can still recapture the mixed feelings of inadequacy and anticipation as the aircraft descended through the night sky towards Khartoum. There had been an awful lot of total darkness below – not a glimmer since Cairo. The Sudan is the Africa of the Movies – lots of wide, (very wide), spaces, deserts and jungles. On disembarkation I was relieved to be met, and welcomed warmly by the First Secretary at the British Embassy – he, of course, was not a secretary at all! In fact throughout my three months stay I was treated very well by the Ambassador and his staff, being, I suppose, a fairly unusual bird of passage. I was invited to a number of Embassy parties, of which there seemed to be quite a lot, including those at the American and German Embassies.

It was a privilege to be able to meet and talk to a number of Ambassadors, including the American, German and Italian. I also palled up with the Dutch Chargé d'Affaires who had a flat stocked with many cases of Stella beer. I was invited to join him and his wife (a former KLM air hostess) on several evenings. They were Anglophiles and fans of the British Police, which was nice. They were posted to London some years later, and I was able to repay their hospitality by an invitation to my home to meet a friend who was by then a very senior police officer. I made a number of other friends among the Embassy staff to one of whom I am still writing every Christmas. As the temperature during the evening was still about 85 degrees, the parties were outside, with 'Red Sea kit' for the men. This is white shirt, bow tie, dark trousers and a cummerbund. People tended to end up in the swimming pool at about midnight, sometimes fully clothed.

At the annual ball of the British Cricket Club I had to borrow a bow tie and cummerbund from the Club President! At one of the Receptions I met the Archbishop of Canterbury, Dr. Coggan, who was visiting the Sudan. During Ramadan there was plenty of time when my work could not be done, so I volunteered to join the working party from the Anglican Church in Khartoum who were decorating the house where the Archbishop and his wife were to stay during their visit. Interior painting in a temperature of 90 degrees was hot work, but I think that I did prove that even expatriate police officers had their uses!

There was a quite big British Army presence in Khartoum, doing an aid mission in a similar way to myself, but rather more involved with training. The theory of the small world was soon proved again as one of the army officers had lived a mile or two away from me in Wolverhampton, whilst posted in the Midlands. This also led to a number of invitations. Shortly after I arrived I discovered that a Mr. and Mrs. M.A.Collins were staying in the same hotel. The opportunity for confusion that this gave the Sudanese hotel staff was huge! As the Collins' had not realised that I was around either the confusion would not have been confined to the hotel staff – small world again. They were a pleasant couple working for the International Monetary Fund, and when we had satisfactorily sorted ourselves out we had a couple of enjoyable meals together. I later found that another Collins had arrived in the Hotel, and wondered if the staff thought that it was a British tribal name. I suppose if you go back far enough it is, Irish anyway!

Khartoum, for expatriates, was a small and closed circle, and everyone seemed to know everyone else. They went to each other's parties, and the main occupation of some of the wives seemed to be to visit each other. An odd sort of life. Pre-war colonial lifestyle? People were surprised that I had been sent on this job without my family, but to be fair it was only for three months, so not worth disrupting the children's schooling. I later refused to do a similar job for the Foreign Office for twelve months in Zambia, as there was no funding for a family.

I had been booked into a Hotel in Khartoum, and the day after my arrival met the Commissioner, at Police Headquarters. The building was somewhat of a culture shock but the Commissioner was a pleasant and impressive man, speaking good English. He may well have been one of those foreign students at Bramshill. He apologised for the fact that I would have to work on Sundays but promised me Fridays off!

After sharing some coffee with the Commissioner I was taken to meet the Sudan Police communications officer, Chief Inspector Mansour Sulieman and a civilian Post Office telecommunications engineer, Abd Almoneim Mohammed Hussein, (Moneim for short). One or both of these two would be with me to explain and interpret as necessary throughout my stay. Both men spoke good English and we got on well together. Moneim was a well-educated man, who wrote to me for some years afterwards, always prefacing his letter with, 'Greetings from the sunny Sudan to cold and rainy England!' Not much interpretation was necessary, among the higher ranks at least, as most spoke understandable English. The Sudan had been, as the Anglo/Egyptian Sudan, a part of the British Empire, and much infrastructure from that time remained, together with many English customs. In fact it was not at all unusual to hear people expressing regret for the old days, 'It was better when the Brititch (sic) were here – it rained more and the camels gave us more milk.'

The northern part of the Sudan is mainly Muslim, so in theory when attending events held by local people there was no alcohol served. However this was observed in the breach quite often, and a preferred drink was known as sherry, but not as we know it! It was served in half pint glasses, with plenty of ice added. Most police officers also seemed to have a bottle of araki tucked away and a favourite party trick was to lay a trail of araki on the table, or, more often the floor, and then set light to it. It was a good idea to be alert to jump back quickly, even if full of very greasy lamb's heels, sheep's eyes, raw liver and other miscellaneous entrails. All this was, shall we say, an acquired taste!

One of the initial tasks I set myself was to discover exactly what the Sudan Police hoped to gain from their new system.

This was not as easy as it sounds, as there was a lot of vagueness about what actually existed, and what it was possible to do. The brief from the Foreign Office had been to advise on the best way to modernise and generally improve the creaking police communications system. In fact the job had to expand into many other associated areas, which could not be ignored. It was therefore going to be necessary to visit each regional province, and as many as possible of the major police stations in each one.

Sudan is a country not all that much smaller than India, with differing problems, and people, in each of the regions. A principle of 'one size fits all' was therefore an impossible concept for police procedures and philosophy. It was also important to visit a selection of the smaller police posts, especially those in border areas, as I needed to understand duties and procedures there. These were, of course, very different to those for which I had been trained or exposed to in my police career in the English Midlands.

I was allocated a Land Rover and two drivers, Fahdel, who was a normally happy-go-lucky young Constable for the longer safaris, and Hassan Ibrahim, much older and more staid, to take me around the Khartoum area. The logical starting place was to visit the police stations in the urban area which made up the capital city, the old towns of Khartoum, Omdurman and the newer area of Khartoum North. One of the Stations had a very large crocodile (a dead one!) mounted over the entrance. I was told that it had left the Nile and was roaming the streets, until shot by a brave police officer. You don't see this very often in Wolverhampton. Or even Birmingham, although I wonder if it would have felt more at home there.

Khartoum, whilst a big city, had few buildings of more than one or two stories at that time, although development was beginning to take place along the banks of the Nile. There were very few women wearing western clothing, and while not hiding their faces fully, most wore a veil of some sort. Whilst quite a lot of men were in army or police uniform, servants, waiters and most civilians wore the traditional white cotton djellabir, over baggy cotton drawers, with a white turban or skull cap. I never tried one, but I guess it was suited to the climate, being well air-conditioned from the bottom upwards! It also eased the problem of finding a public toilet, which is often a problem in a European city. All that was necessary was to find a patch of sand or dust, and pull up the djellabir! Only the main streets in the city centre were all-weather tarmac, the rest were sand and dust. There was a strict curfew at midnight, and I learned that two Sudanese people had recently been shot for failing to stop when challenged.

Omdurman was largely sand, very flat and with practically no trees. Houses were low and surrounded by a mud or brick wall as protection against sandstorms. Khartoum North was a comparatively modern suburb, with more industry and more paved streets. There were many big trees along the banks of both the Niles, attracting large birds, - kites, ibis, the sacred bird of Egypt, river eagles, and always, way up high were the continuous circuit of vultures, looking for death.

The capital city did not pose too many problems to solve, being a relatively small area. An ancient German teleprinter network connecting the main Stations existed, with some radio coverage for the few police vehicles. There had been no attempt to provide radio cover any further afield, and the teleprinters, due to age and the ubiquitous sandy dust, were very unreliable. The requirements were obvious, and seemed reasonably attainable, so I decided that the main priority was to look at the distant regions.

Moneim, Mansour and I decided that the first destination should be the south, over 700 miles as the vulture flies, to the province of Equatoria, which borders Uganda, Kenya and Congo (now Zaire). We flew to the regional airport of Juba, the capital town of Equatoria. During the hours of flight we first saw below the square irrigated fields watered by the White Nile south of

Khartoum. These gave way to vast areas of brown featureless desert and then to the thousands of square miles of the green wetlands and marshes of the Sudd, the Upper Nile.

We flew over the wonderfully named province of Junglei, where flows the Kong Kong River. The contrast between Juba and the area around Khartoum was immense. Instead of desert and a Middle Eastern Arabic culture, Juba was purely green African savannah and jungle. There was the occasional glimpse of a vast green and blue horizon down to Uganda and Kenya, with gin clear air so that a viz of a hundred miles was possible from the top of a hill. Conical mountains like child's drawings rose suddenly out of the bush and the very distant outline of the Ruwenzoris, the Mountains of the Moon, were just visible. They are exactly on the equator, but at five thousand metres high capped, like Kilimanjaro, with ice.

The Chief Officer of Equatoria, Deputy Commissioner Reuben Mac, was a Dinka, who are the prominent tribe in Equatoria and Northern Uganda. Reuben was very welcoming, and had laid on a party in our honour that night. The people of Equatoria are tribal, pagan, not Muslim and there was no inhibition about drinking. I felt that Moneim and Mansour were as much strangers in this environment as I was myself. After a conference during which Reuben told me all his problems and set a wish list for his preferred communication system, which was never going to happen, we adjourned to his quarters.

The party was outdoors, with fairy lights strung among the trees at the back of the house. I did receive the impression that a party was not an unusual event, that the fairy lights were permanent and that any excuse would do! Reuben Mac had, literally, hundreds of small bottles of whisky, gin, brandy, amongst others, which had undoubtedly come from Sudan Airways stocks. He sat, rather as if in state, surrounded by his bottles, regularly through the evening demanding that I should join him in another drink. The constant call was, 'Have another whisk Mr. Michael'.

I was introduced to various local people of importance, apparently as somewhat of a curiosity. I was certainly the only pale skinned person there, and probably the only one within quite a radius. Food, in large quantities, was served onto long trestle tables, at one of which I found myself sitting opposite the daughter of one of the local tribal chiefs. She was about six and a half feet tall, eight feet if you count the large head-dress and quite an imposing person.

Conversation was not particularly easy amongst the almost deafening noise of frogs and other jungle sounds. The frogs were so big that in full song they resonated like tigers! As the evening wore on and the pile of 'whisks' diminished I was quite disturbed to hear across the table, 'I like you Mr. Michael'. After the fourth or fifth repetition of this it began to appear that there were only three alternatives. I decided that the first of these held no appeal at all, the second might have been thought to be unfriendly and the third was, 'Get out of here'. I took the third option and managed to disappear behind the trees. I spent the rest of the evening hiding behind Reuben Mac and the still large pile of bottles. Moneim, being a devout Muslim and also a straight-laced man, had disappeared in disgust much earlier. I had lost sight of Mansour a considerable time before but I regret that I failed to ask if he had become an acceptable substitute for myself as a novelty visitor.

The next day, with both a headache and a need to keep a wary eye open, I was able to find the data that I needed, and feeling that it would be a wise move arranged that we should drive the hundred miles or so to the police post at Yei, near the border with Congo. Armed conflict was taking place in Congo, the forerunner of the banishment of the Belgians, with a consequent effect on police responsibilities. Although at that time I did not see any refugees, smuggling and other cross-border illegalities were commonplace. A hundred miles south west, by Land Rover over very rough dirt tracks to Yei took us to just about the centre of the continent.

The red sand road was so rutted and pot holed that at times even the driver's head hit the roof. Pity about we passengers. We had two armed policemen as an escort in the back of the Land Rover, which also raised the question of whether they had kept the safety catches on. Some of the even more remote posts than Yei are unreachable by motor vehicle in the rainy season, so if necessary the policemen walk – maybe for eighty miles or so. This may be to sort out a tribal battle, or to allocate accountability for a murder; then just part of a Constable's duties. (Shall I suggest either the walk or the responsibility in the West Midlands? I don't think so.)

In this vast and primitive area there was the occasional incongruous touch, for example a man confidently riding an English made Raleigh bicycle, with no bundles or possessions and no visible destination. Perhaps one would see the remains of a British road sign saying, 'Caution' or a barely visible track into the bush guarded by a standard 'No Entry' sign. There was a yellow 'AA' notice at one junction, pointing north west and reading, 'Wau, 420 miles'. Wow indeed! Our arrival at the rest house in Juba had promoted Khartoum to the ultimate in sophistication, but after a day in Yei Juba itself became the epitome of civilisation, with electricity and the occasional flush toilet! Although a notice in the Juba Rest House did read, 'Visitors not allowed in dinning room in shaggy dresses.'

A visit to the open market in Yei was revealing about the poverty and the quality and difficulty of life here. Items for sale or barter were so basic and, in Europe, an everyday purchase. Iron nails, for example, obviously greatly prized, were laid out in bundles of only two or three. Nearly all the women were carrying pots on their heads and babies on their backs, and many were bare to the waist. The predominant Negro tribe, as in Juba, was the Dinka, not Muslim but pagan or Christian. Idi Amin came from this area, and I saw many very big men who resembled him in build and features. Most of the conical huts were just mud and thatch, protruding from six foot high grass and corn, and I saw men hunting buffalo with spears and bows and arrows amongst the banana and mango trees. The rivers were muddy grey, and almost stagnant. Frogs here also provided a continuous night time concert.

We had stopped at the subordinate police post at Lalyo en route to Yei, and came across the 'Juba Express'. This was a rickety old lorry, running as a public 'bus, over the very long, very dusty, very hot hundred miles between Yei and Juba. It was crowded, including livestock, not just on every ramshackle seat but in every inch of space. Three layers of goods and possessions of all sorts were stacked between guardrails on the roof. What a journey. Our Land Rover had been bad enough. It was not air-conditioned, so pretty hot and sticky, but we had not shared it with goats, dogs and chickens.

I found that the Sudan, and many other parts of Africa, were now turning from Land Rovers to Toyota Land Cruisers. Many of the operators and the drivers said to me that they would much prefer the British product, for reliability and 'go anywhere' capability, but found that getting delivery and subsequently spares and service were so difficult that they were now taking the easier option. This was such a disappointing state of affairs – the British product was superior but sales, delivery and service let it down.

On this theme, I also found that the Russians had donated many vehicles and military aircraft to the Sudan, but had not made any provision for spares or service – these were one off gifts. Consequently there were a lot of Russian built 4WD vehicles abandoned in the desert - and every military airfield had its own collection of wrecked or un-airworthy MIGs. The Sudan driver, by the way, is an absolute wonder at repairing vehicles, under the burning sun, and way out, miles from any facilities, in the desert. I have seen them restore an apparently hopeless case to activity, using little more than a Birmingham Screwdriver - a hammer to most people. However, some of the Russian trucks had defeated even their tender loving care! I did discuss the opportunities that were being missed with the Foreign Office on my return, having been described by them as 'the person who probably knows more about the Sudan than anyone else in the UK at present'. It does not seem that the message got through to many of the existing British manufacturers though.

The police at Yei were under the command of Chief Inspector Richard Makurr, another Dinka tribesman, who was again very welcoming, and

Moneim, Mansour and I stayed in his house for a couple of nights. He provided much useful information and he was one who made the comment, quoted earlier, that times in Africa were better when the 'Brititch' were here. The whole of this border area is fairly lawless, with Idi Amin's Uganda next door. We were stopped by a platoon of troops at a checkpoint on the border, all of whom had very bloodshot eyes, and, I suspect, were well under the influence of drink. I would not particularly have liked to be on my own during this encounter.

A number of steps too far in Juba was a little excursion on my own into a shanty town on the outskirts of the township. This was a part of finding out what support the police needed in such places, but I made a fairly quick (but, I hope, dignified) retreat when followed by people saying, 'What you do here?' in fairly aggressive tones.

After obtaining as much data as possible we flew back to Khartoum, in my case keeping a extremely wary eye open for very tall Chieftain's daughters with big head-dresses. Actually I did see the same woman again, a few weeks later, in Khartoum where it was rather easier to dodge and hide. There had been a mass exodus of the privileged from the south of the Sudan, due to a virulent outbreak of 'Green Monkey' disease. For years afterwards I thought this was the beginning of the spread of Aids but recent research suggests that it had originated, in central Africa certainly, but many years earlier. I understood then, and still believe, that there is a link between the two – certainly there was a mass panic in Equatoria province.

After a few days based in the Sudan Hotel to write up the needs and solutions in Equatoria, it was decided that another early necessity was to travel to the Eastern or Kassala province. Kassala bordered the area where a nasty civil conflict was taking place, between Ethiopa and Eritrea. An Eritrean independence movement was trying to break away from the much more powerful Ethiopia, with refugees flooding into Sudan. It was believed that there were as many as 50,000 refugees in the Kassala area. Fahdel, Moneim and I planned to safari due east by Land Rover, aiming for Kassala town, the first place of any size for about two hundred and fifty miles, and nearly on the border of Eritrea. It was expected to be a fourteen day safari. Early morning, before we set off, the air-conditioning unit fell out of the wall into my bath. This, and the daily operation with a swiss army knife on the antiquated water heater was not unusual, in fact part of the pleasure of hotel life, but on this occasion I was actually in the bath. The interrupted bath was well taken, as it was likely to be the last chance for a decent wash. On return two weeks later I kicked the heater and jumped in fully clothed – wow, that was good!

After leaving the grubby outskirts of Khartoum we were soon in genuine desert. The Land Rover was festooned with water carrying goatskins, spare jerrycans of petrol and emergency food supplies. All very necessary. In the vast yellow space of a hot desert there are usually only the tracks of other vehicles to follow. The horizon is often the same in every direction and a compass is a necessity. I have a quiet smile when I see one fitted to a vehicle in the UK. It's a bit redundant, like bullbars. When following these tracks crunch time comes when the light fades or if they divide – as they often do. Then it is compass time.

After a few hours we came across a flock of vultures stuffing themselves on something rather horrible in our path. At this time Fahdel had only one desert driving speed – flat out. If you put a driver with a heavy right foot into the same area as a flock of heavily gorged vultures, which need about two hundred yards to get up to flying speed the obviously predictable can happen. It hit our screen in a cloud of blood and feathers, not doing much good to the Land Rover but rather less to the vulture. While I was quietly suggesting to Fahdel that sometimes 'Shweya Shweya' or alternatively 'Khidder Khidder' (both roughly meaning 'Gently Gently') is a useful concept, Moneim was deep in prayer. I do not think that Fahdel ever really believed me about shweya shweya. His philosophy, as with many of his compatriots was more likely to be 'I.B.M.'. That is not computer speak, but 'InshaAllah, Bukra, Mah Leish.' Roughly translated this is, 'It will only happen if it is the will of God, but it will not be until tomorrow, and in any case it doesn't matter'.

I guess that this is not a bad philosophy to avoid stress, strokes and heart attacks. It also prevents panic in an emergency. On the other hand it also absolves a driver from any responsibility for his actions, or the need to plan ahead. I later found it to be very prevalent in other African countries; it is certainly not confined to the Sudan or any one religion. I wonder if it is now sometimes the mindset of many British drivers. In any event, Fahdel now added another speed to his driving skills – dead slow!

Later that day, tired, hot, blood spattered, feather covered and sticky, we came to a place where the 360 degree horizon seemed to be full of tall ships. The refraction of light that causes mirages had transformed the silhouettes of camels, thousands of them, into the semblance of four masted sailing ships with spread sails. We stopped by a group of Shukriya tribesmen, camel herders who spend the whole of the grazing season with the camels, living with them, and off them. This is the season when the desert can astonishingly go green overnight. They were tall, slim, upright men with ready smiles and gleaming white teeth. They were quick-witted, but so unsophisticated that my camera was a mystery. I showed them my West Midlands warrant card, containing my photograph, which was intriguing. Oh for an instamatic camera, or if they had been invented then, a digital one!

We sat cross-legged in a circle and with the invariable hospitality of the desert people they asked, through Moneim, if I was thirsty. I certainly was, 'Then, if you can drink camel's milk with us, we will give you a camel'. Immediately a camel was milked, and the warm frothy liquid passed round in a battered old bowl. No polite sip would do, but a full draught of at least a pint per man. I took my share, and found it not unpleasant. Rather sweet and soapy, but a great deal better than sheep's milk which can turn an unaccustomed stomach inside out, or buffalo milk which is incredibly salty. It was not unlike goat's milk.

So, after drinking my share I asked, 'Which is my camel then?'

'Ah, but you cannot take it over the ocean to Brittania - we will keep it here for you'.

Did I say quick-witted? By now, I may own a whole herd of camels, somewhere between Khartoum and Kassala.

We next arrived at the first human habitation since Khartoum, a low wooden building made from rough hewn branches, oil drums, mud bricks mortared with camel dung (memories of 'ossmakantar). This was the desert equivalent of a trucker's stop, and very welcome for shi (strong tea without milk of any variety) and a breather. At sunset the tracks in the sand became difficult to follow and we spent the night in the rest house at New Halfa, where there was a police post. The Superintendent in charge had maafi Englezi, and an intriguing situation arose when I tried to explain, Moneim interpreting, how useful an English police rolled cape could be as a defensive, or offensive, weapon in lieu of firearms. It even got to the stage of using a pink bath towel as a cape substitute, but I doubt if he understood our need to carry or wear a cape in the British winter anyway. A kebab steak, washed down with shi, and a rope mattress bed under the starry night sky completed the day.

Night in the hot deserts is usually very cold, frost is often to be found on the vehicle roof and bonnet, but dawn is always very beautiful. The sun rises unobscured by the clutter of civilisation, sometimes big and orange like a Dutch cheese, sometimes shrouded by low cloud, the deceitful harbingers of a cooler day. On this morning it was golden and blue, gorgeous by 6am, hot enough to fry eggs on the Land Rover roof soon after. On our way early for the four hour drive to Kassala I found the desert changing. It was getting more green and less flat, with gullies and humped hills, trees and thorn bushes. The occasional mud and thatch hut appeared as we drove through irrigated areas growing cotton, corn, groundnuts and beans. Dams were being built in this area with European aid, with the intention of providing wide areas of irrigated land as a 'food basket' for the Sudan. There were miles of pleasant country with desert foxes to be seen and many brightly coloured parakeets, and it was not unlike the area around Juba.

Eventually the twisted conical shapes of Jebel Kassala, or Taka Mountain, and beyond that the mountains of Eritrea took shape on the horizon. Humped sandblasted granite, springing three thousand feet directly from the desert floor. It was visible from forty miles away, irresistibly like an old grey elephant resting in the intense heat. Kassala, after the long, hot, dirty drive, was an oasis of blue and purple flowers including bougainvillea, set in, and contrasting with emerald green grass. It was a busy, bustling town with some paved roads, and full of refugees from Eritrea. A pleasant place, and a haven in the middle of not such pleasant places. The bulk of the grey mountain rising directly beyond the town made it visually brilliant and exciting.

We were expected, the teleprinters having done their duty, and after meeting the Provincial Police Assistant Commissioner I was introduced to my local liaison officer, Inspector Khider Ali. He was a middle aged, totally bald officer, whose skull, when he removed his uniform cap, revealed a web of old scars. These, he explained, were knife and sword wounds received on duty. Kassala was, and perhaps still is, a frontier town in the style of the old wild west. Tribal wars, involving many men on each side, were not unknown and smuggling across the Eritrean border was an everyday occurrence. I suspect that some slave trading was still going on, and later, on visits to sub-Saharan Africa, I did some observation for the Anti-Slavery Society, who knew that it was far from dead. Khider Ali was a very professional police officer who had been promoted through the ranks, not joining as an officer, the latter being the normal Sudanese career structure. There was very much an officer caste system in force, and I suspect that it was necessary to be an extraordinary man to break through it. He was totally overwhelmed by being selected to guide a British Police Officer – again I am sure that the days of Empire were not so bad in his view. He pressed several gifts upon me, not the least of which was a lethal swordstick.

All the Sudanese officers that I met would invariably ask, 'How many children do you have?' My answer of 'two' would bring forth a condescending laugh and the comment that he possessed (the word is used advisably) anything between twelve and twenty seven. Four wives of course. Khider Ali was no exception, but in his case eleven wives had been discarded who had only produced daughters, and he was saving up for a medical in Cairo, in the remote possibility that the problem lay with him. Joking, and different customs and life-styles apart, I was impressed with his professional competence and experience. He knew his men and his job and no doubt could have taught many police officers world – wide some of the finer points of police practice. I had been in a sword fight in Wolverhampton, (well, a long bayonet) but it had happened with much more regularity to Khider Ali. It was rather good however to be able to say that I had seen a sharp edge too. Wonder if he believed me? Probably, I think.

In order to make some decisions about the level of communication needed, it was necessary to discover the policing problems in all the areas of the Sudan. This was where the Foreign Office brief to 'modernise communications' became totally inadequate. To recommend appropriate facilities and equipment it was essential to discover the problems and needs of each district. Khider Ali decided to show me the police post at a hill called Abu Gomel (the hill of the camel) near the border. We travelled through wide green plains and banana plantations towards the border, with the mountains of Eritrea reminding me of the Coolins of Skye.

The police post was very isolated – in the absence of vehicles patrols were carried out by camel. Nearby was one refugee camp, just in Sudan territory. There were a number of refugees there from Asmara, the main town in Eritrea, which through the ongoing vicious war of independence was being bombed by the Ethiopians. The refugees were living in flimsy huts, made mainly of straw, and as we approached hundreds came running towards us. I learned that as many as twenty to thirty people, mainly women and children, were living and sleeping in each small straw hut, about as big as my dining room at home.

As I was the only European within hundreds of miles - there was certainly no UNHCR presence - I suppose that they saw me as bringing some sort of help, perhaps from the Red Cross. The best that the Sudanese authorities had been able to do was to provide a water bowser. When I examined this it contained not cool clear water, but, effectively, mud, mixed with dung. As it was a long drive back to Kassala the driver had been filling it from the nearest river bed. Most of these people had no English, but one little woman, a school teacher, could make herself understood. She had two small children with her and all her possessions in a cheap cardboard suitcase. She had no idea what had happened to her husband when their town was bombed.

I have never felt so helpless.

I can still see her, and the children and feel the helplessness. I wanted to give her money, but with so many people there this would have been a lot worse than useless.

On the way back to Kassala we entered Eritrea – the border was not guarded – across a completely dried river bed as wide as the Thames at Henley, and stopped three men in a Land Rover about to enter Sudan. They were obviously men of the Tigre, the Eritrean independence fighters, but had a permit saying that they were refugees, so Khider Ali took no action other than to warn them to go straight to Kassala. We stopped for jabanah (coffee and ginger) and again, being a curiosity, and perhaps because I expressed appreciation of the goat's milk on offer, I was offered a goat. What a picture – leading my goat and camel through Birmingham and tieing them up outside Police Headquarters. (Wish that I could have done it – would have used the Chief's parking space.) I was also just in time to stop a lamb being sacrificed in my honour. This had never happened in Wolverhampton or Birmingham. Although, thinking about it, my wife cooks a very nice lamb chop. Is this the same thing? Room for debate perhaps.

Back in Kassala both Khider Ali and Moneim agreed that something needed to be done about the refugees. We took the Land Rover back to the open market and filled it with dates, rice and whatever bulk food was available. Then something happened which I have always regarded as a small miracle. Several merchants, not normally people noted for their kindness to the weak and helpless, who were drinking coffee in the Market Place, asked what was happening. On learning of the situation at Abu Gomel they loaded up a second Land Rover with bolts of cloth and more food, without payment. Not, I know, a normal response.

Whilst little enough, this was a better reaction than I could get from the UN, the UK Government or the big charities when I raised the matter on my return. The water situation was improved by a word with the Kassala Assistant Commissioner, who was also appalled and pulled strings, but there was little the police could do to provide proper feeding facilities. I wrote to Jo asking her to contact the aid agencies, reported to the British Ambassador in Khartoum and made a lot of noise about the situation on the Eritrean border on return to the UK, but it was not until Bob Geldof got a lot of high profile publicity that any help for the victims of this nasty conflict started to happen. I believe that I may have been the first European to become aware of this particular refugee problem, and have wondered since if Geldof's attention was caught by our comments to the Charities. I shall probably never know the answer to that, but would like to think it possible.

After Abu Gomel we went on to another isolated post at Aroma, north of Kassala. This is the tribal land of the 'Hadendwa' men. They have long shaggy hair, and they are a fierce tribe, all the young men still carrying a long sword slung over one shoulder. Their unusually long arms were very noticeable – perhaps from the use of the sword. I found that battles between related men were not uncommon – son would cut father's arm off if he got upset. Two of these swords now decorate my workshop.

At Aroma the police took me into a dark and dismal local shebeen that supplied Marissa beer brewed from kaffir corn. It was served to me in a gourd. This was a foul concoction, bubbling away in an iron pot standing on the mud floor, from which the men would drink from a communal wooden pannikin. I had to have some, but a ritual sip and an expression of delight were quite enough. It only needed three ugly old women round the pot to be straight out of the Brothers Grimm as adapted by Walt Disney! Italian expressions were common due to the Italian influence in Ethiopia and Somalia and it was strange to hear 'chiow' in such a place.

On the long drive back to Kassala we found a party of nomadic Rachida Bedouin camped in open fronted tents. This tribe are descended from Haroun al Rachid, the Caliph of Baghdad of the 'Sheherazade and the Thousand and One Nights' stories. The women, who by a very rare privilege I was able to see and even photograph, were of course veiled but apparently beautiful, with slim figures and huge tinkling necklaces and rings. Without the police presence even my distant approach would have been very many steps too far, so I was lucky.

On the last evening in Kassala I climbed Taka Mountain with Fahdel, who despite his limitations as a driver, was a friendly young man. Half way up we met a Hadendwa tribesman, who asked him who I was. He was not at all aggressive, merely curious, as a Paleface really was a rarity. When Fahdel explained, he took out the long wooden comb from his mop of hair and presented it to me with a flourish. I could do no other than put it in my own hair could I? A ritual swap, presenting him with my small plastic comb would not have been appreciated, as the fuzzy-wuzzies need at least six-inch prongs to be able to scratch their scalps! The flat plain below, dotted with the lights of camp fires, emphasised just how remote this place was, and how great are the distances in Africa.

Later the same evening I joined a police patrol close to the mountain foot. It was still, quiet and magical, with the bright stars and luminous moon in a velvety sky. The desert is beautiful in these conditions, the temperature comparatively cool and pleasant and the company good. I don't know if the colour grey can be described as 'bright', but that is how the rocks appeared.

Leaving Kassala the next morning I was unexpectedly presented with a Hadendwa sword, which the officers had even been able to have inscribed, in both English and Arabic, 'From the Police Officers of Kassala Province' on a silver band around the scabbard. The trouble that had been taken to get this done brought a lump to my throat. It also indicates the friendliness of the Sudanese people towards the British, and the international mutual respect of police officers. Whilst their police duties are likely to be very different, and often carried out in a very different way, they are always a minority group, and as I have found, with esteem for each other.

I have been a member of the International Police Association, which exists to promote friendship, knowledge and travel among police officers of different countries for many years, and have had some wonderful experiences because of that membership. Perhaps also, we were not so bad as colonial oppressors after all.

Getting the swords home from the Sudan seemed to pose a potential problem, as I ended up with four, plus a sawfish nose bone. I was prepared to put the best ones down my trouser leg but in fact Sudan Airways to Cairo could not have cared less, and the Air France check-in girl at Cairo said 'put them under your seat, cheri'! Couldn't happen now. Those times, like the days of Empire, have gone. The Hadendwa ones rusted quite soon after being exposed to the English climate, and are immovable from the scabbards. Fortunately the scabbards are still in good condition, so when I am doing a talk I produce the inscribed one. The challenge then is for anyone to prove that he or she is the rightful heir to the Crown, like King Arthur, if the sword can be withdrawn.

It hasn't been done yet!

I managed to protect Khidder Ali's sword-stick in time with copious quantities of vaseline, and this is still quite a frightening object. I also bought a beautiful crocodile hide handbag for Jo while in the Sudan, but within a year or so it had turned completely black. They do not of course need to worry about damp climates. Oddly enough my leopard skin slippers are still as new!

On the way to the next town of any size, Gedaref, about one hundred and thirty miles, we came across a tribe of nomadic Bedouin with a 'howdah' built of branches and blankets on the backs of their camels. It was just big enough for one woman and a few children, with their goods slung beneath it, on the camel's flanks. They were really shy, but I was just able to get a photograph, a really evocative one, perfectly illustrating the origin of their name, from the Arabic word Badwiyyin, 'dwellers in the desert'.

Further on we found another group, who were quite happy to let me ride a howdahless camel. One has the distinct sensation, on the back of a camel, that the back legs are going in a different direction to those at the front. There is also a strong sense of insecurity, as it arises from the kneeling position, and a desire to grab at anything available. Being coached by an expert, I had at least to try to do it properly, which is to be perched on the hump (no saddle) with legs crossed, and shouting 'Hut - Hut - Hut'. My preferred position would have been to slide down into the hollow of the neck and clutch at anything to hand. The camel is said to sneer because it knows the one name of Allah that is unknown to mankind. I think however that this one was sneering at me. On the way home from the Sudan I took a weeks leave in Egypt, and did the tourist thing of visiting the pyramids at Giza, and the Sphinx. It is quite difficult to resist the demands of the scarab sellers and the purveyors of rides on a camel, but naturally they expect Europeans to be quite unprepared for the experience of being aboard a camel. It was enjoyable to give them a surprise!

As we neared Gedaref the desert began to give way to more cultivated land. The Sudan Government had put a lot of resources into this area, and several British Companies were involved in development – dams and sugar refineries, among them the company employing my flying friend Mick. The 'road' however was still a deeply rutted dirt and mud track, quite impassable after rain or a flash flood. We got stuck in three-foot deep ruts several times, and Fahdel was showing signs of wear and tear. Moneim, in the back seat, was hooked on my Anadin tablets. As we stopped for a break the country sprang another surprise. A small figure appeared amongst the shoulder high crops. It was an ancient little man, in a straw hat and blue shorts rather than a djellabir, cross-legged on an ancient little donkey that was almost concealed beneath the load of cut crops that it was also carrying. As he passed us I showed off my Arabic by calling, 'Salaam Alaykum'.

With a perfectly straight face he replied, in perfect English, 'Good morning, gentlemen. How are you?'

I was too taken aback to follow and talk to him, and have regretted it ever since. We had left Kassala at 7 a.m. and by mid-afternoon Fahdel was in a temper, never having properly recovered from his encounter with the vulture. He was a city boy – out of his element. Moneim was in the back seat, praying. I was also praying in the front seat, but keeping it to myself.

On eventual arrival at Gedaref at 6 p.m., dusk, we should have been expected, but the communication system, which I was there to improve, had not worked! The Superintendent in charge was away, and his Deputy was deeply suspicious and totally in ignorance about us. As there was no Hotel in Gedaref he reluctantly agreed to find us somewhere to spend the night, and took us to what he said was the Officer's Mess. Not to put too fine a point upon it this turned out to be a brothel, and a very dirty one at that. Fahdel seemed to be quite pleased and in a better temper at this turn of events, but Moneim, the very devout man, took refuge in the Koran. Again. He was incensed at the lack of welcome. Actually it seemed quite funny, because it was so typical of the suspicion of 'people from Headquarters' that one can meet anywhere. As there was no alternative we left Fahdel to his own devices and Moneim and I shifted a couple of rope beds into the courtyard and spent an undisturbed, if hungry night.

Morning brought an interesting development in the shape of a very apprehensive Deputy Chief. His boss had arrived back and was not best pleased to hear where we were. He brought me a peace offering; an ostrich egg in a beautiful red and white jacket. I managed to get it home intact, and very inappropriately it still comes out every Christmas. The Commander of the Gedaref Police, Superintendent Suleiman Daoud Suleiman was a splendid man of about my own age, with whom I had an instant rapport. Like Khidder Ali he was a very professional officer. Both could have fitted into the senior ranks of any British Police Force, with, I think, some benefit to the Force, given some English language training. Useful and productive discussions took most of the day and Moneim and I were glad to settle for an early night in the much more pleasant Government Rest House, to which we had been moved.

It was still the fasting period of Ramadan so Suleiman invited us to join him for the evening meal, at sunset the following day. Twelve of us sat around the carpet in his yard, eleven pairs of brown feet and one pair of very dirty white ones, waiting for the 'go ahead' call from the Muezzin in the nearest minaret. When it comes it is devil take the hindmost. A lot of food is offered and consumed, as everyone stocks up for the next twenty four hours. Cooked meat, kebabs, the delicacies of fatty lamb's heels, entrails and liver, and lots of fruit, straight off the tree. There were the usual proprieties, which I was careful to observe. The left hand is never, ever used to touch food, as it is used for other purposes, and to expose the soles of the feet is an insult to the host. This tends to be difficult when one is sitting cross-legged with shoes and socks off.

Also it is not done to admire anything, as the host would then feel obliged to offer it as a gift. This can be hard to remember for a person brought up to tender compliments in someone else's house. So, to say, 'You have a very pretty daughter' could lead to complications. However, in an Arab household the women of the family are not normally introduced, or if so only briefly, and their presence is apparent only by noises off, in the kitchen. The Sudan, at that time, was, except for a few wealthy and western educated families, very much a man's world. I remember elderly and grave Sudanis clutching their sides and rolling about with laughter and disbelief when I described the workings, and results of the Equal Opportunities Act. They could not conceive that a female police officer could be promoted to Inspector to be in charge of men. In their culture, and to them it was almost obscene, and a world gone mad. As some of the results of integrating male and female officers have been described earlier I will not enlarge on this here.

It was seriously bad behaviour as a guest to fail to eat everything put in front of one. Here, as in many other situations in Africa and the Far East as a visitor I had to stagger through mountains of unaccustomed and unwanted food. It meant struggling mouthful by mouthful and just wishing that it would come to an end. It did of course, eventually, and I managed to avoid disgracing myself at this and subsequent feasts, but I have not been a big eater of greasy lamb's heels since.

Suleiman was up bright and early to present me with yet another gift, a magnificent saw-fish nose, about four feet in length and in much better condition than the one in the Natural History Museum in London. I only hope that I thanked him properly for it, as it must have been a prized personal possession. I wish that he could know that over thirty years later it has pride of place, with the swords, in my workshop, and is much admired – 'No, it's not a sword fish!'

We then headed towards an isolated police post on the Ethiopian border, El Luchdi, where smuggling was a serious and violent problem. This was a four hour drive in a temperature of about 120 degrees. Moneim had long abandoned his Khartoum wear of jeans and shirt for the loose white djellabir. Western clothing in those conditions gets tight, wet and horribly uncomfortable after an astonishingly short time, so I was now wearing my Malay sarong, bought in Malaysia a year or two earlier, and a batik shirt.

We were now passing a huge variety of exotic life – longhorned cattle, buffalo, camels of course and thousands of birds. Five foot tall hunched maribou storks looking in their black and white plumage for all the world like elderly hump-backed clergymen, to tiny bundles of jewelled feathers. Two travellers on foot insisted that we share their jabbanah – coffee made with ginger and boiled in a cut off tin can over a wood fire. I suspected that this was the last that they had, but this is the invariable hospitality of the desert, and it would have been incredibly wrong to reject it. Desert nomads equate generosity with courage, and since to be known as a coward would mark a man for life, welcome and hospitality to other travellers never fails.

We had to cross the Atbara River to reach El Luchdi. It is an important tributary of the Nile, flowing north from the Ethopian highlands of Gondar then joining the Nile south of Merowe and Berber, where the crumbling remains of pyramids more ancient than those near Cairo still stand. The brown greasy river, as wide as the Thames at Chiswick was crossed by means of a low wooden ferry, which with one vehicle on board, via two planks, was hauled upstream by manpower then let go and propelled towards the far bank by rough timber sweeps.

It worked!

We disembarked into three feet of water, which was not a problem but a pleasure. One felt like 'Sanders of the River'. Near here in 1898 during another jihad against the British, the Hadendwa broke a British square at the Atbara. Fierce fighting men, and they looked it.

The police post at El Luchdi was as primitive and isolated as Abu Gomel, but the area was flatter, with many miles of plantations being worked by Nigerians. The Inspector in charge said that the number of foreigners in the district was one of his problems. He advised that it would be safer to travel to the border in his Land Rover, as this would be recognised as a police vehicle. It was again crucial to see and experience the full range of police tasks and problems in order to best decide what level of communication was necessary. The Inspector was quite happy to let me drive over the deep muddy tracks, but insisted on advising me of the best rut to follow. As his command of English was at best uncertain this went something like, 'Left, left, no I mean right, now right again, no I mean left, that's right, but go slow here, that's right, no I mean left' and so on! I ignored him as much as possible without hurting his feelings. Unfortunately he also completely miscalculated the timings, so that we arrived back at the Atbara crossing as it was getting dusk.

As Fahdel was now hungry and tired having had to dig us out of several muddy ruts, I would have been prepared to bet a month's salary on what would happen. It did. The front wheels went on the planks leading onto the boat, but the rear wheels went into the river! She would not move, either way, even in four wheel drive. I have noticed, on several occasions, a peculiar fact of life in apparently deserted parts of the world. As soon as something interesting happens a crowd materialises from nowhere, each member of which has his own solution to the problem. It was time to roll up trousers, take off shoes and ignoring the fifty pieces of advice, in Arabic, organise a series of sideways bounces to get the rear wheels back on the planks. The stars were coming out, the crickets were chirping and the frogs in full chorus, but 'Ham d'il Allah', it worked. I can say, without false modesty, that I was rather pleased by this, and also to have been able to keep a straight face. It was the high spot of the whole fourteen day safari. Fahdel and I swapped seats and I drove back to Gadaref. This was also an interesting experience at night. Physical strength was needed to keep the wheels in the deep ruts, as we drove through an apparent tunnel of high kaffir corn on either side of the track.

We arrived at 9 p.m. to find a party in my honour in full swing, including a mixed couple of English teachers and a female American tourist. As mentioned before, any excuse will do. It was not even necessary for the guest of honour to be there! A Sudanese army Brigadier was chasing the tourist, and a local Doctor was chasing the female teacher.

Moneim retired to bed feeling deeply disgusted by this behaviour and the mismanagement of the timings on the border. He threatened to report all the local people to the President. To make matters worse there was no food until 11 p.m., by which time he had got up again and gone to the Suq to buy some. The party then transferred itself to several Police Land Rovers, for a tour of the Ethiopian quarter. The owners of a thatched hut shebeen were woken up and the party re-started. I can remember the orange painted symbols and patterns on the interior mud and camel dung walls. The combination of whisky and the day's travel hit me suddenly and I subsided into a dignified (I think) sleep on the one and only bed. When I woke at 4 a.m. the drinking and dancing were still in progress, but fortunately by that time everyone else was also getting tired. On return to the Rest House I found Moneim still very cross and Fahdel sleeping in the Land Rover.

By next day both had recovered, and we embarked early on the long drive south and then west to cross the Blue Nile and look at the police procedures at Wad Medani, about one hundred miles south of Khartoum. Although not a big town it was important because of the Nile crossing and I suppose roughly equivalent to Spaghetti Junction in Birmingham! We stayed overnight in a small 'Hotel' which meant a building with a few bare rooms containing only rope mattresses and the ubiquitous oil drum for washing in.

The next day we were eventually within reach of the all-weather road built by the Chinese and which leads, dead straight, and boringly flat, to the ferry across the Blue Nile. The road is narrow, the sun beats down, mirages are frequent, and in these circumstances it is not surprising that the inevitable happens. Drivers go to sleep. One sad sight that we passed was thousands of broken bottles on each side of the road. Two lorry loads of 'Camel' beer had collided. Sad indeed, since a bottle of Camel can be a life saver in the desert.

A problem arose as we reached the ferry, a much larger and more modern vessel than its relation on the Atbara, as the river is hundreds of metres wide here, but boarded in the same way. A lorry driver had made the same mistake as Fahdel and the resulting confusion on the steep and sandy riverbank was a sight not to be missed. Moneim reached for his Koran, Fahdel laughed, hugely pleased and feeling rehabilitated, while I decided that they could sort this one out themselves. Which of course, eventually, they did. I have a nice photograph of a beaming Fahdel! There is now a bridge over the Blue Nile at this point. Easier, but not as interesting.

Finally next day we regained Khartoum, with a lot of useful work done, knowledge gained, a truck load of gifts and a mind full of memories, some unpleasant, some amusing and very many greatly rewarding. The hospitality of the police, and the ordinary simple people that I met was overwhelming, and the beauty of Kassala in particular, so lush and fertile, really got under my skin. Even the goats there fed on green grass rather than rubbish and tin cans as they did in Khartoum. What do I do with the three huge bunches of bananas that I was given? They will improve my reputation amongst the Embassy staff! After more than two weeks on safari, washing in cold water in oil drums, I hastily performed the usual surgery on the water heater and jumped into the bath fully clothed, plus a bagful of dirty shirts.

It was good to lie back in the warm water and plan the next safari.

As I now had a lot of paper work to sort out the Embassy was the first place to visit. I had been promised as much secretarial help as was necessary and decided that I would prepare an interim report to leave with the Ambassador and the Police Commissioner on my departure. I was given two splendid members of the English staff to help with this, Stella and Joan, Stella in particular to help with the typing – computers did not exist! How they ever deciphered the notes made in the heat of the journey well enough to produce an acceptable report is beyond me. I palled up with both girls, plus a third, their friend Lijda who was a secretary at the Dutch Embassy.

As there was quite a bit of necessary time now in Khartoum I spent off-duty time at the expatriate club, the Sudan Club, which was a well sprinkled, green, comfortable place with a swimming pool and a nicely stocked bar. I was often joined there by the girls, plus Gary, a junior Embassy staffer. Occasionally we were joined by another young man from the Embassy, whom I strongly suspected was a security man or spook, although this was never confirmed. His duties were very vague, mainly it seemed to me being that of a gofer, his name was alleged to be Blogg, he did not fit the usual pattern of Embassy staff, and no one was ever quite sure where he was. 'Maafi Blogg' (No Blogg) was the usual complaint from the girls when they wanted him to do something!

I had decided early on that I did not need to conform too rigidly to the Commissioners request to take my rest day on Friday, since I had to choose my work pattern to fit other requirements. As Stella and I were doing my report on Fridays and my group of friends were normally at the Club on Sundays this seemed fair. However, I did warn them that if a police uniform presented itself through the Club entrance, we were having a prayer meeting. In swimming costumes because of the heat. Occasionally the Club was able to show an English or American film, and it was there that I first saw Jaws and Catch 22. Some pleasant times were had there, interspersed with some very hot and sweaty research and analysis around Khartoum and Omdurman.

In the city I had Hassan Ibrahim as my driver. Hassan was a nice old man, elderly for a policeman, but not a very good driver. His preferred method was to start off, get up to about thirty miles an hour then reach over me to open and shut my door, presumably to make sure that it was shut. He then got into top gear, and stayed in it, no matter what the situation was or how many corners lay ahead. I was able to fit in a visit to the camel market in Omdurman, where the top quality pure white camels were bought and sold and to watch some camel racing. I got a ferry onto Tutti Island, in the Nile, which must be one of the hottest places on earth, and saw the land being tilled traditionally by wooden ploughs drawn by a pair of yoked oxen. Watching Dervish dancers, (who do actually whirl!) was exciting not only visually but also acoustically, since all the women present were ululating very excitedly and noisily. This was a sound absolutely evocative of Africa, as was the noise of the haggling in the camel market!

The confluence of the White Nile coming up from central Africa and the Blue Nile coming down from the highlands of Ethiopia is in the urban city. The birth of the mighty Nile itself is a majestic sight with different colours visible for some way after the confluence, although certainly neither blue nor white!

I was also getting a number of invitations to Embassy festivities – being neither a salesman nor a diplomat but slightly unusual. The parties were usually quite high-spirited, officers mess types of shindig, with people ending up in the swimming pool frequently still clothed. No complaints in that climate! I was seated at the Ambassador's table at one of these festivities, and could feel an air of pique among some of the more starchy English expatriates, of whom there were quite a few.

The time passed very quickly, and the festival of Id Al-fitr, marking the end of Ramadan approached, making planning for the next provincial research necessary. The regions of the Sudan are so different, both geographically and culturally, that the facilities had to be individually tailored to the needs of each area. The next research was decided to be to the far west, the region of Darfur, which was then reasonably peaceful but in the early years of the new millennium became a sad, sad, civil war torn country with a vicious ongoing conflict between Government forces and rebels and yet another refugee situation.

This again was long distance, and Moneim and I flew to El Fasher, the Regional Capital of Darfur. This is real desert terrain, bordering Chad and Libya, and over six hundred miles from Khartoum. Not far away the Marra Plateau rises from the desert floor, reaching over nine thousand feet at Jebel

Marra. Up there grow the juiciest, most tender, least stringy grapefruit in the world. It was easy to become addicted to them for breakfast. El Fasher Police HQ boasted a wheeled cannon, painted white and dating from Kitchener's campaign against the Mahdi in the last century. It was also a pretty complex, surrounded by bright flowers that must have required an awful lot of moisture to stay alive. It was rather touching to see them watering the flowers.

I visited the local prison, and had breakfast with the Governor to see what need there was for better liaison, communications wise. The prisoners were not locked in cells, but allowed to sit about in the open, inside the outer security wall. There was little shade, the flies were fierce and as big as bumblebees and it cannot have been an enjoyable experience.

However it was rumoured that there was a queue to get into prison as the food was easier to come by than outside. It is quite pleasing to be able to say that I have survived being inside an African prison. The main, possibly only, occupation for people in El Fasher after breaking the fast in the evening, seemed to be a visit to the Suq. It had mud brick shacks, wooden shanties and tin lean-to huts lit by paraffin lamps and the occasional coloured light powered from the town generator, with a wide variety of goods, mainly pretty shoddy, on sale. No tarmac or paving anywhere in the town, just loose sand, with donkeys, goats and camels everywhere. The whole town stopped to look when I got in some more camel riding experience!

El Fasher was definitely a frontier town, at the end of the railway line from Khartoum, although it was still over one hundred miles to the border with Chad. There was nothing but sand in that hundred miles except very isolated hamlets and a Fort, virtually on the border. Whilst going to and from the Suq (Moneim and I went on four successive evenings, by which time it had lost a lot of it's charm) we were challenged over loaded and levelled rifles. I bought a few bangles for Jo and Nicky, and a revolting mummified baby crocodile for Al!

The work went well, but unfortunately when it was time to leave, Sudan Airways had gone on strike. Since there was no way of knowing when a plane might or might not arrive, this meant camping out at the small, rather remote and totally user-unfriendly airport. A Sudani Air Force pilot was also stranded there, so the world was well put to rights over the next three days and nights. Eventually, and rather joyfully, an aeroplane did arrive and we returned to Khartoum.

Back at the Embassy for some more report writing, Stella and I were getting on quite well with the interim report. With a holiday break due I teamed up again with Gary and the three girls and we had a couple of really enjoyable days out. One of the girls had a British car, of all things in that climate a non-airconditioned Mini! Five of us produced quite a lot of heat, even with all the windows open. Our first trip was the few miles south to the Dam on the White Nile at Jebel Aulia where the river is so wide that it was almost like being at the seaside. We watched the Sudani fishermen casting their circular nets into the river in their time honoured way and fetching out four-foot long fishes. We thought that this was almost a reprise of Jaws. It was cleverly done, certainly not without a lot of practice, and worked well, as those who have tasted a well-cooked Nile perch can testify!

We also, rashly in view of the heat, climbed to the top of the Jebel. This turned out to be more rash than was expected as at the top we heard and felt bullets cracking past. Whether this was deliberate or just bad shooting from a military range we did not stop to find out. It was received wisdom at that time that you were only in danger from an African soldier's rifle if it was pointing at someone else to your left. The theory was that they did not have the training to squeeze the trigger, but would give it a mighty yank. Any road up, on this occasion we survived, although a little surprised.

We also, the same five, took a longer day out to the Gezira Club at Wad Medani, this time on the Blue Nile, and enjoyed a very good and lazy lunch under the trees. I have an evocative photograph of a happy bunch of young people. I also received an invitation to lunch with the Ambassador of the East German Republic, at his residence. This was interesting, but surprising. Did he want to know if I was an anti-communist agent for the West? Anyway he was very pleasant, and his wife served the best apfelstrudel that I had tasted before or since. This was also surprising, since decent flour to make the pastry was pretty well unobtainable in Khartoum, or so my British friends informed me. Perhaps it was flown in from Berlin in the diplomatic bag. On a related theme, it was at about this time that I realised that I needed more shirts, as it was necessary to change at least once or twice a day. My existing ones were wearing out through being washed without tender loving care, probably on the nearest rocks in the Nile. As I was able to 'phone home from the main post office in Khartoum (it entailed pre-booking and a long wait, but was worth it) I asked Jo to send me four white police shirts, care of the hotel. They never did arrive, and for a few years afterwards I had visions of an Arab lady riding a camel around Khartoum whilst dressed in a West Midlands Police shirt!

The north and north-western areas of Sudan were, and are, barren desert with no towns, few villages and virtually no police presence. The Sahrâ Lîbîya, the Libyan Desert, extends into the Sudan, from there expanding westwards until it joins the Algerian Sahara. It was decided that there was no point in lengthy travel to these areas, but it was necessary to remember the need for police radio cover to be provided here in my eventual report. It was, however, worth travelling some two hundred miles north, following the course of the Nile, to discuss communications with the senior police officer at the substantial town of Atbara, the capital of Nile province. The town is where the river to which it gives its name, and which had caused Fahdel so much grief, debouches into the Nile, after flowing down from the highlands of Ethiopia.

Moneim, Mansour and I travelled from Khartoum to Atbara by train, on the British built railway, following the course of the Nile, the Blue and White having united in Khartoum. We arranged for Fahdel to meet us in Atbara with the Land Rover, so that we could call at several remote police posts on the way back. It was an eight hour journey although only a little over two hundred miles. The train was slow and incredibly dusty, but we travelled first class so there was plenty to eat and drink.

There was an excellent working session at Atbara, with once more a very friendly, co-operative and hospitable Assistant Commissioner. I was presented with yet another Hadendwa sword! Moneim, Mansour and I then headed south by Land Rover, with two armed policemen as guards. Although this was a comparatively short journey, about two hundred and fifty miles, it was across real desert, where it is not a good idea to break down. The vehicle was again festooned with goatskins for water and jerrycans of spare petrol, and emergency food supplies.

The route south was through Ed Damer where we looked at the police post facilities. We stopped overnight in Moneim's family home, sleeping on rope beds on the roof of his house, under the stars. So many stars and so bright. Again it was wonderful to see the clarity and brilliance of the night sky. But, nothing is perfect! The flies and the sun got up together at about 5 a.m. Moneim's house was traditional, flat roofed and white, and surrounded by a wall, partly for privacy and partly for security. This was like the majority of private houses at that time. At home, he also became traditional, and again shed his normal attire of jeans and shirt for a djellabir, and small turban, obviously then being much more comfortable.

There was a wedding celebration in the central square of the small town, to which we walked after a meal. I joined in a finger-snapping dance with the men, to the beat of drums, and also found myself much in demand as a dancing partner for the girls who had been allowed to attend. There is a technique to the dancing which was not much like European style. There was no bodily contact, and included the way the woman shook her long hair. I gathered that if her hair was brushing across her shoulders, left to right and vice-versa, it meant that she was willing! This was not, of course, typical Muslim behaviour, and there was not a hijab in sight, as this was tribal country. I am not sure that I totally understand all the nuances of the hair swinging, but it was fun and a very pleasant, non-threatening couple of hours in the little town. Being surrounded by whitewashed mud and camel dung walls, and lit by lanterns and candles was very like being in the middle of a film set. It seemed to me to feel even more what Bethlehem and Nazareth would have been like at the time of Christ.

Next day we drove to the police post at Shendi, diverting en route to look at the spread of many pyramids, at Kebushiya, near the Nile. They are smaller than the more famous ones at Giza, but much older, crumbling and cracking away. It seemed unbelievable that there was no protection against destruction or vandalism – one could wander about and even climb on them if so inclined. I do not think that anyone knew their purpose then, although archaeology is taking place now. Maybe they were tombs like their bigger counterparts near Cairo, or just monuments, built by the Nubian Meroitic Kings.

It was known as the Land of the Black Pharoahs, the Kushites who ruled Egypt and the Sudan from the fourth to the third centuries before Christ. They were covered – on the parts not crumbled away – with hieroglyphics representing birds and warriors. Although not that far from Khartoum they are over a thousand miles from the tourist spots in the south of Egypt. Abu Simbel is not the limit of antiquities on the Nile, although this does not explain the lack of greater international interest in the pyramids at Kebushiya and Meroe.

Since then however there have been a lot of archaeological investigations that have revealed the great extent of the Nubian Kingdom based upon Meroe and Kerma. They were not mere slaves as was thought at one time, and ruled both Nubia and Egypt until forced by climate change to move further south. Climate change is not a 21st century phenomenon, this change was the encroaching Libyan Desert, expanding south and east. It is now thought that the Nubians wandered south to the area of the Nuba Mountains in Kordofan, central Sudan, where remnants of their culture and customs can be found today. I was very privileged to have wandered among the remains of their civilisation in Nubia.

At Shendi the Superintendent in charge was greatly pleased to tell me that he had fourteen children and his Sergeant had eighteen, as against my two! They obviously felt very sorry for me, and had difficulty in understanding that two was not far off average for the UK. He was another man with a great regard for all things British (except our system of one wife per man). Like Khidder Ali he had come through the ranks, having been in the British Army during the war. Another special man I think. The police building was traditional – one storey, flat roofed and surrounded by the ubiquitous wall.

A pleasant camp site was found near to the Nile, and with mosquito nets rigged we spent a good night under the stars, getting up early for a boat journey on the Nile, at Sabaluga, near the sixth cataract. The nets, being less than new, had holes in them big enough for a crow, let alone a mosquito, to get through, but there was not much point in worrying about it. The boat was entirely wooden, roughly hand built and the owner, a fisherman, lived on it, sleeping under the furled up sail. He had his possessions in a wooden chest, upon which sat a fist size rock. I asked, (through Moneim), what this was for and he explained that it was a sacred rock, known as such to all other fisherman, and that anyone who moved it would be cursed. He felt no need for any other security. I have tried this in Wolverhampton. It doesn't work here. He was a pleasant, friendly man, very happy to give me an experience of his life, and this, on another hot and dusty safari, was an enjoyable interlude.

Once away from the green and quite beautiful banks of the Nile this is genuine desert country, stretching to the horizon in every direction. The yellow sandy expanse as portrayed by Hollywood it was not, however. Low hills were frequent, and vast areas of black stony flints, or coarse red sand, carbonised rock and cores of sparkling quartz. These are the flat, wind-graded serir, so dry that not even the flies can find anything to survive on. Then one came to an area of yellow sand, so soft that only a four-wheel drive could cope with it. A desert 'bus', a lorry of course, which passed us, going north, was crammed full of people, others hanging on outside, or sitting on the roof, and all waving madly. This was like the 'Juba Express', which we had seen in the south.

Also travelling north were strings of camels, walking to be sold in the market in Cairo – a month's walk, somewhat like turkeys looking forward to Christmas. We returned to Khartoum through the site of the battle of Omdurman, where Kitchener's modern army killed thousands of tribesmen - Dervishes - in eventual retaliation for Gordon's death in Khartoum, and where Winston Churchill took part in the last British cavalry charge. A dry, dusty, desolate and depressing place it was, although becoming threatened by the encroaching suburbs of Omdurman. The sandy dust was an ever-present, all prevailing fact of life in all the Sudanese towns, as it is in many of the urban areas of north and central Africa. It is usually coupled with windblown dust from open drains which adds spice to the smell and taste.

After a few more days of hot and detailed report writing and much more enjoyable resting at the Sudan Club, a final visit was programmed, this time to the north-east of Sudan, on the Red Sea coast. We flew to Port Sudan, about four hundred miles over the Nubian Desert, the Es Sahrâ en Nûbîya, which is just barren red sand and dust storms. A line of Jebels separate the desert from the sea, some five or six thousand feet high, grim and devoid of life. It was very hot indeed, and, like El Fasher in the west, a great contrast to the southern greenery of Equatoria. Port Sudan is an important town, the only sea access for the Sudan and therefore of strategic significance.

The senior police officer, Ahmed Hussein, held the rank of Assistant Commissioner. The port area was big and busy, with many sea-going ships discharging cargo. Cargo was piled high in the docks, cars and everything else imaginable, all waiting transport inland by rail or dirt track over the mountains and through the desert. A police launch was stationed here for use on the Red Sea. The Sudan police had a proposal to purchase a number of police boats for use on the rivers throughout the country, so there was a need to discuss and plan for marine communications. It was therefore appropriate to make use of the experience here and I was taken out in the launch, which would not have impressed the Thames River Police too strongly. There were a number of useful working sessions with Ahmed Hussein and his deputy Abdalla Hardallo, including a working breakfast when I was introduced to his children, but not his wife.

Ahmed and Abdalla drove Mansour and I some thirty miles south along what would have been a coast road, if there had been a road, to the 'ghost city' of Suakin. It was the base in 1883 from which the Anglo–Egyptian authorities, with an inadequate little army, tried to avenge their first humiliation by the Mahdi. They failed. It was left in ruins after the revolt was eventually quelled. The 53rd Regiment of Foot, the Shropshire Regiment, later to be the Kings Shropshire Light Infantry were in this battle. There is a memorial to those killed in St. Chad's Church in Shrewsbury. In 'The Shropshire Lad' Houseman wrote, 'It dawns in Asia, tombstones show, and Shropshire names are read. And the Nile spills his overflow beside the Severn's dead. 'God save the Queen, we living sing, from height to height 'tis heard. And with the rest your voices ring, lads of the Fifty-third. Oh, God will save her, fear you not: Be you the men you've been, get you the sons your fathers got, and God will save the Queen'. From the side of the Severn to the side of the Red Sea they went, and to many other battlefields as well.

Suakin is now a weird and evocative sight – what used to be a walled city, with little except the town gate now intact, although Kitchener's house and HQ still stands. There are remnants of buildings, but no vegetation covering them, and the colour as white as when they were built. We also saw a boat builder's yard, where dhows were being constructed by the traditional methods of very rough wood nailed together and the gaps filled in with pitch and paint. The dhows so built travel successfully to the Persian Gulf, Dubai, Qatar and across the Indian Ocean. We passed wells eighty feet deep, dug by hand to produce oases. Next day Mansour and I drove forty miles north to Arowsa, where he had arranged some snorkelling with a party of other police officers. Arowsa was a holiday village, built by an Italian firm in the hope of earning hard currency from tourism for diving and fishing. There was a coral reef offering good facilities a mile or so out to sea but nothing else there apart from the tourist accommodation, and a restaurant. Even drinking water had to be brought by tanker from Port Sudan. There was a tremendous sense of isolation. No green anywhere, just red sand with the mountains inland barely visible through the dust haze. There were hundreds of camels roaming wild, with donkeys and goats near the occasional nomad village. These were a few huts made from poles and thorn bushes or tents made from poles and skins. An Hadendwa tribesman riding a camel could be seen from time to time, and beautiful little gazelles, no more than two feet high, which are hunted. Every so often a bleached skeleton, probably a camel, lay in the sand. The heat and humidity were breathtaking. Literally. The car body was too hot to touch with bare fingers.

We were kitted out with snorkelling gear and went out by motorboat. The sea was incredibly clear, deep at first then suddenly very shallow, with the reef only just covered by water, and thus big-shark free.This meant that snorkelling was a better way of viewing the reef than scuba, and the colours were astonishing. With white sand around the reef the sea colour was all shades of blue, varying from the very palest to almost purple. The coral was live and highly coloured – shapes of pumpkins and toadstools to fingers and fragile lace, with visibility of yards to the next high bank of coral. Clams a foot across, which close as anything comes near them, and in which one could easily lose a hand or foot. Many highly coloured fish all around, brilliant blue, red, orange, striped, spotted so that the overall effect is like being inside a tropical fish tank, or perhaps flying around a beautifully coloured garden.

I have since snorkelled and scuba-dived at the northern end of the Red Sea at Eilat, also at the Great Barrier Reef and off Tonga but have seen nothing to beat that time with the police snorkellers! There are shark and barracuda in the Red Sea, but they are rarely seen on the reef, and the guide said it was not a concern as they are afraid of noise and would not attack a group in the shallow water. One did not wish to argue! He did turn away very rapidly at one point though, from what I think was probably a dangerous Moray eel. I fished up, by hand, a shell about nine inches long with six legs or prongs, white on the outside and a delicate pink in the interior. It 'walked' across the floor of the boat in a rather fascinating fashion. I was determined to get it home, and it sits now in my workshop with its previous occupant evicted!

A good day finished in Port Sudan, where there is a swimming pool area in the Red Sea, protected from sharks by nets. It was not particularly inviting but I did enjoy seeing bathers sporting black umbrellas to keep the sun off their heads. We then went to the open-air cinema, where they were showing a newsreel of the state visit of the French President to London, with the Yeoman of the Guard in their full dress. Trying to explain this to the party of police officers was quite difficult. There was then a film about the making of cricket bats. The purpose of a cricket bat was even more difficult to make clear and I have little doubt that they thought it was the weapon used by the Yeomen!

This visit had been very useful, with information gained on the particular problems that the port presented. It had also been extremely interesting, and enjoyable. On return to Khartoum Mansour invited me to his house for an evening meal. This was a signal honour, and I was able to meet his wife, although only briefly as she then retired to supervise the cook. This was so interesting though, as I found that she was the Great Granddaughter of the Mahdi, the 'Expected One', the leader of the jihad in which General Gordon was killed in Khartoum in 1885.

It seems now that Gordon's death was largely due to the lack of support from the British Government, which was nearly brought down by public concern in the UK. I had met other descendents of the Mahdi, and visited his tomb and the Khalifa's House, which was now a museum. The Khalifa was the Mahdi's deputy, and became the leader of the Mahdia after the Mahdi's death. During this evening I had his Great Great Granddaughter, a baby, on my knee. It was fascinating to meet the direct descendents of people who very nearly won a war against the British army during Winston Churchill's time as a young cavalry officer. Mansour had also invited one of the senior diplomatic staff from the British Embassy (this was slightly devious as he badly wanted to get hold of a British Police officer's cap. He felt that they were rather better than the Sudan issue). Stella, who had been working on my interim report, was also present. Her invitation was at my request, so I had my fingers firmly crossed, as it was just not done for women to share a meal with men. However, she was well aware of the potential problems, and became an honorary man for the evening, which went well!

The next weeks in Khartoum were extremely busy. There was a need to discuss the feasibility of my proposals with the Ministry of Post and Telecommunications, to visit the Airport to discuss anti-hi-jack measures, and many Government Departments to confer on other issues including the possibility of terrorism. It was important to liase with the Sudan Air Force over a proposal to purchase helicopters for police use, with the Railway Police for their specialised needs and to consider the requirements dictated by the use of police boats. I had found it necessary to widen my recommendations considerably, and to expand the original brief, in order to suggest ideas common in the UK but not yet introduced in the Sudan. For example, serious accidents were very common on the all-weather surfaced roads outside the towns, through lack of a police patrol presence or speed enforcement. (It is strange to reflect that over thirty years later the same point about the lack of police patrol vehicles could now be made about the UK).

It was also necessary to go into some detail of how the new equipment could be protected from the constant dust and continuous heat. A major existing problem was dust rendering the old German teleprinters unreliable. I was able to use the trains for some of these journeys, which was another experience. Windows were kept open, there was no thought of air-conditioning and the dust and sand were thick enough to eat. People travelled on the roof, or hanging onto the outside of a carriage, and slept on the platforms when trying to be the first to get a seat! I wonder if the organization has changed in the years since. Probably not. The lines were laid and the system operated for many years by British Engineers and back in Wolverhampton I found someone whose uncle had been a Sudan Railways engineer and helped to build the railway line on which we had travelled to Atbara. Small world!

I was invited to lunch at Stella's flat, together with the other two girls and two English couples, to celebrate her completion of my interim report. The party sounds like a massive amount of work for her, but in fact she did not even have to serve it, the suffragis (house servants) did all the preparation, plus the clearing up afterwards! I did think to myself that these girls were going to land back on earth with a tremendous shock if they got married and set up home in Europe. Perhaps they were just enjoying life while the sun shone – literally!

We all went to a concert in the Cultural Centre that evening, which was done very well. Tapes of Mozart, Wagner and Strauss accompanied by slides of Salzburg, the Rhine and the Alps. But all the lights failed as we left the Hall, which was built by the Chinese as a gift to the Sudan. No panic even though the whole town was in darkness, as everyone was used to this happening. Picking our way carefully back – very carefully because it was better to avoid the deep pot-holes and rotting rubbish, we did all snigger at the thought of the President and King Khalid, who was on a State Visit, sitting together in the dark. Regrettably as we passed the Palace their own generator was working!

Joan had made it known that she was looking for a wealthy Sheik, and we had noticed that one of the King's entourage had been looking at her during the concert – she had long blonde hair. The same man was at lunch in my Hotel the next day, so I told Joan that I had spoken to him and had offered to sell my sister with the blonde hair for one hundred pounds:

'Oh no, you *didn't.*'

I think that she half believed me! During my stay I had asked my son, Al, to provide me with as many English jokes as possible to pass on to the Sudanese. Some of these had gone down like lead balloons, as the sense of humour was not a mutual one. In reading some of my report over to Mansour we found that Stella had typed 'smiggling' instead of 'smuggling'. He thought that this was absolutely hilarious. There is no doubt that a sense of humour is a difficult thing to share.

The time to present my interim report to the Commissioner had arrived. It was massive, and he was certainly impressed by the width, but needed a week to assess the quality! In fact he took it with him on an official visit to Darfur, and forbad me to leave until he returned. This, it seemed, was as much because he wished to throw a final party for me as to read the report. (Again, any excuse!) I was now keen to get home, but there was no point in arguing, as I could not have left without permission anyway. I rang Jo, as usual with difficulty, and asked her to tell West Midlands that my projected date to return to normal duty was postponed. (We did add a couple of extra days to the new date, to enjoy at home). I cannot now remember this official party in any respect at all, so it must have been quite a good one!

Ultimately of course my departure time approached, but before leaving I wanted to express my thanks for the company of the three Embassy girls, and in particular for the work done on the interim report by Stella, which had been extra to her normal routine. I had been paid a daily living allowance in Sudanese money, most of which it had not been necessary to spend. As it was not possible to change it into any other currency it had to be spent, so I decided on a really good night out for the four of us, bought them some gifts, and booked a table in the Restaurant of the Hilton Hotel. The Hilton was the hotel used by most of the overseas visitors to Khartoum, although I had been enjoying a stay in a much more ethnic one. The Restaurant was, therefore, host to a very international gathering of salesmen, junior diplomats, plus a few well off Sudani families.

Most of the expat salesmen were men on their own, looking rather lonely. The three young women and I were escorted with great panache to our table. I had more money to give away than I have ever had before or since and had already salted the ground to make sure that the evening 'flowed'. Every male head turned in our direction. This did that fragile organism, my ego, no harm at all.

We had a delightful meal, during which I gave my presents - Sudani slippers and scarves- and then a small orchestra hove in sight. Dancing was obviously not a usual feature of the evening, as apart from local ladies, who could not be asked to dance, there were very few women present. By this time having taken wine, and with the bit firmly between my teeth, I organised a moving of the tables to make a dance floor, to enthusiastic applause from the lonely expatriates. The three girls had a very enjoyable, and busy evening! At one point, while I was dancing with Lijda, a little man from somewhere east of Suez sidled up to me and said, 'You are airline captain, no?' It was a pleasure to reply, 'No, police captain.' I think that I had taken enough Sudani wine on board to be dancing extremely well! An evening to remember.

But, like all things it came eventually to an end, and a couple of days later the three saw me off at Khartoum Airport. Sadly I have lost touch with Stella, who I believe emigrated to Australia, and Lijda, who went home to Holland, but I met Joan later in London and still exchange Christmas cards with her, to Cyprus where she is now retired.

Although keen to get home, I decided to break the journey in Cairo, as I had to fly virtually overhead. This was a culture shock in reverse, as everybody seemed to be very westernised and pale skinned in contrast to Khartoum, only a comparatively short flight away. This impression was however quickly shattered by the taxi from the airport into Cairo – 90 mph in an elderly Mercedes, with the driver seemingly wanting to turn round to talk to me in the back seat. Here is a useful tip for visitors to Cairo; - don't encourage conversation with the taxi driver! Traffic lights were, apparently to the majority of the driving population, optional – suggestions rather than constraints. However I very much enjoyed the few days there, now speaking enough Arabic to survive quite well, - maafi mushkelin – 'no problem', and enjoying displaying my camel riding expertise around the pyramids! I found Cairo beautiful in many ways – bigger of course than Khartoum, and much, much more busy – teeming hordes is, I think, an accurate description. The Nile at night, from the balcony of a comfortable hotel, was a memorable experience. The sound of car horns, continuous throughout the early hours, was also memorable – it was probably better to stay up rather than try to sleep.

Back to work in the Midlands

Back home to a family re-union was another memorable experience, with a lot of press interest requiring posing for photographs with my swords and sawfish bone. It was then nose down to a lot of very careful and detailed work to produce my ten-year plan for the Sudan. I have wondered many times since how much has actually been carried out. Apart from the 'Insha Allah, Bukra, Mah Leish' factor that poor country has been in the grip of fratricidal and inter-tribal strife almost ever since. I also wonder, of course, what has happened to the good friends that I made there. I exchanged letters with Moneim for some time, but have received nothing now for years.

I did receive a very handsome, and ornate, framed certificate of commendation from the Sudan Police, via the Foreign Office, accompanied by a generous letter of commendation from that Office, which said that I had contributed significantly to bi-lateral relations. There was talk of my getting a Sudanese medal, but it never arrived – possibly having gone to the same place as my shirts! My wife also had a very friendly letter from the Commissioner, Abdalla Hassan Salim, which began 'Honourable Lady' and is still a treasure to read occasionally. I wonder sometimes what happened to this pleasant man in the traumas that beset Sudan in the following years. The report which I eventually presented to the Foreign Office, for transmission to the Government of the Sudan ran to 53 pages with a further 31 pages of Appendices. Line drawings of the proposed control rooms and photographs of UK police facilities were included as a guide. A separately bound 'User Requirement Specifications and Estimated Costs' ran to 30 pages. A total of 114 pages – plenty of width then! I was allowed a lot of clerical support and time away from normal duty, which was generous. There had to be a great deal of assistance from firms such as Marconi, (who had visions of a potential sales bonanza) and the local officers of the Home Office Telecommunications Branch, especially with the technical specifications. All this was repaid and the quality confirmed when the police liaison officer at the Foreign Office said that it was the best report from an overseas attachment that they had ever received. Wow!

I have no doubt that it was this comment which led to my being asked, in 1977, to go to Africa again for twelve months to completely re-organise the Zambian Police Force.

During an interview with two Mandarins at the Foreign Office the following conversation took place, 'As the period is for twelve months, could my family accompany me?'

'No, there is no funding for that.'

'In that case I would expect regular periods of leave to travel home, as I have two young children.'

'We would be prepared for you to take one period of leave to the UK, but there is no funding for travel, you would have to pay your own fare.'

'I will discuss the proposal with my wife and let you know.'

Whilst I would have been very interested indeed to do the job, we decided mutually that it was not fair for me to be away for a year, and it was certainly not fair of the Foreign Office to ask it without funding for the family or for travel. It would have been ideal for a single man with no dependents, but those who had enough experience to carry out such a wide-ranging remit were unlikely to fall into that category. Lack of thought, lack of planning and an excess of naiveté on the part of the Mandarins?

I therefore wrote to say that I could not accept this task. The same Mandarins then complained to my Chief Constable that I had said that I would go, and subsequently withdrawn. This was totally untrue. Is it any wonder that I had absolutely no confidence in, or regard for, the Foreign Office of that period? I do wonder, considering the mess made since in various parts of the world, whether their successors have a much better mind set or ability to think ahead, or are even less naïve. I should make it clear here that these rather two faced people were not the ones who had either briefed or de-briefed me over the Sudan job.

With my report work completed and sent off to the Sudan I eventually resumed work at Force HQ in Birmingham. I was asked by the Deputy Chief Constable to work with him to prepare the communications aspect of a plan to deal with terrorism on a hi-jacked aircraft ending up at Birmingham Airport. This was very interesting and enjoyable as I had very much respect and liking for the Deputy Chief, who, although originally a Birmingham City man had been my boss in the West Midlands Constabulary.

We got the plan done and approved by the Home Office, with special equipment (no doubt by now much upgraded) secreted away. Soon after I was advised to apply for a posting as a Sub-Divisional Superintendent to widen my experience. I was posted to the Walsall Division as the Sub-Divisional Superintendent at Willenhall and Bloxwich. The Walsall Chief Superintendent was a former Wolverhampton Borough man, and had been the fast bowler in the Borough cricket team. In the past I had dropped one or two catches off his bowling, which usually put him into a frightening rage, but on the other hand had caught some very good ones, so by and large we were square! This was good, and I think that he was pleased to have another former Borough man working for him. Willenhall Police Station was a former Staffordshire County Station, left for several years without any maintenance and unsurprisingly showing many signs of this.

The Station was, because of the years of neglect by Staffordshire, not a place to be proud of, and consequently morale was not high. There was living accommodation for the Superintendent, who in County times had been Deputy to, and only slightly less important than, God! I found that I had a huge office, which I set about furnishing with unwanted chairs etc from home, and a very ornate bathroom, with a white Victorian porcelain bath, proudly displaying its four little legs. The Station was not a welcoming place to visit, and while we did not go out of our way to offer a welcome to all the visitors I thought that it was necessary to improve the public areas. We were able to beg some huge flower pots from the Council to stand on either side of the public entrance, and the civilian handyman was given severe instructions to keep them filled with colour.

It was also necessary to start a purge on the universal police habit of sticking tatty bits of paper – notices, reminders et al – to the enquiry office walls with untidy sellotape. It still seems to be a police habit, although I more or less stopped it at Willenhall while I was there. (I believe that I confiscated all the sellotape!) I don't think that I have ever been in a police building that was not similarly decorated, and I felt exceptionally pleased to have found enough money to get a corkboard fitted for notices to be pinned to. I would dance up and down in a fury to occasionally find a notice sellotaped at the side of the corkboard. 'Well, gaffer, we ai got nun of they pins with little `eads on left!'

Bloxwich Police Station, a former Walsall Borough Police building, was a hovel, and a disgrace, leading to even worse morale of the officers working there, idleness and rule breaking. It has now been completely rebuilt, about seventy years later than necessary, and houses some specialist squads. Police work at Willenhall did have a few interesting moments, apart from trying to improve conditions there and at Bloxwich. I was called out from home one late evening as a much wanted man was thought to be in our area, where he had relatives. He was also believed to be armed. We had access to a limited number of firearms, so I therefore found myself in command of an armed search party. My biggest concern, I remember very clearly, was not that we might be fired upon, but that one of my troops would shoot himself, me or one of the others, and deployment to minimise this possibility was of considerable importance. As it happened we did not find the guy, nor shoot anyone, which was a relief. It was a reminder of the two armed policemen sitting behind me with loaded guns on a very bumpy road in Equatoria and a foretaste of being escorted by armed Burmese police and soldiers in Arakan a year or two later. It has to be said that training in the use and deployment of firearms was minimal in the British Police at the time of the incident in Willenhall. Like so much else it was left to individual common sense – perhaps in some ways not too bad a thing? At any rate it was a source of pride in the United Kingdom that it was only very rarely necessary, which was commented upon with almost disbelief by police officers in America. Things are different now.

Living and working in a highly industrialised urban area has always meant an involvement with Travellers – gangs of caravan dwellers moving together from illegal site to illegal site, living on scrap metal dealing or stealing and leaving their resting places devastated and dirty. These people are not genuine Romanies but itinerant scrap dealers or tinkers. Not surprisingly they are unwanted and feared by residents and we were often tasked to assist the council in removing them. It was usually a very frustrating exercise, because, with no fixed address it was almost impossible to get them into Court for any of the many motoring offences which took place.

However, on one occasion we did come off best.

A gang had settled near some woodland on the edge of the town, and the local landowner's pheasants were being reduced nightly. We got summonses prepared and went to serve them on all of the male travellers. I knocked on one caravan which as usual apparently contained only a woman and half a dozen small children.

'Where's your feller then?'

'Ah sure he's away working of course, doing the jobs to feed us all.'

'Can I come in?'

No answer so in I went to see the usual extremely well furnished caravan, extra large television set, plenty of whisky bottles and one large cupboard, with a closed door. Suddenly the cupboard door flew open and out jumped the 'feller', who took off across the next field, which happened to be ploughed. I followed him across two more ploughed fields, at which point he fell down and I fell on top of him.

'Ah ye great fat pollisman, harassing me and me with a bad heart!' He did live however to answer the summons at a special Court that day. Whether anyone ever collected the fines imposed I somehow doubt!

The plague of itinerant travellers goes on in the West Midlands to this day. They descend on a site that has not been blocked off, and produce a most tremendous disease threatening filth, with fly-tipping, household waste and anything not remotely sellable. An Irish colleague once told me how the R.U.C. used to deal with people like this in Ulster. An effective, if hard method, which I shall not reveal here but I would be prepared to use it and call it rough justice. In Willenhall we were continually getting requests to move the travellers on, and as the Press were always alerted and involved it had to be done legally. This meant slowly, with days or weeks of distress and fear caused to nearby residents, who suffered theft, vandalism, begging and general harassment. There were ways, short of the R.U.C. methods, of making life uncomfortable for the travellers so that they would move on and at least give the residents a break.

Unfortunately of course this only moved the problem to another area. We were unfortunate to have a partly built motorway access road through the Sub-Division and this was continually seen as the Promised Land by the tinkers. On one occasion, when we had a Court Order to evict from this part-road, the Press were present, and I appeared, once more, on the front page of the 'Express and Star,' surrounded by screaming women (the men were invariably in hiding) and with about five small children all in tears and snotty nosed, clinging to each trouser leg.

I note, with regret but not much surprise, a recent comment made by a West Midlands Police Spokesperson - almost certainly a civilian from the Press Department. This followed complaints and a press report of drug users living in disused Hospital premises, with the consequent anti-social behaviour and vandalism. The comment was, 'This is a matter for the owners'. This may be legally correct, but when Wolverhampton had it's own effective Force I know that they would have been shifted under the 'Ways and Means Act', to the benefit of everybody. The human rights of drug users, squatters and vandals to steal and cause damage, filth and danger would not have been of much concern to me or my colleagues. But then, we didn't have a silly Human Rights Act, did we? And wasn't life better for most honest people?

On one occasion of a tinker infestation in Willenhall it was a real and unusual pleasure to eventually receive, via Police HQ, a letter of thanks for an efficient 'removal' job from industrial premises. I think that most of the unwilling hosts were too shell-shocked to think about writing letters of thanks once the blight was removed! I also treasure an aside made by one of my troops, which I guess I was not supposed to hear. An empty factory was being surrounded, after a daylight burglar alarm, and I happened to be near the scene, so joined in. The remark, as I scrambled over the boundary wall, 'I've never known a Superintendent go in first' is nice to remember! Max Hastings, in his book *Armageddon* about the Allied invasion of Europe and Germany in 1944 states that leaders should not physically lead. He says, 'Experienced leaders placed themselves near the front, but not on point, although this sometimes prompted feelings of guilt. It was better to lose a man than a leader.' However, in this instance police work could not be compared to fighting an armed conflict, and I think that it was good for morale to see the gaffer lead the way.

It was at about this time, April 1977 that I received a request from the Foreign Office to 'host' a relative of the Sudan Commissioner, who was temporarily in the UK with his Wife and small son. He was the proprietor of a Driving School in Khartoum, and was here to find out as much as possible about British driving methods. I must say that this was a surprise, but, who knows, it may be that my work in Sudan gave him the idea. Anyway, the

Foreign Office thought that I was the ideal person! Of course I said, 'Yes', and we fixed a date for the three to travel by train from London. It was a warm Spring day, which later became significant. I had suggested that they take a taxi from Wolverhampton Station. They disembarked from this to the astonishment of the rest of the inhabitants of our cul-de-sac, as both adults were wearing full Arab dress – white djellabir and turban for the man and multi-coloured robes and head-dress for the lady. The little boy, Shabi, was, like many Arabic children, a beautiful child, totally over-awed and very well behaved, and dressed like a British five year old. The lady handed over to Jo a large and aromatic parcel, which she disposed of as quickly and quietly as possible. It turned out to be a large leg of lamb wrapped in paper that had travelled from London under the train seat – and it was a warm day! We imagined, from it's condition, that the heating had still been on! It was a kind thought, but I do hope that the lamb had not been sacrificed on our behalf. It may well have travelled from Africa.

I had arranged for Abdel Ghani el Hag to be taken round the large British School of Motoring in Birmingham, and to have a discussion with the Manager. We talked in my home and had lunch (not leg of lamb) before driving over to Birmingham and he made it clear that he wanted to take back to Khartoum a 'certifical'. As this was neither Arabic nor English I struggled for a bit, but eventually light dawned and I typed up his own certifical saying that he had attended discussions about driver training with the British School of Motoring, and signed it myself. I would not mind betting that this was, and may even still be, worth a good bit of money back in Khartoum. Everything British was flavour of the month, there and then. The visit to the BSM did actually go well, I put them on the train for London with a rather large sense of relief, and our cul-de-sac reverted to its normal tranquillity! Jo had done very well to produce a lunchtime meal which was obviously appreciated, and in the event we enjoyed their visit - especially in retrospect! Actually our cul-de-sac was well used to exotic visitors, as we had had Judge Gill from Malaysia in his huge white Mercedes, Kulwant in his very colourful Sikh turbans, and Amarjeet in her saris. This, however, was new!

In the later part of 1977 I was posted away from Willenhall to be the Deputy to the Chief Superintendent of Sandwell Division, a big, busy and multi-racial area on the north-west outskirts of Birmingham. The Division covered the towns of West Bromwich, Smethwick, Tipton, Oldbury, Rowley Regis and bits of the City. It also had the West Bromwich Albion football stadium, then an established top-flight club. Before the soccer season drew to a close I found myself responsible for all aspects of football match policing, in and outside the ground. The move to act as a Deputy to the Divisional

Chief Officer was a compliment and a move up, although carrying the same substantive rank. I respected and liked the Chief Superintendent and we got on well together. When he was away I acted in his place, as head of the Division. However, I was becoming increasingly disillusioned and felt let down by the West Midlands Police which four years before had seemed to offer great opportunities for the high-quality policing of a key part of the UK.

The Chief Constable was rarely seen outside his office, and would not, I believe, have been even recognised by most of his men. I had absolutely no liking, respect, or confidence in him or his Deputy. I regretted that the very respected previous Deputy Chief Constable for whom I had prepared the Airport anti-terrorism plan had now retired, having been replaced by a man of a very different calibre. The retiring officer felt, I think, along the same lines as myself.

In fact he said to me, 'I always promised my wife that I would go when I no longer enjoyed it. So that is what I am doing'.

Morale was very low in the West Midlands, and in the Police Service as a whole, and there was a continual flow of people retiring or resigning throughout 1977 and `78.

I believe that subordinate officers in a uniformed organisation need to feel that their leaders can be trusted and will support them, though ideally this will be mixed with apprehension over the consequences of disobedience or disloyalty. They should also have confidence that their commanders are capable (within physical limitations) of tackling any task that they themselves are set, and are prepared to do so. Lastly, but essentially, that the trepidation or apprehension is also mixed with liking, or respect. In my view very few of the command structure of the West Midlands Police in 1978 had these qualities – one of the causes of the low morale in that organisation. There was a description of the British soldiers in France during the First World War – 'Lions led by donkeys.' My personal view is that this description could also be applied to the West Midlands Police in the late seventies, or at least to the top command positions.

Another factor lowering morale among officers of Superintendent rank was, I am sure, the amount of time they had to spend investigating complaints against the police. At that time any complaint received was marked out to a Superintendent or Chief Superintendent on a different Division to investigate. It had to be done meticulously, and if a criminal offence was alleged a complete file made up for consideration by the Director of Public Prosecutions. Remember that, for example, an allegation that a police car had been parked in a dangerous position qualified as a criminal offence. I did have to investigate one such. Guess who had made the complaint – the driver who had been stopped for speeding! The file, with plans, photographs, statements and summaries was getting on for an inch thick, and all of us involved, including the complainant, knew that it was destined for the waste bin! I suppose that he felt pleased to have muddied the waters a bit. Whilst no honest police officer wants the 'bad apples' to be whitewashed or protected, this was not what I had joined the Police Service to do.

The serious and worrying side was that whilst an officer was involved for perhaps weeks on a complaint investigation, his own proper job, as far as the legislators or the Civil Liberties Brigade were concerned, could go to hell. This in a sense was a self-generating process, as if the head of the Sub-Division was not able to do his job, complaints could be expected to rise. I always had very able Chief Inspectors to take over from me, but then their own responsibilities were necessarily neglected, and so on. As the Deputy Chief on the Division I had at times to mark out complaints received from HQ to our Sub-Divisional Superintendents, and, in trying to be just, probably took more than my fair share myself. It was not uncommon to have several on the go at once, and I remember even today how frustrating it was, and how shortsighted it seemed. That however was the policy of the time, which I understand is now handled differently by a specialist department. We had to do things differently in the far country of the past, but perhaps the echoes linger on.

It was also quite obvious that things were far from right in the West Midlands C.I.D., and the scandals of the Serious Crime Squad that became headlines soon afterward showed that corruption and bad administration existed. Friedrich Nietzsch had warned that he who fights with monsters might take care lest he thereby become a monster, and that if you gaze for long into an abyss, the abyss gazes back at you. Chief Officers need to take very great care that this is not happening to the personnel under their command.

In my view this situation had continued into the West Midlands Police era at least partly from the poor management and supervision of the former Birmingham City Police. I did not like what I could see happening and decided that it was time to go. Having started to investigate alternative ways of earning a living, I was very quickly 'snapped up' by the British Red Cross. Together with a Detective Superintendent also retiring, and his Wife, Jo and I were given a wonderful send-off party at West Bromwich Headquarters. The local press went rather to town in view of my new job, which was going to be as Red Cross International Disaster Relief Co-ordinator, based in London. One of the headlines read, 'Just the man for a disaster'! A second was, 'Disaster mission for ex-Bridgnorth Sportsman!' I also had many supportive messages from former colleagues in the Wolverhampton and the first West Midlands Forces, and don't mind admitting that it was with tears in my eyes that I closed my office door for the last time.

For twenty one years I had enjoyed my job intensely, the last four which involved the Birmingham Mafia being like the curate's egg, good and bad. I was always proud to wear the uniform, and in fact wore the crown for a total of forty two years. (Yes! Two in the Royal Air Force, twenty five in the Police Service and fifteen concurrently in the Royal Air Force Volunteer Reserve.) I believe that I used the police uniform properly, and was not just a 'uniform carrier'. We had horror, tragedy, fun and drama mixed together in Wolverhampton, where despite being a smaller Force, anything could, and often did, happen.

I was convinced at the time, and still am, that the creation of the huge Metropolitan Forces was a mistake, and a wonderful police system was virtually destroyed by meddling politicians. There is even a call now for Chief Constables to be elected and to be dismissable by Local Authority politicians. Accountability is right and needful, but little power hungry men obviously do not understand that the former would be the quickest route to corruption on the scale of the dishonesty in many countries. Where such a system exists a criminal with a powerful political 'friend' has little to fear from law enforcement, and a Police Chief has to think about the next election to keep his job.

Or do the politicians actually want corruption as it exists in many developing world cities, where the police openly accept bribes to release, or 'lose' evidence against wealthy or influential criminals that they have been forced to arrest? I read that in parts of the United States at regular intervals the need to win the next election takes over from independent law enforcement. In such a system it is also possible for a Sheriff or Police Chief needing votes to retain his job to see the efficient subordinate as a threat. Perhaps these things are what some politicians or the power-hungry here want, but it will not be an improvement. I see evidence of a huge increase in corruption in all areas of life in this country. The police have not been isolated from this. It seems to have paralleled the political cult of personality instead of policies that the media have fostered and the public foolishly accepted.

The containment or reversal of the creeping growth of corruption is one of the most important tasks that a Chief Officer of Police can set himself, and that, it seems to me, is vital, not only for the good of his own organisation and the people that they serve, but for the country as a whole.

A strong, independent, incorrupt Police Service should be a bulwark between civilisation and anarchy. Perhaps a flood barrier is an almost better analogy. The Royal Commission on the Police which recommended the big new Forces formed by amalgamation in 1974 also published a minority report.

This said that about 2000 officers was the optimum size to be administered effectively. This was roughly the size of the West Midlands Constabulary, formed in 1966. Had the Constabulary been allowed to live beyond 1974 it would, I am certain, have become a very successful and efficient organisation. People who were not there, or who do not have the experience, talk about there being insufficient cross-border police co-operation - but it happened!

In the field in which I was often working, targeting and prosecuting car-borne criminals, we co-operated very successfully with our neighbours. More efficient modern communication equipment was in gestation and soon to become available. That tool was all that was needed to provide the advantages of the bigger organisations without the disadvantage of losing local knowledge, local loyalty and local morale. Consider one aspect of enforcement for example; the identification of disqualified drivers who persist in driving. It is recognized that if long periods of disqualification are imposed the person concerned will ignore the ban as he or she will know that there is little chance of being caught. Now, as local knowledge has been eroded this is probably true. But, as a member of a unit covering, and spending time in, a smaller area, my colleagues and I knew who was, or even who was probably disregarding the loss of their licence. They could therefore be targeted. The mechanism was there to circulate that knowledge outside our area if it was appropriate.

A personal example of the problems that large, fragmented areas, poor organisation and leadership can cause happened not long ago. I made a written complaint, in the form of a detailed statement about a serious case of dangerous driving combined with the use of a hand-held telephone that I had witnessed. This included that I was very willing to give evidence and my qualification to do so. The local police station was closed! As I knew that time was important the statement was delivered by hand, inconveniently for me, to the Headquarters of the Thames Valley Police, the correct area, the following day. Thames Valley then managed, by sending it to a series of wrong offices that kept passing it on, to lose it until it was too late to take action.

This was ineffective organisation, poor leadership and management (the three are manifestly synonymous) and uncorrected faults by individuals. It would not have happened in Wolverhampton before 1966. I did eventually receive a fairly abject written apology, but that is neither here nor there. What is important is that the opportunity to give a dangerous, selfish driver an expensive Court appearance and lesson or even to remove that person from the roads around Oxford for a period, was lost.

Also serious is the fact that a person willing to give evidence about a crime, with expert qualifications to do so and a desire to support road safety and law enforcement was left feeling let down by, and annoyed with, the police. If they could make a person with my background resentful, how would an average member of the public feel? Management and personal failures by over-promoted senior officers have helped to diminish the respect that was felt for the British Police fifty years ago.

I also felt that another organisational mistake was being made in the larger Forces. It became the policy to move people around into different departments, rather as some branches of the military do and which they had copied from private enterprise. The theory is that a new perspective, with no involvement in the status quo, would be brought to the post. There is some sense in this, and certainly people can get sluggish and blasé if left for too long in one place. The danger of people who fight with monsters becoming monsters themselves, as Nietzsche warned, has also to be addressed. This is perhaps relevant to those who deal with the terrible things that people can do to each other. However, police work is unique in many ways, it relies very much on information and knowledge of localities and people. There are conflicting needs here which I do not believe were properly considered before the amalgamations were carried out.

It would be wrong to insist that no good came of the amalgamations into bigger independent areas. Of course it has – I know of some positive things about the West Midlands Force, which now seems to have made progress from a very shaky start. For example, specialist squads to target and harass known criminals are a very positive use of manpower and a way of dealing with the sort of anti-social behaviour in my example of disqualified drivers. If one scratches a disqualified driver ignoring the ban there is a very high chance of uncovering a serious criminal. There have been huge successes against organised crime and terrorism. But, it seems to me, that for most people living ordinary lives, the protection provided by the police against burglary, robbery, assault, vandalism, general unpleasantness and 'yobbery' has been downgraded to what we would have thought in 1965 to be an unbelievable extent.

It is also obvious that major crime, intelligence or drugs investigation squads - to lump them all together under one heading - are likely to be an advantage in cross-boundary or international work. Could not these have been superimposed on the basic units, instead of manufacturing artificial and unwieldy new Forces?

I therefore believe that much was lost in the years after 1966. The think-tank body Reform published a report in February 2009 saying that the existing very large Police Forces should be split up, with separate Forces for cities like Wolverhampton and the large counties being divided into several areas. It said that the existing system was not working properly in several ways, was expensive and lacking in public confidence. I am therefore not alone in my views. Back to 1966, or at least to1974, and never mind about all the millions of pounds that have been thrown away in the meantime to pursue political dogma. It may even happen, but I shall not hold my breath while waiting for common sense to prevail.

I am quite certain that in those days the members of each Police Force in the UK thought of themselves as part of a family, with loyalty and commitment to it. They did not watch the clock or think about how much they were earning, and they did whatever needed to be done. I believe that the Fire Services and medical staffs of Hospitals and Clinics felt, and behaved, the same. Of course not everyone was perfect, and there were scandals and failures, but it seems to me that through political interference, personal and managerial failures by Chief Officers, and the recruitment of 'quotas' of unsuitable people that sense of 'family' has been greatly diminished or lost. In future, all NHS Nurses will have a degree. Will that make all of them the caring, conscientious, helpful, likeable people that the vast majority used to be? I don't think so.

I lived through, and can almost pinpoint the decline, deterioration, and demoralisation of the British Police. The round of amalgamations from 1966 and 1974 into the bigger, in some cases huge, semi-autonomous bodies was one trigger. Additionally, by then, the quality of recruits had weakened. This was due in part to a lowering of the physical standards of height, weight and eyesight. Perhaps the relaxation was necessary in order to recruit in sufficient numbers as the pay was so poor, but it certainly led to a lessening of pride in one's own unit. Some of us began to feel that as long as a person had a pulse and could stand up more or less straight they met the new standards.

Moreover the input of people with Armed Forces experience had lessened, due to the ending of National Service, and the shrinking of the Military. Service life is different in many ways from Police work, but the discipline and comradeship that I found all around me in the fifties and sixties was exceptional. It came largely, in my view, because the majority of us had also experienced life during War Service or National Service. It was disappearing in the seventies, but in the first decade of the millennium, we found that it could be remembered, through our reunion and plaque dedication at the National Memorial Arboretum. Although none of us were still serving, the recognisable and distinct esprit de corps of my former colleagues was present and obvious. I have no problem in repeating, 'Once a Wolverhampton Police Officer, always a Wolverhampton Police Officer'.

During the last year of the Borough Force, which had an authorised establishment of 300 officers (the actual establishment being a little lower), a posthumous Queen's Police Medal for Gallantry and two Queen's Commendations for Bravery were awarded. In addition to the three national awards, thirty officers were commended by the Wolverhampton Watch Committee for excellent work in clearing up crimes ranging from murder to stolen vehicles, and two further officers received Certificates of Bravery from the Society for the Protection of Life from Fire. There were, of course, some advantages to both the public and to officers that followed the process of amalgamation. I think that I gained personally from it, but there was, with no doubt at all, a huge loss of morale and a scattering of the talent that had been concentrated in Wolverhampton. I do not believe that the morale lost has been regained in the following years, and I continually read similar views from people who served in the fifties and sixties.

Boswell quotes Doctor Johnson that, 'every man thinks meanly of himself for not having been a soldier or having been to sea'. The Doctor's observations about human nature were often accurate. I agree with him and am glad that I served the ritual of that introduction to maturity through military service. It seemed to me that those who had not done so were of a slightly different order. To be effective an operational Constable, like a professional soldier, has to be a 'man of action', although that action is typically separated by periods of 'inaction', even boredom, which have to be dealt with. But when the moment arrives the police officer needs to be ready and willing to seize it, otherwise he or she becomes merely a person carrying a uniform around. A Police Officer needs to have learned about life from outside the service, before he or she puts on a uniform.

Striving to give credit where it is due, Government did carry out one action to improve policing, by increasing the upper age for recruitment and targeting people leaving the Armed Forces. Therefore the supply of disciplined, toughened people who had experienced life outside school or college was restored to some extent.

Rowan and Maine were the leaders of the first properly organised police body in London. They required that their Constables should be 'men of the people', so that they came from, and understood, the nature of the population that they were dealing with. I suspect that the need for 'men of action' and 'men of the people' (I use the masculine to embrace both genders) has been lost sight of by successive governments, as the best Police Service in the world has been systematically destroyed.

I also feel that we should search very much more closely into the motives of the 'wannabes' the men and women who feel a compulsion to climb, full or part-time, into some sort of blue uniform. In my view this applies especially if they are not able, or not good enough, to become regular police officers.

There may be several reasons for a person to want to be a police officer. There are unquestionably those who genuinely wish to support society and the rule of law, and those who like the idea of a challenging varied life and the chance to specialise. There will be some who merely see today's salary and pension as attractive. I am certain however that there are also a minority who are attracted to the idea of being in a position of authority and also those whose incentives are for even darker reasons. If suspect motivation applies to a minority of recruits to the regular police service, and sadly it does - consult virtually any newspaper, any day, then with how much more relevance does it apply to the recruitment to ancillary positions with I suspect, despite cries to the contrary, less care and fewer checks?

The creeping increase of the civilianisation of many police functions sounds like a good idea. Until you think it through. There was recently an Editorial in my influential local newspaper suggesting that much more civilianisation needed to be done, to get the uniforms out on the streets. It seems to me that the leader writer had lost sight of the fact that civilians can strike, but at present, and I hope fervently that this will not change, Police Officers cannot. Civilian staff in many jobs within the Service could cripple a city, or region, or even the Country, by going on strike, and the thoughtless calls for that to become a possibility worry me.

The Unit Beat Car scheme, universally known as the Panda Cars, was brought in ostensibly to give constables on beat duty more mobility, plus a more interesting career structure with greater job satisfaction. It was intended that part of each constable's tour of duty would be spent in the car, and part patrolling on foot. This was not thought through, and quite failed to take into account the inevitability of human nature taking over on a cold wet night. It also ignored, or failed to anticipate the not uncommon consequence of male and female officers put into the close propinquity of a small car on nights. I do know that as a senior officer I was hearing the worries and insecurity of many police wives, but with the full integration of male and female officers it was impossible to avoid such pairings.

The main achievement of the scheme was to turn the British Police into a Fire Brigade type of Service, scurrying hither and thither in response to radio calls, instead of working as a patrolling body. The former style of patrolling on foot or bicycle meant that you saw and heard things impossible to see or hear from a car. One built up a huge knowledge of the people, bad and good, and the vulnerable targets of criminals, on the beat. Improving the career structure without destroying all that was good about foot or cycle patrols would surely have been possible.

The introduction of the Beat Cars also meant, to quote W.S. Gilbert, that, 'everybody was somebody'. In order to fill quotas officers were put into cars without the really excellent training that we had been fortunate to have. Training to the higher levels was also cut back, apparently to save money. The standard of British police driving, which had been world renowned, sharply declined, manifestly in proportion to the reduction in driver training. Where we had been an elite, the headline now became, 'Crash, here come the police'. There have been attempts to reverse some of the negative effects of the Beat Car scheme by the introduction of patrolling Constables, designated as Community Officers. In my view this is akin to putting an elastoplast on a gaping wound and it is too late to get back to where we were.

I saw a notice recently that read, 'Beware, police officers patrolling on bicycles'. Why, or who should beware was not specified, but it struck me that an appropriate comment might be, 'But we were doing this fifty years ago.' Of course, as with most other police equipment the machinery has been improved, and I would not like to have chased someone very far on the old boneshakers that most of us used. One could on the other hand, on a bike, be very quiet, and see a lot, so there was a tremendous value to it. The bicycle patrolling vanished with the virtual disappearance of the officer on the beat, but now seems to have re-emerged.

In some aspects of police work, women are better than men. For example they are often successful at calming a situation where men may inflame it, or they can and do make excellent detectives and senior or chief administrators. However, whilst there are of course exceptions, I believe that in general they are not suitable for the full range of front line police duties, any more than they are appropriate as front line fighting Armed Services personnel. Max Hastings in his best seller 'Warriors' supports this point of view in relation to military personnel. He writes, 'Only naïve people ignore the inescapable tensions created by sexual relationships between members of combat units.' He quotes a distinguished veteran that it is essential for the close relationship in battle to be uncompromised by sexual tensions, whether these are hetero or homosexual.

Whilst I do not pretend that police and military elements necessarily have the same objectives or methods, there are inescapable similarities between these two uniformed services. They extend as far as the Fire Service, where close relationships in the face of danger are also formed, and where physical strength can be the difference between saving and losing life. A close relationship does exist between police officers faced with dangerous or difficult conditions, and it is naïve to disregard this. Physical strength is nowadays not necessary for many jobs, but policing is still one of them. A six-foot tall constable with a commanding face and presence starts off in many situations with a huge advantage over the less well built or the female. This is something that is, I believe, unique to unarmed policing. Unarmed policing is a system which in this country, until the politicians have devalued it even further, we still largely have. The distinguished author Bill Bryson, discussing William Shakespeare's father, comments that the position of Constable which he held in Stratford was then, as now, one that argued for some physical strength and courage.

Courage certainly does not depend only upon testosterone. Many women have more of Alexander's dynasmus than many men, and are likely to be as courageous, or more so, both mentally and physically. Many, probably most, women are, in their own field, much more courageous, hard working and capable than men would be in a similar situation. But they are usually smaller and physically less strong. Unfair, but a natural fact of life for most. Equal pay for equal work is undeniably right. But equal work between men and women in some policing situations cannot be possible and those who thought that it could were ignoring the basic facts of life. I think also that too many unsuitable people, who happen to be male, have been allowed to become police officers. It is interesting that Hastings uses the word 'naïve'. It has come to the forefront of my mind so many times when dealing with representatives of the Government or the Civil Service, or even in just considering their latest silliness. It is a description that could not be applied to those who have been forced to know, and deal with, the worst of human behaviour.

Other negative aspects of the full integration of men and women officers were mentioned earlier, including the neglect of the specialist knowledge and registers of local sex offenders previously kept by the specialist policewomen's departments. However, there will always be police work that can only be done, or will be done better, by women. During the last year of the Wolverhampton Force Policewomen carried out enquiries for missing persons, and into suspected ill-treatment of children. They also carried out nearly five hundred enquiries into sexual offences, and took nearly a thousand statements appropriate to be taken by a female officer. They gave advice on over seven hundred occasions and cared for twenty three women who were mentally or physically ill, as well as almost four thousand hours of street patrol. This was in addition to the escorting or searching duties that obviously had to be done by women officers. Women are invaluable in any public service organisation, but I do not believe that they should be 'front line troops' in either a military or police role.

The fourth factor in the police decline was, I believe, the big Edmund-Davies pay award of the late 1970s. Police strengths were haemorrhaging away during the seventies and the big award was intended to stop the outflow.

In my own experience, and I think that of others, the cause was frustration at poor leadership, with changing policies and personalities, as much as the inarguably inadequate pay. It seemed to me that a different type of person was being recruited after the award, changing from those who wanted a career that was different, challenging and necessary in a civilised community, to those who were in it for the money.

So, I recognise that there was a paradox. We lost good people, or failed to recruit others partly due to the poor pay scales, but when these were improved to quite a large extent over several years the greed factor seemed to have become much more apparent and universal. Some of the deterioration was due, of course, to shifting social conditions, but not, I believe entirely. Calls for the right to strike, heard again in 2007 and 8 over pay, had been heard in the late 1970s, resulting eventually in the big Edmund-Davies award. I am aware of the police strike that followed the First World War, but am not competent to comment on either the social or police conditions of that time. What I am able to say is that I would have found it unbelievable to hear calls for a police strike during my service before the late nineteen seventies. The Chairman of the West Midlands Police Federation (the police union) complained, in February 2008, on national television, that his members were required to police a Labour Party Conference, after the Government had 'cheated' over their last pay award   I know that I would not have wanted to have that man stand beside or behind me in a dangerous or difficult situation, being aware that he was considering how much he would be paid for it. Mercenaries are rightly held in contempt by regular soldiers. I do not like to think of them in the police service and also hold them in contempt.

I think that it is also fair to point to one way in which the role of Chief and Assistant Chief Police Officers has gone down-market in recent years from the standards that applied during most of my service. It seems that some cannot speak in standard non-accented English. Perhaps they choose not to do so from a false egalitarian doctrine, or cannot be bothered to try. Many people, perhaps even the majority, might say that this does not matter. I think that it does, at least for the head of an important organisation. An indication of intelligence, pride in oneself and at least some level of education can be demonstrated by verbal communication patterns, and construct respect for the speaker. Perhaps current Chief Police Officers, many of whom were recruited in the nineteen eighties or nineties, should take on board Robert Burns' thought, 'O wad some pow'r the giftie gie us to see oursels as others see us'.

While news reports in the media are not always to be relied upon, I do now wonder if some Chief Officers have not become stark staring mad. Two instances, if true as reported, come to mind. In the most serious, a Bristol officer falsely arrested and assaulted a motorist, and instead of being prosecuted and sacked was merely ordered to apologise to his victim.

The second case involved support by the Devon and Cornwall Constabulary for a Gay Pride march in which the Force's Gay Police were involved. Who recruits these people and allows them to call themselves police officers? Yes, I know, Society and morals have changed, but I believe that the bulwarks against chaos and anarchy should not have done so.

I believe that the lack of respect for any form of authority now seen so much amongst the young stems at least partly from the decline of the Police Service. We walked tall, on the footpath not in the gutter, and with pride.

L.P.Hartley, the twentieth century English novelist, wrote that, 'the past is a foreign country: they do things differently there.'

This has always been true, but have we not today, in so many aspects of life, thrown out healthy babies with the bathwater? Of course there are many members – I hope the majority – of today's service, fine young (and not so young) men and women, who do a job which has grown more difficult and dangerous, honestly and without greed, and as well as it was ever done. I regret that, in my experience, there are also some who do not deserve that description and who are not fit to be part of the Police Service.

I do not think that it is too fanciful to relate, in part at least, the decline of English civilised society into the yob-ridden, selfish, unlawful, greedy culture in which we live today to the demoralisation, deterioration and disrespect of the police service of the United Kingdom. Politicians of all parties have, and in the future will increasingly have, much to answer for. Bureaucracy, self-serving and navel contemplation are not characteristics of a bulwark against anarchy.

The culmination of my connection with Wolverhampton Police and the West Midlands Constabulary was at the plaque dedication and re-union at the National Memorial Arboretum in 2007. The support that this received, by former officers (and indeed many widows) from literally all over the country was fantastic and an inspiration. I believe that those of that generation were part of arguably the best police service in the world. I also believe that we of that generation should be prepared to accuse those who, through political ineptness, dogma, malice and envy have reduced the Police Service of the United Kingdom to what it has become.

Another quotation comes to mind. Martin Luther King said, ' You start to die when you fail to speak up for the things that you believe in'.

Perhaps with the twenty-twenty vision of hindsight one can look back and see some truths about the past. Living backwards may have some advantages.

I believe that I understand more about policing now, decades removed from it, than I did when immersed in it.

My viewpoint, allowing that personal experience and history are bound to influence it, is that I am disturbed, unhappy, critical and sad that in general standards of police leadership, recruiting, attitude and behaviour have deteriorated so much. I am still proud to have been 'A Constable, locally appointed, but having authority under the Crown'. In Wolverhampton, or any other city, today, and in need of help, I shall be likely to find only a partly trained person dressed up in an imitation police uniform. This person is unlikely, it seems to me, to have either the ability or the motivation to offer help. This is not progress, nor a bulwark against chaos.

But, in our prime, we were the 'Kings of the City', and I remember and am proud of that.

Chapter 5

Steps In The Dark

After twenty five years in a disciplined, uniformed organisation, it was perhaps time that I experienced other ways of life. There was a considerable culture shock though. I had been offered, and accepted, the position of Emergency Relief Co-ordinator, a moderately senior new post within the British Red Cross. It was based in the rambling old Red Cross Headquarters in Grosvenor Crescent, just off Hyde Park Corner and virtually in the heart (the expensive heart) of London. The intention was that I would co-operate with the two arms of the International Red Cross in Geneva to transport and expedite aid to wherever in the world it was needed. This was likely to be because of natural disasters, through the League of Red Cross Societies, or warfare and civil strife, which came under the aegis of the International Committee of the Red Cross. Some overseas travel was anticipated, and contact with people in other countries. I felt that the job was made for me!

Paul, my immediate superior, also wanted me to plan and organise a control room to be available in Grosvenor Crescent for major operations when the Disasters Emergency Committee was called into action. The D.E.C.at that time was the combination the Big Five of the British aid giving charities, the Red Cross, Oxfam, Cafod, Save the Children, and Christian Aid. This was another job cut out for me after my work in the Sudan and at Birmingham! One of the first tasks was to get to know people in those other organisations, and I went to a number of conferences with Paul. A big surprise was the amount of back-biting and what seemed to be jealousy between the charities. I guess this was the result of the competition for a limited pool of money and the need to interest potential donors in the work being done.

Part of the culture shock was also to find rather old-fashioned attitudes and systems, although the individuals were, with very few exceptions, really nice people. The Red Cross still benefited from the wartime staff trend to have part-time aristocratic ladies, and it is very probable that I was a culture shock to them! Particularly pleasant and helpful to me were the two young ladies, Pam and Sue, who worked in the emergency aid office. Both long since married, I am very pleased that we are still in touch and occasionally meet up at Red Cross staff re-unions.

During my last police leave, Jo and I had toured north London and the

Home Counties looking at schools and houses. Marlow, Henley, Finchley and many other areas were examined, and by the time I started work in London it was becoming obvious that this would be a problem. There were plenty of houses that we liked, but none equivalent to our own that we could afford. We had not properly taken on board the huge gulf between prices in the London area and the Midlands, and in one of my typically over-enthusiastic steps had gone ahead, assuming that we would find somewhere. It also seemed that without putting the two children into private schools, which was an impossible cost, we were not going to find anywhere better than Wolverhampton Grammar School and Wolverhampton Girls High School. Both were then, and still are, amongst the best schools in the country. We were very fortunate to have them there. The fact that later and simultaneously we had one at Cambridge and one at Oxford, both taking post-graduate degrees justified our eventual decision not to move home.

When I started work at Grosvenor Crescent the home decision was still on the back burner, and I found myself a bed-sit in Shepherd's Bush. I do remember sitting in that rather bleak room, comparing it with my normal home life and thinking, 'What have I done?' I felt, I think, dispossessed. However, I was soon able to find a two room flat, right at the top of one of the very high and narrow Victorian terrace houses in Goldhawk Road, which was an improvement. But not much. I guess that it had been a 'tweenies' room, but told people at home that I had a penthouse flat!

Shepherds Bush to Hyde Park Corner was not a particularly enjoyable journey by Tube, so I bought myself a fold-up bicycle, and used this to wander around the West End and even further afield after work. I rather lost confidence in it after it folded up with me inside it whilst negotiating Hyde Park Corner. However, it was easy to lock it to a lamppost, and to stow in the hall with my landlord's permission. Since parking a car in the street in Goldhawk Road was risky, I was travelling home on Friday evening by train and returning on Monday morning. We carried on in that way for the rest of my stay at the Red Cross, eventually having to decide that the move south was unaffordable and unfair to the children.

It was very good to get home each weekend. We had bought a Ford Transit van, already fitted with camping equipment, to which I had side windows added while I was still in the police service. On my weekends at home during the summer we continued to have more wonderful days at Shell Island, on the coast of the Snowdonia National Park, camped on the Great Orme at Llandudno and at Pistyll Rhaeadr, the breathtaking waterfall in the Berwyn Mountains. The weekends were too short!

I did however enjoy a lot of the London evenings, especially in the Summer, when my unfolded bike took me into Hyde Park, Green Park, Regents Park and along the Thames. I was able to visit several theatres, with memories of the emotional experience of Fiddler on the Roof in the Haymarket still powerful, and also went to the Albert Hall on a few occasions. I never felt that living and working in London was much of a privilege. I did enjoy watching the artistry of the pavement 'con-men' with the three card trick and other scams and the soft metal 'jewellery' prizes outside Harrods and Selfridges. The lookout was often suspicious of me and closed down the operation. Clever people. I had to admit that we did not have them in Wolverhampton! I have never been much interested in cooking, so generally ate out in the evenings, but did have a go, not very successfully at producing one or two puddings! Quoting Dr. Johnson again, this time I most certainly do not agree with his observation that, 'When a man is tired of London he is tired of life'. Not true! Not even near true! Percy Shelly, who wrote, 'Hell is a city much like London.' is more accurate. I guess that it is a useful experience to live and work in a world-class city, but I was glad to move away.

The first major disaster that I became involved in was widespread and serious flooding in Bangladesh – little changes in the world of natural disasters. Co-operation between London, Geneva, other National Red Cross Societies and other Aid Agencies was part of my role. The organisation of airfreight, blankets, food for children and the elderly was also a component of the job. At this time I was becoming aware of the complexities of rendering aid. Not all the voluntary donations were entirely charitable since tax breaks could be claimed. A shipload of crates, manifested as footwear, unsourced by the Red Cross, arrived by sea from the USA to Karachi. They were found after unloading to contain thousands of pairs of high-heeled shoes unwanted by the manufacturer. Useful for refugees, yes? Eight tons of alleged food supplies, also unsourced, arrived in Pakistan, for refugees from Afghanistan, taking up valuable space and labour.

Guess what?

Weight reducing powder, from the US of A. When asked about this the President of the donating company said that it contained useful vitamins. Useful for the slimmer refugee. I found, whilst working in London, that it was very difficult to refuse gifts that were genuinely offered, because giving from the heart is good. But the head needs to involved as well.

It is also very easy to obliterate local systems, for example a modern industrial bakery, set up in Africa without follow-up servicing and repairs, caused the ruin of the local one man shops. When it became unworkable and closed down there was a shortage of bread over a wide area. This was rather like the Russian four-wheel drive desert vehicles gifted to the Sudan. When they broke down they were, despite the ingenuity of local mechanics, only good for scrap as spares were not part of the deal. To avoid situations like these it was necessary to work closely with experienced people in London and Geneva. I also worked directly with the then Ministry for Overseas Development, and came to know their senior operatives well. Although we did not always agree about the best method of delivering help, they were a very helpful and generous body, whose work in the developing world has never, I think, been properly appreciated.

One of the big attractions of the Red Cross job had been the possibility of travel. My attendance at Hira's wedding and the work in the Sudan had opened up so many more mountains that I wanted to see over. We had waited until the children were old enough to appreciate other cultures, and had then taken some superb holidays in France, Germany and Italy. We had spent two weeks in the Camargue, all four of us being able to ride the famous white horses. We stayed in an ancient hotel in Arles, with bullfighter's pictures and bull's hides hung on the walls. The choice of this Hotel had been dictated by my wish to meet an Arlisienne. (Only because I love the music!) Unfortunately the first one we met in the Hotel Reception was rather sulky, unco-operative and very French – not at all like the subject of Bizet's wonderful melody. C'est la vie!

At the same Hotel we were very late back for dinner one evening, as we had stayed out to see the beautiful pink flamingos in the marshes. In trying to apologise to the Restaurant staff I gave (so I am told but don't really believe it) the impression that we would like to eat flamingo. It was not on the menu anyway. I do, however, put up my hands to another linguistic howler, having asked, in Rome, by a mere slip of the tongue of course, for a piazza rather than a pizza. My son, rather quickly, asked if this would be a square meal so at least we got a laugh out of it.

We had had another small adventure on that holiday, when Al came running to our room to say that the porter had been trying to kiss Nicky, then aged about ten. I got hold of the man, shouted at him somewhat and told him that I was going to tell my friend the Chief of Police. He locked himself in a bedroom and literally howled for minutes on end! Thinking of the disruption to our holiday if he hung himself with the lavatory chain we hurried out. He didn't, but looked like a badly beaten dog with its tail between its legs for the rest of our stay, which was a reasonable outcome.

Nicky was always (still is!) very fussy about breakfast cereals, and would only eat Ricicles. We therefore carried a box all around Europe and presented her with a box at her wedding reception! Also in Italy Al discovered that when you order prawns they often come with their heads and whiskers still attached and this he did not appreciate. I felt, to preserve our British dignity, that I would have to eat them as well as my own. When the time came for dolce - pudding - he was of course still hungry, so asked if he could have spaghetti. I can still see and hear the owner of the small restaurant saying in outrage, 'Spaghetti – for dolce?'

Refugees in Burma

So, while travel in Europe with the family was always fun and often interesting, I felt a strong pull to see more and go further. Thus, a suggestion made by the Deputy Director that I should take the post of British Red Cross delegate in Burma for three months was gratefully accepted. Jo was agreeable, much to her credit and my gratitude and the kids did not get a vote! The job was to support the Burmese Red Cross, on behalf of the League of Red Cross Societies, in their work to feed, shelter and maintain the health of a flood of over two hundred thousand refugees who were returning to Arakan from Bangladesh. These people were Arakanese, from the north-western state of Burma. They had fled across, or trekked for many miles around, the Naf River, into Muslim Bangladesh. They were in fear of the Burmese Army, then as now an instrument of oppression.

A census had been ordered by the Government and as a result the army was rumoured to be about to massacre all Arakanese. They are largely Muslim and of a different origin to the majority of Burmese Buddhists. These people were old, young, babies and infants, sick and disabled as well as the able bodied. They arrived in Bangladesh after a difficult river crossing by boat or a trek of many weeks to where the river could be crossed on foot. They were not expected or wanted, there was no help, and often starving and ill they had to live in shantytowns with no food provision.

Effectively Bangladesh could not cope with them, it had problems enough of it's own. Of those who had already made the journey back many could go no further than the Arakanese bank of the Naf, while others had trickled back to one of the five hundred villages from which they had fled. The British Red Cross, with the Burmese Red Cross, had agreed to be responsible for organising the feeding of the sixty thousand children of these refugees and if possible other vulnerable groups. It had also provided a very expert British Nurse to work in the Bangladeshi camps and shelters and a food programme there was now in place. Many of the refugees were reluctant to be taken home. Unsurprisingly they preferred food in the Bangladeshi camps to an uncertain future in Arakan. Their rice had not been planted, their houses may no longer exist, the monsoon season was not far off and they still had fear of the Burmese Army. They were now undergoing a forced repatriation. The World Health Organisation Doctor had assessed malaria, malnutrition and diarrhoea and expected a deterioration of the situation. Relief of these conditions or their prevention amongst the vulnerable groups back in Arakan was therefore one of our priorities.

I arrived in Rangoon (now Yangon) in January 1979 to be met by the Secretary of the Burma Red Cross, U Thi La, a retired Lieutenant Colonel from the British Chindit campaign against the Japanese invaders of the Second World War. U Thi La was a splendid man, and a real gentleman, keen to welcome European help in an exceptional task. His deputy, U Thet Swe, a much younger man, was also extremely pleasant, and we had a very good association throughout my stay. U Thet Swe followed the normal practice among devout Buddhists of spending some time each year as a Monk, and I learned a great deal about Buddhism from him. I had not appreciated that one can be a part-time Monk, but it is, I suppose comparable to a Christian going into a Retreat, to think and pray.

The third Red Cross person that I was to work closely with was U Kyaw Saw ('U' is the Burmese honorific, roughly equating to 'Mr'). Also pleasant and co-operative, he was the Accountant, and I was later honoured to be invited for a meal at his home and to meet his Wife and delightful children. The children gave me a present of hand painted papier mâché ducks, which survived the journey home and which I still have.

Burma was, at that time, a country of Monks, who were to be seen everywhere in their saffron coloured robes. Many were quite small boys, and it was strange to see a file of tiny Monks behaving like small boys in any country and trying to trip each other up, or making faces at the white foreigner! I suspect that things are different now in Yangon, or Myanmar generally, and that the boy Monks are not so full of happiness or mischief. I did have difficulty getting a visa to enter Burma – the Bamboo curtain was firmly in place, and it took pressure from Geneva and the provision of a Red Cross 'Passport' to extract one.

It soon became very evident that we were not welcomed or even wanted by the Government. Other European delegates joined me in Rangoon, Jurgen, a Swiss whose normal profession as a deep sea diver was a little bit out of the ordinary – a long way to get to work? The second was a former French journalist, part of whose remit was to get photographs for publicity and fund-raising. I believe that he was quite a good photographer, but in some other ways was a disappointment as a man and a Geneva delegate. Being senior to me in the organisation he was Chief Delegate until leaving in February when I was take over. I disagreed with some of his methods, and he and I disliked each other from the moment of meeting. Journalists and police officers are absolute natural enemies, even when both are 'ex' as in this case, and I admit to often having been very prickly in the face of the arrogance that seems to be inborn in many French males. However, there was a job to be done and we managed to have a reasonable working relationship. I became Chief Delegate after his departure, so was able to correct what I felt had been mistakes.

One of the first problems was the remoteness of Arakan. It was an underdeveloped region, with virtually no infrastructure, having been neglected by the Burmese. There were three ways of getting there – by boat or by air or by foot (the latter not being an option), or a combination of all three. The most efficient means, air and boat, took two days. How we fought the Japanese over country like that has never ceased to amaze me. I bought a painting whilst in Burma, by a local artist, brought it home rolled up in my kit, had it mounted and it lives on our lounge wall. Home would not be home without it. It illustrates perfectly the very early morning scene from a boat on an Arakanese river, probably the Mayu. The mist still covers the surface of the tawny water, a pale golden sun, soon to be red hot, struggles to emerge over the jungle, and the heads of the boat crew are just visible above the mist. The centrepiece is a huge banyan tree; roots above ground on the bank, with little shrines to the Nats, the spirits of the forests and rivers, tied to its many branches. A good time to be travelling, well captured.

The first thing that had to be done was to get to Arakan to assess the situation. We travelled from Mingaladon Airport, Rangoon to the old British airfield at Akyab. Mingaladon was another culture shock. It was rather like catching a 'bus in a very disorganised 'bus station. The aeroplanes, all identical small turbo-prop Fokkers belonging to Burma Airways, were lined up on the apron outside the small terminal, and it was necessary, in order to catch the correct one, to ask the crews where they were going.

Much later in the assignment, I had arranged to take a weekend break on the coast and needed to catch the Calcutta flight. I was having difficulty in the Burma Airways office in Rangoon. Eventually, rather losing patience in the heat and flies I banged the desk and said, 'Look, is there, or isn't there a flight to Calcutta?' The tiny clerk always, like all Burmese, the epitome of politeness, drew himself up to his full height – roughly to my shoulder, and replied, 'Yes Sir, there is certainly a flight, but I do not yet know if there will be an aeroplane on it.'

This made me rather ashamed of my Western impatience. It turned out that there was an aeroplane, and I had a wonderful two-day break, which by then I needed, at Sandoway, on the Bay of Bengal. I rented a thatched beach hut, and spent most of the two days in the beautiful aqua-marine water about a hundred yards from my hut or strolling, wearing nothing but one of the sarongs which I had bought in Malaysia. The sarong is much worn in Burma, where it is called a lungyi, and is the most comfortable and convenient garment, once one has learned how to tie it so that it does not descend at an inconvenient moment. I should add here that the sarong/lungyi is a male garment, the female version is the sarong kabayah, which has a waistcoat as well! Blame Dorothy Lamour and Hollywood for any misconception! This was a resort, for those who could afford it, and it was very interesting to talk to some of the couples there, mainly I think enjoying honeymoon holidays. There were no other Europeans. It was a beautiful place. Perhaps since then has been developed, I hope sensitively, as I could not imagine it with concrete apartment blocks. Perhaps not, however, given the dislike (on the part of the Government only) of foreigners that was so very obvious even then.

Part of the beach was given over to fishing, Burmese style, where a huge net was taken out into the water, then pulled back in by teams of men, always full to bursting with tiny fish. These were then laid out on mats on the sand to dry. As the net was obviously very heavy I joined in to help several times, which produced a round of applause and some banter. This was good to be part of. The most marvellous part of Sandoway however was swimming in the warm surf at night. The water was phosphorescent, so that as I swam glowing drops of coloured fire dripped from my arms, and on standing up a curtain of colour surrounded my body. No other clothing was necessary at night! I think that this perfect weekend is one of my very best memories of life overseas.

To re-wind back to our investigative journey to Akyab, this was not comfortable, even after locating the correct plane. Almost without fail heavy thunderstorms develop in the afternoon at this season, and the small plane was tossed about unmercifully. The crew treated it as routine and we arrived at Royal Air Force Akyab - as it once was - shaken but unstirred. We stayed overnight in a State Rest House, then, very early next day caught a State launch for an eight hour journey along snaking rivers to the small town of Buthidaung. A retinue of cooks, boys carrying live chickens, papayas etc, and numerous armed policemen accompanied us. Whether they were there to protect us or to report on what we were doing was never really established. After several meetings with village headmen and village councils we travelled on for another hour by Land Rover to Maungdow. Wild elephants had been known to crush trucks in these Mayu mountains, so the police bren-guns were appreciated.

Huge piles of elephant dung had to be circumnavigated, as they were too high to drive over. Maungdow was a frontier town in more ways than one.

The overnight stay was in a rest house, whose bathroom consisted of a bowl, a hole and an oil drum full of water. Sleeping was on a bed roll on bare boards. Sleep was not easy, apart from the boards, as every house in Maungdow apparently owned a dog, with every dog in competition with it's neighbour to produce as much noise as possible. I later came across a remote Burmese tribe who bred dogs to be eaten as puppies. The same custom came up years later in a remote part of Africa.

My English colleague at that time in Africa issued a general invitation to anyone who happened to visit London to come to stay in his house. This was before he found out about the puppies! It seemed to me to be a revolting tradition, but I do not quite understand why. Perhaps it is the thought of popping round to the local butcher to ask for a few pounds of stewing puppy with which to feed the guests. Just not what we do, I suppose. We should appreciate how sickening it must be for people of other cultures or religions to think about eating pork or ham. During the evening at Maungdow we were lucky to be there for the performance of a pwe. This is a very traditional form of theatre, where the characters are performed by puppets, whose shadows are cast onto a large sheet, lit from behind. It was very clever, and was obviously much appreciated by the large crowd. We were seen, I believe, as an alternative source of entertainment for them!

Anyway, it was up early again after a sleepless night to get a Customs launch for the three-hour journey to the first of the reception camps. We were now no more than seventy miles from Akyab, - half an hour by helicopter but twelve hours solid travel by boat, Land Rover and foot! We spent two and half days in the hard work of visiting all the camps using the Customs launch and army speedboats. Using a speedboat that went aground in one of the narrow tributaries, U Thi La and I had no option but to wade ashore. On leaving the boat we both sank up to our knees in glutinous and evil smelling mud. This would have been more worrying for U Thi La, who was considerably shorter than me. However, we sank no further, and, both determined not to lose face, struggled to the top of the bank. The armed escort seemed to have been put ashore at a better spot! Firmer ground, and a barefoot trek for two hours across paddy fields, with their traditional raised paths that contain the water, removed some of the mud.

The condition of the returnees in camps and villages gave us an idea of how big the problem was going to be. I see from my notes that at this point I had realised what had to be done, but could not see how it was going to be done. It was also debatable whether we should have the armed escort, in view of the distrust and fear of the army by the returnees. We had however been told that they were necessary in order to be sure of getting to the camps and back again. Guns were kept very much in evidence during the long walks between camps. I remember having the odd thought, as I had had during my command of an armed police search party in Willenhall, and driving with a tooled-up escort on a bumpy road in Sudan, about from which direction the biggest danger of being shot was likely to come! Being accidental would not have been much consolation. We did manage to keep the guards out of sight at each camp until we had established who we were and what we were there for, and as the troops and police did generally behave themselves very well, the suspicion gradually eased.

The Arakan scenery was beautiful - during the journey from Akyab there were mountains on either side, which gradually narrowed into a funnel. Boats there were, of all shapes and sizes, as most Arakanese live by, and fish in, the rivers. From our boat one could see monkeys playing in the trees, parrots by the thousand and water buffalo everywhere, but no crocodiles, as these rivers were tidal. There were no roads or bridges, just the one track through the mountains, sometimes only wide enough for a bullock cart. Getting to one of the camps had involved a night hike, in absolute darkness except for the hurricane lamps carried by our entourage, with a velvet starry sky above and crickets and jackals making very tropical noises.

It was necessary for me to meet the Police Commissioner at Akyab, whose area covered the places where the returnees were arriving. One of our major problems was in arranging feeding and medical treatment for those who had returned to about five hundred villages instead of staying in the Reception Camps. Those who were well enough had walked, carrying their children if necessary. Much discussion between U Thi La, myself, village councils, U.N.H.C.R. and W.H.O. representatives and the Burmese Government was time consuming and frustrating, but necessary. Eventually it was resolved by providing feeding stations with local Red Cross Volunteers in the bigger villages, and getting the men, via a ration card system, to collect food for the children. Not by any means an ideal solution, but the only one which would be possible, given the limited personnel and finance available. There were only the two small towns, Maungdow, and Buthidaung in the Reception Camps area, although Akyab was more substantial, having been the seat of pre-war British local administration. We collected a giggling crowd there when we visited the bazaar and fish market, where shark meat was on sale!

The Commissioner was an interesting man. He invited me to play a round of golf with him so that we could talk, and would take no notice of the fact that I did not play golf! He was very well organised, with a policeman walking in front of us carrying a gun, another policeman carrying his golf clubs and third well behind also with a gun. This did not happen in the West Midlands.

Here it was justified as Arakan, like others of the Burmese States, was subject to a revolutionary independence movement against the Government, plus dacoits, robber groups, for whom the capture of a police chief would give some bargaining power.

The golf course by-passed an old British Cemetery, with graves of colonial administrators going back well into the nineteenth century. It was a poignant thought to see how many of these gravestones bore the names of tiny children. British expatriates suffered much in the cause of Empire, and did more good than is ever acknowledged. This reminded me of how we had been thought well of by the ordinary people, throughout the Sudan. After our golf, I was invited to dine with the Chief and sorted a few things out, including an armed police escort to accompany our river journeys. They would remain with us for the rest of the visit to the camps and protect our personnel at the feeding stations and camps. We were also allowed the occasional use of a police launch. This did work out well, and I think that my background was of help with the Commissioner. U Thi La was able to arrange with some of his former wartime colleagues to get Army support as well. The young Red Cross Volunteers were usually teenagers, sometimes students, always enthusiastic, and enjoyed being involved and wearing a uniform. Organisations like the Scouts had been proscribed by the Government, and the Red Cross was one of the very few organisations open to them. The programme would have been impossible without them.

The arrival by boat at Buthidaung had provided another culture shock. The wooden jetty looked like a bird's nest of branches, although surprisingly able to bear the weight of our baggage and gear. The first place we had visited was the tiny local Hospital. The very limited staff were doing the best they could to deal with the flood of malnourished and ill people, but their drugs and equipment were totally insufficient.

I found that the operating table had a broken leg, and was balanced on a pile of bricks. When this was reported to London, Save the Children donated a new table to the Hospital. They and Cafod, the Catholic Fund for Overseas Development, were two very helpful Charities that I dealt with during my time with the Red Cross. We had brought surgical instruments donated by Christian Aid, similarly a good provider of equipment.

We had also brought, by air and in our launch, whatever medical supplies were then available, plus five outboard motors. The motors were for use with five fibreglass hulls donated by the Japanese Red Cross for quick transport up and down the rivers and rapid transport across to the Bangladeshi camps. Unfortunately instructions for the installing of the outboards did not come with them, or possibly came in Japanese.

One was quickly dropped into the Naf, where I guess it still is, by one of the boat crews, who were perhaps over-excited. It was quite unhelpful to cry over spilt milk, but we made sure that this would not happen again, and took the crews for a training run on the estuary. This was an extra and incidental personal delight as we were surrounded by inquisitive river dolphins, who were no doubt wondering what else might be deposited in their territory!

Some feeding arrangements were in progress but there was much to be done. There were ten reception camps and another nine transit camps, for people trying to get to their home villages. One thing that did make this area easier to deal with was the profusion of building material – bamboo and thatch, with no need to import tents. The downside of that is that bamboo and thatch need constant maintenance, and houses unlived in for a year would either have been taken over by someone else or be untenable. We did identify a need for blankets though. As much as anything this was a psychological need. If people have lost their homes, anything that they can be given as a personal possession helps to restore their self-respect, and thus the will to live.

It was then necessary for U Thi La and myself to return to Rangoon to set up meetings with the other Agencies, work out a proper feeding programme and to report what was necessary. There had been a lot of worldwide publicity about the plight of the refugees, and aid promised from many sources. The British Red Cross was a major contributor towards the cost of buying and shipping five Land Rovers for Red Cross use. One of the early meetings was with the American Ambassador, Mr.Maurice Bean, who presented a cheque for $10,000 that I had been able to negotiate. I appeared on the front pages of the newspapers again, this time the Rangoon ones!

U Thi La was also very keen for us to look at other aspects and areas of the Burma Red Cross work, while there were still three of us. I think that this was partly to emphasise to Geneva how stretched they were by this emergency as well as to discover our view of the work being done. We flew part way, then went by boat on the Irrawaddy, to Myitkyina in the far north of Kachin State, close to the Chinese border. This was a long journey where we slept on deck, and were fed exotic dishes like fried wildcat and turtle eggs, which looked exactly like dented table-tennis balls!

European faces on a boat on Burma's main waterway provoked a lot of interest. Excited children from the riverside villages would swim out to us, and one local travelling downstream steered his sail powered boat straight into the bank in trying to get a better view! It was possible to swim off the boat, although in the far north it was a lot colder than it looked, as it carried the snow-melt icy water from it's source in the southern rim of Tibet.

The wooden Red Cross Headquarters at Myitkyina had been a notorious Japanese prison house during the war, where they tortured prisoners of war. It was one of the areas much fought over by the British protecting the gateway to India at Imphal. Despite its history the house was now a pleasant one and this was an important visit and a big day for the local Red Cross Volunteers. We were greeted by student Kachin girls in their really beautiful national costume – long red patterned skirts, black tops covered with glittering shining metal and round, highly decorated hats. We were also each presented with a bouquet (the first and last time – so far – in my life) by an over-awed little girl, the picture of which made the Rangoon newspapers. Like every other Charity in the world U Thi La had to seize any publicity that was going.

Our return route was to Shan State, in eastern Burma, under the guidance of U Kyaw Saw. Shan was one of the States where an independence movement had very strong support, with continuing long-term insurgency. A view of the Red Cross involvement there was needed. This was a chance to take steps to a part of Burma normally completely closed to foreigners, but permission was obtained, (one way or another) and we flew to the little town of Taunggyi, high up on the hills which climb towards the Shan plateau. This was, and still is, a remote area where, with luck and care, one can meet a shy Padaung, neck stretched to giraffe-like length and slimness by successive necklaces since childhood. I was lucky to meet and photograph cheroot smoking Shan tribeswomen who come to market with golden rings on their legs and arms, and bargain with tough little Tai-Chinese hillmen.

The Shan plateau spreads eastwards, from Burma to Laos, Thailand and China. It is the Golden Triangle, secret, war-torn, drug producing but mysterious and beautiful. Below the western edge of the plateau is the blue-green surface of Inle Lake, the hills mirrored in the calm water. Villages rise literally out of the water on stilts. The fishermen stand like storks on their flat boats, twining one leg around a long paddle to skull, keeping their hands free to cast conical nets. There were no foreigners except ourselves and the only noise in the hot afternoon was the buzz of an occasional motorised canoe, darting like a dragonfly between the floating beds of reeds.

Further west, on the far side of the lake are range upon range of hills, blue or purple in the distant heat. On the top of the first of these, and looking down on Inle Lake there stood a monastery, built of fine-looking seasoned teak. We crossed the Lake by boat and climbed up to the Monastery, where travellers are invited to stay to rest after climbing the steep hillside and to eat. It is traditional that travellers are so invited. We saw the Monks striking a great bronze bell so that deep and sonorous notes soared away over the blue water and stilt supported thatched houses. Little propellers mounted on poles whirred away in the warm breeze, bells tinkled and prayer flags fluttered and the only movement seemed to be cloud shadows gliding over the lake.

The Monks, gentle old men here, tend the gardens or sit cross-legged to talk, to contemplate or pray or perhaps just to sit. The western foreigner feels that he too is part of the peace and wonders why time, and clocks have to exist. We ate, looking over this view, and could not have wanted for more. My peace was brought to a savage end by a red chilli in my salad, the hottest thing that I have ever eaten, before or since. It exploded in my mouth after an incautious bite, and I had to run for water. The Frenchman was of course delighted to tell me that, 'you have to be careful of those!'

Part of the eastern view from the monastery were the hills above Taunggyi, where a white pagoda sat on the topmost point. It shimmered as the sun declined in the west. Burma is a land of pagodas, white and gold, both huge and tiny sitting like inverted bells on every hilltop. They range from the hundreds of ruins at fabulous Pagan on the banks of the Irrawaddy, to the holy and stupendous Shwe Dagon which dominates Rangoon.

Shwe Dagon is a village, a town, a city in itself, guarded at the foot of it's entry staircase by huge stone Chinthes, the mythical winged half lion, half flying griffin of Burma. I had spent a whole day there, wandering barefoot on the white marble, so polished that it looks wet, and found it not time enough. I was by now fascinated by pagodas, and determined to reach the stupa, the bell shape looking down on Taunggyi if possible. It looked unreal in the setting sun, almost floating, as the floodlit statue of Christ the Redeemer looks over Rio, half a world and a religion away. This one was not floodlit, but it was remote, primitive, probably deserted and almost certainly out of bounds to us, and to all foreigners. However, it had really caught my imagination, and it seemed worthwhile to try to play truant for a while. I was so glad, and am still so glad that I did, as it became a time to remember.

The chance came the next day, in a break from work while the others were watching a street game of chinlon. Boys in a circle try to keep a woven cane ball in the air, using only their legs, elbows and heads. Leaving them engrossed I sauntered towards the edge of the little town, accompanied as usual by a posse of small boys, all yelling 'One Chat, One Chat' to the foreign devil. As one kyat was worth about 8 p this was quite hopeful. I had found a useful response to this in Rangoon by holding out my hand and saying 'Chay zu tin bar dai' – thank you, which invariably produced fits of laughter, and a retreat of the posse. Shaking off the kids I passed the ladies rolling cheroots on their naked thighs and the row of little shops where just about everything could be bought, sold or mended, partly in the dusty road, partly in the owner's living space.

I passed the occasional beggar, sometimes horribly crippled, perhaps with no legs and scooting himself along on a tiny trolley, hands bound and padded. Past the sugar cane grinder, selling water in a battered tin cup and the severe soldier guarding the offices of the Socialist Republic of the Union of Burma. Shall I buy water? It is amazingly sweet and clear. Do I give the cripple some kyats? Well, he has a lot less than I have.

Eventually I found a semblance of a path, leading upwards. Soon I was working through secondary jungle, hot work, sweating hot, but not impossible. Every so often there was a little shrine in the trees, a shrine to the Nats, the Lords, the Spirits of the rivers, the rocks and trees and Gods. There would have been many Buddhist worshippers of the Nats up there in the hills as well as animist tribes-people, but the little shrines, whoever placed them, were non-threatening, appealing and I felt no sense of trespassing or being out of place. Tramping upwards after a long, hot sweating time I saw the bell of the pagoda shimmering in the heat of the midday sun above me. The going became easier as I regained a trodden path, and finally, tired but well pleased I staggered into a clearing and found the stupa a few yards away. The hilltop was silent apart from a tinkling and rustling. No engines, no voices, no people.

The view was superb. Blue, blue Inle Lake below, the fragile houses floating like an armada of thatched galleons. Beyond the Lake, to the west, rolls of hills, blue and green and purple, shading into infinity. The sunlight glinted on scores, perhaps hundreds, of bell like stupas, glittering like impossible stars against a blue sky. Faintly the boom, boom, boom of the monastery bell was borne across the water. To the north and east the green and gold undulating jungle clothing the wrinkled hills flowed on into the Golden Triangle and China.

I lay and looked, looked again and felt utterly at peace. The tinkling and rustling was no distraction but a delight as I saw that it came from little yellow prayer flags, home made prayer wheels and metal pennants strung around the pagoda bell. They sang in harmony as the warm breeze touched them, like a silver waterfall. When my eyes were at last satisfied it seemed acceptable to examine the outside of the stupa. Boots off just in case, then a quiet walk round, but keeping off the platform on which the stupa was built. There seemed to be no one within a hundred miles, just the jungle, the hills and the silver waterfall. But, at the far side, hidden from my earlier view, I found a bamboo and thatch hut, no bigger than my garden shed at home, but living space nevertheless. With a slightly guilty realisation that perhaps I was an intruder in this sacred place I returned to the edge of the hill and, with no further sign of life lay down again beside my boots.

Suddenly I felt that I was not alone and turning, saw behind me a saffron robed monk. His powerful shoulders and feet were bare and his old eyes were laughing in a teak coloured face, seamed by many suns. He saw that my boots were off and that I had no gun, and immediately he was a friend. He was the sole custodian of the Pagoda Shwe Pyong Byin, the Pagoda of Shining Gold. He honoured me with an invitation to take plain tea – green tea without milk boiled on a miniature primus stove, and tiny oranges in his minute living space.

How can an Englishman and a Burmese Monk, neither with more than a few words of the other's language, communicate? I do not know, cannot imagine, but we did.

I learned that he existed on food brought up the tortuous trail from Taunggyi below, and the sharing of his oranges and tea became so much more of an honour. There was nothing that I could give him in return, and certainly nothing that he would have wanted, despite my western standard of living and possessions. The bamboo walls of his room, little bigger than a cupboard, were covered with coloured paper pictures, calendars from years past, and newspaper cuttings. On one wall was a rope bed, and on the other a Shan version of a miniature Welsh dresser, tiny but a treasure, containing a few utensils. These few things were, I guess, a lifetime's accumulation, and they made me ashamed.

I learned also, by our mysterious means of communication, that he had been a boxer and a footballer in his youth. Most Burmese men spend a part of their lives as a phongyi, a monk, a week at least in boyhood, often returning many times as adults, as did our Red Cross officer U Tet Swe. My host had opted for a life of continuous solitude and meditation many years before. We talked and drank much tea, corrected the condition of both Burma and Europe, and discussed, within the boundaries of our comprehension, his God and mine. He had worked in his youth for an Englishman named Mr. Robinson, and wondered if I might know of him in England. I am so grateful now for the impulse that guided me to say, 'Yes, I believe that I do.' I tried to understand his life and I think that he tried to understand mine. I felt such peace in that warm little hut, and a rapport that crossed the boundaries of race and religion.

Too soon the setting sun shafted through the thatch, to remind me of my responsibilities below. I wished to stay, but the way had to be westward and downwards towards the now shadowed blue of Inle Lake. A huge golden sun dipped in front of me as I started down, illuminating the old man as I turned and looked back one last time. He was standing above me, one arm raised in the worldwide sign of farewell, the saffron robe fluttering in the evening breeze. I thought that contentment, peace and power radiated from him.

I never saw him again, and probably shall never be able to visit Shan State for a second time. Burma is still a closed land of conflict and despotism, but I fell in love with it during that one afternoon, and with the ordinary people of that beautiful, sad country. I hope that I shall never forget the beauty and quietness up on the hill and the timelessness of the old man's life. I have wondered how it would have been up on the plateau, when the warm sun disappears, the brutal black thunderheads climb five miles high into a sullen sky and sudden savage storms strike the thatch or destroy the primitive path. It perplexes me how a man can be content to live alone, or even exist on tea and oranges, with only his faith for company. I have been privileged to meet many people, all over the world, exotic, exciting, exhilarating, glamorous, bizarre people, but the man of Shwe Pyong Byin is matchless, unique. I like to think that my visit was also for him exceptional, a remembered event in the solitude, quietness and peace of his days.

Down the long, twisting jungly path to Taunggyi my thoughts were still on the plateau, but I found the rest of our team and made my apologies for truancy to U Kyaw Saw. We returned to Rangoon the next day, praised sincerely the work of the Volunteers and reported the state of the States to U Thi La.

Many years later I was to win a place on a trek to Everest Base Camp and Kala Patthar by writing an essay based upon this experience, which is still very clear in my mind.

Back in Rangoon I was staying in the old Strand Hotel, on the Strand - the waterfront. Somerset Maugham wrote many of his famous stories about the East from a room in the Strand. It was a venerable place, fascinating but not exactly five star. I shared a bedroom with a fleet of large, shiny brown cockroaches. Catching one of these I put it down the toilet, only to have it appear from the washbasin overflow pipe, wet but not subdued. After that I thought it better not to investigate the plumbing further. I found some free daylight time as most of the work now consisted of planning, attending meetings, or waiting for meetings to be assembled. Some of these were not chaired exactly expertly, and I felt a huge amount of frustration. Telex and report writing were also daily tasks, but I was able to see a lot of Rangoon.

This I found absorbing, as my Father had served there with the British Army guarding the gateway to India during the First World War. He had been a Territorial soldier with the Kings Shropshire Light Infantry before 1914, and when the balloon went up they had been in a Territorial training camp in North Wales. The Territorial Battalion was immediately shipped to Burma, to replace a regular Battalion brought back to fight in France. He spent the next years there until brought back to the UK with malaria, for which there was then no cure. I guess that he was lucky to miss the trenches, but suffered with bouts of malaria for the rest of his life. Our home contained many souvenirs of Burma and I found it enthralling to be there. Still feeling my own culture shock, I could only guess at that experienced by my Father, transported from a small Shropshire town back in 1914.

Rangoon was a very busy port, and one could see ships from all over the world in a short stroll along the Strand. Large elephants rolling huge logs of teak into position for loading, and large ladies making cheroots by rolling them against their bare thighs to seal them with their sweat were sights to be seen. I brought some cheroots home, but found them to be an acquired taste. They tend to ejaculate sparks like fireworks. I still have some if any reader wishes to volunteer!

Getting around Rangoon was usually by foot or three wheeled motor cycle taxis, 'tuk-tuks' as they are known in some parts of south east Asia. This was interesting; as it was a busy city the horn was much needed but invariably operated by touching a bare wire to the handlebars! Drivers habitually made the 'Nameste' - taking both hands off the handlebars and putting them together - when passing a pagoda. There are a lot of pagodas in Rangoon.

The tuk-tuk drivers were inclined to pester any potential customer, and I was approached by one just as I was walking towards the Hotel entrance.

I said, 'How much to Strand Hotel?' and he did a classic double take and, doubling up with laughter, spluttered, 'Nothing Sir, it is free!'

You can't help being very fond of people like that. Ordinary Burmese people were invariably and incredibly polite. When I consulted a Doctor, who looked about thirteen, he thanked me many times for being allowed the honour of examining me. The politeness made getting onto one of the crowded buses quite difficult, because the other passengers obviously felt it wrong for a visitor to be strap hanging. I usually had to turn down many offers of someone's seat. Eventually, when I was offered a seat that I felt I could accept, there was a heartfelt collective sigh of relief from the whole bus load! Whether this was a spin-over from the British colonial past, or just natural instinctive good manners I do not know, but I had found the same thing in Sudan, found it again years later in Nepal, Vietnam, and even in Tibet in the twenty first century.

I was eventually joined in the Hotel by Alexander, a delegate from the Russian Red Cross Youth Section, with whom I had an instant affinity. His brief was to offer assistance to the Burmese Red Cross other than in our project, and particularly to look at the work done by the young Volunteers. He and I did work together quite a lot, as U Thi La seemed happy to use me as his peripatetic deputy. Alexander and I got on very well together. He spoke good English and taught me a bit of Russian, mainly to do with drinking and toasts! His Grandfather had been one of the last Tzar's personal Cossack Guard. We corresponded for many years, and met when he came to UK on a Teacher's Course. I visited him twice in his home in Moscow, on the second occasion with Jo when we toured Russia. The letters from Moscow dried up some years ago, and I had no answer to those addressed to his home, or to the Russian Red Cross. What happened? Perhaps nothing, but with his family history one wonders.

Alexander's home in a square grey concrete block of flats in Moscow was a revelation. He had his wife were both university teachers but their apartment consisted of two rooms, with niches for the cooking and sleeping areas. They had obviously gone to a lot of trouble to entertain us, and I felt very guilty, as the shops in Moscow had only just started to westernise themselves. I have also found it strange that I could have such an instant rapport with someone with a totally different lifestyle and history and yet an equally instant distaste for my Red Cross colleague from just across the Channel. We flew Alexander to Mandalay, where he could see the Red Cross Volunteers in action at a 'Model Youth Camp' and at a Red Cross Clinic. We saw the Volunteers at work at the site of a fire, which had burned down eight hundred bamboo houses.

I also had the chance to see another 'closed' part of Burma, to visit the remains of the royal palace on its hill overlooking the town and meet some Burmese Doctors and Nurses working in this area. The last royal occupant of the palace was King Thibaw, who was deposed by the British in 1885. He was not a nice man. Disembowelling was not uncommon, and men sentenced to decapitation had to place their head on a tree stump to be stepped on by a royal elephant. I fancy this rather less than the executioner's axe on Tower Green. The Palace was wooden and was burnt to the ground in dislodging the Japanese occupants in 1945, leaving only the walls and the square moat.

We accompanied U Thi La to the site of an important statue of the Buddha. He wished to fulfil the religious rite of putting a touch of gold leaf onto the statue, which over many years and many traditional worshippers had become rather chubby from the layers of gilding. On our return journey we touched down and were able to spend a little time at the enormous and remarkable site of Pagan, on the east bank of the Irrawaddy. Pagan was the ancient capital of Burma, and a thousand years ago was one of the greatest religious centres in south-east Asia. A dense assembly of temples lined the bank of the Irrawaddy for twenty miles, and it is thought that there were over 13,000. In 1287 Kublai Kahn sacked the city, and a few years before our visit an earthquake had continued the destruction. The site was awe-inspiring nevertheless and I believe that work to repair some of earthquake damage has now been carried out. A Burmese will gain great merit by funding or helping to rebuild a pagoda, so it seems that this work will continue. Over 5,000 ruins are still identifiable. Pagan is also known as a haunt of cobras, so some care was necessary – we did not see one. This was a bit disappointing, but I later saw one being 'piped' out of sack in New Delhi.

A high level delegate from Geneva had now arrived in Rangoon. Sven was a former Colonel in the Swedish Air Force and a jet pilot, recently flying the state of the art Saab 'Draken'. He and I had much to talk about socially, and in relation to the project he was senior enough to start putting pressure on the World Food Programme people. Up to now these guys had not impressed me with their enthusiasm. One of my reports said that we felt that they were hoping that the Red Cross would, 'pull their chestnuts out of the fire'. I note that at the time I also wrote to London that in view of the energy of the WFP representatives it was no surprise that half the world was hungry.

It is perhaps worth saying that my estimate of quite a few UN people, both in Burma, Somalia and Sub-Saharan Africa was that they had been recruited to fill a quota of 'jobs for the boys.' This is a huge generalisation, and obviously not true of everyone, but I did feel, then and later, that the cap fitted a substantial minority, at that time. A further visitor of ours was Prince Konoye of the Imperial Japanese Royal Family. He was head of the Japanese Red Cross, and agreed to seek concurrence to send more fibreglass hulls. We had purchased repair kits for the first five that, being in general use showed little sign of tender loving care.

There was a downside to these helpful visits though, in that U Thi La was becoming conscious that the Government resented and were suspicious of so many foreigners. Government permission was required for every journey. He had to be very careful. The Government's preferred option was obviously to do nothing and hope that the problem of the returnees would go away before they received worldwide condemnation. However they were now being prodded, from several directions. This was my first experience of living under an oppressive, dictatorial regime, and it was not a pleasant one. We were waiting for shipments of drugs to combat disease, soap, multi-vitamins, milk powder and baby food for children. It was known that transport between Rangoon and Akyab would cease during the monsoon season, but I managed to get a promise that the Burmese Navy would help if we were stuck in this way. Over 100 tons of rice was now on its way to Arakan.

By March regular supplies had begun to arrive and the mandatory returning programme was in full swing. We had been able to set up a total of 134 feeding stations, in each of the Reception and Transit Camps and in village areas, each serving up to five villages. There were also feeding stations in the two small Hospitals. They were manned by Red Cross Volunteers trained in the field by my Swiss colleague, and U Tet Swe. The Township Councils had agreed to recruit 144 men from amongst the returnees, to help with the issue of milk to children. This, and the porterage of bulk powder and rice had to be paid for, as the men would not work for nothing although their own children were benefiting. A reworking of the budget, with sweat falling profusely onto the typewriter, made this feasible. No one had said that it would be easy!

If possible we intended to include vulnerable groups of adults such as the old, sick, and pregnant women. I do remember jumping up and down on the quayside in Rangoon, waiting for 250 tons of dried skimmed milk. This had been donated by the EEC, shipped from Hamburg in a Greek ship with an Albanian Captain, on charter to the Greek Five Star shipping line! It arrived, but a large percentage was spoiled by salt water. By early April about 100,000 Arakanese had returned from Bangladesh, and the programme was being speeded up, to get them all back before the monsoon season, roughly in May. Jurgen and U Tet Swe were also able to get the volunteers trained in basic health education and hygiene, in addition to the food care and distribution, as we had bulk soap stocks on order.

As I was due to leave in mid-April we got permission for Jurgen, who was staying until later in the year, to travel to the camps area once or twice a month. In view of the attitude towards foreigners by the Burmese Government, and as the programmes were now running with the necessary food and drugs etc coming in, it was decided that he should remain as the sole delegate. Sven was happy with our progress and reported so to Geneva.

An invitation from the Chargé d'Affaires to celebrate the Queen's birthday at the British Embassy arrived for me, but as plans were all finalised to report verbally in Geneva and London I regretfully apologised. I had earlier been invited to, and attended, a working lunch at the Embassy, so the contact for the benefit of the Burmese Red Cross had already been made. I had been working on the project planning with 'Oolie', a very pleasant Swiss employed by the UNHCR, and he threw a final party for me at his house. Next day it was time to say reluctant farewells to U Thi La and his colleagues, then to join the confused crowd at Mingaladon Airport, and try to get on the correct aeroplane to Calcutta. As we took off over the huge stupa, the white and golden bell of the Shwe Dagon pagoda, I hoped very much that I might return, but it has never been possible, and Burma is still in turmoil and beyond the bamboo curtain.

I had agreed with Geneva and London that I would take the few days leave that were owing to me on the way back, and spent a day or two in Calcutta.

This was yet another culture shock, mainly because of the opulence of some Hotels, existing side by side with pavements where whole families were living and sleeping, literally yards away. I made for the mighty Howrah Bridge over the Hoogly River, chatted to a policeman, (somewhat to his surprise) and went down to the Ghats to see the funeral pyres and the ceremonial bathing. Transport in Calcutta, apart from more or less normal cars (invariably the Morris Oxford, made under licence in India) was not by the 'tuk-tuk' but by man-powered rickshaws. Trying this I felt so bad to see the narrow underfed shoulders working away in front of me while I lay back on the padded cushions that I could not stomach it again. I have since realised that to walk instead was depriving rickshaw boys of much needed custom, and I guess that it would be acceptable to take such a ride now that I am older. Then it just seemed wrong for them to be pulling me.

My ticket had included an optional stopover in Kathmandu, and as I did not expect to get the chance to go there again (one never seems to know just what is round the corner) I caught Indian Airways to Patna next day. This was rather different to the intercontinental Air India. There was a change of aircraft there, and after walking across to the new aeroplane was totally surprised to be directed to the cockpit by the stewardess! The pilot had thought that he recognised me, and after we had sorted out who was who and who was not he let me stay there for the whole of the flight. It was that sort of airline! The first sight of the white wall of the Himalaya appearing above the still airborne aircraft was unbelievable and awe-inspiring. I have seen this wall from the air several times since, and once on a flight along the whole length of the Himalaya, from the Hindu Kush to Bhutan, but I think that the initial astonishment that anything attached to the ground could be so high will always stay with me.

We flew down into the Kathmandu Valley over the multitude of terraced hillsides, green against the white wall. Kathmandu was a small town then, in comparison to the metropolis that it has since become, and was the destination of the 'flower children'. It was unsophisticated and charming, the Nepalese Royal Family were admired and revered and communism was a remote dark cloud on the horizon. I was invited to have chikee-chips by the small child waiting on me for my first meal!

Next day I hired a dreadful old bicycle in the city centre, and managed, with a lot of hard work, to get out into the countryside. The traffic and the urban growth would make this impossible now. There were whole families on the move, from the hills down into Kathmandu. The adults and girls wore Nepalese traditional dress, the men always with the hat that was a bit like a military forage cap, but the boys usually in jeans and zippered tops. There was no problem in stopping for a chat, they seemed pleased to talk, and usually had enough English to make this possible. Going to the smallholdings perched on the hillside terraces gave me an idea of the hard life that was lived in order to scratch a living. Being free to move around Nepal like this was a privilege and a delight. Always I was conscious of the great white wall to the north, and of course was eager to see over and beyond it. In the event it took me nearly twenty five years to do so, but it was worth the wait!

All good things come to an end, and after a final meal of chikee-chips I caught a plane for Europe and Geneva. There was one development before we got airborne though, which throws some light on the delightful informality of Kathmandu in those days. An unidentified suitcase had been found. The Nepali pilot came into the passenger section, jumped up and down and announced that he was definitely, with no argument and quite positively, not going to take off until the owner came forward. Eventually he did and we lifted off and turned west, away from the beautiful white wall of fractured peaks.

Geneva was as beautiful as ever, and after three months in Asia a shock! The Disaster Relief team at the League of Red Cross Societies were complimentary about what we had been able to do, and it was with a sense of accomplishment that I returned home. It was very pleasant to get home as well!

The decision had been made that I would have to find work in the Midlands, as the weekly commuting was straining all of us, so I made this clear to the Red Cross, and accepted the fact that, while enjoying the work, and the people, it had been a mistake to think that we could move to London. Both children were doing well at school, it would have been wrong to move them and I felt that I was needed at home. There was however the design and creation of the DEC emergency control room to get on with, plus the never-ending relief work continually necessary in some part of the world. The British Red Cross could not be involved in every disaster, but played some part in providing help in many of them.

At this time I was contacted by Shizuo Sato, from Tokyo. He had been very generous and hospitable to our Malaysian friend Amarjeet when she and her Immigration Officer husband had been posted to Tokyo. Shizuo was now in London for a period for his company, and Amarjeet had given him our name. He was a splendid man, a real gentleman and it is a sadness that he died at quite an early age. I am well aware that there are many English-speaking people still alive who could never forgive the Japanese for what happened during the Second World War. Many people that I have talked to in Malaysia, Singapore and Burma feel the same. However, from the first Jo and I felt very fond indeed of Shizuo who was, I think, one of the nicest, friendliest and most thoughtful men that I have met in a well travelled life.

His wife Nori is a similar character, and though she does not speak much English we are still in touch. I would suggest, indeed insist, that what went on during the war was much more a question of class, education, upbringing, political belief, greed and jealousy than of racial characteristics. I know, and have seen, without any doubt whatsoever, that atrocious wartime conduct by some Japanese, some Nazis and other nationalities since would have been joyfully perpetrated by certain types of British men, and women, given the right circumstances.

I was able to show Shizuo, who was in London on his own, the 'must see' bits of London during the summer evenings when I was back from Burma. He fitted the traditional Japanese tourist role of being handy with his camera, and on one delightful occasion we found a group of Morris dancers, bells, whistles and all, mightily doing their thing outside a side street pub. Shizuo obviously thought that I had been able to arrange this just for his benefit. What was arranged for his benefit was a flight with myself and my flying friend Tony, when Shizuo came home with me for one weekend. Tony had the use of a Japanese four seater, a 'Fuji' from Coventry Airport, which was a very good start. It got better when we came out of cloud overhead Stratford on Avon and the camera clicked away merrily. Shizuo had been a flying instructor in the Japanese Air Force during World War Two, but this was a subject that we kept away from. Nori came to join her husband for a time, and we were very pleased indeed to have them to stay with us for a few days. The cameras were out to capture the Staffordshire pub reputed to be either the family home of Dick Whittington and his cat, or the starting point of their journey. We all enjoyed as well a visit to The Crooked House, a pub so disfigured by mining subsidence that a marble will run apparently uphill on a tabletop. The pub is still open and licensed, but one feels drunk before sampling their wares.

Shizuo visited us also with his daughter Urara when she came for a holiday in London, and we took both of them to see a cricket match at Wolverhampton Cricket Club. I am certain that my trying to explain what was going on would have made a good scene for a Two Ronnies sketch! Shizuo, who was a very westernised man, was totally baffled and Urara's expression was a thing of wonder. We bought her a tea towel inscribed with the rules of cricket to take home to Tokyo. I am certain that it was never, ever understood, and helped to confirm the legend that the English are all bonkers.

Work and pleasure. Japan and Hong Kong

Shizuo and Nori repaid our hospitality many times over when we stayed in their home in Tokyo in 1988, en-route back from a working visit to Hong Kong. We spent three weeks in Japan, and for part of this stayed in their home in Setagaya-Ku, one of the huge Tokyo districts. This was a great honour, and, I have learned, unusual, and not experienced by many Europeans. Urara performed the tea ceremony for me there, in traditional costume, kimono and obi, which was a great experience, and also an honour. Shizuo's niceness was shown by his having met us as we arrived, and a Japanese doll holding a Union Jack placed in our bedroom. He insisted on taking us for a meal into a traditional restaurant to make sure that we understood the menu and the ordering procedures and general etiquette. Thanks to this we were able to cope with ordering Japanese meals for the rest of our stay, learning to look at the pictures of the meals on offer displayed in restaurant windows.

He came to our Hotel the next morning to help plan our visit, and then we explored central Tokyo, walking round the Imperial Palace and getting a meal in the very glamorous (and expensive) Ginza. Traffic was very heavy, but the Japanese drivers actually stopped for pedestrians – this is unique in most big cities outside the UK. There was no litter, no graffiti, public transport ran absolutely on time, and everyone seemed very eager to be of assistance. If we stood looking at a timetable or ticket machine inevitably someone would ask if they could help, usually in good, perhaps American accented, English. Courtesy seemed to be, then and there, a way of life, a culture of kindness and friendship, even in one of the biggest cities in the world.

We had chosen to visit in blossom time, which was breathtakingly beautiful, with cherry and peach blossom, azaleas and irises everywhere that they could be placed. Land was, and I expect still is, very expensive in Tokyo, so green spaces as we know them were few, but every corner had a pot plant or tiny tree or small rocks. And none of it appeared to be vandalised. There were many obviously new multi-story buildings, banks and office blocks, and every so often a shrine or temple, providing a sense of tranquillity in the bustle of the city. They were a mixture of Shinto, Buddhist and Zen Buddhist, tolerant of each other. Shizuo and Nori had a shrine in their home, in memory of their parents, and he explained that if he had worries he would spend time in front of it, to compose his mind. We found that the older, traditional houses reminded us of Victorian British railway signal boxes, very small, taller than they were wide and very close together. In older areas there were no street names and no house numbers, so taking a taxi was a problem if one did not know the way! We did cope unexpectedly well with the Underground, which is of course vast. This was somewhat to the horror of Shizuo's family and friends!

We then took ourselves off on an expedition to Fujiyama, by coach, and were driven up to the snow line. It is a mountain that I would have liked to climb, but this was not on the itinerary, so we had a pleasant night in the Mount Fuji Hotel, over three thousand feet high on the slopes. We had stunning views of the snow capped peak. Next day was a cruise in a 'Pirate ship' on Lake Hakone and then a cable car up Mount Komagatake. This is a resort area, in a National Park, and very beautiful, with the graceful, world-famed, silhouette of Mount Fuji at the head of one valley.

After a night in our hotel in Tokyo we caught the Shinkasen, the bullet train, to Kyoto. At that time it was the fastest train in the world, and we saw the speedometer in our carriage reach 140 mph! Actually this was not that exciting, because the journey was so smooth that the speed did not seem excessive, it was much more like flying low, and it was comfortable to eat and drink.

I had booked a room in a traditional hotel, a Ryokan, from England, by telephone with some difficulty! No web sites in those days! The room was minute, a bit like being in a bamboo tent, with a rush mat floor and sliding paper screens, and of course a futon to sleep on. Our shoes were left at the door, and flip-flops provided, with a different pair for the bathroom. We had breakfast in the kitchen with the family, sitting on very low stools with our knees round our ears. Kyoto was the capital of Japan until the nineteenth century. The city centre is full of temples and pagodas, more than two thousand of them, ranging from the brilliantly decorated ones to the very restrained Ryoanji Temple with it's Zen Buddhist rocks and manicured white sand garden. Cherry blossom and pools full of water lilies were everywhere.

One highlight was to see the Cherry Blossom Dances in the Gion Geisha District, where all the traditional theatres of Kyoto live. Two Geisha training schools and rows of wooden houses with red lanterns also live there. We saw the actresses tottering along in costume, on enormously high platformed shoes. We spent a large part of the two days in Kyoto strolling round or just sitting and looking at the gardens and temples.

We found in both Tokyo and Kyoto that at least in one respect our guidebook was absolutely accurate. It had advised us that Japanese children were to be found in every interesting place, and apparently never in parties of less than a thousand! Those of school age all seemed to be wearing a blue sailor's type of uniform and all intent on practising their English language skills on us, the most visible Europeans around. It was usually the girls who plucked up courage first, then the boys joined in, with choruses of 'Harro, Harro,' followed by fits of giggles. We decided that we should be featuring in several school projects, as we had to sign a number of schoolwork books, with questions to answer, and pose for group photographs. We met one lot in three different places and were greeted like long-lost friends! Of course we were noticeable, being taller than almost everyone else, and a novelty, certainly in the non-tourist areas around Shizuo and Nori's house. I wonder if, through the shrinking of the world by much more tourism and the increase of films, TV and travel by the Japanese, this sense of novelty has been lost. I hope not, because they were so polite and nice. It was great fun, rewarding and good for international relationships. It does seem a little strange that there were so few Europeans to be seen in Tokyo, in the height of the blossom season. Anyhow I think that we were lucky to have been able to make the effort to go when we did, and have it almost to ourselves.

I had particularly wanted to visit Okinawa, the scene of some fierce fighting in world war two, and we managed this next, with the airport ground handlers standing in line to wave the aircraft off! We quickly found ourselves flying in through a tropical thunderstorm. As many passengers did not appreciate the storm one hostess gave a display of origami to keep the children happy. There were only four Europeans on the Jumbo so we got a special announcement in English! There was a big American military presence still on the island, with some pretty disastrous concrete reconstruction work in the towns, where the scars of world war two were very visible. The Hotel that we had booked was delightful however, with a foyer full of orchids.

I was easily able to rent a car for a couple of days, so we saw most of the main island. Everywhere were hibiscus, bougainvillea, - think of a sub-tropical flower and it was there – plus roses and jasmine, mixed in with pineapple plantations and surviving in 95% humidity. The battle sites were now grown over in colour, leaving only the man-made to bear the blemishes. While flying back to Tokyo we had a glorious view of Southern Japan from 25,000 feet, with Mount Fuji well visible. This must have been something like the view seen by the crew of the B25 bomber Enola Gay, 43 years earlier, before they changed the world for ever.

Our first day back in Tokyo was a Saturday, and Shizuo, Nori and Urara met us at the Hotel, for what was an obviously carefully planned day out. We went to a traditional Kabuki Theatre and the Ginza again, then a very glamorous department store, Mitsukoshi, partnered with Harrods. They had timed our arrival to hear the daily lunchtime concert given on a huge Wurlitzer organ, then after considerable giggling between Mother and Daughter we went up several escalators to find ourselves in a replica of Fortnum and Mason's, strawberries and cream and waitresses with frilly lace caps et al! Next day we went with them to join the holiday crowd at the Sensoji Temple. This is an area of old Tokyo, carefully preserved with tiny wooden shops in narrow streets. We were the only Westerners. We had lunch in a traditional restaurant, with our own private room. This had paper and bamboo panels, a rush matting floor, flat cushions and tables about ten inches high! The panels could be slid aside to give a view of the gardens. Food was beautifully cooked at the table by waitresses in kimonos, and eaten of course, by chopsticks. The beef, suki-yaki, was sliced thinly enough to be transparent.

Next day we were on our own before moving to Shizuo and Nori's home, so decided to travel to Kamakura by the Underground and a local train. It is the home of the famous forty foot high bronze Buddha which sits doing what Buddhas do best – looking very inscrutable, ageless and timeless, although he is eight hundred years old. We had a great day pottering around the town, which is a smaller, less self-conscious version of Kyoto.

We were picked up next day by Shizuo to take us to his home in Setagayu-Ku. This was quite a journey. Tokyo is a huge conurbation, dwarfing London, and five cities in one. We were rather apprehensive about the visit, and he was also worried that we would think his home very small. Nori was afraid that we would not like their food. In fact, Jo wrote in her diary, 'none of us need have worried, it was a very special experience. They spared no effort to make us comfortable and to help us appreciate something of their culture - far more than the average tourist would be able to be aware of.' Their home was half western, a fitted kitchen, western plumbing and beds and a large lounge area divided by sliding bamboo panels. One end had comfortable western furniture but the other was a very simple Japanese room, with a rush floor, flower arrangements and their small family shrine.

We met most of their extended family, and some neighbours, at a meal in this room, all of whom expressed their astonishment that we had ventured onto the Tokyo railway on our own to go to Kamakura. Perhaps it was a potential step too far! Everyone was so friendly and seemed to be genuinely pleased to welcome us. We had several more days seeing the beauty of Tokyo in blossom time, and at one temple were lucky enough to see a wedding celebration and ceremonial procession in traditional robes between a Japanese girl and an American man. I wonder if it has lasted. One of the last days out was for all of us to go to Yokohama, to the Chinatown area, waterfront and docks. We watched a Russian cruise liner arrive and disembark and laughed at the elderly (rich) ladies being taken into a store to try on white kimonos. Laughed because Urara explained that a white kimono is for a young virgin! On the way back to Tokyo Urara was keen to visit Tokyo Disneyland, so we did. The nighttime parade, including fireworks and lasers was pretty good and the rest of it was, shall we say, interesting.

We had had a really wonderful three weeks in Japan, and I think that we were all affected when it was time to say goodbye. We only saw Shizuo once again, when he came to the UK to visit Urara and her husband Takeo. We have been able to keep in touch by post with Nori. A pleasing thing was that Urara and Takeo came to the UK for a time as part of his business, during the nineteen nineties and, their son Satoshi was born here. We were able to visit them a number of times and had some enjoyable days out together.

I looked at the Tokyo traffic with a professional eye, and thought that it ran pretty well. It was not too difficult to drive provided that one knew where one was going! Some of the major direction signs were in English but not the local ones. Filling stations were interesting, as there were invariably four or five attendants waiting to serve in order of seniority. No shortage of manpower. We were usually bowed off the forecourt, and seen out into the main road by two more. I wondered if they did this for everyone, or did I just look incompetent? Traffic was very fast between the many traffic lights, but respectful of both signs and pedestrians, rather like German traffic movement. There were some very busy four-lane in each direction expressways. I would very much like to see Tokyo again to find out what has changed, but this is firmly on the back burner. The pleasure was of course, the hospitality and friendship and the very different culture. I think that our main surprise was the unremitting politeness, and tidiness, the fact we seemed to be two of a very few Westerners, and that we both felt so large!

Our route home was the Great Circle Route across the polar ice cap and just to the south of the North Pole. (Everywhere around the pole is to the south!) We stopped for a refuelling break at Anchorage, and were able to leave the aircraft for a substantial time, enough to appreciate the Alaskan scenery at ground level. The next two to three hours after take off were a vista of continuous and blinding white ice and snow, corrugated into great hills and valleys, well visible even from 25-30,000 feet. The weather and visibility were gin clear and by standing up it was possible to get a very privileged view of the Pole and it's environs from one of the rear door windows.

It was not until then that I realised just how big the Artic is. I know that it is getting smaller now, but there is still an awful lot of it. Probably the most difficult thing was trying to get into our heads what day it was. Having changed time zones we were both totally disorientated and it required a lady who had joined the aircraft in Anchorage to tell us what day we were due to reach Heathrow! Funnily enough this did not happen travelling across the International Date Line in the South Pacific years later – maybe I was already disorientated then by being upside down! The route continued over Greenland, grim and inhospitable, Iceland on the horizon away to port and eventually the Hebrides. We did reach the UK on the correct day – the journey was a wonderful end to a wonderful month.

We had been able to arrange the visit to Japan to follow a short visit to one of the largest driving schools in the world, in Hong Kong. It was reputed to be the second largest! I was invited to see their equipment, policies and procedures in 1988 as part of my work as Chief Driving Examiner for the Royal Society for the Prevention of Accidents I had become friendly with the School's Managing Director, Adrian, a former Gurkha Officer, whilst he was on a UK visit. Jo and I decided to kill two very big birds with one stone, flung a long distance!

Hong Kong, with a break in Dubai, is a long way, but flying into the old airport, then still in use, with it's runway out into the bay, and tower blocks above wing tip height was of much interest to me as a pilot. Adrian had shown Gurkha developed admin skills (he had been a member of an Army Everest expedition) and we were met by limousine, taken to our Hotel and found a huge bunch of flowers plus an itinerary for our visit. I remember that we were through immigration and customs and in our Hotel in about fifteen minutes.

Hong Kong then, still very much British, had an overwhelming vitality. Everything was biggest, newest or most expensive. The peace and tranquillity of parts of Japan did not exist. I had trained in the UK with quite a few colonial police officers, going to Hong Kong amongst other Commonwealth Countries like Southern Rhodesia. Although there was no time to look any of them up it was quite comforting to know that they were around. As Adrian had left us a free evening to get our breath back we rushed off to get on the Star Ferry across to Hong Kong Island. This ties for first place with the Staten Island Ferry off the Battery Park in Manhattan as the best twenty five cents value in the world. It had been an absolute priority of mine since reading Richard Mason's 'The World of Suzie Wong'. Staten Island has the Statue of Liberty and the inimitable Manhattan skyline, while the Star Ferry has the Peak rising up behind Hong Kong, Victoria Harbour and the vibrancy of the activity on both shores and the barely believable buildings. Add the watercraft of all sorts, from ocean liners to Chinese junks scurrying around like water beetles, with families living on board, and I'm sure you get the idea. The Star Ferry even has two classes, upper and lower decks for a twenty cent difference. The time to go, particularly from the Kowloon side, is at night when the Peak is a blaze of coloured lights, the buildings are all lit up and the Wanchai waterfront is a riot of activity and movement.

Next morning we were collected from our hotel and driven to the Jockey Club to meet Adrian and his staff for lunch. Horse racing and gambling is a way of life in Hong Kong and the Jockey Club is quite an important place – the last word in affluence. A big party was assembled to meet us, mainly

Chinese, including a senior police officer, a couple of Magistrates and some road safety experts. The RoSPA name obviously carried some weight! After a long oriental meal we went to the Driving School, which had acres of land - manoeuvring and simultaneous training space for cars, motor cycles and large goods vehicles, even some artificial slopes. Indoors were dozens of classrooms all with the latest electronics It was extremely impressive, and very useful to me professionally.

In the evening Jo and I set about trying to see Hong Kong properly. We took a taxi to the top of the Peak to see the view in daylight, then stayed for a meal and watched the millions of lights, on land and on water, come flickering on. We came down on the very steep mountain railway where all the seats face backwards to stop one falling out. The surrounding skyscrapers look as though they have been built at 45 degrees, as the carriages are not stacked but run parallel to the track. One Chinese lady was quite overcome, and covered her face with her coat until we reached the bottom. We finished off a pretty good day with a cruise around the harbour followed by coffee in the Chinese version of a Viennese coffee shop.

I had also wanted to see the old Portuguese port of Macau - reputedly once the wickedest place in the Far East, haunt of pirates and drugs, so we got a hydrofoil from Victoria Harbour. Macau was a contrast to Hong Kong, crumbling and dilapidated, but still bearing traces of faded beauty. It was interesting to see the old colonial houses, very grand at one time, but now declining into their old age. We soon decided that Macau, wicked or not, did not compare with Hong Kong, and returned in time to be collected - again - to meet Adrian and his Chinese wife, his partner and Phillipino wife and his Canadian colleague. Dinner was in the Hong Kong Club in Wanchai, very imposing, very well heeled and very enjoyable. We all had different backgrounds, and different views about nearly everything, so the conversation flowed easily and interestingly, covering most subjects under the sun!

This was part of a way of life that was coming to an end, at least for the expatriate British. I would really like to know how much it has changed for the Chinese. Somehow, I suspect, not too much. Unfortunately to find out has to be back burner again. Adrian could see the way that things were likely to go, and later emigrated to start another company in Canada and sadly we lost touch with him. However, I shall always be grateful to him for what must have been some of our most exciting days, and best dinner parties ever.

After the above digression to Hong Kong, Japan and the Arctic, I have to now rewind to the last year of my time with the Red Cross in Grosvenor Crescent. The Burma job had gone well I believe, and I continued with the relief co-ordination work for the rest of that year, making a lot of contact with various Government and UNHCR departments. The DEC disasters committee control room was also planned and a room adapted for it. However, I did not like the 'penthouse' flat in Goldhawk Road, felt that I was wasting time and that a move back to the Midlands was becoming pressing. As we got into 1978 Shizuo made contact with me, and it was enjoyable to spend a number of Spring and early Summer evenings showing him around London. In June the League of Red Cross Societies in Geneva asked the British Red Cross if they would fund three months for me to act as Chief Delegate in the rapidly worsening refugee situation in Somalia. They said, 'Yes,' and I said, 'Yes,' as this was what I had joined the Red Cross for. Somalia – the fabled and mythical land of Punt.

The War in Somalia

The situation had arisen because of the disputed border area, between eastern Ethiopia and northern Somalia. Ethiopia had launched repeated air attacks to try to end the Somali support for the guerrillas, the 'Liberation Front' in the arid desert region of the Ogaden. The fear of persecution or of being killed had caused the nomadic tribespeople who normally inhabit the Ogaden to leave their normal roaming patterns and head for safety in Somalia. The artificial boundary between Ethiopia and Somalia, like many of the boundaries in the north east of Africa, runs much in straight lines.

Northern Somalia was formerly the Protectorate of British Somaliland, and the south had been Italian Somalia. A belt of land was taken from Kenya and ceded to Italy following the First World War in 1924. The awful artificial boundaries had been imposed by the European powers, and they had now become irrelevant. We, the Europeans, had drawn some straight lines on a map and effectively said, 'That side is Somalia, that side is Ethiopa'. (Naiveté again?) We ignored the tribal distribution, wells, rivers, nomadic patterns, or best grazing and expected it to work. The dissent and bitterness has gone on ever since. For the Ethiopians this was a colonial war, trying to hold onto the Ogaden, supported by Russia and Cuba.

We, the British, were guilty of similar naïveté during the partition of India, when we tried to separate Hindu from Muslim using outdated maps. Half a million died then and twelve million were re-located. We rescued Mesopotamia, 'The land between the rivers' from Turkish domination during the First World War. Then in 1927 we took an amalgam of Shias, Sunnis and Kurds, cobbled them together and called it Iraq. The result is with us today. Individual colonial servants did unbelievably magnificent things in the eighteenth to twentieth centuries. However, time after time one can see how they were betrayed by their political masters by lack of thought, lack of planning and foresight and just – naïveté. I had experienced some of these faults in my own dealings with the Foreign Office in the twentieth century. For thousands of years tribal laws, customs and cultures have developed to suit desert climates and nomadic life, and it is impossible to change these in a generation. One of the great men of the twentieth century, Lawrence of Arabia, tried to warn the British Government of this, amongst other things, and was pilloried and driven into virtual exile as a result.

As a result of the travel that I have been able to do and the people that I have been able to meet, I do not have a great opinion of Governments, of whatever political colour. My notes made in Somalia record that I identified the country as one of the worst places in the world, certainly the poorest. At that time, outside the few towns, there were no schools, no doctors, no law. Boys and girls were likely to be circumcised with a sharp stone, a piece of broken glass or the sharp edge of a tin, and the girls repaired with the long thorns from a camel thorn bush. TB was common, measles a killer and typhus broke out regularly. The educated top class left the country for better conditions in Jeddah and Mecca, and even in Mogadishu there were few modern drugs or effective hospital treatment. The Government was kept in power by the army and police. The bare and arid Ogaden, where the fighting took place, was fit only for use as camel grazing land, with little water, no minerals, no industry, no farms, no nothing. But to a lot of nomadic people it was their home.

In 1978 the whole Ogaden area was disputed, with the complication that Communism was seeking a toehold in Africa. Russian and Cuban advisors to Ethiopia, plus their weapons and military aircraft stirred the pot. Some aid workers were shelled by Communist troops and I found a crashed Russian Mig fighter on one of my journeys. Estimates of the number of people on the move ranged from a million to a million and a half. It was impossible to get a closer estimate, as no reliable population figures had been kept by the Somali Government.

It was thought that uncounted nomadic thousands had moved into Somalia from Ethiopia. Certain was the fact that at least three quarters of a million displaced people existed in the temporary camps set up inside Somalia, with a daily inflow averaging about 600. Many more were living nomadically outside the camps. Some had walked hundreds of miles, even south into Kenya from Ethiopia then east to reach Somalia. Whilst being used to walking they had done so without normal food supplies or their usual watering places, for as much as a month. The elderly and children were malnourished and often suffering from sores and ulcerated legs.

Further exacerbating the situation was the fact that they were used to living in small family groups, or a small village, and suddenly found themselves living cheek by jowl in a camp town of perhaps 60,000 people. Many active men, having seen their dependents to relative safety, then left to join the guerrilla liberation front, or were made to do so by the Somali police and army. Therefore the camps were populated mainly by women, children and the elderly. This was described by the Red Cross as part of one of the worst refugee situations ever, with millions of people on foot, crossing and re-crossing Africa. It was made even more desperate by the drought that gripped much of East Africa. Somalia was, and is, one of the world's poorest countries in terms of wealth and natural resources, and was desperately in need of help and an end to the drought.

The Somali Red Crescent Society (the equivalent of the Red Cross in a Muslim country) were responsible for servicing four of the Transit Camps in the border areas, where newcomers spent a few nights before being moved into a semi-permanent Refugee Camp. The camps consisted of round beehive huts, made of branches and, if they were lucky, sacking or cardboard. A few tents were starting to appear, with bigger tents usable as medical centres.

It quickly became apparent after my arrival that, as in Burma, the Government did not want to know about this major problem at their front door. Heads were firmly in the sand. 'They walked here, they can walk away again' is a fair approximation of common attitudes. The regular Somali army and police were believed by expatriates already on site to be untrustworthy and unreliable. In fact I found that the army had stolen food at gunpoint from the refugee camps and confirmed that the police had forced some refugees to join the Liberation Front. The situation was generally very confused, not helped by a plethora of western aid agencies, in some cases competing with each other, without properly defined roles. People were trying to help the situation, I am sure in most cases for the best of reasons. It was however totally and absolutely uncoordinated, with aid agencies getting in each other's way or each trying to do the same job. Food was being taken cross-country over hundreds of miles of virtual desert, and through an area where the Somali President's tribe and relatives were in positions of influence and power. I found that supplies were being stolen, in this way also but it could not be proved or challenged. Somalia was a very tribal society. Nationalism, the concept of the State, in this case created out of two colonial dependencies, was a comparative irrelevance.

I was asked to travel to Mogadishu, the Somali capital, via Geneva, to be briefed by the Head of the Relief Operations Bureau. The briefing, relating to some of the problems outlined above, did not fill me with any hope that this would be an easy job, but Geneva, as always, was a pleasure. I met my designated assistant at the League offices, a young Norwegian former army officer, Per, (or Peter) and we flew to Mogadishu together.

The town came as a pleasant surprise, not so run down as Rangoon, at least in the newer central area. There was a vivid outlook from my hotel room, with a lot of green trees, and the blue, violet and green Indian Ocean broken by the spray of white waves on a reef. The red white and blue French tricolour flying from the French Embassy was also colourfully in view I was quickly to find that the green area around the town was very small indeed, and the old city was dreadful, barefoot children playing in filth, sewage, and crumbling tenements and many terribly deprived people. It was a snapshot of medieval squalor. Two other Scandinavians, a Danish Major on loan from his army to the U.N.H.C.R. and a Swedish Doctor advising the Somali Government, met Per and I. As we arrived on Friday, rest day, the whole town was comatose and there was nothing to do except settle in. (Twenty Somali shillings to the room maid produced a bedside light)! There are 2000 miles of white beach running down to Kenya, so we had a look at it. It was not very crowded. The reef, about four hundred yards offshore with huge white breakers marking it, kept the sharks out, - mostly. A fisherman was just coming in with his catch, huge lobsters easily a foot long. The Doctor invited us to eat lobster at his house later that day. The evening was a success, and the lobsters, which he cooked himself were beautiful, once the way into them had been found. A peaceful prelude to problems in plenty.

Local people in Mogadishu spoke a mixture of Arabic, Somali and Italian and it was quite strange to be discussing spaghetti in Italian with the very ancient dark skinned little waiter. The hotel, which was a Russian gift before they were ordered to leave the country, had a beautifully laid out swimming pool in the garden. As the filtration plant did not work it had never had any water in it. I did get some hot water in my room after about a month, but the radio set persisted in falling out of the wall!

The Somali Red Crescent Society also came as a surprise, but not this time a pleasant one.

Compared to the strong and intelligent leadership shown in Burma by U Thi La, the Somali Society was weak, disorganised and virtually ineffectual. There were only two full time staff, with the majority of the administration work devolved upon the Accountant who was very much overworked. The General Secretary was a medical Doctor, and obviously thought that this post, and certainly the administration of it, was well beneath him. There seemed to be no effective volunteer structure as in Europe, and neither of the full time men had volunteered, but had been posted to the Red Crescent by the Ministry of Health. They could not be expected to show the volunteer commitment found elsewhere; it was a system that was terribly flawed.

It was also understandable that there was little or no interest in their activities by the general Somali population, for whom just surviving was a continuous day to day struggle. My urgent recommendation was that assistance to the Society should be funded, either by Geneva or by donation from a European Society. This was beginning to happen by the time I left three months later. The Society had no income other than a very small Government grant. No fund raising had been attempted, and on our arrival their only telephone had been cut off due to non-payment of the bill. Other Somali bodies involved in the relief operation were, I soon found, similarly ineffective. The newly formed National Refugee Commission was subordinate to the Minister of Local Government, and the Commissioner, whilst a pleasant man, was not strong enough to press his priorities. When the N.R.C. was set up other Somali Government Departments were asked to supply staff, and it was very obvious that human nature had taken over, and people who were not wanted were dumped there to get rid of them.

It was not a pleasure to find that my French bête-noire from Burma was in Somalia for a time to take official photographs for Geneva. His pictures of the camps and refugees were very professional and evocative, but he managed to upset the Red Crescent personnel by interfering, and was a nuisance in several ways. Fortunately he did not stay very long.

It appeared that the U.N.H.C.R. had not appreciated the seriousness of the Ogaden crisis and had left their mission in Mogadishu struggling with limited staff and resources. This later began to improve, with expatriate secretaries being brought in. The local girls whom they replaced had neither the training nor experience to organise efficient procedures, and when we arrived there was still a way to go.

A further factor which was quickly apparent was that the Somalis had opened the door to far too many organisations on the fringes of charity or relief work. The bigger ones, Oxfam and Save the Children for example, were of course working well with good programmes and staff. Others such as 'Food for the Hungry' started and run by a former Hollywood film star had very suspect methods, and personnel who were seen behaving in a less than desirable manner. They had caused a riot at one point by simply throwing sacks of food off the back of a lorry.

Another problem was that these organisations were all offering different rates of pay to labourers, so this urgently needed rationalisation. There was a contradiction, a paradox in that skilled expatriate workers were needed, but that those already there were putting a strain on services, increasing the high inflation rate and causing damage to the country. The one available outgoing telex in Mogadishu was in use 24 hours a day and flights to the north of the country had to be booked weeks in advance. Prostitution, oddly in a Muslim country, was known to be increasing in Mogadishu, for which expatriate relief workers and journalists were mainly to blame. The obvious solution was to exclude the fringe groups and confine the relief work to the bigger agencies, who could perhaps better control their employees and put donations to more efficient use. It seemed to be too late to do this.

My observations in a letter home soon after our arrival were that the influx of visitors was spoiling the local population. Inflation was at 60%, taxi fares rose every day and there was much begging and obvious prostitution. There were twenty different relief organisations in Mogadishu with ten more trying to get in. Some of these, I commented, were apparently there only in order to wear a uniform and drive a big American car. Neither the U.N.H.C.R. nor the Somali Government, I observed, appeared to have any idea of what was going on or what needed to be done. There was little common sense to be found.

A major problem not caused by the human factors was the very large distances involved. From the capital and seat of Government, Mogadishu, to the main town of the former British Somaliland, Hargeisa, was nine hundred to a thousand miles by surface transport. Because of the way in which the borders had been drawn it was necessary to take a huge dogleg to avoid going into the disputed Ethiopian territory. The transit and permanent camps were spread along the length of this border, currently being fought over. The journey took 22 hours solid driving by four-wheel drive car and over a week by lorry carrying food or other supplies. We quickly decided that Per should be based in Hargeisa to control the Red Crescent operation there, and we flew up to find a suitable headquarters for him.

The activities there were currently minimal, and it was part of his job to build up teams. He was able to rent a house as living quarters and a base. This was actually cheaper that his staying in the very unsuitable hotel accommodation. With only two ports available for food to enter Somalia, Mogadishu and Berbera, getting food and other essential supplies to the remote camps in the north was a huge problem. The shipping lines preferred to use Mogadishu as it had much better facilities, but it was now thoroughly congested. It was hoped that the use of Berbara could be increased by improving the facilities through a Somali-American military agreement but this was some way in the future.

Because of the transport problems, and theft, not enough food was reaching the camps in a consistent pattern to provide a balanced diet. The ill, the old, the children, the weary or injured needed a balanced diet. This should be made up of a staple, usually a cereal, probably maize. Then protein is needed, fish, eggs or more usually pulses. The third part of the food basket is vitamins, vegetables or fruit and finally an energy supplement, for example edible oil. All these constituents are needed to provide satisfactory feeding in a refugee situation, but in Somalia only part of the basket had been arriving regularly. This meant that they could only be fed on perhaps the staple of maize. Over the long term this would bring the people, and particularly the children, to the knife-edge of illness and starvation.

To illustrate the problem of the food transport, imagine taking a twenty-ton lorry from London to the far north of Scotland. There is an all-weather road only as far as Birmingham, and no fuel or repair facilities north of Carlyle. The driver is unreliable, may give up half way or sell the food, and the lorry clapped out. The analogy is correct. The food cannot be flown in sufficient quantity, there are no roads to bring it in from Kenya, and there's a war on the Ethiopian border. It cannot be grown in Somalia. Food, including milk powder for the children, was coming into the country, through Mogadishu, but was rotting in the docks or still on-board ship.

What to do?

It did not take a genius to see that logistics was the over-riding problem to be solved.

One of the urgent priorities therefore was to put a professional transport team in place – people who knew what they were doing and what the problems were. The Disasters Emergency Committee had made a big combined appeal for public donations for this crisis, so I took the unusual and unconventional step of writing direct to Sir Evelyn Shuckburgh, the Chairman of the Council of the British Red Cross. I proposed to him that a British transport team be funded from the proceeds of the appeal. I was never overtly criticised for this direct approach, but I know that it did ruffle a few feathers.

However, it, or perhaps 'it' amongst others, had a result, as eventually we got our professional team, of officers, transport specialists from the British Army. They focused on transport planning, port clearance, warehousing, stock control, and despatching. Most importantly was training their Somali replacements so that a full transport management team could be formed. This took time, of course, to get into place, but it eventually happened, with about thirty camp commodity officers checking on the food train, that food was arriving correctly at the camps, and overseeing the fair distribution. I have always felt that there was so much that it was impossible to do, or to do properly, and so much time was wasted in just trying to tie up loose ends, but I was, and still am, pleased about this result. The British Red Cross was now also donating equipment and funding a very excellent Nurse to work in the camps.

A third port available was Djibouti, the tiny republic of the same name – the country of the Issars and Afars on the northern Somali border. As it was an independent state however one immediately ran into customs delays in getting the vehicles or anything else from there into Somalia at Hargeisa. It could take up to a two months to clear a much needed vehicle through customs, involving visits to no less than twenty six different offices. Each visit must be in the correct order with the sheaf of correct clearance papers, also in the correct order, stamped and signed at the previous office. What drove Europeans into symptoms of apoplexy was the 'one man, one key' syndrome. If a man had not come to work, which was a frequent occurrence, no one else would do his job, or would even touch his desk. It became like a game of snakes and ladders. Up to office number sixteen all was well. But at number seventeen the correct man was not there. He was either ill, having a sickie or just gone walkabout. 'Oh, he not come to work today. Maybe tomorrow, - maybe not. You come back, okay?' The nominated officials for the following forms would not sign, out of turn. And there was nothing to do but slide down the snake and start again tomorrow.

There was however, one quickly learned, a way round it. A payment would miraculously speed up the process. I had flown up to Hargeisa at one point to try to hustle up the release of some urgently needed Toyota Land Cruisers. Seeing no other way, and although it was distasteful, I offered what was in fact a bribe. I had quite a lot of funds available for just such a need, which unfortunately does occur in Africa.

But, I said, 'I have to account for the money to my masters in Geneva.'

'No problem, I will give you a receipt!'

So, I have, carefully preserved and brought out at talks about Africa, the photocopy of a receipt for a bribe. It rejoices in the following words and spellings, 'Jamuruyada Dimoqraada Soomaaliyeed 4.8.80. This expenses under mationed expenses has been paid for the offices of customs of Hargesa 200/shillin, we paid other 200/expenses for the civilian trnsprt offices with out reciet means for the felexcibility of formatives total 400/shillin'.

Stamped and signed! What an absolutely superb phrase 'Flexibility of formalities'.

Job done, with absolutely no bad conscience on my part. One could argue that if no one were prepared to pay a bribe the custom would die out. However as many lives were at stake and the practice was so deeply rooted as to be ineradicable, I have never felt guilty. I will go on shortly to describe how some blackmail was necessary to feed a thousand people in one of the camps, and I don't feel guilty about that either!

There is one other true story involving Djibouti and desert vehicles that happened while I was there. There was at that time one railway line running from the port up to Addis Ababa via Dire Dawa. It carried one train a week. The train passed over only one level crossing. The Djibouti Red Crescent had only one Land Rover. No, they couldn't have? Yes, they did! It must have been very difficult to arrange, but they did. This does seem to be an almost unattainable concurrence of times, lines and angles, but it is also quite possible, if you try hard enough, to have two desert vehicles meet head on at the crest of a high dune, with no other vehicles within fifty miles!

The work that I had been able to do in Mogadishu itself seemed to consist of trying to get everyone to work together. It was obvious that the Red Cross/Red Crescent remit needed to be wider than just dealing with the four Transit Camps, in order to try to co-ordinate the unco-ordinated. It was extremely frustrating since none of the locals wanted, or perhaps to be fair, were able, to work very hard. The representatives of the other big organisations, like Oxfam, saw the same priorities as myself. We had regular meetings of fifteen of the agencies working to provide food in the camps, one major problem always being how to fund the movement from Mogadishu. It cost more per ton to move supplies from Mogadishu to Hargeisa than to ship it to Mogadishu from the USA or Europe. This, until the transport teams got into place, was due to the very long distances involved, profiteering by the private owners of the lorries, theft, corruption and general mismanagement. I worked out that to supply a very basic issue of 595 grammes of food per day to every refugee would need 33 trucks covering over 21,000 km and using over 12,000 litres of diesel per day. Although much money was being donated by Germany, the Scandinavian countries and the USA the shortfall was immense, and at first it was not possible to see how it could be met. The Somali Government was effectively broke, and going into massive debt.

After a lot of arm-twisting in Government departments eventually the situation began to stabilise, with the immediate emergency feeding under control. It was now possible to start making some longer-term plans. The publicity in Europe had resulted in a lot of donations, the Scandinavian Red

Cross Societies being particularly generous. I hosted a visit from the President of the Norwegian Red Cross, who, of course, wanted to see Per, their funded delegate in Hargeisa. We managed to get two seats on a plane and he and I travelled together. The Norwegians wanted to help in other ways, and I remember sitting up, almost through the night, in Per's house discussing what form further help should take. The President was adamant that it should be something easily photographed, like blankets, whilst I was equally positive that it should be training, seeds and tools. His argument was that something easily photographed and capable of good publicity would reassure his donors that positive use was being made of their money. They needed to know that it was not being spent unwisely, and would then be more likely to contribute again. He did have a valid point because due to ill informed, or perhaps even malicious, media comment there was then a public perception of donations being used to fund high salaries or expensive administration.

My contrasting stance was that these people, who had fled with nothing, desperately needed to be encouraged, and to have the possibility, and capability, of taking up their normal life again. Both views were, of course, right. Being the President, and holding the purse strings, he was always going to win the argument, but we did come to some sort of compromise and eventually received both the blankets and the tools, from one source or another. This sort of question is an intellectual dilemma in all relief work. Since there are not that many people with the ability or motivation to spend months abroad without salary, a proportion of the funds available have to be spent on staff costs. With a young family I certainly could not have done so without an income. The salary, whilst it should not be excessive, has to be sufficient to attract the right calibre of person. The old saying that if you give peanuts you get monkeys is as true in relief aid as in anything else.

Also, the dreadful mess of a situation in Somalia before we all got to grips with it shows what happens if the administration is not done properly. Proper admin also costs money. Unfortunately the donors who provide the funds were not encouraged to see it like this. It seemed that they tended to believe irresponsible and untrue tabloid press talk about waste and donations spent on high salaries. The provision of blankets or similar artefacts therefore has much to recommend it, since training is much more difficult to quantify or publicise attractively.

There is, as well, a spin off to this expenditure, as I learned in Burma. If you at least give something personal, even only a blanket, to a person who has lost everything, they immediately start to feel better, and to hope that things will improve. For those men and women rotting in the thousands of little makeshift huts, or tents if they were lucky, this would be a first step to recovery. The delegates from Oxfam, Save the Children, the other major Charities and myself were disturbed and angry about the fringe agencies so prevalent in Somalia. They had the ability to capture some of the pool of donations from both Europe and America (the glamorous Hollywood star was very good at this) but not the experience or the discipline to make it work on the ground. My job in Burma had been much better controlled by the Burmese, who made it almost impossible to get a visa to enter the country. Half way into my stay the Somali Government were just beginning to realise what a mistake they had made in opening the doors so widely.

I made several journeys to the camps, 13 hours in the Toyota to a reasonably near one, and slept out sometimes, on the banks of the Shebelli River, which flows down into Somalia from the highlands of Ethiopia. This is country where elephants, giraffes and ostrich roam, with antelopes and wild boar, storks, vultures, ibis, hornbills and of course monkeys and parrots by the million. Surprisingly one could sleep quite well! The Shebelli was one of the sources of water for the camps in that area, but it was too salty to be properly suitable for drinking. Desalination Plants were available, but at high cost. Oxfam was providing water engineers to install pumps to draw water from usable wells, but with the water table so low there was a minimal flow. There was a promise of twenty solar powered pumps, to avoid the use and carriage of fuel for petrol driven ones. Women and children were digging into the sand in the dried up riverbeds to try to reach a trickle of water below. In some areas they were dependent on water tankers which in turn were dependent on fuel. The shortage of water was most severe in the arid areas near to the Ethiopian border – which was where many of the camps had to be in order to get people to them. There was water in the coastal areas, but it needed tankerage to get it to the camps. It was almost a question of choosing between food and water.

The camps. Dreary, dusty, desolate, windswept. People existed in this windblown dust created by the drought. Pitiful places, with the thousands of beehive huts of branches and sacking or cardboard, so close together. The huts were about four feet high and six feet in diameter. There would usually be just a few semi-permanent buildings, rudimentary clinics or tents for the medical staff to live and work in. Food storage facilities were not a problem, as there was no surplus to store, but some central point to distribute the daily arrival was necessary - usually, with luck, a tent. No toilets, no cooking pots, no fuel and not much food or unpolluted water.

As one approached the children appeared, with the bloated belly of Kwashiorkor, the stick legs and arms and old men's faces of Marasmus and the running milky eyes of Trachoma. Yet they would shout 'Nabat', 'Jambo', or 'Salaam Alaykum' – Hello, welcome, God be with you. The children were usually pleased to see us, although the adults were full of suspicion and distrust of modern medicine. A woman given a course of tablets for a sick child was quite likely to give them all at once, or take them herself, despite instruction from an interpreter. A sickly child was however a source of shame, and more often was hidden away. Treatment for a pain was a piece of red-hot metal placed over the area. There were up to twenty miles of desert around each camp, growing and growing, as the women and children walked for eight hours each day to find wood to make cooking fires.

One of the major things about refugee disasters that I had learned was that people can only be helped in a way which conforms to their way of life, their religion and their own pace. Those in illness, shock or distress cannot conform to a European or American pace, and they can best be helped by trying to restore some semblance of their own culture, primitive though that may be. Forcing unaccustomed food or clothing on them just does not work.

Las Dure camp, in Northern Somalia, the old British Somaliland, was about forty miles from the nearest town, Hargeisa. The town was a broken down flyblown oasis of tin roofs in the semi-arid desert and low barren hills. The pressure was not sufficient to push water up the pipes to the houses on even the lower slopes of the hills, and the queue for a few litres of fuel was over an hour long. It would take about two hours to drive the forty miles, between Hargeisa and Las Dure, over desert tracks through the scrub and low bush. Mountains blocking the way to the port of Djibouti were stark on the northern horizon, the sun hammered down from directly overhead and the monsoon wind from the Indian Ocean blew the sand into every crevice and orifice of vehicles and humans. As a European there were a few compensations though. Beautiful little dik-dik deer, not much bigger than hares leap out of your path, and a hyena slopes away on his baleful scavenging path. As your head bangs against the Land Rover roof for the tenth time you might see a family of baboons scurrying through the bush, or a group of tribesmen with their three or four camels slipping quietly along towards market.

Then you notice that even the occasional bush has been stripped of anything burnable, so the land is a moonscape. The camp is on the banks of a dried up river - the reason for the location of course. There is water there if people can scrabble deep enough with their hands, or perhaps Oxfam will find an available pump to bring up sweet water from the water table below. Fine for now, but what happens if the water table is significantly lowered by over-use? Las Dure was full of flies, swarming, getting in your mouth if you opened it, in your nose, in your eyes. In the clinics not long before our arrival in Somalia one would have found medics dressing wounds using their own supplies of toilet paper stuck down with sellotape, as that was all they had. There had been some improvement since that low point, but not much.

At least one child was dying in Las Dure every hour, from malnutrition, TB, measles, dysentery, malaria or pneumonia. There were five nurses from World Vision and one Australian Doctor, for about sixty thousand people, many of them old or infants. At the time of our visit we agreed to bring in another two Doctors and two male nurses from the German Red Cross, but they would have to come from the front line. Las Dure would still be a death camp. It could have been asked, where are the Government Medical Teams? Answer: There weren't any. Most Somalis go to other countries if they have skills to sell. What about U.N.H.C.R. and the W.H.O.? Answer: There are very many similar camps in Somalia, and numerous others in Karamoja Province in Uganda, to say nothing of other refugee problems in many parts of the developing world.

The big journey was between Hargeisa and Mogadishu, bringing back the vehicles imported through Djibouti. Twenty-two hours driving, and somewhere to sleep, if one was lucky, was in a shanty, or in the open. The roads, having left Hargeisa and until near Mogadishu, were not roads. A track to follow was often a bonus and the drive was very hard work indeed. As August turned into September an increase in the number of lorries available was becoming urgent. This was not only to carry food but other essentials – for example bottled gas and stoves for cooking. One estimate of the critical non-food requirement to be moved to the camps included 50,000 sets of kitchen equipment, 10,000 tarpaulin sheets and 20,000 blankets.

People also had to be transported from where they gathered at the Transit Camps, just inside the Somali boundary, to the semi-permanent camps further inland and away from the fought over border areas. Most of these people, mainly women plus children and old men, had walked for many days or weeks and were in no state to walk further. The inland camps did not offer more than a subsistence-level life, but at least there were medical staff, rudimentary hospital facilities and a regular, if barely enough, food issue. The refugees at the Transit areas were so thankful to arrive at a place where they could rest, under some sort of cover even if this was only by lying down in the dust under a tree, that they were reluctant to be moved on. Perhaps they thought that they were being taken back to the unsafe areas, and they would hide when they saw the lorries. Ill people, particularly babies, would be hidden away, and medication or food which they did not recognise would be thrown away.

We received a very generous gift of lorries and mobile vehicle repair shops from both the German Red Cross and the German Government, which did ease the problem. The German Red Cross teams were very well equipped, down to the last roll of elastoplast. It was still a struggle to get people on to the lorries though. Reprehensibly some of the fringe 'aid' agencies allowed their workers to dress in military style uniforms. I even saw one group marching into a camp, and wondered what they thought they were there for. It did not help to reduce suspicion from people who were frightened of soldiers.

One area that I was particularly concerned about was at El Waq, just over the border from Kenya. This location meant that anyone arriving there on foot had walked for many days, through much of Ethiopia and the north eastern tip of Kenya. Before the Red Cross arrival in Somalia 20,000 refugees had been evacuated from El Waq, as the Ministry of Local Government did not want them there. They declared that this camp was now closed, while the National Refugee Commission insisted that it was still open, and a Red Crescent responsibility. My observations there had convinced me that whatever the Somali Government said, refugees would continue to arrive there. I had made noises and jumped up and down in various Government offices about this situation as it was now reported that again there were over 900 people there and 200 more arriving every day.

No food was available from either local or regional sources and they could not be moved without transport. As the head in the sand attitude still existed I wrote formally to the Commissioner of the N.R.C., with copies to Geneva, the U.N.H.C.R., the Minister of Local Government and anyone else that I could think of, saying that it was a scandalous situation and implicitly threatening an international disgrace. Two days after writing this letter I learned that the Minister was out of contact in Hargeisa, but that the letter had worried his Deputy, the head of the Food Aid Department at the Ministry. I went to see this gentleman and frightened him a bit more about the international consequences of a thousand people starving to death.

He agreed that they should be fed, then moved, and that El Waq should continue to be serviced as a Transit Camp as long as people were arriving there. I copied this agreement to all the people to whom I had just written, and we got things in motion. I believe that when the Minister returned from Hargeisa he was more than offended with his Deputy, but by then could not rescind the agreement without his Ministry losing a lot of face. This was the 'blackmail' to which I referred earlier, and although I am sure that it brought trouble down on the unfortunate Deputy Minister I have absolutely no bad conscience about it. It was a consequence of the absurd splitting of responsibilities between the NRC and the Ministry and the ostrich mentality of those concerned.

I described some of these experiences, after my return to the UK, to senior boys at Wolverhampton Grammar School. I asked them, whatever problems they might have in their life in England, to imagine having been born in the Ogaden eighteen years before. 'You are likely to be dead or dying from TB or typhus or strafing by Mig fighters. If not you probably have gangrene from bumping over non-existent roads in the back of a lorry for a week or more, after collecting a Cuban bullet. If you survive that you will be eligible to be treated at the Martini Military Hospital in Mogadishu. Great. It's pleasant to sit outside under the shade of the thorn trees. Except that you can't get to them, as your leg has been roughly hacked off at the knee, and there are no crutches or wheelchairs. But you have something to lie on indoors. A dirty stinking mattress, with the stump of your leg suspended by string from a rough wooden frame. It's sweltering hot, there are no fans and there aren't enough nurses to turn you over to reduce the pain from the huge bedsore on your back, or even to get you a drink.

If you are lucky there may be a political paper to read, but of course no radio or TV. You have been there for months, maybe more than a year, and sometime the one Egyptian Surgeon will get round to tidying up your leg. You won't have eaten yet today, but never mind, soon they will bring round food. Spaghetti, thrown into a dirty bucket. And that's it. Maybe the lights will be on to enable you to see the food, maybe not. And tomorrow will be like that – and all your tomorrows.

When you do get out of the Martini, if you ever do, you have a future to look forward to. You will have your own little cart on which to push yourself by hand around the streets of Mogadishu, with filthy rags wrapped around your fists and the privilege of begging for scraps of food. And yet when the Red Cross Bwana comes round you will somehow be able to look up and grin, because someone is interested in you, and say, 'Nabat, my name is Sharif'. But when he goes, as he has to, you won't even be able to turn over away from the pain in your back, from the great sore full of stinking pus. Your friends who still have two legs will not able to help you as they have problems of their own, with not much energy left to help others'. And that is a pretty accurate description of what life could be like then for a guerrilla or a Somali soldier. As I have seen it, in the Martini and elsewhere. I hope that it made the English boys think how lucky they were.

To have given a similar talk to a group of English teenage girls – inviting them to think of having been born in the Ogaden, would have been impossible. The sexual mutilation and desperate circumstances of many Somali women's lives would have been unbearable, even for a woman to talk about.

As a result of my several sessions of jumping up and down in various

Ministries my name must have become quite well known, because I next received a request to draft a letter from the President of Somalia, Sayed Barre, to Hendrik Beer, the Secretary General of the Red Cross in Geneva. I knew pretty much what he wanted to say, and was able to set the scene, referring to the 800,000 refugees in 28 permanent camps, requiring 500 tonnes of food each day and the problems with funds, lack of fuel and logistics. I was able to include one or two pet projects of my own, principally the need for bottled gas and cooking stoves. This was now becoming an ecological disaster as well as a human one as the desertified areas around each camp continued to grow through the daily search for wood. The use of stoves was, of course mainly outside the refugee's experience and culture, and was going to be very difficult to get them to accept. However, I felt that it had to be tried, and they could at least be used in the clinics. The Somali President was happy with the letter, into which I also inserted a sneaky paragraph about what a good job the Red Cross/RedCrescent teams were doing.

I was probably also getting a name for being slightly eccentric, as I was the only European to be wearing sensible clothing! I had brought my Burmese lungyi and Malaysian sarongs and found them, as in Burma and the Sudan, by far the best form of attire below the waist in the hot and humid climate. I could not understand why no one else bothered, as something similar could be bought in Mogadishu, and it was very pleasant not to have wet patches around the waist and knees. Perhaps the security of the garment worried people, as suspension is a bit of an art. One problem was that desert boots looked really weird below a sarong, so it had to be flip-flops. I remember one afternoon walking back from the Post Office in the sarong with flip-flops flap-flopping, carrying six feet of telex paper, an empty beer bottle, a book, reading glasses, money and my room key. It took an hour or more to send a telex and there are no pockets in a sarong! A group of expats were playing cards in the hotel foyer, who no doubt were amused. I had absolutely no problem in being regarded as a character as long as we were recognised as being useful as well, which was now happening. However, I do admit that I have never got round to wearing the sarong or lungyi on a really hot day in Europe, except in my back garden. Why not I wonder?

It was at about this time that I was joined by another delegate from Europe, Esa, from Rovanieme on the Arctic Circle in Finland. From the Arctic Circle, Lapland, to the Equator! He was a great guy, well experienced in this sort of work and we got on well together. I was now able to keep up more pressure on the Ministries, as Per was coping well with the Hargeisa end and Esa took up a roving commission on the Kenya border area. This meant my working more or less office hours for a bit, so I was able to join some of the other expatriate workers at the beach club in Mogadishu during some siesta times. The beach club was far away from the sophistication of the Sudan Club, with just a concrete patio and shelter and a few wooden benches, but it did have some glorious water to swim in.

Unfortunately, if the tide was a high one, sharks could get over the barrier of the reef, and a fin could sometimes be seen a few yards out. The locals always seemed to know whether or not it was safe, but one did keep a wary eye open. I saw three big black fins once, about ten yards out, in water three to four feet deep, which rather put me off from then on.

However, it certainly is true that the sharks that one can't see are the ones to be concerned about! Strange and extraordinary denizens of the deep were occasionally washed up, and two locals struggled in one afternoon with a huge ray, about six feet across. I also had the opportunity to go to a local international football match, Somalia playing Zanzibar. The stadium was a reasonably modern one, and a brass band, in full bandsmen's uniform played on the touchline at half time. They were obviously local, since every time Somalia got the ball, or looked like scoring they could not resist striking up individually. The tempo of the drumbeat became frenetic. I think that it added to the atmosphere. Somalia had been losing 2-1, but then scored, nearly at full time and Zanzibar refused to play on. The referee abandoned the game!

While I was working in Mogadishu at the end of August we had several important visitors, notably Fürstin (Princess) Von Sollm, the Vice President of the German Red Cross, with whom I had dinner at the German Ambassador's house. I was also invited to dinner at the American Ambassador's residence. These were very convenient occasions to use to drum up more cash support, and I was pleased to be able to engineer a donation of half a million dollars from the President of the Norwegian Red Cross to support our food transport. As we got into September the Red Cross/ Red Crescent were now, with the help of the half million, being recognised as major players, and I felt that we were achieving something useful. The Scandinavian countries were well represented in Somalia by their Red Cross Societies, and I see that I wrote at the time that I had not come across one of their delegates whom I did not like and respect.

In fact I had received an invitation to visit Oslo, which I regret I never took up. Later during her visit I had a long and productive private meeting with the Princess. She was a very elegant and charming lady, just about old enough to have lost a fiancé during world war two, and we got on well. I also noted at the time that the staff of the British Embassy, as in Burma, were conspicuous by their absence, and thought again how lucky I had been in the Sudan.

It was during this period that I decided that the Toyota that I was using could do with a wash. I had a nice little local woman who cleaned my room, and with whom I had negotiated a few essentials - my bedside light, an extra pillow and an extra chair, but when I tried to get her to find me a bucket she was completely stumped. I tried saying 'maccina' accompanied by scrubbing motions and she brought me a towel. I then got, in succession, a broom and a mop, and eventually the hotel manager! As it was siesta time I was not very popular, but got my bucket and some rags. When ever I saw my little lady afterwards she burst out laughing – the English are definitely mad!

By this time we were starting to have some effect with the Somali and those expatriate agencies who did not seem to me to have done very much. Almost always this was by 'banging the table' and being quite aggressive, or by sneaky means such as my piece of blackmail. Our very good Red Cross nurse, Sue, who had unfortunately had to return to the UK for another commitment agreed with me that some of the U.N.H.C.R. personnel had not been doing much of a job. We found that they had been making nasty comments about our activities. This was fine, as it meant that we were being noticed and having some effect. What was unpopular with them was, I guess, trying to hurry up the bureaucratic process.

However, the U.N.H.C.R. Commissioner did thank me publicly for what we had been able to achieve in getting the Government transport moving. What he could not say publicly was that this had been mainly by threats and lies! My observations at the time about the Somali people were quite harsh, but with hindsight one has to remember that for most of them their life was equally harsh. I wrote that the lower strata of society would cheerfully rob you blind - I had my pocket picked efficiently in the Post Office, mirrors were stolen from the Toyota and I just foiled a bid by two urchins to steal my bag.

The professional classes, with some exceptions, were sly and lazy, but in between, - shopkeepers, waiters, cleaners were some very nice, trustworthy people. A man riding a motor scooter came up behind me in the town and obviously having no horn shouted 'peep peep' as he passed me. You can't help liking people like that. It was sometimes right and possible to give some baksheesh to the children who needed it – not the ones in town who made a flourishing business out of it – one quickly learned the appropriate words for them, 'Imshi towali', shove off! But, I was sitting outside the car, out in the country having a beer, when a poor little thing of about eight came up and begged for the empty bottle. 'Per favore, bottiglia, Signori?' He was stunned to get a full bottle of coca-cola instead, but I probably had more pleasure in being able to give it to him. That's real poverty. Another pitiful child later in the same place was asking for 'mangiare' – something to eat.

These incidents happened at a place I had found, just outside the town, which it was good to spend siesta time in, and peaceful enough to write up some reports. The universal custom when in Mogadishu was to work from early morning until about 12 or 1 p.m. then rest and get on with typing, telexes or more meetings from about 6pm. The place that I found was a bay, very blue sea of course, with low green hills on the two arms of land to give it an almost Welsh aspect, and a small village at one end of the beach. The waves were big and white crashing over the reef half a mile out. Beyond the low hills it became very un-Welsh - desert and savage red dunes. It was always deserted during weekday afternoons except for a few grazing camels and sheep.

The men were all fishermen, and came back to the village about 5 or 6 p.m. to sit in the shade of one of the huts and chew 'qat'. This was an almost universal habit among Somali men, and produced a mild euphoric buzz, very similar to chewing cocoa leaves, as I later found in South America. I don't know if it was addictive, perhaps so as all the men seemed to do it, but it only had a very mild effect (as far as I know anyway!) on me. As the men from the village came home to rest, the women and girls started their daily walk to fetch water, in earthen jars in a wicker framework on their backs or in the time honoured way on their heads. A wonderful photograph if you could get one when they were not looking. Most Somali people objected to being photographed, as they believed that you were capturing their souls. The nearest well was miles away, but this was just an accepted part of their life. Before setting off one of the women empties her jar over a child standing naked in front of the cooking fire. A shiny little brown body in the light of the sun as it begins to disappear in golden and scarlet rays.

As we were beginning to get to grips with the lack of any system or organisation, we were hit with an even more serious problem. Somalia imported all it's supply of crude oil from Iraq, which was refined into vehicle fuel near Mogadishu. The Iraq-Iran war stopped this supply, and the Somali refinery was only able to deal with the type of crude obtained from Iraq unless lengthy adaptations were made. Very quickly there were huge queues for both petrol and diesel. Rationing was instituted and the National Refugee Commission were allocated 600 litres a day. This was not just inadequate but derisory. The requirement to keep the food lorries moving from the docks to the camps was 12,000 litres of diesel a day.

The big agencies, ourselves, Oxfam, Save the Children and the others could see all previous problems pale into insignificance, and that there was no way to keep the refugee population alive if the food transport stopped. It was already known that thousands of children were described by the medical teams as on a knife-edge of survival. A breakdown of the food supplies would leave the children particularly with no resistance to TB, diarrhoea and the other endemic problems of life in the camps. Following some frantic lobbying (including jumping up and down again and banging the table) of the Somali Government, the ration was increased to 6000 litres a day and a bulk supply of 50,000 litres. As this was about half what was needed, the Oxfam delegate, Steve, and I agreed that we had to seek publicity through the world media. Steve, who was American, agreed to stir things in the USA. There was not time to go through formal channels, so I telephoned Jo and asked her to contact Reuters and as many UK National newspapers as possible. We got good coverage in, amongst others, the Times, with headlines, 'Send oil and save lives says Red Cross leader' and, 'Red Cross man's plea on oil supply'. By some miracle it worked, and better supplies of crude oil were secured for the Somalis to refine.

I am not normally a great fan of the media (or more correctly, of some of those who work in it) but used properly it can get things done. Some of their excesses and intrusions could be described as a force for evil, but they can sometimes be persuaded to improve the world. I believe that, through the publicity, political pressure was put on Iraq from Britain and the US. Perhaps also the Iraqis in 1980 were keen to get world support in their very bitter conflict with Iran. I was taken to task quite aggressively by the Press Office of the British Red Cross for not having gone through them, but I felt that I could not care less, we had got a result. It was clear that any indecision, or worries about political consequences, would result in catastrophic delay, so we got on and did it. As in a lot of things in my life, some important, some not, I did it my way, and on this occasion, it worked.

With the Transport Specialists, additional lorries provided from Germany, local drivers being better trained and an improvement in the fuel problem, the beginning of October saw an easing of the immediate worst problems. We had heard that blankets were available for sale in Kisimayu, a small town down the coast, sitting right on the Equator. Abdi, the Red Crescent Accountant and I managed to get seats on one of the small aircraft, and flew down there. He had never flown before, and was totally terrified, gripping my hand frantically as we took off. Kisimayu was a pleasant little town, quite sandwiched between very blue sea and very yellow desert. A small river debouched into the sea here, one side was Kenya and one Somalia, and it was very easy to hop from one to the other with the maximum flexibility of formalities. There was a lot of wild life around, and I have a nice photograph of a large ostrich preceding me down a hillside, looking very dignified and exhibiting a wonderful view of it's tail feathers!

Back in Mogadishu I was nearing the end of my three months stay, and Sven, the former fighter pilot from Sweden, who had taken over in Burma was being withdrawn from Bangkok to replace me. As we were not going to meet in Somalia I prepared a very long typewritten report for Geneva, so that he could be briefed on the problems, personalities and weaknesses. In a personal letter to me later in the year the Director of the Relief Operations Bureau described the report as 'a remarkable summary of the refugee situation' which had helped considerably to depict the conditions. I do remember sweating over the portable typewriter during several long days in the Red Crescent office, and was pleased with the compliment. What to say and, very important, what not to say! I was sorry not to meet Sven personally again, but all the League personnel were very busy, with many earthquake casualties in Algeria and Italy adding to the workload. I was also very pleased to find that the League delegation in Somalia was to grow to twenty two, I like to think because of the recommendations, or demands, that I had made.

I flew back via Kenya, where I took a short period of leave, leaving Esa as Chief Delegate until the arrival of Sven from Bangkok. It was very good to see England and the family again, and I felt, after my debriefing, that it was perceived that the job had been done well. It was said, and I certainly knew, that the Red Crescent was now being run much more professionally and that the basis for expansion had been laid. It was not an easy three months, and I probably upset some of the other players. However, in my view they deserved it. It was good to look back on having got a few things done and dusted.

I think that it will be obvious from my descriptions of work in Burma and Somalia that delegates working in a disaster situation are not exempt from taking a little time off, and trying to find some sense of humour to relieve the stress. This is absolutely necessary and I do not apologise for it in any way. A stressed out and traumatised executive is no good to anyone, the Red Crescent Accountant, Abdi, being a relevant example. This is the same relief that a soldier or police officer may use after, or during, particularly unpleasant circumstances. It may be thought to be unfeeling, morbid or even gruesome, but those of us who are able to react in this way are lucky. The humour may be macabre, but to be able to point to a severed head and say, 'I ain't got no body' is, in my view, better that seeking counselling or compensation for traumatic stress disorder after the event. There is a First World War cartoon by Bruce Bairnsfather showing two English soldiers sheltering in a muddy shell hole in no man's land. The first man there says to the complaining newcomer, 'If you know of a better 'ole, go to it!' I find this a good British example of the same attitude. Laugh or joke to relieve the stress. However some people genuinely cannot cope with this, and the pressure of strain, tension and trauma build up until something cracks. Perhaps if this had been recognised or realised during the First World War fewer boy soldiers would have been shot for so-called cowardice.

The decision to leave the British Red Cross having been made, with sadness and some sense of failure, I had started to make enquiries about alternative work and Jo had continued to process these while I was in Somalia. I felt that I might as well use the driving expertise that I had gained in the police service, and was quite quickly offered an interview for the civil service post of a Driving Examiner. The salary was not much, but it would get me back to the Midlands, which I felt was the absolute family priority at that time. I took the offer, and although I did not enjoy the job much and did not stay in it for very long as another door soon opened, it did help me to go through that door and led into the way that I have spent my life since.

Many years later, in the twenty first century, came a finale of the work for the Red Cross. This was strangely reminiscent of the culmination of my police service through the reunion and plaque dedication that we were able to organise at the National Memorial Arboretum in 2007. I had been invited to be part of the Red Cross Link Group, a twice-yearly meeting in London of former British Red Cross members. Soon after attending such a meeting in April 2008, and totally out of the blue, came an invitation to a Royal Garden Party at Buckingham Palace in July. This was to celebrate the hundredth anniversary of the Royal Charter being given to the British Red Cross, and was to be hosted by the Prince of Wales. Although disappointingly Jo was not invited, we made a weekend out of it, she visiting museums while I hob-nobbed with Prince Charles and the Duchess of Cornwall. Actually, I did only get a smile from her and half a wave from him, but with thousands of people there this was as much as could be expected. The honour and the pleasure was in being invited.

It also led, a few weeks later, to a full page feature in the Midlands evening paper, the Express and Star, describing and picturing the work that we had been able to do in Burma and Somalia. They had dug up, from their files, a family picture of the four of us, so we were able to give Nicky and Al a surprise! On the day of the party I was a bit miffed to be told not to wear my medals, (why not?) but as it rained all day perhaps they would have gone rusty. However, I did enjoy a chocolate cake with a crown in the icing. Does this mean that they were made by the Queen? Perhaps not.

The subject of Prince Charles, by the way, came up while I was in Papua New Guinea, learning a little neo Melanesian (Tok Pisin). He was known there at that time as 'Number wan picaninny belong Missus Quin', but I did not have the chance to discuss this with him. The organisation (or not) in the

Palace Grounds was unbelievably bad. It was obvious that no one had thought that it might, just possibly, rain. The queue for the Ladies toilet was about three hundred yards long in the rain, and I did feel sorry for them all in their flowery hats and flimsy shoes, as I walked past to the virtually empty Gents, well anoraked up. Even thus garbed I was wet to the skin by the time I reached our Hotel. Charles' guests and the other VIPs were looked after rather better, but other mortals, and all the police on duty (serfs) just got wet. Does the Queen have any input into this, or does she also believe that it never rains on the Palace lawns? I did give Camilla full marks for having carried her own umbrella throughout the day, whilst Charles had two serfs to do it for him.

Reverting to my lengthy career as a Civil Servant, I note with some wryness that the Driving Examiner strength have been on strike for more money, and I do not blame them as it is the most boring way of earning a living that can be imagined. This, of course, I did not know until I started doing it. One covers the same old routes time and time again. I used to welcome with pleasure a really bad driver, which meant that I had to wake up. One quickly identified the Instructors who were likely to bring inadequately trained pupils for test. It is a paradox that the pupils getting through the test at the first attempt represent a loss of income to the Instructor. The better and more conscientious teacher he or she is the harder they have to work to attract replacement clients.

I enjoyed the training course at Cardington near Bedford, as the Instructor was also a former police officer, and quickly found the way the Department of Transport liked things to be done. It had both similarities and disparities with police training, but was not too difficult to get hold of. I was posted to the Bilston Test Centre, a suburb of Wolverhampton and a journey that I could do by bicycle (not the folding one – that had folded up for good). As money was a bit tight I decided not to spend it on wet weather clothing – all my equipment was for warm climates, so used plastic bags with rubber bands to cover my shoes on wet days. I understand that this, like my attire in Somalia, was looked on as a little odd. Can't really see why – it worked. After a fashion. (My way again!)

One essential thing that a new Examiner has to do is to learn the routes appropriate to that Test Centre. Each of these has been worked out to have similar numbers and types of driving hazards and the job was so boring because one had to stick to an official route each test, day after day. On one of the first test that I conducted after officially 'knowing' the routes I realised that I had turned left too early and was off-route. It seemed that the easiest way to get back on track was to ask the candidate, a rather nervous middle aged lady, to perform the turn in the road manoeuvre, otherwise known as the three point turn. It was not the thing to admit that I had made a mistake, as apart from the loss of dignity it would give the candidate a good reason to appeal if she failed the test. So we commenced the three point turn.

Unfortunately this lady, as well as being nervous, was pretty hopeless, the street was not really wide enough and not approved for the purpose. The three points were metamorphosing into a hundred and three! Whilst we were sideways across the street, and blocking it on about the twentieth go at turning round, a car approached at speed from the left. An elderly man was slumped and apparently unconscious in the passenger seat. The driver jumped out, sprinted to me and yelled, 'Can you let us past, I'm taking him to Hospital.' Oh dear, what to do? I could see that she had at least another ten minutes of to-ing and fro-ing to complete the manoeuvre, so there was really no alternative. I moved us out of the way and let them through, which then posed another problem. To fail or to pass? If an Examiner helps a candidate in any way they have automatically failed the test. But, it was my fault that we were there in the first place. Fortunately I have never had a problem with making a quick decision, but I am going to leave it to you, the reader, to decide which one I came to! This was probably the most interesting problem during my short stay with the civil service, but I never did get lost again!

It was, in my view, unfair to fail someone by stepping in too quickly and grabbing the steering or using the dual controls. In order to legitimately issue a fail I felt that you had to let them at least begin to make the mistake. This led to one or two remarkable situations, when, for example, a middle aged man who had obviously come too late to driving tried to take us the wrong side of a busy roundabout on a main road. This did wake me up and liven up the day. Not all my colleagues could operate in this way, and when I was posted to another Test Centre I had to sit in with another Examiner to learn their routes. This man suffered from the unpleasant disease of piles – very unfortunate for someone whose job entailed sitting down all day, and he carried an inflatable rubber ring to sit on. If his bottom was playing up he was very twitchy, and I saw him grab the steering on a number of occasions that were not, in my view, necessary. Hard luck on the candidate, who was being 'assisted'.

When one did come across the really badly, or inadequately trained, candidate especially if it was from an Instructor who habitually brought unready pupils on a 'hopeful' basis, there was one way of striking back. This was to stop the test at the furthest point possible from the Test Centre, catch a 'bus back and tell the waiting Instructor, 'Your candidate is unsafe. I have stopped the test. Here are your keys. Your pupil is sitting in the car at the side of the road.' I would then pray for rain, and hope that the Instructor did not know which bus to catch. This was actually quite legitimate within the Civil Service rules, and not, I think, unfair!

Of course, Instructors like this were a minority, but sometimes an efficient one would be pressured to apply for a test by a pupil with an inflated idea of his own ability. That this was the case was usually pretty obvious. It was invariably 'his' own ability by the way! Women and girls are not usually so arrogant when it comes to driving ability. Since the introduction of tables of Instructor's Pass Rates this type of test, at least when using an Instructor's car, has declined. There is, at long, long, last, talk of making a set period of training mandatory. In my view this should have been done years ago.

One feature of the Cardington training course had been the possibility of being assaulted by a disappointed candidate. One was advised to gabble the formula as quickly as possible, not to indulge in debate and evacuate the car post haste. This struck me as pretty feeble. It did not come close to happening to me despite working in a fairly rough area. There are ways of breaking the bad news without giving offence. It seemed to me that the Department of Transport had a poor view of their Examiners, but this advice was perhaps Union led. I also thought it very unfair not to at least try to explain what had been wrong. It was not until an argument began to take shape that, in my view, it was time to bale out. It was also necessary with a candidate, who was, for example, an inadequately educated Black Country lad, to go into the vernacular, and not hide behind the official phrases. So, rather than say, ' I am afraid that you have failed to reach the required standard', I would have been more likely to say, 'Yo buggered it up at them traffic lights ar kid.' I will defend that way, my way, against all comers, because it was relevant to the time and place, and was understood!

An aspect of the training with which I completely disagreed, and which I am pleased to say seems to have been dropped, was the use of the official phrases. We were actually taught that if a candidate said something on the lines of, 'Just my luck to get such a wet day for my test' we should reply, 'It often rains at this time of year, Madam'. The so-called logic behind this was that if you agreed that it was very bad weather the candidate could use it as an excuse for failing! During my period as an Examiner there was a public perception that we had a quota of passes to issue, and when the quota of passes for the day or week was completed no more would be issued. This was strenuously denied by the authorities, but in fact, in a roundabout way due to human nature, it was true. There was no such thing as a quota. However, as the pass rate remained at a fairly steady level from year to year, any Examiner whose rates regularly diverged either way from the average found that he had the Senior Examiner sitting in on his tests to find out why. Since no one enjoys being watched while working this resulted in pressure to keep one's rates to the average.

I was not particularly concerned about the averages, as I had quickly decided that this was not going to be my work until retirement. The low level of salary, slow promotion prospects and general bureaucracy had a lot to do with this, but the principal reason was that I felt that I was participating in a farce. So much depended on luck. A bad driver could sail through if everything went smoothly, whereas someone who was obviously well trained and competent could have one moment of bad luck – often caused by another driver or pedestrian. I felt then, and have seen no reason to change my opinion since, that the British test is nowhere close to adequate, and that it is one of the reasons that we manage to regularly kill too many people on the roads. Whilst a lot of things have improved and the killing rate has fallen a lot I believe that the above comment is still true.

A common question asked of examiners is, 'Don't you feel worried or frightened by being with a learner?' This never occurred to me, and in fact about the only collision that one cannot prevent is being hit from behind. I do nowadays ask my advanced clients, 'Can you tell me the one thing that the instructor or examiner cannot do to prevent a collision?' I rarely get an answer, surprisingly, because it seems to me pretty obvious. It is of course that while one can grab the steering or handbrake or use the dual brake if one is fitted, one cannot pull the driver's right leg off the brake pedal! Learners do brake hard, and this is one of the likely causes of the shunt from behind. All drivers should beware that it is likely to happen if they are behind a car showing 'L' plates.

I served for twenty five years as a Police Officer, the majority of them operational. It has always struck me as strange that whilst there were plenty of threats and 'I am a great friend of your Chief' remarks when arresting or booking someone, not once was a bribe even hinted at, despite plenty of cases where it might have been thought helpful. Although not all my colleagues were angels I am inclined to wonder if this says something about our Force and the Service generally at that time. Yet within a couple of months of being a Driving Examiner, after saying, 'You have not reached the required standard' I had been asked twice, with money in view, 'Is there any way that your decision can be changed?'

One of those offers had come from an Asian Doctor wanting a UK licence. Now here was another example of decision time. There was a set procedure for this situation, which was to accept the money, mark it if it was a note, and go straight to the Senior Examiner. However, it seemed to me that this was a huge can of worms, with the opportunity for all sorts of lies to be told and mud to be flung and a case to drag on for months. So, as in many things in my life, I did it my way, and in both cases said, 'No, there isn't. Don't be a bloody fool.' There were obvious dangers with this as well, but they did not materialise, and I think that I was right.

Apart from the few interesting times like this life was pretty boring and I had learned, after accepting the job, that civil service procedures meant that there was no chance of promotion until I had at least five or six years service. I imagine now, thinking back, that there was also a psychological factor involved, as not long before I had been dealing with, and meeting more or less on an equal basis, Presidents, Princes, Princesses and Ambassadors. I was not overtly conscious of this, but it was not a happy time. However, after less than a year an escape hatch opened in the Spring of 1981. I saw an article in the International Police Association Magazine that RoSPA, the Royal Society for the Prevention of Accidents in Birmingham, were looking for someone to fill a senior post as their Chief Driving Examiner.

Resurrecting the drafting skills that had secured a place on the Police Helicopter experiments I wrote to RoSPA and virtually demanded the job! C'est moi, C'est moi, 'tis I'! Well, OK, but it has worked for me three times! Any road up, after a couple of interviews and a driving test conducted by a former Metropolitan Police Driving Instructor I was offered the post. His comment was, 'I didn't see anything to worry me' which I guess was quite high praise from such a man. Although I had not enjoyed the Civil Service job the experience must have helped me into this one. Advanced driver training and examining were to happily last me for the rest of my full-time working life, and beyond into part-time work, and through the first decade of the new millennium. I am therefore grateful for the Civil Service work and a little guilty that I deprived them of my services so quickly. Having successfully liased with the Department and it's successor, the Driving Standards Agency, for RoSPA on several occasion since I can live with this however, and in 2008 the wheels turned full circle again when I examined one of the Wolverhampton D.S.A. Examiners for his advanced driving test. I'm glad to say that he passed with flying colours.

My remit was very different to that I had had in the civil service, although the title 'Examiner' was common to both. I had been recruited for the immediate task of carrying through an amalgamation between the advanced driver training section of RoSPA and a smaller organisation, The League of Safe Drivers. I guess that my work on the police amalgamation planning team in 1973/4 and as a police class one driver and motor cyclist also fitted me nicely into the frame for this job. I don't think that anyone else was interviewed. The League had an advanced test structure with examiners who were all serving or former Class 1 police operational drivers or instructors. It had been biased towards London, and Hendon instructors, although there were now some examiners in the provinces. It had been started in 1955 under the auspices of the Finchley Road Safety Committee.

At the time of the incorporation with RoSPA it was still being managed, virtually single handed, by a former Road Safety Officer from her home in Finchley. This lady, Mrs Louise Duncan, was awarded a well-deserved MBE by Mrs. Thatcher for her road safety work. I was to bring this organisation under the RoSPA umbrella and recruit a substantial number of examiners, across the UK, all with a similar police background to the original ones from Hendon. A lot more were needed as it was expected that under the RoSPA name applications for tests would increase. An organisation to administer and if necessary train the new staff - all part time, as some would be serving police officers - also had to be set up. Most Chief Police Officers had already given, through the League, permission for serving Officers to act as examiners, as the road safety benefits were obvious. As RoSPA was, and is, an organisation covering the whole UK and also working abroad, this brought a lot of travelling into prospect. Ted, who had assessed my driving was a former Chief Examiner for the League, but now wished to take life a little more easily. He was very well known in police driving circles from his days at the Hendon police driving school, and stayed on our books as a part-time examiner for many years. The police connection explains why the job had been mentioned in a police magazine, and it did, of course, appeal very strongly to me. I have never lost contact with the Service, am still a member of the International Police Association and the National Association of Retired Police Officers, contribute to both and gain benefits from both. I think that it is true to say, again, at least of someone of my generation, that 'once a police officer, always a police officer'.

There was an interesting side issue concerning the amalgamation, which mirrored the police experiences. A lot of people did not like it It was seen by a number of the original members of the League, and some of the examiners, as a 'take-over' by big brother RoSPA. It was therefore an important part of the job to speak to as many of these members as possible, and persuade them that RoSPA did have a human face. The amalgamation had been necessary to keep the League alive in face of increasing financial difficulty. There were a number of local Groups of members, who undertook training for prospective test candidates, and I travelled, and spoke to, I think, all of these. Some man and woman-management skills and 'policemanship' techniques were necessary but I am pleased to say that some of those that I talked to in 1981 remain enthusiastic members and are still in touch personally, so some of it must have worked! I did have one or two difficult meetings where members had expected that a well-known organisation like RoSPA would provide an inflow of much needed funds. There was disappointment when it was realised that it was a Charity, like the League, and that every penny had to be considered. This was rather like the experience in becoming the Communications Officer for the new West Midlands Police in 1974, where police officers throughout Birmingham City had expected that new equipment would be growing on trees.

At the beginning I was up and down to Finchley a number of times to liase with Mrs. Duncan and collect the mass of records that she had amassed. On several occasions I took Gill, who had been allocated as my admin assistant, with me. Gill and another bright girl, Denise, were my office team during the first couple of years at RoSPA. I also had to begin the examiner recruitment campaign, as some of those who had been working for the League had decided that it was time to retire. They were a bit thin on the ground anyway. This was interesting, as it usually meant visiting police stations up and down the country, and meeting people similar to myself.

I was very pleased to find in 2009 that the first new man that I took on, in1981 from the Durham Force, was still a senior examiner for RoSPA in that area, although naturally retired from the police. It was needful to be a bit careful, and try to examine people's motives for volunteering, for expenses only, to do an extra job. One gentleman had been suspended from his police driving role in the Met, for some less than good conduct, and saw the RoSPA name as a way of getting it back. Fortunately I found out about this in time to avoid embarrassment. This was unusual though, and by the time I left full time work with RoSPA we had two hundred and forty examiners, spread throughout England, Scotland, Wales and Northern Ireland. They were all pretty good guys, driving experts, prepared to give up their spare time in the cause of better driving. Not all stayed with us as long as my first recruit of course, but I am very pleased to say that many have, and some have become personal friends.

After the first recruiting effort, by looking at the map of the British Isles, it was obvious that we had a big hole in our coverage, in the Irish Republic. As the Garda Siochana is a national Force we opened negotiations with the Commissioner to see if we could recruit serving Gards as Examiners in Eire. He was not able to agree to this, but made it possible for me to meet a group of recently retired motor patrol officers. There was enough interest for me to run a session of several days explanation and training in how we wanted tests conducted. The Gardai put me up in their training school at Templemore, near Tipperary. (Not quite such a long long way after all, sixty years on from the

First World War). It is a grim grey stone former British Army barracks, from the time of our occupation of southern Ireland. There was a car barrier pole at the entrance, but it was raised, the door to the guardroom was open, it was empty and a radio was playing pop tunes – a 'relaxed'atmosphere was obvious! Eventually a young Constable appeared, whose main concern was that I should not go through any door marked 'Garda Ban' which I learned meant Policewomen! Having promised not to do this I met the seven or eight former Gards, who were also staying in the Centre.

This went very well from the start, and I guess that my name helped. Only a Southern Irishman can say the name Collins, with the proper inflexion and some reverence. The training and discussions went well, and they all agreed to take an examiner's role. One evening, relaxing in a pub in Tipperary, as you do, we got round to talking about the differences between policing in Eire and the UK. I explained the traditional and expected excuse for a damaged CID vehicle. 'Well gaffer, it was like this. I was driving slowly back to the nick, when a big black dog ran straight out in front of me, and I had to swerve to avoid it. That's why I hit the lamp post.' There was an immediate roar of laughter and a chorus of, 'Ah, sure, sure, it's like that with us, only over here it's a pig'! We discovered that damage to CID vehicles almost always happened late at night in both countries, from which certain conclusions could be drawn. Apart from pigs and dogs, and the condition of some Irish roads, there were not too many differences, and in fact some of the Gardai were trained at the Lancashire Constabulary driving school where I had done my motor cycle training. This was another good few days, with nice (if very relaxed) people.

One of my tasks was to strengthen and expand the Local Group system, which the League had in place in London and some provincial areas. This was a feature also of the other advanced driver testing organisation, the Institute of Advanced Motorists. The Groups consisted of enthusiasts who had passed the test and received training to enable them to teach others. They did not need to be driving instructors, although many were, as no money was paid for the training. The Groups of both organisations did, and still do, carry out a magnificent job, and produce very well trained drivers, of a much higher standard than the average. Training a middle aged driver, who is convinced of his own ability (please note the 'his') but full of lazy sloppiness, aggressive attitudes, poor instruction in the first place and overall being a testosterone based life form is a bit like trying to teach an unwilling camel to dance. I know that I have rubbished the concept of women in the front line of the military or the police, but generally I believe, after a lot of experience of both training and testing, that they make safer drivers (See, I try to be fair!) The voluntary, unpaid work done by the local enthusiasts is a rather wonderful thing. I do not believe that it could take place in any other country in Europe. Only in the Commonwealth countries with a good leavening of English blood, perhaps Australia, New Zealand or Canada, could something similar happen.

I did work hard on the Group structure, and am still in touch with many members. Some of us got together to badger the Driving Standards Agency about flaws in the 2007 re-issue of the Highway Code! Later on RoSPA appointed a bright young lady, Maria, as Group Development Officer, and this work still continues, with many very active Groups producing a high calibre of candidate. As this is voluntary and unpaid the success of the Group depends very much upon the dedication, the time that they have available and the expertise of the leaders. Many Groups are supported by their local police traffic officers, in their own time. This, I think, says a lot about the effect that dealing with road casualties can have on individual officers. It is in their own, and everyone's interest, to produce better trained drivers.

The point that I made earlier about male drivers being convinced of their own ability is the reason why we, and the Institute of Advanced Drivers, have always struggled to attract really substantial numbers of members. The cost is not significant - training through a Group is virtually free and the test itself is not expensive. The problem lies in convincing people that the 'L' test is not the end of learning and only the very beginning of being a driver. I have been driving now for over sixty years (started young!), have taken many courses in all sorts of vehicles, and am still trying to get it consistently perfect. I never will, as there is no such thing as a perfect driver.

The former World Formula One Champion Jackie Stewart once said to me that there were only thirty or so top class Grand Prix drivers, and of those, he would only ride with three! Driving on a one-way circuit, with no cyclists or pedestrians is a bit different to surviving public road driving, but nevertheless the comment is an instructive one. A hope for the future is the increasing legislation and attention to company drivers by the Health and Safety Executive. Councils, Corporations and Companies are beginning to realise that they have a duty to put their people through extra training. The 2008 Corporate Homicide Act making prison a possibility for an ineffective manager has sharply focused many management minds. This keeps us busy, but we all wish that we could get more private motorists involved.

RoSPA also ran driver training courses, and in 1981 these were carried out by two full time driving instructors. They resigned soon after my appointment to set up their own advanced training company, with contracts in several African countries. I tested and approved their replacements, two more full time instructors. Whilst carrying on with the expansion of the League – now a fully fledged department of RoSPA, I decided that it would be a good move and an enhancement of my credibility to obtain the Authorised Driving Instructor (ADI) qualification, although it was very inferior to the Police Class 1. It was however necessary to have it in order to give paid professional instruction. There was a theory paper to sit, which was not a problem, and practical tests of driving and the ability to teach. I took the driving test at a Department of Transport centre in Worcester.

We set off, but after a short distance the Examiner asked to me to stop by the side of the road, 'You are a police trained driver aren't you?' he asked. He was obviously ex-police himself to have spotted this quickly - it usually only takes me a few hundred yards and a couple of corners! Getting an affirmative answer he then said, 'Well, bear in mind that the Department does things a little differently from the police.' So, I stopped trying, sloppied it all up to do it their way, and sailed through the test with full marks! Does this say something or not? I think that it does.

To be fair, in the years since then the Department, now the Driving Standards Agency, have come a long way to approach the police standards of the sixties and seventies. The two styles are now closer together. The teaching ability test, with the Examiner role-playing, was not a problem, and quite enjoyable. I have done the role-play myself many times since, and it is interesting and can be good fun. One has to be careful not to be dangerous or illegal on public roads, but that leaves plenty of scope to ham it up, get things horribly wrong and see if the wannabe instructor in the left hand seat actually notices. I usually keep it to things that I have seen other people do, which again gives a big field of potential mistakes. We once, in the job that I went to after leaving full time work at RoSPA, ran a training course with one instructor driving a car while dressed in a gorilla skin and head. This took place on public roads, and no one (including the police) took a blind bit of notice!

The League had been governed by a committee of people influential in road safety in the London area, and this was continued after the amalgamation, with regular meetings in London. I found that again there were a few unreasonable expectations of what RoSPA could do to expand the facilities and membership, but generally the committee was productive. Quite early on I had decided that as far as possible I would run the organisation 'my way' which was not always the way some committee members saw things. There were therefore a few compromises on both sides, but one thing that I had been determined to change from the outset was the name. I felt that 'the RoSPA League of Safe Drivers' was not an appealing one to any age group, particularly the younger generation, which we needed to attract. I proposed to the committee that we changed it to the RoSPA Advanced Drivers Association, which nicely fitted an appropriate acronym 'Road Association.' This did cause a few traumas amongst some of the founder members of the League, and it was necessary to be a bit devious, a bit like getting things done in Sudan, Burma and Somalia.

Eventually the value of the modernisation was seen, and that is what it became for many years, until it was decided to add 'and Riders'. This destroyed my neat acronym, but rightly brought in the importance of advanced motor cycle training. We had asked the Institute of Advanced Motorists if they had any objections to the new name, which brought me into contact with their Chief Examiner, Ted, another former police driver from the Metropolitan Police, who had a fund of wonderful anecdotes. Ted became a good friend, and was, like myself, elected to membership of the Institute of Master Tutors of Driving. He told a rather neat story at a meeting of the latter group, relating to a supposed question in a police examination paper, 'You are on duty at night when you hear an explosion in a nearby street. You find an overturned van in flames, and two people trapped in the cab. In the crowd which has gathered you spot a man badly wanted for an armed robbery. Another man then runs up to you saying 'My wife is nine months pregnant, the noise has made her go into labour and we have no car.' Describe on one line your first actions.' Ted's feeling was that the best one line answer should be 'Take off helmet and uniform jacket and mingle with the crowd!'

An envoy for Mrs. Thatcher

In 1986 Ted and I shared involvement in a major public event to conclude European Road Safety Year. The Prime Minister, Mrs. Thatcher, had prepared a message to the Ministers of Transport of the other eleven countries of the EU. She urged them to take action to cut the toll of road casualties. Eleven people prominent in road safety or driver training had been selected to carry the messages, which were in the form of an ornate scroll.

Ted and I were invited to take part, and of course both our organisations welcomed the publicity. As we were all to be seen off by Mrs. Thatcher from Hyde Park, the media hype was quite intense. Vehicles were being loaned by various manufacturers and companies to do the journeys. I had visions of a Jaguar to drive to Rome. Instead I got a Sherpa van, loaned by Land Rover to go to Dublin! Can't win them all, and there is nothing at all wrong with Dublin, especially as it one of the few places where they pronounce my name properly, but I could have put up with Athens or Madrid in December. Ted got Lisbon in a Daimler, which was very unfair. It led to some mickey-taking for a number of subsequent years. A motor-cyclist went to Madrid, and a pedal cyclist to Copenhagen. A very brave blind man sponsored by the Pedestrian's Association started out on foot on his way to Athens. I did not hear how long it took him to get there - this might let the cat out of the bag, but I don't think that he walked all the way!

An interesting point which emerged later, and which says something about Government efficiency, was that ferry tickets had been bought for someone to take the message to Norway. The Norwegians were not in the EU! We were each teamed up with one or two other people, also well known in the road safety field. My colleague was Bill, a recently retired senior civil servant. It was arranged that I would pick up the van in Birmingham, and drive down to Hyde Park for the send off. It theoretically turned into a Land Rover and back again several times before the big day. Nothing wrong with Land Rovers if you want to cross the Sahara or a muddy field. As Bill, whom I knew quite well, was able to express himself with some force, I did hope that we would not get something with a lot of wind welcoming holes in the back though. I eventually collected a Sherpa van, and as it was December put a shovel and wellies in the back, wrapped in a piece of sacking.

On arrival at Speaker's Corner the van and I were subjected to the full efficiency of a Metropolitan Police anti-terrorist check.

'Open up the back please.'

'OK, but what for?'

'Standard security procedures for the Prime Minister.'

Naturally I expected, as I opened up, that the long bazooka like object in sacking might excite an inspection.

'What's that then?'

'My wellies and a shovel in case it snows.'

'Oh, that's alright then Guv, in you go.'

I do hope that they would do it a bit more professionally nowadays. However, perhaps it was the influence of my International Police Association tie - IPA, (said to also mean 'I Park Anywhere'). I have had the same tie, worn consistently worldwide for about thirty years now, and naturally it looks a bit battered, but I can't replace it as the design has been changed. However, it was once identified by a police officer in the scrum at La Guardia Airport, New York, so it's worth while, beer stains or not.

As everyone got through the security check we were lined up on parade, and inspected and blessed by the PM. She very womanfully climbed up into the cab of an articulated lorry destined for Paris. Mrs Thatcher was accompanied by a cluster of small children, who had won this excitement as a prize for road safety paintings.

As she came to me she bent to the children and said, 'This man is going all the way over the sea to Ireland.'

At that moment a press photographer got a nice shot of the lady apparently closely examining me below the belt! We were handed the scroll, in a long cardboard tube, which had been carried round by an aide-de-camp in a wicker basket, looking exactly like eleven long French baguettes.

So, Bill and I set off for Liverpool, to catch the night ferry. I took the first spell of driving, and all went well until I made an utter botch of a junction in Stratford, which I know like the back of my hand. This, when accompanied by a person very influential in the driving world, is known as the Law according to Murphy (or Sod, depending on one's religious convictions). However, we survived, and arrived at Liverpool Docks to find that (a) we did not have a booked cabin and (b) there was a Force 9 gale in progress. The latter was not the fault of the Ministry, but the former was. Probably the same guy who bought tickets to Norway.

Situations like this call for some police initiative, which is often knowing which string to pull and when, and how hard. Bill had a very nice senior civil servant type melton overcoat, while I was dressed for potential snow shovelling. 'Put your overcoat on Bill, tell the Purser that we are on Government business and need a good night's rest.' The Purser was a simply splendid gentleman looking at the very least like an Admiral in the Swiss Navy, and he reacted to this request in a most gratifying way. A two-berth cabin was instantly forthcoming, as was an invitation to dine in the First Class Restaurant. Bill has this theory that you will not be seasick on a full stomach, so we dined at length on roast turkey, topped up with cheesecake and cream. The theory may be right, it worked anyway, but I do recommend the foetal position on the bunk in a Force 9 storm.

While dining we noticed that the ship had begun to move, but then there was a considerable bump and we stopped, for a long time. On enquiring of a passing steward we were told, 'Ah sure, the little darlin', he's hit the dock wall again. He did it twice last time.' Thus reassured we stopped worrying, and went to bed. The subsequent morning reconnaissance before disembarking revealed that we had been much better off in our lower deck cabin, since the higher a person is on a ship the more the person rolls in a storm. By 6am the lounges were not a pretty sight. The journey actually took eight hours, since somewhere near the Isle of Man I am convinced that the ship was going backwards. The offer of breakfast from the friendly and obviously over-awed

Purser was declined on the grounds that a joke was alright but you know what you do with a pantomime. We climbed into the Sherpa and sped out to the Dublin Docks, Bill driving this time. Although I have never been on a long ocean voyage I do seem to have attracted some storms.

We came back from Cherbourg once in a similar gale. A lady passenger was violently seasick, used her woolly hat as a receptacle, threw it overboard and then had the panache to say, 'I never liked that hat anyway'. A good example of the British spirit! We also had a summer holiday with the children on Guernsey, and came back to Weymouth on a ship called the *Svea Drott* which was on charter from a Scandinavian company. It had been designed to sail the calm waters of the Norwegian fiords, not the English Channel in a Force something gale. That rolled! It was the last one out of Guernsey for a couple of days, and was the time that Ted Heath was shipwrecked in his yacht in the same area. I have some wishful thoughts about this latter incident, but perhaps better not express them in writing.

As we reached the Dun Laughaire dockside we were taken aback to find a three vehicle escort from the Garda Shiochana waiting for us, two motor cyclists and a car. As we were two hours late and the storm was still raging they were bored, cold and wet! Any road up, we got a real VIP escort, done properly, with the motor cyclists leap-frogging each other to control each junction in the city centre, and the speed never dropping below 60 mph. We passed as many red lights and roundabouts as could be found. Either they were showing off, or just wanted to warm us all up. I quite wanted to wave to people, but was too busy hanging on. I have done a few of these escorts at the sharp end, so it was great to sit back and watch Bill coping with it, which he did magnificently. He did say afterwards that he had never before driven through five red lights at take off speed, and I suspect that he enjoyed the experience. It was not until we arrived at the British Embassy that we discovered that the scroll had finished up underneath my shovel and wellies, as a result of either the storm or the drive, and looked more like a French loaf than ever. I did wonder if they might have eaten the one that went to Paris.

We got the opportunity for a wash and brush up and then met the British Ambassador and the Irish Minister of Transport, with some more press interest as we handed over the baguette. After a pleasant lunch we had the chance to explore Dublin city centre, but as the rain was still moving horizontally instead of vertically this took all of two minutes, after which we found a Hotel and slept until it was time for the night boat to Holyhead. This time the cabin had been booked and there was no problem until decanted into the arms of a bored, cold and suspicious Welsh Customs Officer. We finished the journey in good style, and it is a good memory to look back on. A personal letter arrived from the Minister of Transport a week or two later, which was nice, but all in all I think that I would have preferred to roller-skate to Madrid!

North and West Africa and Dubai

The two RoSPA trainers who had left to set up their own business head-hunted me early in 1982 to ask if I was interested in joining them. They had gained some firm contracts for driver training in several African and Middle Eastern countries. Overseas training sessions were scheduled to be of two, three or four weeks duration, so that I could be with my family at home outside those comparatively short periods, but also travel to interesting places. While feeling guilty about moving on from RoSPA so quickly the opportunity to have my cake and eat it seemed to be much too good to miss. I did receive a number of nice letters from members of the Groups, Committee and companies that I been working with expressing regret at my departure. I guess therefore that this period, although short, was successful.

I was asked to take an advanced driving test with a current instructor from the South Western Regional Police Driving School. This went well, with a comment that I would still reach a Police Class 1. As it was twenty eight years since my first course at the Midlands Regional School this was quite pleasant, especially as I was able to tell him something that he had not thought about!

My first overseas assignment for the new company, ISS, - International Safety Services, - was in Nigeria in the summer of 1982, when I teamed up with another former police officer already working for them. It was good to be back with the smells and sounds of Africa, but with these came the realisation that East and West Africa were separated not only by thousands of miles but by very different cultures. Europeans were discriminated against, being pushed to the back of every queue, and it was necessary to pay to be allowed into the country.

I later found that one had to pay to be allowed out again. The country is four times as large as the whole of the UK but at that time had less than half our road mileage, and of that proportion, half again were unpaved. The casualty rate was very high indeed, with even the reported figures suspected of being too low. Road collisions away from a town were known to have led to deaths apart from the impact; vehicles involved being deliberately set on fire with the occupants inside. By ancient tradition those removing a dead or dying person from a crashed vehicle became responsible for the disposal of that person. These two factors, apart from the (to say the least), unsophisticated reporting and statistic gathering would lead to an understandably low reporting of road injuries. A gruesome collection of crashed or burned out vehicles of all types, some still containing bodies, could be seen along most main roads, without exciting much local comment.

I went to Nigeria and other West African countries four times for ISS, during 1982 and 83, and once, later, for RoSPA, and each time found Nigeria to be a deeply corrupt and dangerous country. The major city, and four million strong metropolis, Lagos, is built around lagoons, and therefore the road system requires many bridges as part of the inner ring road. A lot of grandiose road construction projects, the bridges, dual carriageways and flyovers, had been started in Lagos, but many had simply ground to a halt. Uncompleted flyovers were left hanging in the air (a bit worrying in a dark night) and from the air one could be seen heading west out of the city and stopping short just before it reached the sea. I was not able to discover where this had been planned to go. It pointed towards South America! In these conditions collisions were a constant fact of life. Where new roads had been left unfinished or a multi-lane flyover descended into what was effectively a village street, a 'go-slow' invariably took place every morning and evening.

A 'go-slow' meant that one would sit in the car, possibly for hours in the tropical heat, waiting for the vehicles in front to inch through the bottleneck. The local entrepreneurs took advantage of this, and one could buy almost anything whilst stuck in the traffic. Large objects often as big as, and including, a car engine were wheeled along on trolleys and anyone with a vaguely European appearance would be invited to buy a selection of delightful ivory souvenirs. I learned to carry a cigarette lighter and if pestered (for the fifteenth time) to buy ivory, would bring out the lighter at which point the entrepreneur would quickly move on. Ivory does not burn, but plastic does! This could become a game, with the would-be seller usually taking it in good part that he had been sussed out, and quite happy to go look for another sucker! I do feel slightly ashamed of this now, as these guys needed to earn a living, and buying a bit of plastic occasionally would not have hurt me. There was an element of potential loss of face though, since to buy a plastic camel would be seen by the locals as very naïve and hallmark one as a tourist! A sale would also inevitably attract a huge crowd of other would-be vendors, all shouting and pushing with vigour!

However, I had, and still have, another guilty conscience caused by haggling over a beautifully carved wooden tortoise under the palm trees on a beach at Pointe Noire, in Congo. Like many of the similar traders the man had carved it himself, and the amount of work and attention to lovely geometric detail is incredible. I wished that I had offered him his original price. I think though that he would have enjoyed the sale a lot less and certainly would have thought me an idiot. I found that the best way when the situation arose again was to haggle like mad, and both enjoy the game, but when a price was finally agreed to offer an extra, purely as a present.

A unique memory comes to mind of a local driver caught in a go-slow on the top deck of a three-tier flyover. He eventually got out of his car, walked to the low wall and urinated about one hundred feet down onto the bottom tier. I feel that this was probably quite satisfying! When local drivers got tired of waiting in a 'go-slow' they would mount the footpath on either side, or drive for as long as it took on the wrong side of the road.

Arriving by Nigerian Airways (an experience in itself) at Lagos Airport after dark we expected to be met by transport from the client company to the city centre. Invariably we would be stopped four or five times at police checkpoints, each one supported by armed soldiers. 'Have you brought me a present from London?' was the usual demand, with the implication that if we had not it was likely to be a long night. These checkpoints were constructed with black oil drums on either side of the road, and a totally black pole between them. A policeman swung a very small kerosene lamp if he thought rookable Europeans might be on board the approaching vehicle. This was not easy to see in the very dark African night. If one did not stop there was the threat of being shot, but this was not too much of a worry as long as the rifle was pointing directly at us. When aimed at someone else it was more likely to be lethal. Anyone who has fired a rifle will know what I mean – others will have to take my word for it!

On the first occasion we encountered the checkpoints we were in possession of a number of driving manuals intended for the clients, which we handed out to the troops. They were gratefully received, probably under the misapprehension that they were pornographic. On subsequent arrivals we equipped ourselves with some trash to disburse. On one occasion, during daylight, it was possible to see the very scorched high-rise building of one of the Ministries in downtown Lagos. A senior official had been cooking the books, and thought that the best way to destroy the evidence was to set fire to the building. I understand that three employees died in the fire.

We were unfortunate enough to be marooned at Lagos airport on one occasion, when Nigerian Airways, our scheduled carrier, were on strike. It is bad enough to be stuck at Heathrow, Gatwick or even Charles De Gaulle waiting for an aeroplane, but at Lagos this was not funny at all. The place had virtually no facilities (unless one was one of the Nigerian elite), ineffective air-conditioning, unpleasant toilets, one bar and hardly any seats. Nigerian Airways did not believe in making hotel reservations for those held up. I would be interested to see if the facilities are any better, now, but do not really want to risk finding out! We were therefore thrown back on our own resources, and the result was a useful learning curve. We found the fattest, most pompous looking airport officer around and I asked him if it was within his power to get us onto another airline. He swelled up like a bullfrog, said he would find out, and lo and behold we found ourselves transferred to the next flight of Air Afrique to London via Paris! I recommend this form of words as a technique to those marooned in the far corners of the world.

Another experience at Lagos Airport could have been unpleasant. I have been lucky to fly, long haul, on many different airlines, for a good many years, and have never lost an item of luggage. To see the carousel at Lagos gradually emptying induced a very downhill feeling in my stomach, hitting bottom when the carousel was clear and my case had still not appeared. The airline office to whom to report the loss was in the bowels of the building, hot and pokey and the clerks not particularly interested in my problems. After filling in the rather greasy forms, I thought that I had better have another look at the carousel, just in case. Back up the hot staircases to 'Arrivals' and there was my property, going round in solitary splendour, intact and unopened! Back down to the bowels to tell them not to bother, thank you very much!

By this time I was, of course, much delayed, and the man ordered to meet me with transport had got tired of waiting. No answer to a `phone call to the company, so own arrangements were neccessary. An expensive taxi ride got me to the city centre. As it was obvious that I had an accommodation problem, advantage was taken and a tiny top floor room with no air-conditioning in the Hilton Hotel required an up-front payment of the equivalent of one hundred pounds. The going rate for a pre-booked decent room was then about thirty! The Hilton was in the centre, but Nigerian prostitutes congregated a yard or two from the main entrance, and you were assailed the moment you stepped outside. It was, of course, easy and a very good idea to say, 'No', but they could be very persistent, even to the extent of catching hold of your clothing or other bits.

Driving, and trying to train others to drive safely, in Lagos could only be called interesting. The city was, and almost certainly still is (but I do not want to find out) an untidy mixture of modern high-rise buildings side by side with village enclaves where goats, cattle, chickens and children wandered unhindered in the streets. Ducks could also be seen, which was an unexpected hazard, as to Nigerians the duck is the God of Metal. If one kills a duck in a vehicle made of metal much bad luck will follow. The movement of vehicles to avoid ducks could therefore be unexpected, violent and erratic. Most vehicles in African countries are highly decorated, and Lagos was no exception. One would frequently see the legend, 'Jesus rides with me' across the top of the screen. I used to think irreverently, 'Well, He might but I wouldn't!' On the other hand it was an experience to drive to places called 'Tin Can Island' and so on!

One of the training problems was that many junctions had been constructed by British engineers to facilitate the movement of traffic being driven on the left, as it then was. When the traffic was flowing it flowed fast, and these junctions now caused many problems with speeding right hand side traffic streams. The story goes that upon gaining independence from Britain the Nigerian Government had decided to throw away, with many other things, the rule of driving on the left. Drivers were told that on a certain date all vehicles would use the right hand side, but the week before there would be a practice, with lorries driving on the right but cars continuing to use the left hand lane. I cannot prove this without a good deal of research, but I do believe it! The following true fact is one of my reasons for doing so. We were able to get hold of an extremely rare copy of the Nigerian Highway Code, and found that the UK Code had been copied, and partially altered for right hand driving. Unfortunately this had not been done very carefully, and contained unchanged examples of good practice – for traffic driving on the left! Many older surfaces were badly potholed, and water filled, almost to the extent that one looked for a crocodile under the surface. Road humps, known locally as 'speed breakers' were actually suspension breakers, as they were often placed on main roads with no warning, and rose to astronomical heights. The ubiquitous 'push-push', a two or four wheeled pedestrian propelled cart, took up as much room as a big car, but with even more unexpected lateral movement.

One could often see someone on foot behaving very erratically, for example lapping up water from a puddle then dancing into the road waving a panga or a big stick. These were people who had no chance of much needed hospitalisation of course. I once saw a cavalcade of about a hundred prisoners proceeding down a main road to some road works, guarded by one prison officer with a rifle. They all had pangas.

Police procedures at collision sites were rather different to methods in the UK. It was quite a severe offence (for which the offender would be locked up for a long unpleasant time, unless ready cash was available) to move a vehicle after a collision. Since it often took up to three days for the police to turn up and give permission to move, a simple two vehicle collision during darkness would rapidly turn into a multiple shunt of a hundred or so, as they ran into the rear of the ever growing tail-back. If trying to sleep near a road junction a regular thud, crash, tinkle could be heard throughout the night. A factor in this was a dislike of using lights, as it was thought to wear out expensive bulbs and run down the battery. One could therefore be driving outside town on an extremely dark tropical night with no idea of what was coming the other way until suddenly blinded by headlights on full beam. These, and many other examples of different customs and practices had to be researched, learned and passed on to the expatriate drivers who were often our trainees. One that was quite strange was the procedure at a crossroads. If taking the left hand turn the left hand indicator was used, and vice-versa. However, if going straight ahead the accepted custom was to switch on the hazard lights – the four way flashers. This is not done in Wolverhampton. It does however have a certain logic!

A common problem with some of the local staff was an inability to anticipate potential dangers. I found that this is a recognised symptom amongst people who have been raised in poverty. They have never had anything at all to look forward to, as many, or most, of us have had in the richer countries. It can therefore be very difficult for them to think ahead and to wonder what might be - metaphorically - in wait for them. A driver needs to consider this literally as well. Apart from the difficulty of getting guys like this to think, for example, that a vehicle might just pop out of side road in front of them and to anticipate and look for it, there was another very common result. The consequence of not putting oil, coolant or fuel into a vehicle was not appreciated until the problem stood up and smacked them in the face. This attitude, called 'present time orientation', affected almost every aspect of driving, and was one of our major tasks to try to rectify. I have to say here that working to increase better thinking and anticipation amongst much better educated drivers in the UK is not exactly a sinecure. It requires hard work and an ability to nag!

Nigerian traffic law required that a driving licence should always be carried whilst driving a vehicle. This is a good rule, and one that we should have implemented in the UK. It led me into one situation which I still have difficulty in believing - but it did happen, I promise. Nigeria then had a Corps of Traffic Wardens - low level police. As the police themselves were not exactly Nigeria's finest one can draw certain conclusions. These guys were regularly deployed at busy traffic points, ostensibly to control traffic. The signal to stop traffic was a hand at about shoulder height, palm facing the traffic to be stopped. The signal to continue was the hand again at shoulder height, the back of the hand towards the traffic and the only other difference a wiggle of the fingers. This, believe me, is quite difficult to see against a glaring sun and heavy shadows. It required good eyesight, experience, interpretation and knowledge of the system to distinguish between 'stop', 'come on', 'wait by me' and 'I want a present'.

I was training a young expatriate British driver, working for one of the firms with whom we had a contract. We came to a Warden on duty at a busy crossroads. He gave us a signal which my trainee interpreted as 'Stop,' so he did. The Warden left his point, came over to us and said aggressively, 'Why you stop when I tell you to go?'

'You give me licence,' and before I could stop him my trainee had handed over his licence which speedily disappeared into the Warden's breast pocket.

Now he had us, because there was no way we could continue legally without the licence, 'I must fine you twenty naira'- the equivalent I think of about a tenner. Not a big sum, but I knew exactly where it was going! So, we had a lengthy discussion during which I offered to go to the nearest police station, and the traffic became even more snarled up than ever. Eventually it became obvious that we had a situation. He wanted his twenty naira, and I was equally determined not to hand it over.

Eventually the Warden said, 'Okay, you drive with me' and climbed into our car. This was better than arguing outside in the hot sun, so we picked our way through the chaotic traffic and followed his indications. He seemed quite happy to leave his designated duty point, which by now was just a bit frenzied. After about three miles the Warden said, 'You stop here', got out and disappeared into one of a row of small huts. He came back with an English football pools coupon, Vernon's, thrust it at me and said, 'You write this for me'.

I had no problem with this, so put a few crosses on it (marking Wolves for a win I expect) and gave it him back. 'You write name'. Well, this was slightly more of a problem, so I put 'R.Smith, 33 Brighton Road, London' in the appropriate place and gave it back again.

'Okay, here is licence, you go now,' and he disappeared back into the hut. We disappeared also, in the opposite direction, now legal again. I have wondered ever since what he thought that he had got, and if someone in Brighton Road (if there is one) ever received a shock. I suppose one could say that this was a very early example of identity theft! With the benefit of the twenty-twenty vision of hindsight one could also say that twenty naira was probably a very big sum to such a guy and appreciate his reluctance to see it disappear. One tries to understand - Englishmen working for one of the big companies in Lagos, and certainly myself as a visitor, would be seen by him to have so much wealth, status and security. I therefore find it much more difficult to condemn corruption there than I do in Europe.

250

Having recorded some of the down sides of Nigerian life I can move to a rather wonderful experience. We were, of course, training people, sometimes local, sometimes expats, not only in town traffic, but out in the bush. We had been supplied with an elderly Peugeot, and having started apparently with plenty of fuel and the fuel gauge still showing half full discovered that the cupboard was bare. Miles from anywhere, with only palm trees to be seen in any direction and no fuel! After teaching my local trainee a few Anglo-Saxon words, and stamped about a bit I was still wondering what to do (no mobile 'phone in those days) when a small figure appeared from between two palm trees.

'You got problem?'

'Yeah, we got problem, no petrol.'

'Okay, I fix, you give me five naira.'

Well, I thought, five naira is neither here nor there and we shan't be any worse off if he never comes back. But, he did, with a jerry can full of petrol and even cardboard to make a funnel to pour it through. And there was still nothing to be seen but palm trees, in every direction. You don't get service like that on the M1. Rather wonderful, like so many ordinary people, worldwide.

One other fact of life about driving in the bush, which was not so pleasant was that we had to warn expats about the danger of their car being set on fire, with them inside it, if they had the misfortune to hit a sheep, goat or camel. The proper action was not to stop, but to carry on to the nearest town and then report, in comparative safety, to the police. The dreadful thing about the local perception of such a collision was that it did not matter so much if the victim was a child, as a child was less valuable, and easier to replace, than a sheep, goat or camel. Especially a girl of course. Different life styles, opportunities and culture, different attitudes.

As well as the work in Lagos, we went several hundred miles down the coast to the two oil-rig towns of Warri and Part Harcourt. In Warri there is a tree, on a traffic island. For three hundred and sixty four days in the year this is a normal traffic island. On the three hundredth and sixty fifth no Europeans would be allowed, or dare to go near the island, since the tree becomes a ju-ju tree, full of magic and mystery only accessible to one Nigerian tribe. One does not wish to think about the outcome of such an excursion by an unaware European. Warri is a small town compared to Lagos, mainly devoted to the oil industry, and best described as rather less than beautiful. Road conditions in the town centre were difficult and dangerous, with an incredible number of badly beaten up taxis doing unbelievable things, sharing limited space with cattle, dogs, goats, push-pushes and children.

Adjacent to this was a well constructed ring road where speeds of over a hundred miles an hour were possible, and even commonplace. There was the same variation of expertise amongst our trainees as in Lagos, but with a larger group of local staff confidence was higher as they supported each other. Some good drivers were found, and some identified as capable of carrying on in-house training when we left. The general standard of the local staff was much above that of their compatriots who were not employed by the company. This was an interesting phenomenon, possibly caused by good selection, the effects of their job training or a desire to appear competent - perhaps a combination of all three.

The majority of the in-car and large goods vehicle training was carried out in the town or on the ring road. Occasionally we gave ourselves a run of about fifty miles to the nearest oil rig, firstly on the very narrow but dead straight main road, then onto twisting tracks through jungle. The straight roads were dangerous, as they encouraged fast speeds by people with no training for it, often in manifestly unsafe vehicles showing dangerous tyres, sagging suspension, out of track wheel alignment and flapping doors and bodywork. We found, in all the West African countries, an attitude that is shared by most people world wide, including the UK. This is that the vehicle in front must be overtaken, at all costs, whether necessary, worthwhile or safe. It was therefore rare to be followed for long by anything faster than a push-push.

Other factors making the tarmac roads dangerous were the hypnotic effect of the long straights and the heat, causing mirages to appear on the road ahead. An oncoming car would seem to disappear into a black pool, making the judgement of closing speeds and distances very difficult. High speed head-on collisions on these roads were frequent, and I believe the mirage factor to be a prime cause. It was essential to warn new expatriates about this. These roads, identical to those built by the Chinese that I had seen in the Sudan, were still being built. They were still under construction when I worked there again for RoSPA. Very flawed 'aid' indeed, with the dangers either not appreciated or causing no concern to Designers, Donors, Users or Governments.

After completing our work in Warri, and having kept away from the ju-ju tree we drove a company pick-up truck to Rivers Province. This entailed crossing the vast River Niger by ferry – memories of the Nile ferries in Sudan. Our next base was Port Harcourt on the huge delta of the Niger, with its many mouths debouching into the Gulf of Guinea. A large port and town with remnants of the colonial past still visible in the centre, Port Harcourt also displayed much poverty and squalor. One of the districts that we visited was called Bonny, which it certainly wasn't.

We were accommodated in the compound of the French company for whom we were working. Our stay on this occasion covered July 14th and we were invited to a Bastille Day party by the two French chefs who cooked for the company people living in the compound. They had baked a huge cake in the form and colours of a tricoleur. It was cleverly done and looked wonderful, but the usual problem of getting hold of the right ingredients in Africa meant that it was not entirely eatable. More a trifle than a cake! This led, after the consumption of many pastis and a period of maudlin singing of 'Allouetta' and the Marseillaise, into a weepy quarrel between the two, each blaming the other for the baking failure. The quarrel deteriorated into a stand up fight, each armed with a spoon and tearfully flicking lumps of the cake at each other and hysterically screaming French insults.

My colleague Ray and I could also have gone into hysterics over this sight, but did our best to preserve a British straight face. Eventually when the cake ran out, most being on the floor, both the cooks went to bed, I suspect together, and the party came to an end. It is an excellent memory, and had a follow-up the next morning, when the more macho of the cooks came to apologise, and gave us both a key ring with a prominent tag of the International Federation of Master Chefs. I have managed on several occasions since to display it significantly on the table when dining in an up-market Restaurant, in the hope of special treatment. It hasn't worked yet. I live in hope.

The contract which ISS had with a multi-national company operating in Nigeria included work in the nations of the West African littoral, Ivory Coast, Gabon, Cameroon, Congo and Zaire. Ray, a former Wolverhampton Police colleague, had joined me to give driver instruction in these countries. On one or two occasions we were lucky enough to be transported up or down the coast in the company Learjet, a very fast, sophisticated and comfortable small executive jet. This was another flying experience and a bonus which I milked to the full by quoting my RAF experience in fast jets to the pilot. Maybe I did exaggerate just a little (it has been known) but it was usually enough to get me a seat up front. A fascinating experience was flying over the volcano of Mount Cameroon, the vast brown mound of which thrust up towards our aircraft, well visible from the cockpit seat. It was sinister and ugly, a bit like Vesuvius, and revealed itself very clearly, as we were much lower than the commercial passenger aircraft flight paths. It was far less beautiful than the higher ice-bedecked Kilimanjaro, which I was also lucky enough to see from the air, and to climb, later.

One of the problems of working in several different countries was giving lectures on better driving and first aid to guys of several different nationalities. This was compounded by the fact that the trainees were usually a mixture of expatriates, (originating anywhere from Texas to Japan, through Finland) who normally spoke English after a fashion, and local staff. The expatriates were usually graduates, but comprehension of English did vary. The locals in the former French colonies spoke French as their official language of course, whilst those from the former Belgian Congo spoke the Flemish version of French.

Occasionally we had people from one of the neighbouring countries joining in. My French, with a lot of brushing up, was just about good enough to cope, but the mixture could give rise to difficulty. Some special teaching techniques were therefore required, with the whole thing becoming a very interesting exercise. It was necessary to use basic rules on which to hang the lectures – 'Give yourself room to see, steer, brake or otherwise react'. This is still not generally practised in most parts of the developing world, and not properly taught, even where some form of teaching exists. (It is fair to say that neither is it practised very well in the richer and better taught world). We found it helpful to use videos and tabletop model displays to make the necessary points, as standard English technical driving terms, like 'Cadence Braking' or 'Centripetal Force' had to be left out.

One road safety video produced by Walt Disney, illustrating cartoon vehicles zooming about out of control is intended to be seen as cynically funny. In Nigeria it did not even raise a smile. Why? All the local staff thought that it showed a normal way of driving. This is rather sad. Also very sad, I thought, was the fascination that our models had for the local staff. No way had they ever seen anything like these very ordinary miniature cars and lorries, either for themselves as children, or for their own children. They loved to finger them. Just realised in writing this that it was reminiscent of the old craftsmen at BSA and Jensen Motors touching and smoothing their work with love. I felt a strong impulse to give the models away, but they were an invaluable teaching aid in surmounting the language difficulties.

The locals in all the West Coast countries absolutely loved the practical sessions of cadence braking (pumping the brake pedal to retain steering control on a slippery road). They enjoyed the sensation of the vehicle porpoising, and were able to get quite good at it. No anti-lock braking systems universally available in those days. Slippery roads in Africa? Oh yes! Tropical rain turns a slick, cheaply built, hot road surface into an ice rink in seconds. Maybe we saved a few lives through teaching this – I shall never know. Finding a location for practice was a problem for the trainers though, as the noise of tyre squeal was apt to draw a crowd. A mob could get ugly if it was rumoured that someone had been knocked down.

On one occasion I gave some lengthy instruction about first aid, to thirty apparently local staff in Libreville, the capital of French speaking Gabon.

At the end I asked, 'Have you understood?'

There were nods all round, except for one man. I kept him back and asked again, in French, 'Have you understood this?'

No reply, just a blank stare, so I tried the same question in English. 'Not a word,' he said, 'I don't speak French, I'm Nigerian.'

A wrong assumption! In Cameroon another experience could have been embarrassing when I assumed that a young man in working overalls was a local employee. He turned out to be Afro-Caribbean and a graduate of Birmingham University, in Cameroon as a British expatriate expert! Fortunately my mistake had not been explicit, and we got on well together. Ray did not speak French, and being a born and bred Wulfrunian had a fairly strong Midlands accent. This is said, by those who know about such things, to be close to medieval English as spoken by Geoffrey Chaucer and his contemporaries. It was easy to arrange the practical driving so that Ray dealt with English speakers, but we both felt that he should take some part in the theory talks. I selected a group that I thought would understand but suggested that he stick to simple basic English. Leaving the room for a short time I came back in time to hear Ray saying in best Black Country spache, 'If yo goo 'ommerin down the rowd, yo'll feel yer backside going 'alf-crown-thrupenny bit when yer rache the ceurve.' The expressions on the listener's faces were a delight and a joy to behold, but I did all the talks to the French speakers thereafter. I did hear Ray saying later to one of the expats, 'The Gaffer gied me a right bollockin' over that', but I hope that I was not too hard on him. The reference to the historic coins is very much a Black Country expression!

The tasking by the client company to give first aid lectures as well as improving the driving meant taking, as extra luggage, a 'Resusci-Ann'. This is the plastic model designed to allow practice in artificial respiration, particularly mouth to mouth. She was only a top half, contained in a large suitcase, big enough to be a bloody nuisance to carry and get on the aircraft. Being quite realistic she was a reminder of my police helicopter search for the remainder of the murdered girl in the suitcase. She was designed, as a tribute to his daughter, by a Scandinavian man who had been unfortunate enough to lose her in a drowning accident and was therefore young, nice looking and very blonde. The local staff in all the countries rather too obviously enjoyed practising the mouth to mouth resuscitation on Ann, which was understandable, but induced a slightly weird and uncomfortable feeling in Ray and myself. However, a habit of the local urchins in Nigeria was to shout 'Ayeebo, ayeebo' (Whitey) as a provocative insult at any European. We found not long after the initial first aid lecture that we were now called, 'The men with the plastic Ayeebo.'

Having banged on about the problems, particularly in Nigeria, it is only fair to say that generally we were welcomed, with co-operation and interest very high. Local staff, who were after all only products of their environment, could normally be brought to a good standard of competence as professional drivers. They were always very proud of being given a certificate or a badge. It is extremely nice to record that a few took the trouble, and expense, of writing to me at home in England. There were also many interesting experiences, and I have always preferred to 'live in interesting times'. Ray and I were able to enjoy some leisure time on the wonderful beaches of the South Atlantic, Grand Bassam in Côte Ivoire, Port Gentil in Gabon and Pointe Noire in Congo. I have a nice photograph of Ray on a beach surrounded by four Congolese beauties who, no doubt, thought that we were wealthy businessmen worth closing up to. I guess, in their terms, we were anyway. Five local infants, wide eyed and totally in awe at the unusual sight of two white devils on their beach also make a nice picture.

In Cameroon we were based in the big port, and sprawling, hot untidy city of Duala. In the ports of that part of the world, when ships were unloaded onto lorries, the merchandise was rarely stacked carefully, but thrown on untidily in a jumbled mess. Three local trainees and I were following one such lorry laden with sacks of cement away from the docks. I said to the driver, 'Slow down a bit, have a bit more space, because I think one of those sacks is going to fall off.' As I said the word 'off' it happened, covering us with a cloud of cement dust as the paper sack hit the road in front of us. All three trainees, including the driver, looked at me with wide-open eyes, 'How you know that?' I had a reputation as a witch doctor for the rest of our time in Cameroon. Their failure to spot this was part of the inability to consider consequences, yet so obvious if one looked and thought about it. The failure to do this is by no means confined to Africa, it can be found in the richer, better educated countries, but with much less excuse.

Working in Côte D'Ivoire, the Ivory Coast, was another interesting job, as the big port, Abidjan, had a very noticeable ambiance of France. Abidjan had expanded dramatically in the French colonial years, having 700 inhabitants in 1910, rising to well over half a million at independence in 1960. It had a modern and sophisticated city centre, 'Paris by the sea' perhaps. This did, of course, relate only to the centre, but one could find branches of all the Parisian famous name expensive boutiques. Some very glamorous hotels existed, in one of which, quite surrounded by its beautiful swimming pool, we were lucky to stay. An evening stroll along one of the boulevards, enjoying a small cigar, was a wonderful combination of France and Africa. Driving conditions, out of the city, reverted to real Africa. We were able to obtain satisfactory results with both expatriate and local staff from a similar programme to that carried out in the other countries. I have been lucky to meet many interesting people, and one from this period stands out. At Kinshasa in Zaire, in a bar overlooking the Congo (now the Zaire) River, I enjoyed a long and remarkable discussion one evening over many beers. A young local employee of our client company, he was a graduate, and had very positive views about the future of his country and the West African region as a whole. I wonder what has happened to him during the last twenty five years since economic mismanagement, political turmoil and civil war have ruined his country.

En-route home it was normal to fly over the Sahara and Spain to Paris. Hours of nothing but sand or scrub, broken by a landing at Ougadougou in Upper Volta (now Burkina) or Tombouctou (previously Timbuktoo) in Mali. There was often a lengthy stopover at one of these and time out of the aircraft, and I was lucky to see the Presidential guard on duty at Ougadougou. Oh, the fancy uniforms and the colours! The Sahara, even from 30,000 feet is very impressive as it is unrolled underneath for hours, reminiscent in a way of the sight of hours of ice and snow over the Arctic. Despite air travel, it is still a big world. I knew that we might have some work in Algerian Sahara, and was looking forward to experiencing it at ground level, despite the sight of a sandstorm, miles upon miles of it and frightening even when seen from above. The ice and snow capped Pyrenees were the first sight of Europe - home - and another beautiful experience on a clear day. The Spanish and Portuguese sailors completing the long journey by sail from South and Central America in the seventeenth century must have felt this way. A great deal more weary, hungry and relieved than we were, they named the first sight of Spanish mountains on the eastern horizon 'Los Picos de l'Europa'. Part of the Cordillera Cantábrica, they are so known still.

The question should be asked, why did this region, and Nigeria in particular, have such a massive road death problem? It seemed to me that major factors were the lack of proper driver training, inadequate knowledge, poor and corrupt enforcement of traffic law, entirely inadequate vehicle maintenance and the attitude of most drivers. The latter was a mixture of impatience, intolerance and ignorance, and reflected the cheapness of human life. Testosterone poisoning, as mentioned earlier, also had some part to play as then the vast majority of drivers were male. Some traffic laws and local customs contributed to the problem, and mile upon mile of dead straight narrow roads with their hypnotic effect and mirages were a certain cause of many crashes.

I suggested later, through RoSPA, that no improvement was likely until a complete package of road safety training, starting in the schools and with

Government backing, was introduced. Better training and equipment of the police was essential, with driver testing brought to a much higher level and corruption, as far as possible, reduced. None of this was likely in the short term, but is now, perhaps, starting to materialise. It was necessary then to warn any expatriate driving in the region to apply complete and unwavering concentration, develop to as near as possible 360 degrees of vision and 2/10ths of a second reaction times, to stick rigidly to the basic rules of good driving, use a very well maintained vehicle and above all be a pessimist. That advice has not changed. While I was working in Nigeria in the early eighties the number of road fatalities averaged over 10,000 per year. In 2001 it was nearly 10,000, reducing in the following years to almost 5,000 in 2006. Some slow improvement does therefore seem to be taking place. However the Nigerian Road Safety Commission's advice to expatriate drivers using Nigerian roads in 2009 was still to avoid driving at night in view of poorly lit streets, vehicles with missing lights and the increased risk of banditry and roadblocks. Drivers are also advised to ensure that they have ample fuel, carry a charged mobile 'phone and have an emergency contact number. Expatriates are warned that in the event of injury, assistance is scarce outside cities. Even a minor injury may have serious consequences, and mob attacks may be experienced in the event of a fatality or serious injury. Maybe we did some good, as people that we trained could now be in Government or other positions of influence, but there is still a long way to go.

The Managing Director of ISS and I went to Dubai, one of the Persian Gulf United Arab Emirates in October to run a driver training course for a company using expatriate workers. One of the road safety problems in this area was the sudden oil wealth, which made it possible for someone from the desert to abandon his camel and drive off in a Mercedes, untaught, literally overnight. It is necessary to handle a Mercedes or big BMW slightly differently from a camel. Increased awareness of other vehicles and the use of space were therefore a major teaching need. Dubai was fascinating. It was, and of course still is, a thriving entrepôt trade centre.

Displays of tremendous wealth alongside traditional Arabic customs. Gleaming new high-rise office blocks, apartment buildings, and sophisticated and expensive shops within sight of the waterfront. Here wooden dhows were still built in the time-honoured way that I had seen on the Red Sea coast a few years earlier. Dhows built to trade, like those from Port Sudan, across the Arabian Sea to Karachi, Mumbai and the other Pakistani and Indian trading ports. Women wearing elegant and extremely expensive designer clothing walked side by side with women completely hidden and veiled. A shopping expedition, in the cool of the evening, to look for a present to take home, quickly revealed that

I could not afford anything worthwhile! Another contrast, affecting us personally, was that we were housed in the luxury hotel to end all luxury hotels, yet close to the very picturesque old fortress of ancient Dubai.

The weather was fiercely hot, and the cars provided were not air-conditioned. A training run took us across to the RAF base at Sharjah, a few miles along the Trucial coast or east towards the desert. At siesta time it was a welcome change, and worth sacrificing a rest, to visit one of the beaches just outside the city, flop into the luke-warm water or have a go at sailboarding. I found to my surprise, embarrassment and mortification that it needs a lot of practice to stay upright on a sail-board, but it was nice just to fall into the water, which was only slightly cooler than the air temperature!

The time in Dubai was scorching, concentrated work, a useful but strange experience. It was extraordinary to be living in the wealth and luxury of the Arab Emirates but yet to be within easy driving distance of arid country similar to that of north east Africa. It was also a complete contrast to the work and living conditions a few weeks earlier in the western African countries. This made it a very interesting operational experience. It had also provided more practice in the understanding and skills needed for successful desert driving which had been learned in the Sudan and Somalia. I was able to use this knowledge a year or two later in writing a manual on driving and surviving in the desert that was published by RoSPA. This led to my being elected as a Fellow of the Royal Geographical Society, and Jo and I have enjoyed some of their functions in the Midlands, and an annual dinner in the Goldsmith's Hall in the City of London

The next projects that my former Wolverhampton colleague Ray and I were given were in the northern African countries of Algeria, Tunisia and Libya – more desert environment but different countries, laws, beliefs and practices. We had been asked to cover basic first aid again, so Resusci-Ann came with us in her sarcophagus-like plastic case. She was far too big and heavy to be classed as normal luggage, had to be flown as excess and was a bloody nuisance which we could well have done without. However, the contract called for her to accompany us. The first of the North African contracts, in January 1983, was at a base in the northern Sahara, so Ray, Ann and I flew to Algiers. By the time we had found and extracted Ann from the excess baggage pile the immediate rush through Customs was over, so the officers had time to be inquisitive. With difficulty we hauled Ann, still in her big box, on to the inspection counter. 'Open please' said the officer in front of us. I had read the phrase, 'His jaw dropped' often before but had never seen it happen until then. It did, it really, literally, did, right onto his chest! Manifestly he thought that he had found the top half of a real body, and poked a finger tentatively at her chest. The mental processes going on had not yet caught up with the rational perception that we were not really likely to be bringing a body forward for inspection by the Algerian Customs! 'What is this? What you do with this?' were some of the questions when he eventually realised that Ann, like her box, was plastic. Senior Customs men were called in, all very anxious to see the 'body' and it was soon apparent (a) that the Resusci-Ann was not known in Algeria and (b) that we had a problem. Some of the questions and looks directed at Ray and myself indicated that we were suspected of trying to import some sort of pornographic material or sexual objects into the country. Of course, shock and horror, no such conduct existed there! (They said). Bringing the depiction of part of a naked female into an Islamic country did not help very much either.

Trying to explain Ann's purpose was involved and protracted, and input from the company representative waiting for us in Arrivals was not possible as we were sealed off from him, not yet having passed Customs! My offer of a demonstration of 'mouth to mouth' was regarded with suspicion, and declined. Although it was eventually decided that we had not committed any crime, the importation of Ann was firmly banned, and she spent the rest of our stay in Algeria in the Customs compound, never having got out of her box! Fortunately the guy meeting us had a bit more patience than the man who had cleared off from Lagos Airport, and we eventually made contact, sans Annie, and explained where we had been.

It was a four hundred and fifty kilometre drive, well into the Sahara, to our destination, an oasis called Hassi-Massaoud, where the company servicing oilrigs had facilities. The 'road' from Algiers is surprisingly marked on modern maps, but then was no more than a track, which had been roughly smoothed by grading machines. As with many other things from that time, I would love to know if it has been improved. Somehow I doubt it. In view of the length of the journey we set off immediately from Algiers and therefore passed though the lower Atlas Saharien Mountains, the Monts des Ouled Naïl, in darkness. I had hoped to catch sight of the Haut Atlas, whose snow covered peaks rise to well over four thousand metres from the desert floor in Morocco, but this, years later, is still on the 'to do' list! As the sun came up the northern Sahara was revealed in all it's lovely dreadfulness, or perhaps this should read dreadful loveliness. We were following the more or less level and graded road which for many miles was dead straight. The view was monotonous, with a heat and sand haze obscuring the distance. It then became less straight, following 'avenues' of hard sand or gravel between low crescent shaped dunes. These barchans are formed by the movement of sand from a consistent wind direction. They form the common idea of a hot desert, as seen in films.

Near Cwm Idwal

'The Driver of the Year' competition, 1983, with Sarah-Jane, Miss United Kingdom - very soon to be Miss World. Ack. Dunseath-Stephens, Edinburgh

THE ALAN DAVIES GALLERY

Michael Collins.

Myself when young, portrayed by Alan Davies. Acknowledge.

*'Do you **really** want me to fly through the tunnels?' Insp. Mike Collins, Ch. Insp. John Mellor, Sqdn Ldr Tarwid, photo by Derek Johnson*

Reunion at the National Memorial Arboretum, 2007.
Joe's 1950 uniform is still a fair fit!

Iguaçú, falls more wonderful than Niagara or Victoria.

'Hey, man what tribe you from?'

A gentlman of Tarabuco.

X-Ray Tango at Wolverhampton Airport.

A seat with a view. Pago-Pago, American Samoa.

Parasailing over the Pacific.

Sailing in the South Pacific, with John and 'Melinda'.

Rock Guides, Wadi Rum.

A Shan tribeswoman, come to market in Taunggyi.

Hadendwa Tribesman, a 'fuzzy-wuzzy', at a shebeen in Aroma.

Bringing the Hokey-Cokey to the Himalaya, 31/12/95.

Northern Base Camp, Chomolungma.

Ama Dablam - so beautiful. To me, like Uluru/Ayers Rock, not to be climbed.

The magnificent panorama from the top of Kala Patthar.

Southern Base Camp - success after fourteen years!

Joseph - so wonderfully proud to have led us safely - in the dark.

Arrow Glacier Camp above cloud. Fourth night on Kili.

Inspector Khidder Ali and his team.

Superintendent Suleiman Daoud Suleiman.

The Chinese Stones on Chukking-Ri

Sorry, I disturbed you, big guy.

Can you do it, Mr. Foreign Devil? Ten tugriks to try!

Liu Jing Ling and the Li Jiang.

Dinner at the King David Hotel, Jerusalem. 'The Duck!'

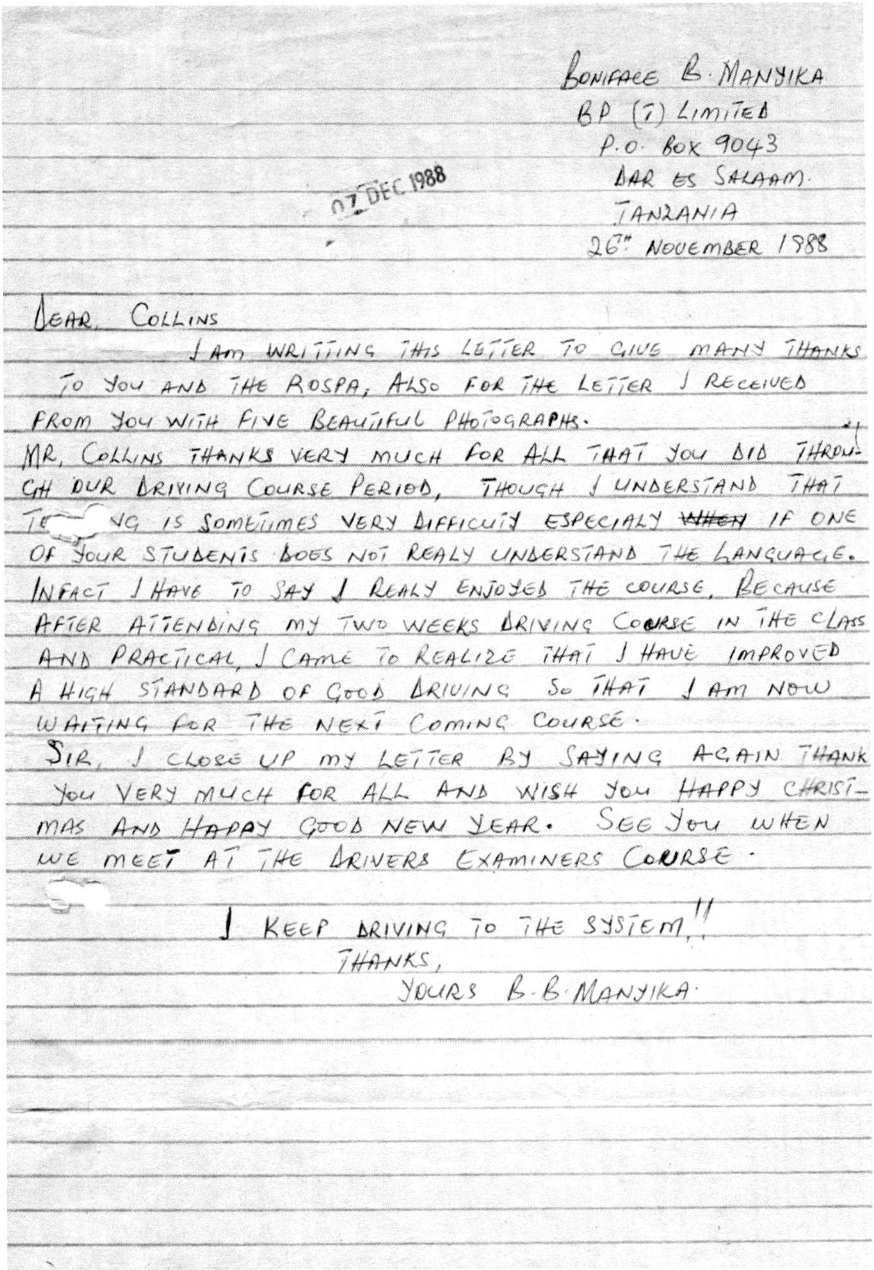

Boniface B. Manyika
BP (T) Limited
P.O. Box 9043
Dar es Salaam.
Tanzania
26th November 1988

02 DEC 1988

Dear Collins

I am writting this letter to give many thanks to you and the ROSPA, also for the letter I received from you with five beautiful photographs.

Mr. Collins thanks very much for all that you did through our driving course period, though I understand that teaching is sometimes very difficult especially ~~when~~ if one of your students does not really understand the language. Infact I have to say I realy enjoyed the course, because after attending my two weeks driving course in the class and practical, I came to realize that I have improved a high standard of good driving so that I am now waiting for the next coming course.

Sir, I close up my letter by saying again thank you very much for all and wish you happy christimas and happy good new year. See you when we meet at the drivers examiners course.

I keep driving to the system.!!
THANKS,
Yours B. B. Manyika.

An appreciated letter from Boniface B. Manyika in Tanzania.

*Santokh Singh, Chief Police Officer and Honorary Prince
of the State of Selangor, Malaysia.*

Face to face with a Maasai Warrior.

The Baroness Anne Gibson of Market Rasen
requests the pleasure of the company of

Mr Mike Collins

at a reception in the
Cholmondeley Room, House of Lords
on behalf of
The Royal Society for the Prevention of Accidents
Advanced Drivers Association
on 19th July 2005 at 12.30pm

Please present this card at Black Rod's Garden Entrance. (Non-transferable).

Jo and I at the house of Lords, 2005.

I did not pose for the cartoon!

"Oh, he's been very sensible about retirement – even gone out to buy a smaller car now there's just the two of us… Listen! Is that him?"

Extra-sensory perception by the artist, I think! Ack permission of Artist, Bill Stott and first printed in Saga Magazine.

A rather dramatised view of my sailing in the South Pacific.
Ack to the artist Terry Halldearn.

Adding to the feeling of being on the set of a film about the Foreign Legion was the occasional glimpse of one of their low, white-walled forts baking in the hot, bright sun, or a Tuareg camp. During a family holiday in the south of France we had found the recruiting depot of the Foreign Legion in Marseilles and persuaded the sentry on duty at the gate to have his photograph taken with Al, then aged about ten. Rather unfortunately for the image of the Legion, they were much the same size, including his kepi!

Barchans are passable given the correct vehicle and tyres and an experienced driver aware of the correct techniques, but otherwise are best avoided. The concave or inside of the crescent always faces away from the prevailing wind and forms a very steep slip face. This can have a thirty-degree or more slope from the horizontal – steeper than most surfaced roads anywhere. We also had to keep a wary eye open for areas of Sabkha or Chott. These areas of salt flats have a brittle crust and a vehicle wandering off a proved track can not only stick but may sink out of sight. I once saw this happen, not on Sabkha but on the edge of a lake in the Cumbrian Lake District of all places. Someone, being too trustworthy about the stability of a Land Rover had wandered too close to the water edge. As the crew scrambled out it disappeared in about thirty seconds!

As we travelled further south, into areas where the wind direction was inconsistent the barchans became seif dunes, formed into continuous long curving ridges with a narrow edge. Seif is Arabic for sword, which describes them well. Seif and barchans can occur as isolated areas of soft sand in otherwise hard flat areas, or merge into a continuous soft sand sea or erg. The northern Sahara has two huge areas of erg, the Grand Erg Oriental and the Grand Erg Occidental, east and west, each many hundred of square miles in area. We had passed through the northern edge of the Erg Occidental and were now travelling through the Erg Oriental, and coming to the mountainous dunes called drâa, sometimes hundreds of metres high. A frightening prospect on foot and impossible to climb by motor vehicle. It was hot, it was tiring and although we were following a well travelled route, not a place to either break down or get off track. The sand was continually scouring into your skin, especially with a little wind, and it is impossible to stop it getting into every crevice and orifice, even in calm conditions. I had been in a small sandstorm, a 'habeeb' or dust devil in Khartoum and its grown-up big brother must be a terrible experience. Not for nothing do the Bedouin and Touareg wear voluminous head cloths.

It was with relief that we arrived at the company base at Hassi Massaoud, which was literally an oasis, a riot of bright flowers of all colours in the burning sand, surrounded by tamarisk and acacia trees. The company existed to keep the oilrigs in production, and our job was to train their drivers to complete the journeys to and from the rigs efficiently and safely. There were a number of vehicles maintained there, and I can make the unusual claim of having driven a logging truck, in a desert. A logging truck, in this context, was nothing at all to do with trees, but a large and heavy vehicle containing banks of computers. I guess that now the complicated material recorded in the truck would be kept on one laptop!

We also did quite a lot of training work in the soft sand, teaching expatriates what to do if stuck half way up a steep slope and especially the special techniques to prevent rolling over going down the equally steep other side! This has not changed. It was interesting to visit the oilrigs, see the heavy work and watch the flares. One consistent problem happened when a rig went off stream and technicians from the coast were called in. They would work non-stop for however long was needed, and then hurry to get back to the more comfortable coast without a rest. Not surprisingly this custom led to a number of rollover incidents when the driver went to sleep and hit a patch of soft sand. It was cured by fitting a cut-out to the engine, so that after a time the driver would have to get out and re-activate the engine, which would then fail again after a set time. This had the effect of breaking the journey and keeping drivers awake. Some years ago Loughborough University conducted an experiment by putting tired people onto driving simulators. Their car management was not improved by either a cold draft of air or loud music. It was only enhanced when they were told to stop, walk round for a bit and have a high-energy drink. Both these ideas are useful advice, even in the UK, where people may try to stretch a journey too far. 'Pressonitis' is a form of disease.

I had a useful experience in Hassi, having developed an intolerance for red wine at home, which had begun to bring on violent headaches. Whilst having our evening meal with the staff, one of whom had the splendid first names of 'Joseph Stalin' I was offered some red Algerian wine. This was local, and very very rough, rather like drinking sandpaper, but it was polite to finish it. I have never had a problem with red wine since. Kill or cure I guess!

Kenya - lost in Amboseli

An occasion of 'pressonitis', where I certainly stretched a journey too far, - a number of steps too far- had occurred after my work in Somalia at the end of 1980. I took some leave in Kenya, before flying home, and rented a car in order to pack as much of the country as possible into a fairly short time. The city centre of Nairobi was, like Salisbury, (now Harare in Zimbabwe) pleasant, shady, and, in my opinion, a tribute to the former British administrators. It was possible to hear lions roaring at night, from the game reserve just south of the city. It did not take a long walk either to find the shantytowns and slums, (not so much of a tribute), which were dreadful by any standards. I was not looked upon there with liking, and it is not surprising, neither are the riots and violence which erupted in 2008 over the disputed elections.

The British had left Kenya, on the surface, peaceful and content and recovering well after the Mau-Mau emergency. Nevertheless it was a simmering pot, bound to boil over, as it did, into inter-tribal violence. This did not touch me in 1980, and I was able to drive through the Aberdare Mountains, around Mount Kenya. The car I had rented was not a four wheel drive and I soon had difficulty with steep slopes on the wet red sand and grit murram surface. I discovered a useful technique here, in desperation, by turning round and reversing up, thus converting the car from rear wheel to front wheel drive. Sort of. Any road up, it then sailed up where it had refused to go front end first!

Despite the tracks, the jungle was fascinating, full of game, with herds of very big buffalo staring at me and obviously not appreciating interlopers into their territory. They were impressed by the reversing technique though. Apart from the game and the roads, the forest was very much like Scotland on the equator, although the Aberdares reach 12,000 feet. Descending to drive along the top of the escarpment of the Great Rift Valley with views towards the ancient volcanoes of Longonot and Ol Doinyo Orok was spectacular. The view to the west from this huge scar on the earth's surface was magnificent. The Valley can be easily seen from space. Despite being forced off the fast all-weather road by the motorcade of Kenya's President, Tom Mboya, who were not inclined to give way, it was good to stop and talk to local people selling fruit and produce at the road side, all able speak English well enough to chat.

Having stopped in a village eating house for a drink on the way back to Nairobi I had an absorbing discussion with a local Kenyan who was an actor. He had just finished filming in a major production by a Hollywood Company, and seemed pleased to share some interesting stories about his experiences with them. I have thought since that this was probably *Out of Africa*, but have failed to recognise him in the film.

After a couple of days like this, enjoying the wonderful scenery and the people, I headed towards Kilimanjaro, with the aim of seeing some big game in the Amboseli National Park. Three more most interesting encounters with local people happened on the way, the first being when I saw a young Maasai girl, in all her tribal finery walking along the road in the direction I was going.

Thinking that she would make a splendid photograph I stopped beyond her and ran back with my camera. She was quite happy to be photographed, and the result was as spectacular as I had expected. Looking at it as a quid-pro-quo I suppose, she was in the back of my car before I could stop her. What to do? I could hardly drag her out, so drove on, becoming increasingly uneasy. To my immense relief we quickly caught up with two older women, who were also very glad to have a lift, offered this time! Sod's law rules, as ever, and a little further on I was stopped by a Kenyan Police Officer, for a routine check. Was I glad to have the two older women in the car! I dropped them all at the market in the next village, and then found four Maasai Moran, young warriors in their traditional short red togas, the colour of dried blood. They each had their head-high spears and the Maasai short sword, called ol alem, which is very like the stabbing sword carried by the Roman legions. Again the photographs that they allowed me to take are spectacular, as they all had the brightly coloured bead necklaces and ear decorations in very elongated ear lobes. Fearsome they looked, but friendly and with enough English for us to understand each other.

The Maasai men are, when young anyway, very good looking, with tall slim physiques. They have been compared, in their physical prowess, with Olympic athletes, and had only recently been stopped from proving their bravery by hunting lions. This was, it should be said, to protect the lions, not the Maasai! The young men still call themselves warriors, ol morani. They were also looking for a lift towards Amboseli, so off we all went. This was wonderful – I had one in the front passenger seat and three in the back. Their spears were too long to go in the boot, and I guess that they would not have been parted with them anyway, so the back seat boys held the four spears, which rested on the back of my seat, on either side of my ears. There was a lovely smell of wood smoke, cattle blood and ochre mud, which sounds unpleasant but wasn't.

Eventually they told me where to drop them, somewhere quite deserted, on the lonely road through the savannah. We parted company, after, for me, a most fascinating experience. I offered them some money for posing for photographs, thoughtlessly pulling out a wad of notes. This, like the whole experience, was I guess a potential couple of steps too far. But, they were respectful, friendly and grateful for the ride, although I did see eyes flicker towards the notes. I would not have missed the experience for worlds. This was not yet the last of the day's events, and it was still early in the morning!

As I left the all weather road for a murram road in Amboseli, I caught up with another lift seeking Maasai man. He was wearing European clothing, and spoke very good English. I learned that he came from a village along this track, and was on his way home for a holiday from his job as a trainee chef in Paris. What a change of life from being brought up as a small child herding cattle. I don't know how it could have happened but I guess that there was a huge intelligence and personality to bridge the gap. I took him, or rather he took me, to his manyatta or village, an absolutely traditional one, inside a boma, or thorn fence, to protect it from lions and other big beasts. The huts were made of a wicker framework of thorn branches, daubed with mud and cattle dung, which bakes dry in the sun. I was privileged to go inside the boma, and saw all the women grabbing children and scuttling inside their huts. I managed, with my friend's permission to get a picture of one lady just disappearing through the low entrance. I was then introduced to a group of the village elders, and again was allowed to photograph them. They had no English, but with some interpretation from my westernised friend we managed. I had managed to learn a few words of Swahili, the lingua-franca of East Africa, and was reminded of my experience, a continent away, with the Monk of Shwe Pyong Byin. No one knows where the Maasai originated. One theory, perhaps far fetched, is that they are one of the long-lost tribes of Israel, like the Falasha of Western Ethiopia. Be that as it may, they are handsome, brave athletic people, a race apart, and I wish them well.

During all this time I had been heading south towards the wonderful silhouette of ice capped Kilimanjaro, 'Shining Mountain' in Swahili. I promised myself that if and when possible I was going to climb it. Kili is a wonderful sight from any angle. Perhaps the most wonderful is as it thrusts violently upwards, soaring practically twenty thousand feet, towards an aircraft overhead. I was privileged to see this when flying south to Rwanda, some years later. Everyone in the aircraft crowded towards the starboard side as we approached, and I am sure that the pilot had to apply some correction to compensate for the shift of weight. What a sight, as the mountain climbs through various temperature zones, from the greenery and trees of the steamy hot jungle through grey rock face to Arctic snow and ice. This experience was before I had had a chance to climb it, but it very much reinforced the desire to do so.

It was with reluctance that I tore myself away from the people of the boma, and counted myself very lucky to have been into their manyatta. The women were still hidden by the way! It could not have happened had it not been for the chance of stopping for the young chef. I hoped that he would enjoy his holiday and enjoy getting out of European clothing. I wonder what happened to him; perhaps he now owns a chain of Restaurants across France. Given the ability to get to Paris from inside the boma, I think that it is quite possible. I was keen to get to the big game areas of Amboseli, and it was no longer early in the day. Following the track, and a fairly primitive map, I eventually reached a tourist lodge, where a beer and a meal served by a very pretty Maasai girl wearing a most splendid bead necklace and not an awful lot else, was very welcome. Amboseli is a huge area and devoid of signposts, so I was now wondering where best to go. While enjoying my beer, a party of European tourists, led by a 'white hunter' arrived at the Lodge. I grabbed this guy, who had a snakeskin band around his terai hat, and asked where I could get the best photographs.

'Oh, no trouble boy,' he said, 'Follow the track to the west until you come to the big swamp. The track turns to the north there, through the swamp, but it's OK at present. Then follow the track'.

Thinking that a man with a snakeskin band around his hat must know what he was talking about, I left the Lodge, it now being early afternoon. The track wound on and after about an hour sharply turned right, and as I had been told, descended into square miles of very sodden swamp. It was far from OK. Amboseli is, at the right season, a dry lake bed, but this bit of it was still very wet. I could see a number of crocodiles with their jaws wide open waiting for me. I later learned that this is a cooling mechanism, not a sign of evil intent, but decided at the time that discretion was definitely the better way. Not a good place for the car to get stuck or break down! So, being too proud to go back to the Lodge and admit defeat, I headed west again, and went on. And on. And on!

Knowing that I had to head north, both to find the big game, the murram road and the beautiful all weather road back to Nairobi, the intended course was to find a viable path through the swamp. With the underside of the Daihatsu protected by steel strips and the usual African heavy-duty springs I was still reasonably happy. The exit barriers are closed at dusk, and it is illegal to drive in the Reserve after dark, but there were still two hours of daylight left. I expected to find the murram sooner or later. So, I went on. And on. And on.

Still heading west the realisation dawned that it would be quite easy to stray into Tanzania, which without a visa or any permission would not have been a good idea. I should, of course, have turned back to the Lodge, knowing that I could find Nairobi from there. However, I was now fully in the grip of 'pressonitis', still hoping to find the big game, and reluctant to give up. But, sooner was now becoming later! Eventually, after what seemed to be hours, and with the sun decidedly lower in the sky, the track made a Heaven-sent turn to the north, onto dry ground. Great. But, the track, which had appeared to be going the right way then disappeared. I was soon, without any argument or equivocation, decidedly lost! The only relief, literally on the horizon, was the great conical bulk of Ol Donyo Lengai in northern Tanzania that I knew lay to the west of Amboseli.

Lengai is a very active volcano, easy to see being well over 9000 feet and sacred to the Maasai, who call it 'The Home of God'. It seemed reasonable that keeping it on my left was the best way of heading north and out of Amboseli, keeping the great beautiful bulk of Kili rising to the sky behind me. I remember thinking, 'If I get out of this I will climb that one day.' Hoping that a track would appear I decided to keep going on this heading. The next problem was that, as no track appeared, the ground became decidedly rough. Then rougher. And rougher. And rougher.

To begin with I was making about twenty miles an hour despite the rutted surface of tussocky grass and mud. But the bumps became bumpier and the thorns thornier. As the Daihatsu was rear wheel drive only and had nothing but the beefed up springs for off-roading it was changing from uncomfortable to quite dangerous. We bounced from hard tussocks of grass to marshy pools, twisting and turning to try to avoid the bigger obstacles. After about an hour, in a wide grove of thorn trees, I was covered in thick dust, really sweating, and praying. Lost, in an unsuitable vehicle in snake, lion, crocodile, elephant and warrior country, the thought was now that a broken spring or two punctures would mean a hell of a long walk in the dark. And only a Maasai or a dead man walks through this sort of terrain in the dark. I was now far past the point of no return. I do remember cursing all men with snakeskin bands on their hats. This was probably the most worried that I have ever been, and I have used the dangers of 'pressonitis' many time since in talking to drivers. Don't do it!

Well, as still able to write about it, obviously I got away with it. Magically, out of nowhere, a comparatively smooth murram track appeared, heading north! I think that I did sit beside the car, say a prayer, and pat it's bonnet. I believe that I had stumbled back to the track from the swamp, having taken a very wide and unknowing loop to regain it. It led to me another wonderful experience, as I did find the big game. It was still light enough, just about, to photograph, and I found herds of elephant, taking their evening water, babies trunk to tail with their Mums. I had been seeing and photographing giraffe, gazelle, zebra and buffalo all day but this was something else. One splendid bull was standing on his own, facing away from me so I got out of the car to photograph him better. He instantly became aware of my presence, and turned 180 degrees to face me, trumpeted and flapped his huge ears. I dived back into the car, he instantly calmed down and went back to whatever he had been thinking about before being so rudely disturbed. This was both disconcerting and instructive, because the guy had turned around so quickly, in almost a jump, and probably faster than I could have completed an 'about turn'. That something so big could move so quickly was frightening. I also saw this agility in quite a different animal by pausing on the raised bank of a small river. Below me, on the other side of the river, half in and half out was a big croc, enjoying relaxation – that is if crocodiles do relax! I tossed a piece of turf, cruelly it seems in retrospect, onto his back. He whipped round and was gone below the surface in a fraction of a second, with only a ripple to show that he had ever been there. That also was instructive!

So, I learned a number of things from this experience – which, I suppose, is what experiences are for. One is never to trust a white hunter, especially one wearing a hat with a snakeskin band. My subsequent trek and climbing guides in Africa and Asia have all been local people, and wonderful they have been. They didn't wear terai hats! Secondly, Africa can bite very hard indeed if you let it. Thirdly, if you press on when it is much more sensible to turn around you can frighten yourself very badly, and finally, elephants and crocs can move very fast!

Driving back to Nairobi, on a decent road was also an experience, as I continually passed, or drove round, the silhouettes of giraffe who apparently take it over at night! It also gave me the chance to wind down a bit after somewhat of an eventful day, but back in the hotel was still so hyped up that I had to ring home despite the hour, and talk about it. Some steps too far, I think, on that day! I have a very beautiful reminder of that day at home. On arrival at the exit to Amboseli, just about to close I was literally mobbed by traders clustered at the barrier, all hopeful of one more sale. I guess that I was the last chance of the day, and I bought an eighteen inch high carved wooden statue of a Maasai Moran, kneeling with his spear and shield, and I suspect, about to go in search of his ritual lion to kill. He is made from polished redwood, giving him absolutely the right colour, and is a true work of art, looking exactly like the four young warriors that I had picked up earlier in the day. I would not part with him for vast amounts of money. Later, giving a talk about Africa to senior boys at my son's school, I produced him and said that his name was 'Affi- an-zoray' which may, or may not, mean, 'May the testicles of your enemy be wrapped tightly around his neck.' This went down quite well, although I think that the Headmaster was slightly shocked!

Back to the Sahara

The work that Ray and I had been doing in Algeria had entailed more flying in the company aircraft, between the oases, each of which had a landing strip, so there are some interesting entries, as a passenger, in my log-book. We had flown another five hundred kilometres much deeper into the Sahara to In-Anémas, near to the Libyan border.

In-Anémas, like Hassi, was an important oasis with a substantial company base and an airstrip. We did similar training and assessment work there.

Ray and I had a change of scenery in March 1983, when accompanied by Annie we flew to Tunisia. This was after a rest period, which Annie did not need but we did. We were not too surprised when a similar performance occurred with the Customs. On this occasion I was at least allowed to demonstrate what Annie was for, in the Customs Hall, to an extremely interested audience. This however cut no ice, and she was again imprisoned in the Customs compound for the rest of our stay. We worked nearer to the coast this time, being based in the town of Sfax, and having the chance to see some of the wonderful remains which the Romans built when they conquered this part of North Africa. What a privilege to drive along the coast road and pass the almost complete Roman arena at El Jem, which rivals the Coliseum.

The next location, for the same oil company was to fly into Tarābulus (Tripoli) for work in the Sahrâ Lîbîya, the Libyan Desert. This was about the time when Colonel Gaddaffi was orchestrating the build up of anti-western propaganda in Libya, and we had to apply for a special visa to go into the desert. The shops in Tripoli that had done a good trade in catering to tourists had mostly been closed by the anti-west policy, which was a disappointment, as I had managed to buy a local doll for Nicky everywhere else that I had been. This had included even the poorer countries like Somalia and even Congo, but in Tripoli there was not a doll to be found, even at the Airport. Tripoli Airport was unequivocally Arabic, with not a word in any European language. They had even removed the male and female schematics from the toilet doors, so you had to guess. The alternative was to wait outside to see who went through which door. This could also be difficult, with the majority of men wearing djellabirs and headcloths! All P.A. announcements were in Arabic so getting on the right aircraft was also a matter of guesswork as it had been at Rangoon, but for different reasons. It may have changed now, with Gaddaffi having softened his stance a bit - I shall try to find out one day!

I was determined to complete the doll collection (it has continued by the way, and is now vast) although the ownership is at present somewhat in question! Having acquired our desert visas we were again flown to various minor airstrips, Zella, Waha, Sarir, Samah, 103-Alpha and Quebec-20 (the latter two oilrigs). At one of these I found a suitable piece of Libyan tree, and concealed it in my kit. At home I had a go at carving two figures, male and female. The man, without much effort on my part somehow turned into a very acceptable replica of the film star Omar Sharif. Jo made him a red tarboosh or fez, and he looks very Libyan. The woman did not matter so much (of course). The couple are Muslim, so she is virtually concealed by her head to toe clothing.

The work again went quite well – we had not even tried to get Annie through Customs this time. The northern Libyan Desert is very different from the black flinty desolate tract of wasteland that I had seen in the south east quadrant while working in the Sudan. This was much more Hollywood style, with rolling yellow barchan and seif dunes, so that we were able to pass on a knowledge of desert driving to the expatriates. The locals had to be restrained by pointing out that it was not at all unknown or difficult for two vehicles to meet head-on at the crest of a dune, in a hundred square miles of sand.

We were accommodated in staff quarters in the oasis sites. Alcohol was, of course, totally forbidden in Libya, and it's possession subject to severe penalties. However! The European oilmen liked to drink, and the wherewithal to make alcoholic drinks on site, was brought back, piecemeal by people going on leave. I found that a cupboard in the room allocated to me, normally occupied by a guy currently on leave, contained all the stocks recently gathered in - enough to found a small brewery. This was a little worrying, but it had not been discovered nor the whistle blown by locals by the time we left! The aircraft used by the company in Libya was not an executive jet, but a quite big and powerful single engined Pilatus Porter, with a very good short take off and landing performance. Having palled up with the two Swiss pilots I was able to log several hours as 'pilot under tuition'. We often flew long distances, well into the desert, between sites and rigs. This was quite exciting as it was possible to fly very low through the wadis, with the dunes rising above us on either side. One I liked particularly was around Jebel Zeltan. Spectacular. No people or animals to upset of course!

Back in the UK for some training work with British Companies I found that I was becoming unhappy with the way that ISS was going. It seemed to me that we were being asked to rush through training programmes with not enough time being given to each individual driver. This meant, in my view, that we were no longer giving as good value for money, and in the summer of 1983 I left the company. Whilst not agreeing with the policies that were developing I remain very grateful for the exceptionally interesting, superbly informative view of North and West Africa that I gained through employment there. By now I had either worked in or visited nearly all the African Countries above the equator, and gained a lot of experience of driving in those conditions. (And even some flying as second pilot.) I should make it clear that the Companies using the same name, as listed on the Internet, are not the one to which I refer above.

After leaving ISS, and while enjoying a holiday at home, the post of Chief Examiner for the Royal Society for the Prevention of Accidents became suddenly vacant again through the tragic and early death of my successor. I was invited to return, and whilst I was certainly not pleased about it happening in that way, it solved the problem of looking for something else. Ron, who had been the head of the Birmingham side of the West Midlands Police driving school, had not altered much of what had been set in place, and I fitted back in easily. I was soon travelling again, with a feature in the Belfast Telegraph in October describing an initiative to improve driving skills in Northern Ireland. Surprisingly during the summer of `83 we had also managed to fit in a holiday in the Lake District, then travel up to Edinburgh to pick up Nicky and her friend Karen. We took them by ferry for a further very enjoyable holiday on Arran, where I climbed Goat Fell.

We had also visited Al in Germany during the summer of `82. He was posted with the Royal Corps of Transport to an Army Base in Northern Germany. I drove over in May, and was able to stay in the Mess. This led to the interesting and slightly worrying incident where I was asked to pull a Base notice pole upright by means of a tow-rope attached to my car. This had been flattened by about five young officers all riding in Al's two seater Spitfire, which he had driven to Germany. I believe that despite my efforts blame was awarded for this escapade, and some extra Guard Duties awarded! Despite this it was an enjoyable visit as I was able to visit an Army exhibition at the Base. We had a very pleasant visit to Hanover with Sue, an Army Nurse with whom Al had become friendly, and also both had a go at water-skiing. This was a very ingenious leisure activity, with a high wire circling a large lake. Hand grabs whizzed mechanically around the wire and, wearing skis you grabbed hold (if possible) as one passed. Al could do this, and was towed around the lake at high speed several times, but I was a total failure at the grab, and was jerked out of the skis and into the water every time. Very frustrating seeing five year old boys doing it with panache!

The Spitfire has possibly featured in the written records of the Royal Corps of Transport, as when making his farewell visit to the Mess it dumped the whole contents of it's sump on the newly surfaced forecourt, just outside the front door. This, however, did not become my problem.

Jo and Nicky and I went over again in July, driving through France and stopping overnight in some delightful places, Gerardmer and Colmar in Alsace. We met Sue again, and had a very pleasant holiday, seeing some delightful places in Germany also. Yes, Spring of `82 to Autumn of `83 was quite a full period! In the Autumn two more interesting things happened, this time in the U.K. Through RoSPA I challenged the Motoring Correspondent of the Express and Star to take the advanced driving test. Others of that profession to whom the same challenge had been issued had declined. Could they have been afraid of being shown up? However, this gentleman sportingly agreed, and we got full page feature treatment with useful publicity which was, of course, the idea. In October, as well as the Belfast visit I was asked to be one of the judges of the finals of the National Safe Driving Competition, to be held in Birmingham. The prize was an Alfa Romeo33 saloon, to be presented to the winner by Sarah-Jane, Miss United Kingdom, who next year became Miss World. Well worth having. (The car). There had been a lot of competition in the early rounds, and finalists had been selected from various parts of the UK. The other Judge, Gordon, who was also one of our Examiners, and I had the pleasure of being photographed on each side of Sarah-Jane (not just once either). I had these photographs doctored to remove Gordon entirely from the picture. Well, why not, he was spoiling it. I possess a tea-plate made to show such a doctored photograph, but this has been banished to my workshop.

The event had been organised by a Public Relations Consultancy in Edinburgh for RoSPA. Two more consequences emerged, one being that I received a very flattering letter from the firm, saying that they believed that no one else could have picked up the details at the last minute as I had done. This was nice for my fragile ego and, I suppose, welcome at RoSPA. The second was that they paid for a new briefcase! One of the competitors had reversed over the original. This had to be, of course, the man from Northern Ireland! I felt so sorry for him, as it was at least half my fault for having put it down where it could be reversed over. He did not win, but in the interests of non-bias both Gordon and I agreed about this and did not hold my briefcase against him. The winner was, oddly enough, a former police driver, who was clearly in a class of his own. It should be said that he had the balls to ask me to stop talking (a deliberate ploy!) and let him concentrate. I gave him a huge brownie point for this.

Road Safety and a red face in Rwanda

After these high spots I continued with the work of building up the Association, and recruiting examiners. In mid - 1984 RoSPA received a plea from Sonarwa, the only Insurance Company operating in the Central African Republic of Rwanda. They were rapidly being driven out of business by the high volume of road deaths and collisions. With the agreement of the

Rwandan Government they asked for two road safety experts to visit the country and design a road safety strategy to help reduce death and injury. As this was a high profile undertaking it was decided that the Head of Road Safety and I would visit Rwanda for up to a month to study the problems and produce a report with recommended action. At last – official recognition as an expert! This was, of course, before the eruption of the horrible series of civil wars, ethnic conflict and genocide that devastated both Rwanda and the neighbouring small country, Burundi between 1990 and 1993.

We flew to Kigali, the little capital of Rwanda in August, via Brussels. Rwanda had been a Belgian colony, and I had needed to radically brush up my French. Mike, my colleague, was content to leave that to me! I had not used any since the year before in West Africa – use it or lose it. En route we had the wonderful experience of flying near to Mount Kenya and the Aberdares, with Amboseli coming up below. My experiences of a few years before in both areas were still very much in mind. Then the aircraft tilted to starboard over Kilimanjaro, as I described earlier. A rather wonderful journey, full of memories. We were both surprised to see how tiny Kigali is. There was, at that time, just one set of traffic lights - that's in the whole country, which is just a little bigger than Wales. It is, or was then before the genocide, a little jewel of a country, known in Africa as 'Le pays du printemps perpétuel', the country where it is always Spring. What a truly wonderful thought - optimism and budding new life all the time.

Traffic discipline was however non-existent and we saw one reason for the collision statistics as early as leaving the airport. Hundreds of 'Mammy Wagons', ancient old minibuses used as taxis, certainly not roadworthy by UK standards, crammed to bursting with passengers. One of these involved in a collision could involve many deaths and injuries. In a poor country they were the principal means of transport for most people. Private cars were not common. The police, we were informed, were also without transport, and walked to the scene of any incident. Shades of the Sudan, but at least there they used camels. We also noticed, during this initial impression of the country, the number of heavy lorries. Rwanda is completely land locked. Goods, and food not grown in-country, came in by big truck, adding to the road problem. The people though, as in so many parts of Africa, were friendly, smiling and wanting to talk to the foreigners.

We were met at the airport by the Manager of the Insurance Company who needed our advice, and he and his wife provided transport all over the little country during our stay. It was going to be necessary, as for my work in Sudan, to see as much of the country as possible, mainly to assess the road structure. They had a nice Mercedes, of which he was obviously very proud, and I was, in due course allowed to drive this. I first came across the Mercedes foot operated parking brake on a steep and narrow murram road in Rwanda, and have never liked them since. I have a strong preference for the old-fashioned handbrake, which does not require one to be able to dance the quickstep, flamenco or tarentella. There were paved roads in Kigali, and some main roads to the coast through Uganda and Kenya were at least partially paved, but otherwise they were mainly murram, narrow and treacherous. There was a dense population of over seven million, compared to less than three million in Wales (at that time). As Rwanda is a country of volcanoes, mountains and plateaux (and one of the few remaining haunts of the mountain gorilla), the human population was squeezed into an even smaller area, increasing the likelihood of pedestrian injuries. At the time of our visit it was depending on subsistence farming, coffee and tea exports, some light industries and foreign aid. Ruanda-Urundi was part of German East Africa before the First World War and was mandated to Belgium, as part of the Belgian Congo, after the war. King Leopold 2nd of Belgium 'acquired' the Congo as a personal possession in 1885 and called it the Congo Free State. Finding it too much to manage he handed it over to his Country to be governed as a colony in 1908.

Another example of how the European powers played fast and loose in Africa. The Congo became unstable at least partly due to the way in which the Belgians scuttled, very much like rats leaving a sinking ship, out of their possessions when the going got rough. At least we, the British, despite being shot at, tried a bit harder to leave a stable country behind us in colonies like Kenya.

Mike and I were quickly invited to a party (again, any excuse) to meet the British Chargé d'affaires, there being no formal British Embassy. I became involved in two interesting conversations here, the first of which involved the British Manager of the local Company. He said that his daughter was coming up for her Rwandan driving test, and boasted that he did not expect a problem, as he would send a case of beer to the Examiner if it became necessary. This did not impress me very much, being similar to the two attempts at bribes while I was a Driving Examiner in the UK. Strange how a driving test can bring out the worst in people. Paying to get vital vehicles through customs in Somalia was not, I think, comparable, or personal. I next thought that I had overheard an unmistakeable Black Country accent, somewhere in the room. Yo conna misteake it. Focusing in on this I found a guy who looked a bit as if he wished he were someplace else.

It quickly transpired that he normally worked in one of the big factories in Wolverhampton. Small world again. I explained why we were in Rwanda, and asked why he was here, especially in mid-August, the start of the Wolves football season. He said, 'Ah'm 'ere to show 'em 'ow to mek 'ose'.

As I had no idea what his trade was, and no detailed knowledge of what his firm made, I asked, 'Oh, hoses for water irrigation systems?'

'No, corse not, 'ose". This left me not much further forward.

Wondering if 'hose' implied setting up spinning or knitting machinery I tried, 'Are you modernising a weaving factory then?'

After some other uninspired guesses, and taking pity on my obvious ignorance he at last revealed all, 'Yo know, 'ose fer diggin' up weeds'.

I did get it in the end!

He was a skilled metal worker, funded by the Overseas Development Ministry to help start a small factory to make 'hoes'! This is a true version of the famous Two Ronnies sketch 'Fork Handles'.

I felt it necessary to look closely, as soon as possible, at driver training facilities in Rwanda. We had found that the driving test consisted of a reversing manoeuvre into a 'box' of cones, a hill start and a turn in the road on a steep murram hill, and a fifteen minutes drive, conducted by the Gendarmerie. There was only one driving school in Kigali, the 'Centre Technique Automobile et Industriel' or 'Cetai'. I thought that I should see how this operated and found that it was being run by a young Rwandan who had been quite successful in several East African Rallies. They were using very small four-wheel drive trucks, miniature version of a Land Rover, practising changing direction on a narrow murram hill. There were a number of Rwandan trainees there. The Instructor asked if I would like to have a go. Foolishly I volunteered. Never volunteer, especially in Africa. It was very cramped in the driver's seat, I was wearing desert boots, my trousers were wet and sticky and it was extremely hot. All good excuses Though the best one is that after I had started the 'turn in the road' manoeuvre on the steep hill I found that the handbrake had been disconnected! This was not easy. Volunteering had been a dive into the deep end, and a step too far, again. I got through it, after a fashion, but very mindful that the Instructor and onlookers had not been impressed. My brown face became red. I walked away from this with the strong feeling that perhaps the Rwandan driving test had hidden depths. I also concluded that Cetai had the potential to train learners well, and our final report suggested that it should be supported and expanded.

After this start we made a detailed study of the problems in Kigali, and with the help of the Insurance Manager and the Chief Officer of the Gendarmerie identified the black spots, 'points noirs'. We looked at the vehicle inspection and vehicle testing facilities and spent some time with the police. They believed that speed, imprudence (carelessness), poor training, drunkenness, overloading of vehicles, particularly the minibus taxis, poorly maintained vehicles, and noncompliance with signals were major factors. Not too different from Europe then. These were factors for me to consider. Mike was an experienced traffic engineer, and assumed responsibility for compiling collision statistics, traffic patterns and examining the road construction in the black spots and suggesting ways in which they could be improved. He had already noted dangerous curves and the narrow streets congested with pedestrians as factors needing improvement.

We spent a very busy three weeks looking at these and many other issues. We were also able, in the process of examining the road network, to see quite a lot of this beautiful little country. I have photographs of a pride of lions (Father, Mother and children) by the side of the track and, in counter-point, a 35 kilometre maximum speed sign nailed to a tree. In the same area, at the entrance to a game reserve was a photograph (also nailed to a tree) of a man being eaten by a large male lion. It bore the legend, in French, 'Eaten under the eyes of his wife'. It was there as a warning not to leave one's vehicle. The photograph had apparently been taken by the victim's wife! The mind boggles at bit – one might have expected hysterics not a photograph, but perhaps she was pleased about it.

We also saw hippos in Lake Kivu, which is tiny in comparison to the big African lakes of Victoria and Tanganyika, but is still fifty miles long and about thirty wide. Maribou storks again, still looking like elderly clergymen as they did in the Sudan! Our eventual report was compiled back home at RoSPA and then translated into French. It ran to fifty one pages, starting with road safety training for children, with educational posters, right through to road improvements to eliminate the points noirs. We were both very pleased with it. With the Desert Driving book and Sudan Report it formed part of the portfolio for my degree in 2002. Regrettably Sonarwa decided that they could not employ RoSPA to actually carry out the suggested improvements. This is likely to have been because of the cost, as it would have been expensive. In view of the carnage to come in a few years time, it may have been for the best, for us at least. I have wondered what became of the happy-go-lucky Rwandans that I met. The young Instructor at Cetai, for example, who hugely enjoyed my ineptness on the steep murram hill - no more East African Rallies for him after 1990 – or the helpful and friendly Gendarmerie and ordinary people. Who knows? The history of individuals from that time in Rwanda are lost for ever.

Despite the resumption of day to day work at RoSPA Jo and I managed to sandwich in another trip abroad in October to Southern Germany. This was to visit Al, who was now out of the army and at Freiburg University, completing the first six months of the year abroad for his linguistics degree. We made the most of it, enjoying a lot of this beautiful part of Germany and making the first of several visits to the Rhine Falls and Mainau and Meersburg on the Bodensee – Lake Constance. I was then asked to run a driving course in Brussels for one of our major client companies in January 1985. This almost led to my being arrested for attempted theft! My IPA connections had been used to arrange an interview with the Chief of Police in Brussels. In order to do the job properly I wanted to know what major traffic problems were faced by the police. There was a rather odd attitude to security as we entered the big building, obviously relaxed like that in Castlemore, Tipperary. Having said at the desk that we had an appointment with the Chief, we were left to wander about and find our own way to his office without proving identities.

However, on being invited in we found that he was having a brick wall built outside his window, blocking off the splendid view of the very grand Grand Place, the centre of Brussels. This was to deter terrorist attacks! I wonder in retrospect whether it was a result of the troubles in the former Belgian African colonies. We had a useful discussion, during which it emerged that he was very envious of my having a police pension at my age. Also, 'Traffic problems, no, it is all the bloody tourists queuing up to see the Mannikin Pis!' We managed to inspect this famous statue later, and were surprised to see how tiny it is - not much to get excited about!

As we were about to leave the Chief's office, I saw my folding umbrella on a table next to his desk. Thinking that I had put it down there I was a fraction of a second away from picking it up as we walked out. Then, by a stroke of very good luck I realised that, 'No, bloody hell, mine is in my brief case' and managed to turn my hand movement into a goodbye salute. Definitely an embarrassing step too far if it had happened. I am fairly sure that Ronnie Barker could have made something of this scenario as well! After that all went to plan, with the usual opportunities on a driving course to see other places of interest. We enjoyed a visit to the battlefield of Waterloo, and drove through the more recent battlefield of the Ardennes. Luxembourg City made a useful training destination. A prowl on foot around Brussels, to sample their speciality, moules marinière, meant using my own legitimate umbrella, but I found moules over-rated. I was also fortunate to get to Ghent in time to see a performance of Eugene Onegin at the Opera House.

I and my RoSPA colleague decided, after seeing many near misses during this visit, that Brussels was probably as dangerous a city as anywhere in Europe. There was a reason for this. The Belgian Traffic Rules specified that an indicator signal was legally imperative whenever the steering was used. This resulted in drivers not looking in their mirrors to see if the intended move was safe, but relying on the signal instead. The consequence was that Brussels, in particular, was full of vehicles covered with flashing lights like Christmas trees, but with no-one worrying about what the other traffic might be doing. This is one aspect of driving that our legislators got right, by making the signal in the UK an option, not an enforceable requirement. It should be obvious, but in many cases obviously is not, that the mirror search is the essential priority, and the fundamental requirement. The signal is only a confirmation, not a carte blanche. Police training specifies that signals should be given only if there is someone, or likely to be someone, who will benefit from the signal. This is not necessarily another driver. The thinking behind this instruction is to make drivers actually look, and think. Automatic reliance on the effect of the signal is not a dependable alternative.

Later that month I was somehow able to sandwich in a winter visit to Freiburg, where Al and I enjoyed skiing on the slopes of the Feldberg. I have never cracked skiing to any successful degree, can manage a straight line but not much else; too late in life to start, I guess. It was good fun though. Personal piloting took place again, in a familiar Cherokee, from a former Luftwaffe airfield near Freiburg. Al and his University roommate Gerhard joined me as passengers to complete a busy month! We enjoyed looking at the snow-covered vista of the old city of Freiburg and the hills of the Feldberg and Schauinsland from above. Gerd and his family are still good friends of Jo and I, as well as Al and his family, and we have shared some enjoyable times in Germany and the UK with them.

With snow still on the ground that winter I was invited to assess the driver training value of a Welsh Mountain Rally School that was due to open in March. A RoSPA journalist and I drove to the School near Carno in Mid-Wales, hoping, with snow falling steadily all day, that we would regain Birmingham before nightfall! The new School was owned and run by Jan, a successful rally driver who had driven BMWs and Porches at international level. He invited my views together with three others, our journalist plus a local Supermarket Manager and a Solicitor who were also invited. He hoped to get a wide range of ability and opinions and to sort out any problems before opening. I sold the idea to RoSPA, as it was obviously going to be of interest, and RoSPA, scenting publicity, agreed our going.

The rally stage that we used was a loose and stony forest track with hairpin bends and steep ascents and descents, through thick mature trees at Coed Ffridd Fawr, high above and well away from the main road. The car in use was the rallyist's special of the time, the Ford RS 2000, a lovely car to drive in a hurry, which I never owned but eventually came to know quite well. This experience was quite different from driving in the desert, a lot colder for one thing, but the disciplines necessary to keep the car heading to where you want to go have similarities.The main sensation, during his demo drive, was one of speed, going steeply downhill on gravel with hefty tree-trunks not far away on either side. After a few seconds though, as it should be with any expert driver, it became apparent that Jan did know what he was doing. I found that the forest track provided ideal conditions for advanced driving practice, provided that it was supervised. Accelerator control, braking and clutch finesse, positioning and observation are all techniques lacking in most road drivers. They have to be learned in this environment, and can be translated into car control in hazardous conditions or collisions avoidance. The ability to gauge the balance and response of a vehicle in extreme circumstances is critical. The comments from the 'guinea pigs' were favourable, and the planned weekend package and training schedules looked good.

I wrote in the RoSPA newspaper, 'The standards of car control, reaction and discipline required by the competition driver are so much higher than those displayed by the average motorist that training of this sort can only be of advantage. If it were possible I would like to see off-road car control practice introduced for all drivers'. I have not changed this view, since 1985, one little bit.

The final word was also mine, 'I believe that the School will be of substantial value, not only to the enthusiastic individual who wishes to improve his knowledge and ability, but also to fleet operators. I have no doubt that the latter would find a reduction in costly collision damage, injury time and inflated insurance premiums after a sharpening up process in the Welsh forests.'

Still no change in my views, but industry, the insurance companies and Government have largely failed to appreciate the value of off-road training.

There was then a change of pace in March. A colleague, Gordon, now appointed as Driver Training Manager, and I were asked to run a training course in Nigeria. The client was one of the oil support companies whose staff I had trained previously, in Nigeria. We were based in Warri, down the coast from Lagos, where I had worked before - the town with the ju-ju tree! Gordon had been, before joining RoSPA, a Warrant Officer - senior NCO - and transport specialist in the British Army. (He is now wearing the splendid uniform of the Chelsea Pensioners.) We caught a small Twin Otter aircraft at Lagos to get toWarri. The pilot of this was Nigerian, female and big enough to completely fill the small cockpit. Well, she got us there. However, Gordon, not surprisingly in view of his background, was unimpressed with the customs facilities at Warri. This entailed putting our opened cases on the extremely dusty airport apron. A so-called customs officer, actually a soldier, then stirred around the contents with the business end of his rifle. I had my fingers very firmly crossed, as I thought that Gordon was likely to hit him. I could feel him wanting to.

After this inauspicious beginning the course went well. It was designed to find local staff who were capable of in-house driver evaluation, and again despite the problems and 'quaint' behaviour patterns of the country the people were hospitable, friendly, interested, and willing to learn. You can't ask much more than that. We did find several guys who were very capable of doing an assessment job, and rewarded them with certificates and RoSPA badges. They were extremely proud of these and enjoyed being photographed wearing them. It was during this course that we went up-country and found the puppy-eating tribe that I mentioned earlier. Gordon's rash invitation to visit his home must have been a source of worry for some time after.

I also managed to get in another visit to Al, who was now enjoying the second part of his year abroad, in Nice. (Germany in the Winter to ski and The Med in the Summer to swim!) He had a small but marvellous flat with a balcony, the Villa Paulette, in the old part of the city. It was good to go out for hot French bread on a blue April morning and have a sunny French breakfast on the tiny balcony. I also found a good place to watch the intriguing local parking technique outside the very beautiful Russian Orthodox Church. This was - find a space a few centimetres shorter than your car. Edge your back end in then shunt backwards and forwards until you have made the space long enough to get completely into. I guess that the logical French consider that this is what bumpers are for. We all enjoyed our second visit to the Côte d'Azur, Monaco and the wild hills, the Gorge du Loup, away from the tourist packed coast, very much. A third visit is unfortunately back burner again!

May brought a couple of celebrities to be tested. This was something that I tried to arrange, as providing that it went well it was extremely good publicity for the Road (RoSPA Advanced Drivers) Association. The first was Paddy Hopkirk, who had been a very successful driver of Mini-Coopers in several Monte Carlo Rallies. I invited him to take a test which I think intrigued him, and he willingly agreed. I enjoyed meeting Paddy, then running a firm making motor vehicle accessories but still a well-known name in motor sport. It is an interesting exercise to criticise someone of that eminence in driving, but fairly obviously he was easily good enough to pass.

The second personality was Ernie Wise, of 'Eric and Ernie', or 'Morecombe and Wise' TV and stage fame. Ernie was also invited to take a test and rather to my surprise he agreed. I met him at his large and beautiful house by the Thames at Maidenhead and we 'rolled' around the town and the adjacent countryside. One advantage of owning a bright yellow Rolls Royce is that everyone scuttles out of the way! No, that's not fair, Ernie was a good enough driver to genuinely pass our test, and I was pleased to drive down again with Paul our cameraman journalist to present his certificate. I then saw a rather remarkable phenomenon. When Paul focussed his video camera on Ernie, he immediately, and I think without realising it, went into showman mode. Whilst on test, and earlier that day, he had come over as a pleasant but fairly ordinary guy, despite being wealthy. The difference in our incomes was not made obvious. As soon as the camera started to roll though he became Ernie Wise the comedian, telling us stories about his partnership with Eric, and funny moments in TV filming, revealing probably unconsciously, why he had been so successful. It was if he had shed or put on a mask. I shall never know which was the mask and which the true personality. Eric had died not long before, so a long partnership had been broken and I think that this was having an effect. I believe that Ernie could not help but revert to his working life when in front of the camera, even our modest one. We did get substantial national press publicity with his test success, which pleased everybody at RoSPA.

The very action packed year of 1985 continued in June with my hosting and running a RoSPA conference of Examiners, for which I was able to beg the use of the West Midlands Police Training Centre in Birmingham. We did run several of these very useful meetings, to which sixty or seventy former or serving police officers would come from all points of the UK. One year this included a former Gardai officer from Eire. Regrettably with increasing cost they had to be curtailed, but were useful and enjoyable brainstorming sessions with like-minded people. With my enthusiastic support a Midlands Regional meeting is now again taking place.

In June we spent a day or two with Jo's nephew Miles, who was then the Organ Scholar at Durham University. He managed to get us a room in the Castle, where we had an arrow slit in the bathroom wall. After killing many besieging enemies in the streets below we also enjoyed dining with Miles in the lovely refectory. We combined this visit with a drive over the causeway to Lindisfarne, a boat to the Farne Islands to be surrounded by seals, Bamburgh Castle and going as far north as Hadrian's Wall. The year continued busily along with our God-daughter's wedding on a beautiful day in Harrogate, and Nicky and her friend Karen setting off unescorted on a European rail travelling 'adventure'.

Chapter 6

Travel writing from Montreal to Vancouver, via Mexico

In September 1985 I was able to take a month's accumulated leave, having reached an agreement with a motoring magazine to write about driving around as much of Canada, America and Mexico as possible. 'America and Great Britain are two nations divided by a single language'. This and other clichés, and perhaps prejudices, about the States were much in my mind as I flew into Mirabel Airport, Montreal. The intention was to see as much as possible, and to use all possible means of travel. In the event my preconceptions were confounded, and I was both delighted and impressed with what is called the American way of life – warts – of which of course there are a few – and all. I had surmised, correctly as it happened, that like the films it would not be! By travelling far and fast I saw something of twenty of the American States, three Canadian Provinces and a little of Mexico, using cars, trucks, trains, Greyhound coach, trolley `bus, airline, small passenger aircraft, taxi, bicycle, ferry, cruise ship, paddle wheel steamboat, seaplane, mountain cable car and my two feet! Seven and a half thousand miles were covered, five and a half thousand of these by a variety of rented, fare-paying or under-delivery road vehicles. North America is a biggish place!

This mileage threw up enough examples to provide reasonably well-informed comments about driving standards, which by and large were better than in the UK and the rest of Europe. The absence of 'hassle' and tailgating was the most noticeable thing at first hand. The similar absence of bad temper on the open road, and to a lesser extent in the big cities, was delightful. Some years later, and travelling across the US from Los Angeles, through the mid-west and into New York, via Chicago I was able to confirm this earlier impression. The Texan motto of 'Drive Friendly' still seemed to be widespread. Europe, and the UK, badly, badly, need to learn this lesson.

I had done some pre-planning and was gambling on being able to find a car rental agency with a car that needed to be returned to New York. This is a good way of avoiding the heavy 'drop-off' charges usually imposed for one-way journeys. It can be hundreds of dollars for a journey even in the same State, so is a useful tip and a cunning plan! It paid off and I was quickly and efficiently installed in a Dodge Aries. It also attracted a fair discount having just arrived from New York and being still rather grubby. It was to return to a Hertz Depot in Manhattan, and I estimated four days for the one thousand mile journey, to leave time to visit Niagara and the Catskill Mountains. The Aries, naturally, was an automatic, with cruise control, the latter not yet seen much in the UK. Both were a boon on the long interstate journeys, allowing complete relaxation of the left foot. The danger with this type of driving aid is that one may relax too much, which needs to be kept in mind. I have never seen much point in cruise control in the UK since, but some people seem to like having it. Perhaps it is more of a status symbol here. I managed a quicker than it deserved look at Montreal, and then headed south. All road signs, menus and radio programmes, and shop names such as 'Henri Leblanc' were in French. Quite a few people that I spoke to would open a conversation in French, and then drop into broken English. Whilst on foot in Montreal, I was asked for directions – in French. Fortunately I could just about cope! Trying to get fairly well on the way before dark I stuck to the Provincial Highway 401, a good standard motorway with a minimum speed limit of 60 kmh and a maximum of 100. Traffic was not heavy, speeds were well within the legal range and spacing was correct. It was quickly obvious that 'tailgating' in the UK style was not popular. In fact, outside the big cities, during the whole month and five and a half thousand miles I was only followed by a 'boot inspector' once, and that briefly. On the highway the heavy trucks were huge, shiny and splendid in their arrogant appearance, but again, not a bully amongst them.

Motels along the North American highways were plentiful, clean and reasonably cheap. Invariably there were en-suite rooms with a colour TV. Particularly useful for the stranger were advance warnings signs 'Food, gas, lodging, next exit'. My first experience of this helpful way of finding a bed was at Coteau du Lac in Quebec Province (or maybe it was Ontario), and made a quick call home to report my whereabouts. I did find that telephoning in Canada and the US, even in remote areas was incredibly quick and easy, with an invariably friendly operator, whose 'Have a nice day' at least sounds sincere. Up early next morning to a bright blue sky and an adequate breakfast for about 50 pence the Aries and I followed the single carriageway 'Kings Highway 2'. We drove alongside the St Lawrence, passing through attractive little towns with evocative names; 'Iroquois' for example. It was now back to English as the first language. The maples were beginning to turn fall colours and combined with the now visible vast expanse of Lake Ontario made it a beautiful and spectacular route, with the chance to visit historical sites, Wellington Fort for example, which was flying a huge Union Jack! There were also a lot of English place names, mainly, perhaps for economic migration reasons, north country ones – Durham County, Leeds County, Liverpool etc.

Driving continued to be good and steady, generally with an upper limit of 80 to100 kmh and notices advising of aerial surveillance. Wow, back to 'Peeler Two' the police helicopter experiments of 1968! After rejoining route 401 I tried lunch at 'Whopper, the Burger King'. Not being a McDonalds or Burger fan I expected something a bit plastic, but in fact enjoyed a cheap but delicious chicken sandwich in a sparklingly clean and attractively decorated restaurant. The sweet was complimentary and the cost about £2. Only the name jarred! I actually did point out the difference between this and the disgusting condition of UK Service Stations, as they were then, to the staff. They were also sparklingly clean and delighted that I had taken the trouble – 'Well, thank you,' obviously liking to be liked!

Also quite surprisingly for someone from the UK at that time, the highway signs advised the distance to the next rest stop before it was too late to take the slip road. We have now caught up in several ways with our motorway accessories, but it took a long time! However, one difficulty with the North American fast route system was now apparent, and needs to be remembered by all visitors. Instead of all exits leaving from the nearside, occasionally a junction would leave from the offside, and cross the motorway via a fly-over. A poor lookout could mean the unwise idea of a sudden lane change. Signing though was pretty good, except that at times they only said that a road number was going North, East, South or West, meaning that compass directions had to be kept in mind. 'Interstate 5 West' for example is only useful to those who do know that they need to go west! The other feature of the road system that I did not like much were the often frequent toll booths. Circumnavigating Atlanta, Georgia was a prime example of this, with a toll every three miles or so, where one had to struggle to find a small coin. Whilst this was not particularly expensive it was irritating and a distraction from the main job of driving. I find that the one UK toll road, missing the problems of Birmingham on the M6, is better organised. (But more expensive). Road signs, although sometimes overdone were generally good, one in particular 'Bridge ices first in cold weather' being a useful reminder of a fact of life which has still not been introduced in England or Wales (there is just one in Scotland). My suggesting them to the Department for Transport was like trying to change the course of the Titanic.

Toronto was an exciting skyscraper city of over three million, with countless high windows glittering golden in the westering sun I stopped long enough in the city centre to get the flavour of it and could not help reflecting that in four hundred miles I had seen only one example of bad driving, even in the city rush hour traffic. The exception was a scruffy guy wearing a cowboy hat and a beard and with a 'No Nukes' sticker on the back of his battered car. What me, prejudices? Queen Elizabeth Way, south-east of Toronto was a busy six lane highway and I enjoyed the lane discipline. Passing on either side, in Canada and the US seemed to work perfectly well, as drivers chose a lane and stuck to it. Weaving from 1 to 3 and back again, as was then common in the UK, did not happen. Weaving, of course, creates collisions.

It seemed to me then that we had got it wrong by generally forbidding overtaking on the inside (nearside) lane. We have improved on this since, and it is now acceptable on multi-lane roads so long as it does not entail weaving. Naturally the ignorant, arrogant or incompetent will ignore this and weave to enter the faster moving lane, but it is not correct driving. It is often not expected, and therefore not forseen by the driver being passed. In this, and some other traffic matters, the Americans had it right first, I think. After an evening meal I found that my waitress had written, 'Thank you, and have a nice evening, Laura' on the receipt. I felt that there was a fair element of sincerity here, but even if not it was very pleasant. Niagara, next morning was very touristy, and to my mind not as exciting as the Rhine Falls. After getting soaked to the skin on the boat trip to the foot of the falls, despite the voluminous oilskin issued to all passengers, I pushed on south-east through Amish and Mennonite country, with my shoes full of Niagara Falls! Here the farmers still used horses and traps and the schoolgirls were wearing old-fashioned long dresses and bonnets. I wonder if this changed in the twenty years since then. Entering the US was no problem at the border, as I had a visa, and was given a six months stay. I usually wear an International Police Association tie for such occasions!

Through the State of New York, State Highway 17 was a convenient route, a dual carriageway with a 55 mph limit. Speed limits were being generally well observed, rarely rising above 60 mph. Indeed it felt anti-social and morally wrong to exceed this. I still do not know how the Americans had managed to cultivate this attitude; perhaps it was the aerial and radar surveillance, which were well advertised. I did not see much evidence of either during the month though, just one driver being booked, apparently for speeding, in Alabama. The other noticeable and pleasant aspect, as in Canada, was the complete absence of close following traffic and 'bullying' heavy vehicles. I still can't believe it! The British reaction to the then countrywide speed limit of 55 mph was, 'Isn't it very boring?' To some extent, yes it was, and it took a long time to cover 800 miles, but one got there and at the end of the day was a lot more fresh and relaxed than, say a 200 mile flog on the M1 or M5. We have been right not to increase our motorway limit, as speeds of

80 to a 100 mph (which is what 70 means for far too many) are for racetracks or for those who have the training, machinery, discipline and authority to cope with them.

On reaching the foothills of the Catskills I left Highway 17 to find a bed for the night in the little backwoods town of Deposit. It looked like a film set, the quintessential American small town. Wooden houses with rocking chairs on the front porches and mist rising off the Delaware River. Here my accent was a decided novelty, people were obviously interested and it carried me through a long chat with the locals over an evening meal. I had to defend my wife for having let me come on my own! Following the Delaware, early the next morning until I got into the Catskills proper, I found myself in Rip Van Winkle country. Tiny lanes through wooded hills and valleys, stopping occasionally to talk to the occasional hill-billy character, who often inspected me as I imagine I would look at a space traveller. Strange that this was less than a day's drive from New York City. Finally locating one planned stopping place, Bear Mountain, and climbing the last few boulders to the summit, a really incredible sight spread itself below and to the south. About forty five miles away, looking noisy even from this distance was the outline of Manhattan. The profile roars up on the horizon and hits you with a knockout blow. If cities could be expressed as having a gender, New York could only be masculine, whilst the centre of Washington is a beautiful gracious lady. New York pounces on you, grabs you by the throat, shakes you and beats you over the head.

Bear Mountain is in 'Sleepy Hollow' country, recalling tales of Ichabod Crane, the headless horseman and the Dutch settlers. There was a superb view down the Hudson River to West Point Military Academy, as well as that fabulous, male, thrusting profile. However, it was far from sleepy nowadays, and I was quickly in a monumental traffic jam as the commuters made their way to the pleasant Atlantic seaside resorts of Rye, New Haven and Bridport.

Becoming totally lost amongst the sculptured lawns and closed hedges of Rye, I eventually found a hotel in Mamaroneck Village, just north of the suburb of Yonkers. A meal in the McDonalds there suggested that my previous experience with fast food had been lucky. Caution suggested leaving the first acquaintance with Manhattan traffic until daylight! At a 7.00 a.m. start it was not too bad, although busier than London at that time on a Saturday morning. The main problem was interpreting the traffic directions, which, as ever, worldwide, seemed to be for the benefit of locals who knew where they were going anyway. I was fairly well supplied with maps, but even so had to go over the Triborough Bridge and back three times before finding the correct exit for downtown Manhattan. Speeds were fast for busy traffic, and fairly aggressive. I have seen much worse in the UK, but it was not the place for a faint-hearted driver. The road between Yonkers and The Bronx varied between two and four lanes, but once in Manhattan the logical rectangular street layout and sequential numbering made it easier.

I was a little unhappy at needing to stop for directions whilst lost in The Bronx, as this area was rather less than attractive. However, no problems and helpful directions. Maybe I didn't look wealthy enough to bother with. One-way streets needed to be watched, as often they were only signed with a small arrow, but again were logical, so if a street was one-way only in the wrong direction the next would almost certainly be usable. American drivers must find our cities like Chester, Worcester or Oxford rather difficult! There was a major disaster in progress on the approach to Brooklyn Bridge, with the whole area sealed efficiently sealed off, but the wide and fast Franklin Roosevelt Boulevard was open and I found a parking place near to the Staten Island Ferry terminal at Battery Park. At nine dollars a day this was the cheapest parking in Manhattan, as unsurprisingly on an island parking space is at a premium.

Finding somewhere to stop was a drawback in Manhattan, which probably has not improved, but once the street layout had been sussed out it was easier in many ways than London or Paris. I left the car and walked up to Times Square where I found a budget hotel, then took the subway back to Battery Park. The token dispenser clerk was surly and impatient - goes with the job maybe – but a fellow passenger went out of his way to be helpful. Grafitti on the subway stations and trains was continuous, rather menacing and unpleasant.

Every visitor to New York should take a return trip on the Staten Island Ferry. It and the ferry from Kowloon to Hong Kong Island are the best value for money short journeys anywhere in the world. This assessment includes Sidney Harbour and the river crossing at Vancouver, both of which are nearly, but not quite, as spectacular. The ferry at 25 cents for a return trip of an hour, with food and drink available and the famous view of the Statue of Liberty and the incredible skyline takes a bit of beating. We even passed fully rigged sailing yachts using the short stretch of water. The visitor must also ride the lift up the Empire State Building, after dark, to see aircraft and helicopters filling the sky, like fireflies, and the glittering gleaming city pulsing with life far below, with the Hudson and East Rivers and Central Park black in contrast. Two hundred years ago all this was a farm!

After the fascinating ride to Staten Island and back I spent an hour watching a rather incredible one man band in Battery Park, who had musical instruments operated by nearly every part of his body. It was time to find the Hertz Depot. Easy on the map, but in the heavy evening traffic I passed it more than once, eventually finding it in an underground car park. Quick and efficient checking in formalities regrettably restored me to Shank's Pony, regretfully since I had developed quite an affection for the Aries. I then walked up Broadway to Central Park, wandered around and introduced myself to a couple of cops in a 'blue and white'. 'Gee, were you a 'Bahby'? Is it right that you guys still don't carry guns'? I was again asked for directions several times. This has been, for me, an experience in many countries; perhaps I have looked as though I might know the answer. (Although this was not always the case). It was therefore quite a pleasure to be asked the time in Central Park - one that I could answer!

The request for directions even happened inside the Empire State Building that I visited that evening. Was I being taken for a New York cop? No, no gun in the waistband of my trousers, and I doubt if Americans ask the time or directions from cops very much anyway! (Just thought, years later in 2009 I shared a 16 day trek with a lady from New York. Should have asked her). The Park was very nice in parts and tatty in others and produced the illusion of being on an island. I spent much of Saturday evening in Times Square, watching the kaleidoscope of flashing advertising signs and other lights, heavy traffic, and a diminutive policewoman on a big horse. Cocaine was fairly obviously on sale and cinemas showing porno movies. A topless bar, tramps asleep in doorways by midnight and plenty of characters from 'West Side Story' and the pages of Damon Runyon. The little town of Deposit, although in New York State, could have been the other side of the world, or even on another planet.

Grand Central Station, with its starry roof was a mixture of a Cathedral and Woolworths. The indicator boards actually told you whether trains were on time or not – this was unheard of in the UK in those days. Once again, we have caught up, but they did it first! My budget hotel, staffed and occupied by Spanish speakers, in the centre of all this was one of the sort where one definitely locked the door at night. I was untroubled and next morning, wanting to try 'Amtrak' I got up early and booked a thirty dollar ride to Washington, from Pennsylvania Station. The cost for the 220 mile journey was about comparable to British Rail, but a lot more comfortable, with better than airline type seats, a helpful conductor in each car, and good cheap food. First class conditions at second class prices. The train had been on the dot on its arrival from Boston. The Station was clean and convenient, with plenty of seats and no struggling or pushing as entrance to the platforms was well controlled. Breakfast of a coffee and a substantial doughnut cost $1. I was approached several times, not for directions but for the loan of a dollar – always the same story, 'I am stranded'. In these cases I was certainly not being mistaken for a cop! I had time for a quick walk around Macey's, 'The biggest store in the world'. UK rail travel has improved a lot since then, but at that time Amtrak was a pleasant and definite culture shock.

Most capital cities are expensive, and Washington was no exception, but the best parts are so beautiful that if possible no visitor to the States should miss them. The gleaming white dome of the Capitol building, just across the plaza from Union Station, with Constitution and Independence Avenues and the Mall area lined with golden white classical facades with Doric columns felt, in my view, what a city should be. Big enough to have everything, but not as overwhelming as New York. I know, of course, that there were, and still are, some terribly deprived and crime ridden parts of America's capital, but the wide streets, grassy parks and trees everywhere were a delight to the eye. People seemed more relaxed than in New York, and certainly easier to understand. I walked around the centre, and found a hotel, then had a rowing boat for an hour on the Potomac basin. An evening visit to the floodlit Lincoln and Jefferson Memorials provided a new insight, and sympathy with American history, and my only superficial knowledge of the magnificent speeches engraved on the walls was shameful. The Avenue from the White House up to the Capitol should be preserved for a thousand years, I think, as another memorial to the best of what men can build.

While in Washington I visited, naturally, the White House, but only to look at the exterior! We burned it down during the War of Independence, and when it was rebuilt it was painted white to hide the scorch marks at ground level. 'White' ever since! I am also glad that I spent some time in the most beautiful Arlington Cemetery. The Cemetery at Bridgnorth in Shropshire, where a number of my ancestors are buried is also very beautiful in a similar way, but does not contain quite as many famous names as Arlington. The perpetual flame on J.F.K's grave, protected by an extremely smart Honour Guard, is very evocative. Whatever might be said now about the man himself, his resting place represents, I believe, like much of Washington, the best of America.

From the top of the 550 foot Washington Monument the views in all directions were excellent, and another visit to the Jefferson and Lincoln Memorials in daylight was well worthwhile, as was the chance to see the Iwo Jima statue and the black Vietnam wall in reality. Having walked around quite a lot I was actually able to give the next applicant correct directions! I found the number of BBC programmes on TV surprising, and doubt if that would be the case now, as our TV has gone so downmarket. The advertising breaks were much more frequent than ours though, so even more irritating. Washington had been a great place to visit, and the parts of the city that I saw conveyed no sense of threat or worries, even walking through the parks at night. Perhaps I was lucky in this as certainly now the city has a high crime rate.

Part of my pre-planning had involved researching the 'Auto-Driveaway Company', which undertakes to deliver cars to any part of the US, using volunteer drivers looking for cheap transport. With such long distances to cover, and air travel cheap and convenient, it is not surprising that a family, perhaps relocating from the East to the West Coast, preferred to get their car delivered by someone else. The Washington office had a Volkswagon drophead coupé, known as a 'Rabbit' in the States, to go to an Air Force Base in Southern Alabama. This suited me nicely, as my next planned stay was in New Orleans. After a thorough check of my credentials and handing over 100 dollars, forfeit if the car arrived in Alabama in more than one piece, I was on my way.

I did ask what the percentage was of cars that 'disappeared' en route, and was told that it was not a problem, as a stolen car that crossed a State line automatically became a Federal crime, on the FBI list. I was allowed four days to do the 900 mile journey, ample time, the only snag being that the route was allocated and not negotiable, except to find food or lodging. However, I travelled the 900 miles at a cost of seventeen dollars, even the first tank of gas being free! I decided, being routed on the comparatively uninteresting Interstate 85, to do the journey as quickly as possible, starting with a transit through Virginia, with the Allegheny, Appalachian and Shenandoah mountains on my right. IS 85 is effectively a motorway, with two or three lanes in each direction. The carriageways were separated by a very wide median grass strip, at times hundreds of yards wide, thus reducing the possibility of crossover collisions.

Very few walkers were to be seen, as hitchhiking was banned on freeways. It was easy to reach Alabama inside the time limit, with only a short deviation off route for a swim in Chickasaw Lake in the Cherokee foothills. Again, driving manners were very good, and regular rest areas were invariably clean, with usable toilets and drinking water. The latter was welcome as the midday temperature was about 85degrees. In fact my left arm and cheek became badly sunburnt through the open car window, whilst I was listening to a report of two feet of snow in the Rockies. It was then that I realised what a huge country America is!

Having crossed the Appotomax River I was definitely in the South, but was a little surprised to be welcomed to the 'Shamrock Motel' in Gaffney, South Carolina by an affable Indian gentleman. (East, not Red!) Taking the chance to look at small town life in the Rebel States, I had a meal in the Snow Drop Restaurant. I felt that here I was definitely a curiosity. Talking to one family, Father could not resist asking my trade, and then we were away into a worldwide discussion. The highlight was, 'That ole Miz Thatcher, she's the best man you got.' I thought, at the time, that he was right! He had been a Crew Chief in the US Airforce at the time I was in the R.A.F. The mother was a real character, they all had very thick accents and all wanted to know what I thought of America, and how was it different from England. Time for tact! Gaffney was south of Charlotte, with the Great Smokey Mountains and the Blue Ridge now on my right.

Deviating a little the next day, onto single track side roads roughly comparable with our 'B' roads I found that these were badly over-signed, with continuous solid lining and warnings about gentle bends, instructing for example that 15 mph was correct for a bend that was comfortable at 30 and possible at 45. The only twitchy moment that I had during the month was through late braking after trying to read a badly placed sign. I eventually deciphered it as 'People have been killed on this bend'. Not surprising. Back on IS 85 the miles of rolling wooded country were spoiled a little by the multiplicity of advertising boards. 'Eat at Starvin Marvins' or 'Cheeky Chink Chinese Fast Foods'. Good alliteration, but 'Piggley Wiggley Discount Foods' offering fireworks, peaches and ice-cream was a bit mind-bending. Firework outlets, big and small, abounded in Georgia and Alabama, often being combined with food stores.

The Rabbit was going really well as we got further south and I became very attached to it. With five manual gears and cruise control it turned in fifty miles per US gallon, good economy for the time for a four to five seater. Those low speed limits maybe? Approaching the big city of Atlanta IS 85 became very busy indeed, at times going up to six lanes in each direction, but the variations came without warning. As the whole of the Atlanta road system appeared to be dug up it seemed reasonable to risk a short cut onto a US Highway, a lesser single carriageway road. It passed through some superb countryside of lakes and forests, but was again very over-signed and double lined. Arriving at Dothan, Alabama at 8 p.m. there was no reply on the `phone from the Rabbit's owner, so I booked in at a motel – never a problem to find one, I had discovered by now.

Here again, people were curious. 'Y'all come from England? My sister-in-law lives in a suburb of London, begins with a 'B'. You know it'?

I tried Battersea, Brent and Bexley but then we decided not to bother any further! Rather sadly delivering the Rabbit to an Air Force Sergeant at Fort Rucker next day and regaining my hundred dollars, plus a ticket to say that the car was in good order and he was very satisfied, was no problem. A taxi from the base got me back to Dothan to pick up a Greyhound 'bus to New

Orleans. Greyhound is a bit of legend and whilst it lived up to it in terms of reliability and convenience it was not really comfortable long distance travelling, certainly no better than National Express. However I am not a fan of coach travel, so maybe bias is showing here. The Depot in Dothan was fairly clean with reasonable food facilities, and the line is very easy to use for city to city travel. Price per distance travelled was about the same as Amtrak. There is of course one vast difference between travel in the States and in Europe. Every city, even of moderate size, has it's own airport, with scheduled services around America, and often internationally. Walk-on ticket buying was easy, except at peak periods.

As the Greyhound coach began it's journey through Northern Florida, Mississippi and Louisiana a rather unpleasant fact of life soon became apparent. For about two weeks each Autumn a phenomenon called the lovebugs occurs here, making driving quite hazardous. They are large insects rather like mosquitoes, flying in thick swarms at windscreen height. They are doing things in public which most of us don't do, hence their name. I guess that they are qualified to join the five-foot high club! The result was a sticky black mess all over the front of the 'bus, which no amount of wash-wipe would clear.

Stopping at intervals to hose off the mess gave the passengers a chance to stretch their legs, or grab a sandwich or a cookie, so it's an ill wind! There was a lot of poor housing visible from the 'bus, many being static trailer homes. I had the chance to walk around Mobile and get a view of the Bay of Mexico while changing 'buses. Confederate flags were flying in a few areas, and a taxi driver said to me, 'Some folks are still fighting the Civil War'. I saw an arrest being made in the manner made popular by Hollywood, the suspect spreadeagled over the bonnet (oops, hood) of the car. I did wonder if this was life imitating the films, as I had seen happening in the UK. Disembarking in the centre of New Orleans, late at night with no accommodation booked was perhaps a step too far, but the usual source of local knowledge, a friendly taxi driver, found me the reasonably priced 'La Salle' hotel not far away. I did think that the interior decoration was a bit ornate, flamboyant probably being the word. However it was not until checking out three days later, having been comfortable and unbothered, that I found that it had recently been changed in function from what may be best described as a bordello.

Three days is little enough to do justice to a very vibrant and exciting city. The vivacity of the beautiful Vieux Carré, with its balconied houses, history, street musicians and conjurers, horse drawn carriages and French, Spanish and Creole accents needed a week to itself. But also English names –

Shrewsbury Avenue and Kent Street were visible.

Over a beer I had an interesting talk with a character identical with the advertisement picture of Colonel Sanders of 'Kentucky Fried Chicken'. People were again keen to know what I thought of the States. They criticised the US themselves but I had a strong feeling that it would be resented if I did so. The remnants of a national inferiority complex maybe? Perhaps some of the international policies and adventures of the U.S.A. could be traced to this as well? Women especially still seemed to be falling in love with my accent – I am sure that with the huge expansion of international travel since then it would not be so common today, but then was rather enjoyable.

Beauregard Park is the place where the slaves used to gather, and became the birthplace of jazz. I spent a day on a genuine rear paddle wheel steamer, the Natchez, cruising the Mississippi and another on a bayou cruise aboard Jean Lafitte, named after a legendary privateer. Both were fascinating, as was the waterfront in the gloriously hot sun. The bayous and areas around New Orleans are the home of the Cajuns – people from the north of America who fled from religious persecution. The Shrimp boats still went out from the Gulf of Mexico shores ('Shrimp boats are a'comin', their sails are in sight') and more Confederate flags were flying. My accent was obviously still of interest and it was not unusual to be asked to say something else! An evening meal, including Filly Gumbo followed by Cajun Jambalaya in the Vieux Carré, and then watching the street musicians - jazz of course - and magicians was another delight.

I did enjoy New Orleans tremendously, and was very sad to hear of the destruction and loss of life in the huge storm damage years later. I hope that by now recovery is happening. However it was time to move on and the Auto-Driveaway office had a Chevrolet pick-up truck to go to Houston, the short American distance of 300 miles away this time, which suited my plan. This seemed like nothing by now! The route, on State Highway 10 went along the shore of Lake Pontchartrain, then crossed 'Old Man River' and I was able to divert into Baton Rouge and Lafayette, all of which was full of history and extremely interesting.

A motel again for the night, one with a pool which, unbelievably after European experiences remained open at night, so a moonlit swim was warm and enjoyable. Entering Texas a cliché came true – vast herds of cattle and multi-square mile ranches. Houston however, I disliked intensely. It seemed to be to be a soulless place, a maze of urban freeways, the whole area devoted to the car. An unpleasant vision of what, unless we are careful and discipline the architects, awaits us in the future. Glass, steel, concrete and plastic. After delivering the truck, with difficulty as the address was number 4000 and something Katy Freeway, I became a pedestrian again, an alien, a dispossessed inferior being doomed to watch the master race zoom past in their Pontiacs and Cadillacs! My researches had suggested that Houston possessed a comprehensive public transport system. All that I can say is that I couldn't find it, and no one that I asked knew anything about it. However, when delivering the truck, I was treated with the utmost consideration and helpfulness, and my rather poor impression of Texas dissolved like an icicle in the southern sun. The Manager of the Company who owned it insisted on transporting me to the Auto-Driveaway office, and then cashed their cheque for my 100 dollar deposit, to save me the hassle. I was so impressed that I insisted that he contacted me if ever in the UK.

I was now aiming for southern Texas and Mexico and had anticipated doing the 200 miles to San Antonio by train. Surprisingly however, for two major cities in the same State, there were only two trains a week. The car rules! So, I decided to rent a car but then ran up against the drop-off charge problem. To leave the car at El Paso, in the far west of Texas would cost about four hundred dollars, and it was cheaper to return the car to Houston and fly west from there, which is what I did.

Texas is big! (Roughly the size of France, Switzerland and the Low Countries combined). To drive across it, at a legal speed takes about sixteen hours, east to west. Signs to El Paso in the west of the State said 850 miles and exits on the Interstate 10 numbered in the eight hundreds! I headed for the Mexican border, and stayed for four nights in the border towns of Eagle Pass and Del Rio.

Texas is friendly as well as huge! I was really overwhelmed with good manners, courtesy and efficiency. At the wheel of every pick-up truck there seemed to be a seven-foot tall cowboy wearing a Stetson, and I expected to be shot if I dared to overtake. But no, it was routine that they pull over and wave me on! After the first few times I found myself doing it as well for the occasional faster traffic behind. Many times I was given precedence by approaching traffic, where I would have given way myself. Every so often there were road signs saying 'Drive Friendly' – something never, ever, heard of in the UK but they do, or did, in Texas. The way to Eagle Pass went through ranch country, single track roads with straights lasting for miles. It was sometimes quite a relief to turn the steering wheel. I was now easily able to understand the comment of an expatriate Texan oil man to whom I had given some training in Scotland – 'Man, if Ah'm gonna overtake Ah want twenny clear miles!' Vast herds of prime Herefords graced the long vistas to left and right and vultures circled overhead. There were vast horizons, indeed it felt rather like Kenya.

Stopping at a little one horse town to phone home, again efficiently and easily, ('You-all have a nice day now.') I was struck by how Mexican the people looked and how rather developing world, as opposed to the glitter of Houston, everything was becoming. Eagle Pass was almost a Mexican town with little difference between it and Piedras Negras across the Rio Grande. My car, a Toyota Corolla, was often surrounded by barefoot kids playing in the dust and the glamour of New York and Washington was remote in time and space. I could not resist a photograph of 'Maverick County Jailhouse' and then walked across the bridge into Mexico with little formality except a small toll. There were some very sharp contrasts with my experiences of the last two weeks. The driving, for example, was less good, and the proportion of beaten-up vehicles much higher and reminiscent of Africa. The under-developed world status of this part of Mexico was obvious. A major earthquake in Mexico City had just happened, and not wishing to add to the problems of an overloaded transport system I changed my plans.

I had wanted to drive south to Chihuahua, but decided instead to stay around the border. After a night in a picturesque and Spanish speaking motel I re-crossed the Rio Grande and continued to the much larger town of Del Rio. It was much more 'American' than Eagle Pass, and I found an excellent motel with a large swimming pool to use as a base. After dark I watched an American film on TV about Dracula 'Love at first bite'. Not an improvement on the BBC! Texas is, I believe, the friendliest place that I have ever been to. People seemed to be genuinely pleased to talk, and touchingly delighted when I praised anything. One tough looking guy of at least six feet six, who could have doubled for the young Clint Eastwood, was quite excited when I enthused over his cactus garden, and the Receptionist at the Motel came back one evening with her husband to meet me and hand over some Texas recipes. That day I was asked several times if I was Australian!

Eventually continuing west, with some reluctance, and crossing the Pecos River, where the two hundred and seventy foot high bridge carries a notice 'No Diving', I entered the little town of Langtry. Judge Roy Bean 'the law west of the Pecos' is reputed to have named the town because of his fascination with the 'Jersey Lily', Lily Langtry, the girl friend of Edward the Vllth. She was also Camilla's great grandmother, but this I did not know in 1985! Roy Bean's saloon, the Jersey Lily, was still standing. One could look out from the front porch, where frontier justice was dispensed with a rope and a six-gun and practically hear the baying of the lynch mob and the crack of the guns.

It was here in Langtry that something rather remarkable happened. Strolling down the only street, which comprises only a few wooden houses,

I saw what appeared to be the rear end of an elderly Morris Minor disappearing around a corner ahead. Thinking that the hot sun was having an effect, I walked on down to the Rio Grande, and spent a lazy hour watching white tailed deer in the gulch below and vultures wheeling in the sky above. Returning towards the main road I then saw, parked in front of one of the wooden houses a genuine Morris Minor, 1950s vintage, a little battered but obviously in running order. An elderly guy was sitting on his porch, enjoying the sun, so I made myself known and said how strange it was to see a Minor so far from home.

The owner, Tom Smith, replied, 'Yup, best li'l car ever come out of Yurrup – I got three more round the back!' And he had – a `58 and a`61 saloon and a `58 Traveller, the rear body of which had rotted and been converted into a pick-up truck. This had been his only major problem, and at one time he had owned a fifth Minor, which he had given to a friend! So, we sat on his porch drinking mint juleps and talking cars. Tom had bought his first Minor in Chicago for four hundred dollars and liked it so much that he acquired the others. He still took one on the two thousand mile return trip to his home state of Missouri every so often. Not bad, for man or machine! When I told Tom that my car, as a young policeman, had been a Minor Traveller, which we took over the Alps to Italy, and that I had toured the Cowley works of Morris Motors we were definitely on the same wavelength. The latter occasion happened during one of the regular cricket matches between Wolverhampton and Oxford City Police. This was rained off so Morris Motors hosted all of us, wives and supporters as well, to a magnificent lunch with many toasts proposed and drunk. We staggered around the works after lunch, none of which we could in the least remember later. I felt that meeting Tom and his Minors was an outstanding experience and I hope that he enjoyed driving them for many years. Remember, that this was the Country, and the era, of the huge 'Gas Guzzlers'.

Rather reluctantly (almost every move so far had been unwilling) I moved on, stopping at Armistad Lake for a swim and then crossed, with no formality, into Mexico again for the fourth visit. Driving along a dirt road for miles I found a statue of the Rain God Tlaloc, then reached the small town of Cuidad Acuna. This was just across the river from Del Rio. The drive had been fairly normal third world stuff – eyes needed everywhere. A pleasant meal of bifstek con papas and tortillas in an outdoor restaurant amongst the fireflies and promenading couples was a great ending to my brief visit to Mexico.

Good time was made to San Antonio early next day. US Highway 90 from Del Rio again crossed ranching country, passing some absolutely superbly named locations, 'Woman Hollerin Creek', 'Turkey Gulch' and 'Eagle's Nest

Canyon' to name but three. A few hours in the delightful river-crossed centre and a visit to the fascinating building of the Alamo where Jim Bowie and the other 'Kings of the Wild Frontier' are commemorated was well worthwhile. The Alamo was defended to the last Texan during the Mexican-Texas war of independence in 1836, and became a symbol of American resistance, 'Remember the Alamo'.

Nearing Houston on 1.10, driving standards visibly declined. The worst piece of driving seen anywhere in the States was here, a man swerving through, and overtaking, heavy traffic quite quickly whilst reading a full size newspaper spread across the steering wheel. Made me quite homesick! The freeways were choked at 3 p.m. and it took an hour to get through the city to the Airport.The arrangements for the car return and flight check-in were quick and efficient though. All this reinforced my earlier impression. Despite the courtesy when I delivered the truck I noted at the time that Houston was an appalling, inhuman place. Dispossessed of wheels one felt like an alien, and it seemed to me how the inside of an ant's nest must be, and the traffic in a continuous rush hour.

 By the time we landed at Phoenix, Arizona, it was dark despite having gained two hours through the time zones, and there was a most marvellous spread of lights enhanced by thunderstorms over the mountains surrounding the city. Flying on to Las Vegas the Captain burst into song as we began the descent. 'Your Captain's now gonna turn off the light. That means we're comin' to the end of the flight,' and so on, culminating in a chorus of 'Fly Western – y'all come back now.' Not British Airways style perhaps, but great fun, and why not?

Vegas is, of course, entirely and completely orientated to the convenience of the visitor, including one armed bandits in the Arrivals area so that no time need be lost in getting rid of spare money. The booking in system for Hotels and cars was so unusually quick by European standards that I inadvertently double booked. I had to explain that people elsewhere do not always keep their promises. Advertising in the centre included 'Classy lassies (and lads) available to the lonely visitor.' On arrival at the Meridian Hotel at 11pm the night was just beginning. I had a limousine from the Airport at a cost of three dollars. A limousine by the way is about twenty yards long with a ballroom in the rear. At check-in I was given a complimentary ticket for the Hotel Burlesque Show (which was absolutely dreadful) and twenty-five dollars worth of chips to use in the Hotel Casino. They did not last very long, and I quickly discovered that the Americans, at least in Vegas, play blackjack (pontoon) a lot faster than we do. Since the object of visiting Vegas was to go to the Grand Canyon, not to gamble, this did not matter. However, it was totally fascinating to walk down the 'The Strip', bright as daylight well into the small hours, during the two nights I was there. No picture or description can possibly do justice to the lights and the opulence. The illuminated statues and fountains at places like Ceasar's Palace were out of this world. I rather liked also, during the six mile walk up and down The Strip, the intensely lighted single storey Church, advertising, 'Immediate weddings, all credit cards taken'.

And over it all the bright desert moon shone down on the gaudy tawdry glitter and the ancient, serious and frightening mountains of Nevada all around us.

The experience of flying over, through and almost under the Grand Canyon in a twin engined Cessna 420 was a fabulous and unusual experience. Vegas Airport was extremely busy, and dealing with everything from Jumbos to single engined Cessna trainers. By once more calling, 'C'est moi' and introducing my pilot experience to the extremely young aircraft Captain, I was able to take the co-pilot's position all the way, which made it even better. I had found Niagara disappointing, but the Canyon was all that I had hoped, and more. It is simply awe-inspiring. An experience, not just a place. The colours of the striated rocks seem to stretch downwards for ever, and flame red as the descending sun catches the canyon tops. We landed for several hours on the Rim, so there was plenty of time to explore a little of this fantastic scenery on foot.

One of the Rangers told me that tourists die on or over the edge of the Rim every year – in fact I now know this to be an average of ten to twelve annually, some of whom succumb to sunstroke. As it is 5000 feet down those who fall off have time to learn to fly on the way down. How on earth do they manage to fall? Wonder-struck perhaps, which is understandable. There is an Indian village in the Canyon, which at that time could only be visited by regular mule train – the only way down for the US Mail! I left Vegas at 8 a.m. next morning, again with some regret. Vulgar and money orientated, and probably then gangster infested it was, but what vitality and life and fun is there, if one has a little cash or a chunk of plastic (preferably with discipline). I liked it. Some years later I drove through Vegas on my way across the States, and found it bigger, brighter, higher and even more vulgar. But Death Valley and the serious old moon-lit mountains were still there.

At San Francisco Airport I was back on schedule, and rented another Toyota to drive through the John Steinbeck country of Monterey and Carmel. It was great to see Cannery Row and the location of some of those marvellous stories. I tried to buy some 'Old Tennis Shoes', the drink that Steinbeck introduced in his tales, but either it had not survived or he had invented it! The Californian weather was, however, in the words of the song 'cold and damp' – not in any way traditional and all the golden girls were wrapped up and shivering! The beaches were windy and some rather scruffy. Monterey, although full of history was also full of tourists, so I travelled on east on the 250 mile journey through Arroyo Seco (Dry Gulch) to Yosemite up in the Sierra Nevada.

Once through the Carmel River Valley, on a single track road with rolling golden brown hills, and over the Coastal Range of hills the road descended into the flat 'salad bowl' country, of mile upon mile of fruit and vegetable fields. The roads were all narrow and oversigned and it consistently appeared that American drivers were not entirely happy, or competent, off the freeways. I stopped for a chat to two friendly California Highway Patrol Officers (the I.P.A. tie works wonders) who had heard about and were interested in the race riots then happening in my former Force area. The police world is quite small. After a meal where free coffee is offered as soon as you sit down, the climb began to Yosemite and into the Sierra. The scenery became spectacular, brown, gold, green and russet and I stayed the night beside the Merced River, which tumbles and chuckles out of the high valley.

Up at 7 a.m. I soon reached one of the most beautiful places in the world, Yogi Bear country, the Yosemite National Park. It is a fertile glaciated valley, carved out of the mountains, guarded by the massive face of El Capitan and graced by Half Dome, Cathedral Rock and the Three Brothers. El Capitan is nearly one mile high and wide, a huge square block of grey stone, and climbers on it look like tiny dolls. The valley is alive with mule deer, raccoons, squirrels and stellar jays and there are mountain lion and black bear in the mountains. I did a six-mile hike to 'outback', the Vernal, Nevada and Yosemite Falls, at 2000 feet above the valley floor. Yosemite was far too beautiful to leave after a day, and I was able to 'rent-a-tent' and sleep well after a talk by a guide in front of a huge log fire. Not bothered by 'b'ars'!

At 6 a.m. the deer were floating along, their legs hidden in the low morning mist. I sat with a warm doughnut and coffee for breakfast and watched the sun beginning to gild Half Dome and El Capitan, flooding the valley with warmth and light as the jays chattered in the tree-tops above. I had already been captivated by Amboseli, the Taj Mahal and the Church of the Annunciation in Nazareth, and would in the future see much more, but knew that this place would remain as one of, if not the, most beautiful.

I wrote in my notes at the time, 'The Indians invested this place with Spirits and Gods, and I know why'. I felt that I would like to call my house 'Yosemite', but have never owned anywhere that would be beautiful enough to justify it. My journey was now becoming a thing of continuing regrets, and it was once again with sadness that I climbed into the Toyota. However, it was impossible to be sad for too long, as heading west were the giant sequoia groves, where one can drive a car through a hole in a living tree trunk. This was an impressive, peaceful and lovely place that I felt to be a natural Cathedral. Then on down through gold-rush country, seeing tarantula spiders as big as my fist walking nonchalantly across the road, and passing little towns with names like 'Lucky Strike' and 'Nugget'. A time machine would have been a great bonus.

San Francisco is well known as another fascinating place. It was an easy city to drive in and to find a motel 'downtown', which made an excellent base. The famous fog came down however as I made an evening run over the Golden Gate Bridge, and quickly became very thick and rather eerie. Sequoia Grove to San Francisco – what a contrast in a day. Next morning was bright and sunny, so I turned in the Toyota, which had served me very well, and with a negotiated drop-off charge, not too expensive. The cable cars just had to be experienced, and they were great fun. The streets leading down to the waterfront really are as steep as they look in the films, and with any loitering driver warned by the clanging bell ('clang clang clang goes the trolley') motorists were pretty spry. Driving was, for a big city, impressive; as good as I've seen anywhere. The streets are very much in a grid, so route finding was easy.

It was now time to seek different transport, so I booked a cruise around the Bay, calling at Alcatraz and under the Golden Gate. What a welcome sight those red towers must have been to the members of the Pacific Fleet in the 1940's. Time was spent happily at Fisherman's Wharf, on an old clipper ship, the 'Belcathra' a Scottish built three master, although it was sad to realise how the ships of Glasgow and Liverpool had once dominated the clipper trade. All through my journey I had been finding connections to Great Britain, but thought that I was now understanding the Americans a bit better – their pride in what they had built, and what they could do. Perhaps this is another side of the inferiority complex that I felt was apparent in New Orleans. Pier 39 has been rebuilt to look as it did in the 1880s when the area was a genuine fishing port. Fish barrels doubled as waste bins! A great collection of shops, some touristy of course, but others up-market. I bought a present for home in a crystal shop where the pleasant girls behind the counter were flatteringly interested in my tour. I really do think that I was very lucky to have done this journey at a time when English people holidaying in the States were not that common.

After a stroll through Golden Gate Park I watched the sun go down blood red behind the Bridge, an experience that I shared with the crew of a cruising San Francisco Police Department car. As in New York and California, they were very interested in our policing problems and could hardly believe our lack of guns. 'Gee, you just had a stick?' I asked about the police chases filmed on the steep streets, and found that at that time they were done at night, with light intensifying cameras to make it appear daylight. There was a special police group paid by the film companies to assist. Now you know! Actually we had, on a smaller scale, done something similar when a film called *Man in the Sky* with the actor Jack Hawkins was made at Wolverhampton Airport. We loaned them a patrol car, plus the two man crew. My friend Jim was the driver, and oh, didn't he get his leg pulled about being a film star with a whole new career to look forward to! Jim had once been photographed by the local paper looking very grim, under the inscription 'He's seen it all'. Another wonderful opportunity for leg pulling! (I should perhaps add that there was just a little competition as to who would be in the film)!

As the sun disappeared, the bridge and the hills of Marin County across the Bay were silhouetted in golden fire. Over the water the lights of the big city of Oakland and Sausalito were coming on, lights were showing on ships and aircraft, and around was all the glitter of the Wharf area and the big houses on Nob Hill. Bells were sounding from buoys in the Bay, and the air was soft and warm. An evening walk around Chinatown was absorbing, it was full of vibrant activity, shops all open until late at night, buskers, imitation waxworks (Is he alive or not? Don't know!) and glowing signs all in Chinese. The area was more Chinese than Singapore, Hong Kong or Beijing. An experience more than a walk. One could spend a week – and a fortune on Fisherman's Wharf area alone, and then a second week and another fortune in Chinatown.

The Auto-Driveaway office failed me this time, with nothing to go north towards Canada, so the alternative seemed to be to try a really long Greyhound 'bus journey – twenty four hours to Vancouver. The coach left at 6am, with four changes of driver, some of whom were very chatty about their job, and all but the last very professional. He talked better than he drove! There were plenty of stops for rest and food, with cheap snacks available at most stopping places. With a front seat so that both the driver and the road could be watched, about 18 hours of the 25 were acceptable!

As we left San Francisco, via Oakland, traffic was already building up, and soon there was immense congestion going into the city. From the east side of the bay the white buildings of San Francisco looked like a tumbled Giant's Causeway – another fantastic view of a very beautiful city. Of course there are problems and crime and deprived areas, but overall I loved it. Lunch was at a little town on the Sacramento River with a lovely view of snow-capped Mount Shasta to the north. At over fourteen thousand feet it was visible for a long time, especially as we travelled more or less all round it. Gold mining was still going on in Northern California and the town of Weed felt very much a frontier. US Highway 97 was giving panoramic views including the Cascade Mountains on the northern horizon. At road works, of which there were plenty, there was almost always a 'flag man' rather than traffic lights, who invariably turned out to be a blonde girl, hair tucked under her tin hat. Klamath Lake, in the wild country of the Cascades, was a blue mirror, with the icy peak of Mount Shasta still showing 70 miles to the south by now. Having swept through miles of prairie, the road now tunnelled through mile after mile of huge fir forest. Occasionally a railroad hove in sight, with freight trains at least a mile long rumbling majestically northwards.

As the sky darkened the seats hardened proportionately and it was a welcome release to stretch legs in Portland and Seattle. Final liberation came at 7 a.m. in Vancouver city centre, a bright blue sky but no doubt at all that Summer had departed up here. I had not made much contact with my fellow travellers on the Greyhound, except the drivers, and I think that everyone was tired and cranky about the long journey. This was much different during my next and later excursion by Greyhound, across the States laterally instead of vertically, when we all chatted incessantly!

I think that the secret with really long distance journeys is to break it at least once, as I did on the later one. However, the Depot provided good facilities for a shave, and general clean up, with cheap storage for my luggage. Once more, as in the US, information was very easy to obtain and arrangements to get the forty odd sea miles to Vancouver Island were simple. A great contrast to, say, booking and getting onto a Channel Ferry, as it was in those days. A coach from the city centre rolled onto the ferry and I was able to enjoy the beautiful tangle of isolated islands and the mountains of the mainland on the 90 minute crossing of the Straight of Georgia.

Victoria, the capital of British Columbia and the only city on Vancouver Island was, then, more like Cheltenham than Cheltenham! (But with a little North American razmataz added). Royal Worcester and Spode china, Harris tweed and Edinburgh crystal were all on sale. It was a very pleasant little city, about the size of Gloucester, and quite delightful at night with the Government buildings illuminated and lined with thousands of lights, seaplanes and a cruise liner in the harbour and sophisticated shops open until late in the evening. However, strangely enough, there were more weirdos, winos and prostitutes visible than I had seen in the cities of America, and noticeably less police. Perhaps the weirdos were more noticeable in these surroundings, or maybe it was the result of less police activity.

I found a hotel in Thunderbird Park, surrounded by totem poles, the carving of which is an ongoing craft amongst British Columbian Indians, and at 7 a.m. next morning, money by now being rather tight, picked up a Chevrolet Chevette from 'Rent-a-Wreck'. It was actually quite a nice little car, with only about 20,000 on the clock. My first destination was Nanaimo, on the east coast of the island, where Bert and Isobel, relations of my flying friends Mick and Maureen back home, made me extremely welcome, and insisted on my staying the night with them. The view from their lounge, looking across the Sound to the mainland, with snow-capped mountains changing shape and colour as the sun moved round, was also their look-out point for killer whales moving south at the right season. A wonderful place to live. Again with regrets I said au-revoir to Bert and Isobel – in fact we corresponded for years afterwards until they both passed away. This then became the last leg of my outward journey, on a gloriously sunny but cold morning, across Vancouver Island to Pacific Rim State Park, on the north Pacific coast. Driving though some of the most breathtaking views of mountains and lakes imaginable, it was impossible not to stop and soak myself in some of the views. Time was, unfortunately, flying and I was relying on 'Rent-a-Wreck' to get me the 100 miles to Pacific Rim and the 160 back to Victoria by nightfall. Still, I could not resist time out to drink in the beauty of British Columbia, wild tumbled mountains, peaceful lakes, boulder strewn crystal clear rivers and trout streams, and everywhere the red and gold maples and majestic firs.

'Rent-a-Wreck' and I arrived in Tofino, the home of the Bald Eagle and Killer Whale at noon, and found a rough sign at the edge of the sea, where the road went straight in and under. 'Pacific Terminal – Trans-Canada Highway'. The end of more than three thousand miles, next stop would be Northern Japan or Vladivostock. In the harbour were two seaplanes, a Cessna and a De-Havilland Beaver, and as probably the only UK policeman who had flown, on duty, in a Beaver on both wheels and skis, the temptation was way, way, too strong, financial problems or not.

Again the scenery beggars description and my few photographs were totally inadequate. To crown it, after a very low run past an Indian Village we spotted a grey whale coming to the surface to spout, a few hundred yards off shore. I suggested to the pilot that he had a pretty good way of earning a living, but he didn't seem that impressed. I guess the grass is always greener somewhere else, but I would have been happy to swap, at that time and place. Turning east for the last time, the car delivered me efficiently back to Victoria, from where I caught the early morning ferry back to Vancouver. I had found the driving in British Columbia to be good, with no hassle, and particularly liked the flashing amber lights, placed one hundred yards before traffic lights to warn that a red is imminent. This really does do away with any excuse for jumping it. Generally, big cities and Houston excepted, as in most areas that I visited during the month, the driving was relaxed, easy, well controlled and courteous.

My flight home was an evening one, which allowed time for just one more expedition – to Grouse Mountain, a famous viewpoint and ski site, looking down nearly four thousand feet onto Vancouver and south to the volcanoes of Washington State, Mount Rainier and Mount St. Helens, which I had passed during the night on the Greyhound earlier. There was a spectacular cable car up Grouse Mountain, with a good restaurant at the top and a terrace where one could look down at the city and Georgia Straits while enjoying a beer. And, of course, it was open and everything else was working! After a hike around for a few hours it was time to descend the cable car, pick up a city 'bus and the seabus across Burrard Inlet, then the 'hustlebus' to the Airport. More, many more, regrets as the long journey to Heathrow commenced. It had been an extraordinary month, begun with preconceptions that melted away, and new sights, new cultures, new enlightenment and new friends. It had instilled the feeling that I had to go back. Maybe North America is the most dangerous country in the world, as I once heard an academic describe it, but it is also a vivid, breathtaking emotional experience, not just three countries. A lot of the people who live there are very peculiar indeed and of course it has the problems of crime and anti-social behaviour commensurate with it's size. Nevertheless, to my mind there is only word to describe the sub-continent, again commensurate with its size and that is, 'Simply magnificent.'

Back to work in Birmingham, nose down but just a little distracted, I was able to get the story of the journey published in both the driving magazine and the RoSPA Newspaper, and to draw some relevant conclusions from it. Then, a year on from the visit to the Welsh Forest Rally School, in March 1986 I was able with the same journalist, Paul, to assess a different type of motor rallying training. This was held at Bruntingthorpe Proving Ground, a former US Air Force airfield in Leicestershire, so very flat, no trees and very, in March, windswept! This was an ongoing school, with paying pupils, six of whom were present, all except myself under thirty. Some had travelled as much as a hundred miles for the tuition and experience. Two of them were seriously considering entering their first rally, and one had obtained sponsorship, so it was a reasonably important business. The instructor that day was Pat, an RAC Rally class winner. The cars were again Ford Rally Specials, with worn tyres so that they could be made to slide on the loose gravel and runway surface.

After a detailed briefing pupils were turned loose to practice cornering by using the accelerator only to provoke oversteer, in a tight circle around a traffic cone, with the steering wheel held rigid. This is practised in both directions but is a lot easier clockwise, as the cone is more visible! It was a useful introduction to the next exercise, cornering at speed on mud or gravel, using handbrake turns and the 'pendulum' effect of a crisp 'on and off' the accelerator. When this had been learned satisfactorily the pupils were taken on a chauffeured drive by Pat around a two-mile mud gravel and banked up 'special stage'. All the pupils then drove it themselves. I found it all reasonably easy, but it was enjoyable to practice and 'sharpen up'. I did prize the remark by Pat after my special stage drive. He said to the group that he had always felt that if chased by a police car he could take to the fields and escape, but after sitting in with me he was having second thoughts! This was nice, as was his surprise that the oldest driver was the most adaptable.

I was sincerely able to give the School some good publicity in the RoSPA newspaper, with similar comments used about the day in Mid-Wales. 'Off-road driving can be of considerable benefit, even to the non-competitive motorist, to help develop car handling ability and flexibility of mind and attitude'. This day led, not long after, to my being asked to instruct at the School in the sudden absence of their regular instructor. This was quite a compliment and a big learning curve to be actually telling paying customers how to do it. The School changed hands and location soon after and I did not get the chance of a follow-up, but it remains a pleasant memory. The techniques learned and practised were useful in the off-road days that we ran later on at the Motor Industry Research Association proving ground near Nuneaton. I did however visit the same School when it had moved to the better venue at Silverstone Racing Circuit. It was renamed Silverstone Rally School and I enjoyed a full day there in rather more stylish surroundings. As I seemed to be reasonably good at it I rather regret that I never had the funds to enter a competitive Rally. One either has to be prepared to drive to destruction whatever one is using to have a chance of competing, or to acquire a sponsor to bank roll the write-offs – the clever trick is to come from a wealthy family! Nevertheless I enjoyed the experiences and saw, perhaps not over, but at least around a few more figurative hills.

Zimbabwe and South Africa

The nineteen-eighties continued very busily, with my ex-Warrant Officer colleague Gordon and I travelling to Africa again. This was to run a course in Zimbabwe for BP to train local staff from adjacent countries. The object was to teach them how to assess BP drivers in-house. We were based in the

Monomatapa Hotel in Harare (formerly Salisbury of course) and very nice it was too. This was before the dreadful days of the Mugabe regime, and the city and country were very pleasant places to be. What a disaster has now come to that sad country.

Our team came from Zimbabwe, Tanzania, Zambia and Mozambique. As we were teaching them to assess, we had to do some role-play as drivers applying for a job, which led to quite a lot of fun and giggling. Quite a lot of shyness as well when it came to describing our hammed-up faults. In fact this, apart from one man, was a well-selected group, and after two weeks they had picked up the idea very well, and could tell us off with gusto! The one unfortunate gentleman, from Mozambique, should never have been sent on the course. It was naturally important that they could drive well themselves, in order to assess others. Gordon took this guy out first and came back shattered, 'We've been 'kangarooing' all over Harare – you take him out and see how you get on!'

I had the same experience of bouncing around with no co-ordination between clutch and accelerator at all. Putting our heads together we found that he normally drove an automatic at home in Maputo, and was constitutionally incapable of moving his feet in different directions at the same time. When the left foot went down so did the right, and vice versa! Imagine! We had to send him home, which was a shame and a disgrace for him, but unavoidable. He was a pleasant quiet man, with tales of the horrors in his country only a short time before. I still feel quite bad about this, but the fault was in the selection by BP. Perhaps politics were at work.

Apart from this the two weeks went very well, and I was actually able to make contact and share a meal with Jo's cousin Peter and his family who were then working in Harare. I also gave a talk about 'accident prevention' to a group of white landowner farmers, colleagues of Ian Smith, the Southern Rhodesia UDI Prime Minister. Interesting people, who did not deserve (in my view) what was coming to them. As usual it was possible, on our drives, to see something of the country, which was still the 'breadbasket' of Southern Africa. I bought some wonderful carvings and saw a wild black rhino for the first time. We went to Victoria Falls, where it was interesting to hold a live crocodile (baby) and learned that a croc with his jaws open is not being aggressive but just trying to cool down. The ruins of Great Zimbabwe and the fabulous rock formations and rock paintings were another bonus, as was a boat on the Zambezi. Gordon and I were quite pleased to be being paid for experiencing these things.

This course brought a rather wonderful postscript to me in 1988, when I received a handwritten letter from Boniface B. Manyika in Dar Es Salaam.

Boniface had been one of the best trainees during the course, and I had sent him some photographs taken during the two weeks. Thanking me for both the photographs and the course, in not perfect but pretty good English the fact of his having taken the trouble to write was a really great pleasure, and I still have his letter. He ends it, 'I keep driving to the system!!' A further post-postscript happened ten years later, when a driving instructor who also worked for RoSPA took on, in the UK, an African trainee to improve his heavy goods skills. He seemed to be very competent, using the advanced system of vehicle control and other UK techniques, so Mike probed a bit. 'Where did you learn?' he asked. 'Oh, two gentlemen came specially from England to train people. They were Mr. Gordon and Mr. Michael.' Putting two and two together - not difficult - Mike learned that our influence had remained strong, since every time a trainee committed a driving fault the company instructor would say, 'Oh, Mr. Gordon and Mr. Michael would not like that one little bit'. Gordon and I were rather pleased about that!

Another co-incidence surfaced in 2007, from twenty seven years previously. Whilst working as an 'L' test examiner in Bilston I had taken, and passed a young gentleman, David. Whilst this was just routine for me, it was his first attempt at the test and being so delighted had kept his pass certificate, with the date and time, 12.15 p.m. on 13th March 1980. When I contacted him in 2007 to fix a rendezvous he realised that I was the same person, now doing advanced tests! Needless to say we did not recognise each other, but after the test David told me the story, and I confirmed that it was my signature on the pass certificate. I am glad to say that again he passed first time, at the top level. It was nice to see, in his letter to RoSPA, that he had felt that it was an enjoyable experience, like meeting an old friend again. Well, not everyone feels that way about their 'L' test examiner!

Following the end of the Zimbabwe work I took some leave and flew into Jan Smuts Airport, Johannesburg. A night or two in that unhappy city was enough (despite being introduced to edible snails – very greasy!) and I rented a car to drive the spectacular route to Cape Town, via Durban and the Wilderness Coast. Durban was classy and a chance to swim in the Indian Ocean was good. A thrill was to stop in Hermanus where the whales come in to calve at a certain season because of the amount of plankton that is available in the bay without effort. I had timed this just right, by luck not judgement, and the bay was full of whalebacks, dorsal and tail fins. Saw one or two breaches out of the water as well – these must have been happy fathers! Something not so enjoyable, but throwing a light on certain South African attitudes was a comment made by the owner of a Hotel in the Drakensberg Mountains.

I had expressed my intention to drive into Transkei, the Xhosa country – 'Why you want to go up to that place, it is all black monkeys there.' I did anyway of course, and enjoyed the experience, with thousands of 'beehive' Xhosa huts and grinning, waving kids. The adults not so sure – I could have been a Boer of course. The Transkei was one of the first more or less self-governing republics set up within South Africa, to provide a homeland for the Xhosa people. Sadly, this did not work and in 1994 it was re-incorporated into the Eastern Province. There was a frontier guard on the border post, not too sure of the validity of my visa but they let me in and out.

However, a trek along the top of Table Mountain, was wonderful, as was the wine country around Stellenbosch, so green and calm, with beautiful Dutch houses. It was rather nice to be addressed as 'Mijnheer', a nice contrast to the Drakensberg Hotel keeper. I was treated to lunch with friends from Wolverhampton, in their lovely white Dutch style house on the way to the Cape. Reaching Cape Point, the southern tip of the Cape of Good Hope, from where there is nothing but sea in a straight line over the South Atlantic to the permanent pack ice of the Antarctic was a unique experience. Sharing the road with a troop of large baboons on Smits Winkle Flats was also an experience – not least for the name!

This had been a great six day break, tacked on to the Zimbabwe work, and a chance to see quite a lot of a different part of the world. It had to be, as usual, squeezed into too little time but I was able, by not sleeping much, to include some of the best. Then it was back to Birmingham. What was it about the sublime and something else?!

In December '86 RoSPA arranged for one of the Examiner Panel and I to go on a two week course with British Road Services in Birmingham to obtain Articulated Heavy Goods Licences, then known as HGV Class 1 - as high as one could get in the heavy lorry world. This was a tough but very enjoyable fortnight. When it came to Test Time though, Tony passed but I didn't! Oh dear! This was terribly shaming, and a kick in the teeth, as I have not failed at much else, driving-wise. However, the Department of Transport Examiner was in a good mood, and agreed that I could retake it the same day with his colleague. This time was a success – what a relief! I think, having been a driver of cars of all types for the best part of forty years, the transition was perhaps another step too far, but I managed to get it rammed home in my brain in the end. I then made it my business to do a lot of 'temping' jobs as a Heavy Goods Driver in my own time, both for experience and to try to get better at it. There was any amount of work available through the temping agencies, but as a 'temp' you naturally always get the dirty end of any jobs that are going. To do forty or so 'drop off' jobs, miles apart on an unknown route, and more often than not in congested city centres, is difficult.

Add to this the fact that some of the loads will have to be fork-wheeled off, and the almost inevitable wait to get onto an unloading bay, and it becomes impossible to complete the task without breaking the hours of work laws and falsifying the records, or speeding, or both. This I refused to do, and therefore collected some abuse from fleet supervisors for bringing back undelivered goods. This did not matter to me in the slightest (one benefit of being a temp) but I feel very sorry for drivers being pushed into breaking the law in several ways by unscrupulous supervisors, - there are plenty of them - in order to keep their jobs. I did do plenty of very big artic rig jobs, some quite far flung, and enjoyed mixing with other drivers. There are some cowboy drivers, either through ignorance or a bullying nature or being under pressure from supervisors, but there are many very fine ones as well, who drive and behave to the highest standards. Those who come to us for training or a test are often very good already. It seems that the word gets round the work force before they come to us, initiating a thinking and improvement process already.

On the other hand I have walked into the driver's rest room to be greeted with, 'Ah know yo'll find some'at to complain about, that's what you'm here for ay it?' Not a good start to the day, but we usually end up friends. (A bit of police cunning helps!) Whilst I did leave RoSPA only three years later I did a number of HGV training and testing days for them first, which could not have been done without obtaining the occupational licence. This has continued on a part time basis since, (now called LGV 'large goods' by the way), so I am content that the course was not wasted. We are getting a lot of Polish nationals now, usually good drivers used to long runs into Russia, but with interesting language.

Not long after this I was asked to take a two week course with Cardiff City Transport to obtain a Public Service Vehicle (now Passenger Carrying Vehicle) licence to drive a double decker 'bus. This again was interesting, and demanding in some ways to remember the live bodies likely to be on board, but as I was now quite used to the bigger vehicles I sailed through this one! On the Cardiff training vehicle the trainee driver sat in splendid isolation high behind the wheel, while the instructor perched on a little stool, sans seat-belt, below and to his left. All went well for most of the fortnight as I learned a lot about Cardiff and it's environs and enjoyed myself in the evenings. Nevertheless the day came when I was negotiating a junction in the city centre, with, I swear, the green light easily in my favour. Coming through the red, from my left was, of all things, a Salvation Army minibus. Definitely nearer My God to Thee, and obviously relying upon Divine Providence. I performed an immaculate emergency stop.

Now, a full blown emergency stop in an empty double decker is quite a thing, and my instructor finished up right at the back of the downstairs aisle, having been bounced off the front end, little stool and all. I already knew plenty of appropriate words of Anglo-Saxon, but learned a few new Welsh ones as well. Unfortunately one cannot chase a speeding minibus in a double decker, even if it is empty. Still, it was a good two weeks.

It was always my intention to do some coach driving in my own time. This is an improvement on shifting heavy goods about, as the load walks on and off itself, although I guess it can be a quite demanding load. It never happened though, as I left RoSPA not very long afterwards, and needed all my time and energies for the new job. However I have been able to train and test both coach and double decked 'bus drivers for them on many occasions since, so once more the course was not wasted. LGV and PCV drivers are very proud of their occupational licences and it is good to be able to speak their language and be accepted as one of them. I have to say that I never enjoyed the bigger vehicles as much as I do decent cars, although there is a je ne sais quoi about rolling down the motorway high above, and superior to, everyone else!

In late 1986 (another very busy year) people that I knew at the Transport and Road Research Laboratory in Crowthorne suggested to the Editor-in-Chief of a forthcoming book that I might be an appropriate person to contribute to it. The book, a major work dealing with all forms of surface transport in the developing world was to be written by a number of authors, each dealing with their own specialty. The Editor, who was at that time the Vice President of the Chartered Institute of Transport wrote to me to ask if I would contribute a section on Driver Training. This was, of course, a tremendous compliment and I was very pleased indeed to do so. The book, *Developing World Land Transport*, was published by the Grosvenor Press International in 1988, and was certainly an important and wide reaching book. My contribution, with three of my own photographs from training work in Africa, was well received by the Editor, and was, I think, if not my apogee as an Author, certainly my widest read text.

The introduction from the Transport and Road Research Laboratory probably came about through the publication, by RoSPA, of my book, *Driving, Navigation and Survival in the Hot Deserts*, the previous year. The book was well received and reviewed, and sold in bulk to various companies operating in desert environments. It was also used by the British Army and the Royal Geographical Society, which led to my becoming a Fellow of the

R.G.S. It is currently, in 2010, being used by companies working in Iraq – twenty five years on, not a bad shelf life! I still get the occasional request for copies, but unfortunately it is now out of print.

I had used the experiences and techniques learned for operating in Africa, and for the general use of four wheeled drive vehicles. Jo wrote the survival part, using her contacts in the Institute of Occupational Health at Birmingham University to discuss the prevention of, and recovery from, exposure to excessive heat. Perhaps one of the reasons that it attracted attention was that, opening at the front it read in English, but opening from the back the text was in Arabic! This, believe me, took a bit of doing, as it was difficult to proof-read! At that time RoSPA had a very good illustrator, who produced some excellent illustrative cartoons, dressed differently, and with different problems according to which end of the book one opened! In the mid-eighties I was also doing a lot of writing for different driving magazines, including the serialisation of the journey from eastern to western Canada via Mexico in 1985, and contributing regularly to the RoSPA newspaper, *Care on the Road*.

In 1983 my flying friend Tony, who was then a teacher at a large school in Tipton, and responsible for the School's Minibuses had realised that there were no written training manuals for driving or operating these vehicles. A proposal to RoSPA that we should jointly write one to be published under their aegis was accepted, and the result has become the standard textbook for schools, clubs, county councils and youth organisations. It has sold very well, been enlarged and improved several times and is now in the fifth edition, being, I believe, a very useful piece of writing. Tony did the technical research and wrote the 'operating' and 'legal'sections, while I provided the driving guidance.

1986 brought an interest in an advanced driving test by the film, television star and model Katie Boyle. Naturally this was not one to be marked out to any old Examiner, so I travelled down to Hampstead, where she and her husband owned a magnificent house in a street of magnificent houses. Katie had been a star for a number of years and was a most attractive and bubbly lady. She is of Italian descent, and this showed both in her personality and her driving. The test was interesting, as I sat in the car in Bond Street while she called at her Jewellers. (Don't worry about the double yellow lines if you are a film star!) I was tempted to disclose that my Uncle and Cousin had been jewellers in the Jewellery Quarter in Birmingham!

As well as being interesting the test went satisfactorily and Katie wrote to say that she and her husband had enjoyed my report. She particularly liked the advice not to incorporate too much Italian panache into her driving and to keep both hands on the wheel. Paul came with me to photograph Katie's Certificate presentation, which was, of course extremely good publicity for

RoSPA as she was very well known and popular. We kept in touch for some time, and she endorsed a card game designed to help people with their driving test in which I had had some input.

In 1988 Katie was given her own Radio Show on Radio 2, and invited me down to the BBC London studio to discuss better driving with her. This was in the first programme, and she wrote afterwards to thank me for holding her hand – metaphorically of course. I am perfectly sure that no handholding was needed, but it is a nice letter to have. It was also rather nice to receive the letter addressed to, 'My dear Friend' from a lady who was widely regarded as one of the most glamorous women of her generation! Another interesting experience and a mountain seen over, especially as I was able to have a few words with an extremely famous film actor, who was 'on' before me! There was some feed back from the interview as I asked the question, on air, 'When is it correct to signal right, when actually turning left?' Not many people (I think only one RoSPA member) got it right. The answer is, of course, when joining a motorway from a slip- road. Correct, but perhaps a bit sneaky! (I allowed 'when turning left in a long HGV as well' as not far off!)

In late 1988, early `89, the BBC World Service asked me to work with them to produce a series of programmes on how to drive safely and more efficiently. The programmes were to be broadcast to South East Asia, the Caribbean and South Pacific Islands specifically, but I suppose, to anywhere else receiving the World Service. This was tremendous fun, and I got on very well with the Producer, Executive Producer and Presenter. We made twelve 'Topical Tapes', dealing with all the basic subjects of car and personal fitness, attitude, gear-changing and steering, then moved on to skid prevention, overtaking, night driving, commentary and emergency action, to a background music of *Joyride*! I had a couple of really nice letters from Kathleen and David, the two Producers, saying that they had enjoyed and learnt themselves from the sessions. Kathleen passed on some instructions that she had seen for Japanese drivers, mentioning the 'Skid Demon' and 'the pressing of the brake of foot while rolling round the corners'! Apparently the broadcasts were very well received. A thoroughly nice experience, which upped my stock at RoSPA.

In 1989 I was head-hunted once more. This time it was by James, an experienced Rally Driver holding a National Rally distinction, who was keen to set up his own Driver Training Company. James, as Managing Director was going to finance the new Company, (although we had to start showing a black balance sheet as quickly as possible) with myself putting in the teaching expertise, as Director of Training. The prospect of adding a Company Directorship to my CV, plus a nice company car (a Peugeot 405) was tempting.

Although RoSPA was safe, and a guaranteed income, (the mortgage was not yet paid off) after discussion at home we decided to go for it. RoSPA agreed that I should stay on the panel of Examiners, which was a good advertising point for the new Company. A lot of rather happy planning work was done by both of us and our one clerical assistant, at a base in the refurbished stables of James' parents home. As this was in the Peak District he chose an appropriate Company name, 'Peak Performance Management'. We had to develop our training strategies, seek and recruit trainers and deliver specific courses. We devised paperwork, report forms and training manuals and handouts and visited potential customers. Another very busy time, as clients began to knock at the door, and we did soon achieve a substantial contract with a very big multi-national firm, which gave me training days all over the UK.

One of the first jobs for James in 1989 was to join his Father-in-law Howard, on an 'economy run', trying, against competition, to squeeze every last drop from the petrol tank. Howard was a well-known journalist at that time, and a previous entrant in this event, which was run by the Northern Group of Motoring Writers. The object was to raise funds for the Charity founded by Simon Weston, the Falklands War survivor. This was naturally good publicity for our new Company, and Howard had raised the substantial sum of £860 through his motoring world contacts. The route was coast to coast (or near enough, being 300 miles), Ferrybridge in Teeside to Workington.

An economy run was new territory to me, and as Howard said in his subsequent write-up, I was clearly uneasy with some of the driving techniques! There was no cheating by freewheeling down the hills, of which there are plenty on that route, but when keeping high gear on the slopes, round corners and roundabouts etc., Howard wrote that he could feel his co-driver cringe! However, we stuck to the task for eight and half hours, averaging 36 mph and over 50 miles per gallon. This was in a Skoda Favrit, to which we had drawn the keys. We were beaten by a Proton with 55 mpg, while a diesel Peugeot achieved almost 70 mpg. Must have been some freewheeling in the latter case I think. It was a quite hard but interesting day, and we were reasonably satisfied with the mileage, but of course the charity donations that Howard had attained were the best result.

Some of the work for Peak was fairly routine bread and butter stuff - training days in the UK to try to expose company drivers to different ways of doing things: sometimes enjoyable, sometimes not. We had an interesting contract with the Inland Revenue Fraud and Detection Service though, which was effectively back to police work. They had to be trained in surveillance and going as fast as possible within the law where it had become necessary. (This is a lot more difficult than it is for the Police, Fire Service or Ambulance drivers.) One of these training weeks, in Glasgow led to a very long night. We set out to do a night run, well in the back of beyond in Stirlingshire. It may have been somewhere near Bannockburn, as this was definitely Scotland one, England nil! The object, using two cars, was to practice both following and overtaking on narrow country roads. All went well until about 2am when my driver allowed both nearside wheels to fall over the very sharp edge of a two inch drop where the tarmac ended. This (which was a big learning curve), ripped the guts out of the inner side of both nearside tyres. Take it on board, it can happen, and not at high speed either!

Now, naturally, we had one spare wheel, and I made the driver change it in the dark, but, and it was a big but, the other car was a different make! We were, at a guess, forty miles from the nearest tyre stockist likely to be open. Mobile 'phones were not prevalent and it was quite a long walk to the nearest box. (The driver went). I think that we limped back into Glasgow at about 7.30 a.m. The Team Admin Manager, obviously a dyed in the wool Scot, went on and on about the cost of his two new tyres until he was in danger of losing his kilt! It was interesting work though, and I have always preferred to live in interesting times. We also had an overseas job, in Sweden in 1994. This was local driver training for a multi-national firm based in Stockholm, and it seemed sensible, as I had done with the Police Chief in Brussels, to make a police contact first. My colleague Eric was also a retired police officer, and we got on very well with the Stockholm officer that I had contacted through the IPA. Naturally, he was English speaking! He was able to discuss traffic problems in the urban area, being a police car driver, and took us on a splendid tour of the city. Stockholm is, of course, a place of ships, islands and sea inlets, and impressively picturesque.

Next day Eric and I got on with the training work, which as it was December was quite cold and rather slippery. I discovered that Swedish drivers, being used to slippery roads, and taking skid prevention courses every year, were much more interested in what was happening behind them than are people in the UK. Stopping in a hurry was a no-no and it was reckoned good policy to risk an amber light rather than surprise the driver behind. The course did go well, and we had a chance to do some shopping for presents in Father Christmas's back yard!

Back home I was able to arrange the use of the Staffordshire Police skid-pan for our clients, as the man in charge was a former colleague from Wolverhampton days. This was a bonus and well appreciated by our clients. I had qualified as a 'skid-car' instructor with the West Midlands Ambulance Department in 1988 so the Staffordshire Instructors were quite happy to take a break and let me do some of the training, which was enjoyable 'hands-on' work. James, through his contacts in motor sport, was able to also arrange for our clients to use the consummate facilities of the Motor Industry Research Association near Nuneaton. Apart from the high speed track, where one can safely train drivers to take fast bends properly, the skid training areas are superb. A conventional slippery round pan was big and safe enough to demonstrate how, by wrong technique, it was eminently possible to be travelling in a straight line with the steering on full lock – a useful lesson. There are also areas of 'wet grips' where wetted slippery areas are adjacent to dry ones giving a good grip. This produces a condition known as a 'split mu' (a divided co-efficient of friction) where heavy braking or sharp moves can spring unexpected surprises, especially with an older vehicle. Another very useful exercise was to come out of a wetted slippery area fairly quickly, brake for an imaginary obstruction (e.g. a wandering pedestrian) on a curving path, and suddenly hit totally dry road. This surprised one client, who was actually a very capable young man whom I had just trained up to win the 'Driver of the Year' competition. We finished up facing sideways, well up on the grass banking, he flabbergasted while I, expecting it and holding tight, was laughing hard! The trick, in areas of wet and dry road, is to release the brakes, straighten the steering from the curved path before reaching the dry road, then brake on the straight. OK in good daylight, but what do you do at night? Only one answer wins the coconut!

We had days of great fun on those, not only enjoyable but, I hope, with benefit to our clients for the winter days, which happen with great regularity in the UK. Neither the DSA not the Department for Transport seem to have cottoned on to the fact that it does get wintry here at times. Apart from a small section in the Highway Code, which is so far off complete that it actually gives wrong advice, we do nothing to train young people how to stay in a straight line and on the black stuff. In partnership with others who actually understand about this, we have made rude noises in the corridors of power about the way young drivers are being failed, but the 'Titanic' took a lot of turning, and so do those bureaucratic bodies.

I stayed with Peak until 1997, when it at last seemed appropriate to step down from full-time work. I'm pleased to say that the Company has grown very considerably since 1989 and is now recognised as one of the market-leading driver development and fleet risk management companies in the UK. James was kind enough to acknowledge the value of my input in the early days through two letters after I retired. My leaving gift was a magnificent Berghaus anorak, which has been to the top of Kilimanjaro and a good way up Sagarmatha /Chomolungma (the real names of Everest) and is still regularly worn in 2010! One of the last jobs in '97 was with a Japanese company who were bringing their own people to work at their UK company base. They needed a lot of familiarisation practice in UK traffic. Like the letter from Boniface in Tanzania, I treasure it still, and am proud of, a written comment from Mr.Y. Morimoto. 'One of the most serious problems for us Japanese is to pass through Roundabout and motorway smoothly and safely. The training course helped me to resolve it, and I could adjusted myself to UK traffic rule and custom. Mike San is a good trainer, so that I got a lot of information about traffic comfortably'. Can't ask for much more than that.

I did however feel, during a theory presentation to some of these guys that I had committed a rather terrible solecism. I was trying very hard to get some reaction to questions about driving but everyone around the table was so ultra-polite that no one would speak before the others. To call upon someone by name was not exactly easy! Eventually I tried, 'You are driving in the country, and a sheep comes through a hedge and commits hari-kiri on your front bumper. What must you do?' There was dead silence and I thought, 'Oh, no this is a sacred rite to the Japanese, I've really blown it.' The dead silence continued for another few heartbeats, then a little voice spoke up from the end of the table, 'I take big knife, I cut off back leg and take home to wife'. There was a roar of laughter, and everything went very well from then!

In 1993, while still working for James I thought that it would be interesting to take the Mensa IQ test. Achieving a score of 161, which is 1 higher than the estimated score for Albert Einstein, may call into question the method of Mensa scoring. Or it may say more about the estimation of his score than it does about the relative merits of our brains. I did guess a lot of the answers but perhaps that was part of the test. However, what is certainly beyond doubt is that I only remained a member for the first twelve months, having quickly come to the opinion that many members were weird. Membership of Interplanetary or Extra-Sensory Perception Groups was not for me. I can still flash the Certificate though, in need! More relevant is the Master's degree in Driver Education gained in 2002.

RoSPA also used MIRA to provide an open day for members, and on one such occasion a man turned up very impressed with, and proud of, the ABS system fitted to his car. The ABS was a lot newer and more rare than it is today. 'We'll take you on the slippery bits,' I said, 'Oh, this will not skid, it's got ABS.' I knew that this was optimistic, so got my friend Tony to jump in the back with his video camera, 'Now, get up to about 50 mph, and centre over the drain so that the nearside wheels are on the wet and the offside on the dry. Now brake hard.'

We have him nicely on video saying, 'Oh hell!' as the scenery spins round 180 degrees to the right. A bit cruel perhaps, but a valuable lesson that not all the new aids were perfect, and that if you are brutal enough to a car it might do anything. It might be said that this combination of wet and dry at MIRA was artificial, and unusual. This is partly true, but I have experienced conditions exactly like this many times high in the hills in winter, where the low sun has melted the ice on one side of a narrow road only, the other side being in the shadow of the hedge. I had a passenger ask once, in such conditions, 'Why are you driving on the wrong half of the road?' Well, if you don't know!

There is a very high speed track at MIRA, which is so banked that it is hands off at 150 mph and used by the companies producing fast cars. The MIRA staff are proud of the fact that there has only been one fatal accident – a drowning! This requires an explanation. One of the test drivers got it wrong on the banking, flipped over the upper edge and landed upside down in the lake on the outside of the track. Pity, as it spoiled a good record. We never used this track, as it was appropriate to vehicle testing only. I was promised a ride on it, but unfortunately it never came off, so 140 mph was my maximum, and now likely to remain so! RoSPA continued to use the ground for 'Members Days' for some years after I had left Peak and we had some very enjoyable, and companiable days there. Regrettably, because it was very useful training, this has now been discontinued on grounds of cost, but it is a good memory.

After retiring from every day work I did not want to sit by the fire in slippers, so set up my own self-employed Driving Consultancy. RoSPA were pleased to have me back as a part-time trainer, also remaining as an advanced test examiner, and for years I was working almost full time for them. The great benefit of being self-employed was that if one didn't fancy a job one didn't have to do it! I have continued to provide these services ever since. I have had to come to terms with many changes, including computerisation, electronic booking and reporting procedures, not all of which seem to me to be an improvement. Something about new tricks and old dogs? More tests to retain my driving instructor rating also became necessary. 'Hazard Perception' caught out a lot of experienced instructors, some former police trainers, through their observation skills being too quick to spot the problem on screen. Believe it or not, this resulted in a penalty! One had to learn to play this game, and fit into their time frame, which was not the DSA's finest hour. It does, of course, illuminate the low standard that the DSA expected of the 'ordinary' driving instructors. Nevertheless, I was pleased to be able to provide some training and testing days so that RoSPA's standards could be assessed by DSA senior staff. I was rather pleased with one comment, 'Thank you. Very relaxed, very expert, correct and very professional'. I have invariably got on well with, and respected the 'hands-on' DSA staff, many of whom have a similar background to mine. It is the theory and business 'experts' who seem to a lot of us to be living in another dimension.

I attended some RoSPA courses on managing occupational road risk and manual handling training, and helped to devise 'Banksman Courses'. These are to train lorry drivers and their assistants in manoeuvring big rigs in confined spaces. I find it fascinating that the word goes back over a hundred years to when all heavy freight was moved on the canals. Helping to manoeuvre the barges was a Man on the Bank! In 1997 the President, Lord Astor of Hever presented me with a Certificate of Life Membership, only the fifth to be awarded in almost one hundred years history. In 2005 Jo and I were honoured to be invited by his successor as President, The Baroness Gibson of Market Rasen, to a Reception in the House of Lords. This was to celebrate fifty years of advanced driver training, started by 'The League of Safe Drivers' and continued by RoSPA. It was a nice summer day in July, and it was pleasant to stand on the Terrace with a drink and see the passengers on the river tour boats all aiming cameras!

Rewinding to 1990, another very pleasant occasion in London had come our way. This was the annual dinner of the UK Malaysian Law Society at the Cumberland Hotel, to which we were invited by a friend of our friend in Ipoh, Perak, Hira Singh. The dinner was in the presence of His Royal Highness the Regent of Perak, Rajah Nazrim Ibni Sultan Aslan Shah. A scintillating occasion, which I believe that we both made the most of. A further glittering evening in 2005 was the President's Dinner of the Royal Geographical Society, to which I had been elected a Fellow in 1986. Two hundred and fifty guests were present in the Goldsmith's Hall in the City of London – virtually in the shadow of St. Pauls. The main speaker was the film producer David (now Lord) Putnam. We again made a week-end of it, and whilst perhaps amongst the least distinguished there thoroughly enjoyed it. It was quite nice to be announced in ringing tones to Princess Anne, the Society's President, even if it was only as, 'Mr and Mrs' following Lord and Lady Somebody and preceding the Honourable Somebody Else! Being present in Goldsmith's Hall, amongst all the wonderful displays of the Goldsmith's art was an added privilege.

It seems appropriate to continue with some of the steps that I have taken around the world, for leisure and pleasure. I have to say here that I have been very very lucky to have been fit enough to take them, to have the opportunity to do so and to meet with support instead of objections from Jo. We have, of course, continued to have holidays together, and as well as the major ones described earlier have seen a lot of Italy, France, Ireland, the Outer Hebrides, Germany, Austria, Spain and the Mediterranean. We have both been very lucky, and privileged.

Chapter 7

Some more true traveller's tales for Jan and Max, South America, Atlantic to Pacific coasts and back, 1991

Having wanted to see the 'bottom end of the American continent 'since travelling around the US and Canada six years before, in March 1991 I persuaded James to let me take a long accumulated leave and flew into Caracas, the capital of Venezuela. Publicity describes Venezuela as 'The Adventure', and I have no quarrel with this. I was about to join, in Rio, a fourteen strong group making a six-week safari across South America, from east to west, Rio to Lima, but I wanted to see the 'Lost Worlds' of Venezuela first. The Hotel Avila, in the very modern, busy and teeming city centre of Caracas was, in a word luxurious. Having been founded by Nelson Rockefeller in 1942, I suppose that this follows! The discovery of oil made Caracas one of the richest and most modern cities in South America. Interesting to note though that the Hotel was obviously proud of its Colonial Terrace restaurant, in 'a real colonial setting'. I wonder what this meant.

I was up at 4.30 next morning to get a flight to Cuidad Bolivar, where I transferred to a small twin engined Dornier to fly over the lost world. This should be worlds, as there are several of the flat topped, sheer sided and very high mesas. Mesa is Spanish for table which describes these spectacular rocky outcrops well. They gave rise to the stories and films about lost worlds, cut off from ground level, where dinosaurs roamed and other extinct species and plants thrived. The Dornier flew south towards the Guyana Highlands, a land of gold and diamond mines. A major object of the journey was to fly over the highest waterfall in the world, three thousand, three hundred foot Angel Falls, seventeen times higher than Niagara! The Falls were originally named not for Heavenly beings but after an American pilot, Johnny Angel, who discovered them literally by accident, crash landing at the top earlier in the century. One way of getting up the sheer cliffs! The Falls have now been renamed Kerapakupai-Merú, by order of the Venezuelan President Hugo Chávez. This means waterfall of the deepest place in the indigenous Pemon language, and is part of an initiative to remove Western influenced names. Since Venezuela is very far west of Europe this is political rather geographical! The cliffs are the edge of the 45 mile diameter tabletop mountain of Auyantepuy. The cliffs are so sheer that the river falls without interruption for a large part of its drop. Quite a sight and quite a site. We also came close to Mount Roraima, which at nearly ten thousand feet was thought to be the site where Conan Doyle placed his story of the 'Lost World'.

Our flight was magnificent, and was completed by landing at a Missionary Community at Kavac. Pemon Indians, wearing only loincloths, unloaded the plane, then we trekked to a river, where they produced a boat to navigate through the canyon of Kavac as far as a hidden waterfall. The canyon was so steep sided as to be almost in darkness, and too narrow for the boat, at the top end, so we swam to, and under the waterfall. It was extremely hot, so getting in the water was a bonus. There were several other people on the tour, fortunately all young and active, including a couple of off-duty air stewardesses, so the swimming and trekking bit was not a problem but enjoyed by everyone. After a barbeque lunch we flew back to Cuidad Bolivar and a meal on the banks of the Orinoco, getting another vista of beautiful Angel Falls on the way.

This had been an extremely good day, all arranged in the UK by a company in Kensington, and considering this ran incredibly smoothly. A tremendous amount was seen and done in less than twenty four hours. The Indians in loincloths were a bit touristy, but they looked cool – perhaps it was genuine clothing for the job! The mesas and Angel Falls could not be anything but genuine though, and were not only lost worlds, but out of this world! Arrival back at the Hotel Avila by midnight and up at 4am to ring Jo before she went to bed! With a day to spend in Caracas before joining people in Rio I wandered round the city before a much needed snooze in the warm sun in Los Chorros Park. The city centre was superficially American but underneath definitely Spanish, exemplified by the taxis being big American models, but rather beaten up, with bald tyres. Traffic was heavy, fast and close to each other. The Hotel staff and people in the city that I spoke to were all very friendly – perhaps I was lucky, but I felt at home and attracted to this teeming, busy place. A country to re-visit for longer – some day.

I met Sarah, the Group Leader at breakfast in Rio the next day. Not all the group had yet arrived in Rio, so a few of us walked to the base of Pão de Açucar, the Sugarloaf, in the Bay of Guanabara, and took the cable car to the summit. The view, from the 1200 foot summit, down to the city and the long beaches of Copacabana and Ipanema was superb. The Sugarloaf itself looked unclimbable, with great grey smooth slabs of rock glistening in the rain It was all enhanced, I think, by the low cloud which swirled around Corcovado, Hunchback Mountain, where the huge statue of Christ the Redeemer soars over the city. The clouds hid but occasionally revealed all the lesser sugarloaves out in the wide bay surrounded by green hills. Big ships were continually coming in and birds as big as pterodactyls flew around. There was a jungly bit full of bright blue butterflies half way up where we stopped, plus a macaw and a toucan in a cage.

I enjoyed the view and a beer and cigar for over an hour, coming down into the gathering darkness through streets vibrant with life. Although we had been warned about the dangers of Rio and South America generally in the pre-trek briefing, it did not feel particularly dangerous. Following the suggestions I had lined my rucksack with chicken wire, to prevent it being slit open. This made it difficult to pack and heavier! We actually had no trouble throughout the journey except for one of the girls being hassled, which I and other men in the party had soon been able to sort out, but after one week back at work in the UK my car was broken into and quite a lot of property stolen. Sod's law rules!

We had planned to stay in Rio for two more days, and on the Sunday afternoon I walked back to Copacabana. The beach was nice and fairly clean, but, I thought, not really deserving of its reputation as one of world's best. Shell Island in North Wales is better! Then in Copacabana town I was nearly run down by a bus, which mounted the footpath behind me, totally out of control, demolishing twelve concrete posts and killing one pedestrian. Now that really was dangerous! Traffic in Rio, like Caracas, certainly had a Mediterranean flavour being dense, too fast, too close and not under proper control.

By Monday morning the whole sixteen members of the group had assembled and we got to know each other in the close proximity of the Funicular railway up Corcovado Mountain. It wound very steeply through thick green jungle, disturbing clouds of blue and yellow butterflies, and giving tantalising glimpses of the city below before bursting into sunshine, above the clouds. The Redeemer is huge and white, floodlit at night when He floats serenely with his arms outstretched over the streets below. After lunch we all went for a swim at Copacabana. In March it was still pretty cold, with big breakers, extremely salty water and a very strong undertow. However, it was nice to be able to chalk it up – a world class beach!

After a dinner in Copacabana, much later, to which we all went by bus, I walked back to the Hotel on my own and was able to really appreciate the illuminated Redeemer hanging in the dark sky, and having no problem with hassle or threat. Next morning, after taking the subway to the city centre we got a clanking old trolley up a winding hillside track to the reputedly dangerous suburb of Santa Teresa. This was where Great Train Robber Ronnie Biggs was then hanging out, and it did look to be the sort of place where the police would not have easily found him, had they got the extradition order they were seeking. There were plenty of rough buildings, and rough people clinging to the outside of the trolley, and some questioning stares, but no trouble. It was the sort of area where credit cards were useless but one should not carry too much cash, and quite a contrast to the smarter areas of Copacabana.

Late that evening we all went to a city centre club, where the floor show – tall girls alternating between carnival costumes and virtually nothing except head-dresses – was very good. I was photographed by one of our party doing two show-off dances with one of the girls on the stage. Well, we were invited! I think that the costumes were into virtually nothing by this time. I have a vague memory of all the show girls being taller than myself, but that might have been their head-dresses! (No, they weren't, by the way)! It was all good fun anyhow, and I have the photographs.

We were up at 6.30 next morning, myself with quite a head, to start our cross-continental safari by travelling south by bus along a winding coast road through lush green vegetation and beaches that stretched as far as the eye could see. Makeshift stalls sold clumps of bananas, pyramids of papayas and the green sweet juice of sugar cane. The overnight stop was at Parati, a small pretty old town with cobbled streets, original houses with white plastered walls, wrought-iron balconies, terracotta roofs and legends of colonial piracy. The clear calm waters of the Baia Ilha Grande are dotted with palm-clad islands – one for every day of the year according to local legend. It had been raining on and off ever since I arrived in Brazil, and next morning we found that the road from Parati to São Paulo had been washed away. This entailed a twenty five hour diversion back towards Rio, through the Serra da Mantiquera mountains, and a pit stop in the most crowded and busiest bus terminal in São Paulo that I have ever experienced. Probably the washed out roads had something to do with it, but it was horrendous. The rain streaked windows of our bus afforded glimpses of the megalopolis, which vies with Buenos Aires for the unenviable title of the biggest city in the Southern Hemisphere and showed, in the darkness, the lights of skyscrapers stretching to the horizon. Inviting it wasn't! These were conditions where it was rather nice to have a leader who was fluent in both Spanish and Portuguese particularly as bits of broken Spanish, which several of us had, were not much use in Brazil! Then pit stops in a series of one horse towns as we crossed the red soil of the Paraná plateau and eventually reached our next destination of Foz do Iguaçú. By this time we had got to know each quite well and whilst, as ever, there were one or two people that I did not rate too highly I was very impressed with Sarah.

Foz was a two-night stay in order to see the stupendous and spectacular Iguaçú Falls from both the Brazilian and Argentinian side. Iguaçú means

'Big Water' in the Guarani language – and it is! By now the rain had stopped, and cloudless blue skies became the norm. The falls are the meeting place of three countries, Paraguay the third one, and they are one of the sights that every traveller should see. Far more beautiful and exciting than either Niagara or Victoria, they simply take your breath away, from any angle. They occur where the major Parana River and several smaller ones converge at a series of cliffs, so that there are a number of separated falls. There was much white water, horizontal and vertical, and like Victoria, clouds of air-borne spray. The rocks are reddish brown but with a lot of bright green vegetation. We were able to walk from spectacular view to stunning view to magnificent view, and then take a flat bottomed outboard motor boat to close up on an even more impressive sight, the fall of the main cataract, a mile across, - the *Gargantua do Diablo*, the Devil's Throat, with very choppy water, and plenty of spray! We were even able to walk to the top of one of the falls, and watch the water boiling and bubbling on it's way down. There were plenty of pretty little long-nosed, ring-tailed animals around, tapirs I think, and a couple of toucans. Iguaçú is, or I suppose are, an abiding memory of this journey, blue and white water, red cliffs, greenery and the thundering noise of the falls. They surpass any other waterfall, anywhere. Instead of dinner in the Hotel, which was not very wonderful the previous night, I led a breakaway group to a very nice Italian Restaurant and then for drinks in a bar and a disco. A pretty good day!

Next day was Easter Sunday, with chocolate rabbits en masse on the breakfast tables. We arrived in Asunción, the capital of Paraguay, after a five hour drive through rolling green wooded country. There were many herds of fine cattle and big haciendas with horses obvious at each one, the lush green grass making it evident that this was good cattle country. The outskirts of Asunción were very third world though, reminiscent of towns on the African west coast. Bullock drawn carts and mud walled shacks were commonplace. The Hotel where we were booked was really old colonial style, huge rooms, terraces looking over the very wide Paraguay River, and a lizard in my bathroom!

Easter Monday brought a chance to stroll through the city centre, which was an enjoyable mixture of skyscrapers and old buildings, all the latter with balconies in the Spanish style. Shopping, even for postcards, was in the old Mediterranean method, involving three separate stops – one to choose, two to pay and three to collect. Just a bit inefficient! I managed to lose the rest of the group and enjoyed myself watching Indians selling curios in a shady park, after a gentle saunter through the pleasant avenues. The real highlight was a Presidential procession, with about four hundred young soldiers in smart white uniforms with fixed bayonets, all singing while slow marching, and accompanied by a band and regimental colours.

The Cathedral was long and dim, not as ornate as the Brazilian ones with a Spanish ambience rather than Portuguese. After lunch in a twelfth floor restaurant, with a splendid view over the river, and feeling very appreciative of Asunción, I found a funny little railway station, where a wood burning locomotive with a cow catcher on the front took me on a one hour for forty pence trip to Arequa. The wood-burner got up steam with tremendously important hooting and hissing, a real event worthy of the Orient Express at least! It ran across and along streets, more like a tram, with people waving – it obviously was an event. (Maybe it only ran on Bank Holidays!)

Arequa was a sleepy little town by a lake, and after a stroll I found a bus back to Asunción. This was again reminiscent of West Africa, the bus being full to overflowing with people, luggage, sheep, cockerels and displaying notices to 'Señor Pasajero'. It bumped over cobbled roads and past some very deprived housing en route to the back streets of the city, where I suddenly realised that we were on the way back to Arequa! Eventually re-gaining the Hotel I felt that this had been the best day yet, and that I had really fallen for Asunción. Many years later I can still see and hear the young soldiers singing as they marched.

Our destination now was Salta at the foothills of the Andes in Northern Argentina, via Resistencia. Using local buses we followed and then crossed the wide Paraguay River. This is the Chaco, cattle country again. Sections of the road were just dirt surface. There was the occasional view of a gaucho, with his wide brimmed hat, baggy horizontally pleated trousers and medallioned belt. The image was a powerful one, uncompromising, silent, stoical, masculine and proud. A cowboy, but without the gunslinger connotations of the North American West. This is well below the equator, summer is December to March, and it was hot. The Falklands War was obviously still remembered in Northern Argentina, as a lot of the conscripts came from this part of the country. Posters saying 'Islas Malvinas' were not unusual and I saw a few streets called 'Belgrano', but there was no unpleasantness. Resistancia to Salta was fifteen hours overnight, by local bus, passing some very prosperous farms, in a violent thunderstorm.

We descended into Salta with the Andes rising high behind the small town, a seemingly sheer wall, looking as high as the Himalaya beyond Kathmandu but speckled grey, not pristine white. After a sleep in our rather spartan Hotel, I went on another solo expedition to see as much of Salta as possible. Many of the people showed signs of Indian or part Indian ancestry, being very brown. I bought a 'face in a head-dress' from an Indian carving them with a very sharp machete, and holding the wood against his leg! The driving, as in

Asunción, was surprisingly polite and careful. The 'Mediterrean style' (gas and brakes, and get as close as you can!) from nearer the east coast seemed to have disappeared. Salta was another town that I really fell for – the view over the town towards the Andes from the hill that I climbed was fabulous. There were some beautifully ornate buildings in the town centre, including the museum, which was quite a good one, and some equally ornate rock formations outside. Red cliffs with profiles weathered into grotesque silhouettes, and a series of llamas painted on one cliff face – Indian art, I think?

I made a reservation for a hire car for Friday, as I was set on a solo expedition to San Salvador de Jujuy (Huy-huy), just because of the wonderful name, but before that we went as a group on a local (very local) bus to Cachi, 90km away in the Andes. We climbed up through clouds on a graded (dirt) road, breaking through the clouds into an area of huge cacti, most at least twenty feet tall. Cachi was about 6000 feet into the mountains, but surrounded by much higher ones, up to, I guessed about 10,000 feet, but still no snow in sight. The mountains were very grey and sandy brown instead. There was a surprisingly good museum here, with Inca and pre-Inca pottery.

I got away from the group again for a time, and enjoyed the mountain views. Our return journey, also by local bus was via some real mountain roads, with several rivers to ford. Two more passengers joined the bus, one quite elderly but still in his wide brimmed, silver-buckled black hat strapped under his chin, worn over a balaclava, a bright red poncho and a wonderfully impassive expression on a face like a starving hawk. He could have been a former gaucho, but also perhaps an eccentric aristocrat like Don Quixote. The latter idea became irresistible when it became obvious that he was accompanied by Sancho Panza. Sancho was short and fat, with a moustache, a brown sombrero, a scarf and culottes. As I mentioned earlier, you meet some interesting people on a Greyhound Bus. Well, there are interesting ones on Argentine buses as well.

Early Friday morning I made my excuses and collected my Renault 12 rental car. The spectacular road north of Salta climbs steadily through multi-coloured canyons, with more of the huge cacti, towards the border of Argentina and Bolivia. The jungle was continuous and the road frequently blocked by fallen trees or rocks. I was stopped once or twice at police checkpoints. This may have been because I had washed a pair of long blue woollen stockings the night before and thought that having one hanging out of each rear window was an efficient way to dry them. Maybe it was being taken as a political statement. I stopped at the little Jesuit town of La Caldera where there is a huge figure of Christ overlooking the road, rather like the Redeemer in Rio. On arrival at Jujuy I found that their time was an hour behind that of Salta – difficult to understand as they are on virtually the same longtitude. Maybe that was a political statement! An enjoyable walk round, a view of a very ornate wedding and the purchase of a doll for Nicky's collection, then a different route back, and another visit to the top of San Bernadino behind Salta. This was a good day, principally to be able to drive on my own and please myself.

After a lazy morning and a ten-minute shoe-shine on my boots in the Plaza, next day was scheduled for some horse riding. Six of us had opted to do this, and it was really enjoyable. From where we picked up the horses on the pampas, the high snow capped Andes were in sight, tops well above cloud level. It was good to feel a bit like a gaucho, as the horse could actually be persuaded to gallop - downhill! Could have been a hoof too far, but wasn't.

Afterwards I climbed the hill behind Salta while the light lasted, for the fourth time I think. It was about an hour's climb, but well worth it for the views. Sarah had arranged a visit to a folk show and dinner for the last evening in Salta, in an ancient room with cow skins and bolas on the walls. This was a little like the hotel we stayed at in Arles – also cowboy country. By 7 a.m. next morning we were en-route to Bolivia via the border crossing at La Quiaca, and climbing up into the mountains. We had abandoned local bus transport and had packed ourselves and belongings into the backs of two Chevrolet pick-up trucks. It was a beautiful day with spectacular scenery, more twenty foot high cacti and yellow sunflowers. The rock shapes were tortured, with red yellow and orange mineral deposits overlaying the basic grey.

I had a late breakfast on a bench looking west towards the snowy peaks. Lunch, after about a hundred and twenty miles, was at Huinahuaca, on the bank of the Grande de Jujuy, and still in Argentina. The country then became flatter, the road surface dirt, and generally reminiscent of Southern Texas and Mexico. At a border passport check point buses were being filled up with Bolivian people – short, swarthy, very Indian features, the women in thick brightly coloured woollen clothes, bulky voluminous skirts and nearly all with bowler hats, hair parted in the centre, as decreed by a Spanish monarch over two hundred years ago. The land was now almost desert, with dunes of pure sand. Herds of brown and white llamas were roaming free. The short downhill walk from one customs point to the next was a trip from the twentieth to the nineteenth century. The clothing was traditional – stout Bolivian women in their bowlers and woollen ponchos sat in small groups selling tiny pyramids of potatoes or beans, ignoring the frontier line to make best use of the wealthier shoppers on the Argentine side.

All the villages were one horse dusty little places, with hotels best described as a cross between a prison and a motel! Lunch was chicken soup, with a whole leg of chicken, including the claws, in it. After descending a really steep hairpin-bended unsurfaced road into a beautiful valley we stopped by a river, where there was a school that we were able to visit. It seemed to be very very poor – dusty like almost everywhere else. The kids, aged about five to eight, were excited and pleased to have visitors, and we handed out sweets, coins and postcards. There was then a long long climb out of the valley – sheer drops of about a thousand feet and hairpins on the dirt road, but almost no other traffic. We passed tiny villages, the houses with mud-brick walls and thatched rooves. There were some local hitchhikers on the track, and we picked up and squeezed in several adults and children. I have a splendid photograph of a Bolivian lady sitting regally in the back of one of our trucks, wearing her bowler hat, and woollen cloak. She was surrounded by various bags that she had been carrying to, or from, market.

We were now at about 15,000 feet, sometimes above cloud level. The superb view all round included canyons, valleys and folds of rock. The tangled mountains extended for forty to fifty miles to the horizon, with the snow capped peaks in Chile being more like a hundred, but looking nearer in the clear cold air. At this height it was not surprising that some of the party were showing signs of anoxia - some silliness - even though any walking we did was relatively easy. Arrival at the town of Tarija was a welcome relief after a long journey – the back of a pick-up truck is not four-star comfort, even if one is squeezed against a well-padded Bolivian lady! The Hotel Bolivar provided hot showers, and then it was good to go for a drink in the rather nice Plaza and watch a sort of local carnival! This had been a very good day indeed, a wild journey but being able to set our own pace in the pick-ups and with wonderful views, virtually all round, all day.

We had a day in Tarija which is a pleasant town – very civilised and obviously better off than most of the small villages that we had passed through. I walked to the village of Tomatitas, having a beer en route. This was definitely not on any tourist route, and I thought that Sarah had done very well to show us a bit of the real Bolivia. The whole area felt nineteenth century, narrow streets, houses with balconies and narrow openings for shops, with certainly no modern shopping centre. I spent the afternoon on a river beach near to women washing clothes in the river. Next day I found a place to swim in the river – cool clear water, great on a very sunny hot day, then sat in the Plaza seeing a gardener carefully brushing the grass and collecting fallen leaves. And this was not for the benefit of tourists, because apart from ourselves, there weren't any!

At 5 p.m. we all caught the overnight bus to Potosi, being advised to wear our warmest clothes for the journey. The bus was small and very crowded, so that at first it was very hot then became very cold as we climbed up through several mountain passes. It took until 6 a.m. to arrive at Potosi, a pretty horrible journey, as the seats were too small, with no legroom, so no chance to sleep. A bit more real Bolivia I guess, especially as we had to wait for two hours for our rooms to be ready! Potosi is a bleak town, at 12,000 feet, so there was a feeling of breathlessness. It was once the treasure house of the world, where the Spaniards mined silver, and was the home of the Bolivian Mint.(A lot of the gold and silver mined here was stolen on it's way back to Spain by Francis Drake, Walter Raleigh and their buccaneer colleagues, for the glory of Queen Elizabeth!) The 'Cerro Rico' (Rich Hill) is a national monument, and appears on stamps and coins. It looks like a small version of Fujiyama – a child's idea of a mountain shape. The mining is now mainly of tin, although it seemed doubtful that conditions for the miners had changed very much since Spanish times. Donations of warm clothing left for their dependents were gratefully welcomed. It seems that opencast mining would have been better both economically and in terms of human cost, but this would entail demolishing the national monument, so had not then been even considered. 'Del mundo soy el tesoro. Soy el rey de los montes', 'Treasure of all the world. King of mountains I am'. Perhaps a sentiment left over by the Spaniards.

Although bleak, Potosi still had some splendid buildings, including the former Mint, now a National Museum. The Potosinas wore slightly different clothing, with black or brown hats more like Welsh ones than bowlers, and the skirts less voluminous. It was hot in the sun, but at that height very cold out of it. Traffic relied mainly on the horn at blind junctions – not much change there then! We had an evening meal with Eduardo, a very articulate self taught mine guide.

On Friday, 12th April we had a private mini-bus for the five hour journey to Sucre. On a map Potosi and Sucre look quite close, but it was only when travelling the roads that one realised the determination and grit of the Spaniards to conquer this part of South America, greedy and rapacious though they were. Sucre was at that time the legislative capital of Bolivia, although no more than a small University town. On arrival we had a party in a pizzeria for one of the girls, whose birthday it was. 'Journey Latin America' had provided a cake. The kids outside with their noses pressed to the window, watching the funny foreigners thought that Christmas had come early when they got balloons, paper hats and chocolate cake! Sucre is a very attractive town, with all buildings in the centre painted white by law. We were stopping two nights here, and on the next morning, Saturday, the town was full of Indians from the village of Tarabuco, here to sell their wares to people like ourselves. Tarabuco has a very specialised market, and the people, the men in particular, have retained a distinctive style of clothing, which made them very identifiable. Bright orange red and black ponchos, knee length woollen breeches and black conquistador helmets, decorated with coloured clumps of wool, fur or silver. The helmets covered their ears, and they were extremely photogenic, but I thought that they were sad, poor, hungry people.

I enjoyed listening to one man playing a guitar, and bought some presents for home from them, then took myself off with some food on a longish walk up to the Christos above Sucre. There was a church, La Recoleta, from where there were wonderful views down to Sucre and beyond to the mountains that we had travelled through. There was a rite involving fire at the foot of the Christos, and I was waved away, not unpleasantly though, as one Indian man did call out 'Buenas tardes Cabellero'. It may have been a private funeral rite. It is necessary to bear in mind that a high proportion of the people in this part of Bolivia are pure Quechua Indian, who have retained much of their own culture in places like Tarabuco. Many of the women wear hats that define their race, a white trilby denoting a mestizo or person of mixed blood. Next day we had a two hour journey in our mini-bus over winding twisty dirt roads to the market at Tarabuco, crossing a railway line many times – what marvellous engineering to build a line through these mountains, as we were now firmly in the Andes, this part being the Cordillera Central. The market was enclosed in a walled arena and was bustling – absolutely humming. Every local person wore the traditional dress. Older women wore a very elaborate winged head dress, but the younger ones- perhaps the unmarried- a silver fez type of hat. Sandals, bare legs but the extremely colourful ponchos.

My overall, rather disturbing impression, was again that they were so poor, not very healthy, and the elderly even haggard. It was very hard to refuse to buy things, and by now I had a large collection of dolls, taking up enormous space in my rucksack! They did all get home eventually, and have pride of place in Nicky's collection. I went into a small Church and tried to understand the Service. All the people were wearing what was obviously 'best clothes' and there were many babies and children. Afterwards, sitting in the rather poor little plaza I had an odd thought, 'This suddenly reminds me of Myitkina in Northern Burma'. The buildings were not unlike and the silver decoration on the red and black clothes like that of the Karen tribespeople. Rather strange.

We got back to Sucre in time to say goodbye to our quite comfortable mini-bus and catch the overnight local bus to La Paz. I have done quite a number of overnight public bus journeys around the world, and they are rarely occasions to look forward to. Interesting, with sometimes intriguing fellow passengers, but comfortable - no! We were advised to wear warm clothing again, as the route took us over La Cumbre pass, at five thousand metres – nearly sixteen and a half thousand feet. This is high enough to give serious breathing difficulty, but we were by now beginning to be acclimatised. I did wonder if the driver was!

We left Sucre at 5 p.m. and stopped for breakfast next day from a pavement stall in Cochabamba at 6.30 a.m.! I managed to get a wash and shave in front of an interested audience in the Plaza Central. Then on a different local bus at 9am which climbed steeply onto the Altoplano, an immense plateau. The views were yet again spectacular – fifty or sixty miles of high peaks in the clear air and under a bright blue sky. We found a tarmac road for the first time since leaving Brazil eight days ago. The Altoplano was not bare, there were herds of llamas and cattle, and some healthy crops of cereals. On the horizon ahead were the peaks of the Cordillera Oriental – seriously high at eighteen to twenty thousand feet. We passed through the La Paz suburb of El Alto, which was rather a downer to our group of tired people. It was a dingy and depressed shantytown, with chaotic traffic, potholes and mud. Then suddenly we were on the edge of a deep canyon, and able to look down a thousand feet upon a mosaic of tin, slate and tile roofs and modern skyscrapers in the city centre. Although sitting in a deep bowl La Paz is the highest capital city in the world, at about twelve thousand feet. It is surrounded by mountains, the most imposing of which, Mount Illimani, catches the last rays of sunset most effectively. The modern city centre cheered everyone up as it promised the delights of civilisation, and the Hotel Rosario was very welcome at 5.30 p.m. – a journey of twenty four and half hours from Sucre! This was a good hotel, with several courtyards and a rooftop restaurant giving a great view of the city lights. As one might imagine, after visiting the restaurant, not much else was done that night.

I was very impressed with the Prado, the main shopping street next morning, but only a short way off it were dirty, broken down cobbled streets, and an Indian Market selling literally everything. I found that at that time 60% of the million plus population of La Paz were full blooded Indian. Now we were back to the bowler hatted ladies with their voluminous skirts, still following the ancient royal Spanish diktat. The centre was choked with traffic, all adopting normal big city driving habits. There were a variety of cars, including Ladas, and, big surprise, some Ford Escorts and Sierras. The Transit Police had a big display on the Prado of vehicles involved in fatal collisions. No lack of contenders for a space on the display. I managed to have a talk, of sorts, with one policeman, who seemed very impressed with my International Police Association card. As the IPA was not then so well known he may have thought that I was there for Interpol!

Ever since entering Bolivia I had found myself liking the country and the people, and this continued in La Paz. There were no tourist traps, or at least no more than to be expected in any big city, and some people showed considerable courtesy. One Bank Clerk actually left his counter to point out directions from the pavement – you don't get that in Birmingham. During my walk however I did see another face of Bolivia, a student demonstration with riot police in full gear, armed with visors, helmets, shields, Mace and dogs. I watched for some time, with no one taking any notice of me, or bothering about my use of a camera, and it eventually subsided without any violence on either side. The camera would have been seized in many countries, certainly in Tibet.

That evening, after a museum visit, we went as a group to a peña, a folk music show in a small upstairs room, with exotic costumes, drums, zampoña, pan pipes and flutes. This was great. Next day Sarah had laid on transport to get to Chacaltaya, which at 17,000 feet Bolivians claim to be the highest ski-run in the world, and the home of the Andean Ski Club. It was snowing and our mini-bus had to give up on the lower slopes of the hairpin-bended track. I wanted - as usual - to get to the top of the mountain, and with a couple of the others climbed alongside the piste towards the top. The view on a clear day north to Lake Titicaca seemed to be snowed off at first, but it suddenly cleared and was as good as promised, through broken clouds, and included the Altoplano and Cordillera Real. I had been advised that any skiers on this piste needed to be extremely accomplished and this was borne out during the climb up when I saw one appear suddenly out of the clouds above, and disappear, just as suddenly, on the very steep slope into the clouds below!

However, the climb and the views were exhilarating. Another valuable piece of advice had been to chew some coca leaves while climbing, which were available and actually do provide a boost – a bit like chewing qat in Somalia. Reducing the leaves to pulp is the first stage in the lengthy process of manufacturing cocaine, but more unpleasant liquids than saliva have to be added. I was the only one of our party who reached the top, so there must have been something in it. A Bolivian gentleman said to me at the top, 'You have got good condition!' Despite being the Andean Ski Club base the ski lift was rather primitive – just a moving wire, where you carried your own T bar and hooked on by friction! I decided that I was probably better off walking, as this was, like the piste, definitely for experts in practice! This was not only the highest ski-run in the world, but perhaps the oldest lift, being built in 1941(And not improved since!).

A 7.30 a.m. start next day, by local bus to the Straits of Tiquina to cross Lake Titicaca by small boat. Titicaca is the highest navigable lake in the world, with plenty of quite big steamers crossing and re-crossing it. Some of them were brought from Europe piecemeal, and re-assembled in Bolivia. Being half in Bolivia and half in Peru there appeared to be a lot of cross-lake travel. At about 12,000 feet I had expected the lake to be black, cold and forbidding, but in fact it was a beautiful blue, surrounded by mountains on either side, snowcaps in the distance, and very beautiful. It seemed huge, but is not as big as the Great Lakes of North America, or Baikal in Siberia. I have a nice photograph of a Bolivian Border Guard at the Peruvian border. He was flat on his back in the sun, cap over his face and snoring well! When we reached Puno, our Peruvian lakeside destination, there was no problem in arranging a two hour steamer cruise.

Peru seemed less prosperous than much of Bolivia. There did seem to be an increasing amount of poverty as we had travelled west from Brazil, Paraguy, Argentina and Bolivia to Peru. Here both men and women were wearing the same clothing style, down-market European, with none of the exotic local costumes seen in Bolivia. Some houses had thatched roofs, some with tin, and three-wheeler load bearing bicycles were much in evidence.

Puno itself was cold and bleak, and has been compared to Watford Gap – many passing through but few staying! A contrast to La Paz. Next morning we took a small boat to a traditional settlement of the Uros Indians, floating islands made entirely of tortora reeds well out in the Lake. There were many islands, the biggest with several families living on it, with huts made also out of reeds and straw, including a small school and a small Christian church and a square tower made of reeds and straw. What happens in a storm? I suppose that they just rebuild it. It was a peculiar feeling to be walking quite safely and solidly on what was just a platform of floating thatched reeds. The reeds rot quickly from the bottom up and so have to be continually replaced at the top. The reeds grow around the Lake shore, are used to make furniture as well as huts, and their tender root areas are also a source of food. We were able to visit the Church, which was decorated with pictures and texts pinned to plastic sheets pinned to the walls. The school had about twenty infants, being taught by a middle-aged Indian lady, and seemed to be rather better run than the generally squalid surroundings.

The children did not seem to be as excited by our visit as those at the little school in Bolivia – I think that they were used to tourist visitors. Apart from some fishing and hunting the Uros people seemed to be dependent on tourism, living in unpleasant conditions, with all the children not in school begging, and their parents needing to sell souvenirs. I did buy a model reed boat, and a large embroidered rug (how to get it home?). So, I did contribute to their economy – it was difficult to refuse. I did carry the rug home, and had it framed as a wall hanging, and it is a beautiful part of my souvenir collection – highly coloured and having entailed a great deal of work. In a way the settlement was similar to the straw houses out in Inle Lake in Shan State, Burma, and the Coral Sea coast of Papua New Guinea, where huts are raised on stilts above water levels. The Uros were forced onto the lake dwellings as the Incas pushed further and further into their territory, but they choose to live in this way still? Tradition? No taxes? No interference? Privacy? Many have now left the islands for the mainland, and intermarried but there were still a few hundred afloat. Their canoes were also made of cleverly woven reeds. Thor Heyerdahl, the ocean explorer, co-opted Uros Indians to help build his ocean going 'Ra' rafts. The first one sank because he chose to ignore their advice on the finer points of construction!

After the islands we went to Sillustani, pre-Inca ruins on a hilltop overlooking pastures and a tranquil lagoon. There were herds of llamas and their smaller cousins, alpacas, running free on the pastures, many having beautifully white fur. The giant funeral towers, called chulpas, are wider at the top than at ground level, and made of stone blocks cut so that the edges are perfectly aligned with hardly room to push a knife blade between them. Good design, and clever construction, but by whom? A tribe who were conquered by and assimilated into the Incas during the 12th to 15th Centuries, but, like so much of South America, the architects are unknown.

Our next destination was Cuzco, by the local train – although local it took twelve and a half hours on the journey! Rather more comfortable than the local buses, as it was possible to move around but far from warm. It climbs through mountain passes to about 13,000 feet, with plenty of visible snow. Many men were clinging to the outside of the carriages – I hate to think what that journey was like! The train never got above twenty miles an hour, clattering through fields worked by children in homberg hats, and stopped at innumerable stations. The first was at Juliaca, which is a Peruvian Crewe junction, where one can change to go to Ariquipa, or stay on board for Cuzco. Like Crewe, there was a delay, which the locals are used to, and take advantage of. The local knitting collective bombards passengers with alpaca hats, slippers, jerseys, cuddly toys and chichi drinks in tin buckets. They were not allowed onto first class, so throw merchandise through the window, and wait for one to throw money back! At each following stop itinerant salesmen, and women, get on and off, eventually visiting each carriage selling brass llamas, hot potatoes, suckling pigs and lottery tickets. They can then be seen boarding a train going the other way, for the same process. There was plenty of snow around and Brazilians on the train were excited enough, never having seen any before, to jump off whenever possible and play in it like children!

Cuzco was, for me, love at first sight. Our hotel was, again, a reminder of the cowboy country of Arles and the Camargue, really old, huge rooms, big old carved doors, carvings on a balcony around a central courtyard that was bright with flowers. Cuzco derives it's name from the Quechua word for navel and was the Inca capital and the centre of their civilisation – about the time that we fought the Wars of the Roses in England. We spent over a week there, visiting some fascinating sites, but coming back each evening to enjoy the café culture. I quickly found my own spot where I could - more or less - mix with the local people. A group of men, 'Los Monarchos' were regular entertainers in this café, playing hauntingly memorable music on a guitar, pan pipes, a drum and flutes. The leader was quite young, but blind, and led by the hand by a small boy. I enjoyed them on several evenings, having avoided the rest of our party. On the final visit I bought a tape of their music and gave them a substantial tip, for which I was charmingly thanked by the boy and one of the group. They knew that I was appreciating it very much.

The wide central plaza had a big church on one side and the cathedral on the other. Both were floodlit at night, and then were particularly beautiful. Also floodlit was another finely sculptured white Christos, on the summit of a very black mountain. As in Rio, it hung in the sky, floating above the town at night. I climbed up to the Christos and enjoyed the view down to Cuzco, seeing, oddly, what seemed to me to be a Moorish influence in the buildings and layout of the town. Cuzco has a similar geography to Bath, being in a bowl surrounded by hills, and is of roughly comparable size. There were a few obvious villains about, and some whiny begging, an American tourist influence I wondered, but also some very friendly, smiling, helpful people. I joined in one game of football in a back street! On a spur of the hills overlooking the town are the remains of Sacsayhuaman, the walls of this Inca fortress still largely intact. Like the Chulpas it was built with huge blocks of stone, fitting so precisely together so that a knife blade could not penetrate the joints. It was probably earthquake proof. I met an Indian guy up there who was selling carved items – and had enough English to chat. It was here that the Conquistadores tricked the Incas into relinquishing control of Cuzco. Also here a great battle was fought between the heavily armed and mounted Spaniards and Indians using little more than Stone Age weapons. Yet - when they had won - the Spaniards were quite unable to demolish the great blocks of stone, most weighing many tons that formed the defensive wall, although they did pull down the towers. A great sense of history in this place – guess who I felt sympathy for.

The first full day excursion was into the Sacred Valley of the Incas, stopping in three Quechua villages, Pisaq, Chinchero and Ollantaytambo.

Pisaq retains its Inca layout and is renowned for it's market and the terracing behind the village. The original engineering and the preservation of the terraces are unrivalled in South America, and certainly looked as good as those in Nepal. The green hillside rises from the flat valley floor like a staircase to the sky. At the height of the Inca civilisation they enabled the farmers to create micro-climates within each valley, and exotic crops that would not grow at one level would flourish at a different one. The market was bustling and busy and very like Tarabuco. The women's clothing was different though, black skirts and black hats with a coloured fringe like a lampshade. Men wore shorts and ponchos, with a saucer shaped reddish hat, with the bowl of the saucer facing upwards, or sometimes a woollen helmet covering their ears. Nearly all the local people were wearing the traditional dress, but those of mixed race with the white trilby instead of the decorated hat. A winding path up a hillside led to the Temple of the Sun above Pisaq. It was superb – just right in it's location, with a huge stone sundial in the courtyard. On this day one wonderful photogenic view followed on the heels of the last. After a fascinating time in Pisaq we moved to Chinchero in the next valley, with splendid views of rolling hills and the ever-present backdrop of the Cordilleran peaks. Chinchero market was similar, although because it is more remote and had only recently become accessible by road, we were the only non-locals. The market was held within the Inca built walls, still in excellent condition, big blocks of stone looking as if nothing would shift them.

Then it was on to Ollantaytambo, a fortress that was never conquered by the Spanish Conquistadors. Their horses could not cope with the steep terracing, and the Indians diverted the river Urubamba to flood the surrounding fields. Ollantaytambo also had a magnificent Temple of the Sun, although this was in ruins, and an Indian fortress, reminiscent of Mycenae. Although the Incas had eventually abandoned the village the terracing was still spectacular, and it was very peaceful to sit at the top, and enjoy the view along the fertile and beautiful valley of the Urubamba. I took the chance to have a run at 12,000 feet, bearing in mind the coming three day trek to Machu Picchu. There was a chance to ride horses again at Urubamba on our return journey to Cuzco. Altogether a magnificently enjoyable day, with people who could not have been met or seen anywhere else. We finished it off with dinner at a restaurant in town. The menu included pancakes wrapped around fruit and coated with honey.

Seven of the group had decided to walk the Machu Picchu trail. The trail follows the route that the Incas would have used to reach the long forgotten outpost of their empire. Thirty five miles over three high passes, with two overnight camping stops. We had four local porters to carry camping gear and cooking gear, and Auriello, a local guide. The porters were very cheerful but skinny and looked under-developed, but easily carrying loads that I could hardly have lifted. So much like Nepal. The heavy gear was bundled into blankets, and carried on their backs. This looked very unergonomic and certainly did not conform to RoSPA's advice for lifting and carrying, but seemed to work for them. They were all wearing primitive sandals, cut from old tyres, but had kept their decorated hats. Auriello led us first along the Urubamba valley, through well tended fields, with the high snowy peaks on either side. Some were conical, hanging over a layer of cloud in the valleys. There was a magnificent view of La Veronica, at 18,000 feet one of the most shapely peaks. The local method of crossing the river was by means of a basket, suspended from a wire. We started to climb, to heights from where the Urubamba shrank to a ribbon winding sinuously in its narrow gorge through jungle covered hills. The trail wound through jungle as well, and was absolutely a wilderness – no villages, just beautiful wild scenery. We were surrounded by flights of green parakeets, which were noisy enough, but as it grew dark they were joined by frogs to provide the bass and baritone. Our first campsite was in an open clearing, where after the tough climb a supper of soup, sausage, carrots and maize stewed over an open fire was very appreciated.

As it was dark by 6pm we were in bed by 8.30, but up in time for a 6am start after a breakfast of porridge and coffee, a wash in a cold stream and a visit to the woods to do what the bears do! During the day we ascended to and descended from the three passes, all between 11 and 14,000 feet. Quite a hard slog again. The second camp was within the enclosed walls of an Inca ruin, from which there was a beautiful view down the Urubamba valley. Washing arrangements next morning were slightly different, as there were five stone built 'cubicles' with a flow of water from a mountain stream running through each one. Auriello reckoned that they were Inca built, for travellers on the trail to the city. The porters had happily slept without tents, obviously used to doing so. One thing that did make me happier about the massive loads that they were carrying compared to my rucksack (even that was by now feeling quite a burden) was that they were used to the altitude, and, like Sherpas, far better adapted to it than we were. Machu Picchu is the top of a mountain (it's name is 'Old Peak' in Quechua, which suggests that it was a known site before the Incas) at nearly 9,000 feet. The trail dipped and climbed but certainly at times we were well above that – certainly high enough to feel the thinning air. There was exhilaration in the late morning of the third day as we climbed the final flights of one thousand steps cut from the living rock to the Sun Gate, and saw the city one and a half kilometres beneath us. It made the exhaustion of the trek through dense sub-tropical undergrowth, over precarious log bridges and glistening ice fields well worthwhile. We joined the rest of the group, (the softies), who had come on the little train which runs along the Urubamba Valley, and only walked two thousand feet up the many hairpin bended path from Puente Ruinas station. After several beers and fruit there was time to explore the city in it's incredibly photogenic site. We walkers then headed for the hot springs at Aguas Calientes a couple of miles away.

We stayed overnight at Gringo Bill's, which was an adventure in itself, and fully lived up to its name! My feet were quite sore, but on Gringo Bill's advice I walked for a further ten minutes up to the springs. They were natural, open-air, really hot, and a boon and a delight after the three day trek. We were up at 4.30 a.m. for the 5.30 little train back to Cuzco next morning. There was a surprising amount of pushing and shoving to get on, and the first display of bad manners that had been seen. It was a very little train, and I suppose that it was important to get to market early for the genuine locals. I suspected however that they were more likely to be well-heeled tourists from Lima or other cities, as this was so unusual. Sarah expected it however, and had cash ready to get us on board! In Cuzco and enjoying the hot sun in the Plaza, I was found by Albert, a shoe-shine boy. He had a little English, and told me of his ambition to go to University, but could not see how to raise the money. I gave him 1,000,000 Intis (not as much as it sounds) to start him off, and a lecture about opening a bank account and saving. I wonder if he did? Nice if he was now a Professor of Something in Arequipa or Lima. If you should read this Albert, please let me know! Then it was an enjoyable walk, on my own again, past the Christos and up to Sacsayhuaman where I bought two Serpentine carvings from the Quechua Indian who was still there.

For the last day Sarah had arranged some white water rafting on the Urubamba. The river is an important one, navigable in parts and eventually arrives in the Atlantic, having joined with the Rio Ucayli, which is one of the main headwaters of the Amazon. It flows through valleys where the crop of coca leaves is used mainly in the production of cocaine. The leaves are pulped in laboratories hidden under the tree cover of the forest, rather as grapes were historically treaded to make wine. In the early nineties the main source of cocaine was Columbia, but now it is increasingly made in the foothills of the Andes in Peru. I had chewed coca leaves while climbing Chacaltaya, and found that it does give a lift. Traditionally it was used by the Indian tribes as a medicine and to combat the effects of long journeys at high altitude. It is possible to buy an infusion of coca tea in both Cuzco and La Paz, this being regarded as not harmful. It was also an ingredient of Coca Cola in the early years of the Twentieth Century, until banned by an American Act of Congress. To turn the coca into cocaine after pulping, a cocktail of unpleasant chemicals, including kerosene and sulphuric acid is added to produce the drug and make huge amounts of money for drug dealers on the streets of American and European cities. Because it is illegal and uncontrolled the 'run-off' from the mixture is allowed to flow directly into the rivers that eventually form the Amazon. There is therefore a serious ecological problem for the Region, in addition to the terrible consequences of the drug trade. The peasant farmers get comparatively very little for using their crop in this way, but it is possible to understand why they risk prison sentences if caught by the police or army. It is one of the few ways in which they can make enough to live on. I have sympathy with them, but sincerely believe that the drug 'barons', dealers and middlemen should be subject to a death penalty – as painful a one as possible. I know and regret that effective enforcement or punishment is not going to happen however – too much money finds it's way into the bank accounts of politicians in various countries, the US, EU and UK amongst them.

The Urubamba contains some serious white water rapids, as it flows through the Sacred Valley, and ours were great fun. After the series of rapids the guide said that anyone who wanted to could jump off the next footbridge into the river, as the water was deep enough. Most of us liked the idea, and it was not worth bothering to strip off as we were all totally wet from the white water. The bridge was about fifteen feet above water level, so it was a fair jump, and we took action photographs of each jump. One of the girls was so excited that she forgot to take her glasses off – they may have finished up in the Atlantic. Fortunately she had a spare pair. After the excitement we were able to dry off in the hot sun on the grassy riverbank, and were met by the inflatable's owners with two pick-ups and a very welcome picnic. Another very good day, and for the last night in Cuzco we had a fairly hysterical party in a town centre restaurant, where the local kids pressed their noses to the window to see the funny foreigners all wearing each other's hats!

The next destination, with a beautiful flight over the Andes, was Arequipa, an elegant and beautiful University City. It is famous for the Convent of Santa Catalina, which is almost a medieval city in itself, with narrow streets, bright flowers and tree-lined cloisters, all enclosed in a massive sillar (white lava) wall, and the 18,000 foot volcano, El Misti, in the near distance. Misti, shaped like Fujiyama and with a similar snow capped peak flanks the city, and is a child's idea of a mountain, an elegant triangular silhouette. Even higher are a group of 20,000 peaks to the north and east, the nearest to El Misti being Chachani. They had sandy coloured, almost invisible, slopes and white peaks, so that the tops seemed to hang suspended against the blue sky. I spent the day enjoying the city centre, which was certainly the most beautiful that I had seen in South America. Sarah had enjoyed being here to obtain her degree in Spanish. However, the highlight was to go to a restaurant run by a friend of hers where roast guinea pig - cuy - was a staple part of the menu. Now, not everyone can face eating something that looks like a grilled rat, but the paws were nice and crunchy. James' brother owned, at that time, an up-market restaurant in Derbyshire, and also possessed a rather odd sense of humour, so I got him a photograph of a guinea pig being consumed, had it enlarged and framed and it was exhibited in the restaurant – for a time anyway!

There were two more fascinating items on the itinerary before reaching Lima, the capital of Peru. We took a local bus along the coast road through a moonscape, ugly and depressing, with mean little villages, as poor as anything we had seen so far. This was an almost unbelievable contrast to the beauty and peace of Arequipa. The bus was dangerously overcrowded, with people sitting or lying in the aisle during the eleven hour journey to Nazca, the site of the inexplicable and intriguing lines in the desert. There were people selling everything, singers and food vendors at almost every stop. Because the annual rainfall here is virtually nil Nazca was full of very ancient American cars, Dodges and Chevrolets etc, ancient since they don't rust away!

Cessna six-seaters were available to fly over the lines from which the geometric lines and designs of hummingbirds, lizards, whales, monkeys and many others were superbly visible, easily recognisable and very photogenic. This was a cost not included in the journey, so not everybody did it, but I had to! For those who did not fancy the twisting and turning in a small aircraft there were climbable towers where at least some of the designs could be seen. The markings are captivating and unexplained. There have been many theories, ranging from landing instructions for visitors from space to solar calendars or astronomic observatories. One theory is that they were religious totems made by lines of people trudging through the reddish pebbles that form the surface to expose the lighter coloured sand beneath. The latter does not come near to explaining to me how such accuracy of the birds and other shapes could have been achieved from ground level, or even through observers on nearby low hills. I prefer the visitors from other worlds! Explainable or not, this was perhaps the most interesting way of spending forty dollars that I have ever found, and leaves a mystery, probably over two thousand years old, which is not yet solved.

We then went to the nearby site of the Nazca open-air cemetery. This is one of the driest and least windy places in the world, and bodies had been left clothed and unburied to become dehydrated and desiccated. Skulls abounded, full skeletons and isolated arm and leg bones. Some shrivelled shrunken bodies had been arranged cross-legged in a half circle, like a macabre picnic party. There were hanks of hair left on this group and some unrotted clothing. One suspected that this particular arrangement had been done, not by Nazca people but by very much post-Nazcas. The word cemetery suggests a properly marked private site, but this was just an area of dry, dusty, desert desolation. Like quite a few other things seen in Bolivia and Peru, this was a reminder of the other side of the world – the sky burial sites in Tibet, but here there were no birds to pick up the pieces. The Internet suggests to me that both the lines and the cemetery have become much more commercialised since my visit in 1991 – no surprise there then! In '91, although known about for many years, no protection and little commercial activity had taken place, and we were able to just wander anywhere. I took a photograph of the 'picnic party', and presented it to James' brother after framing. Knowing that his sense of humour was almost as odd as my own, I suggested that it could be labelled, for display in the restaurant alongside the guinea pig menu suggestion, as a picture of his regular clients. It was, too!

Only a mile or so away, in Nazca town, our hotel had a very nice swimming pool shaded by multi-coloured trees. This was a pleasing contrast to the desert, which we all enjoyed and used for the rest of the day. Sarah had been able to arrange a boat journey into the Pacific, from the fishing port of Paracas to the Ballestos Islands. It was two hours on the boat, so the islands are far enough away from the coast to be a safe haven for sea-lions, pelicans and penguins, and we saw hundreds – particularly sea-lions and diving sea birds. The incredibly crowded beach favoured by the sea lions was irresistibly like sun-bathers on a Mediterranean beach in high summer, but the noise of grunting, roaring and fighting from the beach and the rocks all round was a cacophony of definitely non-human sound. Oh, but perhaps I am not so sure! They were all sizes and all the shades of dark colours from pale fawn to black.

From the boat we could see another design like the Nazca lines but on the sloping surface of the sandy dunes facing the sea. It was shaped like a candelabra, and the origin was, and still is, not known. The design and manufacture is much easier to understand though, as the face of the dunes was visible. The boat captain suggested that it was a homing device for boats coming in during bad weather. This seems as likely as anything. Then it was back to a local bus for the overnight run to Lima. This was the time of the 'Shining Path' Maoist revolutionary guerrilla movement, and one had to be wary, as there had been a lot of violence by them since the party was founded in 1980. We were not troubled however. The outskirts of Lima were scruffy and grubby, and the centre dull and run down – perhaps because of the communist activity.

If Arequipa had been the most beautiful city on our journey, Lima was the most uninteresting. This is probably unfair, as I was only there for the drive in and an evening walk around the centre, but it felt grim, unwelcoming and fairly threatening. It was time to say goodbye to the rest of the Group early next morning. I was quite touched to find that they had all got up early to see my taxi off to the airport. I had decided to finish the journey in the Caribbean, whilst the others went on to Equador. An overnight stay in Caracas gave me the chance to rent a car and drive to the Caribbean coast at Maiquetia. Venezuela has a string of beautiful beaches along it's northern coast, and I spent a lazy beach day. Caracas has a lot going for it as a holiday destination, apart from the treks to places like Angel Falls that I had done the month before. It is only ten miles from the coastal beaches, and despite having been founded in the sixteenth century, is a modern sophisticated city, - in the centre at least. Nestling in a long narrow valley in a mountain range, it is also exciting visually. I enjoyed being back there, even for only a day and a very enjoyable evening again in the Hotel Avila.

The West Indies

My flight to Grantley Adams Airport, Barbados, crossed the intensely blue Caribbean Sea, calling at tiny airports on Grenada and St. Vincent en-route. Both are such beautiful tiny islands, ringed with white beaches and rising green and so volcano-like from the cobalt sea that from the air it seemed impossible to even think about landing on them. Whilst not having been a particular admirer of Princess Margaret, I did feel envious of her private island of Mustique. I was able to rent a car easily at the airport and found a place to stay in Bridgetown which called itself The Home of the Daiquiri. With a constantly manned bar by the side of the swimming pool, and a few yards from Rockley beach and the breaking waves, both of which were snow white, I quickly found this to be true. The Barbadian hotel owner, who doubled as barman, initiated me into the mysteries of a real daiquiri. I spent the next few years making them at home, using Jo's blender, but they were never quite as good as his! A swim in the rolling breakers, followed by a banana daiquiri by the side of pool was a very good way of passing the time, and a serious temptation to spend the rest of my life there!

However, I wanted to investigate the island, so did my own tour, all round the coast. Whilst only about sixty miles, this took all next day as there was a lot to see. Sheer one thousand foot high cliffs on the east coast, Bathsheba where the Atlantic rollers foam over masses of detached rocks, and Sam

Lord's Castle, a mansion built by a notorious buccaneer. He made his money, so the story goes, by plundering ships that were lured onto reefs by hanging lights on the coconut trees, so that captains mistook them for the lights of Bridgetown. Savannah Garrison and St. Anne's Fort was also full of history, British soldiers being stationed there at the end of the seventeenth century. This was a good day, beautiful views, stopping wherever I chose to talk to friendly people. The east coast was very rural, with huge fields of sugar cane, not affected by tourism, and people waved as I drove or walked past.

I also got myself an underwater voyage from Bridgetown into the Caribbean, in the commercial submarine 'Atlantis', yet another new experience. I had an invitation to visit the home of the sister of one of Jo's Barbadian nursing colleagues, Sister Nicholson, and spent a pleasant evening, dining on flying fish and other interesting specialities. She was a music teacher, with one of the famous members of the West Indian Test team as a pupil, so was able to talk about cricket – as I believe any Barbadian, male or female, can do! After leaving the pleasant company I sat on the beach for an hour and enjoyed the phosphorescence, the luminous waves a reminder of the Indian Ocean coast of Burma. To finish off a good day, a final banana daiquiri in the ever-open bar.

At the Airport next morning were a very pushy crowd of packaged Europeans. I enjoyed falling out with them! Flying to Port of Spain, Trinidad, was only a comparatively short flight using a L.I.A.T. small turbo-prop, and passing overhead the island of Tobago and the Grenadines. Trinidad, it was quickly obvious, did not have the international appeal, nor the visible wealth of Barbados, but cricket was still a common interest. I joined in a game with some local boys in Savannah Park, and spent a day wandering on foot, thinking that I had probably spent more than enough on rental cars! It cost $65 by taxi to go into the city, and $1.50 to return by local bus! It was extremely hot, and a coconut, bought and sliced in half from a cart at the side of the road, was very welcome. Port of Spain was then a vibrant city, quite different from the quieter Bridgetown. There was a mixture of beautiful old colonial houses, concrete monstrosities and dreadful shanties. It was also time to get a haircut before I got home, and so tried out a local barbershop. This turned out to be probably the worst one that I had ever had, as the guy was obviously not used to dealing with straight hair!

However, once done, it was fait accompli, and I enjoyed some repartee with him, and the other customers. He admitted that he had been surprised to see me come in, and had not dealt with WASP hair before! All the locals in Barbados and Trinidad had been friendly, welcoming and happy to talk. There was some (but not enough to worry about) begging, prostitution and attempts to work a con-trick in Bridgetown, but not in Port of Spain. Why? Was it the influence of packaged tourism in Barbados? All the older people that I spoke to said that it was not like it used to be – the universal lament!

It was then home, Trinidad to Heathrow after a wonderful safari, taking eight weeks in total, covering eight countries and a multitude of sights, experiences and memories, and meeting interesting, beautiful and bizarre people and cultures. I felt myself very lucky indeed to have seen and experienced it all and had the privilege and opportunity to do so. I also felt tremendously indebted to Sarah, who was a fund of knowledge and expertise. I enjoyed meeting her at their London Office to show off my photographs. I was also very grateful to Jo, who had supported my ambition to travel, again.

The Hashemite Kingdom of Jordan, with Petra and Wadi Rum

I have been fascinated by the history of El `Orrance, Lawrence of Arabia, for many years, and had tried to get into Jordan over the Allenby Bridge whilst on earlier visits to Israel. At that time I was very firmly refused permission to cross the River Jordan from the West Bank. However, in 1992 I was able to arrange a visit to Jordan to include the rock carved Nabatean city of Petra. The many centuries of settlement in this area have left archaeological riches that range from Neolithic statues and four thousand year frescoes to the Graeco-Roman splendour of Jerash and the mosaic riches of the Byzantine city of Madaba. A Bible would be a good guide book to take to Jordan, as it's pages record just about all the tribes who have occupied or journeyed through there. Canaanites, Moabites, Assyrians, Persians, Philistines, and Babylonians followed by the Romans, to mention just a few. For a short time it was even under British rule after centuries of repression under the Ottoman Turks. Look anywhere on a map of Jordan and you will certainly find place names familiar from the Old and New Testaments.

But, despite the jewels of the cities of these ancient civilisations, the desert comprises more than two thirds of the country. The place that I most wanted to experience was Wadi Rum in the south of Jordan. This was where Lawrence based his operations during the Arab Revolt that he orchestrated in 1917-18. Despite beating the Turks he and his Arab partners were let down. Deceit and betrayal are words not too strong for the policies of the politicians of Britain and France. They did what I have commented upon earlier in Sudan and Somalia, ignoring the promises made to Lawrence and the Arabs. They drew straight lines on a map, considering only the vested interests of Britain and France. A single glance demonstrates how they used a ruler with no thought for history or tribes. Sykes and Picot and their associated politicians of both countries were much the same, during and after the First War, as their successors are nearly one hundred years later. Untrustworthy and untruthful. We are still suffering, now in the Middle East, very much so, for their broken promises, mistakes, ignorance, naivety and hubris.

I joined a small group in Amman in early September, for a very packed tour led by a Jordanian historian, Samir, who was a splendid guide. Amman is full of history and was inhabited by prehistoric man from the Palaeolithic Age. From much nearer our time, the Roman Theatre is one of the best preserved I have seen anywhere. It seats 6,000 spectators, and is still used! The Roman Forum nearby is spectacular. Some wonderfully complete Byzantine mosaics are displayed at the Theatre, beautifully displaying a leopard hunting an antelope, birds, including what seems to be a pet bird in a cage, and kilted men. Their faces are so untarnished and astonishingly modern! This reminded me of how lucky Jo and I had been to see a mosaic being discovered, and the sand carefully brushed away to reveal its perfection during a holiday in Greece. The Group spent a very full time in Amman, and found it not enough, because there was so much to see.

Amman is a modern city despite all the history, but it is possible, perhaps on a bit of remaining grass, to find a traditional shepherd with his sheep and probably black goats, maybe even carrying a lame lamb on his shoulders in biblical fashion. Amman was first mentioned in the Book of Deuteronomy as Rabbah of the Ammonites, and became Philadelphia under the Egyptian Ptolemy Philadelphus, who was apparently not a very nice man. He was one of the succession of Ptolemies squabbling over the custody of the tomb of Alexander the Great, the location of which is now shrouded in mystery. It seems that Philadelphus copied the Alexandrian policy of naming cities after himself!

Jerash, a few miles north in the hills of Gilead, formerly known as Antioch on the Golden River, was founded in the second century B.C. by the Romans, and is now the best preserved Roman city in the Middle East, probably in the World. Two more wonderful theatres with the stone backdrop to the stage still standing, a main colonnaded street, the Cardo Maximus, and the Temple of Artemis with magnificently tall columns were all so visible. Other colonnades and the lovely oval piazza at the south end of the Cardo must have made Jerash a city to be proud of, in it's time. Shall we be able to say the same of Wolverhampton or Birmingham in two thousand years time? We are lucky that so much of it remains to remind us how civilised (in some ways) Roman life could be. I was thrilled by the mosaics in the Church of St Cosmos and, still it stands, the triumphal arch built to celebrate the visit of Emperor Hadrian (yes, the Emperor of the wall). The hills of Gilead are pastoral country, producing olives and sheep, with Bedouin farmers moving their flocks to graze on the grass that follows the highly erratic rainfall. A group of Bedouin with their camels and flocks can sometimes be seen on the move, time having stood still as it does in Sudan and other Arab countries.

Jordan has been, like Palestine and Israel, a crossroads where for centuries travellers and armies have passed and repassed, to buy and sell, to dominate and to aggressively promote their own religion. It is therefore a land of castles, on hilltops and in the desert, and many almost defensible still. Some are Crusader castles, other look like Crusader castles but were built by Salah al-Din in his stand against the unenchanting Europeans, and others were Roman Barracks. Some were built by the Caliphs of Damascus, long after both Saladin and the Romans, to protect the trade routes. They helped to enforce loyalty from the Jordanian tribes as well, as a side effect, I'm sure. Qasr el-Kharanah, south east of Amman, is one such. It is an uncompromising quite square block of undressed stone that looks unbreachable, with just one small entrance. It may have been used also as a caravanserai. It is surrounded by hostile desert, but oddly is only a few miles from Queen Alia International Airport. We were lucky to be able to visit several different castles on our journey south towards Petra.

Not only castles remain in the desert, but palaces also and religious sites. God told Moses, so records the Book of Deuteronomy, that he could look at, but not enter the land of milk and honey. Mount Nebo, in the hills of Moab, is where he looked out on Canaan, the Promised Land. The ruins of a Church and Monastery lie on a ridge overlooking the Jordan Valley, with a panoramic view of the Dead Sea and the Judean Hills. Moses, given a clear day, would have had an extremely fine, and perhaps frustrated, hurt and rueful view of Canaan. It was absorbing to be looking at that same view – not very much changed. The Church has beautiful mosaic floors vividly depicting a variety of animals and trees. It is reported that an intrepid Roman lady traveller reached Mount Nebo in A.D. 394, and struggled up the steep hill partly on foot and partly by donkcy, and was assured that Moses had died and was buried there. Deuteronomy says that Moses died and was buried in the land of Moab. Perhaps this is not surprising, given the disappointment that he had. The lady, Aetheria or Egeria, must have been a character, a spiritual ancestress of some of the intrepid 19th and early 20th Century Englishwomen travellers. Dame Freya Stark maybe, and I admire them equally. But, one cannot help but feel terribly sorry for Moses, desperately trying to shepherd his gang of unruly stiff-necked Jews in some sort of order through the Wilderness, only to be told that he could go so far but no further. According to the Bible he was one hundred and twenty years old, yet his eyes were not weak nor his strength undiminished. I guess that the trials of the Exodus journey had been punishment enough for wanting to do things his way. I have sympathy with him for this. His grave or tomb has been lost for centuries.

Madaba, a little south and east of Mount Nebo is a seemingly modern town. It was built on an artificial mound or tell, that rises above the tableland to the east of the Mountains of Moab. But, it was known at the time of the Exodus, and is mentioned in the Books of Numbers and Joshua. It is called the city of mosaics, because of the number of wonderful floors in the Churches and private houses. Mosaics flourished here in the Byzantine period, during the fourth, fifth and sixth centuries A.D.and are amazingly detailed and intricate. We were fortunate to be able to see the most famous, the wonderful map of Palestine and Jordan, in the Greek Orthodox Church of St. George. This mosaic contains a fascinating plan of Jerusalem, clearly recognisable and showing the north and east gates and the domed Holy Sepulchre. The map is dated to the sixth century, and was not discovered until about 1880, when a group of Christians found it underneath some rubble. Imagine the surprise and delight – one could feel it pulsating around the Church still.

Further south and west on our journey towards Petra was Machaerus, a dramatic hilltop fortress ruin, and the traditional site of the execution of John the Baptist. We were now back into the wild and beautiful mountains of Moab. The historian Josephus says that Herod the Great built the fortress over an earlier Hasmonean stronghold. Herod's son, Herod Antipas put aside his Nabatean wife to marry Herodias, the wife of his brother, and John spoke out strongly against this as sin. After which Herodias'daughter Salome demanded his head. It is said that all this happened at Machaerus, now known as Mukawir, and it is a site where one can easily believe that such drama has happened. But, recently, a much more positive result has been achieved by 'Save the Children'. They developed rug weaving, the traditional craft of the Bedu women, and improved the colour combinations and design. The rugs are now in demand abroad, and result in more money becoming available for education, better food and health.

It would be strange to visit Jordan and not see a Crusader Castle. Kerak, - Crak des Moabites - was known to the Crusaders as Le Pierre du Désert, the Stone of the Desert. Whatever one may think about the Crusader's motives, attitudes and lust for domination, there is no denying their military skills. Kerak is built on a hilltop, and also commands what was known as the King's Highway. The garrison could have power over and levy tolls on the north-south traffic travelling between Mecca and Damascus. It is so strong, still, that it is beautiful in strength. Jane Taylor describes it as 'a great ship riding waves of rock'.

The little town, largely a Christian one, sits beneath it and one can look up at the castle and feel how the people were protected – or perhaps at times threatened. It soars above the town on the rock. We had a little extra time to spend here, so I enjoyed sitting with a cool drink and was surrounded by a group of local boys, eager as ever to talk to a visitor, to them I guess one almost from outer space. Many of the local Christian families trace their ancestry back to the Byzantines. Kerak has known Iron Age people at the time of the Exodus, the Crusaders who made the name Kerak synonymous with strength, Salah al-Din, the Mamluk Sultans, the Ottoman Turks, and finally the British who eventually handed it to Transjordan in 1921. Walking up to the castle it is impossible not to visualize, even experience, how dominant it would have been. The western side is protected by a deep dry moat, and strong stone walls help still to defend and isolate the site. Long stone vaulted galleries lit only by narrow slits and rooms entered by heavy arched doorways are typical Crusader construction, and add to the sense of bygone strength, dominance, supremacy and clout. I felt privileged to sense and glimpse it.

Petra and Wadi Rum

Peter, Pierre, Petra – Rock. Petra is literally carved from the sandstone and granite mountains that have hidden it from the world for centuries. It is an area of wild and bizarrely shaped rocks by the side of Wadi Arabah, the section of the Great Rift Valley that runs from the Gulf of Aqaba to the Dead Sea. The Rift Valley was originally described as reaching 6,000 kilometres from Lebanon to Mozambique, although parts are now believed to be systems created by other rifts. What is sure though is that these violent cracks in the crust of the earth have created much of the dramatic scenery of Palestine and Jordan.

For over a thousand years the weird rocks were thought to be impenetrable, inhabited only by the Bedouin. The great extent of Petra is not yet fully revealed, and many mysteries are still to be solved. Apart from the twisted tortured shapes, striations in the rocks are vividly coloured, purple, deep red, white and grey against the ochre background. Dean John Burgon's poem, although beautifully phrased, spread the myth of the 'rose-red city'. The words 'half as old as time' also helped to create a rather wonderful legend. He had never been there when he wrote these lines, and had second thoughts about the 'rose-red' after seeing it! My overall impression was of a light yellow and very pale red. Petra can without doubt look rose-red in some sunlit conditions, but there are sandstone areas of Shropshire that do so more emphatically. However, there are none, anywhere I think, that can compare with the majesty of the carved rock, and the mystery of how the Nabateans, a nomadic tribespeople from Arabia, constructed them, during the centuries before and soon after Christ. The Nabateans began to settle on this land vacated by the Edomites. They had moved west to the greener lands on the other side of Wadi Arabah after King Nebuchadnezzer transported the Jews to Babylon. How and why a nomadic tribe settled and made Petra their capital in the Wadi Mousa could be another epic story, which I believe has not yet been told. Part of that story could be the tradition that this was where Moses displayed the impatience for which God punished him, by striking a rock with his staff for water to gush forth for the Israelites to drink. The tradition may even reflect the historic fact that the Nabateans constructed an artificial oasis for the city by the use of dams, aquifers and conduits, to enable it to live and flourish. A further tradition lives on, that the brother of Moses, Aaron, or Haroun, is buried close to here, on Mount Hor.

The entrance to Petra, from the modern buildings that accommodate the tourist crowds, is through the Siq, the gigantic mile long cleft between two high mountains. Travel through this narrow defile, in shade and comparative coolness is either by camel or pony - we had ponies. Emerging from the shade of the slender crack in the rock, to find oneself face to face with the sculpted columns of The Treasury was an astonishing experience. The two story facade, in contrast to the shadows, was bathed in sunlight, and was actually glowing as pink as a rose. It is probably the loveliest and least eroded of all the monuments. How on earth they made something of such perfect proportions and with what tools was a continuing puzzlement to me through our long visit. The Treasury was more likely to have been a tomb, or perhaps just an extremely impressive entrance portal to the city. Many of the carved monuments are tombs. Petra is therefore, to some extent, a city of the dead, but there is a magnificent Theatre and paved streets with the remains of columns on one side. Houses carved out of the rock reminded me of the rock dwellings in Shropshire and Worcestershire, but these are very much older. We spent a day in Petra, which has been invaded, of course, by entrepreneurs selling relics of the Nabateans. Actually this was pretty well under control, and not objectionable, and within the valley it was so hot that anyone selling bottled drinks was on a winner. I did buy the head of a Nabatean King, and watched a man filling bottles with sand, which he cleverly shook into coloured bands to reflect the colours of the rock striations.

Perhaps the best area was, via steps cut into the rock, the 'High Place', where obelisks were created by digging away the top of the mountain to leave standing columns. It is thought that the two obelisks were in honour of the God Dusares and Goddess Al Uzza, the Nabatean's greatest deities. The huge labour of cutting away a whole mountain top could only have been undertaken to serve great Gods. This also a place of sacrifice, with a stunning view down to the buildings in the serpentine valley below. The Turkmaniyah tomb bears an inscription, in Nabatean, 'This is the property of Dusharra, the Nabatean God.' In a sense, I suppose, the whole site resembled a sandcastle, but built with solid rock, not shifting sand. It was almost possible to see where a builder - carver - architect had said, 'I can merge this design into that one,' like a child adding towers and buildings to his castle before the sea, or in this case time, rushes in.

There was so much to see within Petra that we had an extra day here, but I badly wanted to go to Wadi Rum. Fortunately I was able to rent a car (but only with a driver!) and spent the free day there. It was quite a long drive down towards Aqaba, but the driver spoke English well enough for us to have an interesting conversation, and we enjoyed each other's company. He gave me a set of prayer beads at the end of the day, which I still have.

Wadi Rum, is described as one of the world's outstanding desert landscapes – a desert of mountains. Rum is small compared to the Sudan, Libyan or the Sahara or to the Central Asian wastelands of the Taklimakan and the Gobi, and is not as colourful as the great red Simpson in Australia, but, it has mountains! Great sandstone and granite blocks and crags of mountains rising suddenly and individually from the flat desert sand. They often show sheer faces, and rise to nearly 6,000 feet, so are quite serious. Lawrence has written beautifully about Wadi Rum in the Seven Pillars of Wisdom, far better than I am able. If I dare to steal one of his phrases he says that it is 'greater than imagination'. The Bedouin have lived here in their black goat hair tents for centuries. Some are now settling into villages but others still prefer a nomadic existence, carrying the portable houses of hair in their traditional wanderings.

I was lucky to be able to find a Bedu guide to take me through, up and over some of the narrow rock clefts and to find the rock drawings. I also joined a Bedouin Police detachment at one of their bases – whether they were able to disentagle my very limited Arabic explanation that I was a former English Police Officer I am not sure, but they were very hospitable and friendly. The concept of a policeman having enough money to travel was, I am sure, a strange one to them. The hospitality is traditional in all the deserts that I have been in, even when, as here, there was little danger of dying of thirst. t was yet another privilege to drink tea with them. The Bedouin Police are the modern inheritors of the traditions of the Arab Legion, the legendary Force raised by Glubb Pasha in the early nineteen thirties. They won a celebrated reputation during the Second World War and I was proud to meet their successors.

El `Orrance is still a legend, and I felt a little of what he obviously felt for the desert and the mountains and Wadi Rum, although without his extraordinary ability to put it into words. Being there was extraordinary enough. It remains a great memory of a unique part of what was a special journey, through Jordan. I have been helped with some of my descriptions by the wonderful book High above Jordan by Jane Taylor, who produced some marvellous photographs of marvellous places.

Chapter 8

Some serious safaris - The South Pacific, Australia, New Zealand, and round the world, 1994

We had been receiving invitations to visit Kulwant and Mohinder in Tasmania for many years, and after both of us enjoying good holidays in Italy, Spain and Germany we decided in 1993 that it could be fitted into 'round the world' travel in 1994. With an itinerary arranged by Wexas, the World Expeditionary Association it would cover much of Indonesia, Papua New Guinea, Australasia, New Zealand and the Pacific Islands and back via Hawaii and the USA, west to east coasts. By some careful timing it could be done between January and the middle of March. As we had discovered before, Jo cannot deal with a really hot climate. Australia in January is hot, she was still working and could not take that amount of leave and in any case did not want to be away from her other interests for so long. Again therefore it was just one ticket - or series of tickets.

Indonesia

I was still working for Peak Performance, and had plenty of accumulated leave due, so on New Year's Day 1994 I landed at Soerkarno Hatta Airport, Jakarta, Java. The long non-stop flight on Garuda Airways, the Indonesian national carrier had left me pretty tired, but I was able to book a room at the Hotel Permata Harmoni from the Airport. This was rather a pig in a poke, but eventually, after trouble getting to it, quite reasonable. A town bus into the city centre was rather an adventure on it's own, as the streets were flooded after an exceptional tropical storm, and traffic was horrendous. I then agreed with the driver of a three-wheel single passenger tuk-tuk (luggage balanced on knees) that he would try to find the Hotel (maps and local knowledge were non-existent). The driver became totally lost trying to wend his way through the flooded streets and it took a long hour to find, with relief, a bed! The tuk-tuks or bajaj were banned from the city, but have started to creep back. They are a dreadful method of transport, but, I suppose, provide a cheapish way of getting around. Jakarta is nowadays notorious for its congested traffic, disregard of traffic laws and wholesale corruption. Four or five lanes of traffic on a two lane road are not uncommon. Not much change there then! It is now classed as the twelfth largest city in the world and part of a megalopolis of 23 million. I am glad that I went earlier.

Next morning was hot and still very damp, so humidity was high and walking, in a tired state, felt rather like being under water. The Jakartan climate was rather like being very close to an extremely hot fire, whilst being sprinkled with a hosepipe, and inhaling traffic fumes! However I was very keen to explore old Batavia, for a few days whilst in Jakarta, which now encompassed the old port area. Batavia was the capital of Java when it was a Dutch East Indies colony, and a port full of the mysteries, surprises, vices and tales of the Java and South China Seas. The Dutch were driven out by the Japanese in 1942 and never came back, but some of the old culture still remained, with grand houses of typical Dutch design. Bugis schooners were still being built in the harbour, gracefully rounded wooden sailing ships that sailed the South China Sea, carrying cargoes of timber, trading, smuggling and pirating. They looked too beautiful to have been involved in the activities that the stories told of them. They are the last fleet of wooden cargo ships operating in the world. The crews were, and are, feared. Women told their children that if naughty they would be given to the Bugis men. This is believed to be the origin of the word Bogeymen!

Although Indonesia is a mainly Muslim country, big and little Father Christmases were everywhere with people still saying Happy Christmas. The area around the old port was very run down, with broken decrepit shacks bordering a river so dirty that it was almost black, and so unpleasant that even the small boys, unusually, were not larking about in it. It did not seem that the Soerkarno regime had done much for this part of Indonesia, as yet, although he did have grandiose plans to make Jakarta a world-class city. However, as I have experienced in so many places, including the UK, the politicians were a disaster but individual people were friendly, helpful and anxious to supplement their own income by offering their services. After the largest coldest beer that I could find I accepted an offer to be shown around Batavia, which by now was reminding me very strongly of the dingiest back streets of Rangoon. It all seemed very deprived, apart from the showcase skyscrapers in the new centre – the beginning of Soerkarno's ambitions. Other than these I felt that there had not been much change since the Dutch were running things.

Next day I shared transport with an Australian couple to the town of Bandung. There are a number of volcanoes in the area, spectacularly ten thousand footers or more. There was the opportunity to climb to the crater of one that is still active, and then down to some very hot springs. The countryside was green, trees well up the mountains, but bright with flowers. It is a great experience to taste a pineapple cut from the side of the road while you wait! Huge tea plantations, where women wearing mushroom hats waved at travellers, and rice paddies with a man ploughing by ox and wooden plough were all a flashback to Burma. A motorway returning to Jakarta was surprisingly modern, with 'two-second gap' chevrons and barriers on the overhead bridges. This was something of a contrast with both the wooden plough and the slums of Batavia.

Borneo

After an interesting few days I got myself back to the Airport and picked up a flight across the Java Sea to Banjarmasin in Kalimantan, the Indonesian two thirds of the island of Borneo. The remaining part of Borneo, Sarawak , is where my wedding-speech pupil at Hira's marriage came from, and belongs to Malaysia. Surrounded by Sarawak is the tiny Monarchy of Brunei, whose Sultan is reputed to be one of the richest men in the world. I wanted to explore into Dyak country, the legendary headhunters and longhouse dwellers of Borneo. The island is a fabled country of jungle, deep gorges, mountains, diamonds, savage tribes and has fascinated me for years.

Banjarmasin is built on the delta of the river Barito that flows into the Java Sea from the highlands of central Borneo. There is a network of water throughout the town, with several smaller rivers and canals, and many people live in shanties near, or in, the dirty orange coloured muddy water. The river and canal culture was very like the klongs of Bangkok. Shanties were cheek by jowl with a small mosque serving roughly every forty dwellings. Naked boys, seeing my paleface, showed off by diving in for small coins, amid huge laughter, waving and grinning from the water. The canals and riverside were, and probably still are, a mutual laundry, toilet, bathroom, rubbish disposal area, a source of food and drinking water, transport and fun for the kids. We grumble about the cost and inefficiency of Severn-Trent but thank Heaven for it! Being one of the very few palefaces among 300,000 people, I was persistently shadowed all around town. The shadows either wanted to stare or to 'help' while the smaller ones, of course, hoped for baksheesh. A strong impression was of overmanning in almost every phase of life, with people competing for work and space.

Indonesia, with a population of around 200 million, is the fourth most densely populated country in the world, and it certainly showed, both here and in Jakarta. I felt quite ashamed at needing to brush the shadows off, but they soon became a pest if you didn't. With the increase in tourism and therefore more palefaces this may not be such a problem now. Away from the ever-present water I found plenty of noisome back streets and alleys, but also a very acceptable hotel. I was joined by a 'friend' over dinner who spoke good English, and we had an interesting discussion, but then he spoiled it by trying to sell me some jewellery. Should have expected it!

Banjarmasin is a big town and possessed a Government Tourist Office, catering it seemed mainly for Australians, and I arranged for Jimmy Kapoh to show me around for the next couple of days. He was waiting for me at 6am next morning to travel by klotok, (a slow boat propelled by a paddle), to the Kuin Pasar Terapung, the floating market, where, he promised me, we could buy breakfast from a floating take-away! Jimmy, whom I got to know quite well, was a pleasant and intelligent young man, wearing a T-shirt with the inscription, 'When money speaks, truth is silent'! The market, where the Kuin River joins the much bigger Barito, comprised literally thousands of small boats, both traders and customers. The wholesalers, in bigger boats, had stocks of just about everything that could be grown, and what was needed was taken away by smaller boats, for retail selling.

The boat people were mainly women, some extremely old, and most wearing umbrella sized hats that covered their faces. The hats were straw coloured and from above, or at an angle, looked exactly like huge mushrooms. The women wore a paste on their faces made of a mixture of meal, which looked similar to, and, I guess, did the same job as the sandalwood used by Burmese women and children. Although the expanse of water was at least half a mile wide the boats were crowded together, rubbing against each other in a monstrous jam. An excuse for boat rage, but I didn't see any, and everyone seemed to be happy and busy despite the obvious poverty. There was considerable skill involved as mixed in with the small paddled boats were motorised passenger carriers and a few large river steamers. We travelled to the market from the town centre along the Kuin River, which was only just wide enough for our boat. A sort of one-way stream.

The shanties on either side almost met, like a Dickensian London street. Ramshackle footbridges were low over the water, so close that mostly I had to duck, and usually covered with grinning and waving boys who jumped into the water at every opportunity. They loved to get towed, by holding onto the stern until beaten off! Life was being lived on and in the water. At 6am people were washing, furiously scrubbing teeth and breaking off to laugh and wave at me. Jimmy pulled in at the side of the floating restaurant and as he had promised we did get a good breakfast of fried bananas, kassava cakes and coffee (made from the river?). The technique was to have a long pointed stick and 'fish' for what you fancied on the bigger boat, taking care not to drop it in the river! This was a terrific, memorable, satisfying experience, but hygienic not! Jimmy told me that the market had developed as an opportunity to trade by bartering, but that it was now strictly cash purchases. There was also a floating clinic, sponsored by the Banjarmasin Rotary Club, and what appeared to be a floating mosque complete with a small tower. The three or so hours that we spent there absolutely justified alone getting to Kalimantan, but we also went, by the klotok, to the island of Pulau Kembang which is effectively not much more than a mangrove swamp. The object was to visit the old Temple. It was quite bizarre to see a swastika displayed, but this was an ancient Asian symbol long before the Nazis stole it. It means 'wellbeing', from Sanskrit. The Temple was surrounded on all sides by macaque monkeys, the island being also known as 'long tailed monkey island! There was a visitor book in the Temple, the last entries being two girls from Calgary, so I was not the only visitor from far away.

That afternoon we also went by a different boat down the Barito to the delta, a two hour journey to Pulau Kaget, the home of the long-nosed monkeys. The river was busy with tugs, big boats, Bugis Schooners and prahus by the thousand. We even got a wave from a police boat! The island is again a mangrove swamp, with small waterways only just wide enough for the boat, which was now being poled, with the engine off, as the monkeys are very shy. The swamp was silent, but alive with insects, kingfishers, fish eagles with the monkeys just visible in the trees, jumping, swinging, nursing babies. Their faces are weird, with the long nose swinging loose almost level with their chins. They are extremely rare and only found in Borneo, so to actually see them was a privilege. Zoologists know them as Proboscis Monkeys, but the locals call them Kahau, from the sound of their calls. They live on mangrove leaves that are toxic to most other creatures. What would Charles Darwin have thought about those long noses? A really great day, easily comparable with many that I have been so lucky to experience. I enjoyed sharing a beer with Jimmy back at my hotel, and we had a long and interesting chat about our different life styles. I still had my boots on as we sat in the hotel lounge; they were an old pair, comfortable but scruffy and getting to the end of their days. Jimmy looked at them and said rather wistfully, 'Those are very nice boots'. This rather disturbed me, but they would have been too big for him and there was no guarantee that I could buy big enough replacements. I did give him a good tip later when we parted though, enough to buy his own.

We made arrangements to take the public bus the next day, to get into Dyak tribal country.

The bus was very crowded as we took a two hour drive through flat paddy-fielded country, very wet and a lot of it mangroves at the edges of streams or rivers. The area for a hundred kilometres around Banjarmasin is shown on the map as marshy. I was an object of interest on the bus and a very large lady offered me a sweet! We left the bus at the village of Kadogan, and walked through the market to get a meal in the local eating house. Girls were squatting on the floor in the kitchen area, cutting vegetables into bowls, but the fried fish also on offer was very good. The next transport was a Mitsubishi pick-up truck with a canvas roof, into which crowded about twenty men. Fortunately Jimmy and I were just able to squeeze into a seat at the fresh air end. It stopped regularly for people to get off, but always more got on.

We were now travelling on a graded track through thick jungle on either side, and climbing into dramatic hill country, I guessed about two thousand feet up, with higher ground still in the distance. I saw a man ploughing with oxen and a wooden plough. There was the occasional shack at the side of the road, but not many people, in contrast to the town. After a long drive through a tropical rainstorm we came to an orange coloured river, swirling, fast and with a set of rapids just downstream, and some bamboo rafts. It was crossed by a wooden footbridge suspended from wire ropes. This was Loksando, the Dyak village, almost hidden in the palm trees. There was one muddy street, with cattle looking miserable in the heavy rain, and one-story houses roofed with tin which was covered with vegetable mats. The latter would be necessary to absorb the sound of the rain and protect the metal. Jimmy and I got a drink in a teahouse, and watched a form of snooker being played on a table with flat sliding discs instead of balls. By now it was beginning to feel that we were taking part in the play or film based on Somerset Maugham's story 'Rain'. I described it to Jimmy, saying that it was about a prostitute and a very inhibited preacher, trapped in one room in never-ending rain in tropical Samoa. He was highly amused. Eventually it cleared and on the way back over the bridge we met a Dyak villager, whom I guessed was about fifty, going on eighty.

What a fascinating face. I did wonder if he had been a headhunter, but could hardly ask. He had a splendid straw hat, and bare feet, but the ambience was rather spoiled, as he was also wearing a sheet of blue plastic as a cloak, but he did tolerate a photograph. I understood that he had walked for four hours to come down from the hills into the village. We caught the pick-up and the driver and passengers were extremely kind enough to make a special stop at a long house on our way back and wait for me to see it, as I had missed the one in Loksando. It really was long - many yards – and two stories high with the ubiquitous tin roof. Two ladders from ground level got you up to a bamboo veranda, one ladder being homemade but conventional and the other just a log with notches cut into it! There were eighteen families living on the top floor, with a 'holy' communal area in the centre and small living quarters for each family around the outside walls. They were separated from each other by bamboo and curtains, with beds made of bamboo raised up on stilts. The ground floor was just empty space, the top floor being raised up on stilts. This design protected the living quarters from snakes and other unpleasant jungle inhabitants. There were only a few adults in the house, so I was able to go in without a problem, but several babies were there, kept safe and out of mischief in cloth bags suspended from the ceiling, with just their faces showing. Cooking was done on the veranda or outside. I wondered what a Fire Service Prevention Officer would have suggested!

The long drive back to Banjarmasin got us back late, but it had been a good fourteen hour experience. Jimmy and I had a final beer and a chat and said 'Salemat minum' (Cheers) then 'Sangan bagus' (very good) to him while he replied 'Samey Samey' (you're welcome)! I parted from him with some regret, as he been a cheerful, knowledgeable companion, and I put this on paper to the Banjarmasin Tourist Office later. He hoped to start his own tourist agency.

Bali and Lombok

Next morning I sat slowly cooking in Syamsuddin Noor Airport, while the loudspeakers played, 'While Shepherds Watched' and 'White Christmas'! It was about five hundred kilometres back across the Java Sea to Ngurah Rai Airport at Denpasar, the capital of the island of Bali, and an interesting flight as my seat was next to a Colonel in the Korean Army, the military attaché to Indonesia and his family, enjoying their Christmas break. Strange how non-Christians do seem to have hi-jacked our holidays as well as their own! The Airport advice desk found me a hotel in Denpasar, with the Dutch inflence still obvious in it's old colonial style. The lizards on the wall were pure Balinese though. I walked by mistake into a local wedding reception in the hotel, and was invited to take a photograph of the couple in their gorgeous costumes. Gold fabric, red head-dress and white coral necklace – and that was just the man!

During breakfast on my first full day in Bali I was asked for advice on where to go and what to see by a German couple. Having done my best I gave myself a tour around central Denpasar, which is very attractive with beautiful flowering trees, Banyan trees and temples with Chinti and Shizuo statues. The Museum had ferocious masks, ornate and colourful costumes and cages full of fighting crickets. I stayed for two hours, a long time in a Museum for me. Bali was, of course, quite different from the other parts of Indonesia that I had seen, being full of tourists, although later I and the two Germans were the only Europeans at a performance of gamelin music and dancing, and we were awarded special status. I had decided that the climate and the atmosphere made wearing my sarong appropriate – perhaps that had something to do with it. I was invited on stage to join in the dancing anyway! Memories of Rio! Before this I had been out in the afternoon to go to the Kechak (monkey) Dancing in the Arts Centre, which was good and not at all touristy. Walking back I chanced upon a funeral procession, with dozens of people carrying palm leaves, banners, statues and flowers and beating gongs as they marched. It was colourful and noisy – a good send-off I guess.

I was quite surprised to find that next day was still only the 10th of January – a lot seemed to have been packed into ten days, and I am so glad now that I made notes and photographed it all. I ordered a rental Suzuki jeep that turned up at 8 a.m. as promised, the intention being to now see some real Bali away from the tourist packed beach and town areas. The jeep and I headed towards the mountains - as ever - and enjoyed a lovely morning, finding a spectacular waterfall at Gitgit, which was so like the Falls of Pistyll Rhaeadr in North Wales as to be almost it's twin, except that it was approached over a bridge made of four bamboo logs. We found genuine farming people working the fields, (wearing the mushroom hats) bullock drawn carts, men carrying heavy loads in a yoke, bare breasted women, vast isolated statues of the Buddha, volcanic lava, tiny peaceful villages with smiling children and great mountain scenery. The views were very like those in Borneo.

I stopped for lunch in the old Dutch port of Singerama on the northern coast, turned east for a while then made my way back on a different route through the central mountains and volcanoes of Bali to Kintaman and Batur. I stopped at a wayside stall selling durians, manned by a nice family, Mother, Father and two children, who were all very proud to be photographed while displaying gleaming smiles. Durians smell absolutely awful, but once you have got into them taste like banana custard! There was a violent thunderstorm through the mountains, and a long descent from the rim of a volcano to the village of Bangli, seeing huge butterflies in the rain forest, hearing a multiplicity of crickets and finding thousands of temples. Bangli had a sort of venerable triumphal arch marking the village entrance. Each temple had at least one Chinte like statue, usually decorated with chequered cloths and sometimes an offering of food. They appeared eerily in the mist formed by the rain. Eventually back to the hotel for a beer and a swim, the weather having turned to a lovely evening. A great day, plenty of effort and over 200 kms in a small island, but seeing the

Bali not of the package beach holidays.

I had located the site of Barang Dances at Batu Bulan, held at 9.30 a.m. next morning, so by keeping the Jeep, this was a decided opportunity. The dances, with a huge variety of masks and monster costumes were held outdoors with an old temple as a background. A lot of effort was put in and again I was, I think, one of the few Europeans. After buying a couple of carvings I found the road to Ubud. Unfortunately this had also been found by the package industry, so I quickly shook off the dust and took a long lonely uphill track to Penelokan Kintamani. Emerging as the clouds broke was beautiful timing as there was a great view down to the crater. Mount Batur was now visible, with a lava flow gently steaming. After buying some rambutans, which are a bit like lichees for lunch, it was possible to drive down a winding path from the rim into the crater and drive onto the black pumice of the most recent cooled lava. Out of the crater and driving around I picked up a little man on his way home. He was a Civil Service clerk and spoke excellent English. I had a pressing invitation to stay at his home and climb Mount Batur tomorrow, but I wanted to go on to Bangli again and watch the Fire Dances. These were held in the dark, and were spectacular.

Wednesday 12th January was an easy day! Had a swim, visited the museum in Denpasar again and appreciated it more this time. While walking around the town centre, looking at the fighting cocks in their cages I found a ceremony at a shrine near a banyan tree. Women processing, wearing very colourful sarong kabayas and the men in white shirts and turbans. There was a beautiful display of fruit and incense at the shrine, and as far as I could understand from a friendly local onlooker this was the rough equivalent of our harvest festival.

I was still being approached for information and directions by other visitors – three times now on Bali. I suppose that I was a bit tanned, but also about a foot taller than most locals! After a peaceful evening, solo in the dining room but with my own live music I checked out next morning to move to another area, and was given a gift of a little Balinese monster statue. It survived to now live in my garage! I had found a very nice little Hotel, right on Semawang Beach. My room opened directly onto the sand – pretty good at $20 a night. The sea was not as blue as Barbados, and the beach not as evocative as Sandoway on the Bay of Bengal, but it was very very pleasant! There were outrigger fishing boats, white, yellow and blue, painted so well that they looked like fibreglass, but were in fact tree trunks. After several swims and a laze with a bottle of beer I walked through a totally quiet bit of the town, just the sound of birds in the trees. It was good to watch the clouds rolling across Gunung Agung and the sun shining on the cliffs of Nusa Penida island.

A couple of pineapple juices were better than those from a tin. A rather sad little man wanted to buy my sarong – he spoke Italian and wanted one day to travel to Italy, but had no money. I noted that he was quite a philosopher, so I guess that he did not seek a donation! As it grew darker the sound of gamelan practice came from a Temple. The sky was soft velvet and the stars of the Southern Hemisphere very bright. The only sounds from my private veranda looking onto the beach were the lapping of waves and the crickets in the undergrowth. I had a good night, undisturbed by the fan, but something heavy jumped onto the roof at midnight! The few days on Bali, despite too many other tourists, were a great experience.

I was very sad to hear years later of the terrorist bomb near to where I had stayed. I could have lingered here for a long time, but was itching to see over the next mountain, so on Friday morning I caught the Mabua Express, a very streamlined, space-age jet foil catamaran to the next island, Lombok. The jet foil travelled at 60 kmph for the 120 km journey, arriving at Materam, the small capital. Bali and Lombok are separated by a very deep water channel, and have different flora and fauna. The channel is considered to mark the division between Asia and Australasia.

I got - again - a self appointed guide, and visited the Water Palace, built around a lake for the King of Bali in 1744. Bali and Lombok had fought, and Bali won! I also got some interesting wooden masks from a wood carver, and visited the Meru Temples, where the Temple Guardians Subili, who is a force for good stands on the left and Suriva, a force for evil on the right of the entrance. Both carried sticks over their shoulders – police staffs? Meru is the collective name for the Holy Hindu Trinity of Brahma, Vishnu and Shiva. After all this I had lunch in a Kentucky Fried Chicken shop! Lombok is a very beautiful island, with a high volcano and many tree covered hills and smaller mountains. There was a great view of the coastline from the catamaran, tropical and mysterious, and a lovely view in the setting sun of Bali as we returned, with the Gunung Agung standing clear of cloud and holding his head high above the hundreds of blue triangular fishing boat outrigger sails. A really good day, completed with an easy transfer to the airport, where I had left my heavy luggage.

Australia

Arriving at 4.30 a.m. in, Darwin, Northern Territories, there was a long queue for immigration into Australia, but surprisingly I was able to book both a Hotel and a Kakadu overnight tour at the airport. The Hotel was a former police training centre well restored with a brilliant swimming pool. After a quick sleep I went for a walk into Darwin. The town centre was very modern, very American, but with Aboriginal people wandering around, a couple, man and woman looking sad, disorientated, without hope or future. The first Abo that I spoke to was bloodshot eyed, unsteady and very drunk – how sad. Darwin was a mixture. Modern shops adjacent to warnings of maurauding saltwater crocodiles (the most dangerous sort) in the streets. Also 'Stage' Aussies, even down to the man with corks around his hat! One group of women out on the town, in the bar where I had my evening meal were described in my notebook as, 'Ugh!' All very friendly though – too much so. I did my best not to be a sniffy Pom, but the Restaurant group were rather like Dame Edna. Difficult to take seriously!

I was picked up as arranged at 7 a.m. by Ben in an OKA four-wheel drive Australian built minibus. After picking up four other people we headed for the wetlands of the Kakadu, which occupy a lot of the tropical monsoon country of the Northern Territories. Kakadu is a world heritage site, named after the first Aboriginal inhabitants, the Gagudju people. Ben was a very competent leader and obviously enjoyed imparting information. He spotted and stopped by a frilled lizard by the side of the road, which was beautifully photogenic, and we saw wallabies and goanna lizards while still on an all weather highway, together with ten foot high termite mounds. We stopped at Humpty Doo settlement, to get a drink at the Humpty Doo hotel. What a wonderful name!

After leaving the road entering the National Park it was time to do it properly and trek. It was hot and the flies were terrible, but Ben, who was a proper Aussie did not subscribe to the corks on hat theory. Perhaps the man that I saw was a tourist! We walked to Nourlangie Rocks, through millions of Eucalyptus trees and red rocks. It was hard work, but the rock paintings made it very worthwhile. This was an aboriginal resting place, a place for 'dreaming time' for perhaps 40,000 years. There were paintings in ochre and white, thousands of years old and recognisable as animals, humans, spirits and 'X-rays' showing bone structures. Some were partly protected by railings, others not, but had been painted on smooth cool surfaces under the overhanging rocks, so were still legible, even those of an estimated age of 20,000 years. Nourlangie is a massive outcrop of rock, part of the Arnhem Land escarpment. It would have been a place of major significance, sacred to the abo people. We had been briefed to bring swimming gear, and although crocs up to ten feet long had been visible in some of the billabongs Ben found us a place under a waterfall where it was safe - he said - to swim. As no one became a crocodile's breakfast I guess he was right, and it was a wonderful thing to do.

We stayed the night in tents at Cooinda camping ground, which had a restaurant and a pool. It was a relaxing meal after a great, but tough, day and a chance to chat to the others, Mark, a lawyer from Melbourne, an English couple from Bideford and Sandra, a librarian from Wadham College, on an exchange post in Darwin. All very 'getonwithable'! There were wallabies all around the site, no kangaroos, but dingoes howled through the night. Up at 6 a.m. to get a small boat on the Yellow Waters Billabong, famous for its crocs. The boat travels through narrow waterways then out onto the floodplain. This is the wet – and green. There were fish eagles, kingfishers, red legged Ibis and of course the pale basilisk eyes staring just above the surface. Not a place to swim, but after breakfast back at the camp site we trekked to Baroalba Springs, through the trees with weirdly shaped rocks rising hundreds of feet on either side. The rocks were multicoloured, red, grey, yellow, with nothing man-made in sight, or perhaps even in memory! Swimming was fine again, three pools, one with a waterfall and a set of rapids. This was a bit like Pistyll Rhaeadr in North Wales, but a lot hotter! Picnic lunch was at a great rock with a view to 'Lightning Dreaming' site on the escarpment.

The Aboriginal people think of spirits as natural phenomena like lightning. 'Whistling Duck Dreaming' is another sacred site. Then Ben drove us to Jabiru, the only town in Kakadu, where there was a small airport, and a hotel that is built in the shape of a crocodile, and looks very much like one from the air. An hour's flight over Kakadu and Arnhem Land showed how huge it is and how green to the horizon in all directions. We flew over Jim-Jim with its twin falls, the wall of the escarpment, red rocks and broken pillars of standing stone, and, like Angel Falls in Venezuela, totally remote and accessible only on foot or by four wheel drive. The escarpment is the ancient coastline of northern Australia. Then it was the long drive back to Darwin, and, after two great days in good company a nice meal in the Pancake Palace!

I rented a little Dihatsu next morning, to get some driving in myself. It was very easy. Visiting a post office I was struck by how clean, bright and efficient it was – an improvement on ours. The Stuart Highway took me to the Adelaide River – which is nowhere near the city of Adelaide by the way, for a two hour cruise to experience the jumping crocodiles. There were over 400 in this stretch of the river, some up to fourteen feet in length and persuaded into jumping almost completely out of the river to snatch meat held on poles from the boat. The passengers were warned not to stand near to the rail when the big ones jump. This was a fascinating sight, fourteen feet of snapping crocodile literally seeming to stand on its tail. Some of them can be identified by the boat crew, 'Magnum', 'Popeye', 'Tiny Tim' and so on!

Whilst I had seen plenty of crocs up and down Africa, this gave me a new respect for them. I saw one with a whole feathered cockerel between his jaws.

After the cruise I drove back to Darwin in a tropical rainstorm, but called in at the Humpty Doo Hotel again. What a line up of characters at the bar and playing pool! One would not care to order anything but a beer and I did not dare to take a photograph. The women were only identifiable by their lack of beards. Then last evening in Darwin, so I went for a stroll in East Point Reserve, an attractive park with palm trees running down to the shore of Fannie Bay – watch for saltwater crocodiles again! Finally another tropical electrical storm, so another visit to the Pancake Palace. I was able to leave the rental car keys in a slot in the desk at the Airport next morning – very relaxed and easy. It was still just less than three weeks since I had arrived in Jakarta – wow! It was another example of how big Australia is during the flight in a small aircraft. We landed briefly on Groote Eylandt, a mining settlement in the Bay of Carpenteria and then across the northern end of the Great Dividing Range to Cairns, in Queensland.

I had decided to spend one night in Cairns then go on to Port Moresby in Papua New Guinea for a few days. Cairns is very different to Darwin, which then was practically all new, having been flattened by a cyclone twenty years before. Cairns was a fascinating mixture of new shopping malls and Victoriana, when, I guess, it became popular as an Australian resort. The sea was very blue, lots of palm trees and high wooded mountains behind the town. After a swim I spent time in the bar, talking to an 'old-time' Aussie, who was politically well to the right of Genghis Khan!

Papua New Guinea

There was a good view of the Great Barrier Reef as Air Nugini flew me towards P.N.G. and the approach was exciting. The Coral Sea was so blue, with the tree covered mountains, all green and mysterious rising straight out of it up to over 12,000 feet. The meal, however, did not arrive until we had started our descent to Port Moresby. I felt bolshie enough to insist on finishing it as we taxied in! My seat companion had been Neil, an Aussie working in P.N.G. He told me of worrying fears of escalating violence and crime in Moresby, but I doubted if it was worse than Lagos. Actually it was much less of a problem.

On Neil's advice I booked into the Airport Hotel, which was nice, with a superb pool, where I met Moses Yamaga, the Security Supervisor, who was very keen to show me around – my mistake I think in tipping him four Kina too quickly! Actually this is not a fair comment, as he was very friendly, well informed and helpful. He began to teach me some 'Tok Pisin' (pidgin). I had wanted to fly into the interior, as there were no roads up-country at that time, but all flights were fully booked, so I settled for a rental car. There were no effective tour operators, - what a difference from Cairns and Darwin! The atmosphere in the Airport hotel was rather West African, i.e. a bit chaotic, but with an overlay of Australia. The men were very dark skinned. They all seemed to be short and stocky, with broad powerful jaws and mostly bearded. Most looked as if their Fathers had been Headhunters – their Grandfathers almost certainly were! Moses explained that these men were Highland – interior – stock, come to the coast to work. They had a similar build to police officers from the Solomon Islands whom I had met at the Police College. After a good swim I had dinner by the side of the pool with a beautiful view of distant wooded mountains. I later found that P.N.G. was very green and wooded, jungle I suppose is a better description. Dusk came very quickly and with it the mosquitoes, so a hasty change into trousers and a long sleeved shirt! The hotel had quite strict dress regulations, no shorts even by the pool after 6 p.m.!

My rental car next morning was a quite nice Toyota, but there was no map to be had and no road signs. Driving was on the left, but in very African conditions. I stopped to ask the way to Sogeri from a group of men lounging by a hut, obviously unemployed. Three piled into the back – this could have been another step too far! However, they put me on the right road, and then asked for the bus fare back. Don't know how long they had to wait for one, but they seemed happy enough, and all spoke enough English and combined with the pidgin already learned from Moses we were able to have a conversation, of sorts. When they got out I discovered that one had been sitting on my wallet! The road was quite delightful, with lots of hairpins as it climbed up the Laloki River Gorge, with sheer cliffs on either side. It then entered the Varirata National Park, with views of high mountains, the Owen-Stanley Range.

I diverted to the Bomana War Cemetary, where the white military gravestones of four and half thousand Allied troops, mainly Australian and Papuans stand in disciplined straight lines. The names of many members of the Royal Papuan Constabulary whose bodies were never found are inscribed, with numerous others, on a rotunda. After about 8 km I reached the Park HQ where the walking trail started to four lookout points, Gares, Variramongare, Varira rata and Lifiliwasowaso. Very evocative names. Thick jungle to start with, and oh for a tape recorder! Shrieks, crickets, birds and 'what can that be?' The muddy undulating path was on the edge of an escarpment, with good views to the coast and the tall office buildings of Port Moresby, and the high mountains from each viewpoint. There was a tree house that had been used by the ancient Koiari tribe, about sixty feet from the ground, reached by a primitive ladder tied with rattan, and a platform of split bamboo pieces. A great view of tree tops! The houses were originally used as sentry boxes, to see and warn of an enemy approach.

A good two hour hike got me back to the car, then I continued on to the Sogeri plateau, the sealed road now becoming a gravel and murram track. I had a lunch of bananas from a roadside stall and then decided to have a go at finding the Kokada Trail, used by Allied troops in World War 2, where they defeated the Japanese, and Hombrun's Bluff. No signs but found the track with a bit of persistence. The driveable track came to an end, so I walked on for a while, and came to the edge of the Bluff, where I found a nice little family living in a stilted house right on the edge of the steep drop. A ladder led up to the living place, open fronted for coolness, with a few chairs and a table in the shade under this deck. The house – I'm sure home built, was a mixture of local wood and corrugated iron, not very beautiful, but functional. The family that I met were two twins, twelve year old Noreen and Jackson, their older sister Aileen and her baby. No sign of Mum or Dad. They were pleasant people, Jackson in particular speaking good English. I think that they were as surprised to see me as I was to find them. After a chat I took photographs which turned out to be really good ones, and again, as in the Sudan, I wished that I had one of the old Instamatic cameras or that modern digitals had been invented so that I could show them how they looked.

Returning to the Hotel, I met up with Moses, who gave me a guided tour of Port Moresby The town was founded by Captain John Moresby RN in 1873, and named after his Father and in 1994 had a population of 150,000. It was the main base for the defence of northern Australia against the Japanese in World War 2, who had invaded New Guinea and Papua. Since the war it had developed a reputation as a dangerous place, and from the areas I saw with Moses it looked as if that could be justified. Again, the ambience was West African and I doubted if it was worse than Lagos. The harbour, identified by Captain Moresby as a naturally protected one was very busy. The day was finished off with a floodlit swim and dinner by the pool. A very good day. Next morning started early with a swim in the hot sun – this was 22nd January! Moses guided me around a bit more of the town, and when he had to go to work I started to drive wherever a side road would take me. I ended up in Tobugeria fishing village, where there had just been a wedding in the Baptist Church. I poked my nose in, nobody minded and I was invited to photograph the reception. The bride wore a traditionally English white dress and the men were in dinner jackets. The photographs show some nice looking ladies smiling at me, and the children were certainly intrigued. I understood that the food was provided by the whole village. The wooden church actually had a small steeple, and was painted white. The village was quite pretty, if one ignored the piles of rubbish. No bin lorries?

Many of the houses were on stilts, and this continued out to sea, where they rose out of the water for a hundred yards from the beach. It was very similar to the houses in the water at Inle Lake in Burma, but here they formed streets, with pathways of wooden planks, also on stilts between the houses. OK as long as the sea stayed calm I guess. Kids were, of course, showing off, with little brown bodies splashing merrily around. Outrigger canoes were drawn up on the twisted mangrove shoreline – this was Saturday. Further inland bright red bougainvillea bushes coloured the scene, and with a couple of bottles of lemonade from the village Trading Store I sat for an hour and let it wash around me. This was good – what I had hoped to find.

Back to the Hotel for another floodlit swim and poolside fish dinner, an excellent Barramundi. The waiter, who spoke very good English told me that he also spoke 35 of the 700 different P.N.G. languages! This had again been a very good day, and although I did not reach the Central Highlands felt that I had now had a good experience of the culture and life. Also a little idea of what it had been like to fight the Japanese over those hills and jungle. Next morning started well with a swim and a poolside breakfast then Moses and I drove out of town to the Brown River, where again the kids were showing off, more little brown bodies jumping off high bridges into the muddy water. We then went to the P.N.G. Museum, a good experience again of culture and history, with fierce masks, feathered headdresses and figures in full anatomical detail! My flight was late afternoon, so I checked in the car and said goodbye and thanks to Moses – in Pidgin of course! Papua had been great – expensive but I had done a lot in a very short time, and seen many new things.

Back to Oz

Flying back to Cairns I found a backpacker's hostel on the Esplanade, which was garish with bright lights and quick-eateries, but interesting. I caught the Seastar at 7 a.m. for a voyage to scuba dive at the Great Barrier Reef. A marvellous day, starting with a three hour ride on very rough seas. Some people were sick, but I had learned the technique of keeping my eyes fixed on the distant horizon. This tricks the brain in forgetting the motion, and it worked! The instruction about Scuba diving was very professional, with a medical for those who were taking part. We stopped first at Michaelmas Cay, a tiny flat island full of sea birds - a bit like the Farnes, then snorkelled from a small boat. There was then a training scuba dive down to about 24 feet. I coped well enough to be allowed to do a second dive to 35 to 45 feet.

After lunch on board we went on to Hastings Reef and jumped straight in and down to about 30 feet and stayed for about thirty minutes. The coral was not quite as good as in the Red Sea or at Eilat, but still very colourful, with hundreds of brightly coloured fish wearing football shirts, some quite big. It was also enjoyable to be able to say that I had swum with sharks, even if only the small reef variety. Probably big enough to remove parts of your anatomy though – but they don't, or didn't that day! It was very very rough on the way back to Cairns, during which we were given a certificate and invited to buy a video of the diving. One of the other divers was Mike, from Stourbridge, a former member of Halfpenny Green Parachute Club. Small world, again. Finally to end a pretty good day: I saw a flying fox while having a meal on the Esplanade.

Next day, Tuesday, 24th of January `94 was also terrific, with a coach trip to the mountains behind Cairns to Rainforest Station, where some aboriginal boys taught people how or try, to throw a boomerang. I could do it reasonably well, finding it was much like throwing a cricket ball. I still prize the remark, 'Man, what tribe do you come from?' These were smart intelligent young men, so different to the drunken wrecks roaming the streets of Darwin and Cairns. Then onto an amphibious DUKW, ex-army, built in 1940 in Michigan, for a ride through the rainforest with a commentary about the different trees, and forest flora being pointed out. A bonus were a couple of kangaroos in the bush.

Then onto the lake to see big turtles, eastern water dragons and twenty five foot long pythons. Regrettably the latter were shy and did not appear, but gee, you can't have everything! Next stop was Kuranda Village where some Abo dancers in traditional war paint provided a pretty wonderful photograph. The Kuranda Scenic Railway returned to Cairns on a one and a half hour journey down the Barron Gorge, with spectacular views of the forested mountains and gorges from the observation platforms on each coach. The bridges over the gorges were apparently built from meccano and scaffolding, but they did the job! The railway was built in the 1880's, virtually by hand and largely by Irish navvies. It had become necessary as the tin miners on the plateau were often isolated and starving, with impassable roads. After nine years, landslides and thousands of tonnes of earth moved by handpicks and shovels, it was opened in 1891. The length was 75 km, and it climbed over a thousand feet.

My arrival at Cairns was also good as I found that my wait-listed seaplane flight was on after all for that evening. Rushed to the Marina to catch another De Haviland Beaver on floats, as I had found on Vancouver Island. The pilot was a very ancient warrier, who after hearing (of course) of my flying history let me sit up front with him, and put the other three passengers in the back. Yes, I know, but sometimes one has to make one's own good fortune! The short flight, to Green Island, on the inner reef, was great – over the blue Coral Sea to the tiny cay, which is green with lovely white beaches all round it. It is a resort for the resort of Cairns!   So tiny that I had time to walk all round it, buy Dave the pilot a beer and still be back in Cairns for a Hawaiian fish meal in the Pier Mall, looking out on five pelicans on the beach. Another really wonderful day and I was sorry to be leaving Cairns so soon. But, there were many more places to see!

My flight to Alice Springs next day was at 12 noon, so with a relaxed morning I phoned home and woke Jo up. This was the first time that I had got the timing wrong, but no doubt I was anxious to share the experiences of the last few days. Cairns to Alice was 900 miles; after the blue sea on take off and the rain forested hills and tableland, nothing but red and grey desert with straight-line fences and a few wriggly tracks for two hours. We overtook a thunder squall, preceded by a dust storm. After landing it arrived, despite the fact that it is one of the driest places in the world. It is also one of the hottest, and walking out of the air-conditioned airport terminal was really like sticking your head inside a hot oven. The temperature was 43 degrees, and opening the window of the airport bus let in a blast of hot air – it was much cooler with it closed, even at 40 mph. Toddy's was a backpacker bunk house, six to a room with a pool and a Barbie. Very Australian, free and easy, but just what I wanted. Walking into Alice that evening it was still very, very, hot, but more pleasant than, say, Jakarta, as it was a dry heat. There was a modern mall and shops, but I was sad to see the Abos wandering around, apparently with nothing to do, and, I think, looking for a drink or a handout. I felt that they had been abandoned by both local and National Government. Despite it being quite late I was able to book a camping trip to Ayers Rock. Try to do that in the UK!

Once again the pick-up early next morning was on time and efficient. There were ten in the party, half of whom were from the UK! Two Nurses from Newcastle, a Farmer from Ludlow, a girl from Shrewsbury and myself. Bill the leader was the mythological Aussie outbacker - he did not seem properly dressed without a beer in his hand. Bill stopped for us to look at a Thorny Devil by the side of the road, which looks exactly how it sounds, but not big enough to be worrying!

He then ran a competition for the first one to spot Ayers Rock, but with a catch. I won, but the catch was it was Mount Connor. Not Ayers Rock, but quite similar. The correct name for the Rock is Uluru, the Aboriginal name. This is very similar to Europeans and the ignorant media referring to Chomolungma/Sagarmatha as Mount Everest, but I am really pleased to see that the Australian Government has decided that it should be officially known as Uluru/Ayers Rock. Well done Australia. After a five hour drive we reached our camp site in Uluru National Park for a Barbie lunch, then continued to the Olgas, a series of 36 domed mountain humps, west of, and just a little higher than the Rock. They are now correctly named KataTjuta/Olgas.

They reminded me of Kassala Mountain in Sudan, as they jumped straight out of the desert, but were red – very red in the setting sun, as is Uluru itself. Climbing on them was forbidden, but we had a good two hour walk through the red canyons, then returned to Uluru to watch the sun setting behind it. This was really spectacular, the huge sandstone rock glows a fiery red, almost as if illuminated from within then becomes silver as the light fades. The substantial crowd watching were, I think, awestruck. This was the counterpoint to watching the sun rise over the mountains of Saudi Arabia, from the top of Mount Sinai, which Al and I were to experience a few years later.

We were in a tented campsite at the modern Ayers Rock Resort, and after a good meal cooked by Bill, and plenty of beers, I tried sleeping outside. It was beautifully warm enough, but with the dark had come the insects, so the tent was better! Up at 4 a.m. for those who wanted to climb up the series of tethered ladders to reach the top in more or less cooler weather. This was not climbing as such, but just an hour long slog up to over a thousand feet. There were several notices put up by the Aboriginal Council of the owners of the land, the Anangu and Yankunytjatjara Tribes, asking visitors to respect the fact that the Rock is a Holy site to them. I found them rather sad and poignant since thousands – millions - of visitors take no notice, neither it seems do the tour operators. The Australian Government however, in 2009, considered banning the climbing. Good on yer, Aussies, again!

Eight of our group wanted to climb, but Marie from Switzerland and I decided that we would respect the wishes of the owners and the Tribes who live there. We walked around the complete base of the Rock, and I reckon that we had the best deal, as a bonus for being respectful. There is no view of anything from the top except flat desert all round, and the Olgas, which we had already seen, a few miles away. It was an easy two hour walk, as the Rock springs sheer from the desert, it lies there like a crouching beast, red, light brown or silver according to the sunlight, and the track around it is flat. It was interesting though, passing many Abo Holy Sites that we were asked not to walk upon or photograph. I felt that the Aboriginal Council have a pretty hopeless task to request respect. However, Marie and I did our bit, which I felt that Bill approved of, although obviously he could not comment.

How do I know that there was no worthwhile view from the top? Well, rather wonderfully there was a light aircraft flight available, over Uluru and the Olgas, and feeling that this did not show disrespect but interest, I took it. What a unique bit of land formation the monolith of the Rock and the Olgas are. Like icebergs, the majority of the bulk is hidden below the surface. No wonder that they were felt to be Holy. After this it was a quite hard five hour drive back to Alice. The group had mixed well, all nice people and I kept my mouth shut about my feelings over climbing. It was a good two days, very well run, lots to see and learn, but my credit card had taken a severe beating. I rather wished that I had known the names of those Tribes while learning to boomerang!

Next morning I was up at 3.30 a.m. for a booked balloon flight. We drove out to the take-off site, and got the balloon inflated, but the pilot then decided that the wind was too high, so both the balloon and I were deflated. Pity, and I have never got round to managing one since. Still, to repeat, one cannot have everything, and the two days in Alice had been great – if expensive! My flight to Sydney landed at both Melbourne and Adelaide, my only acquaintance with these two cities. They looked pretty good from the air.

Kulwant and Mohinder had travelled from Tasmania to meet me at the airport, and this was wonderful to see them after so many years. We went to the Navy quarters of their son Roshan and his wife Esta, and found a very Australian house-warming party going on next door; in other words plenty of beer. I got to bed about 2.30 a.m., almost 24 hours since getting up in Alice! We took the city train line to Paddy's Market next morning, an efficient system, partly underground. Paddy's is not just a Market, but also an Australian Icon! It has been a feature of Sydney life since the early years of the 19th Century, and was also a fairground site. Why it is called Paddy's is a bit obscure, but there was one in Liverpool, and with 40,000 convicts being transported direct from Ireland, plus those of Irish descent from England it is not really a surprising name! It was certainly a great place to visit. We then went to Circular Quay, with its wonderful view of Sydney Bridge and the Opera House. We had lunch in a Thai Restaurant in China Town, which is very much like China Town in San Francisco - just the other side of the Pacific! The Opera House was open to visitors, and we also were able to walk onto Sydney Bridge with magnificent views of the harbour and bay. The Opera House is, of course, better than everything that has been written about it, I don't think that words can do justice to the inspired design. To continue a pretty good day we strolled to the Royal Botanic Gardens, which can only be described as beautiful, even though I am not a garden enthusiast. I think that the snatches of views of the teeming very blue harbour made it for me. It was probably at this point that I fell in love with Sydney! Considering that it was founded as a penal colony it is a pretty nice place!

The next few days were also marvellous. On Monday we drove up to Katoomba National Park, in the Blue Mountains, about fifty miles inland from Sydney. More spectacular views of gorges, sheer cliffs, rainforest and mountains that were really blue, although tree covered. The blueness is in the atmosphere. I enjoyed a walk on my own along the cliffs, then joined Kulwant and Mohinder for a Devonshire cream tea – a very traditionally English summer pastime! We finished yet another very good day with a meal outside Roshan's house, a long philosophical discussion and a phone call to Jo so that she could talk to Kulwant and Mohinder. On Tuesday we drove south for an hour and a half along the coast road to Wollongong, with many bays, very white sand and white breakers rolling in from the blue sea. Sublime Point was well named. On Wednesday Mohinder was due to give a long reading at the Sikh Temple where I met other Sikhs and the Leaders. Then we took the train to Circular Quay, went to a Guitar performance in the Opera House and then one of the world's great Ferry rides to Manley Beach. Definitely on a par with Staten Island in New York and the Star Ferry in Hong Kong. Have I been lucky, or what?

Back in the city, the Centrepoint Tower, at over one thousand feet from sea level in the Harbour was the tallest building in the Southern Hemisphere. It has since been overtaken by towers in Kuala Lumpur, but is still no pygmy, and had to be visited. The lifts reach the top in 40 seconds, not a bad rate of climb! The view from the Observation Level really was fantastic, from Wollongong in the south to the Blue Mountains in the west and the magnificent Harbour, with its almost continual fleet of white sailed boats almost below. The Restaurant revolves, and Mohinder, who had never been there before was fascinated. We stayed until it got dark to see the city lights around us come on. The tower is again comparable to New York, the view at night of 'fireflies' – actually air liners, below similar to those seen from the top of the Empire State Building.

The next morning we took our trip to Bondi Beach, that I mentioned earlier. To be honest, I did not find it too different to Perranporth, except that the weather was so good. Good weather is much more plentiful at Bondi than in Cornwall! Friday was the end of my stay in Sydney, and it was with mixed feelings that I caught the flight to Auckland. I wanted to see New Zealand, but Australia had been great everywhere, and particularly with the wonderful hospitality from Kulwant and family and the beauty of Sydney. They saw me off and gave me a small kangaroo – inanimate fortunately! I did not see them again for a number of years, but fortunately that did happen eventually, in Wolverhampton!

New Zealand

Aotearoa, the Land of the Long White Cloud, is unquestionably the most beautiful country out of the many that I have been lucky enough to visit. It is also perhaps the most civilised, although having so many isolated areas that lend themselves to remoteness and adventure. It is also a fact that it is the only country in the world to have had women simultaneously in all the main positions of inflence. The Queen, the Prime Minister, the Speaker of the House of Representatives, the Chief Justice and the CEO of the largest company, Telecom NZ, all during 2005-6. No doubt some people would find that relevant! New Zealand is also one of the most comfortable to live in, with an area a little bigger than that of the UK, but only 4.3 million inhabitants (2008 population statistic-much less in 1994). However, Aukland, my first stopping place, whilst still an enjoyable city in a beautiful location, suffered a little in comparison with Sydney – but then I thought, and still think that at that time Sydney was virtually incomparable.

Before leaving home I had arranged to contact the NZ International Police Association representative, Norah Crawford, a retired and widowed police officer. She was a lovely person, very hospitable and pleased to meet me, and we corresponded for years afterwards, until her death. We had several meals together. Norah arranged for me to meet Bob, also a retired Officer, and he and his wife Hilda drove me around Aukland, with some great views of the city from the rim of an extinct volcano, a Maori sacred place. I was also able to get a ferry to Waiheke Island in Hauraki Gulf Bay. This was beautiful and peaceful, and it was good to sit for a time looking north across the blue South Pacific to Great Barrier Island. It was strange to think that I was almost exactly opposite Scotland, as, apart from the colour of the water, the scenery was like that of the Lower Clyde, and Arran. I completed two walks with splendid views, in weather much like an English Summer, cool when cloudy but hot in the sun. Norah had also arranged for me to meet Keith Riley, an officer of the Auckland Police Traffic Department, who was able to show me, using his patrol car, a bit more of Auckland from the Traffic Police point of view, and also to visit his Headquarters. I noticed that there were a lot of quite elderly English cars around – Morris Minors, Morris 1100s and Avengers, which added to the 'English' feel of the city.

On Monday 7th February I rented a Toyota Corolla and was onto a good road south by 9.30 a.m. This was through lush, rolling, farming country, with mountain ranges on the skyline. As the weather was warm but not hot it felt a little like driving through Lowland Scotland or Mid-Wales on the best of British days! By 12.30 I was at the Wautoma Cave system and took a boat ride into the spectacular Glow-worm and Armani Caves. Another beautiful two-hour drive on virtually empty roads took me to Rotorua, the 'Thermal Wonderland'. The hills had become more and more volcanic in appearance and three or four miles out the smell of sulphur became obvious. It was a very pleasant town, on the edge of the lake of the same name. Rotorua was a bit like Cairns – too much to do! I settled on a 'Mud and Mountain' trip for next morning, found a bed and went for a Hang-Maori meal and Were Hake war-dance and war-chant display. The concert party contained some very pretty Maori girls and handsome big men. They did the vigorous stamping and shouting and the tongue display, the Haka, which the All Blacks use on the rugger field and then the Honga, noses touched - touched, not rubbed! It was a bit touristy, but nicely ended another very good day.

The pick-up next morning, was, as in Australia, on time and efficient, using a big Toyota 4 Wheel Drive. The driver/leader was Darren, who was all of twenty one and obviously fancied himself as a Whiz-Kid, but who did know how to drive it. The 'Mud' part of the day was in Wai-O-Tapu, the New Zealand Thermal Wonderland. Apart from Darren and myself there were six others, one German, two Americans, two Danes and a Canadian. We started by being on time for the Lady Knox geyser, which erupts daily at 10.15 a.m.! It is a hot chloride spring, discovered in 1893 by prison labourers trying to wash their clothes. They were amazed when, after soaping their clothes, it violently erupted, taking their clothes with it! The soap disperses an upper layer of water in the underground pool, allowing the super-heated steam and lower water to erupt. In 1903 Lady Knox, the daughter of New Zealand's Governor General soaped it, hence the name. It is spectacular, but I was rather disappointed to find that it had to be bribed to perform! We walked through the thermal area, having to keep to signed and guide-railed tracks. Since the area is full of boiling pools of mud and steaming fumeroles this is a good idea! The visitor can see only a small part of the area, which covers 18 square kilometres, and is full of magnificent colours from the different chemical elements. The colours included yellow, red, purple, white, orange, green and black, from sulphur, arsenic, iron oxide, manganese, silica, antimony and carbon. Must be a painter's delight. We then saw the sulphurous collapsed crater of Devil's Home, and had a swim in a hot and cold pool – hot on one side, cold on the other, with two inlets. It was important to keep heads out of the water, obviously!

The Mountain part was struggling part way up Tarawera Mountain, a still active volcano which last erupted in 1886, burying the village of Te Wairoa. Struggling, because it really was, even in the 4WD Land Cruiser. As we were not yet clear of the mud we all had to help with a push from time to time. Abandoning the car eventually we climbed to the shattered peak and crater rim from where there was an excellent view to the coast and Mount Edgecombe, another volcano that had been recently active. We all then did a scree run into the crater, about 300 metres down, led enthusiastically by Darren. I was quite pleased to keep up as the others were all in their twenties. This was steep and exciting, but hard on the feet! Lunch was in the 'Mud and Mountain' jungle camp, which they kept hidden from other tour operators, and was followed by a jungle walk with bush-craft instruction thrown in, passing more boiling mud and sink holes. Next a view of Angel and Tarawera Falls, which emerge through the side of a cliff from their underground course. This led to a swim in the river that leaves the Falls. Four of us did this for several hundred yards downstream. It was cold, but crystal clear and fast flowing. It was quite deep and as wide as the Severn at Bridgnorth, say 30 to 40 yards. It was enjoyable to look up to the sheer cliffs on either bank while floating downstream on my back.

Finally a drink together in Rotorua when we got back at 8 p.m. after a long day. It had been a very good wilderness trek and the Company lived up to the claims in their brochure, which ended, 'It's Wicked, Mate!'

I was able to get a flight from Rotorua to Queenstown on South Island with Air NZ. The views were spectacular in gin-clear visibility – the blue sea, wooded mountainous fiords to the north, then the snow capped Southern Alps coming into sight. As we arrived at Queenstown by 3.30 p.m. there was time for a longish walk by the side of Lake Wakatipu before finding a bed for the night in a backpacker's hostel. Queenstown is a place with everything to do, quite beautiful, sited on the northern shore where the 52 mile long mountain-walled lake does a double dogleg. The town, like Cairns and Rotarua, is totally given over to tourism with challenges to do this or do that or do both shrieking out from every window and street corner! No problem in finding a bed in a back-packer bunk-house, four to a room, and as there was plenty of light left took the 'sky lift' up to 2,500 feet on Bob's Peak. This gave a superb view of the blue lake, which changed magically to green as the sun went down. With mountains all round, and the snowcapped Southern Alpine peaks of Mount Cook and Mount Tasman on the northern horizon this was a view to die for.

At 7.30 a.m. next morning the pick-up outside the bunk house was, once more, on time and efficient. This was a coach to travel through Fiordland to

Milford Sound, the fiord from the Tasman Sea which is the most renowned for its mountain scenery, seals, dolphins and penguins. The whole of Fiordland is beautiful, with ice carved valleys, waterfalls and unusual birds and animals. New Zealand was formed when, over a hundred million years ago, it broke away from the huge ancient continent of Gondwanaland. As it became an isolated island there were no large predatory animals. Consequently many birds gave up flying or developed strange characteristics and sizes. Despite man bringing in predators such as rats, cats and ferrets, non-flyers still exist like the famous kiwi and moa. Also still existing is the lizard-like descendant of the dinosaurs, the tuatara.

We travelled along the shoreside of Lake Wakatipu, under the ridge of the 8,000 feet 'Remarkables' and through lush rolling country of sheep farming with glimpses of wapiti and deer. Also seen, demanding attention and strutting around at our coffee stop was a Kea, the mountain parrot indigenous to the Alpine areas of South Island. They are called cheeky, being known for their intelligence and curiosity, and are quite capable of working out what best to steal - this one looked it! The Otago Peninsula was settled by many people of Scottish descent, and almost every name had a Scottish ring - Dunedin, Invercargill, Atholl, Lammerlaw, but mixed with Waikouaiti or Hauroko from the Maoris. There was even a Snowdon, but at over 5,170 feet it is a bit higher than the original!

Other names were very evocative - Bligh Sound, Preservation Inlet and Doubtful Sound on the Tasman Sea coast. At Mossburn - this must be from the Scottish settlers - the coach turned north west towards Lake Te Anau, and I was at the most southern point of my round the world journey. Rather a sad marker in retrospect, but this was all so beautiful that it was impossible to be sad about anything. After the lake we were below really big mountains with snowcaps and icy glaciers, and in towering beech forests. In a true rainforest like these, the trees grow on rock, and are nourished by water and sunlight.

We climbed up through the mountains to the Homer Tunnel, which had been cut through solid rock for nearly a mile, then descended to Milford. It was only accessible on foot, taking three days over the mountains until they built the tunnel. Named after Milford Haven, the small town stands at the head of Milford Sound, which opens into the Tasman Sea. To get there it passes glaciers, high waterfalls, sheer cliffs with fur seals swimming, diving and sunning themselves on the rocks, and dolphins swimming in front of the boat. Penguins also live there, but they were shy! There was also the spectacular view of a very lovely mountain, the conical Mitre Peak, rising to nearly sixteen and a half thousand feet sheer from the icy blue/grey water of the fiord. The North Face of Mitre Peak is a contender for the disputed title of the highest sea-cliffs in the world! The fiord is called Piopiotahi, 'a single thrush' because of a legend that a thrush flew there to mourn it's partner. This was a really great two hour fiord cruise, with a coach ride back to Queenstown on a lovely clear and blue-skyed evening. Views of the Eyre, Livingstone, Franklin and Stuart mountain ranges - Scottish again - many of which were snow capped. Passing under the 'Remarkables' again, this was truly a Remarkable day.

I treated myself to a private room for the night in 'McFee's Hotel' and walked around this pretty, lively town again, looked up to the floodlit Restaurant on the top of Bob's Peak and watched the Earnshaw, a really lovely old fashioned steamboat come in to the jetty. As dusk was falling the mountains all round the lake were silhouetted against the setting sun on one side and the last rays lit up the eastern mountains on the other. A beautiful evening, finished off with a pleasant chat with a Korean man on the jetty, and the best fish and chip supper ever!

Next day was another first! By coach to the Shotover River canyon, the world's richest gold producing river. Gold was discovered in 1855 and is still mined there today. The Shotover jet boats are very fast, specially designed with no external propeller. Water is drawn in from the bottom of the boat than driven out with great force by an impeller. This result in high speed with direction controlled by a swivvling nozzle so that the boat can spin in it's own length. This, believe me, is exciting! Power came from a Chevrolet V8 engine running on LPG. Ten people were in each of the two boats, going through the canyon at 40 to 45 miles an hour and just missing the rocks on either side. Photographs show all the women screaming - and some of the men!

The ride lasted about forty minutes and was all that it was advertised to be to be - as everything else in New Zealand had been, so far. I was so hooked on this that on arrival back at Queenstown I booked another ride - for an hour this time, with one other passenger, on an Alpine jet boat on the lake and the Kawarau River. This was faster than the Shotover jet, as there was more room to throw it about, and very choppy on the lake. The boat bounced well, which was a bonus. Having already taken two jet boat thrills before 3pm I was picked up to do some white water surfing on the Kawarau River. (Queenstown is exactly that sort of place - don't let a minute escape in idleness!) Fitted with a wetsuit, flippers, life jacket, helmet and surfing board, one was well prepared. Again, as was becoming usual, I was the oldest in the team of ten people, but I coped with the four pretty rough rapids fairly happily. It was yet another first! We travelled downstream for about 7 km, and there was no photography of course, but I was able to buy a video, shot from the bank, which looks quite dramatic.

I was back in Queenstown for, believe it or not, the 7.30 p.m. sailing of the T.S.S. Earnshaw an ancient but beautiful steamer, all brass and polished wood, that plies around Lake Wakatipu. It was built in 1911 to supply remote places on the lake. This was yet another pleasure, nowhere on the boat was out of bounds, and it had been maintained, cleaned and polished to perfection. It was dusk as we returned to Queenstown, with the mountains silhouetted blackly this time in contrast to the dark blue sky. I had been on the water all day, one way or another, including three totally new experiences and totalling a wonderful day, so I finished with another excellent fish and chip supper!

I had seen notices offering flights over Mount Cook from Queenstown, and felt that while I was there it could not be missed. Obviously the weather was critical, but once more I was lucky. My three fellow passengers were a family from Hong Kong, whose small son had not seen snow before. The flight, in a Cessna 185 on skis was very professional and could not have been bettered. Although I had flown on skis before it was another first to land on a glacier - the Tasman Glacier, at about 6000 feet. Dave the pilot, who knew people that I knew at Coventry Airport, flew very close to the mountainsides, but it was a calm clear day, making this possible and enjoyable. I was familiar with the Cessna, having flown this version at Halfpenny Green, and the landing did not seem to pose any problems, although it could certainly become quickly impossible if conditions changed. I noticed that Dave put a sort of anchor on the tailwheel to stop the aircraft leaving us behind and sliding down the glacier! The peaks of Mount Cook form a rough circle around the head of the glacier, and Dave was able to get close to many of the gullies and faces by a bit of twisting and turning, which was really interesting flying. The same can be done near the Shropshire Hills, but not so dramatically, and with more chance of scaring the wildlife! Mount Cook is a big lump of rock, with three summits, the highest reaching over 12,300 feet. It was first seen by Abel Tasman the explorer. The Maori name Aoraki, meaning 'Cloud Piercer' has been incorporated into the official name, which I think is a good thing, in the same manner as at Uluru/Ayers Rock. Mount Cook Ski Planes is a part of Air New Zealand, and still operates the only aircraft permitted to land on the glacier, so I was very lucky to be able to do this. The future held that I was going to be unlucky not to reach Everest Base Camp in 1995, but very fortunate to have been on a glacier only a year previously.

The Tasman Glacier is 29 km long and as much as 4 km at it's widest. The greatest depth is estimated as 600 metres. What a lot of ice. But, if global warming continues it is estimated that it will have disappeared in less than twenty years - perhaps much earlier. The 7km X 2km by 245metres meltwater lake at the foot of the glacier was not there in 1973 and scientists believe that the glacier will now disappear into it. This is a terrible thing that we are now having to accept as a fact.

New Zealand held one final new experience before leaving, but for this I had to fly back to Rotorua and pick up my car from the Airport. There was then a very pleasant drive to Whakatane, south of the Coromandel Peninsula, where swimming alongside dolphins was virtually guaranteed in The Bay of Plenty. The Bay runs from Coromandel to Cape Runaway. I was rather intrigued with the latter name, wondering if there was a story hiding there about a slave's desperate bid for freedom. No, the name was bestowed by Captain James Cook, who fired a cannon at a Maori canoe that had approached too closely. Not surprisingly they ran away!

Having made contact with 'Dolphins Down Under' and found a rather splendid old fashioned house now being turned into a Bunk House, a Spanish barman appeared who was very delighted to talk about Europe. Maybe he was homesick. I walked to the edge of the Pacific and looked out at the vast expanse of water. A plaque inscribed with the fact that 1000 million people live in the countries bordering the Ocean sits on the shore of the Pacific. It was named for calmness and perhaps suggests that we should pray for peace. The tiny waves breaking on the shore here are a reminder of the vast distances and power implicit in this ocean. Whakatani was the site, at the Pohaturoa Rock, sacred to the Maoris, of the 1840 Agreement of Waitangi which at least tried to give them some rights. There were small islands out in the Bay. Whakaari/White Island is volcanically active, and displayed a distinct cloud of steam that evening. It was therefore another reminder of the power in and under this ocean. I walked back to the Bunk House in a rather thoughtful mood.

Today, Sunday 13th February was the first day that everything had not gone like clockwork and perfectly to plan in New Zealand. Despite the 'guaranteed' result the Bay of Plenty was very deficient in dolphins. The guys running the boat said that they could not understand it! I and several other hopeful swimmers stayed out in the boat all morning and then tried again in the afternoon, but there was not a whisker of a dolphin to be seen. However, it had been such a brilliant week that it would have been quite wrong to be disappointed, and it was a pleasant day in lovely weather on the water anyway. I reluctantly turned in the car next morning in Aukland, and was picked up by Keith Riley - in a police car - and given another tour of the city, before a very pleasant final meal with Norah Crawford and Bob the retired officer and his wife, Hilda. I was pleased to be told that hundreds of dolphins had been seen yesterday off Coromandel! They were all flatteringly interested in what I had been experiencing, and were, I think, very pleased that it had all worked out so brilliantly.

The next leg of the journey was Aukland to Tonga, and I left New Zealand with quite a lump in my throat. The incredible scenery, the nice efficient, well organised people and ordered opportunities and the sense that everything is there waiting to be done, resonated with me very much. It would be ridiculous to say that there is no crime, or unpleasant people or muddle – of course there is, as everywhere, but in my view it is well outweighed by the good bits in Aotearoa, the Land of the Long White Cloud. Because I have travelled and worked abroad a lot I am often asked which, in my opinion, is the nicest or best country in the world. Out of the developed countries, my answer has been, since 1994, and now always will be, with not a flicker of doubt or hesitation, New Zealand. I felt as though I had been there for months, and it was a very wonderful week.

Pacific Islands wandering, Tonga and Vava'u

The Kingdom of Tonga is still well away from the rest of the world. The mountain tops of a drowned continent rise from the iridescent waters of the South Pacific in a cluster of miniature jewels, some of which have been populated since at least a thousand years before the birth of Christ. James Cook named them The Friendly Isles, which I found to be still so true. East of Fiji, west of Tahiti, and perhaps on the same latitude and longtitude as Heaven, the islands stride across the International Date Line, and are the first to see the dawn of each new day. There had been nothing to see but sea since leaving Aukland, twelve hundred miles to the south. It was a long journey.

My Royal Tongan Airlines tiny twin engined aircraft descended into the equally tiny international airport and decanted me into a sauna. There had been much recent rain, so that it was hot and humid. A venerable taxi took me into the capital, Nuku'alofa, which sits in the largest island, Tongatapu. We passed palm trees, chickens, children, pigs, flying foxes but not an advertisment hoarding in sight. Tiny tin and wooden houses led into the centre, where the Royal Palace, also tiny and tinny, adjoins the Pangai, the town football and cricket field. I had not booked ahead, so got a room at Breeze Inn run by a tiny (everything so far seemed to merit that word) Japanese lady. This turned out to be a mistake, as it was a backpacker type hostel, with a bare and very hot room. I walked the short distance to the town centre for a meal in a very friendly and pleasant café, and then retired to the 'Breeze Inn' but not to sleep!

On Wednesday morning I found an air-conditioned room in the Pacific Royale Hotel, and then, as this part of my journey was very much an unscheduled ramble made some enquiries to decide where to hop to next.

Fiji was too expensive, but the Vava'u group of islands were described as wonderful, with the best snorkelling and scuba in the Pacific, and so they were. There was plenty of opportunity to get in some more scuba practice beforehand, so I booked a session with Beluga Diving, run with a one to one ratio from a rubber boat by an energetic Aussie, Matt. The reef, only a little way out from Nuku'alofa, was superb, better than the Great Barrier, with canyons and caves descending to a hundred feet and coral of all colours and shapes, shelving and plate, mushroom, brain coral and the rare and much sought after black fans, plus crowds of inquisitive and colourful fish. With good professional instruction from Matt I stayed at over thirty feet for half an hour, about which he was complimentary and awarded me an initial PADI international scuba proficiency certificate.

I decided to stay on Tongatapu for at least two more nights – no planes to catch, no clocks to worry about! So, on Thursday 17th February I set about organising transport. A scooter seemed to be the best bet, for which I needed a Tongan licence. The main police station was very typical of the developing world, reminiscent of Africa, but much friendlier. It was also very relaxed, as I walked through some open doors into a senior officer's office, where he was sitting with medals and lots of pips! No problem, he showed me to the right office! I still have the licence, which is a treasure, and which I am quite sure is the only one in Wolverhampton and possibly in the Midlands! It was easier to rent a Yamaha scooter, which had no gears, but worked well enough, and to set off to tour Tongatapu. This was not going to be a lengthy journey, as after all this is all on what is really a mountain top! The place to see more flying foxes was at Kolovai, only eleven miles away. There were hundreds hanging from the trees like seagull-sized bats. My friendly taxi driver from the airport had pointed out some in flight, so I did not disturb their siesta, but carried on to Abel Tasman's landing place, marked by a rather beautiful plaque. The first Missionaries also landed here and brought Christianity to Tonga. In 1826 a Weslyan Mission established deep roots in Tonga, initiating a set of laws based on the Ten Commandments and a deep reverence for the extended family. The Royal family led the congregation every Sunday at the time of my visit, and still there is no work or business done that day. Are the Christian principles the reason for the friendliness I wonder, or is it the island's remoteness? I believe it is more likely to be a natural feature of the Polynesian people, since Captain Cook's description pre-dated the Mission. Although there have been mistakes made by the Government in the last twenty years I do so hope that the attitudes and friendliness have not been diluted by increasing travel.

I had passed pretty tended gardens, bright frangipani and bougainvillea, yellow and red flame trees and little wooden houses where everyone waved, and went on to Ha'atafu beach for swim in the very blue warm sea, off a white beach with no footprints except my own. From here I turned the scooter onto the south coast road to see the blow holes, where waves force their way through holes in the hard coral rock, sending geysers as much as fifty feet into the air, creating a wonderful natural spectacle. Got a drink at a little roadside shack here, served by a very friendly good looking girl, who gave me a bunch of bananas and posed for a very giggly photograph! (Most of the girls in Tonga are very good looking!). I was still less than 15 miles from Nuku'alofa, but feeling distant from even that remote town. Then slowly back to the northern coast, to call again on Matt at Beluga Diving, who seemed pleased to see me, and gave me a diving contact on Vava'u. A thirty minute swim and a picnic with bananas under tall palm trees on the waterfront went down well. From here one can look out at many cartoon type tiny islands with just one or two palm trees, and expect to see a marooned shipwrecked sailor launching a bottle into the sea! The National Cultural Centre in Nuku'alofa hosts a kava drinking ceremony - a little bit akin to a Japanese tea ceremony and I went up on the stage to take part in this. It was followed by a buffet of roast sucking pig, octopus, crayfish, clams and beef marinated in coconut oil which was then followed by traditional Tongan dancing (the Lakalaka) and exciting music.

I got a seat right behind the pilot on the Twin Otter to Vava'u next morning. Looking down at the chain of atolls and reefs during the hundred and fifty mile flight the colours were spectacular, the sea navy blue to aquamarine and always snow-white sand. The Vava'u archipelago is part of the Kingdom of Tonga, but different. Life was simple, - people found time to walk, although most modern conveniences existed. It is hillier than Tongatapu, so more picturesque, with glimpses of the blue sea around every corner. Here were about 20,000 people in some of the fifty or so islands, most living in the little town of Neiafu and four villages on the main island of Uta Vava'u. The beautiful harbour at Neiafu was full of yachts and trimarans. Vava'u has been described as the nearest thing possible to paradise, and although I have been lucky enough to see many unusual and beautiful places, I have no quarrel with that description, at that time.

Not surprisingly the only place with vacancies was the Paradise Hotel, on a small hill overlooking the harbour and after booking in I got a lift into the small town, finding the tiny tin roofed Anglican Church of St Andrews and the much grander Cathedral of St Josephs. Given the names, apart from the weather, the scenery, the sea and the people it could have been

Wolverhampton! I fixed a sail in the yacht 'Melinda' for tomorrow and then enjoyed a swim and a meal in company with a young German, Rolfe, who knew Freiburg, Schauinsland and the Feldberg so I could boast about my 'extensive' skiing experience on the latter. (Extensive in terms of falling over). The Hotel was totally laid back, dinner took a long time, but it didn't matter. On my own (Rolfe had probably rumbled my skiing experience) on the terrace with a cigar after dinner completely made up for any minor shortcomings of the Hotel. The sea was molten silver, the palms were whispering, the lights of the little town below twinkled and the stars were bright and clear in a velvet sky. Magic, quite magic.

Next morning brought another new experience, described in my notes as a truly wonderful day. I met John and Julia, partners and the owners and crew of 'Melinda' which is (I do hope still 'is') a fifty foot overall gaff-rigged ketch, like the old Bristol Channel pilot boats. She was built in New Zealand by an Englishman, had a snow-white hull and tan sails, (five when fully rigged) and was very beautiful. Julia is from Surrey and also beautiful while John is a Kiwi, a good guy but not quite so beautiful! I liked them a lot and believe that it was mutual. They were interested in my journey anyway. We left Julia on-shore as she was preparing for a big charter the next day, and got under weigh, using the diesel engine to get out of the harbour. As I was the only passenger John told me to regard myself as part of the crew, and after helping inexpertly to get the sails aloft he entrusted the wheel to me for the rest of the day. There was not much to hit after leaving the harbour!

We had safely passed a Russian cruise ship, the *Odessa* which may have been the one that Jo and I and the Satos had seen disgorging elderly ladies to try on unsuitable saris in Yokahama! Outside the harbour there were many little deserted islands, all fringed with untrodden white beaches, some volcanic, some coral atolls. In fact, it was a riot of colour all round, with the indigo sea, blue sky and tan sails against it and the islands covered by green palm trees. And no noise, just the lap of the waves against the dinghy towed behind us, and no one else in sight. We sailed until lunch time then anchored off an atoll in about ten metres – it had been very deep until then. There were many hues of colour in the water, shading from navy to aquamarine in the shallows over the coral. The atoll, deserted, beautiful and totally isolated was two to three hundred yards away, so John sent me to snorkel to it while he prepared lunch. After a zig and a zag I found it and enjoyed the feeling of being on a desert island without even a Man Friday! On the far distant south east horizon was a volcano, in the area where the mutiny on the *Bounty* had taken place. After about half an hour I got a wave from John, and swam back passing over shoals of damsel fish, moorish idols and butterfly fish, to find a hammock and an orange juice waiting. Lunch was a steak and veg, and a fruit salad after – just right. Then slowly back to Vava'u, feeling that I was more or less getting the hang of the steering. Well, it was a lovely calm day! By now the rapport between myself and John was good enough for him to accuse me of nearly ramming the Russian ship, which we passed again, and for me to accuse him of being a lousy fisherman. He had promised to catch a yellowfin tuna but could not live up to it! The passengers were returning in small boats to the *Odessa* and I admit to feeling very superior to them. John and I walked up to the Hotel, and shared some beers with Rolfe – no alcohol on board *Melinda*. Rolfe, who had a coca-cola franchise in Mannheim, invited everyone to a feast on Monday. To finish the day I spent some time on my perch on the terrace balcony with some enjoyable music and dancing by the side of the pool.

Next morning, Sunday, I made my way to the little St Andrews Church. It was very bare, but surrounded by bougainvillea and frangipani. There were only a few local people and no travellers, but it was a traditionally Anglican communion service, with all the words repeated in Tongan. The priest, a huge man wearing a white robe was Polynesian, and seemed very pleased to welcome me, with thanks for coming and wishes for a good stay. He seemed to be very sincere, and was obviously widely travelled. On Sundays, as in Nuku'alofa, the shops closed down, and I learned that it was not even permissible to swim until very recently. The men were wearing lava lavas, - black or blue kilts – with jackets and ties. After a lunchtime swim in the Hotel pool I was picked up by Patty Vogan who ran Dolphin Pacific Diving. We went out by launch with four other divers. As they were all fully certificated she was able to keep tabs on me, so I got good one to one tuition down to forty feet. A great experience was to go into the underwater entrance of Mariners Cave. It is possible to come up above the surface whilst still inside the Cave, and breathe normally. (For a bit, until the air ran out!) Then on to the Haunted House rock formations and another forty foot dive, with beautiful coral and all the wonderful tropical fish. I had now done five Scuba dives. Like John and Julia, Patty and her husband Grant were nice people, both American. The visibility under water was incredible in that extremely clear sea – as much as thirty metres downwards and many feet horizontally and I enjoyed it tremendously.

Next morning I was picked up by Patty on the beach for some further dives, just myself this time. We went down to fifty feet for the first time, at the Swallows Cave. After a second dive, further out, down for forty minutes I was really feeling that I had got the hang of it. You use the breathing equipment like a throttle, breathing out to descend and inhaling hard to ascend. Patty said that I had the potential to be a very good diver, but don't kick so hard, use your hands more – it worked! The beautiful coral and multi-coloured fish were everywhere again, and it was another and delightful world. That evening was Rolfe's feast at the Hotel, and included Ulie from Stuttgart, John and Julia and myself. Patty and Grant joined us and she was very complimentary about my diving. 'It would be fun to certificate you.' This was definitely not a sales pitch, as they knew that I was moving on to Samoa next day. I liked her very much, and think that it was mutual – 'Don't you dare come back here again without looking us up'. I wish! After Rolfe's feast we all went to the Neiafu Club, not too different to those seen in Africa, with some weird characters, but an amazing fiery sunset over the bay.

Next day, the 22nd of February, by rising early I had time before my flight for one more Vava'u sea experience, by borrowing the Hotel Kayak. Round the bay was another beautiful beach, isolated except for a black and white sea-snake. This was a chance to say goodbye to Vava'u and Tonga privately, goodbye to perhaps the most delightful small place in the world. I said earlier that New Zealand was my choice for the best and nicest of the developed countries, but little Tonga, undeveloped but very civilised, is, I think the most delightful. I left, as I had almost everywhere on this safari, with great reluctance and have never had the chance to return. Perhaps this would not be wise, as I can still see it as it was sixteen years ago, and hope that it has not been changed by us, the visitors, too much.

Why have I not continued scuba diving, as I had reached a certain level of experience? I enjoyed it very much, but could not bear the thought of cold and murky European seas compared to the incredible visibility and warmth of the South Pacific. But, I did use the experience to do some scuba swimming with dolphins in the Red Sea at Eilat in 1999, which was almost as good, as was the snorkelling over the lovely coral at Eilat. It is not possible to appreciate how big and (apparently) friendly dolphins are until you are alongside one! On arrival home from the South Pacific I got one of my friends, a talented artist, to create a cartoon showing all the experiences on Vava'u and sent copies to Julia and Patty. I believe that they were appreciated.

The Samoan Islands

It was only a short hop (for these waters) of about 500 km to Western Samoa – not comparable to the more than 3000 over nothing but sea, to Hawaii! Immediately, even from the airport bus into the capital, Apia, there was an air of greater development than in Tonga and the feeling of a Western influence rather than Australian or Kiwi. The Samoan Island Group was first discovered for the West by the French Navigator Louis de Bougainville (he of the flowers) in 1768. As in Tonga the big influence for change came from Methodist or Wesleyan Missionaries. The Group was split into Western and American Samoa through whaling and USA commercial interests and in 1899 Western Samoa was annexed by Germany. During the First World War Germany was expelled by New Zealand troops, and the island became the first self-governing nation in the South Pacific in 1962.

I found that there was still a strong Western European influence – Heineken in all the Hotels! I got myself a bed in the Kitano Tusitala in Apia, which is on the island of Upolu. Tusitala is from the affectionate Samoan name for Robert Louis Stevenson, the 'teller of tales', who lived there with his family from 1890 until his death in 1894. He wished to be buried at the top of Mount Vaea, and a trek to his tomb was one of my reasons to be here. Apia was a pleasant town of 30,000 population then, now grown to 37,000, and not too much changed I hope. English is one of the official languages, so no problems at all in Banks or shops. Even the policemen wore a uniform slightly reminiscent of England, white helmets, light blue tunics but lava-lavas – blue kilts. I found two who were very happy to be photographed as I walked into the town. As in Tonga, the people all seemed to be good looking, and well built. Perhaps lucky, but I did not see anyone unpleasant looking in either country. I was lucky to be up early enough next morning to see the Samoan Police Band, some twenty strong, followed by a contingent of officers, including four policewomen wearing skirts, not kilts (very different!) marching extremely smartly along Beach road. They were marching to the daily national flag raising ceremony outside the historic Courthouse, where the National Anthem was played. This was an impressive sight, traffic and pedestrians being required to stand still. I would like to see this happen in Wolverhampton, but fear that I shall not. Samoans are proud of their country. I write between the lines here. I was delighted, and surprised, to find that this daily weekday custom still goes on in 2010, and that the police uniforms have not changed.

After photographing the two smiling policemen I drew some money (an ever-growing necessity) from a Bank, later finding that the Bank had telephoned Jo to ask if we knew that our card was being used in Samoa – quite a good service! I then walked along Beach Road to the legendary, very picturesque (and expensive) Aggie Grey's Hotel. It is one of the world's great Hotels, the *Raffles* of the South Pacific, where fresh bananas grow in the verandas and your waiter becomes a fire dancer in the evening. It has a wonderful history, being host to Somerset Maugham, James Michenor, British

Royalty and too many famous Hollywood and British film stars to list. It was where Maugham did some of his writing, in particular *Rain*, the story of a prostitute and a missionary on a South Pacific island that was made into a well known film starring Rita Hayworth. Aggie Grey was herself a very well known lady in the islands, daughter of a Western father and Samoan mother, and the Hotel is still owned and run by her descendants. It is rumoured that Michenor based Bloody Mary from *South Pacific* on her, although she was definitely much uglified in the film!

It had rained hard today, first time I had seen any for weeks, and was very hot and humid, but there was another fiery sunset. I had dinner in a small café, very atmospheric, with cockroaches biting my ankles! I was up at 6.30 a.m. to photograph the police band and breakfasted on fresh, just picked, bananas. By 9 a.m. I was able to book a flight to Pago Pago, in American Samoa, and then started the long and hot walk to Vailima, the house that Robert Louis Stevenson built. The weather was still very hot and humid and I needed a litre bottle of Fanta en-route, arriving at midday. The old house was in considerable disrepair, having been damaged by weather and time, but I was able to contribute to an appeal to help restore it, and I am very pleased that it is now complete and functioning as the RLS Museum. Workmen pointed me towards the bush trail up Mount Vaea, which is only about as high as the Clee Hills in Shropshire, but a great deal hotter and stickier! I met a German guy at the bottom who had given up, which for me was not on the programme.

The RLS tomb was very emotive, with a beautiful view down the 1,800 feet to Apia and the sea in one direction and to the inland hills in the other. Carved on the cement tomb are his lines, 'Here he lies, where he longed to be; Home is the sailor, home from sea, And the hunter home from the hill'. I stayed there a long time, thinking about this man, and his tales, then down the long way, through very wet bush and slippery mud until near Vailima I found the pool and waterfall where he used to swim. It was a great sight after that trail, where I had fallen twice. Three teenage Samoan boys were larking about in it, so I stripped off and joined them, to their great delight, and an offer to share their bar of soap! Then back to the road and through banks of hibiscus and frangipani to the Tusitala for a hot bath: - total safari time six hours, but it was very worth it. That evening there was a Samoan floor show at Aggie Grey's. This was a bit touristy, obviously, but interesting, especially the man walking over blazing coals.

I was up early again next morning to photograph the police band once more; it was difficult to resist more 'photos as they were so serious and proud – but late comers came running to join in today, including bandsmen! The rain had cleared and it was a beautiful morning, so I walked to Palolo Deep where I was able to hire fins and snorkel gear and spent two happy hours on the reef. Then, intending to catch a bus to travel across the island I was approached at the little bus depot by a young Samoan man who, not unusually, asked where I was from and my name. He literally danced with delight in telling me that he was Robert Collins, whose Great Grandfather had been William Collins of Liverpool who married a Samoan girl in 1901. He was delighted to meet a 'relative'. Well, who knows? I later sent him, from home, 'photos of my family, and a map and pictures of Liverpool.

I did not get a reply, so don't know if they ever reached him. The bus to Siumu, on the other side of Opolu was an old crate, very like those in Burma. We crawled around the town, then stopped and everyone got off. I thought that I now had it to myself, but no! Everyone had gone shopping, and all returned carrying a variety of packages, bottles etc. At last we crawled, creaking and groaning, up the steep mountain road, past Vailima, and into clouds and a tropical downpour. After a scheduled thirty minute ride which actually took two hours I found Siumu to be a pretty little village, and walked in very heavy rain to the famous Coconut Beach. This was nice but I only stayed for one beer as it was full of a coachload of fat European tourists. (Yes, I know, but on a solo safari like this one through the South Pacific, I consider myself a traveller, not a tourist). Then still in heavy rain, walked on to Maninoa. This was totally beautiful, unchanged for hundreds of years and surrounded by green, yellow, crimson and white trees, flowers and bushes. Everbody is so friendly, and wants to stop to talk. The rain continues, but so what? No one bothers! Upolu's mountains obviously bring down the rain, probably the reason for the island being so extremely lush, colourful and beautiful. Maninoa was a peaceful, delightful village with a splendid old Catholic Church and many Falas, the traditional Samoan house with thatched roofs and open verandas for coolness. I was able to take a lot of photographs of people, who agreed with pleasure; no suggestion of worry that their souls were being stolen, as in the more remote parts of Africa. Getting the last bus back to Apia I found the Tusitala full of noisy, overbearing and (in my opinion) rather horrible tourists, all wearing leis, the welcoming collar of flowers and looking rather silly in them. Having discovered that they were from the *Odessa* which had followed me from Vava'u, I was now pretty sure that this was the one that we had seen in Yokohama - maybe even the same Russians! Regular annual clients maybe, as happens in the UK! Firmly rejecting a lei I made myself scarce and dined in the cockroach café again, the roaches being better alternative company. I have met some wonderful Russians, but en masse and in tourist holiday mode, solitude was preferable.

Up early to see the flag raising again, then to Aggie Grey's to meet Robert

Collins' sister Lelani, who was one of the staff. She was charming, but I am sure totally confused about who I was and why I was there. Robert had insisted that I must meet her as well! Then to the little airport to catch the Polynesian Airlines Twin Otter, to American Samoa, another small (for these seas) hop of about 200 km. The small aircraft was quite full, and as mentioned before, Polynesian people tend to be not only handsome, but also large. One lady was too big to fasten her seatbelt, and they all had piles of baggage. How does it get off the ground! I guess that a shuttle between Western and American Samoa made a good shopping trip, perhaps with some duty benefit. Anyhow, we did get off the ground, and once more it was a glorious ride, with wonderful views of American Samoa, which has rather higher, very shapely and more dramatic mountains as we approached the island of Tutuila where the capital, Pago Pago is sited. Lata Mountain, the highest is over 3000 metres, no mean hillock.

I was able to get a room at the Rainmakers Hotel, afterwards catching a bus towards Leone on the south coast, and then walked to Scenic Point, allegedly a viewpoint for turtles and sharks. Like the dolphins in New Zealand they were on holiday, but it is a lovely spot. Creamy waves atop a blue blue sea, breaking with a crash onto black volcanic rock against the backdrop of green tree clad mountains. I had a chat to a local man on his way to work at the airport, then watched a cricket match on Vaitongi village green. Cricket, in American Samoa, which I had not seen elsewhere in the islands. I was able to get involved by rescuing the ball that had gone into the sea! The batting was of the haymaker type, but some very good catches were taken, in the deep and behind the wicket. The teams wore white shirts and dark blue lava-lavas. I talked to a lot of people, all very friendly and all wanting to know my name. Friendliness is in fact a known characteristic of the Polynesian people, and I found them pleasant and honest as well, although I had noticed a different reaction by a very few New Zealanders, where the 'islanders' were blamed by some for importing dirt and disease into the country. We have overheard something similar in the UK as well.

I got a local bus to Ilili Village, and talked to a Deacon of the Samoan Christian Church and the 'family' bus back to Pago Pago – no charges on either! After a meal I got a night swim on a deserted beach next to the Rainmakers. There was no phosphorescence, but lying back in the warm water, looking at the lights across Pago Pago Bay, with outlines of the mountains against a full moon was pretty good. Palm trees, pale sand, a whisper of surf, and warm air. Then a walk into town and a beer in Miss Sadie Thompson's Bar (the name of the prostitute from 'Rain') which was a pick-up place if ever I saw one, but denuded of tourists as a cruise ship had departed while I was swimming. I had made the most of this day, ending with finding a lizard in my bed!

Up for a dawn swim on the same beach, still deserted and still beautiful, and after breakfast a bus to Afono scenic pass, with great views 2000 feet down to Pago Pago Bay and town. Decided to walk back down, which had been an inspired choice, as I found a village feast in preparation, with three roast pigs, big ones, each after the roasting decorated with bright flowers, and being carried on a litter by two hefty men. I did not find out why the feast, but it was Saturday, probably another cruise ship was due in. No problem with photographs of the roast nor of the village man with full body tattoos. This is a Polynesian tradition, displaying really intricate designs still observed very much in Samoa, who cling to their traditions, and were lucky not to have been invaded by the Japanese. The American army had a base in Samoa during the Pacific War, and the people of American Samoa are classed as American citizens, but in 1994 their historic traditions were still much alive. Advice to visitors included not to talk or eat in a Samoan home before sitting, not to eat while walking in a village and if chiefs were gathering not to walk past their meeting house while carrying a load at shoulder level. Even an umbrella should be lowered to hip level. It was also advised that heavy labour was avoided on the Sabbath and that it was normal for a ten minute hymn and prayer service to be held in houses each evening. One custom that again had resonance with countries thousands of miles away was that it was impolite when sitting to stretch out one's legs – they should either be folded underneath or covered with a mat. In Arab society it is very rude to point the soles of the feet towards another person.

After this too short visit I caught the twin otter back to Savaii, the biggest island of Western Samoa, with the dramatic mountain views again. The landing was onto a short airstrip, and was too fast and rather bumpy. The young female second pilot apologised, so I told her that I was still trying to get it right after 25 years! I had booked a room at the Ocean View Hotel but took one look at it and decided to try elsewhere, and got a fale of my own on the beach in the grounds of the Savaii Hotel, with a great view across to Upolu island. The owner of the Hotel was English, Roger, who was married to a Samoan lady, and obviously had quite a nice life style! Sunday morning started with a pleasant cup of tea on my veranda, watching the sun rise beyond Upolu, followed by a swim on my own beach. Roger's son then brought me a 4wheel drive Suzuki Samurai for the day – no licence, no paperwork, no deposit! As the centre of Savaii is totally occupied by the volcano Mount Silisili which rises to nearly 2000 metres-not far off 6000 feet - there is no way across the island; all the villages and population are on the hundred mile circular coast road. Silisili's twin peak Mount Afi erupted hugely in the eighteenth century, and the lava flow buried villages on the north coast, ten miles away. I headed west, with really beautiful flowery villages. This was like the south coast of Upolu, not surprisingly, but there was no rain today.

I am conscious that I have overworked the adjective beautiful while trying to describe Polynesia, but cannot find anything more appropriate. People were going to church, women in long white dresses and big white hats. Everyone waved! I had to keep stopping for the view across to Upolu, and then at the dark sand (from lava) beach at Nuu. This was dramatic, blue sea, white surf and black sand, then stopped again at the blow holes at Alofaaga. These were terrific, as the waves crash into the rugged lava cliffs and propel jets of water, like steam, hundreds of feet into the air, with incredible power and noise. A coconut dropped into a blow hole will shoot out with the next blow. A local guy, who was probably waiting there for the opportunity, demonstrated the technique, and fired off several towards Tonga! Carrying on towards the western tip of Savaii, I picked up a local youth, who was apparently hoping for a lift. I think that he was slightly defective and did not seem to know where he wanted to go. He was totally unfamiliar with the concept of a map, as so many local people - all over the world - are. We struggled with this for some time and eventually I dropped him near a local man in one of the villages. There was little English spoken here. The boy then tried to offer me money, with a pathetic search in his ragged bag. I felt bad about leaving him, and hoped that he would get where he wanted to go, but felt that I could not do anything better for him, as he might even have been hoping to go in the other direction.

On the northern coast the sea was an unbelievable shade of pale blue in Asau Bay. Stopping at a shanty advertising Ice Cream and Sprite I noticed a police officer's cap on a shelf inside. This turned out to belong to Inspector Henry Tiata, who was having lunch, very definitely off-duty, wearing only a colourful sarong. I could not decide whether he had just stopped for lunch and borrowed the sarong, or whether this was his home and off-duty source of income! He spoke good English and was happy to chat when I introduced myself to him. I promised to send him details of the International Police Association from home, and did so, but again did not get a reply. Maybe the postal service in Samoa was as unreliable then as ours is nowadays. The road became a rough track after this so I retraced my steps, and picked up more people, without problems this time. It was just as lovely a drive in reverse, and a picturesque white church with a tall tower and surrounded by flowers at Falealupo village made another good photograph. I was back at my fale in time for a chat with Roger's very pretty Samoan wife, a swim, dinner in the

Hotel and a view of the moon rising out of Upolu. It was a golden orange ball, with a track of the same colours stretching back across the Apolima Strait towards me.

Another dawn swim next morning on my private beach, and my extremely relaxed car rental allowed me to keep the Suzuki until I caught the ferry after lunch, so I drove up the north east coast, anti-clock, to see the lava flow that I did not reach yesterday clockwise! This was from the last eruption, recent in geological terms, which buried five villages and half buried churches. This was still very black, hard, rough and utterly desolate and horrible. Back at the Hotel lunch was interesting, as I was watched and fanned by the large female Hotel cook! The little ferry was as crowded as an Indian train, people lying on the deck, as there was no seating to be had for the hour and a half journey. I met the German guy who had failed to reach Stevenson's tomb, and made sure to tell him that I had reached the top. Also bumped into, again, Rolfe, the provider of the feast in Vava'u. We were obviously following an identical wandering path from Aukland to San Francisco! We had another beer. Of course. As we arrived at the ferry terminal I saw a huge Manta Ray swimming alongside the boat – magnified I guess by the refraction of the water. Very impressive though. Rolfe and I joined a party of eight other Germans who were, surprise surprise, having a beer party in the Airport Departure Lounge. This was, I guess, as good a way of any of saying farewell to the Samoas. Although I was now looking forward to getting home, once again I was leaving the friendly islands of Polynesia with genuine regret.

Hawaii

There are about 2,600 miles between Samoa and Hawaii, over, apart from a very few isolated dots of land, nothing but sea. This is when the voyages of the 17th and 18th centuries, in leaky claustrophobic sailing ships, and, centuries earlier, the expeditions in outrigger canoes become vividly real in the imagination. It was about 3.30 a.m. when I was met by Police Officer Maggie Hirakawa at Honolulu airport, on the island of O'ahu. Maggie was the Hawaii representative of the I.P.A., and I had arranged to meet her before leaving home. As it happened she was on night duty driving a patrol car, and asked if I minded if we went to the Central Police Station, before she found me a bed. The Traffic Department was interesting, with a good welcome and everyone was very friendly. Then Maggie had to go to the scene of a fatal traffic collision, and I held her gun belt, pistol and holster by the side of the road, while she and two colleagues looked inside the cars.

By this time the early commuter traffic was about, and, still wearing Samoan beach clothing, (slightly more than swimming trunks, but not much) I did wonder who they thought I was! Maggie was now using her own car, which broke down, but after a bit of chaos we got to her home by 11am, where eventually she rigged me up a temporary bed. Shortly after I was wakened by the tow-truck taking her car away. Later I was awakened by two very small boys, who were extremely intrigued, and needed me to play a Super Mario computer game. Super Mario is not my favourite character! Maggie, if slightly disorganised (not at all surprising with two small boys and a full time job on shifts), was extremely hospitable and helpful, and by that evening had arranged a small flat for me near to Waikiki Beach. I treated her and her Japanese/American husband, also a cop, to a meal in a Japanese Restaurant. I did get the feeling that he was not so welcoming – perhaps he did not like the visitors that she was bound to get as the I.P.A. rep in a place like Hawaii. The I.P.A is very strong in some of the U.S. States, and I am sure that they did get many police officers on holiday, even from Europe. Anyway, we had a pleasant meal, and then I fell into bed with relief. The terms of my flat short rental were extremely good, and I did get a strong impression that anything that the police wanted would be made available.

Next morning Maggie picked me up in her mended car and took me to Pearl Harbour. This was a tremendously evocative visit, and a wonderfully well organised Visitor Centre and Memorial. It is of course, one of the defining areas, and times, of modern U.S.A. history. I was able to talk to a veteran survivor of the attack, and then a Navy boat took us across the harbour to the U.S.S. Arizona Memorial – which is built over the battleship that exploded and sank after a direct hit by a Japanese bomb. It was extremely moving to know that the bodies of the 1,177 drowned sailors were still beneath our feet. Deliberately their final resting place is where they died, and I think that to leave them there was a brilliant decision. You can't forget them. The Memorial commemorates all the personnel killed by the Japanese attack on 7th December 1941 - 2,395 killed and 1,178 wounded. Two other ships, the USS Oaklahoma and USS Utah are still sunken in the harbour. The other eight that were either sunk or beached were salvaged, repaired and later saw action in the Pacific.

Maggie then drove me up into the mountains, from where there are spectacular views of O'ahu island, then left me in the city as she was due on duty. I spent the afternoon on Waikiki Beach, which is beautiful, fringed by both palm trees and skyscrapers. Like the other famous beaches, Bondi, Copacabana, the Riviera, all are urban, and with too many people. I prefer Shell Island, in North Wales, which is actually more beautiful than any, but does not have the weather! I watched a Hula show, and have a note that I was called up on stage to perform, but I have absolutely no memory of this at all – must have blanked it out, or got drunk! Or both.

Next day I did a tour of Police HQ with Maggie, including their Control Room and Union shop, where I bought a T-shirt emblazoned with the SHOPO logo (State of Hawaii Organisation of Police Officers), which has since proved to be of interest in other parts of the world! Lunch was on the sunlit terrace of the police canteen – it seemed that they did themselves pretty well. We then did another tour of the island before she went on duty at 6 p.m. We spent time at the Byōdō-in Japanese Temple, up in the mountains. This was a beautiful building set in beautiful flower filled grounds. I had dinner in a very sophisticated revolving Restaurant at the top of a 275 feet tall tower. Marvellous views of the lights of Honolulu, which is a big, confusing at first, and very American city. The water was still blue from the beach at 11.30 p.m., with luminous waves, and earlier I had caught the 'green flash' which can be seen in the Pacific if one is in the right place at the right time and also lucky, a moment before the sun disappears below the horizon.

On Friday, 4th March I was booked on a whale watching cruise with an early start, and not having to go far out to sea to find them. There were plenty of Humpbacks, displaying backs, dorsal fins and tail flukes. Getting a photograph with an ordinary still camera proved to be extremely difficult though, as you have to be very quick. However, better photographs were easy in the afternoon, during some parasailing from a fast launch in the harbour. This is terrific, slightly frightening at first, as you climb to about 250feet, strapped under the parachute and being towed at speed by the launch. It is the speed which keeps one aloft, and the slightly frightening bit came when, unexpectedly the launch crew reduced speed so that the parachute drops towards the surface. One wonders, having just seen all those whales, if the boat's engine has failed! During my turn they let my feet actually touch the water before picking up speed and sending me aloft again. The group was only four people, myself, a Mexican man and two young Japanese girls, both of whom screamed loudly as they were dropped towards the sea. They were treated more kindly than myself! This was a great experience, not only for the pleasure of having done it but also for the views of Honolulu, the blue sea, the shoreline and Diamond Head Mountain beyond. I was able to get some excellent photographs, of both the others being 'reeled out' and from under the parachute myself towards the tiny looking boat below. The experience was like being a kite on the end of a string, rising higher as the person on the other end of the string reeled it out, or ran faster or both!

America, by Greyhound bus - West to East this time

At 2.30 a.m. next morning, an arranged pick-up to the Airport was on time, smooth and efficient, but again I was leaving a Pacific island with regret – this time for the last time before rejoining the Western world. It is about another 2000 miles to the Californian coast, and again over virtually nothing but sea, so a very boring ride – like being above total cloud cover.

We arrived on time at 1.15 p.m. at Los Angeles Airport, with the famous smog hiding much of the city on the approach. A helpful 'Traveller's Aid' kiosk fixed me up with a room at the Airport Century Hotel, and then I took a public bus to Santa Monica, which was rather disappointing, not very glamorous despite being adjacent to West Hollywood and Beverley Hills. The beach was grotty, and the sky was overcast and smoggy. This was not an improvement on the islands! That night was the first time I had needed a blanket since being in Jakarta more than two months ago!

Next morning, over a nice breakfast I skimmed rather than read a gigantic Sunday paper, then got a taxi for a tour of L.A., including Beverley Hills, Century City, Hollywood and the Hollywood bowl and the famous sign on the hillside. Also the Avenue of the Stars, 20th Century Fox studios, the U.C.L.A. and downtown L.A. My driver was a Russian from Kiev! This part of the huge city (130 separate municipalities) contained some beautiful houses and streets, but between downtown and the Greyhound Bus Depot it became rather unpleasant, with Negro and Hispanic young men lounging at every street corner, and not looking very welcoming. I had to pay the driver extra to go to the Greyhound Depot, as he was reluctant to go through these streets. However, the Depot although very busy was efficient and easy to understand and by 2 p.m. I was on a Greyhound bus to Las Vegas and Salt Lake City, the start of a six day Greyhound journey across America, west to east.

The north eastern suburbs of L.A.were, and, I guess still are, interminable, and not very pretty, with the mountains of the Sierra Nevada only just visible to the north through the haze. It was here that we picked up Black Maria and her daughter Ebony, whom I described earlier when discussing Prison Vans. The occupants of the bus were pretty mixed, but Maria definitely the most interesting. Little Ebony was fine but the other two kids were a pain, obviously having decided that I was both interesting and tormentable. I put up with it as I really did not wish to fall out with Maria! The bus stopped for a while at Barstow, in the Mohave Desert, where the driver entered into a dispute about how many passengers had paid. In the end he threw three off, and Maria and kids left of her own accord. We were now two hours late, but I had had the chance to get a snack and buy a postcard in the Depot. The Mohave is as fierce as depicted in the films, miles of nothing but scrub, or sand, and weird cacti shapes. The roads passes, in a very straight line, not far from the southern end of Death Valley. It was good to be sitting in air-conditioned relative comfort. The Greyhound seats are reasonably comfortable when you first get on, but as we got into Monday morning I was beginning to hate them. Transit through Las Vegas, where I had stayed, gambled and flown nine years previously broke the monotony – it was even more illuminated, gaudy, glitzy, and tawdry than before. Interesting though. And the bright desert moon still shone down from the velvet sky onto the ancient, serious mountains of Nevada.

The bus arrived at Salt Lake City at 7.30 a.m. – my, was it good to get off, stretch and have a wash. The sun was coming up behind the pinkly snow-capped Rockies. I booked onto the next bus to Cheyenne in Wyoming State, then had plenty of time to walk around the very gleaming white stone city centre, with both the State Capitol of Utah, and the Mormon Temple being very beautiful buildings. Salt Lake City is in a valley, so there were snow-capped mountains all round, white now that the sun was up. There were a lot of expensive shops and clean-cut young people, like the Missionaries that knock on our doors at home. I found a group of friendly girls in the Temple Courtyard who been on one of those missionary expeditions to Europe. They were happy to talk about their odd religion and seemed to have no problem with the prospect of being one of several wives. Salt Lake is a beautiful city - in the centre at least, but there were a lot of beggars. I did wonder if they were imports, perhaps hoping that generosity was part of the religion of the Church of Latter Day Saints as well as big families!

It was a comparatively short hop of about 400 miles to Larami, but slow, as we negotiated a steep winding road up into the Rockies, which are divided into many ranges, the Uinta, and Medicine Bow and Bighorn among them, which reach about 13,000 feet and several National Park areas, with Yellowstone not far away. ('Not far' in American terms). The mountains got smaller as we reached the flat High Plains and cattle country of Wyoming, a big, empty State, the least populated State in the U.S. with only about half a million people. We passed not far from the National Dinosaur Monument as this area, actually in Utah, is home to two of the largest dinosaur graveyards in North America. The occasional herd of farmed buffalo also made the views interesting. This is Indian and cowboy country; I would have loved to be here when I was about ten! Now I was just conscious of the Greyhound seat getting harder. There was a blood red sunset as we reached Laramie at about

7.30 p.m., with some snow about, and frozen rivers. Different to the Pacific! We passed some weird eroded rock formations in the Laramie Mountains, recognisable from films, and arrived at Cheyenne in a snowstorm, on time at 8.30 p.m.. It was now very cold, as we were, of course, much further north than L.A. I found a good room in the Plains Hotel. Some of the characters in the Hotel had come straight out of the films! I needed a sleep but was up at 3.30 a.m. for the bus to Chicago.

There was a stop for breakfast in Ogalla, the snow being now quite deep, but the roads were kept clear. Better than we do, but they are used to, and equipped for, it. Lunch was in Grand Island, Nebraska, on the Platte River. The road had descended to the plains and flat farmland, and there was not a lot to look at. It was becoming a long journey! There were plenty of interesting characters on the bus, but I had real difficulty in understanding some of them, although they thought that they were speaking English! We reached Omaha at 6pm for a break, and change of drivers. This gives an idea of the distances involved in the U.S., 3.30 a.m. to 6 p.m., about five hundred miles as the crow flies, and the Greyhound was definitely not a crow! The route was via the State of Iowa and Bill Bryson's hometown of Des Moines (he says one would not notice it, and I didn't!) to arrive in Chicago, blessed relief, at 5.20 a.m.. It says a lot about American standards of customer service that I was able to find a room and a usable bed in the Harrison Hotel in the city centre. Try doing that in an equivalent city, Manchester or Birmingham before 6 a.m..

Waking rather bleary-eyed at 11am I got breakfast easily in the café next door that was full of obvious students, and found that there was a college next door to the café. A very bracing walk got me to the Lake Front. Lake Michigan was blue but cold, my frequent swims of last week were now only a happy memory; a thing of the past. There was a great view of the city skyline, containing the Sears Tower which was then the world's tallest building, and also the 3rd and 5th tallest. Another bracing walk to downtown, did some shopping for souvenirs in the Marriott Hotel and went to the Visitor Centre. They had an excellent display about Alphonse (Al) Capone, Dillinger, Elliot Ness & Co, and a moving film about Lincoln.

I had, of course, to get to the top of the Sears Building, 110 stories, nearly 1500 feet, with a fantastic view all round. Even with the Lake it did not quite match the view from the Sydney Tower, but I was already getting very fond of Chicago. I had not liked L.A. much, but this was different. Before eating I walked to Police Headquarters, flashed my I.P.A. card and was allowed in to see their Museum, Roll of Honour and had an interesting chat with the cop on duty. Next morning I went for a long held ambition, a ride on the 'elevated rapid transit system', the Loop, which was a great experience, and all that I had expected, clattering around the city centre, partly at street level but often high above the street.

I was totally hooked on Chicago by now, and had a lot of conversations with locals who seemed keen to talk – I was still wearing hiking gear, so was obviously different to the people in city clothing. And I could understand the accents! Chicago, a very big city, was yet so different from New York. I loved Chicago, could tolerate New York and disliked L.A., and am not really sure why. Maybe I was lucky with the people that I met. Somehow the skyscrapers were different, everyone seemed to be proud of the city, and keen to know if I liked it. Chicago has had a chequered history in the 20th Century, so maybe there was an element of defensiveness here, but this was never expressed in that way. After a visit to the Fort Dearborn site, where there had been an Indian massacre, I checked in for the New York bus – last leg of the Greyhound safari, with about 400 miles to Cleveland at the southern shore of Lake Erie where there was a break for an hour. Then in deep snow through Pennsylvania for another 400 miles plus to arrive in New York from the north west, and getting the view of the Manhattan skyline as a final bonus, after thirteen hours.

Greyhound had done me very well, but there was absolutely no wish to repeat the experience, and the pattern of their seats was well imprinted on my backside. People did lie in the aisles to try to sleep during the long night stages, but room to do this was limited, so regular passengers got down early and hogged the available space. But, it was cheap, provided a little knowledge of eleven States and an introduction to the towns and people of the central U.S., which it would be difficult to do in any other way. I am glad that I did it. Experiences do not necessarily have to be enjoyable! There was an easy transfer to the JFK Airport bus, and as I had plenty of time checked in to the BA Executive Club Lounge. I had the whole bar at my disposal, but had to remove my, by now rather disreputable, boots, which were labelled and put out of sight! The final picture in my album of this trip is of my boots, still bearing the BA label, outside our front door!

This was a wonderful 'round the world' journey, from the beginning of January to well into March, an appropriate time to be away from Europe and swimming in the Pacific. The memories, though now sixteen years old, of the countries, the people - some bizarre, some wonderful – and the seas are still very strong. I do, of course, owe a huge debt to Jo, for both realising how much I wanted to do it, and for not objecting. Not many wives would have been so supportive. But, it was good to be home.

Chapter 9

The Himalaya, first, second and third time and a few other high places! Sagarmatha/Chomolungma, 1995/6

In May 1995 Jo and I called at a remote farmhouse in the Cumbrian Fells, to meet Doug Scott CBE, the first Englishman to summit Everest. She, the highest point on earth, is known as Sagarmatha, The Goddess of the Sky to the Nepalis, and Chomolungma, The Mother of the Universe to the Tibetans. I am quite sure that these are much more appropriate names for her than that of a Nineteenth Century English Surveyor.

Doug set up a Charity after his successful climb, which is now called Community Action Nepal, to put any money made from organising treks in the Himalaya into building schools, medical centres and many other projects in Nepal. His object was to help the Sherpa and Tamang people, who make the magic of the mountains accessible to climbers and trekkers. This seemed to us to be a wonderful philosophy, and the only legitimate way to explore this glorious part of the world. We have been contributors to CAN ever since. I wanted to see if Doug thought that I could cope on one of his treks at high level, as I was then just sixty four. He was a most interesting man, satisfied that as long I could do the Snowdon horseshoe in a decent time I could cope with some of the Himalaya! He was also flatteringly interested in Jo's MA which she had then almost completed. So, James being happy to let me have leave over the Christmas period, I reserved a trek to Everest Base camp starting that December, to join four other English people. This was not for Jo; she intended to complete her thesis! The five found each other at Kathmandu Airport Arrivals lounge and were met by our guides, Pemba Gyalzen Sherpa and Serap Jangbu Sherpa.

Serap later become a well-known guide, reaching the summit of Everest himself, and participating in a well-known rescue. He corresponded with me for several years. Pemba was also well known, having guided Sarah Ferguson, The Duchess of York, on the same route the previous year. He had been to stay with the Duke and Duchess in the UK since, and was very proud of the fact that he had his own green wellies kept at their residence! Both were pleasant and interesting young men, very expert at their jobs. The other four trekkers were Rachel (a Doctor), Louise and Robert, who were an item, and John, a well built young man who looked quite capable of reaching the summit on his own. All were much younger than myself! The Hotel Mountain was a very comfortable place to acclimatise for a couple of days, with the chance to wander round the ancient centre on foot and enjoy the evocative atmosphere again since my earlier chickee-chips visit.

Whilst the outer city had grown a lot, the very old Buddhist monuments had not changed. The plan was to leave Kathmandu by helicopter for the airstrip at Lukla, where the trek began, but there were a couple of false starts before this actually took place. Waiting at the airport for the weather to become flyable is a customary occupation here. When we did get going the helicopter turned out to be a very big ex-Russian military machine, incredibly noisy and excessively vibrating, with passengers sitting facing each other and all luggage piled in an untidy heap in the middle! Not ultra sophisticated, but we arrived, despite some still heavy cloud. Lukla, at over 2,800 metres (more than eight and a half thousand feet), was really interesting, as it is built on a steep slope. The Twin Otter aeroplanes which use it as well as the helicopters land uphill of course, so passengers waiting by the small terminal building are well above the point where the aircraft touches down. We could hear the aircraft before it appeared dramatically from between the cloudy mountains that ring the airstrip, and could look down on it as it approached and landed. Slightly, but not very, reminiscent of the field near Wolverhampton that my friend Mick and I used to fly from!

After disentangling our bags from the pile we met our porters and cook-boys, and started the trek, through the one street of Lukla village. Being well used to urban poverty, in the UK and Africa, the most deprived parts of Kathmandu had not been a surprise, but the poverty of these villagers was. The porters also were also poor, with an assortment of cast off clothing, plastic in use as socks and string for laces. Nevertheless carrying big loads cheerfully, and pleased to have the work. We gave them big tips and some of our own clothing at the end of the trek, and their condition is part of what CAN has tried to improve. They were very like the Peruvian porters that I had seen on trek to Machu-Pichu in '91, not paid particularly well, but glad of the work, and cheerfully carrying loads that seemed impossible.

The Sherpa people are born to thin air, and like the men at Machu-Pichu are adapted to it, and can perform physical tasks that people from lower altitudes struggle with. The cook-boys, being better paid, were better off and were irrepressible, seeming to spend most of the trek singing. They also carried heavy loads of cooking utensils, dishes, plates etc. It was noticeable that food was always prepared properly, although usually being cooked in cold, dark and draughty places, while they squatted on earth floors. Places were always laid, with hot washing water prepared and the food invariably well made and enjoyable. The red dustbin bubbling away in front of the stove always smelled good! Being woken by a scratching at the tent flap or hut door at 5.30 a.m. and a cheerful face offering 'bed-tea' was a pleasure throughout the trekking days!

It was an easy trek to our first camp site, Phakding, about four hours only, a site in a pleasant green valley, actually lower the Lukla. Our heavy baggage was carried on Dzopkyos (pronounced dubchuks, which spelling I will stick to in future!). They are crossbred between cattle and yaks, short haired, but very tough. We were joined by a boy of about twelve walking home to Namche Bazaar for the school holiday – only a two day walk home from school! He carried a very big rucksack, and was fascinated by my retractable walking pole. The path was already spectacular, with plank and rope bridges, some scrambles up and down and generally reminiscent of Highland Scotland. We were sharing tents of course, and the mix meant that Dr. Rachel was lucky with one to herself, while I shared with John, but they were a good size, with plenty of room for kit as well. We quickly got the hang of helping the porters to put them up. John told me that this trek was something that he had dreamed about doing since he had been a boy. It had been obvious though that he was not finding it easy, and was lagging even on this first stage. I was disturbed by the amount of equipment that he was carrying, including a large video camera. We had already come across the carved or painted rocks, which along with Temples and Shrines should be passed following a clockwise path, if possible. It is a religious and cultural tradition to follow the left hand path but as a sometimes-forgetful foreigner one was never told so, but just heard a polite cough, or saw a reproachful glance. In honour of the Himalaya I do this now when climbing in the UK, but the left hand path is not so well trodden here. We had also made the acquaintance of the Nepali type toilet, a usually ramshackle wooden hut, suspended, just, over a high drop, and with a hole cut in the floorboards. They require practice and flexible knees. We passed a lot of settlements at this altitude, all looking pretty poor.

Next day, up early (very) after 5.30 a.m. bed-tea we continued along the fertile valley of the Dudh Kosi, called the Milk River, because it is snow melt. It is also fast, tumbling over and carrying rocks, not to be trifled with, and beautiful in very blue and very white colours. We crossed the Dudh Kosi several times, the bridges of rope and wood never looking very strong. But they functioned. One was about one hundred yards long and high over the Dudh Kosi, and some of the dubchuks did not like it at all. They often had to scramble with difficulty up some of the steep climbs, but somehow kept going. The long bridges sway well with two or three people on them, but no dubchuks fell off, and no people either. We were now climbing significantly, passing ice formations on the riverbanks, and getting tantalising glimpses of high snow capped mountains through the occasional break in the valley sides.

Rachel, Louise, Robert and I were walking well and enjoying it, but John was now really having problems, and had handed over his video camera and other gear to one of the porters. Before reaching Namche Bazaar we passed into Sagarmatha National Park. This was the point where we had to obtain a Nepali Climbing Permit, issued by the Nepal Mountaineering Association, which tries to keep track of who are in the National Park. Arriving at the small town after a six hour trek John more or less collapsed. We were now at nearly three and a half thousand metres, well over ten thousand feet, and he may have been suffering from the thinner air, compounded by his heavy kit.

Mountain Sickness is no respecter of youth or fitness, and this may have been his problem. After a day in Namche Bazaar acclimatising, and two nights rest in a rest house he still felt quite ill. Pemba decided that he had to go back to Lukla, and arranged for him to be escorted back there, one of the porters carrying his kit. This was very sad in view of his long held wish to see the Himalaya, but sensible, as MS can be a killer if allowed to become acute. We spent the acclimatising day around the big village, which is the most important of Sherpa settlements and a former trading centre with Tibet. I walked up to the airstrip above the village, and to the best viewpoint, being rewarded by the first distant view of Sagarmatha and it's attendants, Lhotse and Nuptse, both looking even higher because of the perspective.

The air was clear and the visibility wonderful. The night sky was usually wonderful, with the stars so unbelievably bright and not spoiled by the light detritus that is inescapable in Europe. The nights were cold though by now, with frost on the inside of the tent and the outside of sleeping bags. The trick was to get the cooks to fill a metal water bottle with almost boiling water, which also provided warmish water for a wash in the morning! It was a long night if one got cold.

On trek day four we quickly began to see, and be amongst, the high peaks. Thamserku and Kantega, over 6,800 and 6,600 metres respectively soared in shapely profile behind us. To the north-east we began to see the twin peaks of Ama Dablam towering magnificently to a height of over twenty two thousand feet. In my view it is one of the most beautiful mountains in the world. Ama Dablam is sacred to the Sherpas, and should not be climbed, certainly by any other nationality. One expedition to climb it ended in disaster, but it has since been climbed by Europeans. I am not pleased about this, - we should surely respect the sites sacred to other people. I felt the same about Ayers Rock, which is a sacred place to the Aborigines. Two of us refused to climb it but walked all round instead, hoping that those Europeans insisting on climbing up the ladders would fall off. Enjoying the view of Ama Dablam, which photographed beautifully, and is enlarged on permanent display at home, we diverted to Khumjung Gompa.

The Monastery keeps an alleged yeti scalp. It lives in a locked box, with a glass front, over which is thrown a cloth. For a small fee a monk will withdraw the cloth with a flourish, and leave one to draw one's own conclusions. It's a reddish brown fur cone, more or less the shape one would expect, but it cannot be handled. The Dudh Kosi was now crossed again, as it became the Imja Khola. The river descends from high glaciers and certainly looked it, being almost totally white now. There was then the seemingly interminable climb up to Thyangboche, to complete a six hour trek. Our third campsite was in front of the rather beautiful, and substantial Monastery.

It was now snowing, quite firmly, with a covering on the ground, although not yet difficult to walk in. It was necessary here to pay our respects to the Head Lama, a wise looking old man – perhaps a re-incarnation? It was correct to present him with ceremonial white silk scarves which we bought from one of the monks, passed to the Lama and then received back, with his blessings. One could, I suppose, if cynical say that this was a form of tourist tax. But it did not cost much, their lives were certainly not privileged and it was a nice and meaningful ceremony. We were shown the different rooms of the Gompa, with, of course, a large cross-legged Buddha, and much colourful, if rather dusty, decoration, prayer wheels and wooden masks. I have my own wooden masks now in my workshop, bought through CAN. Scarlet and gold were colours much in evidence in the Gompa. It was not even approximately comfortable, rather like the rooms of the Potala Palace in Lhasa, which I saw later. I felt that Buddhism was not exactly encouraging a life of luxury, in either of these places anyway.

Next day, trek day five, we continued to climb, but first descending through rhododendron trees to the river. We were now passing many prayer flags and prayer wheels, and it was appropriate to give each wheel a spin, clockwise of course, as one passed. The prayer flags and tinkling metal ornaments were reminiscent of the Stupa of Shwe Pyong Byin in Burma, years earlier, the same religion but different cultures. And a different climate!

The overnight stop was at Pheriche, and in heavy snow we were glad to find accommodation in a teahouse rather than the tents. We were now amongst high peaks all around, all snow covered, with quite deep snow covering the tracks. Trek day six was Christmas Eve! The plan was to trek to Dughla, where a stony waste normally marks the terminal moraine of the mighty Khumbu glacier. The stones of the moraine were now covered by deep snow however. It was becoming difficult to walk on the track, which was covered in ankle deep snow, making it difficult to recognize. I kept slipping off into much deeper snow on either side, often thigh deep. It became more and more tiring and difficult to pull ourselves back onto the track. The snow was much earlier and heavier than normal, and this was the season when a number of people had to be airlifted out, or died, in the National Park. As we reached Dughla Louise felt that she could not go on in these conditions. I am sure that this was sensible, rather than try to struggle on, and Robert agreed that they should both go back to lower levels. This meant splitting the party, and Pemba decided that he must lead them back, to sleep in Tea Houses en-route and with enough supporting porters to reach Lukla.

This was hard luck on Robert, who was fit enough to continue, but the correct decision. Serap was left to carry on as far as possible with Rachel and I. The planned destinations were the two peaks of Kala Patthar, which gives a superb view of the black south west face of Sagarmatha, and Pokalde, the latter being nearly nineteen thousand feet. We were not able to achieve either of these objects because of the snow, but Serap found a very acceptable alternative, after we had been marooned over Christmas! The scenery, despite the difficult trekking conditions was spectacular. Blue sky, unlimited visibility, and the panorama of peaks, pure white where the snow had lain, or very black on the sheer slopes. The peaks were invariably shapely, Nuptse, being closer, seemed to dwarf Sagarmatha. We struggled towards Pumori in the distance at over 23,000 feet with Lobuche to our left and Mehra to our right. Late on Christmas Eve we arrived at the collection of shepherds huts and teahouses at Lobuche village, at 16,000 feet more than high enough for anyone except a Sherpa or a Tamang to feel the lack of oxygen. The blue sky had disappeared and it was now snowing heavily again. We were fortunate to find refuge and bunk beds in a teahouse. The village is shown as a summer settlement only on the National Park map, and I think that it was fortunate to find it still open. The few remaining porters and cook-boys obviously thought that this was luxury!

Christmas Day was a white-out, with blinding snow. Moving was not even thinkable. Jo had packed me a small Christmas cake, and some messages. I shared the cake, but not the messages! It was reasonably warm, quite cosy in fact, but one wondered how long we were stuck for! However, Boxing Day was blue, bright and clear again, so Rachel and I decided to try for Kala Patthar, with Serap and the junior guide, (also Pemba) Sherpa. I had not climbed very far when the altitude hit me. I struggled for a while, but it became impossible to continue and Pemba came back with me to the Teahouse, having to stop and sit down in the snow every few yards. At one point he disappeared in snow up to his shoulders. Rachel was much less affected and she and Serap carried on, getting quite close to Kala Patthar before having to return. Mountain Sickness is a strange thing. I felt really ill, and was very grateful for help from Pemba, who looked after me in the best traditions of the Sherpas. On reaching shelter I could only lie flat for hours. Obviously the exertion in the snow had caused much of the problem. When several years older, I reached just under twenty thousand feet, to the summit of Kilimanjaro, perhaps not easily, but at least getting there. Whilst feeling ill I noticed physical problems. My eyelids and left hand swelled and my heartbeat was irregular. My right hand felt, although actually was not, frostbitten and both thumbnails broke right back. All these symptoms vanished as we descended to lower altitudes.

Next morning we made a mutual decision that we were not going to be able to climb either Pokalde or Kala Patthar, and left Lobuche, with many thanks to our hosts, under bright blue skies. After a good night I was fine, and wanted to at least climb something! I think, having heard later how many climbers and trekkers did get into difficulties in the unusual weather that year; we were quite lucky to have found shelter and warmth for two nights. This was the year of the film *Into Thin Air*, when a lot of people (eight from one American expedition) died on Sagarmatha. They had continued, where we did not. We made good time down to Pheriche in the better weather, and there Serap asked if we felt up to a climb onto the ridge which leads to Chhukung. Chhukung is a higher peak than Pokalde, but he thought that we could get onto the lower ridge, despite the snow.

Our fifth camp was therefore at the summer settlement at the base of Lhotse Nup Glacier, tented as the settlement was deserted. Our trekking day ten was again blue and bright. The four of us, Rachel and I, Serap and Pemba climbed up to the steep ridge, Chhukung-Ri, in substantial snow but strangely without too much difficulty. There was a superb viewpoint at the top, where a Chinese expedition had built a series of cairns leading up the ridge. Rachel took an outstanding photograph of Serap, Pemba and I with the panoramic background of blue sky, pure white peaks, contrasting jet black cliffs, and cloud below us further down in the valley. We also had a terrific view of Sagarmatha, Nuptse and Lhotse, with Makalu, one of the other really big peaks, partly hidden behind Lhotse. I think that the hour up there made the whole three weeks worth-while alone, and compensated for not gaining our objectives, and it is a precious photograph. We were so pleased by all this, and at having arrived at something worthwhile, that we tobogganed on our bottoms down the lower, less steep bit of the descent. Uncomfortable for the rest of the day, but good fun! We camped at Pheriche, where we had spent the night in the Teahouse on the way up. This was still at nearly 13,000 feet, so cold, but the snow rather less than it had been.

Next day was the long descent following the Imja Khola valley down to the quite large village of Pangboche, for our next campsite in front of the three hundred year old Monastery. As at Thyanboche the Gompa had magnificent wall paintings, and Tibetan manuscripts. We were also getting probably the finest aspect of the sacred mountain, Ama Dablam. We stayed in a Tea-House again for the next night, by the side of the Imja Khola, and as it was New Years Eve showed the several women and girls who lived there, and our porters and cook-boys how to do the Hokey Cokey! The women seemed rather mystified, except for one very old lady who was nearly blind but was obviously loving it. Our team, being rather more used to the peculiar habits of Europeans, really took part with Rachel and myself, and then they showed us some Nepali dancing. Quite a good party. It is noticeable that all the people who live at these high altitudes have conspicuous red patches, caused by blood flow, on their cheeks. It was also visible by now on the faces of Rachel and myself, and shows up strongly in the photographs of the party – altitude, not wine!

New Year's Day brought the sound of Tibetan horns above Namche Bazaar, and then the long descent as the deep valley of the Dudh Khosi dropped away below us followed by the climb up to Lukla. There was a chance for a last (and lingering, as far as I was concerned) look at the tip of Sagarmatha just visible between the nearer peaks. We said goodbye to Serap and Pemba and the rest of the team with some sadness, and flew back to Kathmandu on the Twin Otter, taking off downhill of course!

Pemba Senior met us at the Airport; relieved I think to see us back. Louise and Robert were at the Hotel having arrived safely back several days before. They were keen to find out what we had done, and I think, did not feel so bad about their early return, on learning that we, and a lot of other people, had had difficulty and curtailed plans. Next day was a spare, before flying home, and after a good rest, and a very long, very hot, bath, I took the rattling old trolley bus to the former Nepali capital of Bhaktapur. This has been neglected by the tourists in comparison to Kathmandu, and was therefore less altered, perhaps better preserved, certainly more peaceful and a fabulous old red brick town to stroll around. There was a huge amount of traditional crafts and trades in the centre, plus a view of the mighty Himalya, which one does not get from Kathmandu. A very good winding down day, then back to the Hotel for an evening visit to the unique Yak and Yeti restaurant, with it's open fire and magnificent copper chimney in the centre of the main room.

Doug Scott, in his description of trekking in the Himalaya says that it will not be just a holiday, but an experience, and possibly a life-changing one. He also describes how the Sherpa and Tamang people are his old friends whom he wishes to see fairly reimbursed for the hard work, responsibility and risk that they take to provide the enjoyment and experience of the beautiful Himalaya. This is why he organised them into a Trekking Agency, giving proper pay and completing many building projects as well. Doug also warned that the reality of trekking is not for everyone, and how unexpected delays, tummy upsets and, as exactly as happened to us, heavy and unseasonable snowfall can disrupt plans. Expect the unexpected he says, which is an honest assessment, perhaps not always given in some other glossy brochures. For me this trek was certainly a wonderful experience, possibly not a life-changing one as I had long been bitten by the bug of exploring the blank spaces on the map, but certainly a very memorable and rewarding one. I liked the people very much, and loved the country, and resolved to be there again somehow, sometime.

Chomolungma again, 2004

In April 2004 I was privileged to trek again in the Himalaya, as I had resolved to do in 1996, and to climb as high as possible on the highest peak of all. Chomolungma to the Tibetans, Shangri-la, The Roof of the World, The Land of Snows to me. There were four of us, all English, Husband and Wife Howard and Peta, another man, Kim, and myself, all English. I had decided to go again with Doug Scott's Trekking company now running in partnership with Community Action Nepal, as we were supporting CAN and very much in sympathy with their objectives. Since '96 I had taken part in several excellent reunions in the Lake District, and done a number of great climbs with groups of like-minded people, struggling with Helvellyn on a dreadful Lakeland Day – almost as bad as the Welsh mountains! I also have a nice photograph of a Sherpa enjoying a Lakeland molehill (to him!).

We were met at Lhasa Airport by Gelse Sherpa and Dawa Sherpa with a Land Cruiser, and got an immediate taste of altitude problems as we walked out of the air-conditioned terminal building. I felt disorientated, woozy, weak, wobbly and breathless, and I believe that the other three were much the same. This was not surprising, as the Tibetan plateau has an average altitude of 13,000 feet, well above the height at which Mountain Sickness can start to kick in to those not yet acclimatised. The plateau is roughly as big as France Germany and Spain put together, yet it is still remote and one of the least explored places on earth. The writer Joseph Conrad described empty regions on a map as 'Blank spaces of delightful mystery', and I very much agree with that. The two hour journey to Lhasa city seemed interminable, although it was on one of the few stretches of reasonable road in Tibet. Fortunately our driver was, by Tibetan standards, pretty good. This meant that he did actually look to see if it was possible to overtake, and not rely on intuition, optimism and aggressive use of the horn. The horn is much used in many places east of Suez, and especially so in Tibet!

We entered the city past the simply huge, and from a distance, beautiful Potala Palace, the former home of the Dalai Lama. A traffic island, on which were two Golden Yak statues was spectacular. The traffic also was spectacular. The Chinese have built a mini-Beijing around the ancient city, with brightly lit and signed shops, and wide avenues often composed of four lanes. The Chinese forcibly 'liberated' Tibet in 1950, and in the process destroyed the entire religious and civic infrastructure. The Tibetans do not like this much, and neither did I, as much of the old city has been destroyed. The streets were incessantly filled by bicycles, motor bikes, rickshaws, taxis, very dilapidated buses, and yaks. Lots of Nissans and Toyotas as well, but not one European manufactured vehicle. The heart of ancient Lhasa, encapsulated by the garish new town, was a contrast, a relief and an instant reason for sympathy for the native Tibetans. This was the not-so-long-ago 'forbidden city', where tiny streets were lined with hundreds of small stalls and literally crammed with pedestrians. Many were pilgrims from other parts of the country, following the spiritual left hand path around the Jokhang Temple, which all Buddhists must visit as it is one of the most holy places in Tibet.

Traffic, in the old and new areas, was totally undisciplined and driving is not an occupation for the nervous. Overtaking, which appeared to be mandatory, even if impossible, required a steely jaw, and a sincere belief in re-incarnation. Par for the course I suppose. Lhasa has, however, a useful device that I had seen before in Chinese cities – a highly visible digital countdown at major junctions controlled by traffic lights. This showed the number of seconds remaining to the next colour change and probably helps to avoid 'jumping the gun'. The police, or Public Security Bureau as they are called, seemed quite incapable of exercising any other traffic management. This did not stop them two days later from arresting me for trespassing on army property! The Chinese security services were and still are, as we have seen recently, paranoid about the possibility of another Tibetan revolt against their occupation of the country, and have built surveillance camera posts all over Lhasa.

I had a Rough Guidebook which told me that I could get a good photograph of the Potala Palace by following a particular path up a small hill. It seemed to peter out into a dead end, and I did walk around for some time trying to work out just where the book meant one to go. Eventually the path was barred by a gate that said, 'No Foreigners' (in English, so no excuse). However, it was open, and no-one was in sight, so I thought to myself, 'If

I'm going to do it I might as well do it.' I walked through and a few yards further on took the splendid photograph that I had been seeking. The guidebook had obviously been overtaken by events! Although no one had been in sight, Sod's Law then operated, as a figure in army uniform appeared below, hurrying up towards me. Caught on candid camera obviously. The soldier, young and of low rank was extremely polite, even saluted, but made it clear that I had to go with him. We ended up at the bottom of the hill in an Army Barracks, with no one speaking any English and I trying to explain, with the aid of a phrase book, that I had been photographing the Palace. Army officers in increasing orders of seniority appeared, but still no English speakers.

My level of concern rose as they were joined by police officers, all with an immense amount of shoulder decoration. It peaked when I saw one writing what was recognisably a Charge Sheet, even in Chinese! Eventually, with the welcome arrival of an English speaker I was able to display my belongings – no guns or explosives or secret plans and to express my admiration for all things Chinese. Nevertheless my camera was impounded and with it I was driven, in a dreadful old boneshaker of a police car, to the nearest camera shop to have the film developed. I was then taken to our hotel in the old city to check my address. 'You get camera tomorrow,' was the promise, which I did. The officer I saw at the police station next morning spoke good English, (a relief) was as big as a sumo wrestler, but was quite friendly, and rather amused. I guess that they were relieved not to have an international incident! We parted on the best of terms, with lots of advice on trek security, but they kept my photograph of the Palace. Not being an expert on Chinese police procedures I have to guess that this was to attach to the file to justify the arrest. Whilst the latter was in progress at the Barracks, and despite the extreme politeness, my concerns were raised, on a scale of 'one to ten', to about ten! (Equivalent to my being lost in gathering darkness in Amboseli!) It was nonetheless an experience, from which again I learned. Firstly I learned not to necessarily trust a 'Rough Guide' as I had learned not to trust the word of a 'White Hunter' in Kenya. Secondly that it is not a good idea, in a country where the language is a mystery, to go through a 'no entry' gate, even if it is open!

During the three days in Lhasa we got acclimatised to the altitude, and also had the fairly unique opportunity of visiting the Potala Palace with it's more than one thousand dusty, unlived in rooms. Unique because Tibet was still a comparatively empty space on the map, only open to visitors for the past fifteen years. We saw very few other Europeans in Lhasa. The Palace is beautiful, viewed from below on its high hill, Marpori, the Red Mountain. It is huge and layered with stacked terraced rooms that have white walls picked out in brown, fawn, green and gold. Built of mud, stone and timber it is thirteen stories high. No nails were used in the woodwork, and all the materials were carried by either mules or men, as the wheel had not reached 17th century Tibet.

Inside and in close-up it was depressing and rather a culture shock. As I had thought previously about the Gompas in Nepal, Buddhism seems to instil the ability to manage with no luxury, or even minimal comfort, amongst its monks. Or perhaps that is just the reaction to bare boards by my well-padded Western lifestyle. I guess that they feel the cold less than I do anyway! After the hundreds of cold and dusty rooms the view of snow-capped mountains from the roof was beautiful though. The Dalai Lama must miss that in his exile. It was quite a surprise to find a kettle boiling merrily away in one of the lower courtyards. Being suspended over a section of curved and brightly polished steel, the ensemble obviously caught and concentrated the sun's rays brilliantly. A little comfort then, at least! Whilst not being described as a Museum, this was apparently why the Palace still exists, and is kept more or less untouched. Perhaps the Chinese felt that destroying it would be a step too far even for them.

Our Hotel was comfortable, if rather cold, and was splendidly ethnic. It was right in the old city, and from the roof we could watch the crowds of chanting pilgrims circling the Jokhang Temple, from morning to night, always clockwise of course. Every so often individuals would stop to prostrate themselves fully on the ground, in an act of worship. There were small stalls around the Temple, the Barkhor Bazaar, and I enjoyed visiting 'Ancient Thing Store'!

Tipping was not expected in Tibet, but bargaining skills had to be honed up and practised. I found two splendidly dressed gentlemen, in what I believe were traditionally colourful ceremonial robes and fur hats. They were delighted to pose for a photograph in the Square in front of the Palace. This was rather a contrast to the MIG fighter on display in the same Square. In fact the old city, the Temple, stalls and pilgrims were all in huge contrast to the mini-Beijing a few hundred yards away, and the frenetic traffic passing the Golden Yaks traffic island. Whatever the rights and wrongs of the Chinese occupation it was impossible not to feel sympathy for the Tibetans, as almost their entire religious and civic structure had been destroyed.

We were also able to visit two Monasteries in the Lhasa area. At Sera there is a well-publicised debating hour in the courtyard where the monks debate and argue about philosophy and the teachings of the Buddha. When they make a point each monk slams his fist hard into his other palm, and as many of them are young and vigorous, (indeed I think most that I saw), the whole courtyard sounds like one huge prizefight! This reminded me irresistibly of young Hebrews in a Yeshiva college, half a world away, studying and debating the Talmud and Torah with the same devotion to the subject and emphatic gestures to emphasise a point. I have found that lots of similarities like this occur despite languages, cultures and distances. For example, there is a mountain in the Alps and another in the Himalaya, both named in the local language 'Virgin'.

The monks at Sera have a reputation for skill in martial arts, and were once hired out as bodyguards. I have wondered since how many of them were involved in the uprising against the Chinese in 2008. Having seen and enjoyed their delight in debate, it is difficult not to feel a lot of sympathy for their action. Drepung Monastery, like Sera dating from the 15th century, is perched on the side of a steep mountain. It was once the largest Monastery in the world, housing ten thousand monks. Beautifully painted boulders lead above the buildings towards the summit of the mountain. Many monks from there took up arms against the Chinese in 1959, and the Monastery was badly damaged. One could not help feeling the history.

Now acclimatised, cleared of being a spy, and getting some feel for the culture, we drove south on the 920 km Friendship Highway, which is designed to stretch from Lhasa to Kathmandu. It was still not finished, and many sections were almost literally mountaineering on wheels. Howard was virtually concussed by having his head bounced against the Land Cruiser roof, and the journey, even with three overnight stops, was very tiring. The first planned stop was at Gyantse, but most of the day seemed to be taken up in climbing the fifteen thousand feet Khamba La Pass. Hairpin after hairpin after hairpin!

A 'truck-stop' marked arrival at the shores of Yamdrok Tso Lake, high in the mountains, yet surrounded by even higher peaks. After a welcome break we followed the astonishingly cobalt blue waters of the Lake to the Pass of Karo La at over five thousand metres, and finished the day at Gyantse. Accommodation at Gyantse was adequate, but the small town itself was a treasure. It became the base camp of the ill-advised British Expedition to invade Tibet under Sir Francis Younghusband just one hundred years earlier. The expedition was driven out of Tibet, after they had managed to take the Dzong or fort, which is still impressive on its prominent hill. The main attraction of Gyantse is the Kumbum (which means ten thousand images) Monastery. It is an unmistakable landmark, with a circular pathway leading around the building, from the ground to the gold dome at the highest point. The path gives access to many small rooms, each with it's own image of Buddha. One is supposed to keep walking round until all have been visited. I did feel that I may have seen ten thousand images!

Next day we drove to Shigatse, the second largest town in Tibet, the site of the vast Tashilhunpo, the largest working Monastery complex in Tibet. This was fortunate to escape most of the ravages of the Cultural Revolution, and thus contains some wonderful works of art. One life size golden tiger seems to spring snarling off the wall on which it is painted. We were privileged to see the monks at prayer, and to look at much that is normally private in the maze of alleys, courtyards, temples and chortens. Our Hotel in Shigatse was the most sophisticated yet, with a Banquet Hall and even a Night Club. Finding a Reception Desk and a Bar was an enhancement of previous experiences. The Hotel brochure, which I kept, is a wonder of 'Chinese English': 'Willing to live here without doubt, it is best choice for tourist and business-man. Trust us and choose us, without hesitation! Just a phone, we always keep around you.'

Anyway, best night so far in Tibet! The third day's drive on the Friendship Highway was to Tingri where we continued our trek on foot next day. The Highway had been very busy, despite all the re-building, mainly with heavy trucks. Passing technique through the ever-present veil of dust was to be heavy-handed on the horn, and have blind faith coupled with extra-sensory perception. I have a photograph, taken from the back seat, showing us overtaking a truck in complete lack of viz, after taking which I think that I shut my eyes. Strangely, this method seemed to work, although I think that Tibet's collision statistics have to be treated with a great deal of reserve. I do not blame our drivers, who were very cheerful chaps – I think that they had to be. This was the way that they had been taught to drive, and the modus operandi that all their peers used. If they did not get quickly past the lorry in front the lorry behind would overtake both it and ourselves, certainly creating more danger. But wow!

Tingri is a one-yak town if ever there was one, but had accommodation with cabins round a central ground, a bit like a motel. It did however have a splendid view of Cho-Oyo, at over 8,000 metres a major Himalayan massif. Three eight-hour days on the Highway had produced bruises in all sorts of unexpected places, but the views of gigantic walls of ice, glaciers and snowy peaks, and Lake Yamdrak-Tso had been memorable. The reliability of the Toyota on such 'roads' was pretty good. Only one flat tyre, which was remarkable, and a bit of trouble with the cooling system. As in so many developing countries, the Tibetan drivers are expert improvisers, and I never had any doubt that we would complete the journey. Maybe late, but completed. Perhaps the regular groups of prayer flags have something to do with this. No European vehicles were seen until later when we entered Nepal, where there are plenty of Mercs and BMWs.

The sixty kilometre trek to reach the northern Base Camp for Chomolungma involved four nights in tents – extremely cold, with snow on the night that we arrived, but very satisfying. It was well within the powers of us all, as we were well acclimatised. I think, with hindsight, that this had been the problem with the 95/6 trek, apart from the unusual snow, as both here and on Kili I had no problem with 18-20,000 feet, given time to get used to the thin air. The snow was greeted with pleasure, as it changed the scenery completely, the lower slopes at this time of year being grey, brown or dun coloured and uninviting. The villages looked bleak and cold. Our support lorry, with cook-boys, tents etc was able to follow a more or less navigable track to the Base Camp, while we walked diversions with Gelse and Dawa our two Sherpas, up and down, to make a more interesting route.

The first camp site was at the windy village of Ra-chu, on the banks of one of the main branches of the Ra-chu, which flows down from Cho Oyu. Tingri to Ra-chu had entailed crossing a huge plain and following a bluff alongside the river. In the warmer months this plain is green and supports extensive flocks of goats and sheep, while the glittering white massif of Cho Oyu is visible to the south-west. At Ra-chu the children came out in force to inspect the foreign devils. The whitewashed houses were decorated with red, white and blue stripes, with blocks of dung stacked, I guess to dry out, on the roofs between prayer flags. Here Kim revealed unexpected depths by producing a skipping rope from his rucksack, and we had fun teaching the kids to skip. It was a new game to them, I guess because of the absence of skipping ropes, and perhaps an absence of playtime as well, but the oldest girl picked it up like a veteran and helped the smaller ones – perhaps instinctively. This was good to see.

After another campsite in the Rongphu Valley, looking south to the Rongphu Glacier, next day brought us to the ruins of Rongphu Monastery, where we had our third camp. At just under five thousand metres it had been the highest in the world, until it was sacked during the Cultural Revolution by local villagers, who had been fuelled by tales of exploitation and corruption of the monks. Since then it had been partially repaired and a new rest house built. It provided a wonderful view of Chomolungma, which had become visible at the end of the Valley the previous day, wearing its brilliant scarf of cloud and wind-borne ice crystals. This view, with the highest mountain of all wearing white in contrast to the lower slopes, was a compelling incentive to complete the journey. On this section I had been walking with Peta, and found her interested in some of my tales about the Police Service – well she said so anyway! It was during these two days that it struck me that I could write some of them down. Hence, for good or for ill, appears this book, all down to Peta! It helped to shorten a rather long walk, for me at least!

The trek between Tingri and Base Camp is described in the 'Lonely Planet' book about Tibet as taking three to four days, so we completed it well on schedule. It is also described as 'medium to difficult' with the highest point at Nam-la being 5250 metres – over 17, 200 feet through remote country where one has to be absolutely self-sufficient. I have no quarrel with that description!

Arrival at Base Camp for our fourth night was quite late in the afternoon, as we had spent some time at a Sherab Chöling, a Sky Burial site. These are places on rocky locations, holy to the Tibetans and available for funerals of devout Buddhists. The body is placed on a special rock, and after a service is left for the birds to carry away in pieces. I understand that it is a privilege to be so treated. Of course, we would not have been welcome with a service in progress, but it was an interesting place to see, and reflect upon. We just had time to get the tents up having chosen a reasonably peaceful spot away from the herds of yaks when it started to snow heavily and a Tibetan trader with a large yak herd decided to park himself next to us. Sod's Law rules, even in the Himalaya! These were yaks, by the way, not the half-breed dubchuks, quite noisy, not constipated and not exactly dainty footed!

However, we had a good, hot and substantial meal prepared by the cook-boys and retired, in heavy snow, rather pleased to have all achieved Base Camp in good order. Next morning we made our way to Base Camp Village, where there were a lot of interesting stalls selling a wide variety of bits and pieces, some trash mixed with good souvenirs, set up by Tibetan and Nepali entrepreneurs. This, at 5,500 metres, over 18,000 feet, was the starting point of many of the early attempts to climb the mountain, including the ill-fated Mallory and Irvine expedition of 1924.

So it is an historic, evocative site. We were made welcome by a large Indian Navy team, there in preparation for an attempt on the summit, and shown their gear and planning strategy. Having paid some sort of levy at the Chinese checkpoint, we were allowed to proceed higher, by Yak-Trak, onto the Rongphu Glacier Moraine. The higher one wishes to go the more money has to be paid to the Chinese, which explains the cost of summit attempts, then about 30,000 dollars. It was pleasing that we were able to continue for some way, seeing laden teams of yaks both climbing and descending. Eventually, at about 5,700 metres the two Sherpas decided that we should not go further. I think that we were all satisfied that we had got some way past the Base Camp, without difficulty. The group photograph, with the summit in the background is a nice one. That evening two of the Indian team visited us, with a couple of bottles (they were well supplied with all necessary luxuries) and we drank each other's health, crammed into one of our tents.

Returning to Tingri by truck was quicker than trekking, although not so interesting, but on arrival we found that our Nepali transport had been held up in Communist roadblocks and toll extraction, and its appearance time was debatable. Nothing to be done about this, until the guerrillas opened the road, and it was another day before they could get through. Exploring the delights of Tingri took about three minutes, so this was rather an anti-climax, but it was a frequent occurrence at that time in Nepal, and at least there had been no violence. We eventually started on the three day journey to Kathmandu, a stunning drive with two overnight stops. There were wonderful views to Cho Oyu and Chomolungma from the high passes of La Long-la and Tong-la, both over 16,000 feet. The Sherpas described the Friendship Highway as lying on a clenched fist, with the back of the hand the plateau and the knuckles the descent into Kathmandu. There was an unbelievable log-jam of lorries at the Frontier post, but fortunately this coincided with one of our planned overnight stops. The road descended, via a series of incredible hairpins like the climb up the Khamba La, starting with the bare plateau and gradually becoming more and more like the Scottish Highlands. We followed the valley of the Sun Khosi, which eventually joins the Ganges, and found, as tourists became more plentiful, that it was even possible to bungee-jump down to it.

This journey is almost an adventure in itself, especially with the chance of being taken hostage in the mix! Our Hotel, definitely in New Kathmandu, had a swimming pool on the roof, and this was a very enjoyable way to relax, feeling reasonably warm after the Tibetan plateau. We were also all very lucky to get a flight with 'Buddha Air', which operates a Beech 1900 twin turbo-prop along virtually the whole range of the Himalaya, from Langtang in the north-west to Makalu in the south-east. The flight lasted an hour, and everyone was invited into the cockpit – one at a time of course! The views were out of this world, but I think that the thing that impressed me most was the time it took to get up to Himalayan summits height, even at turbo-prop speed, and the sight of the majestic white peaks as they came into view. This was a really wonderful end to the whole experience.

Community Action Nepal had warned, in the trek briefing, that Hotels and Guesthouses in Tibet would be basic, and that exposure to fleas, mice and the occasional rat was a possibility, together with revolting toilets. Because of the newness of tourism in Tibet it was necessary to expect the unexpected and that in reality one would have stepped back in time three or four centuries, with services and attitudes not comparable to Nepal. It concluded that the briefing was not designed to deter anyone from visiting Tibet, but to describe the likely conditions. 'The visit should be approached with an open mind and a sense of adventure – a step into the unknown. It will be a never to be forgotten experience, for whatever reason'. I found Doug Scott's CAN briefing about Tibet to be totally accurate, and whilst sometimes uncomfortable, frequently tired and often cold, would not have missed Conrad's 'blank spaces of delightful mystery', with good companions, good guides and totally new experiences, for anything.

Success this time! Base Camp in 2009

In late 2008 I entered a competition set by the magazine of the Royal Geographic Society to write a five hundred word essay on That Special Moment – something that had been a life-changing experience. I have been lucky enough to have several special moments, but the one that really meant something was meeting the elderly Monk in the hills above Taunggi while I was working in Burma. I have tried to portray this meeting in the section above describing my International Red Cross employment. Making something readable and sensible in only 500 words was the challenge of course, but in February `09 we were very surprised to hear that I had won the Mountain category. The prize was two-fold – an excellent Gore-tex Arc'teryx climbing jacket and a highly subsidised trek to Everest Base Camp and an ascent of Kala Patthar for the incomparable view. - Decision time!

The offer to have another go at completing the 1995/6 trek and to experience those beautiful mountains again, was balanced against the facts that I was now 14 years older, would almost certainly be with a much younger group of people and the personal expense, which was quite significant. However, surprise, surprise, the thought of completing the earlier effort won! In fact, on meeting the other eleven members of the party, I was about twice the age of the next oldest!   Jo put up no objections, which was very good of her, although I know that she was somewhat worried about the physical effort involved.   Eventually, I did get home very tired, but this was mainly on account of the last leg of the return journey between Heathrow and Wolverhampton! My contact at the UK office of the Australian company, Intrepid Travel who donated the prize was very helpful, and it was all booked for me to travel on Qatar Airlines, on 25th September.

Before hearing of the prize I had decided that `09 would be the year to complete the 'three peaks' challenge of the UK; Ben Nevis, the Snowdon Horseshoe and Scafell Pike, so this became the routine to prepare for the Himalaya. Nearly all my gear was already in hand, so in June, hoping for good weather, we booked a weekend in Ambleside, so that I could climb Scafell

Pike, using one of Alfred Wainwright's wonderful book guides. Hopefully Jo would enjoy a leisurely day while I climbed. The day started reasonably well, but rapidly turned into positively the worst day of the summer. As I reached the tilted grass plateau of Esk Haus, at 2,500 feet, the rain was horizontal, blowing extravagantly in from the Irish Sea, visibility was not much better than zero and it had stopped being fun! From Esk Hause to the summit is normally not difficult, although 'AW' does point out that at this point 'many hearts have sunk into many boots' as the summit, although in evidence, is still a long way off! As nothing further than ten feet away was visible to me my heart stayed where it should be, but with hindsight I now know that 'pressonitis' dictated the rest of the day. Goethe's comment, 'Es irrt der Mensh so lang er strebt' - 'Man will err while yet he strives,' seems appropriate!

On a good day the view from here is described as spectacular, and I would love to see it, but, good days come at a premium in Lakeland! I did press on and eventually, certainly more by luck than judgement found the summit cairn, where I met four other wet and weary climbers from Wolverhampton! They took a just barely visible photograph of myself in my Gore-tex jacket, which was in course of being christened. After descending a short way we parted company, as their car was in a different location to mine, at the foot of the mountain.

It was now quite impossible to use either a map, a compass or 'AW's' book. The jacket was working well, but anything handheld would have been instantly jet-propelled over to the East Coast! I did in fact 'err' and in trying to follow the path that I taken up to Esk Hause got it totally wrong. The viz was such that I was well down the mountain before it became obvious that all was not well. In those conditions the only sensible thing to do was to keep going downwards, on what, in reasonable weather would have been an easy and enjoyable path. After a long, long time, by now wet and cold everywhere, outside and inside, even under the Gor-tex, I joyfully saw buildings ahead and below. This turned out to be a very isolated farmhouse in Wasdale, with the occupants sympathetic, but not surprised. Apparently my mistake is not unknown, and 'AW' even warns about it. There was no way to return to my car on foot except to re-climb Scafell Pike, since my car was on the east side of the mountain and I was now on the west. The second option was to take a very long drive by taxi back to Ambleside.

The first option was not an option!

Fortunately they had a `phone, (vital there I imagine) and with some difficulty found a taxi driver in Cockermouth, who was prepared to do the drive. After many cups of very hot tea, and letting Jo (who had had a pleasant dry day at ground level in Windermere!) know that I was going to be rather late, the sight of the taxi negotiating the muddy track was extremely welcome. I have to say that I felt very foolish before the farmer, his wife and the taxi driver, but they decently assured me that I was not the first, nor would be the last! The route to Ambleside seemed to go on for ever, as it does when you are wet and cold, went a long way north through Cockermouth and Keswick before we could turn south to Ambleside, and cost the best part of £200. I had seriously wondered at one point if the driver had mistaken my accent and that we were headed for Scotland. This was not the best day that I have ever had on a mountain. However, I would like to do it again, but shall watch the weather exceedingly closely.

Next day we were able to recover my car, by 'bus, it now being reasonable weather and headed for home. This experience helps me to understand how Cockermouth and Workington could have been so devastated by floods in November '09.

The next part of the preparation was the full Snowdon Horseshoe, from Crib Goch, the knife-edge arête (in Welsh 'red ridge'), to Crib y Ddysgl, Y Wyddfa, Llewedd and Llewedd Bach in August. This route is 11 kilometres long, with a gain of height fractionally under 3,000 feet and a summit height of 3,559 feet. Not much by Himalayan standards, but a real mountain, strenuous and dangerous to the inexperienced. The ridge and pinnacles require some skill and care, especially in poor conditions. The weather was fairly Welsh, but a lovely day by comparison with the Lakes, and although it took a lot longer than usual, and was approaching darkness when I reached Pen-y-Pass, the day was a success.

I had been wanting to 'do' Ben Nevis for years, and found a three day, two nights break available through 'Explore', with whom I descended the Cretan gorges in '08, and knew were good. I booked this for early September. On this occasion the weather really was lovely and although a long, quite tiring climb the view from the summit, well above cloud and including most of the 'munroes' made it well worthwhile. The next day was a trek into Glen Nevis, where we saw a golden eagle zooming over the lower slopes, and enjoyed crossing the river on a single foot strand wire bridge! A good weekend, and good training.

On 27th September, feeling that I was up for it, I met the other eleven trekkers, plus our Sirdar, the trek leader, at the Kathmandu Guest House. This was after a good ride with Qatar Airways, via Doha in the Gulf, where I was able to buy a Bedouin on a camel (both inert ones) for Nicky's collection. This, quite a large Hotel, despite the Guest House name, is an historic building that used to be the mansion of the Rana, the 19th –20th Century oligarchy rulers of Nepal. The extensive garden, regularly patrolled by a drinks waiter, was beautiful, but some of the building did not seem much changed since then! Meeting the rest of the team, in the garden, with a beer, Chitra the leader went through the do's and don'ts. Chitra is not a Sherpa, but a Tamang, one the other racial groupings in Nepal who are involved in the trekking business. He is a very pleasant man, and full of local knowledge, as were our Sherpa guides in '95/6 and '04. He had one idiosyncraticy soon discovered on the trek – to call, 'Come, Come, Come,' when he was ready to move on, usually the last thing one wants to hear after a too short rest break!

It was intriguing to find that of twelve trekkers, four guides and four porters I was the only Brit. Eight were Australian, with three Americans, one of whom lives in Honolulu, so quite a mixed bunch, with five men and seven women – all much younger than myself. Intrepid Travel is an Australian Company based in Melbourne, so the Southern hemisphere contingent was not surprising.

There was also a mixture of jobs, including two members of the Australian Air Force, one male and one female, whom I liked very much and hope to meet again if she gets a hoped for attachment to the RAF. My background, and current work, were the subject of verbal investigation, and seemed to attract interest! With a little give and take and patience we all got on very well together. In a mixed party like this, particularly during a physically demanding 15 days, one is exposed to the pleasures and frustrations of travelling in a group, but on this occasion the dynamics were great – better than some that I have been on. My being slowest on the steep hills, a point that had worried me when deciding whether or not to go, did not cause a problem, not noticeably anyway. Of course it could be that everyone except the guides was happy to have a good excuse for a slightly longer break! We always got to places on time anyway!

Early (very) next morning, Sunday, we arrived at the internal flights section of Kathmandu Airport, which was the usual chaotic scene that local flight check-in areas often are. Chitra, obviously having done this many times before, got our bags weighed and checked in one enormous pile, and we boarded the twin engined Dornier with only a short delay – waiting to get to Lukla can be days! These are times when it is good to have a local leader. The flight was still a great experience, and rather more comfortable in the small aircraft than it had been in the ex-Russian helicopter in 1995! What was not particularly comfortable for me as a pilot of over thirty years was seeing the approach at flying speed onto a tiny, upwards inclined airstrip, apparently only a few yards in length and ending in a sheer cliff face. However, they are good at it! After claiming our bags and meeting our porters and the three Assistant Guides, we were on the march by midday. First day on a trek is usually an easy one, and we did only about seven kilometres, slowly and comfortably, to Phakding, following the Milk River, the Dudh Kosi through green fertile country, reminiscent of the Scottish Highlands.

I noticed a big increase in the number of Teahouses and Lodges since '95. Tourism was obviously booming, with a service industry to match. This was a pleasure - good for Nepal and good for us as well! The Tea-House was comfortable with twin rooms – I shared with Mark, a young man from Sydney who had been working for Barclays Bank in London, and was now trekking around the world on his way home. Washing was a bit primitive, a cold tap in the garden. However, the night was better than one in a shared tent! Next day was a festival so we all had a 'Tikka', the red forehead spot for good luck, before setting off on the 9 kilometres to Namche Bazaar. Over six hours to cover 9 km seems slow, but I found this to be one of the hardest days. The climb up to the town from the bank of the Dhud Kosi was steep, rough and long! It did take up most of the six hours, with a gain of nearly 3,000 feet. I remembered it well from '95, although it was not a problem to me then, but I think now, with hindsight that it was this effort which ended John's Himalyan adventure. Anyway it was a relief to shed the rucksack and sit on soft cushions!

We were sharing the Hotel – rather bigger than a Teahouse, with a group of Monks, in town to celebrate the festival day. This was great, and interesting, although none of them spoke English, but we were woken at about 5 a.m. by their horns – sounding rather like Swiss Alpenhorns. The Hotel was comfortable, with a hot shower room and western toilets! Namche Bazaar is a small town but with no motorised traffic at all – except perhaps a motor bike or two but I didn't see one either now or in '95. It has many substantial buildings, the material for which has been carried up either on the backs of men or animals, or found locally or perhaps flown into the tiny airstrip above the town. I suspect that most of it was carried up by men, as we had already seen porters bent under huge loads - things like sheets of corrugated iron or double sized bed frames.

Later both I and Shane, the Australian soldier (Air Force Regiment) tried to lift the 'smaller' ones carried by our own porters. I could not lift one at all, while Shane could just about stagger with it on the flat. Obviously there is a lot of technique as well as strength and endurance involved – but what a way to earn a crust. The streets of Namche are narrow, paved in part, with many inclines and steps; it is built into a corner of the mountainside. Instead of cars one found dubchuks, half yak, half cow, around every corner! We were staying two nights in Namche, for acclimatisation. I spent the evening badgering Chitra for Nepali words, and ended up with at least a survival vocabulary. Next day, after the Alpenhorn arousal we discovered that his idea of acclimatisation was two strenuous climbs to local viewpoints, allowing first views of the Everest

Group, Nuptse, Sagarmatha and Lhotse in the far distance.

When recovered from this exercise and taken lemon tea – very refreshing and available in every Tea House (sadly I can't find any of the right flavour in the UK) I enjoyed a gentle stroll without backpack, and experienced something which says a lot about Nepali people. I had decided to buy another towel and a few other things, and finding these in one of the many shops catering for people like us, asked the lady in charge if I could use a credit-card instead of rupees. 'Yes, of course,' she said, 'but we have to go upstairs to machine'. After quite a climb to the top story (funny place for the machine, but that is neither here nor there) we found that it was not working, as the telephone line had crashed.

'Okay,' I said, 'no problem, then I would like to pay with dollars. But I will need to go to Hotel to fetch dollars'.

'Yes, you take things to Hotel, and come back with dollars to pay!'

Wow! Wouldn't happen in Wolverhampton! How nice. I wonder, did she think that all trekkers were trustworthy, or have a fondness for the English, particularly after Johanna Lumley's campaign for the Gurkhas, or did I look so honest? Maybe a bit of each and I do so hope that she never gets taken advantage of. I had been told that my mobile phone would work in Nepal, but no! BT also assured me that their charge card was usable from a public telephone. Only trouble was, no public phones, even in Kathmandu. Annoying, as I have used the BT card from many parts of the world. However, the Internet cafés could do it, at a price in rupees, which was why I needed to preserve them! I got through, to the intense interest of the other occupants, and had a rather public discussion with Jo!

On day five, Wednesday, we started early for the six to seven hour trek to Phoriche. Four hours on, and a lot of Nepali flats (ups and downs) and also a lot of 'Come, come, comes' we had lunch at Nom La, a handsome village high above a Gorge, with a long rough descent to the foaming white river. By now I had realised that in Nepal every 'down' is followed by an 'up', so that as you welcome the release from the pull of gravity, you know that you will have to pay for it soon! And so it proved, again. The village of Phoriche was a welcome sight at the top of the climb from the river, with the opportunity to get a photograph of people threshing grain that was laid on tarpaulins in the fields. I had earlier got a nice picture of two four year olds fighting over a balloon in the Tea House at Nom La. Not much difference there then! The Lodge at Phoriche was again comfortable, the stove in the dining room was lit and after a good meal Mark and I spent a good night. The owner of this Lodge looked about sixteen, but was an experienced guide, had summitted Everest and was due to do so again in 2010. He knew one of our leaders from '95/6, Serap Jangbu Sherpa, who is now also an established Everest summit guide. It was good to be able to send him 'Regards from Mike'as we left next morning for the 8 km trek to Dingboche.

We were now getting high, and the weather reflected this, being cold with some rain for the first time. On the plus side we were getting some wonderful sightings of Ama Dablam, the most beautiful mountain in the world – in my view anyway, as I said earlier about 1995/6 when we were on a similar route. I have had two pictures of it at the top of our staircase since then, so that visitors to our house climb up to it! It has twin peaks, in perpetual snow and ice since the mountain, at 6,812 metres, 22,350 feet, is one of the Himalayan big ones. It stands remote from the Sagarmatha group, like some of the other beautifully named high peaks, Kantega, Thamserku and Makalu, and is, I think, the most beautiful of all. It also changes shape as you trek around it, with the smaller of the twin peaks seeming to shift from right to left.

Our Lodge at Dingboche was not the most comfortable, as it was cold with poor lighting, but better than a tent in the snow as we had used thirteen years ago. While crouching round the stove I broke my specs, one arm coming adrift! Remess, one of our assistant guides, saw what had happened and said 'Super glue, I fix!' Where the tube of glue came from I cannot imagine, but it does seem that most things have been carried up to these remote villages. Anyway, he did 'fix', and it lasted for most of the rest of the trek! Dingboche was another acclimatisation two night stop, and next day, with lots of 'Come, come, comes' we climbed to Ama Dablam Base Camp. This was a challenging scramble on a steep winding turf and gravel track, gaining about a thousand feet. It was icily cold on top, but spectacular, with a lake fed by streams from the mountain. I dread to think what a dip in the lake would have been like. I found an Internet café as we returned to the Lodge, and was able to 'phone home again, this time without the audience! This acclimatisation day was hard work, but I was really pleased see Ama Dablam at closer quarters.

Next day, Saturday, 3rd October was a comparatively easy one; 7 km to our Lodge at the tiny village of Lobuche, where we had been marooned by snow for two days over Christmas 1995. This was Nepali easy – lots of ups and downs, but we were now getting high. Lobuche sits at 4,900 metres, well higher than most of Europe at over 16,000 feet. The weather was cold, and cloudy, with an occasional unveiling of the ice-bound peaks surrounding Nuptse, Sagarmatha and Lhotse to keep us going! Kala Patthar was now and again visible, as a black, rather ugly and sinister triangle, like a child's drawing of a mountain, crouching near Nuptse.

Next day was the big one! It was a long trek to the Base Camp, passing Gorak Shep and the foot of Kala Patthar, often in or just under cloud, so no beautiful views to encourage us. The scenery was mainly grey scree and rather grim, until we actually found Base Camp and then it was all grey granite, ice, boulders, grit and large scree and very grim! There is nothing there, except a cairn and some prayer flags and a home-made inscription, giving the height, 5369 metres – 17,614 feet. What a difference to the Northern Base Camp, coming in from Tibet, where there is practically a village, semi-permanent shelters, Chinese Army/Police post and lots of souvenir stalls. Also, I believe, some crime and prostitution! However, the difference did not matter, the achievement was all, and lots of fists punched the air.

The one spectacular sight was the Khumbu ice fall, with huge pinnacles, or seracs, of ice, grinding their way from just above Base Camp to where the glacier can thaw and flow into the Milk River, the Dhud Kosi. This becomes the Imja Khola, then the Kosi River and eventually joins the Hindu Goddess Ganga, the Ganges, and thus into the Bay of Bengal. The ice fall is one of the most dangerous parts of the western ascent, as it is moving at 3 to 4 feet a day, and the seracs collapse and crevasses may suddenly open. Blocks of solid ice as big as houses have crashed down on climbers. We were able to get a good photo of our whole group, as there were several other people there.

We then had quite a long walk back to our Lodge at Gorak Shep. This used to be the site of the first Everest Base Camp, and the Lodge is a good sized Hotel, warm and comfortable, sitting at the foot of our next objective, Kala Patthar, or 'Black Rock' in Sanskrit. This is an ugly mountain, very correctly named, with no permanent snow or ice but giving incomparable views from the summit towards the Himalya, north, east and west. It is the point from which many of the famous photographs are taken. At 5645 metres – 18,516 feet, if we reached the summit, it would be the highest point of our trek. This is small fry by the standards of it's neighbours, but still much higher than anything in the Alps. The latest measurements have placed it three metres higher than Mount Elbrus in the Caucasus, which is the highest mountain in Europe.

The backdrop as one approaches the summit is the beautiful, symmetric southern face of Pumori, frozen, white and looking down on her little brother from 7,145 metres, nearly twenty three and a half thousand feet. Pumori is 8k west of Sagarmatha, and is considered to be her daughter by the Sherpas. Her name means 'unmarried daughter' in the Sherpa dialect. Kala Patthar is an outlier of Pumori but is too ugly to be her daughter! I find it quite fascinating that a mountain at the top of Europe - the Jungfrau, is also named to mean maiden, or virgin, in German. She is not so tall as the Nepali lady, at thirteen and a half thousand feet, but still very cold, icy and impressive. Jo, Al, Nicky and I visited her as a family, in 1981, via the Jungfraujoch mountain railway.

I spent a pleasant evening in the meal room at Gorak Shep talking to some German trekkers. After getting to bed early we were woken at 4am, and started the climb up Kala Patthar in the dark, aiming to miss the early morning cloud and be at the summit for sunrise. This was not real climbing or scrambling, just a long, very steep winding gravel and grit path in clouded darkness. I found it really hard, and was certainly the last of our group to reach the summit. But, we all but one got there – one of the girls had decided to stay in the Lodge. It took two and half hours, not enjoyable as there were no views. But in those conditions you just keep plodding on, and suddenly as the summit appears, I was above cloud with unlimited visibility and the view, all round was glorious – the only word for it.

The lovely face of Pumori rose so close as to be almost touchable, Nuptse, Sagarmatha and Lhotse were now visible as the triple conjoined sisterhood only a few kilometres away, with Ama Dablam and Kantega standing heads up to the south east. To the north, into Tibet was a range of tumbling icy peaks against the dark blue sky, and a layer of white cloud beneath me foaming up from the valley below. My photographs are spectacular – they cannot help but be. Kala is a twin summit mountain. From my position I was able to look across and down a little and see the tiny figures of other insignificant human beings on the northern peak against the distant snow and ice. This gave, and gives on the photographs, a realisation of the immense, gargantuan scale of it all.

A place for the Gods

The gravely path had given way to big rocks at the peaks. They were iced over and a lot of care was needed to keep ankles intact; a broken ankle or leg up there is unthinkable. The only way to descend is on foot or on a stretcher. Maybe helicopter rescue is possible, but it would not be easy. But we all survived, and too soon really, 'Come come come', was heard, and it was time to descend to the real world for breakfast at Gorak Shep. The views of the three sisters continued on the way down, the clouds had shifted, and Sagarmatha, hiding a little behind her companions, was easily identifiable by the crown of cloud around her head. Mark took a splendid photograph with my camera on the descent which is only spoiled by my presence in it! It had been a truly wonderful experience, better even than reaching Base Camp.

After breakfast we began to trek south, now downhill on average, but still with plenty of ups, reaching Pheriche for the night. A long tiring walk next day brought us to Thyangboche Monastery, which to my surprise was now surrounded by Tea Houses, a Lodge (we had camped there in `95) and a quite sophisticated Restaurant for lunch. Then on to Phakding where we had stayed on the way up.

Day Thirteen, Thursday, was an easy trek to our last Lodge at Lukla, giving a chance to explore the village and to shop for those who wanted to. Early next morning, Day Fourteen, was the return to Kathmandu day, not at all the end of the enjoyment, as the view of a substantial part of the Himalayan range was visible through the Dornier windows. I had worked out which side of the aircraft would be best to sit, and fortunately got it right, as my photographs, in unlimited visibility, even through the windows, are superb. Take-off from Lukla is also interesting, as the pilot has to use the short take off technique. This is to get as far back as possible to the cliff face at the upward end of the runway, and brakes on hard with full, or very high, revs. Brakes off and the aircraft leaps forward over the point where the runway takes a sharp downwards plunge, and she is flying very quickly. It must be a little like driving a car over the edge of a cliff, or taking off in a jet from an aircraft carrier – in both cases I can only imagine! The ride up from, or down to, Kathmandu rivals anything available at Alton Towers!

The city has grown so much since 1996, and even since 2004. The traffic is unpleasant, and in Thamel, the district where the Kathmandu Guest House is, was distinctly dangerous. Narrow streets filled with a multitude of pedestrians, trekkers trying to spend their rupees, Nepalis trying to earn a living, and all manner of wheeled and four legged transport. The pedestrian is at the bottom of the pecking order, and fair game for anyone. Cars meet head-on, and of course neither driver is willing to lose face by giving way. I took some interesting photographs of the chaos to illustrate a road safety article, one with a policeman admonishing someone under a 'Yeti Airways' sign.

It gets even more exciting after dark. We had another night in the Guest House, and all went out for a final party to Rum Doodles! (I had hoped to see the Yak and Yeti again, but was not in the majority)! Rum Doodles is well known however, and is the place where one is expected to boast of trekking or climbing feats on a very outsize cardboard footprint, which is then stuck to the walls or ceiling. Rumour has it that Sir Edmund Hillary was the instigator of this tradition, and that the footprint is an outline of his climbing boots! We all took part, and my contribution was a Union Jack (necessary to counter-balance the Stars and Stripes and Southern Cross). On second thoughts I added a tiny Michael McGillicuddy climbing up a very steep mountain, and an 'Up the Wolves', neither will mean a lot to subsequent patrons, but never mind.

Home by Qatar Airways, early next morning. This, although not physically demanding, was definitely the most frustrating part of the whole journey. We were very late leaving Kathmandu, not surprising given the chaos of the Airport, and missed the connecting flight to London at Dohar. This was an occasion where an ability to make my presence felt was necessary, and after some obfuscation and procrastination I extracted a free 'phone call home to say that I probably would not be home today. And a free lunch. That there is no such thing as a free lunch is a well-known aphorism. This one was actually free but turned out to be dreadful (perhaps on purpose) and I felt it's effects for a couple of days. It was rather strange that the staff at Doha, Qatar's home base, were much less pleasant than those at Heathrow, who were excellent.

The later flight did miss the last train home from Euston, annoyingly by 10 minutes, so I settled down to make the best of a long cold night partly in the waiting room but mainly in the toilet! However, at 1.0 a.m. a ferocious female Station Manager told me that the Station was now closing and that I would have to leave. This did not go down very well and my words were 'I have not had a good day, and if you want me to leave you will have to carry me out. And if you do I will ensure that the Chief Reporter from my influential local newspaper will be on the first train to Euston in the morning to interview you about it'. She went away to think about this, and shortly came back to say 'Yes, you are welcome to stay in the waiting room!' It was still a long cold night, but quite interesting to watch the Station coming to life at about 4.0 a.m. To add injury to insult I had to fork out £69.50 for a ticket for the 6.30 a.m. train, having missed my booked and paid for one. It was nice to be home! I should say that Qatar did well to ensure that my luggage did arrive at Heathrow at the same time as myself, and that they promptly, and with no quibble at all refunded my £69.50! I would fly with them again, but perhaps not to Kathmandu!

The 'Express and Star' did do a feature on the trek, making quite a lot of the disparity between my age and the others in the group, and the fact of the winning essay. It was obviously discussed in Wolverhampton, as I received many comments and being asked, by people that I did not know, where the next climb would be! I have dined out on it a few times since. The trek and climbs were a great experience, and so rewarding and satisfying to have completed what could not be completed in '95/6. Many good memories, of the guides, the Nepali people and the mountains are left and will remain, plus the wonderful photographs inspired, even for those with no artistic skill, by the mountains.

Chapter 10

Round the world again, the other way this time. Russia, Mongolia, China and Vietnam

Jo and I had visited Moscow, St Petersburg, Kiev and Odessa as part of a Group in 1990, and had an exciting and memorable time. She has written this up so I shall not pirate any of her work except for two true stories which are not quite to my credit! The first is about going for a walk on my own, quite late at night, from our Intourist Hotel near to St Basil's Cathedral in the centre of Moscow. As in foreign cities I enjoy looking at the back streets and prefer not to stick to main roads it did not take long, in flying terminology, to become unsure of my position. (Alternatively totally lost).

I had a Russian phrase book but, 'Where can I buy some toothpaste?' and so on did not quite meet the situation. I thought that the 'Pressonitis syndrome' had been eradicated by my experience in Amboseli in 1980, but proceeding on foot this time an attempt to reconnect with the River Moskva seemed to be the best course. I had not fully appreciated that the Moskva proceeds from a point close to Red Square in a series of loops and bends. It got later and later, the City Centre lights got further and further away, the streets got dimmer and more deserted and my heart sank lower and lower! I was aware that I might be closing on the Lubiyanka, which was very much, in 1990, a place to be feared. Luckily, I got away with some steps too far again, and was able to stop one of the extremely infrequent and reluctant taxis by walking in front of him. He spoke enough English to recognise, 'Red Square, pazhalasta', and got me there for a substantial number of roubles, without being arrested for lurking near the back entrance to the Kremlin!

Later the group reached Odessa on the Black Sea, and as I had not yet been able to drive myself in Russia, decided that we would try to rent a car for a day. A notice in the Reception area of our Hotel said, 'Car for hire'.

'Oh, good.'

'Can I hire the car today?'

'Niet, it is not free today.'

This was repeated precisely every morning, until the last day of our visit, and it was rather obvious that they did not want to rent me their car!

However, at last, 'Da, the car is free today'. So, I produced every document that I had, including many roubles, and was then shown to the yard at the back of the Hotel, where there stood a very nice and quite new white Mercedes. I now began to understand the Niets! The man in charge was obviously not happy, but we had been allowed to pay for it at the Reception Desk, so he no option. I could sympathise with him, as it was a beautiful car, - probably the best in Odessa, and I was an unknown quantity. We had intended to drive along the Black Sea Coast to the Summer holiday resort of the Tsars at Livadia, near Yalta, a respectable distance of around two hundred miles. But, you can't beat the Russians on their home ground! Having been carefully instructed on which was the brake pedal etc, we were about to drive away when he said, 'You have a visa?'

We had visas to enter Russia of course, and I said, 'Da, I have Russian visa'.

'But do you have visa to leave Odessa?'

He then explained, with pleasure, that it was not possible to leave Odessa by car without having a visa giving permission to do so. What to do? The car was paid for and the cost was extremely unlikely to be refunded, but to get the apparently necessary visa would probably entail a bureaucratic nightmare taking all day, so we just drove off, and when outside the Hotel yard decided that as we were stuck with the car we might just as well enjoy it. I drove along the coast road to the city boundary to see if the warning was true. It was! So, refusing to be completely beaten we drove round and round and in and out of Odessa until getting giddy, to put as many kilometres on it as possible. Odessa is not a particularly large city. Still, I guess we saw quite a lot of it that the rest of our group did not see! Some you win….!

Despite these hiccups we did enjoy this Intourist holiday, learned a lot and saw some beautiful places, including taking photographs (with an ancient camera) at midnight from a boat on the Neva in St. Petersburg. But I did want to see as much more of Russia as possible, and seven years later in 1997 I was able to arrange through Wexas, the World Expeditionary Association, a journey on the Trans-Siberian Railway, from Moscow, going on to Ulan Bator, Beijing and Ha Nôi. I suppose that it is obvious that this was quite a complicated journey, covering Russia, Outer and Inner Mongolia, China and Vietnam, partly by long distance train and partly by local transport, including boats and motor cycles and even a bit on foot! The correct visas were critical – something that Marco Polo did not have to worry about. In the event Wexas and their associate agents did a wonderful job and it all worked incredibly smoothly (probably better than did Marco Polo's) even down to my contact at one Chinese railway station waiting on the very long platform opposite to my carriage door. No, I don't know how she did it!

On the 8th September `97 the trek started with Finnair to Sheremetov Airport in Moscow, via Helsinki. The welcoming Russian inspection took over an hour, and the Intourist Hotel was not unlike those seen in other parts of the world – prostitutes in the lobby, pre-payment for the mini-bar and no bathplugs. However, the experienced traveller does not worry too much about either problem! Moscow itself had changed a lot in the last seven years however, being much more cosmopolitan, smarter, brighter and better dressed! It was early enough for me to wander into Red Square, without getting lost this time, and once more, as happens to me so often, was asked several times for directions. 'Isveneeta, niet Rooski!' Dinner was in a 20th floor Mexican Restaurant, looking down upon the Kremlin whilst eating spicy Mex food, chatting in sort of Spanish to the waitress and watching with one eye a Marilyn Monroe film over the bar! I then enjoyed a saunter along Tverskaya Street until nearly midnight and encountered Valeri who said, 'England very good, I would like to drink with you'. My notes describe him as 'un veiux moustache' (after Napoleon's troops) and while I am normally happy to see other bits of life this had all the appearance of becoming expensive, vodka already having been taken. We therefore parted with expressions of mutual affection!

I had a wander round the G.U.M. complex next morning after checking out of the Hotel and another walk after lunch. The store is rather extraordinary with ornate galleries and some excellent shops. Then it was time to get to Yaroslavski Station for the 21.15departure of the Trans-Siberian train. In my large sheaf of documents I was warned to carry my own supply of soap and toilet paper for the four night - three and a half day journey to Irkutsk in Siberia. The food was described as 'standard Russian fare' whatever that meant! But, there is always a samovar in each carriage, which means a constant supply of hot water for tea, soup and coffee – provided that one has the constituents, or can buy them from vendors passing through the train. I found that there was a quite reasonable Buffet car, despite the warning.

The Trans-Siberian is one of the World's great railways. The Atlantic and the Pacific were joined by rail in 1904. Before then travel across Siberia (meaning 'sleeping land') was by sledge, cart or horse on the Great Siberian Post Road, which was dusty, soggy or snowbound by season. The climatic conditions have always varied immensely. A modern traveller reported 4degrees in Vladivostok, snow in Irkutsk and 36degrees in Moscow! Milk is sold in solid blocks in the market in Irkutsk during winter! The Post Road crossed 53,000 rivers, each one a test of strength or ingenuity. Convicts and political prisoners walked. Despite it's problems it was an artery, carrying tea, silk and spices from China. The Silk Road by rail. The line now, across the broadest plains, the largest forests and four of the world's longest rivers and through some of the harshest conditions in nature, is indispensable.

After the warnings the itinerary goes on to say that the next three days will be spent in getting to know your fellow travellers, relaxing (plenty of that) reading and watching the changing scenery. Trouble with the last promise was that it doesn't change very much. First was mile upon mile of flat grassland, bare of trees, a small taste of the vast Eurasian steppe that followed in Mongolia. Then the Taiga, the huge boreal coniferous forest. Hours and hours and hours of fir trees, each looking like it's neighbour. Passing a clearing with a little wooden house in it every fifty miles or so was a wonderful transformation and break. Something to look at!

And a station building – wow! The accommodation was in four berth sleeping compartments, and here arose the first problem, before leaving Yaroslavski. I found that I was booked to share with a young woman, and her child, both of us being rather horrified. This turned out to be a mistake however, and I was quickly re-installed with two young German men and a young Russian man, who smiled. Occasionally. The first night in the bunk was not at all bad – a bit lumpy but nobody snored excessively, and we co-operated quite well in the manoeuvres necessary to get up. We three foreigners were keen to see out of the window when the blinds were up – more fir trees! About every hundred miles was a village or small town, looking completely like Anatevka from *Fiddler on the Roof*. They were all absolutely like the film set – muddy lanes, wooden shacks, only Tevye's horse and cart missing!

The dispenser in the carriage provided chocolate and coffee for breakfast, but would not provide change. However there was a fairly continual patrolling trolley in the corridor. Two female guards in smart blue uniforms per carriage kept the corridor and compartments clean, with so far, a steady supply of toilet paper. The bulbous decorated samovar supplied hot water in my mug for shaving. All pretty civilised, but only one toilet and washbasin in each carriage. The Russian, Dmitriy (Dima), was travelling to the big city of Omsk in connection with his business as an optician. As Omsk was on the far side of the Urals (the very far side) all of us in the compartment were keen to get there.

The first day passed slowly, with a break in the Restaurant car, the pectopah, for lunch. I had thought of the train as the Trans-Siberian Express, but it an express it isn't. My mistake! The Restaurant and Bar compared very favourably in décor and comfort with British Rail, but the menu was a bit restricted. The car was presided over by a Russian lady with a wonderful full set of gold teeth. I badly wanted to photograph her smile, but this was a non-starter. She held up a newspaper in front of her face whenever she saw me camera in hand! I noticed that she was looking with interest at my gold wedding ring – perhaps seeing it as an extra molar! We stopped for twenty minutes at the big city of Perm, in the western foothills of the Urals, now two hours ahead of Moscow time, and nearly nine hundred miles away. I took the chance to stretch my legs on the platform. This required a considerable degree of alertness, as being left behind with no money or luggage or passport was not a good prospect. As the trains were incredibly long it was also possible to be cut off from the correct reboarding area if careless, as the lines were crossed on foot without benefit of platforms or bridges.

Amanda and Adele, part of a small group of young people from New Zealand had been laughing at my efforts to photograph the gold teeth, and it was pleasant to share quite a lot of the journey with them. Regrettably the train passed over the dark, wooded and mysterious Ural Mountains during the night. I had been looking forward to seeing them, because they feature in *Doctor Zhivago*. Also they are reputed to be the first high ground one hits when travelling eastwards from Sedgely Beacon, near Wolverhampton. As the direct line of sight between the two passes over East Anglia, the Netherlands, the Vistula Delta, the North European Plain and the Pripet Marshes before crashing into the western Urals I was prepared to believe this, but would have liked to assess them for myself. Another disappointment due to the timings was to miss seeing Yekaterinburg, where the last Tsar and his family were murdered, but there would have been no chance to explore anyway (even if permitted).

Morning on the second day, Thursday, 11th Setember, still travelling east at a ponderous pace, was bright and sunny, but the scenery was altering a little. This was joyful. There were birch trees which were starting to change into some beautiful colours amongst the firs. Somehow there was a more Asian feel about the settlements and small towns. This was almost like park land, different to the Taiga. And I saw Tevye's horse and cart - absolutely – and flocks of geese which had been missing from the Anatevka villages yesterday!

We rolled majestically into the very big city of Omsk, crossing the Irtysh River, which is a tiny thread on a map but actually hundreds of yards wide, and were about 800 miles from Perm, on the other side of the Urals. The time was now three hours ahead of Moscow. It was beginning to dawn just how big the Russian Federation is! Omsk, as far as was possible to see, is a beautiful city, a metropolis of over a million people and the second largest city in Russia east of the Urals. We lost Dimitriy the Optician here but gained another Dimitriy or Dima, a River Policeman, who had enough English to explain that he had also been in the Air Force. He and I had some shared experiences, but we talked mainly about football! But some sketches in my notebook try to show the relationship between London and Wolverhampton and the comparison between my police rank and army ranks and badges! I have little doubt that I bragged about Wolves beating Spartak! By now I knew the two Germans, Frieder and Stephan, quite well, and found that Frieder was in possession of a Langenscheidt English/German dictionary, which Al had helped to prepare and which bore his name. I was given some totally undeserved credit for this. They were also impressed with his study at Freiburg University and I discovered that Stephan was a traffic-engineering student, with a special interest in railways. A four night journey was perhaps the equivalent of a painstakingly researched thesis!

Dinner was a rather enjoyable omelette in the Restaurant car with Amanda and Adele, but still no success with the gold teeth. It was a mere 400 miles between Omsk and the next major city Novosibirsk, which, despite the short distance we did not reach until the early hours of Friday morning. It is a key industrial and transport complex, the third largest Russian city after Moscow and St Petersburg and with a million and a half people is the biggest and most important in Siberia and east of the Urals. It was dark of course by the time we pulled into the very impressive Station, so I did not see the great Siberian River Ob. The city owes its existence to the Trans-Siberian Railway, being founded as a regional transport hub. It grew into its present importance with rail connections to Central Asia. Novosibirsk means, New Siberian City, named as part of Lenin's New Economic Policy in 1926 and the very fine Station, shaped like a locomotive, reflected the railway connection.

I had got into my bunk before we reached the city as there was nothing to see in the black darkness of the Russian forest, but had not been able to sleep. As we shuddered to a halt it seemed appropriate to get out. Many families were boarding here and despite the time it was very busy. The importance of the railway line to this whole region had been obvious all day, with crowds at each station, passengers boarding and leaving and vendors of all sorts of goods, both local and travelling with the train. The history of Novosibirsk, since the revolution, short though it is, is interesting and in order to see more of the Station I rather thoughtlessly stepped down from the carriage. My pyjamas, dark blue and not too different in appearance from a Chinese Cultural Revolution boiler suit, did not have any noticeable effect on the busy crowds, but it then dawned, rather late, that I was off the train with only pyjamas, no money, passport, identification or specs, so I reboarded, just as the train began to move. (There is the beginning of a novel there). This had been interesting, and I slept well after regaining my bunk!

Friday morning was again bright and beautiful, but it was feeling distinctly colder, which was odd as we were still travelling east, well within Siberia but still on roughly the same latitude as Moscow. The scenery was nice – open spaces and pretty trees. More large flocks of geese inhabited the village streets. The families boarding in Omsk had included children, who were now playing in the corridor. One boy, obviously intrigued by my strange language, wanted to show me all his toys. Not so different from home. A real old character paraded up and down the corridor, a little Matrioshka, carrying a basket full of sausage rolls and other eatables. She used the word 'Moos' to indicate which was beef – I hoped that it wasn't, but don't really know why. We were now two and a half thousand miles east of Moscow, and about to enter another time zone, four hours ahead. The train was still running on Moscow time though, and it was shown on all the station clocks. We had not seen a major road, (except in the cities) since starting the journey. The very few roads of any sort were narrow and unsurfaced. The scenery now began to change, with more mixed forest and hills in the distance – what excitement! My main impression so far had been of flatness, trees and ugly buildings. Some of the older (pre-revolution?) wooden houses were beautiful though, with painted and decorated shutters and eaves, and adjoining wells. Small figures could be seen trudging across vast landscapes, or bent at work in small gardens or fields. The occasional vast factory appeared, isolated, with no apparent support system for the workers.

Then Krasnoyarsk, another very big city of around a million people, the home of the Siberian Cossacks and once more the city and the railway needing each other to prosper. Another place also of history during the years after the revolution. I thought of Alexander Bondar, my Russian colleague in Burma, regrettably no longer in touch. His Grandfather had been a Tsar's Cossack. Krasnoyarsk is a centre for ski and climbing sports, in the most beautiful country seen so far – hills, and forests of pine, larch, spruce and fir.

After travelling east for so many hours (actually east north east) and two and a half thousand miles from Moscow the line now swung towards the south, to reach Irkutsk, near to the western shore of Lake Baikal. While sharing a meal with the Kiwi party I tried once more to photograph the gold teeth. This had now become a game between their possessor, and myself and she was greeted with applause every time she got a newspaper up first! This was not at all like trying to steal a picture of someone who did not understand, and thought that their soul was being captured – she was happy to play along! We arrived at a warm and sunny Irkutsk at 2 p.m. on Saturday. It was quite a wrench to be leaving the train after three thousand two hundred miles, thirty five stops and three time zones. I did manage to get a photograph of one of our carriage attendants cum guards, who was smart and quite pretty in her blue uniform. She had worked very hard to keep everything in order, and I parted with a good tip with pleasure. After disgorging passengers here the train was going on to Vladivostok, on Russia's east coast, only another 1400 miles plus!

I had to get to the Hotel Baikal in Listvyanka, forty miles away on the shore of the Lake. The enquiry point was a pleasant walk along the Gagarin Boulevard (named for the first spaceman) to the Intourist desk.

'How may I get to Listvyanka please?'

'There is a hydrofoil down the river to the lake.'

'Oh, great.'

'But it often does not run because they have no fuel.'

So I settled for a taxi to the bus station and a bus, which was interesting as I was able to assess some driving techniques. Interesting but not impressive. It was not easy to find my seat on the bus, as the seat number was on the ticket – in Russian. However, there was generous help and I enjoyed the ride through pleasant wooded rolling country, failing to get off at the correct stop for the Hotel and ending at the terminus. Again the offers of help were plentiful, and I got a free ride back for the three or so miles towards Irkutsk. The Hotel was excellent but almost empty, with the feeling of being a very welcome guest. It was high on a hillside, looking down on the lake, with snow-capped mountains behind, the Khamar Daban Range, south of the lake and crossing the border into Mongolia. They are largely unexplored and unclimbed mountains, several up to 7000 feet, hunting territory for Sable and Elk and appearing very beautiful behind the lake.

Having just got myself settled with a beer in the sunshine on the terrace, thinking that I would appreciate a trek in those mountains I heard a call of, 'Mike!' This was unexpected! It was Amanda and Adele, who had also booked a room in Listvyanka, having beaten me here by sharing a taxi with their several Kiwi mates.

The next surprise was an approach on the terrace from Sergei, 'You like fine ride on Lake Baikal? I take you to boat in very fine Russian car.'

I had wanted to get out on the lake so this seemed fair enough. The very fine car turned out to be an elderly Lada, with a windscreen criss-crossed with cracks like a spiders web – more cracks than glass. Autoglass Repair apparently did not have much business in Siberia. I wondered if the boat would be in better condition. However, it was, and gave me an enjoyable hour, going out to where the lake is a mile deep. It was very cold, but the water was very clear and the view across to the snowy Khamar Dabans was spectacular.

Baikal is the most voluminous freshwater lake in the world, contains more water than the Baltic Sea, is the deepest lake with an average depth of 2442 feet and is amongst the cleanest. It is also the world's oldest lake and was made a UNESCO World Heritage Site in 1996. It has well over a thousand species of aquatic animals and fish, many of them unique. I was able to go into the Museum the next day, which would have been interesting if all the signs and descriptions had not been in Russian! As I walked back to the Hotel in the setting sun I got a friendly wave from a man who had been on the bus from Irkutsk – this was nice, and not part of the pre-conceptions about Siberia, almost like a friendly wave from one of my neighbours at home. The Hotel had filled up during the afternoon, and I shared dinner with Killian Mullett from Dublin. There was a band and dancing after dinner, perhaps the liveliest so far in Russia!

After an early breakfast Killian and I climbed the 1500 foot Chersky's Peak behind the village, which gave a lovely view down onto the lake. The woods up to the peak were silent and peaceful, there was no litter but two signs near the top advised against smoking, drinking and going with bad women! As these were in Russian but illustrated with cartoons perhaps the interpretation was a bit loose – or maybe Killian had enough Russian to construe. Perhaps the inference was that if you did not obey the signs you would not be able to struggle to the top! You don't find signs like these on the Wrekin or in North Wales! There were hundreds of paper twists tied to tree branches: - prayers I think or requests for good luck. This was somehow reminiscent of the shrines to the Nats in Burma. I found it a very special place.

During a wander round the village I was able to buy two dolls for Nicky's collection, a Cossack and a Buryat, from the girl who had carved them. The Buryats are an ethnic group, the northernmost Mongol people, traditionally from around Lake Baikal. I also caught up with a girl who was struggling with some very heavy luggage. She had enough English to gratefully accept my offer of help, and explained that she was going on holiday to the Sanatorium. I failed to get the full meaning of this, but saw her to the gates of what was evidently a Hospital - of some sort. A Russian puzzle contained in a riddle wrapped in an enigma! Maybe it was some sort of work experience.

A pleasant meeting then was with a man and his wife who been very helpful on the bus the day before. They were nice people, out picking herbs by the roadside to go with their lunch. Most of the meetings in Siberia had given me the feeling that, once the ice was broken, the people were not much different to those in the West. A smile and a 'Good Morning' in Russian usually brought a good response. Most of the younger people had some English, learned in school, but a response in German was more usual with older ones.

I walked to the Church of St Nicholas, enjoying the planked wooden or log houses painted in vibrant colours, especially decorated around the windows. The Church had some 18th Century paintings, that seemed to me to be valuable. They were not protected. This part of Listvyanka, away from the main road was peaceful and far from the 20th Century.

Then, surprise surprise, I met Amanda and Adele and the rest of the Kiwi gang, yet again. We were now getting quite pally! A beer and two Hershey bars in the sunshine on the terrace made a good lunch, and then it was checkout time, once more with considerable regret, as I have repeatedly found when moving on. The overnight in Listvyanka had been very good indeed, and I was (and am) grateful that it been included in the itinerary. The Irkutsk Hotel (formerly Intourist) for the next night was not so good, but hey, you can't have everything!

Monday gave me enough time to look at Irkutsk before catching the south-bound Trans-Mongolian train at 6 p.m.. The sun was bright but the wind was cold. It was not difficult to imagine it icy cold. Irkutsk has a subartic climate, with warm summers but brutally cold winters. It seemed that I had, more by luck than judgement, chosen a good time to be there. Many artists and aristocrats were exiled there in the early part of the 19th Century after the 'Decembrist' uprising against the Tsar. The cultural heritage of the city has reflected this since, with some beautiful wooden houses decorated with ornate hand carvings in contrast to the drab post-Revolution apartment blocks surrounding them. By 1900 the city had become known as the Paris of Siberia. Not surprisingly there were some bloody clashes between the Reds and Whites in Irkutsk in the years after the Revolution. Once again reflecting the importance of the railway, the Station is a rather beautiful and impressive building. Irkutsk is perhaps the fur capital of the world, and I was delighted to see, in the bustle of an open-air market, amongst extremely expensive fur coats and hats, a gleam of gold teeth! The guardian of the Restaurant Car, doing some shopping before, I guess, working on the return journey to Moscow. We had a smile and a laugh, but still no photograph!

Mongolia

The Mongolian train was rather more like my preconceptions of this whole journey. It was old and dirty. My ticket was for carriage 13. It had required some ritual uncertainty to find the correct train to go south and rather more to discover that there was no carriage 13! I was then hustled, by a very large lady, into a compartment with a young Mongolian woman and two small girls who regarded me with very wide eyes. She had no English at all, so conversation was impossible, but she seemed not to be upset to share the compartment with a foreign devil! Perhaps it was par for the course. They were being seen off by a man who could have been Husband, Father or Grandfather. He had tears in his eyes as he stood on the platform waving goodbye to the girls. Of course I could never know, but I did wonder what that story was.

I had been warned that it was wise to provide my own food as far as Ulan Bator, as a Restaurant or Buffet car was unlikely, with a probable delay at the Russian border exit of eight hours! There was a corridor trolley with black bread, chocolate and squash. It looked like Snickers and Bounties until Wednesday morning! Both I and the little family across the compartment slept well, untroubled by each other. The landscape next morning was very different to that seen from the Trans-Siberian. It was rolling bleak - very bleak – hills with the occasional huge factory with tall chimneys. Maybe steel production. We were still in Russia, and I was aware of and had regrettable experience of cars made with poor but very cheap Russian steel. The small towns en-route were also terribly bleak, at least from the railway. However, to be fair, the view from the train between Birmingham and Wolverhampton is also pretty bleak! My strong impression however was that this was a bit of Siberia that no one wanted very much. This was reinforced after we reached Mongolia and things cheered up a great deal. The train was even more ponderous than the Trans-Siberian, and stopped at every station. From Irkutsk to Ulan Bator is less than 700 miles but it took from Monday evening to Wednesday morning!

We arrived at the border at Naushki at 1.30 p.m., and as the book said, we stopped. And waited. It was forbidden to leave the train except to visit the Bank on the Station to exchange roubles for Mongolian Tugriks. The book describes it as a shuttered fortress – absolutely right! Whilst in the inevitable queue in the Bank it was a bit disconcerting to discover that the train had disappeared! An American girl in the queue who spoke good Russian said that it would return, and it did! My passport was collected at 4.15 and we moved off again at 7 p.m.. After about five miles we stopped again at the Mongolian customs at Sukhbaatar until 10.15.. Whoever wrote the book about this border got the timings spot on! I have been through Russian border controls several times and think that it is fair to say that they and the Israelis are the only ones who do it properly. I know that I could easily smuggle anything I wanted through the sloppy UK security, short perhaps of a gun, and I have, with no problem at all, taken bank notes concealed in an empty toothpaste tube though a border check which I shall not identify. The Israelis squeeze the tube, to make sure that it does contain toothpaste! I think that, on the whole, it is better that it is done properly although the delay is extremely irritating, and on one occasion in Tel Aviv led to a stand-up shouting row where I was perhaps lucky not to be arrested.

Having said all this, we arrived in Ulan Bator at 6 a.m., thirty minutes early! There are many versions of the spelling of the Mongolian Capital of the Mongolian Republic, but I will stick to the simplest, meaning Red Hero. The Wexas system worked well, and I was met on the platform and directed to the modern and pleasant Edelweiss Hotel. The Edelweiss is not a flower that one would associate with Mongolia, but it does grow there and is a protected plant. The only criticism of my room was the hipbath designed by and for a tiny Mongolian! I was able to book an immediate journey to the National Park outside Ulan Bator, first to the site of a Monastery destroyed in the Socialist Revolution of 1921 where most of the five hundred lamas were killed. Despite the history it was a beautiful place, with a new building looking like a Nepalese temple and wonderfully ornate inside. This is not so surprising, as following the fall of communism in1991 a return to Tibetan Buddhism is taking place. Shamanism continues to be practised though. Historically it was a main form of worship, and is now regaining strength.

I did not expect at this time to be travelling through Tajikistan and Uzbekistan two years later. The Mongol nation was founded by their leader Temujin (he later took the name Genghis Khan, meaning Universal Leader) in the thirteenth century, and I was able to see the tomb of his descendant Tamerlane in Samarkand and relive today's experiences. I am not sure that Genghis Khan or Tamerlane would have been prepared to accept that 20% of their countrymen now survive on the equivalent of little more than a dollar US a day. I think that they might have done something, probably violent, about it.

Despite the obvious poverty and difficulties of life I liked what I had seen so far. It was so different to the backside of Siberia that had followed Irkutsk. Mongolia has a population of under two and a half million, a quarter of whom live in Ulan Bator. Being 1500 miles from east to west and roughly 700 from north to south, it is easy to see why there is a lot of space. The National Park did indeed contain vast areas of grassland, and it was also easy to understand why horses have remained an essential ingredient of Mongolian nomad life. There were wide rolling grassy hills rather than mountains around Ulan Batar and out into the Park, although snow capped mountains reared their heads in the distance. There were several white gers, the moveable traditional home of the nomadic herders. It is sometimes known as a yurt, but that is only the generic Russian name for a tent. They are in use across Central Asia, as far east as Turkey, and have changed very little. Genghis Khan or Chingis Khaan would not feel out of place in a twenty first century ger, although he might be pleased to see the wooden door instead of a felt curtain and the stove and chimney pipe instead of a hole in the roof! The wooden frame and wool felt covering are easy to erect and collapse and can be carried by only three horses, camels or yaks.

I felt very privileged to receive permission to visit a genuine family in their ger home. They were friendly and welcoming and I have a beautiful photograph of beaming Mongolian faces – male and female and solemn children, around their stove. The men are wearing brightly coloured wrap-around coats, the del, secured with a crimson or orange silk cummerbund. The sleeves were huge – wide and long, no need for gloves! The women had a similar style, but not so colourful. Both men and women had knee length boots. Some of the men wore the traditional decorated Mongolian hat that I can only describe as looking like a bit like a miniature Burmese stupa or pagoda! I enjoyed koumiss, fermented mare's milk with them and was also treated to an appreciation of their precious and valuable herd of small horses – ponies I guess really, and an impromptu display of riding.

The Mongolian taxi driver who had brought me from the city into the National Park was a townie, wearing western style clothing (obviously much easier for driving) and he looked as totally out of place amongst the nomads as did I! This was a totally splendid experience – there was much laughter on all sides and a lot of shaking of hands. I am quite sure that it had not been 'provided' for me, but was genuine hospitality. My main impression was of the green vastness of the space in which they lived, and their apparent health, contentment and relative comfort and well-being, despite that one US dollar a day statistic. Many showed the red cheeks typical of mountain people. Another photograph which I prize shows one of the women milking a mare, and looking up at her husband with obvious affection and laughter. The families did seem happy together and it was quite apparent that their simple life did not prevent love and affection.

There were two contrasting things of interest on the way back to Ulan Bator, which is a big and, in some areas, modern city. The first, while still in the grassland, was a standard 'No Entry' sign standing upright in a wide area of grassy plain, with no track or path visible anywhere. The driver could not explain this. I have seen an identical sign and situation in a fairly uncivilised part of Africa. I suppose that they may mean something to someone, but I have not been able to work who or why! However, after all, this is not much more bizarre than some of the ridiculous creations of Highway Engineers in the UK. Second, as we approached the city outskirts was a large pile of small stones with a few flags on it. This was an 'owoo' a holy site, and similar to the prayer flag cairns to be found on both Nepalese and Tibetan sides of the Himalaya. Both the latter would have been festooned with prayer flags to a much greater degree though, and built of rocks, not stones.

Ulan Bator had the wide streets typical of communist town planning and it was interesting to see modern police cars in black and white livery, but also some beautiful temples that had been preserved. There were plenty of illustrations of the Russian influence – square and ugly concrete tower blocks but also some gers side by side with small houses in the older areas. I had time to enter a big department store in the centre and managed to knock over a big pile of dolls to the great amusement of Friedur, Stephan, Killian, Amanda and Adele, who were also shopping for presents. This was a reunion of the 'Trans-Siberian gold teeth appreciation society!' A rather good goulash dinner finished what had been an absorbing day.

Over an early breakfast I met an American who was in Mongolia to hunt Ibex. His local guide told me that this was very big business with the US. A long way to come to shoot goats I thought, but presumably they don't shoot back or otherwise defend themselves. The train for the day and a half journey to Beijing was clean with male Chinese attendants in each carriage in very smart military style uniforms. My compartment, with the same four bunks was shared with Killian and two Mongolian ladies who again seemed quite unperturbed to be sharing with us. There was a restaurant car and the train snaked along quite quickly through miles and miles of nothing but flat grassy plains. By 10 a.m. it was a fine day, although looking very cold outside. Lonely clouds in a blue sky. There was snow on distant hills, which at times reached down to the track. This was the Gobi Desert, uncluttered beauty in its current green phase. By 11 a.m. the two ladies were fast asleep, but the view now included twin humped camels - interesting and rather weird to see them on grass, not sand.

I found two Dutch guys, Jan and Kobus, whom I had met in Ulan Bator next door with a bottle of Vodka. Not a favourite drink of mine, but this was better than some I have tasted, and helped to speed the journey! Killian was well equipped with various tins of food, including a tin of peas, which we managed to open with my Swiss knife and share for lunch! By 5 p.m. the scenery had not changed, it was still green and flat. There was the very occasional house in the vast distances, with a herd of horses or cows and the even more occasional small figures.

By 7.30 p.m. there had been two Station stops in eleven hours! We were following the line south east, still in Mongolia and still travelling through the Gobi, which now began to resemble a traditional desert a little more, with thin scrub and more camels. At the last Station stop a gang of Mongol kids perhaps six or seven years old put on an impromptu display on the platform for the foreign devils. They had small tyres and a metal hook to roll them with and were, of course, quite expert at it. Several of us got down onto the platform and were quite unable to roll them in a straight line, which caused great amusement and earned them quite a bit of loose change for which there was a huge scramble. I expect that the two trains a week were a looked for event in their lives! It was good to see that they all looked healthy, cheeky and well nourished. The town looked like most towns seen from a railway train; not too impressive, with mostly small square low white houses.

Killian and I shared a cooked meal with Jan, Kobus, Freidur, Stephan, Amanda and some of the other Kiwis. At 9.30 p.m., after a full day in the Gobi, we arrived at the Chinese border. There was much interest in our passports from the two ladies, neither of whom spoke any English. This puzzled me until I realised that Killian and I would appear to them as compatriots, yet with two quite different passports. Impossible to explain! At the border it was necessary for the train's wheels to be changed to the narrower Chinese gauge. This was an imposing procedure. Everyone had to get out of course and then each carriage was lifted from the bogies by a huge set of lifting apparatus, a bit like immense forklift trucks and moved along to the smaller track. I know that the Chinese invented many things, including gunpowder etc etc, but this was mighty impressive. Amanda and I shared a beer in the Station Restaurant, still open at 12.30 a.m., while keeping a very close eye on the movement of the train. Having eventually regained my bunk I woke to a bright morning, but the totally different scenery of Inner Mongolia, Nei Monggol Zizhiqu, an Autonomous Region of China, with over twenty two million inhabitants compared to the two and a bit million of the Republic.

China, north west to south east

The flat grasslands had gone and the train was travelling south east towards Beijing through a wide valley with truly beautiful mountain ranges on either side. There was neat cultivation, maize, other cereals and vegetables. Men and women wearing the peasant's conical hats were working in the fields, but there was heavy pollution by chimneys belching smoke from big factories, built I thought in the 1930s. Then came the first sight of the Great Wall running for miles at the foot of a mountain at Zhangjiakou. Beijing was only about a hundred miles and two or three hours away as we followed the general line of the Wall, which passed in and out and over the mountains. It was spectacular, looking like a gigantic white ribbon snaking over the hills, apparently undamaged here. It disappeared as we neared Beijing, the environs not being very pretty and the air polluted, although the mountains were still visible all around until we reached the high rise apartment blocks nearer the city centre in mid-afternoon. Beijing Station – one of several large termini, was chaotic, but a driver from the Qiamen Hotel was efficiently present to welcome Friedur, Stephan and I. We left the Kiwis with a reluctant wave – it did feel rather as if we had been, in the words of the Cockney song, together now for forty years!

The Qiamen, very much in the city centre (if such a huge metropolis can be said to have one centre) was a sort of Hilton, not to my taste really, but having the advantage of a desk where the two Germans and I could book an early trip to the Great Wall tomorrow.

There was then time to walk to Tian An Men Square through the extremely busy and wide streets. The traffic, cars, vans and millions of scooters and motorbikes was ferocious and as far as I could see there was no help for pedestrians to cross. I doubt whether zebra crossings would have been respected anyway. The need was for agility, speed and 360 degree vision. Tian An Men Square and the buildings around were floodlit by the time I got across to it. It is vast of course, as everyone in the world who had access to TV had seen in 1989, following the deaths of hundreds of people. This brutal reaction to a protest by students and intellectuals is described by the Chinese Government as, The June 4th incident, but to the rest of the world as the 'Tiananmen Square Massacre'.

There is in fact no evidence that the mass killings happened in the Square itself, but were in the surrounding streets. Nevertheless it retained an air of subdued menace, and was a decided reminder that China was, and is, a military authoritarian Government. Tonight however it was thronged with peaceful people, children flying kites and all enjoying a warm autumn evening. Back in the Restaurant at the Qiamen, an Italian meal was accompanied by an episode of Rowan Atkinson as Mr. Bean, dubbed in Chinese! I woke with a start several times during the night – the bed is stationary, why has the train stopped?

Early next morning a Minibus picked up Friedur, Stephan and I to join two other German men, two Brazilian women, two Chinese, one Indonesian and Craig, an Australian of Greek ancestry! The lingua-franca was basic English! The first call, after an interminable drive through a lot of Beijing was the Ming Tombs. We then left the city to reach the entrance to an accessible part of the Great Wall at Badaling. This was absolutely a tourist site, very commercialised and buzzing like a hive, with a variety of people, many of them Chinese. Chinese philosophy says that the only true Chinese is one who has seen the Wall, and until he has climbed the Wall a farang has not seen or understood China. Despite the commercialisation, it seems appropriate to me to dignify it with capital letters. Fortunately for me not many people wished to trek along the wall as the steep bits, up or down, were quite hard work, with very deep steps, giving ratios of 1 in 3 or 4. I was able to outwalk the crowds and really enjoyed an hour or so on my own to an unreconstructed section.

The Wall here afforded splendid views of the distant white line twisting, climbing, meandering and zig-zagging over the wooded hills for part of it's thousands of miles. The regular square squat watch towers, spaced every 500 metres, and with the same concept as those at Hadrian's Wall appeared solid and defensible even today. It was fascinating to think that only a few days before I had been in Mongolia from where Genghis Khan and the Mongol Horde had charged into Beijing despite the Wall. It was very old even then. I was even able to find an exit passage to the ground, which in places was thirty feet below, and view it, from Barbarian territory, as an attacker would have done. It did not look like a pushover. I have to say that it was with a little nervousness that I went out, via steps and a hole, in case a spring-loaded barrier prevented re-entry. However, the Chinese had not yet got round to that to repel modern invaders! It was good to sit and look at the Wall on the way back to the Minibus, and consider the history since well before the Christian Era. We stopped at a Cloisonné Factory on the way back to Beijing, and although this was obviously a sales ploy it was interesting to watch the girls, in rather Spartan conditions, applying the wire to the copper base, and then many layers of paint. I did actually allow myself to be persuaded to buy a jar! An interesting day finished with joining Craig, the Greek Aussie, in a 'Beijing Duck' Restaurant. As Peking Duck is one of China's national dishes I thought that it better be tried. The crispy duck can be chosen from a row of corpses before being cooked, but I was not terribly impressed. However the use of chopsticks, under the eye of experts was going quite well. Fortunately it was not a completely new skill!

Next morning I again took the thirty minute leisurely stroll to Tian An Men Square, the world's largest public place, enjoying the variety of shops lining the wide roads. At 25 degrees it was already a hot day. I noticed many German cars in the street, VWs, Audis and Mercs, all seemingly in good condition and showing no apparent shortage of money. Where were our sales people? There were also many taxis and thousands of bicycles! Families were again flying big kites in the Square which was literally filled with people. It was noticeable that there were very few beggars. Female street cleaners were numerous in the street and parks, and litter was being ruthlessly despatched. There were also plenty of public toilets and, surprisingly, plenty of information in English. (It was actually normal English too, which when one considers the strange instructions on using TVs, Mobile Phones and other implements of Chinese origin is even more surprising!)

My agenda for the day was to spend as much time as necessary in the Forbidden City, the former Imperial Palace of the Ming and Qing dynasties from 1420 until the abdication of the last Emperor in 1912. It is the largest surviving palace in the world, with 980 buildings embracing (by at least one estimate!) 9,999 rooms. It is a World Heritage Site and the largest collection of preserved ancient wooden structures. The entrance through the Gate of Heavenly Peace was once the preserve of the Emperor only but is now a celebration of the Republic and Communist Movement.

The roof decoration, colours and shapes were immediately stupendous. Fit for an Emperor perhaps? What was not so quickly seen is that it is indeed a city inside a city inside a city. The River of Golden Water wanders through the complex, with a delicate garden also, wide squares and pools. In fact it took me three hours just to get an overview of the complex – and that was plenty in the 25-degree heat! It was very full, like the Great Wall, of tourists of all nationalities although here they were lost in the acres of space. One Chinese man insisted on being photographed by his family shaking hands with me! Hall upon Hall and Palace upon Palace – the Hall of Central Harmony, the Hall of Supreme Harmony and the Hall of Preserving Harmony. The Palace of Heavenly Purity, the Palace of Earthly Tranquillity and the Hall of Mental Cultivation!

After three hours the mind definitely boggles. Huge squares, vibrant colours resplendent in the hot sun, especially on the upswept roof gables and columns, statues of Shi Tzus (Chinese dogs originally bred as Temple dogs) lions and giant tortoises. Inside the wooden carvings, gilding and colours emphasised the power, wealth and privacy that had been here. The most obvious signs of religion were, to my eyes Buddhist, but Taoism and Shamanism were part of the culture, but more difficult for an unskilled foreigner to recognise. The Chinese people, in the twenty first century, objected to the commercialisation of the complex. A Starbucks, opened inside the walls, was forced to close in 2007 and has not been allowed to re-open. I rather approve of this, although a cold drink would have been very welcome after seeing the 979th building!

Eventually, by now tired as well as hot, I emerged through the Gate of Divine Might into the lovely Jingshan Park that borders the Palace at it's northern end, opposite to Tian An Men Square. Jingshan is also called Feng Shui Hill or Prospect Hill, as it is an artificial hill, once an Imperial garden, erected during the Ming Dynasty. There are five peaks, each with an ornate pavilion. There was an immense view all around, of the Forbidden City and central Beijing. The extent of the Palace could be seen from here, something impossible to grasp at ground level. Many ordinary families were enjoying the once Imperial splendour, all noticeably with only one child. There was a very ornate sedan chair in which people could dress as Emperors and Empresses to be given a ride, carried by servants dressed in the Imperial livery. How are the mighty etc etc, and sic transit gloria mundi! There was a great atmosphere though despite the history, with a small band playing and children learning to draw and paint.

Managing my usual challenge of trying to find my way to the Hotel via the back streets, I succeeded this time! People there were surprised to see a farang, but not at all hostile, merely curious, and quite prepared to smile a greeting. I am sure that they would have been happy to talk if it had been possible. I did receive a lovely smile from a barber who was cutting a small boy's hair in the street. There was a tricycle laden with three very big boxes to a height of eight or nine feet, some sort of delivery service, being pedalled with dexterity but difficulty in the traffic. Back at the Qiamen a much-needed hot bath was welcome, and I was relaxing and thinking that this was first day since Moscow when I had not seen anyone from the train when Friedur and Stephan knocked the door to say, 'Auf Weidersehen'. There were flying back to Frankfurt early next day, and I was sorry to see them go, having enjoyed their company. The Hotel Restaurant was again showing an episode of Mr. Bean, and I was meticulously shown to a table where I could watch it.

On Monday morning I woke up to another glorious day. At 8 a.m. the Restaurant was not showing Mr. Bean during breakfast! My overnight train for Xi'an was not until 6.40 p.m., so there was time to enjoy more of Beijing, and I wanted to see Behai Park. I have found that with only a short time in a foreign city one should start to get a basic feel for the layout, then make sure of survival words, 'Yes, No, Please, Thanks, Where,' etc and then get familiar with the money. I had now done Roubles to Tugriks to Yuans, with Dongs to come, but it was necessary to mentally convert these to dollars and then sterling in order to have an idea of what I was spending. Since our first holidays abroad I realised that traveller's cheques are a snare and a delusion, and always take cash, if available and be very careful of it, with a variety of concealed waist belts. So far, no problem! If it cannot be bought in the UK then US dollars are pretty universal. Euros are certainly easier now in Europe, although personally I do not want us to join it. I now had a feeling for downtown Beijing and found the Behai, another former Imperial Garden to the west of the Forbidden City and Jingshan Park with the aid of a pedicab ride. The pedicab is the pedal driven version of the rickshaw, and it was a lot more acceptable to sit back on the cushions than it had been in Calcutta, where the underfed man struggling to pull me had aroused deep feelings of unease and selfish privilege. This is, I think, a dilemma. Do you refuse to take advantage of his need to work, in which case you deprive him of much crucial income? I do not know the right answer, but the pedicab or the tuk-tuk with a small engine are less worrying. Mind you, in each case the ride is exciting, if not hair-raising!

Behai Park is, or was in 1997, a truly beautiful place. The adjective is one that I know that I have overworked in the above pages, but even allowing for the interest and exhilaration of being in a different culture it is the only one that fits the Behai, as I saw it. A very large blue lake lies in the middle of landscaped gardens, coloured statues of dancers on an island, pavilions, temples, an arched marble bridge across the narrows. It is dominated by a small hill upon which was a magnificent white and gold stupa – pagoda. Even early on a Monday morning the Park was again being enjoyed by a multitude. No problem, of course, in finding patrons in a city like Beijing. I enjoyed the Yong Temple, the Five Dragons Pavilion and the Jingxinzhai – Heart-ease Study. It was a delight to see that small motor boats were offered for hire, and I thoroughly enjoyed one on the water in the hot sun, for an hour. A lot of local people were also afloat, smiling and waving. There was a distinct air of mutual enjoyment, irrespective of nationality or religion.

A stroll up to the white and gold Pagoda got away from most of the crowds around the lake, and an ice cream and a beer - both easily available - under a shady tree with gentle background music just audible brought me calmly back down from a fairly high high! I returned to the Qiamen through Zhongshan Park, another of the Imperial Gardens; the Emperors certainly had no problem in going for a nice stroll as a change from the sedan chair – close to the Forbidden City Palace! One can imagine that they would not have been accompanied by an Empress or concubine, they having had their feet cruelly bound since childhood and therefore unable to walk. Zhongshan was attractive and well cared for, but not comparable with the Behai, being more an area of buildings where religious ceremonies had taken place. The Ming and Qing Emperors made offerings to the Gods of earth and agriculture at the SheJi Tan Altar – the Altar of Earth and Harvests, built in 1421 and looking as good as new. The Park was renamed Zhongshan in honour of Sun Yat Sen, the revolutionary who inspired and organised the downfall of the Manchu dynasty in 1911.

It will have been obvious that I had enjoyed Beijing very much, and like so many places where I have been I left it with some sadness. But Xi'an and the Terracotta Warriors called! A taxi organised by the Beijing Overseas Tourism Corporation turned up on time, and the driver was very pleased with a $5 tip, 'You please to come back!' I had been warned that the crowds at this huge new Station were unbelievable, and to beware of pickpockets. It was much more like an Airport Departure terminal, with multi story ramps for loading and unloading, and a 'soft seat' louge to wait in. Despite being such a big station the train was easy to find, and I was booked to share the same sort of four berth sleeper with Patti, Martine and a Chinese lady. Blankets and linen were provided again, with a lamp, a table and even a hand towel. Very reasonable apart from the mixed sleeping.

There was a Restaurant car, but the train was due to stop at many stations on its journey south west towards Xi'an. It was said that food would be available from vendors, but warned that each stop would be very short, and departures would not be announced

We left on time and as it was still light it was worth studying the scenery. This could not be more different to the grasslands of Mongolia, with snowbound hills and valleys. As it got dark the best place to be was in the bar, with a beer!

Sleep was rather disturbed as there were a lot of stops. Martine left at about 4 a.m. and her place was taken by a friendly, and English speaking Chinese man. Settled down again until 7.30, to awake to a misty morning, terraced intensive farming on both sides, with oxen and hand ploughs using every possible bit of land. It was broken countryside with hills, gorges, gullies and caves, rivers, dry river beds and a lot of small towns. We then ran alongside a mountain range, up to about 3000 feet. A lot of farmers were in the fields tending maize and paddy fields – the crops all very neat and well looked after. Despite all the stops we arrived at Xi'an ten minutes early at 10.20 a.m. I shared a taxi with Patti to the Tang Cheng Hotel, and as it had turned into a thoroughly miserable day (the first since Moscow fifteen days ago –(not so bad then) spent the afternoon watching some dreadful American TV! I was also able to easily book a day tour for tomorrow and collect my onward rail ticket to Guilin from the very nice Miss Liang Ling Ling at the Xi'an International Travel Service. The Tang Cheng was a comfortable Hotel, but not much English was spoken. There were few Westerners about: I was the only one in the Hotel Restaurant. The meal was good, except that the soup arrived after the main course!

Xi'an is a very big city of eight million people, and is said to be one of the richest cultural centres in the World, not even counting the Terracotta Warriors. It was the eastern starting point and terminus of the Silk Road to Istanbul, and ranks with Athens, Rome and Cairo as one of the four great capitals of ancient civilisations. It was home to the Qin, Han, Sui and Tang Dynasties from 221BC to 908AD. The Chinese say, 'Go to Shanghai to see modern China, go to Beijing to see one thousand year old China, but go to Xi'an to see three thousand years of China'. I was picked up absolutely on time by 'Panda bus' which then negotiated huge traffic jams to pick up at other Hotels. The first stop was at the Big Wild Goose Pagoda. This was a fabulous place. I lost the others from the bus and the guide (deliberately) and wandered round the grounds listening to and enjoying Buddhist music and the scent of incense. It was just a few chords from string instruments repeated over and over, totally different to anything Western, but somehow mind grabbing and hypnotic. I can still hear it clearly over a decade later. I loved it, and the whole experience.

The Pagoda was built in 652 AD by one of the Tang Emperors and is a simple but imposing Buddhist temple, over two hundred feet high and about eight stories, tapering at the top. It was called the Wild Goose Pagoda as a story tells that a group of hungry monks saw a flock of geese fly overhead. One of them wished that he could have a meal of goose, and the leading goose promptly fell dead at his feet. Well? It was a gift from the Buddha of course. Why the Big Wild Goose Pagoda though? Easy question – because there is a Small Wild Goose Pagoda! This one was built in 707 AD in an area of temples outside the city wall; being newer it is less important than its larger cousin. It is in fact a pretty, dainty building. The next stop was at a Silk Carpet factory. Two girls had been working manually for two years on a carpet that would sell for $4,000. Even if I could afford it I don't think that I would have wanted to buy it to walk on. At some point on the tour I was congratulated by the bus driver on my Chinese. I had picked up some bits in Beijing and on the train, but have no idea what type or quality it was. Might have been high class Mandarin, or argot from the docks! We eventually left the urban sprawl of Xi'an, which despite the culture and long history is a Chinese Birmingham or Manchester - not pretty, with huge traffic jams. We also made the obligatory 'please buy something' stop at a ceramics factory, where I met my erstwhile sleeping companion Patti on a similar tour!

Eventually clearing the urban sprawl we arrived at the Warrior's Museum, and stopped for lunch at the very busy Museum Restaurant. At the start we had picked up from one of the Hotels an obnoxious fat man from Southern India and his wife. He had been trying to browbeat our very inoffensive tour guide from the moment he climbed, with difficulty, onto the bus. I had already reached the point of disliking him very much as we sat down for lunch at one big table. His conduct then became completely unacceptable as the lunch was not instantly forthcoming, so I fell out with him big time. It was embarrassing to be sitting at the same table. He was swearing, banging the table and shouting 'We are hungry!' in an attempt to bully both the waitresses and the tour guide. After too much of this I told him that he was a disgrace and an extremely unpleasant person, and I required him to shut up. He did, more or less, but I thought that it was interesting that none of the other ten or so people of various nationalities at the table was prepared to speak up. They might almost all have been embarrassed British! Eventually, and not in too bad a time at all, the lunch did arrive. Later the Guide thanked me for my intervention – he could hardly have said anything himself, and was only about half Fatso's size anyway. I later gave him a note for his Company to say that his behaviour had been perfect, in case he was complained about – I was pretty sure that that was going to happen!

I had been involved in a similar situation in an expensive London Restaurant a few years before. A man at a nearby table was being unpleasantly objectional in a very loud voice. No one, including the people at the same table, seemed to be prepared to do anything about it, so I went over and told him to shut up. Somewhat to my surprise he did. At an adjacent table, with a party of friends, was the current British and European Heavyweight Boxing Champion, Joe Bugner. He was big enough to tell any normal sized person to behave, but also did not seem inclined to do so. Perhaps being very big is not quite enough! I shared a lift from the Restaurant with Joe, who later became WBF world heavyweight champion, and we exchanged a grin about the incident. It is not until one shares a small lift with a world-class heavyweight that his huge size becomes obvious! He was at that time ranked amongst the top ten world heavyweights, with Ali and Joe Frazier.

Back in Xi'an, and losing the rest of the Group after lunch I wandered around the environs of the Museum, which were attractive, with pomegranate and small fruit trees and many souvenir stalls. I got a lovely grin from a wizened old man selling the Chinese equivalent of 'Kiss Me Quick' hats. But, like the lady of the golden mouth, no photo! There is a strong belief among primitive people that if someone is in possession of their likeness that person will have power over them, but I had not expected this in China and certainly not on an International Train. One always asks anyway – or should do so. I was able to photograph some younger men playing a big board game on the sidewalk, which seemed at first sight to be more like draughts than chess. However, watching for some time I was totally unable to grasp it, so it was rather more complicated than either!

A great deal has been written about the eight thousand terracotta warriors and horse pits, the first of which were discovered in 1974. I cannot improve on these descriptions, so will just record that they are fabulous, wonderful to look down upon from the viewing platforms, and that, as far as I can see, each of the eight thousand does have a unique face! After shaking off the rest of the group I was privileged to meet and shake hands with the elderly peasant Yang Pie-Yan, one of those who discovered the pits. He and his companions were given sacks of grain as a reward by the local administration. I wonder how much money has been taken by the Museum since? What a reward for finding something described as the eighth wonder of the world and the most famous cultural relic of China.

After a couple of hours we went on to the Huaquing Palace, a truly beautiful building and gardens, built in 644 during the Tang Dynasty. An Emperor brought his favourite concubine the Imperial Lady Young, who is said to have bathed her creamy skin in the smoothing waters of the warm fountain. I bet she did. In a less romantic period of Chinese history General Chiang Kai Shek, who fought the Japanese invasion of China was arrested there by some of his own Generals in 1936. It is still a beautiful place, despite the bullet holes, with a cable car running up the mountain behind it.

The traffic in Xi'an was even worse than it had been in the morning, and it took us two hours to get back to the ancient Bell Tower. The tower or Zhong Lou is geographically in the city centre, with streets running from it to the North, West, South and East Gates in the still existing Ming Dynasty city wall. It was built by the Emperor Zhu Yuanzhang in 1384 to dominate the city and surrounding countryside, as Xi'an then was very much a military town – as evinced by the Warriors of course. The painted wooden tower looked wonderful in the floodlights and it was in a very contented frame of mind that I asked the driver to drop me here, to walk back to my Hotel. The poor young guide, who really had not had a good day, was rather horror stricken by this decision, but I calmed him down and gave him the note to say that he had behaved very well with Fatso! The Restaurant in the Hotel was closed by the time I got back, so I found a really Chinese one, with no English menu, little spoken and no other European in sight. I ordered from my phrase book and gained credit from the Head Waiter by liking plain tea! There was a great series of smiles from the waitress and a group of five young men at the next table were, I think, betting on (a) could I order it and (b) could I eat it! My meal arrived exactly as ordered, and in the correct sequence, for 40yen - $5 - £3! My tip was smilingly and politely refused.

Next morning was an early start for a 6.40 a.m. taxi. My offer of a tip was once more smilingly refused by the check out girl, who insisted on carrying my case to the taxi, and handed over a beautifully packaged takeaway breakfast. I left the city with a wonderful impression of Xi'an. Overall it is not beautiful but it had been full of helpful, smiling people and some fantastic individual sites. The train was another four berth sleeper, clean; was found with no problem and left on time. There was pretty Chinese embroidery on the pillow cases. At first I had the compartment to myself, but then was joined by three Chinese men, who after eating a lot of pot noodles all went to sleep. However, this was a lot better than the Indian from Hell! We stopped several times at small towns, always with smart salutes from the Station Guards.

About midday I decided that the last of Killian's tins of salmon would be welcome. (English salmon, given me by an Irishman in Mongolia, and eaten whilst travelling across southern China. Small world). The pot noodle fans, having woken by now watched with great interest while I opened the tin with my Swiss knife and hoped very much not to make a mess of it. Following precedent they were all interested in my phrase book, via which I found that they were Engineers – sketches helped! There were no signs of any other Europeans on this train. We were now travelling through an area of intensely cultivated terraced hills, with mountains in the distance. Ox or bullock drawn farm vehicles and ploughs were universal, and some sowing by hand of a winter crop. We were now definitely headed south, towards my destination, Guilin. I felt that during this day the train had afforded an excellent picture of the peasant face of China, from dawn to dusk working in the fields, weeding, digging, planting, sowing and harvesting in their conical hats.

I woke to a misty morning, still in an area of intense cultivation, but now of flat paddy fields with the occasional water buffalo, evocative of much Chinese art. It was very rural, with poor looking houses. I was now onto my final map of south China, at Qidong - 400 kilometres still to Guilin. When the others stirred we shared breakfast – I did not record what but it was probably more pot noodles! It was noticeable that there was a substantial police presence on the train looking for stowaways - smugglers? After a stop at the substantial town of Lengshuitan the train entered the beautiful valley of the wide Li River that we followed to Guilin getting there by mid-afternoon.

I had tried to get off at a minor station, Guilin Bei, which caused some amusement, but I feel it was understandable! By bargaining with a taxi driver at the main station from 40 to 20 yen I restored some confidence in my burgeoning Chinese – but I expect that he would have come down to 10! The Ronghu Hotel was good on an attractive lakeside setting not far from the city centre so after a wash I was able to walk to the China Travel Service office for my onward tickets. Guilin has a comparatively small but very busy city centre, but a population of well over a million. It is famous for it's natural beauty, the sugarloaf hills on the Li River and the Cormorant fishermen, all of which I had come to see. Guilin translates as 'Forest of Sweet Osmanthus' because of the number of fragrant osmanthus trees. It has been a settlement since well before the Christian Era.

Once more I felt that I was probably the only European in the city, (although I am sure that this was not true) - there were no signs in English and no maps to be found - after all this was now deep into southern China and only about three hundred miles as the cormorant flies from the South China Sea and the Gulf of Tonkin. Young people on bikes were keen to practice their English, and a young teacher helped me to find the Travel Service Office, which was hidden in a dingy building. He was then joined by another young teacher and I found it difficult to avoid meeting them tomorrow for a bike ride. I was a bit wary at first but these two, Li and Tang, turned out to be very good guides, with a genuine interest in improving their English. They did cost me a few dollars, but the experience was worth it.

After parting from them I was stopped by a young female teacher, also on a bike, who wanted to talk. She had very good English already, but asked what I would like to do tonight. I thought that this was definitely a step too far, and pleaded tiredness. I don't know what I might have missed while having a relaxed meal in the Hotel Restaurant! The meal, ordered in Chinese - after a fashion - was as expected, as I avoided the more exotic items on the menu - cock's testes, penis of ox and cold seaweed. Fish and chips I could not have!

It was raining at 7.30 a.m., but Li and Tang turned up as arranged (principally by them), well shrouded in oilskins. As it was Saturday they had no school, so we hired a bike for me for 40 yen for the day - not a bad price, although it creaked a bit. We had a comprehensive tour of the city, including Folded Brocade Hill, Solitary Beauty Mountain, Diecai Park, Wave Subduing Hill and an 800 year old banyan tree. Then for lunch where both were very keen to have snake, mandarin fish and noodles. I discovered why when the bill came - $75! I guess that snake was too expensive for their own pockets, as I found that it is a costly delicacy. Interesting though, as one chooses one's snake from amidst a writhing bunch in a glass tank before it is killed. The taste was not at all bad, but the skin was a bit of a problem with the chopsticks. I was nowhere near a beginner with these, but under the eye of professionals?

However I managed and we finished with sweet water chestnuts. I think that we all enjoyed the lunch, as did the waitresses, and I got some nice photographs of a group of Chinese giggles. We then went to an artist's shop as I wanted to buy a painting of the Li Jiâng, with its miles of the incredible and beautiful sugar loaf hills. This is now a treasure at home. How good to be able to buy direct from the artist, with no middleman. He was very proud to show his work and for me to choose a painting The rain had eased off so we continued the bike tour to Camel Hill with two humps, and Seven Stars Park and Cave where there was a newly built wall showing the thousands of years of Chinese history. We returned my bike at 4 p.m. and I actually got some change. Wow!

By now I was definitely cast in the role of provider of a good time, as they suggested that I might like to go to a theatre that night. I had decided that they were not at all a threat, and was at the stage of thinking, 'What the hell – it's all good fun,' so off we went at 7.30 p.m., again by bike, with myself using Li's machine and he on the back of Tang's. No lights, but again, 'What the hell'! The show was good, acrobats and a contortionist but a bit expensive at $30. Back to my Hotel at 10 p.m. where we said goodbye. They had obviously enjoyed themselves, and so had I. I wonder if it formed the subject of a later lesson (perhaps how to get a good meal and a night out – no I think that is a bit unfair. I may be wrong but I believe that they were genuine and enjoyed showing me their city. It was a sine qua non that I had more money than they did). I would like to think that they remember the day, as I do.

I had a quiet walk round the lake before turning in, and then received a phone call from my tour guide Liu Jing Ling on the river trip booked for tomorrow. This was real devotion to duty, but I later found that I was her first client and she was determined to make a good job of it. At the end of the day she told me that she would keep the tip I gave her for ever, which was a nice thought, if not too likely. Like a lot of the young people to whom I spoke in Guilin she had good English but wanted to improve it further. I wonder if this came about through an enthusiastic teacher at the University? JingLing arrived on time next morning in a private car with a driver. She was so enthusiastic and keen on her job. We joined the cruise boat at the city quay, where for the first time I saw other Caucasian faces.

There were many many boats and the view from the top deck quickly became very dramatic. We were surrounded by the small boats of the fishermen, using cormorants that love to dive under the river surface for fish. They are prevented from swallowing what they catch by a cord tied around their throats. But, are given one occasionally as a reward!

The riverside scenery included Elephant Trunk Hill, where a section of rock hollowed out by the river does resemble - with some imagination – an elephant with its trunk in the water! The cruise, through the wonderful scenery of the multitude of sheer, narrow, tall hills, some rounded some pointed, is described as being through the most scenic area of China, and a poem has described the river as, 'a green silk ribbon running beside the jade hairpin hills'. This is a very good description. The hills standing in row upon row to the horizon, almost like the Terracotta Warriors, were dramatic, unusual and fascinating. Adding to this were the still present fishermen, small villages and glimpses of buffalo wallowing in the shallows.

After four hours and an included meal which I shared with a retired Pakistani Dentist from Bridgewater we arrived at Yangshuo, which was infested with Europeans! After Guilin this was an unpleasant shock. There were some nice views in the town, but it was very touristy, so I was not sorry to rejoin Jing Ling for the drive back to the city. She had been a very good guide, but the driver was terrible! Overtaking in all the wrong places, the first reaction to anything being the horn, and also placing complete reliance on it. Sometimes it might be better to be ignorant as a passenger! This was a foretaste of driving in Tibet, the reliance upon hope and gritted teeth. I believe that the culture of this sort of driving is deeply embedded in the Chinese psyche and would take generations of proper training to remove.

However, the drive gave me a chance to have a wide ranging discussion with Jing Ling and I learned a lot about Chinese family life, society and customs, that certainly would not have been given by a European Guide, or even an older local one. She was a very nice girl, and I enjoyed talking to her about England. I was most surprised to receive, later at home, a Christmas card and a letter saying how much she had enjoyed the day with her first client. I must have recounted my trick of hiding sandwiches in my uniform cap for Al when policing the West Bromwich Albion matches, as she mentioned this in her letter. Obviously it was not done in China! Jing Ling, if you should happen to read this do please contact me and tell me if you still have my tip in your purse for good luck.

Monday morning was unbooked so I had a wander round, visited the Market, bought a shirt for $3 which has only just been demoted to a painting smock for Jo, and two yellow baseball caps (still in use) for wear in the Jensen! I climbed Elephant Hill, then with weather improving from drizzle to sunshine, sat by the river, watched the fishermen and talked to more students, all keen to debate in English. As the Ronghu Hotel Restaurant was a bit dreary I was not too hopeful about the packed breakfast very early next morning, but they excelled themselves; there it was beautifully packed and a good start on the next leg by train, from Guilin to Nanning.

I had by now grown used to the reasonably comfortable four berth sleeping compartments, so it was a shock to find that the train to Nanning was a very crowded 3rd class carriage. The seats were described as 'semi-soft'! However the map confirmed that we were at least travelling south towards the Vietnamese border. The special Guilin and Li Jiâng scenery was eventually left behind and became more traditional Chinese small fields, mountains in the distance with intensive farming by peasants in conical hats and many water buffalo. There were several beautiful river scenes, but scruffy towns and villages, mud and straw huts sometimes on stilts in pools, with a mirror over the door to keep away bad spirits. I was quite enjoying this journey except for the continual habit of the other passengers of spitting on the floor. However, I had come to see the customs of other countries!

The train arrived at the one million plus city of Nanning precisely on time at 2.40 p.m. and the system worked again. My contact for onward tickets into Vietnam, Miss Ling (Maria) was waiting on the platform, and by some magic was exactly opposite the door of my carriage. How she did this I do not know, as I had changed seats to find one that was better than semi-soft! I had five hours to spend in Nanning, so I took her for a meal. Like Jing Ling she was a very pleasant girl, with good English and able to discuss many subjects. I then had a stroll into the city centre, which was quite modern, with plenty of high rise office blocks. It had a very different feel to both Guilin and Xi'an, strangely more Western and less traditional and was tremendously busy. I felt that all the million inhabitants rode a bicycle.

It was interesting though to see the extra signals on the traffic lights, which gave a count down to the next change of colour. This was useful going from red to green but could prompt drivers to try to 'beat the change' from green to red. I found no tourist traps, and received some nice smiles and comments, but had seen no other European face since Guilin. However, the *Sound of Music* was being played on the Station loudspeakers! In the waiting room (soft seat this time) I found at last some European faces, two Danish guys also on a round the world safari, and we were then joined by some Norwegian girls, also doing r.t.w. The girls had no onward tickets and the guys had no Vietnam visas!

The train was eventually open for boarding at 8.45 p.m., so we had a party – the long wait was never explained. I pushed the Norwegian girls into getting tickets, as they seemed inclined to hope for the best – I felt that I was rather better organised than both sets of Scandinavians. We were joined by a Japanese girl travelling on her own, who was grateful to hear my few words of Japanese. At the Chinese border at Pingxiang the Chinese border officials left and a Vietnam officer joined. Passports had been taken by the Chinese and were not returned until the train started to move – a slight reason for panic! The first stop in Vietnam was a mile or two on at Dong Dang, where all passengers had to change to a Vietnamese train because of the different rail gauge, and go through the usual customs and passport controls. The two Danes, without visas, marched off with all their kit and were never seen again!

Vietnam, another World Heritage Site

Eventually, after the usual bureaucratic nonsense the train moved off at 3.30 a.m.. This train had reverted to the four berth sleepers, which two of the Norwegians and a Chinese man with a huge amount of luggage and myself shared until arriving in Hà Nôi at 11.30 a.m.. This train was pretty basic and very slow. There was a squatter toilet at one end of the carriage and a washroom at the other, which seemed to be a bit illogical! The scenery was more jungly, but then became flatter and more cultivated, with lotus fields. There were grilles on the windows – to prevent escape? The entrance to Hà Nôi was not impressive, but then, what city railway approach is? My very well organised journey arrangements had ended at the Chinese border, so now it was up to me although I had booked ahead to a Hotel. The usual Asian scramble to provide a taxi took place in the station concourse, and I selected the most honest looking young man and said. 'OK'. This was a minor mistake as he turned out to have not a car but a small Honda motor bike – like almost everyone else in Hà Nôi! However, I rose to the challenge, carrying my rucksack on my back and the driver with my suitcase on the tank between his legs. Unconventional in Europe, but not at all so in Vietnam.

The capital city of Vietnam, on the Red River, has been around since 3000 BC. It has changed hands and names, being at one time called Dragon's Belly. It was captured by the Chinese Ming dynasty in the 15th Century but then recaptured by the Vietnamese and was renamed Dông Kinh. This was the name that became Tonkin to the West and which still survives in the Gulf of Tonkin, Tonkinese beautiful women and music. The French made it the capital of French Indo-China in 1887 and although their hold on Indo-China ended in 1954 during that short time French culture, language and elegant architecture became a vital part of the city. I quickly found that most old people would reply to a question in French, and during a walk around on the first afternoon enjoyed coffee and cake in a chic café by the shore of the Hoàn Kiém Lake – this was a reminder of the Bois de Bologne except that either the prices were cheaper or I had more money to spend! Hà Nôi is a city of beautiful lakes within the central area.

Hoàn Kiém is literally and figuratively the centre of the city, which has a population of well over six million, most of whom, like the Chinese, seem to ride either bicycles, scooters or motor bikes. Probably every owner of a motor bike operates it as a taxi! I found it delightful. There is always a downside of course, and in this case it was very persistent shoeshine boys, postcard sellers and the incessant noise of vehicle horns. Away from the old city and the French area it was more like Burma and Thailand than China. I walked around the lake and met my Norwegian travelling companions! In a city this size it was a bit strange, but I guess (a) that we gravitated to the same spot and (b) were easily recognisable!

The narrow streets around my Hotel were a bustle of activity in the dark as I walked back.

I was hailed lots of times – on the whole in a friendly way (I think!). Next morning was fine and hot, so I got a motor-bike taxi to the ancient Tây Cám Gardens, where Ho Chi Minh's Mausoleum was guarded by a soldier and was not approachable – by myself anyway. This was not too upsetting as the Park was quiet, peaceful and beautiful, and also contained the Chùa Môt Côt, the One Pillar Pagoda, which was my main objective. The Pagoda is exactly what it is named – a wooden temple sitting on a single pillar of concrete.

The pillar was originally, when built in 1049, of stone, but the French destroyed the pagoda when they withdrew in 1954, so it was replaced with a more modern substitute. It sits in the middle of a lotus pool, and is designed to resemble a lotus blossom. The King Ly Thái Tông was childless but dreamed that a Goddess handed him a son seated on a lotus blossom. He then married a peasant girl who bore him a son. Naturally he then built the Pagoda to resemble the flower – as you do. Whatever the truth of this, even the reconstruction is a beautiful little building and I was pleased to be able to carry a model of it home as a very relevant souvenir. I was then not too surprised to meet the Norwegian girls again in the Park!

While still in the Park I was assailed by three girls of about 14, who had been sent out from School to find an English visitor and complete a long questionnaire about the UK. I got into terrible difficulties trying to describe my son's job! After finding the nice Bois de Bologne café again I was able to get to the Ngoc Son Temple, (Jade Mountain Temple) on Jade Island. This is reached by a picturesque red wooden bridge – Hoc Bridge, or the Morning Sunlight Bridge, and watch soft shelled turtles swimming below. A wander then through the old district to the Red River, which is – wide! A young man reading an English book asked me to explain two words 'rival' and 'amicable' to him and when thanking me said 'You make it easy for me to understand'. This easily made up for the Shoeshine boys and postcard sellers! Vis à vis shoeshine boys by the way, I have, in many parts of the old world had to vigorously stop them polishing my suede desert boots!

In the old quarter, while consulting my map, I was twice very politely asked, 'Que voulez vous?' by elderly men. I would have loved to talk to them about the communist war and the old days of Indo-China but my French would not have stood the strain. Pity.

I found the Cathedral during the afternoon, which was in use. Children were being taught in groups but I could not interpret the subject. The exterior was a bit grim and the interior was rather bare by English standards, but the altar area was being redecorated with a silver trellis. I had booked a car to take me to Ha Long Bay for the next day, so after a visit to the Air France Office got a motor bike back to my Hotel and an early night.

Friday turned out to be a wonderful day. The car was a Toyota Carina (what else!) and the driver a young man with a few words of English. I had not been able to rent a self drive. He had the capability of being quite a good driver if trained and removed from his peers, but as it was I noted a dangerous fault about every thirty seconds of the four hour, 190 km, drive. However he was pleasant, and we got there! We were never out of sight of cycles, motorbikes, buses and lorries, but no really big vehicles, as the bridges were too weak for their weight. There were some terribly broken roads, but also a stretch of new toll motorway. Ha Long Bay is such an important tourist site that I guess that this has been finished by now – hope so anyway. The countryside was pleasant and green, fields being worked, lots of buffaloes and boys herding ducks. Little girls on scooters or bikes wearing straw hats with flowers on them. We were passed by one small motor bike with the whole family on board – Father, Mother and too many children to count, all hanging on somehow.

We stopped for a drink by the side of the road, and the driver would not let me buy him one. I had a fruit a bit like a small durian – probably it was, but a long way away from where I had the last one in Indonesia. Suddenly the Bay, part of the Gulf of Bac Bo, appeared, so much amazingly better than the photographs, with 3000 conical islands, covered in green vegetation and like the hills of the Li Jiâng, but rising sheer out of the emerald waters of the South China Sea. The Bay was made a World Heritage site in 1994, and most assuredly this was justified. People have been visiting it, painting it and writing poetry about it since the 13th Century and the Bay has been part of a number of films, including at least one of the James Bond saga.

The Russian poet Pavel Antokolsli wrote, 'To have a concept of the seductive beauty of Ha Long Bay we should multiply our Crimean coast with the south Caucasus, and then cube the product'.

That is a pretty good testimonial to the Bay of Descending Dragons. The name comes from the legend that the Jade Emperor sent Mother Dragon and a group of Child Dragons to help the Viet to fight invaders. They descended from the skies and spat out innumerable pearls that became the jade stone islands and smashed the invader's ships! There are many beautiful beaches and grottoes created by the wind and waves, and most of the islands are named for their shapes; 'La Vong' – the old fisherman, 'Ong Su' – the praying monk, 'Ga Choi' – the fighting cocks, and so on. The islands are limestone, probably 250 million years old, so that the greenery divides to display the white rock beneath – another aspect of beauty.

We arrived at Bai Chay beach at 1.00 p.m. and by 1.30 I was on a boat, leaving my driver, Nguyên Cao Phong, to his own devices. It was a holiday for him as well, and wonderfully cheap as he was thrown in with the car. The firm obviously did not trust a European to cope with Viet road manners – perhaps they were right! I had the boat, apart from the three man crew, to myself as I had earlier on Lake Baikal, but this was a lot, lot, warmer. Could it really be for only $6? They had seemed very happy to have my custom - no suggestion of waiting for more clients. This was all wonderful, to sit in the prow, with a beer and all but the essential bit of clothing discarded. It was a gorgeous day, and I ran out of film shooting islands, turquoise sea, beaches, grottoes and other boats.

Nguyên was waiting for me with the car, and we found a Hotel for myself, and one more to his taste for himself. Out for a walk after a meal whom did I meet but Agathe and another of the Norwegian girls! They were pushing their luck as usual, short of cash and in a very poor hotel, so I took them for some drinks, a chat, some advice and promised to send them a photo of the Jensen!

Next morning, I had booked a longer voyage with the same boat, Captain Tuan, and once more had it to myself. This was wonderful again, with my film stock replenished and able to get nicely sunburned in the prow, surrounded by squadrons of flying (or jumping) fish. Breakfast on the boat was good coffee, fried eggs and oranges. I was not surprised to see, and wave to, the two Norwegian girls on another boat. It was extremely good to lie back in the prow, and think about the island of Bali Hi in *South Pacific* which was probably filmed at Ha Long, 'You gotta have a dream.' I had brought my trunks today, and was able to swim, diving in off the boat and at one of the perfect beaches. It was easy to look down many metres through the translucent water. Lunch, bought from a smaller boat, was Vietnamese, using chopsticks. It included baby squid and fresh complete crabs that had to be shelled, a fish, big prawns and pancakes. It was quite a relief to finish with an orange and a number of cans of beer. Like everything else, just about perfect however. Revisiting my photographs now, I can hardly believe how perfect. One, from the inside of a grotto shows a perfect round shaft of sunlight coming in to illuminate the cave. Another picks up the dark red double sails of a working junk against the white limestone and emerald water. Life was, of course, going on for the Viet people amongst all this tourist pleasure, and there were many working boats around, some selling food, others fishing for shrimps, most with some sort of living accommodation, maybe just a cane shelter. There were floating villages of fishing families near some of the monolithic islands. After hours spent watching the islands and the sea the day, very regretfully, came to an end. I tipped Tuan and the boat boys generously and took their photograph after a perfect day, and walked gingerly on sunburned feet to the Hotel. It was worth the sunburn!

Breakfast on Sunday morning was at a roadside café – surprisingly good coffee and a pineapple pancake – well, the French were here for the best part of a hundred years! The ride back to Hà Nôi was as equally busy as coming, even on Sunday. Passengers in buses and lorries waved as they overtook, apparently demanding to be allowed precedence. I wondered if they employed people especially to do this! Four people on a small Honda motor bike was not unusual, all wearing conical hats, not helmets. How do they stay on, short of having a conical head? People were flying kites in the villages, as we stopped at a workshop producing needlework, stone earrings and silk wear on behalf of a charity for orphans and the disabled. I bought a few things as this was unexpected and a pleasure to see. Nguyên got us safely back to my Hotel and I also tipped him fairly generously, plus a letter for his boss. He had, I am quite sure, enjoyed his mini-holiday, but what he was doing I did not want to ask!

This was the end of my four weeks round the world safari, apart from getting myself by motor bike taxi to Noi Bai Airport, and a very comfortable but uneventful flight home with Air France. The last day at Ha Long had been a wonderful climax, and the whole journey, from riding the 'Iron Rooster'- as described by Paul Theroux - to the Mongolian Gers to the Big Wild Goose Pagoda to the French ambience of Vietnam, had been a kaleidoscope of experiences and memories, with perhaps one of the best days of my life at Ha Long to complete it. I am very grateful to all those who made it possible, took an interest, helped and co-operated and of course to Jo, for not objecting to my desire to take a few steps more.

Israel, the Negev, St Catherine's Monastery and Mount Sinai

In April 1999 Al, Nicky and I decided to visit Israel together, to safari around the country and meet again our friends Eliezer and Hannah Ben-David at Kibbutz Ma'anit. Nicky and I had both spent working holidays at the Kibbutz some years before, but this was the first time for Al. We stayed first in Nahsholim, a holiday village not far from the ancient remains of Caesarea and enjoyed swimming in the warm sea and wandering around the ruins of the Roman Capital of Palestine. Ceasarea, despite its name, was actually founded by King Herod. A Crusader Fort gazes down on the turquoise water as it ripples over 2000 year old ruins. This is the well named Sunshine Shore of Israel. On the coast where once Samson wooed Delilah, Solomon reigned and Cleopatra enchanted Anthony, the sand turns from gold to purple as the sun goes down, the blue sky becomes velvet and the sea is deep with blues, violets and greens. A great few days there, during which we contacted Eliezer and spent time with him and Hannah and their son Eldad and his family at

Kibbutz Harduf, near Haifa. Sadly Eliezer and Hannah, who had both suffered terrible trauma in Europe between 1939 and 45 have now passed away, and I am grateful that we were able to see them again. We are all still in regular touch with Eldad. We were able to take them to the beautiful white cliffs of Rosh Hanikra, on the Lebanon border, and have a long enjoyable meal in Akko – Acre of the Crusader battle.

Nicky, Al and I then set off on our Safari, by rented car in this corner of the world where so many things happened in such a small area. I had suffered greatly on my previous stay while walking from the Kibbutz at Ma'anit to the ruins at Ha Megiddo (Biblical Armageddon). On a very hot day, Israel is not that small, but this time we did it in comfort! The ruins of King Herod's stables, built on top of the hill where the final battle between good and evil is forecast to take place are fascinating, and the Church of the Annunciation is very beautiful. The Church in Nazareth is built on the spot where traditionally Mary was told by Gabriel who her baby would be. We were also able to travel to the Crusader Castle at Belvoir, that looks down from on high to the valley of the Jordan. The settlement of Bet She'an began five thousand years before Christ and in the late Caananite period - from the 16th Century BC, became the seat of Egyptian rule of Palestine. The city saw most of the Kings and Conquerors (up to the British during the First World War) who have trampled through the Holy Land since then. After the battle of Mount Gilboa the Philistines displayed the bodies of King Saul and his sons on the city walls.

We enjoyed the almost perfect Roman circus arena and extensive historic ruins that have now been restored and made into a National Park. Going on to Gan Ha Shlosha which is beautiful enough to been the true site of the Garden of Eden, as the mythology suggests! We also got ourselves to Tabgha, the Church of the Multiplication beside the Sea of Galilee and by following the Jordan south, to Jericho, where, outside the modern city is the site where Joshua made the walls fall down, or didn't as the case may be. Excavations have found walls, thousands of years old, but intact! Jericho is the lowest permanently settled and continuously inhabited site anywhere. It's Arab name means fragrant, and the Hebrew name is thought to come from the same root. Perhaps that explains why it has been inhabited since perhaps 16,000 B.C. and why Mark Anthony gave it as a gift to Cleopatra. We found the modern town to be very hot, dusty and bit run-down, and decided not to accept it as a gift if it were offered!

From Jericho we continued south to the Dead Sea, and, of course, had a 'swim' at 1300 feet below sea level-although a real swim is not possible. It is an 'immersion'and an experience of being able to sit in the water and read a book without sinking, rather than exercise! We then ascended the long steep road through the Judean Desert to our destination for the next few days, Jerusalem. En route the road passed the area of desert where I had made myself violently ill by accepting Bedouin hospitality years before – sheep's milk in tea! This was not a place that I wanted to linger in or remember, although their generosity and warmth were wonderful reminders of the traditional desert welcome.

What can I say about Jerusalem that has not been said better hundreds of times? Jo and I had visited the city in 1986 when we picked Nicky up from the Kibbutz, but again it was a new experience for Al. I think that it must be wonderful to go there for the first time, and wish that I could do so again. We got comfortable rooms in the Hostel run by and attached to the English Cathedral of St. George. These were an improvement on the room which Jo and I had found near to the Damascus Gate in `86, best described as cheap and cheerful! This had led to a problem when we flew out from Tel Aviv, as I had kept the Hotel card in my pocket, which, mainly in Arabic, made it very clear that it was a Palestinian Hotel. The Israeli Airport Security people are the only ones in my experience, which is world wide, who do the job properly. The Russians, back in the time of the USSR came close, but not to quite the same level. The Israelis found the card, which led to our being suspected of terrorism, which led to an interrogation, which led to me getting furiously angry as we were being made to stand, and Jo was hot and tired. After a shouted exchange about the way they were doing their job - politicians describe it as a 'frank discussion' - she was allowed to sit, and we were eventually allowed to board the aircraft, but it was not a pleasant experience.

St George's Cathedral was very English, but I was surprised indeed to find a plaque on the wall in honour of an ancestor of the car dealer who had just sold me the Jenson-Healey in Burton on Trent. A unique name, so no mistake! We had time to visit all the places that are 'must see' – Gethsemane with its two thousand year old olive trees, and a climb in the blazing heat through the Jewish Cemetery to the Mount of Olives. Also of course the Temple Mount, the Western Wailing Wall and Mea Shearim, where every man seems to be wearing a fur hat and an ankle length coat, the traditional European Hassidic garb. The walk around the city walls brings into view sites that resonate with history, Arabic and Christian, buildings that are white and brilliant in the strong sun and at a multitude of levels, the narrow alleyways running like dark rivulets through the old city. We walked the Via Dolorosa from the Damascus Gate to the Holy Sepulchre. My view of the Church and the so-called sepulchre inside it is that they are horrible places, and I have no belief at all that they are the genuine site of the crucifixion and burial of Jesus. In my view it is a myth, originated by the Emperor Constantine and his Mother

Helena on scanty evidence, and followed at the time, and since, because of who they were. The beautiful and peaceful (even with hundreds of visitors) Garden Tomb, a few yards from the Damascus Gate seems to me, for several reasons, to be the real place. One of them is the huge rock behind what is now a bus station, and which does look like a skull. General Gordon of Khartoum thought so, and his judgement was pretty good in many ways, so I go along with him. The Church of the Nativity in Bethlehem was also founded by Constantine and Helena, who was, I believe an hysteric, determined to 'find' evidence of Christianity, so I am doubtful about that also.

We enjoyed our wanderings around the city very much, and on the night before leaving I decided that we would have a slap-up meal in the King David Hotel. This is definitely up-market, so we dressed as well as possible for travellers, and enjoyed the evening, and were treated well. One incident though, which in retrospect I am a little remorseful about. English TV had been showing the John Cleese series about the dreadful Torquay Hotel 'Fawlty Towers'. In one episode Cleese was trying to boost the Hotel by having a Gourmet Evening, the main course being duck. Naturally everything possible went wrong, and the episode ended with Cleese bringing in a large dish with a huge domed cover and announcing in triumph, with a flourish as he took off the cover, 'The duck'. But it wasn't! Now, we had not ordered duck in the King David, but our main course was brought to us in a similar plate and dome, which the Head Waiter removed with a comparable flourish. We looked at each other, burst out laughing and said in unison 'The duck'! This was very unfair, and the poor guy was totally astounded, but it would have been completely impossible to explain to him, so we just got on with enjoying our meal, and gave him a good tip at the end. I have always felt just a bit ashamed about this, but I guess it followed the typical legend that all the English are mad!

Our next destination was the Gulf of Eilat on the Red Sea, via the Negev Desert. Eilat is about 200 miles south of Jerusalem, and the Negev covers most of this distance. It was once thought to be a fearsome desert, whose name means 'dry' and which few travellers wished to penetrate. It is alleged to rain once a month between November and March and never at any other time. Now with modern roads, settlements and accommodation it is still an exciting journey of rugged beauty and the traveller's tales need not be of superhuman hardship. Jo and I had journeyed through it in 1986, which I had enjoyed but she had not, being much affected by the heat, and having to stay in the Hotel room at Eilat during the day. The Negev fits, in part, astronaut's descriptions of the moon' surface, but in others more like Alpine glaciers, but coloured in hot reds. Our first stop on this safari was also at

Be'er Sheva which has been known since the fourth millennium before Christ, and has some remarkable remains of sites from the time of the Biblical Patriarchs. Unfortunately parts of the modern city resemble Milton Keynes. The Turkish Old City does not deserve this description of course, but I could not feel any liking for the place. It is thought that Abraham lived in this spot for twenty six years, and Isaac after him. There is dissent about the translation of the name, but the most likely seems to me to be 'The Well of the Oath' after the oath of agreement sworn between Abraham and Abimelech, the King of the Philistines. After Be'er Sheva the desert got real, and drinks were welcome at the Ramon Crater, the edge of a mountain escarpment with views over the Wilderness of Zin towards Mount Sodom, the end of the Dead Sea and Jordan. Towards Eilat, the desert becomes even wilder, with strange violet mountains, orange rocks and jade cliffs and gigantic sculptures in the rocks carved by nature. Gazelles race away and Ibex haunt the rocks, and occasionally there is a Bedouin camp pitched near a well. Black clad women can be seen walking, probably for miles to borrow a cup of sugar from her nearest neighbour. It was a long tiring journey, but on a well used route, so safe enough these days.

Nevertheless we were very pleased to arrive at Eilat and check into one of the excellent Hotels which line the Gulf coast. This caused a slight trauma at the Reception Desk as they failed to understand at first that Nicky wanted a room of her own, while Al and I were sharing, assuming that he and she were husband and wife. However it sunk in eventually and it was good to find cold drinks and international food at this modern resort, the Mecca of all watersports enthusiasts and snorkel and scuba fish watchers. There is so much to do in Eilat and it's neighbour Sharm El Sheikh across the bay in Jordan that it needs a lot more than the day or two that we had. Nicky had to fly back to Tel Aviv to return to the UK and Al and I were booked to meet a guide to take us across the Sinai to St Catherine's Monastery. However we enjoyed some excellent swimming to enjoy the crystal clear water, coral and the multitude of incredible fish. It was during a beach afternoon that they went off and bought me, without my consent, a new pair of swimming trunks to replace the very ancient black and white striped ones to which I was attached. I felt that while scuba-diving or snorkelling I had fitted in, and would not frighten the striped tropical fish! However, I have had the new ones almost as long now, and have used them from the Red Sea to Santiago, Kathmandu, Tanzania, Crete and Austria, so I guess that it was a good deed after all!

We also had a dive in the yellow submarine *Jaqueline* in the Gulf. This goes down into deep water, with good views of the changing coral and fish, and the sea cliffs. At the shallower part of the journey scuba divers were tapping on the portholes like strange underwater ghosts. The sub was designed in Finland, built in Belgium and now lived in the Red Sea! We took Nicky to Eilat Airport, and saw her off back to work at home, not knowing that she also was going to have a very disagreeable experience with Security Staff at Tel Aviv before boarding the international flight. She was examined as part of the routine checks, but then interrogated very closely as her documents showed that she was going home alone, leaving the two of us behind. This was apparently thought to be very suspicious. She was questioned for a long time and all her belongings searched in detail by a male Security Officer, and it was apparently very unpleasant. However, as I said earlier they did then do the job properly, perhaps still do, and it might be that some of the incidents that have happened since on aircraft would have been avoided if other countries were as thorough.

Anyway, while Nicky was suffering, unknown to us, Al and I left the car in a long term park and crossed the barbed wire border into Egypt to meet Ayman Abu El Saud, our guide through the Sinai. Ayman, whom we knew nothing about until now, turned out to be a very pleasant and helpful man, with a 4WD car and a driver, so we were able to head south without worrying too much about staying on tarmac. We stopped for drinks and a swim at a Hotel on the coast before heading inland. This offered a great contrast between an ultra-modern and expensive resort Hotel, and just out to sea, on Pharoahs island, the two castles of Salah El Din, built in 1170 by the Muslim warrior whom we in the West know better as Saladin. The castles, covering most of the small rocky island played a major role in the Crusades.

We then drove into desert proper, through huge tumbled rock formations, where chiselled inscriptions proclaimed the existence of tribes and people who passed through here during the course of history. There are about ninety miles between Salah El Din and Mount Sinai, during which the desert was broken by low mountain ranges, infrequent clusters of date palms, and when we reached an all weather road the occasional trader's stall. The high mountains beckoned in the southern distance. We had booked a room in the modern village of St Catherine's, near to the Monastery and found that the pilgrim chalets had been built to replicate Bedouin tents, and were comfortable and cheerful. There is a continual torrent of visitors and pilgrims to the mountain and Monastery, and the modern village supplies all their needs.

The mountains above the Monastery are neither grey nor grim. They reflect the sun, golden at times, briefly sandy when the radiance decreases behind cloud. There is fertile greenery in the valley where the Monastery nestles beneath the protection of Mount Sinai, Jebel Musa - the mountain of Moses. Winter snow descends upon Musa and his big sister next door, Jebel

Katherina. It trickles down into the valleys and waters the oases and orchards that provide oranges, dates, olives, apricots and grapes to the tending Monks and Jebelliyah Bedouin.

Despite our plunge into the sea at Salah El Din before leaving the coast, the green oases were Heaven-sent. I wondered if Moses and the quarrelsome, grumbling, stiff-necked people of the Tribes had felt this and had agreed that the snow-melt valley was a wonderful place to rest. Some doubt has been expressed that this part of Sinai is the true scene of the Biblical ascent by Moses. The prophet Isaiah taught that God lives 'in a high and holy place', and I have felt the ambience of an infinite personality in other high places where I have been privileged to stand. I am, years later, still very content to believe that this is such a place.

The Monastery stands foursquare, hidden within an encircling high wall of golden stone, the many treasures securely preserved for over a millennium. Traditionally without entrances, bona-fide visitors were once hauled in a basket up the wall – I guess medieval Monks were martial, not meek. Disappointed not to be basket-cases, we crept in through the miniature door and found ourselves in a fascinating Byzantine warren of roofed and unroofed corridors and tiny ancient buildings. Especially, growing from the building that was built to protect it, was the bush that is held to be, not a descendant, but the very one where God told Moses he was on Holy Ground. Our Greek Orthodox guide allowed us into the Library, where we were permitted to hold a very ancient codex – long quiet centuries of painstaking scripture in our twentieth century European hands. Finally, we saw art treasures and icons, exquisite even when unsophisticated, and every one a venerable antique.

Dawn seen from a mountain top is always an extraordinary event, and so we met our mountain guide, Suleiman, at 2 a.m. Siket El Bashait is a tortuous snaking path climbing to the summit of Jebel Musa. There were a collection of camels at the foot, waiting for those who would rather sit than walk, and hundreds of pilgrims beginning the ascent. At 7,496 feet Sinai is a not insignificant mountain, and at times, finding the hindquarters and tail of a passenger carrying camel in front I was tempted to strap-hang. Everyone showed a light of sorts, and, gaining height it was rather wonderful to see the snaking tail of glow-worms beneath us, twinkling like earth-bound stars against the desert floor. Enterprising locals had set up rest stops on the path, and it was tempting to buy a Coke or a warm tea. Moses did not do this, but we did. After two and a half hours climbing, the summit was already packed with people, gathered around the tiny Greek Orthodox Chapel that traditionally encloses the rock from which God made the tablets of stone. As sunrise was due at 05.11 everyone was facing east, where the coastal mountains of Arabia were dimly visible against the slowly lightening sky. We weaselled through the crowd to a prime position, and waited – extremely cold but eager to see the night-dimmed ranges illuminated by the miracle of sunrise. And it came – on time precisely, not a moment too early or late! The first shining sliver of orange appeared, then levitated itself into a glowing fiery ball and as it cleared the distant mountains the enthralled audience shouted spontaneously, 'Do it again'! The rocky heights around us and across the Gulf brightened into gold, - violet or purple in the valleys; colours that no human artist could match. With the sun created splendour came welcome warmth, and Louis Armstrong who sang to me alone, 'The bright blessed day, And the dark sacred night, And I think to myself, What a wonderful world'. The sun quickly warmed the mountain top and Al and I enjoyed staying, looking at the view, the colour and the vast distances all around, before eventually racing each other down the path, through the golden sunlit rocks, that had seemed so difficult in the cold dark. Maybe there are other contenders for the site of the tablets of stone. Maybe the Byzantine Emperor Justinian was wrong in the sixth century. Maybe Moses did not ascend any of these mountains. But, fourteen hundred years of pilgrimage and unbroken religious history have left a legacy, an impression, an after-effect, and to me a consciousness that this is a very special place. This had been a wonderful shared experience.

Ayman got us safely back across the Sinai to the Israel border, where we were quite sorry to part from him. Al was due to fly home, while I was staying to see Eliezer and Hannah again, but we both enjoyed another of Eilat's offerings – the Airodium! This is a vertical wind tunnel, about thirty feet high, with the updraught capable of supporting a human body. We had about half an hour of careful instruction, then put on a 'flying suit', a plastic overall with bagginess around the arms and legs so that it spread out into wings. You then step off over the thirty foot drop and enjoy the feeling of being weightless! The instructor could, of course do various aerobatic manoeuvres, which we attempted, in a clumsier way to emulate. After finding that the updraught and suit did actually work it was great fun, and another new experience. The instructor said, 'You can fly!'

After Al had left, I decided to stay on for one more day, and had, at last, the experience of swimming with dolphins that had not happened (due to their reluctance, not mine) in New Zealand. Amongst all the other exceptional things, Eilat had 'Dolphin Reef', where it was possible to hire Scuba gear and a wet suit. The dolphins had been trained to return regularly to the reef. Perhaps lured is a better word, since I believe that they are intelligent enough to make up their own minds. They were free and unconfined and had the whole of the Red Sea as their territory and playground. It was however possible for the managers of the site to virtually guarantee the chance of swimming with them. They did look as if they enjoyed visiting the reef – perhaps they enjoyed the dolphin/ human contact as much as we did. I was OK with the gear, and this was comparatively shallow water, but there was some instruction by a professional lady who reminded me of Patti in Vava'u. It is not until one is alongside a dolphin that it is apparent how big they are! But very friendly, and unconcerned. I did think at the time how good it would be to ride on a dolphin's back, following a Greek legend, but this was one step too far that I did not take! However, another unique and wonderful experience.

Close to Dolphin Reef is the Coral Reserve, the most northern coral reef in the world. The Red Sea is a tropical sea, and although the Gulf is it's northern extremity it qualifies as tropical. This latitude does not prevent it being a delight of richly coloured coral and the home of a multitude of fish. The chance to snorkel again before leaving Eilat was therefore too good to miss, and after saying goodbye to the dolphins I said hello to the coral again. The Management of the Reserve have imposed some strict rules on swimmers, partly for their own protection and partly to preserve the coral. Marked pathways have been laid out on the reef table, which in the crystal clear water are easy to follow, and it is forbidden to move or touch anything. This would be a remarkably silly thing to do anyway, because Lionfish, Scorpionfish and Stonefish are all present on the reef, are extremely well camouflaged, merge into the reef rocks and have a sting which can cause paralysis or death. Sounds a bit worrying, but as long as the rules are obeyed it is another great experience. Blue Trigger fish, Clownfish with their rather comic faces, Sergeantfish wearing the stripes of their rank, multi-coloured Parrot fish and many others, all beautifully coloured, perhaps especially the dangerous ones, to match their coral homes. Even common Goldfish, which look so much more right in the clear water and amongst the coral than in a tank in an English living room. The water over the reef table is only a foot or so deep, so one has to be careful of scraping knees on the sometimes very sharp edges – in fact it is a rule to wear sneakers. The reef wall then drops sharply to about 20 – 30 feet and continues to descend to the open sea and maximum depth of about 6000 feet, and occasional short visits of Sea Turtles, Barracudas and Sharks are not unknown. Blood in the water from a scraped leg is therefore not a particularly good idea. This reserve is one of the most impressive and famous in the world, we were very lucky to see and swim in it and I am so glad that it has not suffered the deterioration of some coral reefs due to the dirty habits of humankind.

Approaching the end of a wonderful stay in Israel, there was one more site that I wanted to visit before reaching Kibbutz Ma'anit. This was the Nahal Zin Ravine in the Ein Avdat National Park, in the northern Negev. The Avdat Mountains rise to only about two thousand feet, but are composed of spectacular hard white limestone. The Ravine can be trekked, following a stream and passing the mouths of caves where Monks lived during the Byzantine period. There are magnificent views of the white cliffs as the ravine, or canyon, winds through the mountains, and with ladders set into the cliffs at some points it is possible to climb up and get a complete view downwards as well. Herds of Ibex, wild mountain goats, skip about happily from crag to crag, impervious to the heat and the height! The Ravine is subject to some very firm, and enforced, rules, i.e. you must either wear or carry headgear, you must carry water but cannot carry food, and don't annoy the wild animals! Oh, and the ladders are one-way - up - only, so when you are up you are up! However, despite the rules, it was a great trek of about three hours, and a good way to leave the Negev.

I drove north through the West Bank, following the Jordan, and through Nablus, the Palestinian City which has been the scene of repeated unrest. The city is a large urban area, definitely not a tourist site, but I had no problems at all, and reached Ma'anit to spend a couple of days with Eliezer and Hannah. I am so very glad that I stayed on to do this, as I did not see them again after leaving Israel, and they were both people that I thought a lot of, each with an incredible, perhaps unbelievable, history during the 1940s and 50s. After a pleasant time, culminating in a stroll and an enjoyable meal on Mount Carmel above Haifa, it was time to say Shalom, and return home.

I don't think that it could have been a better visit to Israel, with some wonderful experiences and memories. It is one which none of us have been able to repeat, although it remains as one of the places that I would want to, but may not see again.

Chapter 11

Trekking in Uzbekistan, Tajikistan and the Pamirs - Kilimanjaro, Mount Meru and Ngorongoro

Uzbekistan, Tajikistan and the Fann in the Pamir Mountains

The Pamirs are among the highest mountain ranges in the world, with Stalin's Peak (as it was known during his years of despotism until 1962) reaching 24,590 feet. It is now renamed Ismoil Somoni. Two other mountains, one still unofficially known as Lenin's Peak, are over 23,000 feet. The range is snow covered all the year and has bitterly cold winters and short summers. The source of the historic Oxus River is in the Pamirs, which lie in a knot or junction of the Western Himalaya, the Hindu Kush and the Karakoram. They have long been known as the 'Roof of the World', which is a perceived translation of 'Pamir'. The northern Great Silk Road crossed them, en-route from Xi'an to Kashgar. They have been a strategic trade route for hundreds of years, an area of conquest and territorial campaigns in Central Asia, and the location of much of Rudyard Kipling's *Great Game* between England and Russia in the 19th Century. Kipling's great character Kim (Kimball O'Hara) carried out his espionage here during the Great Game. The Pamirs were crossed by Alexander the Great and his army, and Lake Iskanderkul is named after him (Iskander is the Persian name for Alexander, and kul is Tajik for Lake). The ancient cities of Bokhara and Samarkand, with the tomb of Tamerlane and memories of the Mongol tribes lie on the edge of the Karakum Desert to the west of the Pamirs. Afghanistan, the North West Frontier and the Khyber Pass are to the south, and the Taklimakan Desert in Chinese Turkestan to the east. An area absolutely overflowing with famous names, famous locations and history, famous stories, ancient and modern.

The English diplomat and poet, James Elroy Flecker, who was more or less contemporary with A.E.Houseman although dying at the terribly early age of thirty, wrote *The Golden Journey to Samarkand*. Often referred to as the Golden Road, this has been a hymn to travellers to Central Asia and the

Far East, and a call to travel during the twentieth century, now continuing into the twenty first. Its most enduring extract is that written on the clock tower of the barracks of the 22nd Special Air Service Regiment at Hereford. 'We are the pilgrims Master; we shall go always a little further; it may be beyond that last blue mountain barred with snow. Across that angry or that glimmering sea'.

In July 1999 I had the chance to join an expedition run especially for the Royal Geographical Society in the Fann Mountains, the western ridges of this intriguing area. This was much too good to miss, so I flew into Tashkent, the capital of Uzbekistan on 17th July 1999, arriving at 2 a.m. local time, after a six hour flight. Several of the group were on the same plane, and we were met by our Russian guide, Andrei Kroussanov, and his colleague 'young Andrei'. I have known quite a few Russians during my work and travels around the world, and there are two who stand head and shoulders above other people of their own and other nationalities. One of these is Alexander Bondar, whom I met and worked with in Burma and the other is Andrei. It is a sadness that I have not been able to climb, or trek with him again. Both Alexander and Andrei are, or perhaps were, quiet men, not in any way the typical vodka drinking boisterous Russian of popular myth. It was obvious from the first moment that Andrei enjoyed his job and loved the mountains and his style of quiet unobtrusive leadership helped us to appreciate and love them also. 'Young Andrei' was about eighteen, on holiday from St Petersburg University, a pleasant helpful young man and an experienced climber already. Galena, the female Doctor appointed to travel with us I do not know so much about, as she spoke only a little English, but she treated my spectacular head wound during the trek very effectively! Achmet, who drove us wherever it was possible to drive, was an Uzbek, very cheerful, and helpful. He was responsible for a fairly elderly Russian minibus that took us up some 'interesting' gradients on the dirt roads to the start of our trek. From time to time this needed a bit of help. I have a nice photograph of all the men in the party – about eight of us (except myself, who was otherwise occupied taking the picture) pushing the bus up somewhere where it did not want to go!

However, at our arrival in Tashkent, this was in the future! There was a five hour bus ride to Samarkand, after the normal Russian bureaucratic hassle at the airport. A city tour had been planned immediately after an extremely unpleasant breakfast at our Hotel in Samarkand. The temperature, by the way, was about 40 degrees and dusty! The others and I were tired, but the Registan, the centre of Samarkand made the journey worthwhile. Samarkand, the second city of Uzbekistan, now with more than half a million people, is one of the most ancient inhabited cities in the world, at least 3000 years old.

It was contemporary with Babylon and Rome, and had a position on the Silk Road midway between China and the West, thus was a crossroads, a mixture of cultures, religions and people. It has seen Alexander the Great, the Mongols under Genghis-Kahn, Tamerlane also known as Timur, and of course in modern times, the Russians. It would be unthinkable to be in Uzbekistan and fail to see Samarkand. The Registan, the ensemble of three Madrassas facing each other across an open square of blindingly white stone blocks is a world site not to be missed. Alexander, in 329 BC, found it even more beautiful than he had imagined. I thought so also. Unfortunately the tour so soon after arrival was an indigestible surfeit of history and glorious buildings. It could perhaps have been better timed, and the lady who was the city guide was grimly determined not to let the smallest detail go unexplained! I should say here that this itinerary was nothing to do with our climbing leaders, Andrei and Andrei, it may have been inspired by the Kremlin! However, the photographs that I somehow managed to take stimulate a memory of what was, in retrospect, truly a wonderful experience. The Madrassas are tiled in glowing flowing colours, blue, red, purple, brown and yellow, with architecture that inspired the building of the Taj Mahal by Shah Jahan in the seventeenth century. In the West Madrassas are commonly said to be Radical Islamic Schools, teaching anti-western propaganda. Politicians, particularly in the USA, who should have been briefed much more carefully, have used the word in a perjorative sense. In fact it means a school. It is, I think, an interesting exercise, to compare the history, architecture and objects of the Madrassas, which were certainly superior schools, with, let's say, Oxford Colleges. Grey stone against bright tiles, battlements against domes, spires against slender minarets – the contrast of just the achitecture could provide a thesis in itself.

The tomb of Tamerlane, who was the descendant of Genghis-Khan, and one of the most brutal but most effective military leaders in history, was different to the colourful Registan. The Gur-e Amir is quiet, a low grey dome externally with no celebration of power or Empire. It is tiled in the shadowy interior in intricate but muted colours. This is the resting place of a man who, in his time, was the most powerful in the known world, and with Alexander (and perhaps, nearer our own time, Napoleon), one of the most effective military leaders ever. The low stone tomb is covered by a slab of jade on which is carved, in Arabic, 'When I rise the world shall tremble'. The tomb was opened by the Soviet anthropologist Mikhail Gerasimov in 1941. It is said that Gerasimov, who moved the body from the tomb, found a second inscription reading, 'Whoever shall open my tomb will unleash an invader even more terrible than I.' This may or may not be true, but what is historical fact is that two days after the opening of the tomb was commenced, Hitler began Operation Barbarossa, the invasion of Russia. I felt that there was a huge sense of ongoing ceaseless history here, and even looking back can feel the hairs on the back of my neck rise.

The guide, eventually satisfied that she had given extreme value for money, decided to release us to rest. Anything on the itinerary, had to be done! The two Andreis had released themselves earlier, so it had not been possible to appeal to them for help, but it was a blessed relief to stagger back to the hotel, minds reeling a little with medieval Central Asian history. The plan was an early start for the two hour drive to trek commencement tomorrow morning. It was at this point that I made a bad mistake. Andrei had warned everyone not to even think about drinking water from the bathroom tap, but I had decided that it would be safe to brush my teeth. It wasn't. I wandered alone around the city in the afternoon, but the bad mistake was now making itself apparent. It could have been the breakfast as well as the tooth brushing!

After another rather horrible meal and a disturbed night we set off early in the minibus and crossed into Tajikistan through a not entirely impressive border post, into the town of Panjakent. The Tajiks love vivid colours and this was apparent on some of the public buildings, although the shape and style was iron curtain concrete. The children's clothes, boys and girls, were colourful, despite the fact that there was obviously not much money around. The kids were all delighted to wave and pose for photographs. History was again all around, as in some of the more remote villages the Sogdian dialect, that Alexander the Great would have recognised, is still used. There was a genuine sense of welcome among the Tajiks in the summer camps where the whole family, parents, grandparents and children, bring their sheep and goats for the abundant grazing. It occurred to me that the love of colour was reflected in the surroundings, the mountain tops brilliant white in year round snow, intensely blue lakes like little jewels, juniper forests on the lower slopes and lush alpine meadows with a profusion of bright alpine flowers.

In Panjakent we were joined by Galena and the cooks who would travel with us, and then, in the somewhat reluctant and often struggling bus, followed the Shing River by graded dirt road into the mountains to our first campsite by the sixth Marguzor Lake. The Shing was snow-melt racing downhill, very much like the Dudh Kosi, the Milk River, as it races down from Sagarmartha via the Khumbu Ice Fall. White topped high peaks were visible all around, at last it felt like mountain trekking country, and the heat and tiredness of Samarkand were leagues away. There was not at that time a tradition of portering among the Tajiks, although economic necessity may have changed that now, so we were joined next morning by a team of donkeys, all naturally given names by the ladies in the Group! The first trek was a steep climb up to 10,000 feet, to camp below theTavasang Pass. This was pleasant walking, with easy tracks passing local people in the summer camps. Nearly all were wearing traditional Tajik clothing, women in coloured dresses and wide trousers tied at the ankles and a small hat or coloured headscarf. The men were usually less colourful, with a shirt, wide trousers and a scarf round the waist. Next day was more strenuous, as we were getting close to the higher peaks of the Fann, which now arose magnificently to Chimtarga at over 18,000 feet, capped with snow and ice even in July. She was surrounded by her slightly smaller but snowy sisters, Energia and Zamok. Eventually we camped in a magical meadow below the icy north face of Gardish. Our cooks produced the first meal that I had enjoyed, and the toothbrush episode was now an unpleasant memory. This was beautiful country, with glaciers, alpine meadows, juniper trees and blue, white and yellow flowers. An occasional avalanche could be heard, or was even seen on one slope. There was often a smell of thyme, mint and sage. There were several days of trekking, all with steep climbs and descents, and a swim in Chukurak Lake. This was a very beautiful spot and the lake was alleged to be warm enough to swim in, but it turned out to be a very brief swim! I was leading quite a lot of the time, as Andrei seemed happy for me to follow my nose. As we were following well-used trails this was no problem. We passed a few villages and were invited to take chai with one Headman in his mudbrick and stone house. There was also the chance to do some enjoyable ridge walking and scrambling, amongst the broken tumbled crags for those who were energetic enough, and to see golden eagles soaring over the valleys.

By the sixth trekking day, some of the party were showing medical problems, sore feet and tiredness. Andrei was also having trouble with his left knee, - an old injury I imagine, so I lent him one of my trekking poles and led with young Andrei so that he could take it easier at the rear. There had been some hard but beautiful days, twelve miles on one, following a really rough white water stream cascading downhill. There was a clever irrigation system rigged up here, with pipes going uphill at an angle of 45 degrees, the water travelling up them by the pressure of the stream rushing down. We had been lucky with fine weather up to now, but on the sixth day a torrential thunderstorm hit us with hail and heavy rain and everyone got soaked, so we camped at 2.30 p.m., got the tents up and into the sleeping bags. It didn't stop until after seven, but the cooks did a splendid job in providing soup and potatoes. Next morning was beautiful again, so we got drying lines out and enjoyed what was, in the sunlight, another beautiful site. Geoff, one of the older men in the party was really not well, and had got lost trying to find the latrine tent during the night. He wandered around for an hour in the dark before finding his way back to his own tent. It was now that the wisdom of having a Doctor in the party was apparent, as we were far away from any other medical help. We had a rest day here, and Geoff took it very easy, and improved. I did a short trek to enter a disused fluoride mine, sunbathed on a boulder in the afternoon, and then watched a goat being killed and skinned for our evening meal.

The trekking was very similar to the Himalaya further east, with tumbling white mountain rivers crossed by ramshackle bridges. The main difference was the colour of the many lakes, which could not have been more blue. Some of the lakes were also incredibly clear, and reflected the surrounding mountains in very accurate detail. The blueness from height is, I suppose, due to minerals in the ground. Juniper trees seem to thrive on it, so there was often some greenery somewhere in view. Particularly beautiful, seen from Alaudin Pass at over 12,000 feet, were the two deep blue Alaudin Lakes. There was a suggestion that Alaudin was the same name as Alladin, which seems possible but I cannot confirm it. However, I did not find much relevance to the pantomime plot! Mutnye Lake, surrounded by the high peaks, was alleged to mean 'Murky', and in contrast to most of the others, it was, a bit. Perhaps more like Glaslyn high in the cwm east of Snowdon on a 'Welsh' day. Actually 'Glaslyn' means Blue Lake in Welsh, but it isn't, often! As we got higher wind sculpted pillars of rock appeared, assuming strange shapes. The mountains themselves regularly changed colours from gold to grey to white, and were now invariably wild and savage. Some were attracting a plume of cloud, or ice crystals, as does Sagarmatha, further East. We had a long wait for the donkeys to catch up at one campsite, as 'Rambo' had fallen off the track! Fortunately he survived! The last camp before tackling the Kaznok Pass was at the Eagle's Nest, a hollow in broken rocks, high and very cold. The cooks did a splendid job in providing hot food, before a cold night and an equally cold start at 6am. The donkeys left us here, including the disgraced 'Rambo', to take a much longer route back to Panjakent, as they could not climb the Pass.

There was a lot of snow to cross from the Eagle's Nest, but Kaznok Pass, at 13,250 feet is a permanent zone of snow and ice, so Andrei cut steps to make the climb possible without everyone needing to have an ice axe. This was quite hard climbing, and although some of the Group had been less than 100%, everyone managed it. The steepest point was near the top of the Pass, so there was an air of triumph from everyone to have got there. We received a fierce blizzard as a reward at the top, but when it cleared the panorama was spectacular, with Chimtarga, although over 4,000 feet higher, looking almost attainable.

The central mountains of the Fann are spectacular, great soaring pinnacles like a child's idea of a mountain. One in particular reminded me strongly of the icy white needle of the Matterhorn, or perhaps, more fancifully, the opening advertisement scene of Paramount Pictures.

There were some wonderful photograph opportunities, but then it was a long long scramble down a very steep scree slope descending the southern side of the high peaks. I think that everyone fell over at least once. Finally another twelve mile walk towards Lake Iskanderkul and the last campsite at Sarytag Kishlak. When we had completed the difficult descent, and were on a flat track towards the Lake, I disgraced myself like 'Rambo' by tripping over a small rock and cutting my head open. Obviously getting too relaxed. Galena made a good job of treating it, and it looked impressive all the way back to the UK, but was not as bad as it looked! Somehow, and I am not quite sure how he managed it, Achmet met us at the campsite with the minibus and our kit and tents, and we were able to set camp at 7.30 p.m. – a long but fantastic thirteen and a half hour day!

The final day was a lot less tough, about eight hours by minibus. We passed the side of Lake Iskanderkul, and I found it a humbling experience to think of Alexander and his army making their way over these mountains, marching from Macedonia to conquer the known and, to them unknown, world, more than two thousand years before. No doubt he was carried; – no, wrong, I believe that he walked or rode his beloved white-starred warhorse Bucephalas, if he was the man that I think he was. Most of his army certainly walked though. We had it easier, crossing the Zeravshanski Ridge and following the Zeravshan River valley to Panjakent and then on to Samarkand, and a soft Hotel bed!

As with Samarkand, it would have been unthinkable not to see Bokhara. The four hour drive was hot and rather dull, but at least the Intourist coach was an improvement on the minibus. The city has an ancient history, having existed for two to three thousand years. The region is known to have been inhabited for more than five thousand. It was on the Silk Road and therefore a city of scholarship and culture, with many Mosques and Madrassas. It is deservedly a World Heritage Site, and although in Uzbekistan, has an ethnic majority of Persian speaking Tajiks. We were taken through fascinating narrow twisting alleys in the old quarter, to see the Kalyan Minaret, also known as the Tower of Death, from whose 150 foot height criminals were once punished by being thrown off. They did not offend again. Despite its gruesome history the Minaret was beautiful, golden in the hot sun, contrasting with the bluey-green domed roof of the mosque next to it. It is said that the Kalyan stopped Genghis Khan in his tracks. It was 40 degrees again, and I think that everyone was exhausted by the end of our walking tour. Once more we had a lady town guide, who insisted on giving her full schpiel at every site!

However, after a shower, and teethbrushing from a bottle this time, we had a good dinner together in a Caravanserai in the old city with local dancers, which was a good show. We enjoyed expressing our appreciation to Andrei and his team – I was elected to buy some gifts and present them, which was a privilege and pleasure. Then at 3 a.m. coach to Samarkand, a final breakfast together on a Hotel terrace before coaching on toTashkent for flights home. This fifteen day expedition, with thirteen campsites, almost all exceptionally beautiful and memorable, and glorious high snow capped mountains, and above all so full of history and famous personalities, was a wonderful trekking experience. It was made by Andrei. I very much regret that it has not been possible to meet him again and hope that his life since in St Petersburg and on the mountains has been good. Andrei, how about another climb some time?

Kilimanjaro, Mount Meru and the Ngorongoro Crater

Kili, the top of Africa, the World's highest free standing mountain, and one of the world's largest volcanoes. Who would not want to stand on Uhuru Peak? I certainly did, having seen it in two very distinct aspects and conditions, first while worried, sweating buckets, and lost in Amboseli, on the Kenyan, northern side of Kili. Secondly, in much more comfort, from a southbound aircraft as the mountain soars gloriously up nearly 20,000 feet to meet the clouds. It is as if it is reaching up to touch the impudent aeroplane trespassing on its territory. There was a chance to know the mountain properly in Millenium year, in company with one other Englishman, David, younger than myself and a regular trekker and experienced climber. We met on the aircraft en-route to the small Kilimanjaro Airport, south of Kili, having been booked in adjoining seats, in February 2000.

There are several established routes to the top of Kili, some comparatively long but easy, effectively steep walks not climbs, and they have been tackled by very brave disabled people, and even by someone in a wheelchair. However David and I opted with our guide to do a climbing/scrambling route, via Arrow Glacier and the Western Breach and it became one of the best trek/climbs that I ever completed. The plan we had both opted for was an acclimatisation climb on Mount Meru, before the thinner air of Kili. Meru is no pygmy itself though; at a fraction under 15,000 feet it is the fifth highest mountain in Africa and an active stratovolcano.

Having had long stops at Rome, Cairo, Addis Abbaba and Nairobi we were very late arriving at Kili Airport and there was no one to meet us. The plan was for David and myself to stay at Momella Lodge, a Hotel that used to be the African home of actor John Wayne. Feeling that the spirit of Wayne, when we turned up obviously not expected, might be 'The hell you are', we got ourselves onto a minibus with some German tourists (who had been met!) and stayed at Springlands, another Hotel, for the night. No problem, this is Africa! Zainah, a very forceful Tanzanian lady re-arranged everything very well, and we enjoyed a pleasant open-air dinner at Springlands. Momella Gate, in Arusha National Park was the starting point of our trek to the top of Meru, and next morning we got there, eventually, getting some wonderfully enticing views of the snow and ice on Kili en-route. There we met our guide, Joseph, an armed Tanzanian Ranger, and the two French couples from Provence, with whom we were sharing the climb. Momella Gate is a gate in theory only, although it does have a sort of Rugby football goalpost to mark where it is. It is in very green, lush parkland, not trimmed and disciplined like an English Park, but wild and beautiful, with Mount Meru rising in the background.

Three hours very pleasant walking through the grass land where giraffe and buffalo co-existed happily (apparently!) and then into forest where Joseph reminded us to keep an eye open for leopards sleeping (or pretending to sleep) in the trees, brought us to the Miriakamba Hut. At nearly 8,000 feet the Hut is a comfortable stopping place, providing a good dinner and plenty of beer for those who wanted it! We spent an enjoyable evening talking to the several other trekkers and guides there. Sleeping was in a mixed dormitory with bunk beds, which I think rather surprised the two French ladies but it allowed a comfortable first night. Breakfast was toast, fruit and coffee, then a steeper ascent to Saddle Hut, at 11,800 feet, but still walking not scrambling.

David and I climbed to Little Meru peak at 12,000 feet and enjoyed wonderful views in the late afternoon light across to Kili, 70 km to the north-east. Kili was lit beautifully by the setting sun behind us. Looking down upon the miles of tree covered plains between the two mountains was also beautiful, and exemplified the vastness of Africa. It was good to be here again. Saddle Hut was more bare than Miriakamba, with not so many people, but we got a good cooked dinner of soup, meat and rice, and went early to bed, ready for a 1am rising! There were no lights in the hut, so it was lacing on boots by torchlight, with cold fingers! Coffee with biscuits was excellent and we started the hard part of the climb at 2.30 a.m. The object was to get to the summit by sunrise. It was extremely cold now, with a strong wind, but we were able to leave our main gear at Saddle Hut, and just carry a day sack with water and food. We started with a steep climb through forests and then onto rock slopes, still in total darkness apart from our own torches.

This was not easy, and would have been dangerous without an experienced guide, but Joseph, and his colleague who had joined us last night, knew what they were doing. We got onto a narrow ridge leading to Rhino Point, where the last rhino living in Arusha had died, then some scramble-climbing over big rocks. We reached a ridge leading to the summit at about 6.30 as golden streaks were beginning to appear to the east, south of Kili. The sky lightened, the climbing became easier and gradually a glorious golden sunrise appeared as we tackled the steep rock climb to the final peak, reaching it at about 7.30. Lights had been showing in the semi-dark from the villages and shambas at the foot of Meru, and Kili was now highlighted and silhouetted by the rising sun. I have been on a number of mountain tops for sunrise, but this, like Mount Sinai, was one of the most beautiful. As the light increased white mist filled the distance between ourselves and Kili, and I have a wonderful photograph of Joseph, with Kili in the background over his shoulder. He is giving a hugely delighted wide smile, teeth very white against his skin, obviously very proud that he had done his job properly, and that we were all so happy to be there.

The peak of Meru is marked by a permanent metal Tanzanian flag, and a book in an all weather box for successful climbers to sign. At the age of 68 I was quite impressed that someone of 76 had signed in! It would not be a difficult climb in daylight, but in the dark it was quite something. After enjoying the splendid scenery for a while we made our way down to Saddle Hut for lunch, to congratulations from the staff there. They seemed genuinely pleased that it had been successful – how nice. On the way down there was one incredible sight, being able to look down into an ash cone – one of the volcano's vents. It was a perfect circle, a huge hole in the centre, and the view was as if we were flying over it. The climb down was long and hard, and slightly worrying was the thought that it had been done in the dark of an African night on the way up!

Continuing down in the afternoon we reached Miriakamba Hut about 4.30 p.m., with the two French ladies being now very slow. Climbing Meru had been quite hard, cold and windblown and they were tired, but after a good meal and a restful night we said goodbye to Joseph and continued down to Momella Gate with another armed Ranger, Burra. Burra kept his rifle accessible, warned that leopards were a real possibility, and even found some footpad marks and droppings, but to my regret we did not see one. Burra said that if they were in a tree we probably would not see them until too late! However, this was a most beautiful walk in the morning sun, with herds of giraffe and buffalo again and bushbuck and the occasional elephant. Two had come very close to the buildings at Miriakamba Hut and there was a loud sound of trumpeting, but no herd. (I cannot resist saying that they were seen but not herd.) This morning walk was a gorgeous African experience.

At Momella Gate we were met by transport to take David and I to Momella Lodge Hotel, and our French friends on to Moshi, the town at the southern foot of Kili. Apart from the mix up the night we arrived everything had worked very well and the acclimatisation for Kili proved to be well worth while. I had felt a bit breathless at the top of Meru, but not uncomfortably so. I felt that Tanzania had made the very best of promoting the country to visitors, and this feeling was strongly reinforced in the following days. I hope very much that this has not changed, and that porters and guides still have ample work and are treated properly by the tour companies.

Momella Lodge was unquestionably beautiful – bright flowers, green tended lawns, and pleasant staff with a series of two person huts outside the main block. One did have the uncharitable thought that this was due to a number of third-rate films, as well as a few good ones, but what the hell, as we could hear John Wayne saying! A number of people focussed on Kili were staying there, and I talked to Stuart who had walked on two artificial legs on a sponsored charity walk up one of the easy routes. He had not reached the summit, but got as far as the Shira Plateau, which was pretty impressive, and David and I felt it was worth a decent donation towards his sponsored target. We had dinner together, during which Stuart's colleague asked the waiter for a plastic chair so that Stuart could take a shower. The waiter's face was interesting, as the prosthetics were hidden by trousers and not obvious, but he did not bat an eyelid!

At 8.30 a.m. we were picked up to collect our climbing permits from the office in Moshe, interestingly being caught in a speed trap on the fast surfaced road from Arusha! Then it was a very dusty track to Umbwe Road-head to meet our two guides, Richard Meeza and his assistant Nestor. We were all booked in, so that our presence on the mountain was recorded – again demonstrating the professional approach of Tanzania. With four porters to carry the camping equipment it was a six man support party for the two of us, but that's the way it is done! Good for the local economy as well. Richard asked me to lead the trek to the first campsite in the rainforest, and in retrospect I believe that this was not a compliment but a very sensible way of assessing what I would be able to do, showing his experienced mountain leadership. In fact, I was feeling very fit, having done a lot of preparation up and down the Wrekin, and we covered the normal six to seven hour trek in four. This was a bit too fast for both David and our guide Richard! It was like home to me, quite like the lower slopes of the Wrekin, with many fallen trees, some scrambling over rocks, quite hard work but not difficult, and we got to Bivouac 2 for the night, rather than

Bivouac 1 as suggested in the guide book.

Bivouac 2 was a pleasant site, still in the rainforest, with rock overhangs or caves, so it was not necessary to crowd into the tents. We were now at twelve and a half thousand feet, but no sense of height yet as there was no view through the trees, either downhill or of Kibo, the peak. We had a good night and awoke to porridge and toast and were off by 8.30 a.m. Richard said that he would lead this section, but he had told David that he was impressed with my speed, and felt that we could tackle the Western Breach, via the Arrow Glacier Route. This would be slightly shorter, but harder and more interesting, and that the final ascent at night would definitely be a hands and feet climb.

We agreed and although I did find the final metres of height gain at the top very tiring and breathless, Richard's judgement was right, and we made it! The Kili Guidebook recommends this route only for the very fit, so we were flattered by Richard's assessment. In fact we got to respect him a lot for his knowledge, helpfulness and professionalism during the next few days, and also the same in respect of Nestor. Perhaps I have been lucky, but I am sure that this has applied to, perhaps not all, but most of the expedition leaders that I have travelled with, and whom I remember with pleasure.

We quickly left the rainforest and emerged onto an exposed ridge by the side of the Great Barranco Valley, and suddenly there was a breathtaking view of the snow and ice of Kibo, far above against a cloudless blue sky. Kili (the full name is shrouded in mystery, and no adequate translation exists. It is possibly two corrupted Swahili words, perhaps meaning White Mountain or Shining Mountain. Maybe it comes from 'njare' meaning 'source of water' in Maasai or 'njaro' an east coastal word referring to the demon who creates cold!). No one knows, and I suspect that the Tanzanians do not really care. They just describe it as awesome and magnificent, inspiring wonder and respect through history. It is difficult to argue with that. The mountain is unique, being divided into five distinct ecological zones. The lower slopes, inhabited and farmed, the rainforest, then heath and moorland followed by highland desert where the seasons meet, summer by day and winter at night, and the icy summit with artic conditions, blistering sun by day and sub-zero freezing temperatures at night. Oxygen at this level is half that at sea level, and there is little protection from the radiation of the sun. The ascent, climbed or walked, by whatever route, is literally a journey from the Tropics to the Arctic.

The forest had been dense with grey/green streamers of lichen (old man's beard) hanging from the trees, and mosses, ferns and orchids encrusting the branches. Moving out onto the heath and moorland this changed, with giant varieties of plants that have adapted to the environment. Heather trees grow to twenty five feet, giant groundsels and camphor trees, lobelias and yellow proteas abound and multi-armed giant groundsels, fifteen or twenty feet high look like aliens amongst the abundant clumps of tall grass. There are three dormant volcanoes on Kili. Kibo, generally regarded as at the peak of the mountain, Mawenzi, to the east and Shira to the west. The three distinct cones can be seen from many aspects, and over the millennia vast eruptions, growths, subsidences and the ebb and flow of glaciers have created Kili as she is today. Occasional puffs of sulphur and steam can be seen, and smelt, from the fumaroles or vents. It has been decided, by those who profess to know about such things, that Kili is dormant, if not extinct, but the Earth has a long history of surprising us, and I would not exactly write her off.

We arrived at Barranco campsite in nice time for lunch. This was the point where I lost my trousers – a story, 'The day when I lost my trousers half way up Kilimanjaro', upon which I have been able to dine out a few times! Sounds good, but in reality it was nothing dramatic but a prosaic bit of forgetfulness. I had a rather good pair of 'action trousers' (that I have never been able to replace), which had suffered during the night climb on Meru. As we were staying two nights at Barranco I begged some hot water from the cooks, and washed them. I spread them out on a bush to dry, and for all I know they are there still!

We spent two days at Barranco for further acclimatisation before our climb into thin air, the breathless zone at Kibo, the crater rim at nearly 20,000 feet. There were splendid views now of the Kibo glaciers, and the Mawenzi ridges and peaks at 17,000 feet. By climbing a little way the view across the seventy kilometres to Meru, bathed in morning sunshine, and then silhouetted by the setting sun was splendid. Our route was the Western Breach, where the ferocious Western Wall is broken, scattered and tumbled. The Western Wall is a serious technical climb, including an icefield and the Diamond Glacier. It has been likened to the North Face of the Eiger, requiring a full support team and ice climbing equipment. We shared Barranco during the first day with a German team who were tackling this climb, and saw above us the lights of their bivouac half way up the Wall during our second night.

Arrow Glacier campsite was the next day's destination; we were now trekking through the Highland Desert, barren and forbidding from 13,000 to 16,500 feet, hot in the sun by day but wintry cold as the sun sets. The mammals that occupy the lower regions; colobus and blue monkeys, porcupines, baboons, the occasional lion and secretive leopards do not inhabit this inhospitable terrain. Elephants, giraffe, eland and buffalo have been sighted in the lower moorland, but most are transient only. Even birds find the thin air and the strong shifting winds a challenge, but the larger raptors, buzzards, crowned eagles and lammergeier vultures are able to soar in them. As the altitude increases life diminishes, until only humans and a few insects share the highest levels. Is this maybe some sort of parable?

Our fourth night campsite near Arrow Glacier was another stunning experience. It was a relatively flat rock-strewn shelf, only a few square yards in size but spectacular because we had climbed through the clouds and were now looking down onto their rolling foaming white tops with clear blue sky above. From time to time they rolled away for a moment and then the villages and farms below revealed our height. There was once a Hut near this site, but it had been destroyed by an avalanche. It was here, much too late, that I remembered my other trousers left on a bush some three thousand feet below! Richard confirmed that we could do the Breach, graded at 1+, with a 12.30 a.m. start to reach Kibo for sunrise, so it was early into very cold sleeping bags.

It was a beautiful moonlit morning. One upside of Africa is the staggeringly clear stars that light the sky at night. The climbing guide likens them to Christmas tree lights in a darkened room. Only Richard and Nestor came with David and myself, as the porters needed to take a longer descending route following Kibo south circuit, and meet us at our fifth night camp, Mweka. It was cold, and I had put on all available clothing, which at least made things easier for the porters. The moonlight made the climbing fairly straightforward at first, and it shone on the glaciers to our left and right. We were following a ridge, which the guide describes as difficult to descend, and needing ice axes when snow covered. It was dry and clear of snow and ice to start with, but getting increasingly hard work by both hands and feet in proportion to the decreasing oxygen. Crater Rim was reached at 5.0 a.m., with the sun beginning to cast a golden glow behind Mawenzi. The last thousand metres or so to Uhuru Peak was extremely steep and partly iced. It was now hard work, and I needed frequent rests on this last bit. Richard and Nestor made repeated efforts to carry my rucksack, but I just about managed to hang on to it and reached Uhuru in one piece. After getting my breath back (or some of it) it was mandatory to pose for a photograph by the 'Welcome to Uhuru Peak, 5895 metres amsl' sign. Like the top of Meru with it's permanent metal flag, the board was nice to see, with what I felt was a genuine 'Congratulations' message. Uhuru, at a little under twenty thousand feet, means Freedom, and is a symbol, with a very special meaning, of the struggle of the African nations to liberate themselves from the brutal colonialism of some obdurate white European countries. I just love the mountain, and the area, and am very proud to have climbed it, even breathlessly.

It was very cold, and the extra clothing was welcome but the views from Uhuru of the ice walls, hundreds of feet in depth, and to look down on the crater itself made the temperature seem irrelevant. The glaciers have spectacular ice pinnacles, rearing up many metres high. White clouds, snow and ice contrasted with the dark lava rocks. As the sun rose one beautiful sight to the west was the triangular outline of Meru, the peak just surfacing out of a white mist tinged with gold, while to the east were the shattered peaks and pinnacles of Mawenzi. They were formed when liquid lava was forced up from the earth's mantle into the vertical cracks in Mawenzi's cone. The softer rock eroded away, leaving the hard black lava walls and spires. The Saddle, which connects Uhuru and Mawenzi is Highland Desert, bleak, inhospitable and strewn with boulders, lava gravel and parasitic cones. Not a picnic site!

After gorging on photographs, and with the sun now warming up, it was time to leave. There were a lot of exhausted walkers now arriving at Uhuru from the 'normal' Marangu 'easy' route. As many of these people were not experienced climbers or trekkers they were to be congratulated for having the persistence to keep going. Some are not able to make the final two to three kilometres to Uhuru and have to turn round at Gilman's Point, approximately two hours from Uhuru and about 700 feet below. Because this is so common a special certificate naming Gilman's Point is awarded to them. This must be devastating, after struggling for five or six days, but altitude sickness can kill, so a good guide will insist on giving up if the symptoms are apparent at, or before, Gilman's. I do know how disappointed I was at having to give up on the first Himalayan trek, and anyone who gets to Uhuru, by whatever route, has done well.

We were taking an easy way down, on the Mweka Route, a lot of which although steep, long and dusty, was capable of being taken at a run, and we reached Barafu Hut, at 15,000 feet for lunch. Kibo, and the southern glaciers five thousand feet above, was still visible in majesty, as were the forest and plains below. It was good to think that we had done it. People were making the ascent up on this route, and I do admit to a sense of superiority as we greeted and passed them. There is, I think a variant of Schadenfreude at work here, the German word for enjoying the misfortunes of others! There were a lot of people on this walking path, and we were both grateful to Richard for starting the ascent on the much more isolated and interesting Umbwe route. From Barafu, meaning 'ice' in Swahili, the route became a pleasant three and a half hour walk to our fifth campsite at Mweka, on the edge of the rainforest, and congratulations from our porters.

After an enjoyable lazy evening the sixth day was downhill for three or four hours through the forest to more congratulations at the Park Gate, near the College of Wildlife Management. After checking out and being awarded our nice certificates, signed by Richard and the Park Warden – ('successfully climbed, right to the Summit') we regretfully said goodbye and many thanks to Richard, Nestor and the porters, and rewarded them, appropriately I hope.

Transport to Springlands Hotel was waiting for us at the College – again all very well arranged by Zara Tours!

David and I had both opted to extend our journey to Lake Manyara and the famous Game Conservation Area of the magical Ngorongoro crater. The Crater of the Rain God was formed millennia ago, in the same sort of tumultuous explosion that raised Kili and the other Tanzanian volcanoes towards the skies. The fires died and this volcano folded back inside itself, with the caldera walls forming a protection against the outside world. The flat crater floor is about nine miles in diameter, thus a huge bowl, and full of just about every major African mammal and bird – lion, leopard, cheetah, elephant, buffalo, wildebeest, hippo, ostrich, and giraffe. Even the rare black rhino, struggling against extinction is there.

Also in profusion, and providing food for the predators are zebra, eland, many sorts of gazelle and antelope, down the tiny and pretty dik-dik. All this, and much more lay in wait, and we went out for our garden dinner at Springlands with great anticipation. Over dinner we palled up with two pleasant twin sisters, Ineke and Marloes van Bilsen, who had not been climbing but were also going to Manyara and Ngorongoro. I am afraid that my urge to tell stories, some of them quite tall, took over, but they seemed to enjoy them, while David kept quiet! Next morning we had a Land Rover and guide, with the sisters also sharing another vehicle, and we shadowed each other, for the hundred and fifty miles to Lake Manyara, then embarked on a three hour safari through the game reserve, the two vehicle's paths crossing and re-crossing as we saw a wonderful variety of game, including lion, regiments of elephant, big and small, which we had to keep dodging as they insist upon precedence! Also coming out for inspection were impala, warthog, baboons, monkeys, eagles, storks and pelican. It was, I suppose rather like being in a huge wildlife zoo without bars or walls, and so lush and forested that even the elephants could hide and spring a surprise!

We stayed at Twiga Lodge for the night, and had a birthday party for the twins. They wanted to `phone their Mother in Nymegan, but there was no service to Holland so I rang Jo and asked her to pass a message on that her daughters were fine! A nice evening, with plenty of Dutch beer to be drunk in both toasts and relaxation! Next morning, after another safari though the reserve was the drive to Nogorongoro, with a climb through beautiful forest to the crater rim and our campsite for the next two nights. From here the view is 2000 feet down to the crater floor, and about 16miles rim to rim. As lights began to come on around the campsite and shadows lengthened down in the bowl of savannah grass it really was a most beautiful place. Tens of thousands of herbivores keep the grass in submission, and knolls known to the Maasai as Hills of the Red Earth swell up to provide an alternative to the level prairie. In the north Kitati Hill, a miniature defunct vocano seems flat-topped, but has it's own shallow crater. Its Maasai name means girdle, as it resembles the garment worn by their women. There are acacia forest thickets on the crater walls, and on the plain, and alkaline Lake Magadi, with its resident flock of flamingos. The interior of a collapsed volcanic crater does not sound very attractive, and, for example, the crater of Vesuvius certainly is not, but amongst the grandeur of the places that I have been privileged to see, Ngorongoro has a wonderful claim to world pre-eminence.

We were up at 6.30 for the very steep descent by Land Rover down into the crater. A herd of cattle carrying tinkling bells were being led down age-old trails by a Maasai boy so that they could lick the salt rich margins of Lake Magadi and drink from the freshwater streams that trickle down the walls. Officially they need a Government permit to do this, but as they have been doing it for generation after generation I suspect that the permit is not always seen as necessary. There was an early morning mist, and the crater was as gorgeous as the night before from the rim. Tiny dots below slowly magnified into game, of all sorts. It was so easy to find spectacular sights. A rhino and her calf, thousands of zebra, wildebeest, buffalo, hippos, some wallowing in a freshwater pool and others apparently undecided whether to go for a bathe or not. The Maasai seem to have no problem with being on foot – after all they do hunt lion as an initiation rite, but it would not be a very good idea for a visitor.

We soon found a pride of lions, a big male and his harem, who took absolutely no notice of us a few feet away in the truck, except for a lioness who lazily walked round inspecting us. Lions are inherently lazy – they seem to enjoy lying in the sun as much I as do, but this can be a shade deceptive as they can clear a thirteen foot barrier or a thirty foot chasm with one leap. This I can't do. I suspect that the indolent lioness would have a different attitude if she saw us on two legs. Strange. Maybe the overlaying smell of metal and fuel masks the human meat recognition. There is a PhD resting on this question, but who is going to research it?

We had lunch, ours, not theirs, surrounded by the lions, continuing the safari afterwards and seeing many gazelles, hartebeest, giraffe and ostrich, jackals, lots of hyena, eagles, white Egyptian vultures, cranes, pink flamingo in Lake Agadi and a convocation of elephants. The high spot was finding a cheetah, stalking something small in the grass, his belly close to the ground until he was spooked, probably by us, and took off with that beautiful fluid motion. He was pretty fast, but not, I think at top speed, which can be as much as 70 mph. Nevertheless it was a real privilege to have found and seen him in his own natural hunting ground. That you do not get in a zoo. The whole day was a privilege, and hardly believable in retrospect. It was literally like being in the middle of a wildlife film and as on Meru and Kili I was deeply impressed with the attitude and work of the Tanzanian Conservators. I hope that it continues.

All good things come to an end, and after climbing a very steep track up the crater wall (a one-way system is sensibly enforced) we returned to Twiga Lodge where a cold shower was very welcome after a hot, dusty but enthralling day. With a 6.30 a.m. start we spent next day in the Tarangire National Park, seeing more animals in a different setting, more open country than Manyara, and without the volcanic history of Ngorongoro. Again a great opportunity to see Africa in reality – no infrastructure, very few other people, just animals being animals, red in tooth and claw.

Finally back to the Springlands Hotel, where we caught up with the twins and confirmed that their Mother had been reassured of their safety! Up at 3.45 for the early flight from Kili Airport, and getting wonderful last views of Kili and Meru in the sun-rising light.

David and I have kept in touch ever since, swapping trekking destinations, and even managing to be in the same part of the Himalaya at the same time in 2009, but on different routes. This was a truly wonderful seventeen days, that I am very lucky to have had.

Snowshoes in Bulgaria

In 2003 I did something different! I saw an advertisement for a trek on snowshoes in the Rila Mountains of Bulgaria, a country not yet fully recovered, despite the passage of time, from the tender loving care of the U.S.S.R. Jo having decided that this was not for her, I got a fairly easy flight into Sofia at the end of January, with the snow looking eminently suitable for snowshoes!

If ever a case needed to be made about the despoilation of a country by the Russians, I think that this was it. The Rila, in the south west of Bulgaria are beautiful, serious mountains, and once one had the knack - two days at least required - of keeping the snowshoes on, the trekking was a delight. The knack to manage two trekking poles was also needed by those who had not done it before. We did not camp on this holiday, but trekked through the great green coniferous forests each day, returning to the very spartan Hotel each evening. By the end of the week the seven of us were completing a full day up into the higher mountains, which was pretty good. The sensation of using the shoes was quite different to skiing, more of a push and slide, but with the poles it worked. Well, I suppose having been in use for thousands of years, it would! Actually, it was quite good to think that we were using one of the most ancient forms of transport. The two highest peaks in the Rila are Malyovilsa at nearly nine thousand feet, and Mousala at nearly ten. Serious mountains but not climbable in snowshoes! Primitive man could probably have done it in bare feet.

Another thing that was quite enough to make any English person despair – the ease with which quite elderly cars were being driven up and down steep hills in deep and often falling snow with not the slightest problem. Yes, they had chains on, but they all knew how to use them.

There were a few decent restaurants, showing what could have been achieved instead of the square concrete blocks of flats and 'co-operative' housing in the villages. These were depressing – may be better in sunshine but I doubt it. I have a cynical feeling that the more attractive eating places were placed where better off people tended to go for their snow sports, as there were plenty of well dressed and well fed children around with skies, and toboggans. Also rather sad was the occasional old-fashioned hostelry in a village street, rather like one good tooth in a dreadful mouth, that had survived the years of communism. Great to go in and enjoy their form of glühwein but not so good to look at (or live in) the concrete next door.

Rila Monastery, a World Heritage Site, where we went by coach on the final day was staggering. It was founded in the reign of Tsar Peter of Bulgaria in the 10th Century on an outlier of Rila Mountain. It stands at over three thousand seven hundred feet – higher than Snowdon, alone in the dark green forest, apart from a cluster of subsidiary buildings and trader's stalls. The white-capped peaks can be seen not so far away. Rila is the largest and most famous of the Eastern Orthodox Monasteries of Bulgaria, and famous for Saint Ivan, a medieval hermit. The Monastery is very big - quite easy to get lost in. It has cloisters, towers, domes, colonnades, courtyards, archways and several series of arches. I am not quite sure if 'beautiful' is the word, but certainly 'striking, impressive, imposing, eccentric or extraordinary' would all fit.

Every so often a Monk would step out onto a open platform 25 feet up the Hrelyo Defence Tower, and smite a large bell by the side of a wooden clock with it's workings visible behind glass. The tower was built as a refuge to retreat to in times of need. The overall impression of all these disconnected corners is of horizontal stripes in both brown and white and red and white, and this is the main theme of decoration on the brick and wooden walls. Inside, murals depict Bible scenes from Genesis to Revelation. The interior rooms that I saw were baroque - very - but I don't suppose that this carried over to the living quarters. Most Monk's cells that I have seen were not luxurious.

We all had a fascinating time wandering round, with no hindrance, and some interesting souvenir shopping at the stalls. Rila gets a lot of tourist visitors, and I doubt if any of the traders were in need. Then it was back for an early night and to Sofia, the capital of Bulgaria to reach the Airport next day. Sofia was not impressive! It is a city of well over a million people, and while there are some beautiful houses, and wide streets, the latter are the Russian variety – a street nearly as wide as Red Square or Tian An Men Square makes one feel a bit lost. Despite the fourteen years that had passed since the end of Communism in Bulgaria, the city still looked very institutional and uncared for. Throw in the pot-holes, dead dogs, concrete flats, wandering pedestrians and erratic signposting, and I just could not feel that it was a place to love.

But, I have been critical of aspects of the country that did not appeal to me, and perhaps I have not been fair. They have lived through bad things and come out the other side. Living under Communism was never easy. The people, our guides included, were mostly great, the scenery in the Rila is wonderful and it was another good experience that I was lucky to have.

Chapter 12

The Pilgrimage to Santiago de Compestela

Having read an article describing the long walk, or Camino Francés, from St-Jean-Pied-de-Port to Santiago de Compostela in Northern Spain, I decided, with Jo's approval once more, to give it a go while I still could. In the event, I wore my feet out up to the ankles, but got there! The camino is well researched and travelled, and in a much more accessible part of the world than some of the odd corners that I have been in. The walk can be as long as a piece of string – start from Trömso in the Arctic if you wish. However the last 100 kilometres have to be on foot (or 200 by bicycle) carrying your own pack, to qualify for the Compostela, or parchment certificate of achieving the pilgrimage. This has been a goal for pilgrims of hundreds of years, and an itch of mine for some time.

I am still not entirely sure why I did it. A challenge certainly, a chance to do something new and different and perhaps an interest in the medieval religious legend – was it really the bones of Sant Iago, Saint James, a companion of Christ, in the great cathedral at the end of the trek? I was not very likely to find the definitive answer to that question, but it was in the back of my mind. There are many routes, official and not, to reach Santiago, and I would not be at all surprised to hear that someone did start from the Arctic Circle, or Tierra del Fuego!

I met men and women who had travelled many more miles than myself; one Englishman had started from Newcastle, caught the ferry then walked down from Northern France. People spend every summer trekking the camino, perhaps doing it all in one gigantic go, or coming back year after year to do another hundred miles! I decided, because as usual time was a bit squeezed, to take six weeks, and start from the French side of the Pyrenees, at the Pass of Roncesvalles, just before my 74th birthday in 2005. The intention was to walk for about five hundred kilometres more or less, depending on deviations and sight-seeing. Because the camino is such a well travelled, historical and popular route there is every advice and guide book possible, and I got everything that I needed from the 'Confraternity of St. James' in London.

As this was going to be a solo effort, unsupported, it was also necessary to think hard about what to carry. In the event I took far too much, and my progress through northern Spain was marked by paper parcels of unwanted clothes sent home from every village post office! A wonderful thing, for me, was that while some of the camino is on public roads, much is on mountain or valley tracks, rough, flinty, often cobbled and crossing streams by ancient Roman bridges on the medieval pilgrim routes. These are, of course, only accessible by foot, cycle or horse. Thus, I could talk to people when I wanted to, or not. In fact it soon became de rigeur to call out 'Buon Camino' - have a good walk - to those that one passed, or who passed you.

The passing and re-passing was a continual source of interest, as of course everyone walked at different speeds, or took an extra day somewhere, and I found that I was continually meeting fellow travellers for the fifth, sixth or tenth time! It was unusual, even at 5 a.m., not to find a humped, rucksacked, limping figure in front, and a similar one behind! Some it was nice to walk alongside and chat, others not so enjoyable, but it was very easy to either lose someone or keep up, according to preference. This suited me very well!

St-Jean-Pied-de-Port, is a beautiful little town literally at the foot of the lower slopes of the Pyrenees and surrounded by green mountains. A toy train, up through the hills from Biarritz was a delight, and I arrived in superb late May weather. The very French Hotel Ramuntcho found me a room, and I dined on a west facing terrace in the evening sunshine. Unfortunately the weather changed and I woke up about 2 a.m. to a most tremendous thunderstorm, which was a little worrying as by now it was walking day. The bar that evening had been full of a variety of walkers from different parts of Europe – all speaking reputable English of course. And all experts. 'You will walk yourself into fitness' quoth those in the bar, but for some reason that I still do not understand, I actually walked myself out of fitness – feet wise at least, perhaps through all those extra clothes. However, this was yet to come, and the early morning was beautiful again, with tendrils of mist clinging to the hills, and the higher Pyrenees soaring away to my left. The climb was by a track, shared with plenty of others, human and sheep, and very steep. The green lower slopes gave way to a quite grim real mountain ambience, leading to Col Lepoeder at about 5000 feet. Although not very high, these are serious mountains, snow bound until Spring, with snow still in the shadowed pockets in May. There are a few isolated villages and the occasional Inn, but it is wise to bring food on this leg over the mountains. The guide book warned not to start after ten am. even in Summer, and to postpone if the weather was showing low cloud or high winds.

The frontier between France and Spain is marked here by a barbed wire fence! No passport worries! A similar route was used by prisoners of war escaping into neutral Spain in both the World Wars. My father's cousin, Patrick Collins, also in the Kings Shropshire Light Infantry from Bridgnorth, escaped from German custody in France during the First War, and got away into Spain this way. What a story that must have been, back between 1914 and 18, and I felt privileged to be following a similar path, although in very different circumstances.

Once across the border fence at a cattle grid crossing, and up to the Col, it was possible to look down on the roofs of Roncesvalles Abbey. Roncesvalles – a name to thrill the imagination, since I was a small boy. I had a picture in my Children's Encyclopaedia of the dying hero Roland blowing his great horn to summon aid from Charlemagne – too late. Basque mountaineers nowadays say that ghostly echoes of the horn can be heard on stormy nights in the Pyrenees.

The Song of Roland is one of the earliest and most famous French epics, but does actually have a basis in fact. In the Eighth Century Charlemagne, called The Great, was fighting the Saracens in Spain and had left Roland and a rear guard at the Pass of Roncevalles. This force was destroyed by the fierce Basques of the region, Roland refusing to sound his horn until he was dying, to prevent Charlemagne being also trapped. Roland was Count Hruodland, a Frankish name which in time became Roland, and the horn, given him by Charlemagne, was said to be so powerful that birds fell from trees, the earth shook and chimneys fell when it was sounded. Well, maybe, but it is good to believe that the heroism and sacrifice is basically true, and I was excited to be there.

It was here though that I found the first of the sleeping arrangements on the camino that were less than satisfactory. Because of the numbers of pilgrims in the high season, many beds have been crammed into very small spaces. They are in very short supply anyway, but if one is lucky enough to secure one, there will be no personal space at all – just the bed, and if it is a bottom bunk the floor underneath it. If it is a top bunk, tough! This was unpleasant, and very similar to sleeping in the Salvation Army Hostel in Walsall when I was in the Air Force, as mentioned earlier! Apart from the space, smells and noise were much about the same. Anything valuable is best to be worn! After a 27 km climb up and down the Pass, this did not appeal. Some official Hostels, or Refugios, which were at least inexpensive, were not so bad, but most, all along the route, were. In fact I had my very good sunglasses stolen, about four nights later.

I think that many of the Refugios have not changed since the days of the first and genuine pilgrims – tougher, harder men than ourselves, and certainly with fewer valuables! Hot water – they didn't need it! The dormitory at Roncesvalles was very large – felt like hundreds of occupants and I was allocated a top bunk! Seeing that the chance of a decent night was minimal I checked out again, and went into the Auberge opposite with my fingers crossed that they had a room. They did, and it was worth it! I quickly discovered that if you wanted a cheap hostel room, the only chance was to start walking very early, like dawn, and get to one before it became full. Sometimes it was necessary, and sometimes it was just nice, to splash out for a B&B or hotel room.

Next morning breakfast was early, and there was time to look at the Abbey, which is a handsome building, but of cold grey stone, not welcoming at all. It was consecrated in 1219 and is alleged to be a fine example of French Gothic (if you like that sort of thing). The important errand, to get my 'Credential' stamped had been done the night before. This has to be produced in Santiago to obtain the Compostela, and the stamps are ornate, coloured, very varied and rather beautiful. It is quite a treasure and makes a worthwhile pilgrim passport. Mine has sixty multi-coloured stamps, providing a rather wonderful record of places that I stayed in or visited. My aim was to cover the 25 km to the village of Zubiri on the second walking day, and this was now going to be through the Basque country, that extends to beyond the city of Pamplona, which most Basques regard as their capital.

The Basques are a very old people, speaking Euskara, an ancient language, sometimes decribed as one of the oldest in the world. There is doubt and debate about their origins, which may even be Indo-European. The name Barscunes, found on 1st Century BC coins from the region has been translated as, ' the tall ones', 'the proud ones' and 'the mountain people'. This may even be of Celtic etymology. As Celtic words are found all over Brittany, and ancient Celtic style dwellings on the camino, this does not seem to be too unlikely. Interesting. Anyhow, very soon after leaving Roncesvalles I found two Basque policemen wearing their unique uniform – very large and floppy red berets and grey tops. One gave me a smile for a photograph, but the other hid under his beret!

An eight bunk Refugio was available at Zubiri and seven other snorers were just about acceptable. I covered the 23 km to Pamplona by 1 p.m. next day after an early start. It was a long hard drag uphill into the old city, through interminable modern industrial suburbs, having crossed a photogenic medieval bridge at Trinidad de Arre. I have a photograph with my rucksack standing on a low wall at the end of the bridge, and being absolutely dwarfed by the bag. It was about now that I was beginning to realise it was too full! The old city, enclosed by a high wall was ancient and beautiful, having been a fortress town ,founded by the Romans in 75AD, and the capital of Navarra since the 9th Century. I decided to spend the next day enjoying the city, and found a really nice hotel. It was good to get out of several days dirty clothes and wear some of the better ones that I had been carrying round, to dinner in their nice 'Hemingway' Restaurant. A good look at Pamplona and the Cathedral de Santa Maria took up most of next day, and set me up for an 8 a.m. start on the fifth walking day, with a lovely exit from Pamplona via the University. Everyone wants to stay in Pamplona because of the Bull Run, which is in July, but it was very full and busy even now. In fact I found that the bulls are run in a number of the Basque villages. It was begun as a means of getting them to market.

The next destination was Puente la Reina. The Queen's Bridge, over the Rio Arga, built by Royal Command for the increasing number of pilgrims in the 11th Century is gracefully built of light coloured stone and unstained by time. The Knights Templar founded the Iglesia del Crucifijo in the 12th Century, the porch being decorated with scallop shells, the symbol of St. James and the Camino. The Hotel Rural, where I got a room, was old but refurbished, while near to it was the original pilgrim's hospice. A little town full of history, but after looking at it all I watched Liverpool playing Milan in my room!

From Pamplona to Logroño took two days, with the weather now really hot. The scenery was lovely though, surprisingly green and a lot of vineyards. This was now La Rioca, renowned for the making, selling and drinking of wine. The occasional bodega has installed a wine tap, where a push of a button delivers refreshment! I found the first of these before even crossing out of Navarra. It is literally a fountain, near to the 12th Century Cistercian Monastery of Irache. It starts running at 10 a.m., and the guidebook advises discretion on hot afternoons! I got a 'bus into Logroño, which was part of the plan to get me to the Church on time, as I had to be back home for early July for my Godson's wedding. This is a fine city, the capital of La Rioca. A statue of St James appears here in the guise of Santiago Matamoros, the Moor Slayer. This is in recognition of his supposed appearance on the Christian side, mounted on a white horse, at the battle of Clavijo in the ninth century. The makers of the statue would, of course, have expected him to be on the Christian side!

From Logroño there were several days walking to reach the next major city, Burgos, a distance of 114 km. I found a variety of beds, in a variety of villages and small towns, and a variety of Churches! One bed was in the Hospiteria Santa Teresa, run by Cistercian Nuns. They locked the doors very early, but as my feet were now hurting quite badly this did not matter and I had no desire to sightsee! The condition of my feet was very surprising, as I was wearing my good, well run-in trekking boots, and had not been rushing. However, large blisters had appeared and the end of one small toe had disappeared. It may have been the rough tracks, but it was surprising, and did not improve much until I was back home.

Inside the Cathedral of Santa Domingo de la Calzada a live cock and hen are kept in cages to celebrate a rather complicated local legend involving a young German pilgrim, an Innkeeper's daughter and a miraculous intervention by St. James. Don't try to understand it! I also enjoyed sitting in an outdoor café with a local family, the son of whom had a tiny tame bird that seemed to like perching on my shoulder! There was some rain on this section of the Camino, but generally it was pleasant walking weather. The route now left La Rioca and into the region of Castille and Leon. On a section of forest paths there was a monument to a group of local people executed during the Spanish Civil War.

I got a 'bus in through the industrial suburbs of Burgos, which were traditionally unpleasant, but then fell in love with the city centre. I had enjoyed Pamplona and Logrono, but Burgos, the heart of old Castile was full of shady squares, fountains, trees and an equestrian statue of the warrior El Cid, who did actually look a bit like Charlton Heston. The Cathedral of Santa Maria is described as an extraordinary Gothic achievement. It is of white stone, and literally covered with all the extra decoration, tracery, arches and pinnacles beloved of the 12th to 16th Century.

I thought it superb, and enjoyed walking around and photographing it, feet notwithstanding. (Although they were!) An evening meal in a medieval restaurant in the Cathedral Square, and a bed for two nights in one of the better refugios finished a good day. A great experience was spending all next morning in the Cathedral. I am not known for appreciating museums, but this was something else, vast, white, cool, and beautiful. The tomb of Roderigo Diaz de Vivar – El Cid, and the Papamoscos, the 'Flycatcher' clock are there. This is an articulated statue which opens its mouth when the bells strike on the hour. It is quite fascinating, and easily explains how several hours can be spent there, if one misses a strike! The Cathedral was made a World Heritage Site in 1984, and is the only one in Spain independent of the surrounding city centre. Wearers of shorts are not welcome, and quite right too. Do-nuts and beer were good for lunch, then the Telegraph and beer in the sun for the evening. Another good day.

Leaving Burgos at 5.30 a.m. next morning got me breakfast at a truck stop at Villabilla. Then it was a long gentle climb onto the 3000 foot meseta. The meseta provided probably the loneliest of walking, as there are long dry dusty stretches, with few villages, but also rolling arable land with cornfields, speckled by poppies. The sight of the occasional golden eagle broke the uniformity – it was a bit like being afloat on a wide rolling green sea. Bed was in a Church Hall, and a pleasant meal in the village with a lady from Eastbourne and a man from Holland, fellow travellers.

A late start at 7 a.m. next day! I found a peculiar little chapel, the Hostal St. Bol, where breakfast was being served – felt a bit weird and rather odd people, so I was quite pleased not to have slept there. The guidebook advises against it unless desperate! The meseta went on and on, more green sea, with oddly shaped piles of white stone, like the tors on Dartmoor. The next place of interest was a refugio and bar, that the guidebook advises women travelling alone to avoid and to use the Town Hall refuge. The mind boggles! A little further on are the ruins of the Convent of San Antón, with an Arch stretching across the road. Monks here once specialised in caring for pilgrims suffering from St. Anthony's Fire. Perhaps that was the problem in the refugio? Castrojerez is a straggling town built in layers on a hill. It is believed to have been founded by Julius Ceasar. I found a single room in a pretty little hostel, and decided to walk into the town. This was a mistake, as although having fewer than one thousand inhabitants, it straggles on, and on and on. It was about forty five minutes before I got back to the hostel, very hot with very sore feet! I stayed put for a meal, enjoying bocadillos and do-nuts in the garden with a view of the 13th Century Castle above in the evening sun.

Next day was a limp as far as Frómista, about 25 km, crossing some high steep ridges, and signing an autograph for a little man coming the other way. Aparently an Englishman was a prize! Stopped for a beer - very hot again - at Boadilla Del Camino in a welcome shady garden, where I met the man from Newcastle mentioned earlier, and a 74 year old from Maastricht. The Pension in Frómista had a bath – wow, a real prize! This was a handsome small town, with San Martin described as one of the most perfect Romanesque Churches in Spain. Storks were nesting on an adjacent tower. At this point a rest to my feet was indicated, and this part of the camino was more flat and boring cornfields and meseta, so I caught a train into León, the next big city en route.

I had enjoyed Pamplona, enjoyed Logroño more and Burgos even more still, but León was the crème de la crème! The 13th Century stained glass in the Cathedral is as magnificent as anything in Europe, and I was very taken with a life-size statue of a man with his hand on the shoulder of his small son in the square outside. The sculptures at the main door are impressive. I was very lucky to find what was visibly a wealthy wedding in progress, with ladies wearing lace mantillas over their hair and shoulders. Dinner was outside again, looking at the many beautiful buildings. I was joined by a middle-aged American couple who were on a motor-home tour of Spain. We set the world to rights over a lengthy meal and they insisted on paying for mine. I am not sure whether they were so impressed that I was doing it mainly on foot, or were just sorry for me! Very pleasant anyway, and they later posted an elaborate brochure of the Care Home that they owned to my home.

A reasonable night in a reasonable bed improved my feet, and I was up early to walk around the city and around the Cathedral. It is Gothic, but less so than Burgos, and in fact is considered the most 'French' of the Spanish Gothic ones because of the slenderness of the exterior and the transparency of the interior. I was able to join a service, and even take part in the singing, as hymn sheets were provided. By now the Spanish pronunciation was coming on quite well! Communion, just bread, no wine, was brought out to the congregation who stayed in the pews, but then left, followed by the 100 plus choir. The Bishop (I think) under a canopy, and a number of priests and the choir and congregation then processed very slowly, singing, to the Church of San Isidoro, rose petals being thrown down on them from upstairs windows.

In the evening sun this was rather wonderful, and as the choir stayed singing outside San Isidoro for over an hour I was able to get a meal nearby and remain listening to them. I regret that I did not find out what the procession was for, but it was obviously of significance. San Isidoro was a compulsory 'halt' for pilgrims, since the bones of the Saint are kept in a reliquary on the high altar. I really liked the Cathedral, which somehow more resembled an English one than the previous three – maybe it was the tall and slender tower. Another difference between it and Burgos was the red tiled roofs, which were common not only on parts of the Cathedral, but also in much of the city centre. This gave a feel of the terracotta roofs of Italy and Southern France. I went happy to my bed, burst a large blister and felt even happier!

Astorga is a small town not far from León, and there was time for a beer and a do-nut before heading there, leaving once more with some regret. One description of the journey out of León is of bleak moors being very testing for pilgrims, while another describes the sight for sore eyes after the meseta, the green and beautiful Montañas de León. Beauty is in the eye of the beholder! Personally, the hills beyond Astorga were beginning to attract my attention, where the camino climbs to five thousand feet, so that the hills must be higher, and patches of white could be seen. Snow? Maybe. Astorga is a pleasant small town, with a huge Cathedral, and used to be the chocolate centre of Spain in the 19th Century. There is still a chocolate museum! Here I found a bunk bed in one of the best hostels, if not the best, the Albergue de Peregrinos San Javier, run, and run very well indeed, by Felix. Plenty of clean space, plenty of toilets (with paper, wow), a clean cold drinks machine and hot showers!

The most striking building in Astorga is the Palacio Episcopal, known to everyone as the Building Gaudi, due to it's architect having designed either a Disney cartoon, or a horror film according to one's point of view! A great contrast to the dignified, peaceful and graceful Cathedral opposite. The paved central plaza, as in nearly all the small towns so far, was free of traffic, so that children could ride their small bikes, or play football while parents enjoyed the sun over a coffee, or whatever. It was in marked contrast to the centre of most English towns, where traffic has been allowed to dominate, and was rather as if the town centre of Wallingford had been paved over and totally pedestrianised. I also enjoyed a coffee, and could not see that the kids were either coming to, or causing harm. But as I wrote those words in my notes, a football landed on the balcony of the Town Hall, at one end of the plaza, where it remained! Perhaps it was the job of the Town Clerk to collect them next morning! At the front of the Town Hall tower were two full sized and well dressed Maragatos, who swung hammers at a bell between them every quarter of an hour. The Maragatos are said to be related to the ancient Phoenicians, or possibly Berbers.

Next morning was day 21, the 7th June, with enjoyment of the sight of the hills ahead, lots of broom and gorse, purple and gold in the distance. There were many storks to be seen. The camino was now quite clear of motorised traffic, just a narrow pebble and sand track and starting to climb into the Montañas. By afternoon I had climbed into the medieval village of Foncebadon where I had hoped to find a bed. The village is, however, still medieval – the road through it of unmade stone, dating to the Middle Ages. Apparently the village is being restored, but most of the buildings were crumbling ruins. There was a long queue waiting for the refugio to open it's door, and the one modern hotel was cashing in and ripping off right and left, so there was not much doubt about the way to go. It was a long way further up into the hills, but led to one of the most fascinating nights yet and I am really glad that I carried on to Manjarin.

Manjarin is a refugio, built by hand by Tomás, who was a big city architect until deciding to devote his life to caring for pilgrims. This is a high desolate spot, where fog, rain, cold and snow are almost the norm. (In fact during the evening, night and morning while I was there it was beautiful, but I quote from the guidebook!) It is a few metres from the highest point on the whole camino, at 1517 metres, a shade under five thousand feet. We were given a mattress each to use in an old cowshed, with Andreas, (German) Ian (English), two Dutch and one American girl. The rest of the buildings were stone and wood, hand built by Tomás. This was very much private enterprise on his part, and when the local authority threatened to cut off the electricity he went on hunger strike in front of their offices in León, - and won! Although in a previous incarnation Tomás was an architect, the buildings of Manjarin expressed, shall we say, his flip side!

We got a respectable meal, and payment was by donation only. But after dinner, we were commanded to stand for a dedication to the four Archangels who guard pilgrims. Tomás, two other men and a girl processed, extremely solemnly, through the open air dining area, wearing white tunics with red Templar Crosses, holding swords vertically and singing a Gregorian chant. Fabulous. A photograph of this would have been wonderful, but quite, quite impossible to even think about. I remember it, and wish that I could paint.

An eccentric guy though Tomás is, I rate him and what he is doing. I have to say that the toilets were a bit makeshift, but I got a satisfactory wash in a pond. I would not have missed this for the world.

Just before Manjarin I had passed the Cruz de Ferro, a huge iron cross put up originally to help pilgrims to find their way across the hills. Traditionally each pilgrim adds a stone to the cairn below the cross. I had passed the highest point, but it was not yet all downhill to Santiago, - far from it!

At the crest of the hills this was good walking country, rather like the Rhinogs in North Wales, but higher. Rolling hills of purple and gold, and very enjoyable. I caught up with two very elderly people from Oxford, husband and wife, she in a voluminous tartan skirt. We talked, they had obviously been doing the camino for years. Probably both Professors! Coming down off the hills via a hard rocky descent to Moliniseca, I wondered how the two old people behind would manage, but decided that they had probably done it more times than I could imagine.

Then it was a rather long drag along a busy road into Ponferrada, where the Castillo de los Templaros is everyone's idea of a medieval Templars Castle. I treated myself to a Hotel in Ponferrada, intending to have a good look around the Castle tomorrow, having walked 60 km in the last two days. My feet were now enjoying themselves, although a bath and a laundry session before a walk around this elegant town centre was nice. Only 60,000 people, but like so many of the small Spanish cities the centre manages, and I don't quite know how, to give the impression of being very big and very important. This is much more pronounced than in the UK. It is a bit like Bridgnorth, with a High Town and a Low Town, old and new respectively, but regrettably a lot of graffiti. Perhaps this goes along with the new industrial area.

The day spent here in the centre and in the Castillo was worthwhile. I thought it crazy that so many on the camino had to push on, day after day without stopping to look at things, even apart from the bonus of a rest from time to time. I enjoyed Ponferrada, and the arrow slitted, keyhole windowed Castle, despite the graffiti.

I was on the road by 6 a.m. for the long industrial road out of Ponferrada.

Soon the country became very rural again, with smallholdings, lush vegetables, more storks and hills all round. Those behind were the Montagñes de León that I had walked through, and ahead were the Cordillera Cantábrica, looking irresistibly like a much higher version of the Malverns. Twenty two km, and a number of villages further got me to Villafranca del Bierzo and the Hostal Ave Fénix.

This was another idiosyncratic and unusual place, called Fénix because the remarkable owner, Jesús Jato and his family rebuilt it themselves after a disastrous fire. Villafranca is a beautiful little town, clustered around two Churches, in a valley where two rivers meet. It seemed to me to be a mixture of Switzerland and Lynmouth! The obligatory castle is big, formidable and still lived in. Near it is the Romanesque Church of Santiago, with its Puerta del Perdon. Pilgrims who had made it this far but could not carry on were granted the same indulgences and benefits as if they had completed their pilgrimage, once they had crossed through the 'door of forgiveness'. The Hostal had every facility, including a pay phone, an evening meal and, incredibly, a special quiet room for seniors to sleep in! Jesús Jato and his family devote their lives to taking care of pilgrims on the camino. He charges six euros for breakfast, but will only accept a donation for the bunk bed, and for two euros will transport rucksacks further into the mountains, for those who feel in need. He is reported never to turn anyone away. It was rather wonderful to sit outside, after a substantial dinner which included several glasses of red wine with a beer to follow, and chat looking down on the lights of the little town and up to the dark hills above. There were thirty or forty people staying for one night or more, so plenty of company to choose from. A good night and a most interesting personality.

Next morning I followed one of the little rivers up it's valley towards Vega de Valcarce. This was a bit like following the River Lyn up the Lyn Gorge except that every so often the Madrid to La Coruna motorway swooped hundreds of feet over the valley – something not seen at Lynmouth. I stayed overnight at a private albergo, where all ten or so guests were expected to help clear and wash up after dinner. As there were several women to take command of this it was not a problem, but everyone did help!

The next destination was O Cebreiro, which is a tiny village developed from, and for, the pilgrimage. There was a Hospital run by Monks here, from the 11th to the19th Century, and in the Church of Santa Maria lives a statue of the Virgin, who reputedly inclined her head after a miracle had taken place. However, when I reached there she was not inclined to do it for me – but I had to get there first. The path was described as very beautiful but very steep, and needing plenty of time, so I left Vega de Valcarce at 5.30 a.m., continued up the gorge through chestnut woods, then eventually into the more open hills, covered in gorse and broom. They began to look very beautiful as the light strengthened. Despite the early start, I knew that there would be someone ahead, and there certainly was, so we took each other's photograph against the backdrop of the Cordillera.

They are a range of mountains - green and pleasant at this point – which stretch almost from the Pyrenees to Cape Finisterre. This was an enjoyable, if very steep, climb up for me but there are a number of serious 8,000 ft peaks, the highest Torre de Cerredo being 8,687 feet. Skiing and winter sports are possible here. The central block of the Cordillera were named Los Picos de l'Europa, because they were the first bits of home that the Spanish sailors saw over the horizon, as they tried to evade the English pirates, Drake, Hawkins, Raleigh and company several hundred years ago.

Suddenly, when I had almost given up hope of ever getting there, O Cebreiro was dramatically ahead. The miraculous statue in the old grey Church was rather beautiful, but a bit touristy, not feeling sacred. I believe that the village has been reconstructed to give the feeling of a genuine step back in time. There were some of the old Galician thatched houses, of Celtic origin without chimneys, the smoke emerging through the roof thatch. There was a nice shop and hotel, and the whole atmosphere - not necessarily the worse for it - was much more touristy than earlier parts of the camino. Just before reaching the village, the camino crosses into Galicia, the fourth Region it traverses. Galicia is brilliantly green because it is so often wet! It also has it's own official language, Galician, and signs are often in this rather than Castilian (which we call Spanish).

It was useful to have a rest here after the steep three to four hour climb, and enjoy a cake and a drink in the shop, with other walkers that I had been seeing on and off for a few days. Then in increasingly sulky weather, downhill for a bit on the 21 km to Triacastela. The path had gone through several poor villages, and these continued, until in one an elderly woman who had been herding a bunch of pigs ran after me – 'Señor, Señor'. She offered me two pancakes, which were nice and hot. I had thought that either she was very kind, or very motherly, or very sorry for me, as by now it must have been obvious that my feet were hurting again. However, after I had eaten both pancakes it transpired that this was a commercial transaction! Must have been a nice little earner, with daughter indoors making the pancakes and mother outside using the pigs as an excuse to spot the next bit of cash limping down the track. Or perhaps I am too cynical. Anyway they were welcome!

There is a dramatic sculpture of a medieval pilgrim at the top of a windswept hill at Alto San Roque. He is larger than lifsize, relying on his stick, and holding on to his hat, which he needed to do here. I was not able to discover the name of the sculptor, but it is very good, very spectacular and in an extremely well chosen bare, isolated site. I hope that nothing is ever built near to it, as it does incorporate the feeling of a lonely hard journey, which it was, and can even be still. He looks tired, he looks lonely and he meant something to me.

Triacastela appeared at about 3.30 p.m. and the Refugio looked very good. It was now far too late to get a bunk there of course, the 4 a.m. starters were all ensconsed, but I found an expensive private one nearby. Unfortunately it was up six flights of steps but the adjoining bath made the climb worthwhile. I decided, feet notwithstanding again, to take the longer route to the Benedictine Samos Monastery, so next morning took a route through a Gorge again. This time it was more like the Wye Gorge, with steep tree lined hills and the occasional rock face. Eventually there was a beautiful view down to the enormous Monastery, which sits by a river in a valley.

The Monks seemed very pleased to welcome visitors, and a young American man and I had a special team of guides! I could actually understand the Monks more easily than the American! The cloister walls were covered by quite weird murals, biblical subjects but difficult to see what the artists were getting at. Interesting anyway. It was a long walk to the next stop, Sarria, but through pleasant countryside, which was still like the rural West Midlands, - Shropshire Worcestershire and Hereford. I had been passing, repassing and spending time with Gerda, a lady from Cape Town for the last few days, as we seemed to be averaging about the same speed. She had started originally with her husband, but he had given up and gone home! We shared a few meals and walks over the next 100km, as unbelievably we were now inside that magic distance from Santiago! There had been times when it did not seem possible. The distance marker had been a target to photograph, but it had been so covered in graffiti, I guess in an understandable excess of enthusiasm, that it was not very photogenic. I got the next one, Km 99 instead!

Portomarin is a new and pleasant town, built when the old one was drowned by the waters of the dam on the Rio Miño. Journey's end was in sight, and the sun was out again! One problem though, my Galician was not as understandable to the locals as my Castilian had been, in particular the essential order at the end of a trek, 'Cerveça, por favor'. Eventually it appeared that I was not rolling the 'r's' enough! There were five more overnight stops before reaching San Lázaro on the outskirts of Santiago, through pleasant walking and flourishing villages. The nearness of the big city, and the end of the camino were now becoming obvious.

Two priests were standing outside one little Church, and virtually hijacking travellers to enter! In fact that this a good move, because, (a) it was extremely hot, (b) they provided lemonade and, (c) there was a most unusual statue of Christ on the Cross. He had His right hand, not nailed to the crossbar as usually portrayed, but extended downwards as if appealing to, or perhaps, blessing, those below. This attitude made His whole body twisted and painful and it was a striking portrayal. I have mentioned this to several Ministers, but have not yet found one who had seen anything similar.

The camino had been steadily, but not entirely, downhill from O Cebreiro, but from here on it crossed numerous small river valleys, making a more arduous final section of ups and downs than might have been hoped for! It was mixed farming country after the hills, and it looked very prosperous compared to the poor villages I had been passing through. The agriculture, topography and way of life still seemed much like Shropshire or Worcestershire. The regional food speciality in Galicia by the way is pulpo, - octopus - which is apparently recommended by many pilgrims, but not by this one! I think that this is more to do with the Galician name than the taste, which is not bad.

At Lavacolla, the nearness to the city was evinced by the cost of a bunk, so at only 11 km away from the Cathedral it was worth carrying on. This village was the place where pilgrims stopped for the traditional washing and purification before entering Santiago. Nowadays it is better known for the site of the city Airport. Times, and habits, change! Whilst I was now expecting to make use of the latter soon, it was not enjoyable at this stage to have a hell of a long diversion around the end of a runway! All things come to an end however, and at Monte de Gozo or Monxoi (Mount Joy) it was possible to look down at the centre of Santiago, with a vague hint of the Cathedral towers.

As a complete contrast with experiences en-route the big official refugio at San Lázaro was quite empty, and it was nice to stow my rucksack, and get a shower before making my way to the city centre. This was all that one would expect – big, very touristy, and completely given over to the pilgrimage. I liked it, and it was a great pleasure to find the Camino Office, hand over my Credenciale and receive the Compostela after a wait while my name was, as far as possible, written in Latin. The Credenciale was checked, quite thoroughly, to make sure that I had walked at least the hundred kilometres, and there was an inquisition to enquire my reason for the journey. This is good, as the Cathedral Authorities try to ensure that the Compostela is not granted indiscriminately, and only to those who have at least an element of spiritual reason. It was all very organised as well; I was able to get my Compostela laminated and put into a cardboard tube next door!

The old city was full of pedestrianised narrow alleyways, stone arcades, some nice shops and, of course, somewhere to eat on every corner. I decided to leave the Cathedral until tomorrow, and just enjoyed wandering round the old grey streets – and met Gerda, again! I walked back to San Lázaro- and got totally lost! However, the refugio appeared eventually, with a few more inhabitants now, including Anne, whom I had last seen on the toy train as we started out from Biarritz thirty four days ago!

A bus was appropriate into the city on day 34, and I found accommodation for the next few days near the Cathedral at the Hospedaje Santa Cruz, a sort of semi-private B (sans the second B), in one of the stone arcades. Breakfast – maafi mushkelin, hundreds of places! Hospedaje is the Galician word for Hostal or Hostel. This was an odd place, but it was a private room, with a bath, and I got on famously with the landlady, who gave me a box of chocolates for Jo when I left for home. In fact I did find that most of the people of Santiago were keen to be helpful and friendly – it is their livelihood of course.

The final walk of my journey was to the Cathedral for the noon Mass. The entrance to the Cathedral is a series of steps up to the elaborately sculpted doorway, the Pórtico de la Gloria. Then the centuries old tradition is to place a hand on the Tree of Jesse, under the statue of St James. The thought comes about how many hands it has taken to wear the stone into its particular shape. The tradition is then to descend under the altar to the silver casket in the shrine where the remains of St. James are said to be kept. There was an almost never-ending queue to do this and to touch the statue of the Saint via stairs above the altar.

The Cathedral is, of course, huge and being of grey stone the interior is rather dark. Although lit by many candles and small lights there seemed to be much less light than at León and Burgos. I was very lucky to have gone at this time on this day, because the botafumeiro was about to be swung. This huge censer takes six men to get it going. They pull on a very long rope from which the censer swings from the Cathedral roof. I was lucky as it is only swung on St. James's Day, 25th July, and other special feast days or days of significance. It is a fabulous and impressive sight, and absolutely without any regard for the health and safety of the congregation! The censer is several feet high, fat, obviously extremely heavy, and fastened to the end of the rope with what appeared to be a fairly casual knot. At it's full travel it swings smoking over the heads of the congregation for almost the full length of the nave.

Definitely awe-inspiring. A rumour was going round the several pilgrims with whom I was now well acquainted that it had been swung because Mrs. Cherie Blair was in the congregation. Whether she would have qualified to make it a day of significance I know not, but I can say that, if true, it is definitely the only thing of significance that she or her husband did for me, and I forgive them other matters because of it!

After the botafumeiro it was nice to hear my name read out as one of the numerous people who had been granted the Compostela the previous day. I spent a lazy afternoon, enjoying the city, which is enjoyable but somehow failed to grab me in the way that Pamplona, León, Logroño and Burgos had done. I spent a couple of days enjoying the sun and getting a tour of the Cathedral tower and roof with Antonio, a pleasant young student, and also meeting the American girl from Tomás's place at Manjarin. She thought that the others might still be there! I also went to the noon Mass again in the hope that the censer swing would be repeated, but this was obviously not a significant day. It was interesting to note that during the Mass the Priests took wine but not the congregation, who were offered wafers only. This seemed to fail to underwrite the Catholic belief of transubstantiation, but I may not have understood the proceedings properly. Although the Cathedral, under a dull sky, can look quite grey and grim, caught by the evening sun it was beautiful and golden. I found a place in a wooded park, where the three main towers can be photographed to advantage quite late at night. This is the best view of it from anywhere. And 11 p.m. was still very appropriate to enjoy an ice-cream!

By day 38 I had decided to finish the journey properly and get myself to Cape Finisterre, Cabo Fisterra in Galician. The edge of the known world in medieval times, and therefore the final achievable destination for pilgrims on this earth. It was also the spot, on the cliffs, where pilgrims traditionally burnt the robes and boots in which they had made their journey to Santiago. It was traditional to walk, taking three or four days to cover the 90 plus km. It would have been good to do this, one way at least, but I was now running out of time, so the 'bus journey of about three hours was a convenient substitute. I found a room in Fisterra village, and did walk up to the cliffs and Monte Facho, the small mountain upon which is the lighthouse. The 'bus journey had been rather beautiful, a bit like Devon which then turned into the South of France, although the walk up to the cliffs turned back into a rocky Lynmouth! This was a very enjoyable place to be in the afternoon and evening sun. There is a sculpture of an outsize pilgrim's boot at the top. A young Spanish couple asked me which way was west (perhaps they were thinking of conquistador ancestors sailing into the sunset), which information was quite easy to supply. Having decided not to burn my clothes, although the fire scorched traditional rock is very visible, a walk back was attractive. The long way down the mountain through pine woods and enjoying the beautiful blue bay led to a terrace bar overlooking the little port, where I enjoyed a beer and a battered, very fresh, haddock. A good day, made even better by learning from Jo that we had both been invited to a reception at the House of Lords, soon after I was due home. Impeccable timing for once!

Then back to Santiago and home the next day, with no problems. Plenty to think about and, despite the dilapidated feet, some very good experiences and memories, and perhaps even lessons learned. I received a package about their home from the American couple who bought me dinner in León and a postcard of the Cape Winelands from Gerda in South Africa. She lamented never having said goodbye, and said that she had not been concerned until getting on her homeward aeroplane, having been convinced that we would meet up yet again! In fact she had spent five days resting in Fisterra while I was there – obviously another who did not burn her clothes!

The Samaria Gorge in Crete, and a cruise around Greek Islands

It was fairly unusual for me to be joining a group to go down something, instead of get to the top of it, but this is what happened in September 2008! I had done a few treks with 'Explore' and liked their style, and never having been to Crete I liked the idea of trekking the famous Gorges, followed by a lazy week cruising around the Gulf of Evia in a Caique, a traditional Greek small passenger boat. Once again with Jo's agreement, I booked this in early '08, and then promptly fell ill with a double infection! She got me fit again during the summer, but it meant that we did not get the July holiday to which she was looking forward in the West Country. This was a great shame, but could not be helped, and we made up for it with a wonderful holiday cruising down the Danube from Vienna to Budapest and back in 2009 - something that we thought was a great experience.

I flew into Khaniá Airport to join a small group of people in this little town on the northern shore of Crete – famous as the location for the film *Zorba the Greek*. This part of Crete, before it joined Greece, was a centre of Minoan civilisation, followed by the Romans, the Byzantines, the Venetians, the Genoese and the Ottomans. There are remnants of each, particularly of the Venetians and the Turks, and it is an attractive little town, with narrow alleys leading up from the circular harbour, whitewashed houses, and the massive Venetian walls. Fishermen can still be seen bringing in octopus, and the taverns around the harbour were doing a good trade in the very hot sun. A good start! After lunch we took a local bus up a precipitous escarpment to Somalis Plateau. The bus climbed well over three thousand feet from sea level, through hairpin bends, and I would have preferred to be driving!

Next day was a reasonably long trek in the White Mountains, the Lefka Orin, which are fairly wild, and a quite serious mountain range, with 58 peaks higher than 6,500 feet. The Lefka Orin are described as having to be taken seriously, with proper experience and equipment necessary in winter, and heat plus lack of shade a problem in summer. This was a good preparation day for the Gorges however, as we did not try anything too difficult, but enjoyed the views of mountain scenery, which were excellent. I had been a little worried about being sufficiently recovered, but found this day no problem. Our English guide, Kat, had planned that we would get lunch at a mountain hut, the Kallergi Refuge. When we arrived there however, after a three hour or so climb up from the plateau, it was locked and bolted, with a note on the door saying, 'Sorry, come back later'!

This might be described as an illustration of relaxed Mediterranean attitudes! Kat was not at all impressed, and we heard her giving someone a dreadful telling off via her mobile phone! She received a promise that a man with keys would be there in about an hour. It was quite cold up here, and two of the ladies in the group were not very happy about the hour's wait outside, so I scouted around, and found an old car at the back, which was not too difficult to get into! They decided to wait in the car, at least out of the wind, while the rest of us walked on further. More splendid views, with the whiteness of the mountain name well justified. Hundreds of beehives in the valleys, obviously a flourishing local industry.

Eventually the man with the keys turned up, rather shame-faced, and provided very hot soup for everyone! This was, apart from the wait, a good initial short trek, and our hotel on the plateau was pleasant, with a good dinner and a good bar.

The Samaria Gorge is a mountain climb, but downhill! Depending upon who one talks to, it is either 16 or 18 km long, but will certainly take up to eight hours to walk, descending from 1.250 metres (4,100 feet) to sea level. It was created by a river running down through the Lefka Orin to the Libyan Sea, and is the longest and described as the most spectacular gorge in Europe. The village of Samaria (Santa Maria), part way down the gorge was abandoned in 1962 in order to make the area part of the National Park that bears the same name. The gorge varies in width from 150 metres to 3metres, with sheer cliffs over 1,600 feet high at the Sidheroportes, the Iron Gates, which are neither iron nor gates! This is where the mountainsides narrow to only a few feet. The trek starts with the Xilioscala, the 'Wooden Staircase' which is neither wooden nor a staircase! It is a series of rough steps and a zig-zag path which descend about 2,500 feet in a very short horizontal distance into the gorge itself.

It provides some wonderful views of Mount Gingilos, which at just under 7,000 feet and limestone white looks quite spectacular. There were lots of cypress trees and alpine shrubs and an attractive forest as the descent flattened out a bit. The descent is quite hard work, and it is easy to see why the gorge is officially closed during winter. It becomes blocked by snow and fast flooding torrents, and is quite dangerous. In fact there have been a lot of restrictions placed upon trekkers in the gorge, for their own safety – it is only open, even in summer, between 7 a.m. and 3 p.m. and it is strictly prohibited to camp, light fires or swim! We had started as early as possible, bearing in mind that there was a chance of a swim from the beach before catching a ferry to our next stopover. Once down the gorge, by the way, there are only three routes out (1) walk along the coast paths – no motor road, tracks only (2) climb back up the gorge –not possible, not enough time before it is closed. (3) catch the ferry, or a (very) distantly possible (4) – swim! Timing is therefore quite important, and there are some horrible stories about those who have not got it right! Anyway, the prospect of a swim or a paddle was a totally inviting one when halfway down and very hot! Of course, because of the steepness of the gorge walls the path is much in shade, but hot it still was! Our heavy baggage was being taken down to the coast by truck, on an extremely roundabout route, but Kat had warned everyone to take swimming gear. It really was very surprising how difficult the descent was. Considering that it is a descent. I ruined a pair of boots in the Gorges, which had been to the top of Kili and Sagarmartha Base Camp!

It is only 7 km from the top of the Xilioscala to the deserted village of Samaria, but it took us a good three hours. The little 14th century Church of Sacred Mary of Egypt is built of rough stone, and has survived the desertion of it's former congregation. It is possible to go inside, although it is necessary to obtain the key, and to be awed by the array of Byzantine mosaics, wall paintings and icons. A rest was definitely needed here, and then a continuation towards the Iron Gates.

The track gets distinctly rough from here, with huge boulders and some mountaineering descents, but the thought of the sparkling blue Libyan Sea below was a spur to get on with it. The Gates really are dramatic, with the distinct feeling that it is possible to touch both rock faces at the same time. It isn't of course, but the cliffs, well over one thousand six hundred feet high here add to the illusion. In a sense it was a little like walking through the pre-demolition old streets in Wolverhampton at night. Looming overhead, the upper stories of the 17th-18th century houses were almost within reach of each other, and my right hand stayed close to the staff handgrip, ready for a quick draw! The Sidheroportes were positively a happier experience!

Another deserted village, Old Ayia Roumelli, appeared after passing through the narrowest part of the Iron Gates (incidentally, this is a description applied to locations as widely separated as the gorge of the Danube between Serbia and Romania and the legendary barrier erected by Alexander the Great in the Caucasus, to keep out the northern barbarians) and then it was an easy walk to the sea – at last! New Ayia Roumelli is a very pleasant little seaside resort –although access is only by foot or by ferry, and after about eight hours of quite hard and very hot labour the Libyan Sea was very welcome. The ferry between Ayia Roumelli and our next stop, Loutro, eastwards along the southern coast is, not surprisingly, well patronised, but there was no problem with boarding. It was extremely good to relax on board and watch the coastline slipping easily past.

We had a hotel in Loutro right on the waterfront, very much part of the little harbour. Little, but very busy, with a constant stream of ferries going both east and west, as this coast is so inaccessible otherwise. A very enjoyable dinner in a waterfront restaurant finshed off a strenuous but successful day. Loutro lies nestled in a cove, surrounded by high crags, and is very picturesque. Every house is painted white, with blue shutters. No individualistic owners! As the lights began to come on around the small bay, and we shared the company of local people, it was like being in a film set. Next morning Kat announced that another gorge, the Aradena, was lying in wait. For those who wanted to! I think that everyone did, and we scaled the steep crags behind our hotel, climbing literally up from the waterfront. The Aradena Gorge is shorter than Samaria, but equally steep, descending from two and a half thousand feet to the sea at Marmara. There is a warning that it is easier and safer to climb up rather than walk down. Inexperienced walkers, or those suffering from vertigo, should take the bus – only there isn't one! It is legs, helicopters or nothing, like much of this coast. We had decided to make a day of it, climb up to the deserted Aradena village on a track that bypassed the gorge itself, then trek down for a swim at Marmara. The top of the crag from Loutro had a quite spectacular ruined monastery, and a wonderful view down to the cove of Finix (Pheonix). This is a tiny very sheltered inlet, with two luxury hotels – again accessible by boat, foot or helicopter! They are advertised as providing an idyllic 'get away from it all' stay, with the nearest shops the best part of a thirty minute walk up and over the hill to Loutro, and the night life consisting of listening to the sound of the sea and the chapel bells. There is also a beautiful chapel that we were able to visit, full of icons and paintings of white bearded Greek Orthodox priests. I felt that a couple of nights in one of the hotels, with the hire of a canoe thrown in would be wonderful, but not for much longer! I had stayed at Ave Fénix during the long walk to Santiago – rebuilt after a disastrous fire, and I guessed that this was Finix for the same reason.

So having completed a Himalayan type 'flat' (steep up and just as steep down) to the sea there began the long climb up a zig-zag path to Aradena. The gorge is particularly spectacular when seen from the sea, looking like a great gash in the cliffs created by a giant butcher's cleaver. Strangely this was a reminder of looking down on Loch Ness from the air; another massive slash in the Grampian Mountains created by a colossus. There is a bridge over the gorge between the deserted Aradena village and Anapolis, which had typically Cretan village houses, white stone walls and red roofs. The downwards trek was, like Samaria, quite hard work, but provided gorgeous views of the so blue sea through the thick oleander bushes. Soaring above were large birds that we hoped were eagles, not vultures! Marmara beach was tiny, but a delight, with a cliff top café overlooking the strand, and loungers with umbrellas for which, apparently anyway, there was no charge for café customers. Unbelievable, and possibly not entirely true, but no one asked for money and I think that we all enjoyed a swim and a free lounge!

A tiny ferryboat back to Loutro gave an opportunity to once more relish the effortlessly moving coastline, with an enjoyable meal in one of the harbour restaurants to follow. The plan for the next day was a ferry, again moving eastwards to the popular resort of Khora Sfakion, after lunch. There was time to rent a single seater canoe from the waterfront before the ferry, and take it out of the cove and round the point to look at the Aradena Gorge from the sea, the pretty beach of Finix and dodge the incoming ferries on the way back! Khora Sfakion has a reputation as a one-time haunt of brigands, smugglers and pirates. Although having fewer than five hundred inhabitants it is the capital of the remote and mountainous region of Sfakiá, and somehow the waterfront of tavernas and shops seemed quite sophisticated compared to our previous stops. Although it is isolated, there is a road out of Khora Sfakion, but the almost impenetrable White Mountains and rocky coast had made the village an historic centre of struggle against both Venetians and Turks, with sea caves used as bases of resistance. Despite the road out of the village towards the Idi Mountains and the centre of Crete, the harbour was busy, with ferries travelling both east and west, like Loutro. The minibus that had somehow managed the very long round trips to reunite us with our heavy luggage at each stop was here again, and took us out of the village towards Zaros, our final two night stop. There were marvellous views along the route, looking backwards and downwards towards the Libyan Sea until we reached Preveli Monastery.

Preveli, or to give it the proper and deserved title, the Holy Stavropegiac and Patriarchal Preveli Monastery of Saint John the Theologian and Saint John the Baptist is a very important and historic place. It is one of those special places that I have been lucky and privileged, not just to read about but to see and visit, and I am grateful to 'Explore' for having arranged enough time for proper understanding and appreciation. Firstly, the magnificent sites of the upper and lower buildings (the two Saint Johns) are hard to believe. It perches on the cliff edge, white walls, red roofs above the so blue sea, surrounded by greenery and palm trees, with views southwards towards Africa. It is not too difficult to believe that Daedalus and Icarus might have spread their feathered wings and striven to fly from a place like this.

The origin of the Monastery was probably in the 10th or 11th Century, and from the 16th to the 19th Century the present site was a centre of resistance to the Venetian and Turkish invaders of Crete. In the 20th Century Second World War the Nazis invaded Crete with what they expected to be their unbeatable weapon, airborne and parachute troops. Their huge losses in the battle for Crete together with their defeat during the Battle of Britain were probably what persuaded Hitler not to agree to Goering's demand for an airborne invasion of England. The losses and the time taken to gain control of Crete also delayed the Nazi invasion of Russia until the most advantageous time was past. Thus the battle for Crete is likely to have been an important factor in their eventual defeat. Preveli Monastery played an important role in the battle.

In 1941 a substantial number of British, Australian and New Zealand troops had had to be left in southern Crete by the retreating Allied Forces. They were given help, food and shelter by the Monks, and a number were evacuated by British submarine from the coast below Preveli, with their assistance. That this support was given certainly caused grave risk, danger and not least expense to the Monks and the Monastery. The Monastery became a rallying point for hundreds of Allied soldiers, in defiance of ferocious reprisals against the Monks and local population. It continued to be, following the tradition of earlier centuries, a centre of resistance to the occupation until the Nazis were driven from Crete.

There are beautiful tablets in Greek and English, describing these actions, where the sun shines on the wall of the Monastery Courtyard. A little way along the cliffs is a moving war memorial overlooking the beach where the soldiers swam out to the submarine, and guarded on either side by the figures of a British soldier and a Monk. Both are carrying automatic firearms, which I believe is a wonderful illustration of the truth of this inspiring story. No turning a religious cheek here. It is dedicated to all the countries that believe and fight for the idealism of democracy and freedom.

The visit to Preveli was much appreciated, an important part of the stay in Crete, and remains, with me, a valued memory.

Zaros, the location of our hotel for the next two nights is a pretty village, straggling a long way up a ravine (what else in this area?) in the rugged Idi Mountains. This hotel was without doubt more sophisticated than the previous three, with an excellent swimming pool serviced by a bar, and enjoyable shady gardens to spend the evening in. Perhaps, 'Explore' thought that we had earned it! Next day was our fourth trek, down Rouvos Gorge, five kilometres long and just as steep and rugged as Samaria and Aradena. It is, perhaps, even more dramatic and definitely prettier. Eagles were seen again, and we enjoyed a four hour descent, this time having been driven up a rough track to the head of the gorge. The Idi Mountains are very scenic and this descent provided some excellent views of the Psiloritis Range instead of the sea. The Hotel pool provided an excellent relaxing place for the afternoon, followed by an enjoyable final dinner. The after-dinner entertainment by a local dancing group, two men and two girls, was really good. An invitation to join in on the stage was accepted with pleasure, as I have long believed in, and acted on, the Latin encouragement, 'carpe diem'!

Our faithful minibus took us to Iraklion Airport early next morning, where we parted company with some regret, as it had been a successful and enjoyable group, who had mixed and co-operated well together. I had particularly enjoyed the wildness of the gorges and the mountains and the unusual experience of struggling to climb downhill! It had been an excellent eight days. The timing again was good because there was an opportunity to catch a local bus and explore Knossos, the city of King Minos, before flying to Athens.

Knossos was a Neolithic settlement perhaps as long ago as 7 or 6000 BC, but it is difficult to distinguish fact from Greek myths, with contributions by Homer and Ovid. The Palace or city, as it became, may have had over a thousand interlocking rooms. It has certainly been destroyed by both earthquake and fire several times. Sir Athur Evans, a British historian uncovered much of the present site during the early years of the twentieth century, but is now generally thought to have jumped to far too many wrong conclusions.

However, the myths abound, one being that the half man, half bull called the Minotaur was kept by King Minos in a labyrinth, or maze, at Knossos, although the site of the maze has not been discovered. The Cretans exacted a tribute from the people of Athens, which was seven young men and seven young women annually, chosen by lots, to be fed to the Minotaur. The Athenian hero Theseus volunteered to kill the Minotaur, and was helped by Ariadne, the daughter of King Minos, who had fallen in love with Theseus.

She arranged for a ball of silken thread to help Theseus to find his way out of the maze after killing the monster. This was a 'Clew' and the Oxford English Dictionary suggests that it is the origin of our modern word 'clue'. One would, perhaps, like to think that Theseus and Ariadne lived happily ever after, following such trauma, but sadly this was not to be! Even Daedalus, the architect of the labyrinth, fell out with King Minos and tried to escape from Crete with his son Icarus by manufacturing wings for them both. No happy ending there either!

The one part of these myths that is still with us is that of the 'bull leapers', young men who would dice with death by leaping over a charging bull, from head to tail, in defiance of his horns. They are pictured in many frescoes, and the sport is continued today in Spain. Teams of leapers gather in cities like Valencia and Barcelona. With three bulls in a ring at once they infuriate the animals until they charge, and then use courage, quickness of reaction and eye, and athletic dexterity to leap over the head and horns. I have seen bull fighting, but not the leaping, and it is on my personal agenda for the next visit to Spain, as I think that this displays far more courage, skill and integrity. The bull does not die a sad, grubby, one-sided death in the ring as he does in the traditional fight. It seems however that the Spanish thirst for blood in the sand from bull versus man is not quenched.

The excavation at Knossos is huge, and certainly cleverly displayed. The uncertainty of what was or was not true detracted a little, but nevertheless it was a couple of hours well spent, thinking, 'Well, perhaps?'

I had been sharing a room during the Gorge treks with Chris from Grantchester, and he was also joining the next part of the Odyssey - cruising around the Gulf of Evia on a traditional Greek small boat, a Caique, for eight days. After flying from Iraklion to Athens the itinerary was to join the Caique at the port of Rafina, on the eastern coast of Attica - the Greek mainland. In theory there was transport to Rafina, about thirty km distant. The Greek talent for disorganisation now made itself apparent, as the transport did not exist, and we learned that the Caique would now be sailing instead from the port of Marmari on the island of Eubeoa. Jo and I had experienced this talent on an earlier holiday, on a cruise around the islands, when chaos erupted over totally inadequate arrangements for mealtimes, and the crew hid themselves away rather than deal with it! They had to be told. And were! We did wonder what a real emergency would have been like. On this occasion Chris and I discovered another lost soul bound for Rafina at Athens Airport. With a bit of haggling I was able to convince a taxi driver that he would enjoy taking us for a sum, which split three ways, was not too outrageous! However, all was eventually well, as the company had booked us into a very nice Hotel in

Rafina, where we met the other fifteen passengers. We were even refunded the taxi fare!

As our Caique, the M/S Isidorus was in Marmari, not Rafina, next morning we took the regular ferry to Eubeoa, or Evia as it is now better known, and were welcomed aboard by the skipper and owner, Thanos, who was hugely likeable and very efficient. I hope, with the Greek economy in ruins as I write, that he has not been forced out of business. The Isidorus was a beautiful little boat? Ship? Well, Caique, any road up! It has been in Thanos' family for generations, and was crewed by him and two assistants, one of whom was the cook and bar-tender. There was a lounge with just enough room for the sixteen of us to squeeze round a table for meals, a sun deck with a good supply of mats, and what I can describe totally inappropriately as the ground floor contained the eight cabins and eight toilets. The cabins were not exactly luxurious, being pretty small for two grown men, but cleverly arranged with a small washbasin and shower, and Chris's bunk above mine but at right angles to it. Fortunately we got on quite well! Most of the others were either couples or friends, so there were no problems for Aphrodite, who was the Goddess of Harmony (amongst other things)!

The first cruise was south along the coast of Eubeoa to the little town of Karystos. (Castello Rosso) where there is a red Venetian Fort dominating the town and harbour. We then cruised north along the coast for the next six days, taking breakfast and occasionally lunch on board and going ashore in one of the enjoyable little towns for dinner. These included the marble mines near Marmari, and Eretria, where the Gulf of Evia narrows dramatically. The myth is that this narrow channel, which makes Eubeoa an island, was caused by the God of the Seas, Poseidon, having a hissy fit and striking the earth with his trident. Maybe! But history, as distinct from myth, is enshrined in the coast. The museum at Eretria is full of sculpture and pottery, and is close to the site of a school where it is said that Alexander was a pupil and Aristotle a teacher. Beat that! It is a fact that Aristotle died in nearby Chalkis, and was a tutor to Alexander, so maybe they were here together for a time.

Another site, going back to his time, has marvellous mosaics which are enclosed, covered and secured. Well done Eretria, which was also mentioned by Homer as having sent 40 ships to the Trojan War, and is known as the birthplace of the Greek alphabet. Eretria contains many historical sites, just too many to walk around in the midday heat. Apart from the history, the weather had been arranged very well, and a lot of time was spent on the sun deck. Thanos had promised some superlative swimming time, so that was good to anticipate. At Panagia there is a Church with beautiful colourful ancient paintings that is home to two and half thousand year old olive trees.

A branch from one of these trees is sent to every opening ceremony of the Olympic Games. Nea Styra had lovely beaches where there was the opportunity to swim and snorkel. On our way back to Marmaris we entered the Bay of Marathon, where one of the decisive battles of the ancient world was fought in 490 BC between the Athenians and the invading forces of the Persian King Darius 1st. The Persians had captured Eretria, but were beaten at Marathon. Plutarch wrote that a Greek soldier, Pheidippides, who had fought in the battle, ran from Marathon to Athens without stopping, burst into the Athenian Assembly and cried out 'We have won' before collapsing and dying. The story is now shrouded by the mists of time and argued over by academics, but I am happy to believe it. What an exit line!

Our final day was pretty wonderful, because Thanos fulfilled his promise of some excellent swimming and anchored off the seven tiny Petali islands in the Gulf of Evia. They were the private summer residence of the Greek Royal family, and are now in the hands of the Picasso family and Greek shipping magnates. We could not land, but it was a delight to anchor in the warm blue translucent water and dive off the side of the boat. This was the first time that I had done this for some years, so received some applause! This was a truly beautiful place, with the tiny wooded islands rising from the blue sea and the mountains of Eubeoa beyond them. Oh, the water was good!

The return arrangements worked well, so perhaps I was a bit unfair about the connections from Athens. After all, we had all arrived at the Airport from different directions and at different times. After an enjoyable dinner in Marmari we got the regular ferry to Rafina next morning, and a minibus awaited to take everyone to Athens. This had been a most enjoyable, relaxing cruise, with glimpses of ancient history available for those who wanted them, plus some wonderful scenery and good company. I would like to do it again.

Steps still to take – Badee badee bukra, yimkin

I have been asked many times for my opinion of the best country in the world. What an impossible question to answer properly. Best for scenery, for adventure, people or Society? I think that it depends upon where you stand. New Zealand has to be, all-round, the most wonderful place overseas. But I have always been grateful for, and appreciative of belonging to the countryside of Houseman, Elgar and Shakespeare. Tried living in London, and didn't want it. Longed for rain, lazy rivers and green fields when in the Sudan and Libya. Enjoyed the tranquillity of the Shropshire hills after the excitements of Chicago, Singapore and Rio. It has always been good to come home.

I have to say a big thank you to Jo for never objecting to my travels and keeping the home fires burning when I was away. She and I had some marvellous far-off travels together, as well as those described earlier. We stood under the Lion Gate of Mycenae and on the slopes of Mount Parnassus, above the sanctuary of the oracle at Delphi. Kissed the Blarney Stone, drove over the Alps in an elderly car, strolled through the marble ruins of Rome and Ephesus, cruised up the Bosphorus from Istanbul to the Black Sea, and joined the audience at the New Years Day concert in Vienna. We stayed in traditional houses in Tokyo and Kyoto and were able also to join audiences in the opera arenas at Verona, the Baths of Caracalla, and the ornate theatre in Odessa. A step, hopefully still to come, is a cruise past the castles of the Rhine in 2011, to follow our enjoyment of the peace, the history and the beauty of the Danube. A few more steps, mumkin Insh' Allah, to be taken on my own are on a climb to Jebel Toubkhal, the high point of the Atlas Mountains, which rise from the desert to snow-capped peaks. We, as well as I, have been very lucky and privileged to have been able to seize the moments. Carpe Diem. I have been so lucky to meet, and make friends with lovely people in remote and beautiful places. There is only one thing that I regret – not having taken in the beauty of the world from outer space. That really would have been seeing over the mountains.

I am very happy that Al and Nicky, and both their partners, have all had the opportunity to travel as well, for work and pleasure, in each case to far-flung places that I have not experienced! We are the temporary custodians, not owners, of the genes that have been handed down, and I hope that they have been passed on to the two boys Jan and Max. Jan has, already at the age of eight, done something that I never have, and never shall, do! He 'steered' a cross channel ferry from the Captain's Bridge – very well organised by his Father! Max is already an experienced traveller with his parents! I hope that they will both wish, and have the opportunity to travel or work in those far-off places, and enjoy the world in their turn. That has been, at least partly, the aim of this book.